SOCIAL SCIENCE AND URBAN CRISIS

Vicious Circle

Vicious Circle — copyright 1969 by Herblock in The Washington Post.

SOCIAL SCIENCE AND URBAN CRISIS
Introductory Readings

VICTOR B. FICKER

AND

HERBERT S. GRAVES

The Macmillan Company, New York
Collier-Macmillan Limited, London

The Macmillan Company
866 Third Avenue, New York, New York 10022

Collier-Macmillan Canada, Ltd., Toronto, Ontario

Library of Congress catalog card number: 71–125410

First Printing

With Appreciation to Our Wives—
Merle and Rae

FOREWORD

by Senator Charles H. Percy

"Urban crisis" is an often heard phrase, glibly used to describe a whole gallery of ills.

To the businessman-commuter, it is the traffic jam he faces every morning and evening. It is crime in the streets, making him fear to take his wife out for an evening in town. It is drugs, which are now common even in the suburban high school his teen-ager attends.

The black parent in the ghetto shares with the businessman the worries over crime in the street and over drugs. But the ghetto resident also contends with bad schools and dilapidated housing, poor employment opportunities and insufficient medical care, racial discrimination, and the general frustration caused by living in poverty while the majority of the country lives in unparalleled affluence.

The blue-collar worker suffers through an urban crisis that is all too real. Inflation stuns him. He carries a heavy tax load on a salary that, as recent reports have shown, becomes less and less adequate as he gets older and as his family grows. He labors daily at an often unsatisfying job; the American dream of comfort and security continues to elude him, and college students tell him his goals are mistaken. The urban crisis for him is a series of threats to his safety, to his financial stability, to his value system.

The affluent young professional is one type of individual who seems to be moving back into the city. Proximity to cultural and intellectual pursuits is a major inducement. But the problems are still there—crime and traffic jams, and all the rest.

Yet there is another characteristic of our big cities that particularly affects the young person. It is the anomie, the facelessness, the lost-in-the-crowd feeling. Our cities too often lack warmth; they seem to provide facilities for shelter, for business, for shopping, for transportation, but not for human sensitivities, not for encounters between persons.

Although certain problems may be more obvious to certain people, all of them in combination make up the urban crisis. None of these problems exists in a vacuum.

Each is aggravated and intensified by others. The crisis of our cities is this complex web of ills, this intricately woven network of social, psychological, economic, governmental, environmental, and simply human problems, all interacting, all affecting each other.

The effort to find solutions is particularly frustrating, for there is no single, simple answer—not to the complex of problems, not even to any one problem, for no one problem can be tackled alone successfully. The attempt to solve one must take into consideration the effects of others. The resolution of the urban crisis can be achieved only through a multifaceted attack based on a thorough understanding of the variety and interconnection of the city's problems.

The essence of city life is interdependence. In an article included in this volume, Walter Lippmann asserts that "Robinson Crusoe, the self-sufficient man, could not have lived in New York City," and that is true in a sense, unless Crusoe could have learned a marketable skill, found a job and an apartment, mastered the subways or buses, learned to shop for his food and clothing, and accustomed himself to city crowds and city air. He would have had to learn to be patient when the subways stopped, or the garbage wasn't picked up, or he was laid off from his job. He would have had to resign himself to the fact that he was seemingly impotent in these matters, probably the cruelest blow of all. Again Lippmann, from the same article: "There is no way of evading the fact that in a city as big as New York only the garbagemen can collect the garbage . . . the individual citizen does not have his own incinerator."

The 1970 census clearly indicates that the population shift to the suburbs is increasing. The flight from the city became a marked trend in the late 1940's and has continued ever since. Returning veterans took advantage of Federal Housing Administration programs, which discriminated against ghetto dwellers, in effect, by refusing to insure in "unstable," or integrated, neighborhoods. Moving to the suburbs always has required some expense, limiting this opportunity to the more affluent.

The cities have been left too frequently with the poor, the black, the old, and the latest rural migrants—the bulk of those persons who have the most need of public aid. But the cities have lost the affluent persons and businesses that can provide the tax resources necessary to support that aid.

The city supplies the business, cultural, and public facilities utilized by the entire metropolitan populace, but it has difficulty reaching for taxation purposes those persons outside the city limits. In an article in this volume, Harvey Cox—speaking of Boston, but it could be any large city—states, "Technically and sociologically, it is a metropolitan region, interdependent in every respect. Politically it is a congeries of fiefdoms and protectorates engaged in the legalized looting of the center city. . . ."

There is hardly an urban problem that does not demand for its solution either the tax resources or the organizational cooperation of the suburbs. Lack of finances and coordination has left many a sore to fester—housing deteriorates, roads jam, schools worsen, city services decline, downtown retailers suffer, hopelessness reigns, and drugs proliferate. In this atmosphere crime increases, causing even more of the affluent to leave the city and further weakening the city's base. This cycle must be stopped.

The interrelation of urban problems, the interdependence of city life, the mutuality of interest between city and suburb—all of these require that a valid understanding of the urban crisis be based on a study that is broad in scope, and is perceptive of the cause and effect relations of city activities.

An academic study of the urban crisis calls for an interdisciplinary approach, including sociology, psychology, government, economics, history, ecology, and architecture, among others. This book of readings is an extremely valuable volume, for the writers examine the problems of the city from all perspectives and lead the reader to a realistic conception of the urban crisis.

It is extremely important to the future of our country that we attain a fuller appreciation of the variety and complexity of the urban crisis. Only with increased knowledge and deeper understanding will we recreate our cities as places of beauty, vitality, and opportunity for all.

PREFACE

This collection of essays, its organization and arrangement, is a result of a year-long study in which the Division of Social Sciences of Polk Junior College attempted to find out exactly what was needed and useful for today's college freshman. We were all aware that significant problems were encountered by students as they began their formal college study. We also recognized that, for many of these students, this might be their only contact with the social sciences.

In compiling this book, we were presented with a twofold challenge: first, to provide a scholarly, workable, and in-depth introduction to the social sciences; and second, to equip the student who was going no further in the social sciences with knowledge and skills immediately useful and relevant to him. It should be obvious that these two goals would become one if a significant curriculum change were to be brought about.

As the first part of the study, the authors did an intensive examination of courses traditionally offered to high school students across the country. To check these findings, an examination was conducted of Florida's students. Three principal findings emerged from this study. First, students were receiving essentially sound training in the area of history and national government. Traditionally, students take courses in world history, American history, and, perhaps in their senior year, choose an elective such as problems of American democracy. Knowledge of national government tied in closely with that of American history, as the students seemed to know about the national executive office but knew increasingly less about congress and the supreme court.

The second major finding was in the area of identifiable weaknesses in the social sciences. Again a direct correlation exists between courses traditionally offered and students' performance. Knowledge was significantly low in the areas of sociology, geography, anthropology, psychology, and local government. The discipline that scored lowest was economics. Clearly then, traditional high school courses do not present a balance in the social sciences.

The third finding arose somewhat by accident. As the investigation proceeded, the authors observed the high level of correlation between reading proficiency and proficiency in the social sciences. As we pursued this further with professional reading specialists and counselors, we discovered that if the student had trouble reading he also had trouble in the social sciences.

Armed with these findings we began to study how we might best deal with these problems. Traditional survey courses were found lacking in that they often offer only a brief and somewhat shallow look at each of the disciplines. Professors objected because they felt they could not do justice to their area of specialization in a two- or three-week treatment. Findings of the National Council of the Social Studies also indicated that standard survey courses were on the wane. In further discussions we also rejected treating a series of social problems, feeling that this approach was too scattered and failed to provide appropriate depth. However, the problems approach did offer the advantage of relevancy. As an attempt to combine the best features of both the survey and the problems approach, the authors decided to focus on one social problem from an interdisciplinary perspective.

The students, as always, were eager to offer their suggestions as to which problem they wanted to study. In a survey of over 400 Polk Junior College students, the two social problems most frequently suggested were urbanization and race. It was decided to study urbanization with special emphasis on the problems of ethnic groups and ghetto life.

The selection of urbanization indicated the level of national awareness exhibited by students. By showing their concern for this trend of urbanization, it became apparent to the authors that these urban regions were the areas in which most of the college-educated would live.

Having selected the social problem, our next concern was choosing the reading matter. While it would be possible to utilize select books, it was evident that the students needed a broad study available only by reading internationally recognized articles by experts writing in their field. Likewise, we felt the necessity to provide an interdisciplinary look at the social sciences. Certain articles are clearly identified as to their disciplinary emphasis. For example, readings on ethnic groups, crime, and ghetto life fall most naturally in the field of sociology. Similarly, attention focused on taxation, unemployment, and poverty indicate emphasis on economics. However, we realized almost immediately that nice, neat divisions of the disciplines were impossible. Therefore, while the authors did attempt to identify certain disciplines for emphasis, the attempts to treat the material are clearly interdisplinary.

The readings have been arranged so that the student begins work immediately on the causes of urban problems and the manner in which they have developed. Part I focuses on the historical development of the city, while Part II presents many of the contemporary problems. Nothing stifles a student's interest more than having to spend what seems to him an interminable amount of time getting to the problem. Nevertheless, a full appreciation of the social problem cannot be gained without this important background.

Parts III through X take a close look at areas of specific concern in urban life. These selections clearly show the absolute necessity for all the social science disciplines to bring their expertise to bear on the urban problem. The concluding articles present hopeful projections and concepts for the future. The student is not simply presented with a dilemma and left to consider it with no solution in sight.

This book, therefore, is designed to provide material that is both scholarly in content yet readable for the student or lay person beginning his study of the social sciences and the city. Care was taken to assure that a number of top scholars in our country would be represented. The discussion questions are so written as to demand that each of us take a look in our proverbial "own back yard." Hopefully these questions can lead to some practical research.

A list of suggested readings is provided to enable students and faculty alike to pursue further study. An almost unlimited amount of supplementary material is available and can be used to provide even further emphasis on needs identified locally. A number of audio-visual materials are available for school and community use, and the authors particularly recommend much of the recent work done by the National Educational Television Network.

Finally, we wish to stress the importance of classroom discussions with the students. The opportunity to think and talk about new ideas is a necessity. The success or failure of an approach such as the one advocated in this book may well hinge on this point. Students must be involved and the opportunity for give and take, real feedback from the instructor as well as other students, is essential. Two major concerns must occupy the attention of all of us. First, we need to begin long-range planning to deal effectively with urbanization. Second, we need to make cities desirable places in which to live. Cities are for people. As one commentator recently expressed, "Unless we make our cities livable and safe, they shall become jungles unfit for normal human habitation."

We were very free in utilizing the professional skills of the reading specialists of our faculty. Theirs was the task of testing each piece of material for readability, but, more important, working with us from the very beginning. We wish to thank Mrs. Carole Wines, Mrs. Mary McIver, Mrs. Claretha Carnegie, and Mrs. Jeanne Lasater for their most valuable assistance.

We would also like to express our appreciation for their clerical assistance to Mrs. Pat Partin, Miss Wini Murdock, and Mrs. Marilyn Caldwell.

V. B. F.

H. S. G.

CONTENTS

III URBAN ETHNIC GROUPS

IV GOVERNING THE CITY

V POVERTY AND WELFARE

VI EDUCATION AND UNEMPLOYMENT

VII   URBAN TAX TANGLE

VIII   DEVIANCE, CRIME, AND THE POLICE

IX THE URBAN GHETTO

X   UNIQUE URBAN PROBLEMS

XI   THE CITY OF TOMORROW

SUGGESTED READINGS

THE CITY IN HISTORY

The development of urban life seems a peculiarly modern one. A look at both the ancient and medieval worlds illustrates this point. While it is certain that large cities did exist in ancient and medieval times, the concept of urbanization is relatively recent.

Historically, cities have developed for a variety of reasons. Initially man found it necessary to locate in groups for mutual protection. Being social by nature, man responded to a group situation. Once the concern for protection was met, he turned to other areas, perhaps less vital but, in the long developmental pattern of cities, equally important.

High on the list of priorities was the need for suitable food and water. The necessity of natural resources is obvious if life is to be sustained. Land suitable for grazing and agriculture brought people together. However, such necessities do not foster large cities. These early agricultural communities find their modern-day counterpart in the midwestern farm community in which the farmer comes home at night but spends his days in the fields.

The concept of size took on meaning as cities became centers of commerce. The location of cities at crossroads provides a good insight into this development. But equally significant, it marks a shift of emphasis in society. The essential factor is that man no longer needed to devote his full human resources to the task of simply providing enough food and raw materials. It is significant to point out that as society depends less and less on its agricultural output, it tends to become increasingly urban.

City life remained essentially unchanged throughout ancient times, and as far as the western world is concerned, city life experienced a decline during the middle ages. Europe became isolated when it cut itself off from the Mediterranean and the society became essentially rural again.

The twelfth and thirteenth centuries favored a return to town life. With the beginning of the industrial revolution in the 1800's, the transformation from town to city to metropolis became complete. As industrialization spread, so did urbanization. While not all metropolises are centers of industry, their relationship to industry via commerce is unmistakable.

The cities have meant for man many things. They have been the centers of culture where the great playwrights, artists, and thinkers have gathered. The first modern university, the University of Paris, was fostered by the city and in turn fostered the growth of the city as Peter Abelard's fame spread throughout Europe. Similar patterns emerged at Bologna, Oxford, and Cambridge.

Major trends in social thought likewise were given birth in our cities. Historically the centers of revolution, cities have become gathering places for young radicals anxious to found a new social order.

But as these cities developed, man's lot did not significantly change. In fact, its growth seems to have taken its toll on those very areas the cities should have fostered and nurtured. Where man turned to the cities as a place of increased economic opportunity, the cities became for him the centers of the cruelest forms of exploitation. As man searched for greater learning, the cities became the home for deep educational deprivation. Man looked to the city as a place to develop new friendships, develop new ties; yet as the city grew, it became more impersonal, more alien, more apathetic.

Where the cities once served as the brightest hopes for modern man, today they are the centers of his greatest frustrations. The cities are beset by innumerable problems, and it becomes incumbent upon the student of today's urban scene to reflect and to look back at the development of cities to see what went wrong. Where should changes have been made? What should have been done differently? How should we have planned better?

For western man, our problem is saving the shambles that we call our cities. For most of the rest of the world, the problem is quite different. Those portions of the earth we term "developing nations" are undergoing the same processes of urbanization that we have over the past century. The major difference is that these countries will very likely complete the process in a much shorter time. What advice then can the historians offer these developing nations? What must be done to our own modern metropolis to make it a place suitable for living?

Perhaps Kenneth Boulding in his article *Where Are We Going If Anywhere? A Look at Post Civilization* offers us some insight. He claims that the major emphasis in post civilization is that of increased stress on human resources. The history of urban development points to incredible strides made in the fields of technology, commerce, art, learning, and science. Particularly difficult to comprehend is the progress made over the past one hundred years. Not even our most severe critics can say we have not been spectacular in our progress.

But in our progress, viewing it historically, have we significantly bettered the lot of the downtrodden or has progress widened the gap? Have we made it possible to say that today we are maximizing the human potential, the humaneness in all men? Or have we utilized man's inhumanity to man at the expense of fostering this humaneness? On this front, we have little to sing praises about.

Might this not be the lesson in the history of urbanization? An examination of the development of urbanization can foster no more positive results than the awareness that man must return again to the center from which all this progress came—himself—and see to it that he once again takes his rightful place in today's ongoing history.

THE NATURE AND RISE OF CITIES

Ralph Thomlinson

Today's citizen takes urbanization for granted yet it is, historically speaking, a very recent development. The great cities of history are dwarfed by today's metropolis. The great population increase of the last century gives evidence that we have had precious little time to come to grips with this movement of urbanization. Yet understand it we must if intelligent, progressive planning is to replace the stop-gap measures of today's cities.

WHAT IS A CITY?

The initial observation pertinent to defining a city is that neither social scientists nor governing bodies in various countries agree among themselves on a definition. Disagreement often exists even within a nation, as in the United States, where the Bureau of the Census has had to set up a special category for urban places not classified as cities by the relevant state governments —a condition found in several states in the Northeast and a few in the rest of the nation. Although officials and scholars agree in defining a city in contrast to the surrounding countryside, this urban-rural comparison is made by means of many different criteria.[1]

A common approach is to specify a minimum number of inhabitants; above a certain number of residents, a community is called a city. Minimum population has been set by legislative and other bodies at 200 in Denmark; 300 in Iceland; 1,000 in Venezuela and New Zealand; 1,500 in Ireland; 2,000 in France, the Congo, Israel, and Argentina; 2,500 in the United States and Mexico; 5,000 in Belgium, India, Ghana, and the Netherlands; and 10,000 in Greece. In the nineteenth century, the United States favored 8,000. Some countries—Japan, for instance—define two or more "urban" categories with different minimum sizes. Therefore no one can fix an absolute figure that will meet with international unanimity. This definition possesses the further weakness, that there are many areas larger than 2,500 (or 10,000) that do not seem urban in character, and smaller communities that we do regard as urban.

A second type of quantitative definition uses density as its criterion. Mark Jefferson said that a density of 10,000 people per square mile is indicative of a city. Other scholars have suggested smaller figures. Although not agreeing with Jefferson in other respects, Hope Tisdale Eldridge wrote that "urbanization is a process of population concentration." The same criticism applies here as to the first kind of definition: It does not always agree with our conception of what a city is.

Historical criteria are used in the third method: A community is a city insofar as its role in the past has conferred this title upon it. We thus refer

[1] Georges Chabot, "Introduction," *Les villes* (Paris: Colin, 1948).

to earlier times to decide what is a city. But it is just in this way that people accept a number of places as cities. The historical criterion takes us back to a time when city and country were much more distinct than they are today, thus ensuring a less arbitrary definition. Unfortunately, use of this criterion entails the risk of including many now-defunct cities. And how are we to treat newly founded communities?

A fourth kind of definition is based on administrative law: A city has privileges and obligations not possessed by unincorporated rural areas. In this case, a government decision is necessary to place an area on the list of cities. In the United States, state legislatures grant municipal charters, officially declaring that a place is a city, town, borough, or whatever else they choose to call it; this charter provides both rights and duties. In some European countries during the Middle Ages only a city had the right to open a market. To a lawyer a city may be a municipal corporation endowed with a legal existence that enables it to own property, to sue and be sued, and so forth. Juridical factors are central in this definition: A city possesses a charter guaranteeing it certain rights and privileges and imposing upon it certain obligations. But these legal distinctions are breaking down as suburbanization surrounds corporation limits with a juridical haze.

Fifth, the exterior aspect of a community is relevant, for it is by physical impressions that we recognize and classify places. An urban area is built up; a rural area is not. A city is a man-made landscape of buildings, streets, water mains, and other contrived appurtenances. Richard L. Meier defined a city as a place where "artifacts have accumulated to such an extent that they have extinguished most features of the natural environment." But some built-up places are essentially rural, the tall structures

being grain elevators and the elongated ones being storage sheds for various agricultural products. Furthermore, say sociologists, cities should be defined in terms of people, not things. And some critics insist that the appearance is only the manifestation of a more profound reality—the way of life—and that phenomena should not be defined by symptoms.

The type of life then supplies a sixth criterion: modes of living and feeling. Some styles and attitudes are appropriate to the city and others to the country. When people contrast the city and the countryside, this difference is usually what they mean. A city is more than just the physical accompaniments of high density—busy streets, skyscrapers, and crowded subways; it is also a style of living and a culturally different manner of regarding life. A stereotypical urbanite talks fast, keeps close track of time, lives in an apartment, and does not know his neighbors. In short, as Louis Wirth said, urbanism is a special way of life. But this way of life is not susceptible to precise definition, which makes it difficult to use as a principle of classification.

A seventh point of view is that the dominant factor determining urban or rural way of life is the occupations of the inhabitants. Stated simply, the urban habitat is made up of workers who do not cultivate the soil. The 1938 Congress of the International Statistical Institute recommended adoption of a definition based on the percentage of the population engaged in agriculture; in a city the most frequent means of subsistence are service, commercial, and industrial occupations. Also, the division of labor is more varied in cities. But by this definition some large towns in Hungary and Bulgaria would have to be labeled "rural," yet a tiny cluster surrounding a railroad coaling stop in Kansas would be called "urban." This criterion also leads to difficulties and ambiguities in the case of mining areas: Extractive activities are not farming, but they are not urban either.

The eighth criterion is insistence on commercial character as defining a city, emphasizing the distributive function of the marketplace. The market element is paramount in Friedrich Ratzel's definition: A city is "a permanent collection of men and habitations which covers a large area and which is found at the crossing of large commercial routes." Arthur Smailes regarded a city as a place having banks and shops. This criterion appears too narrow, for business plays only an accessory part in the activities of many cities.

A ninth approach uses the industrial occupations as the sole criterion: A city is where factories are. But a few factories, or one large one, in a rural area do not constitute an urban enclave worthy of the designation "city." Both this definition and the objections to it are similar to those of the seventh and eighth approaches.

These last three criteria imply a tenth standard: the dependent or even parasitic nature of cities. Werner Sombart spoke of cities as "aggregations of men dependent on products of outside agricultural labor for their subsistence." The daily need to bring in food and other necessities places the city in the position of relying upon rural areas for its existence. Traditionalists often proclaim rural areas as the source of life and cities as parasitic, hypercivilized, and degenerating. In return, these decadent cities usually supply the luxuries of life to rural regions in exchange for foodstuffs, or they may simply exploit the surrounding countryside through military dominance. This view of urban-rural relations often brings forth such virulent criticism as Henri Bordier's "cities represent points of ossification of the social organism." In any case,

definition by dependence is not fully satisfactory because, in modern countries, rural and urban areas are interdependent in their industrial, agricultural, military, educational, medical, and artistic needs.

Related to dependence is an eleventh basis for definition: A city is a central place for transportation. Anyone who has traveled the French railroad system knows that nearly all routes lead to Paris and that one often cannot go directly from A to B even though they are only 50 miles apart; rather, he must ride 150 miles to Paris, change trains, and ride 175 miles back out to reach city B. Similar conditions prevail in the hinterlands of New York City: To go from one place in metropolitan New Jersey to another late at night, it is sometimes advisable to cross the Hudson River into New York City, ride the subway, and then recross the Hudson to New Jersey. Rural areas are places that buses pass through; where they stop is usually a town. And if a community is too small to merit a bus station, it hardly deserves to be designated a city. Charles H. Cooley theorized that stops or breaks in transportation provide nuclei for the founding of cities. But, without denying the indispensability of transport to modern city functioning, it is not sufficiently central to urban existence to adopt as the primary defining criterion.

Commuting is becoming common enough to be regarded as the twelfth defining attribute of cities. Most city dwellers commute—but so do many farmers in various parts of the world. Jean Brunhes and Pierre Desfontaines used commuting to distinguish a city from a village: "A city has the majority of its inhabitants employed most of the time inside the agglomeration; a village has the majority of its inhabitants employed most of the time outside the community." Then is a suburb a city or a village—and is a village urban or rural? But this commuting phenomenon may be more closely related to the cost and rapidity of transportation than to the extent of urbanization and therefore is not a fully satisfactory test for urbanism.

A thirteenth criterion is government or religious functions: Cities are essentially church or political centers. In a few countries these two criteria are appropriate now, and in a large number of nations they once were excellent defining criteria. Henri Pirenne described medieval cities as "distinguished by gates, churches, and population density." But this kind of definition is no longer suitable, for religious and government activity are of slight importance in many modern urban communities.

A fourteenth approach is that a city has a central focal point, a place where "things happen." This nucleus, known in Chicago as The Loop and in many cities as Main Street or Downtown, is a markedly congested, massively built-up area in which no one lives but to which many persons come for work, shopping, and entertainment; consequently, the highest property values in the city are found there. Although a central business district is characteristic of many cities, quite a number of old ones have several such districts, and a few very new cities have remarkably little central concentration. The degree of downtown development appears to be largely a result of the type of transportation that prevailed during the formative years of a city's growth; cities that came of age in the automotive era often have highly dispersed businesses, shops, and entertainment facilities.

The fifteenth and final criterion is diversity: Cities are undoubtedly more complex and varied than are rural areas. The variety is evident in the appearances and functions of both buildings and people. Hans Dorries said: "A city is known by its more or less orderly form, closed, grouped around a nucleus which is easy to find; and by its very varied appearance, composed of the most diverse elements." This approach, though containing considerable truth, is not conducive to precise demarcation between urban and rural modes.

The most likely way out of this maze involves a sixteenth possibility: using several of the already-listed criteria. A modern city is

1. A large agglomeration of people living in a contiguously built up area,

2. Who function to produce non-agricultural goods and services, and more particularly, to distribute all manner of goods and services,

3. And who, as a result of carrying on such functions develop a way of life characterized by anonymity, impersonal and segmentalized contacts with other people, and secondary controls.[2]

Yet even this compromise approach is not without blemish, for it more closely resembles a definition of a complex metropolitan area than of a single city.

Although scholars have failed to agree upon a universal definition of a city, largely because cities themselves differ in different culture areas of the world, their points of disagreement have shed considerable light on the urban dweller and his habitat. Furthermore, a formal definition is probably less valuable, albeit far more succinct, than is this sixteen-part description of the fundamental properties of cities and qualities of city living. A precise definition of the word "city" that would be legitimate and useful in all regions of the world is

[2] Abram J. Jaffe, "Summary of the Proceedings of the University Seminar on Population" (New York: Columbia University, 1951), mimeographed, p. 15.

not possible, but we do know approximately what cities are like.

In sum, cities are built up of large quantities and varieties of edifices offering physical contrasts and requiring transportation facilities to relieve congestion and permit flow of materials and people. Urban centers are characterized by rapidity and fluidity of life, specialization of activities, complex social organization, and intensification of opportunity. Compared with inhabitants of rural areas, city residents are more heterogeneous, often anonymous, and given to impersonal and secondary relationships as a result of their far more numerous recurrent personal contacts.

THE EARLIEST CITIES

Cities came into being with man's emergence from a primitive to a civilized state. This simultaneity was not a coincidence, for the first cities provided seats of government, bastions of defense, altars of worship, markets for exchange of goods, and meeting places for the interchange of ideas. Among the most commendable achievements of human history, the development of the city ranks with that of fire, agriculture, and printing.

Cities appeared first in the Mesopotamian basin, probably about 4000 B.C. Whether by diffusion or independent invention—archaeologists disagree on this matter—they were found in the Nile Valley by 3000 B.C., the Indus Valley by 2500 B.C., the Huang Ho Valley by 2000 B.C., and in Latin America by A.D. 500. The region now known as Iraq can thus claim to have housed the first known city, and Egypt, West Pakistan, China, Mexico, and Peru can stake legitimate claims to having exhibited a similar early capacity for urban ingenuity. Archaeological excavations and reconstructions of these ancient cities

lend invaluable support to the few written records that have survived.

The Sumerians established their cities on the silted plains of the Tigris and Euphrates Rivers and extended their agricultural land by an intricate irrigation system. Although milestones in man's history, these cities were small by modern standards, having generally 5,000 to 20,000 inhabitants and reaching an estimated maximum of 34,000 in Ur early in the second millennium.[3] Heavily fortified walls protected the generally wealthy and privileged residents of these cities, and temples and palaces were the most prominent structures, with private residences scattered helter-skelter along narrow, twisted paths used for both pedestrian access and disposal of refuse.

The emergence of cities in Mesopotamia may possibly have stimulated city growth in the valleys of the Nile, Indus, and Huang Ho, but the sparsity of data makes this diffusionist inference questionable. Whatever their inspiration, urban centers did spring up along the lower Nile and in the delta at various times between 3000 and 2000 B.C., although even the largest communities were little more than shrines and market centers serving the rural hinterlands. Next came the urban settlements on the alluvial plain of the Indus Valley, where archaeological unearthing of Harappa and Mohenjo-daro gives evidence of their having been capitals of empires dominating scores of small towns and villages. The valley of the Huang Ho, or Yellow, River was the first host to cities in eastern Asia, but precise dating and accurate description await further excavation. The earliest New World cities were those of the Mayas in the Yucatan peninsula, followed by those of the Incas in what is now Peru, both

[3] Leonard Woolley, *Excavations at Ur* (London: Benn, 1954), p. 193.

cultures are insufficiently documented to establish dates with any certitude. Like the Sumerian cities, the Mayan and Incan urban centers were small, generally with populations of about 10,000.

Turning from the great cultural centers of the ancient Orient to the classical civilization of Greece would have seemed to the Syrians, Persians, Egyptians, Minoans, and other luxury-laden materialists of the time a lapse into barbarism. These sybarites, whose orientations were comparable with modern American standards, lost out both in power and in intellectual acclaim to the relatively ascetic tastes of Athens and Sparta, the most powerful of the Greek city-states.

The Greek *polis*, or city-state, was an autonomous and self-sufficient unit comprising a city and its hinterland, from which it drew sustenance. The term "city-state" is somewhat misleading, for the *polis* did not consist solely of a city, and the rural hinterland was fully as important to the Greek as the city was. Except for a few merchants, most inhabitants of the city owned and operated farms. As Max Weber reminded us, "the full urbanite of antiquity was a semi-peasant."[4] Topography greatly influenced the political system, for Greece is predominantly mountainous, and settlements were located in small valleys. Communication among the valleys was slow, hampering development of an integrated economy and fostering hundreds of small *poleis*, each fiercely protective of its independence. Emphatically contradictory in their temperate philosophy and their actual highly contentious behavior (both of which have contributed unquenchable legacies up to the present time), the Greek city-states provide vivid historical vignettes of urban dominance, a fact often obscured by their remarkable contributions to aesthetic, democratic and intellectual endeavors. With a population that apparently never exceeded 300,000—of which half were slaves and aliens—the Athenians made ineradicable impressions upon world history.

Ancient urbanization reached its apogee under the Roman Empire, when a vast state controlling the destinies of more than 50 million people was concentrated at Rome. At the peak of its power, in the second century A.D., Rome may have housed as many as 1 million people, making it the largest city to exist prior to industrial times. But thereafter its population diminished, dropping below 20,000 by the ninth century. No other city reached Rome's maximum population until London attained 1 million early in the 1800s.

THE MIDDLE AGES IN EUROPE

From the fall of the Roman Empire to the sixteenth century, a Dark Age of cities prevailed. The few large cities dwindled drastically in size and function, and no new ones arose as replacements. Because western Europe sank into an essentially agrarian civilization for several centuries, there is a question whether or not any medieval community was a true city. Before the end of the first millennium, "burgs never consisted of more than a few hundred men," and "towns probably did not pass the figure of two or three thousand souls."[5] Greatly reduced in size, the few remaining cities consisted of mere clusters of dwellings grouped around a monastery or castle and serving mainly as administrative foci for religious, political, or military jurisdiction. Weekly markets were held, to which peasants from

[4] Max Weber, *The City* (1921), trans. by Don Martindale and Gertrud Neuwirth (New York: Free Press, 1958), p. 71.

[5] Henri Pirenne, *Medieval Cities* (Princeton: Princeton University Press, 1925), p. 77.

roundabout brought their produce, and there was an occasional annual fair. Otherwise, towns served the dictates of the bishops or military commandants. "Neither commerce nor industry was possible or even conceivable in such an environment."[6] These circumstances, and the fact that daily necessities generally needed to be within easy walking distance, ensured that few medieval towns extended more than half a mile from the center.[7] During the Renaissance, even towns of considerable prominence often housed only 10,000 to 30,000 persons, and lesser towns generally had fewer than 10,000.[8] Throughout the Middle Ages, only Paris, Florence, Venice, and Milan are conjectured (in the absence of reliable data) to have reached 100,000 population.[9]

As long as each region was broken up into numerous small fiefs held by feudal lords with their vassals and serfs, each suspicious of other fiefs and refusing to cooperate even when not waging intermittent wars, cities were not likely to spring up. For cities to prosper, peace and cooperation are necessary so that merchants and teamsters can bring in food and supplies and move out salable commodities. The breaking up of the feudal system thus facilitated the rise of cities initiated in the Renaissance and coming to fruition in modern times.

URBANIZING THE WORLD

Some city growth did occur after about A.D. 1000, and by 1400 many vil-

[6] *Ibid.*, p. 76.
[7] Lewis Mumford, *The City in History* (New York: Harcourt, 1961), p. 313.
[8] Frederick R. Hiorns, *Town-Building in History* (London: Harrap, 1956), p. 110.
[9] Pirenne, *Economic and Social History of Medieval Europe* (New York: Harcourt, 1936), p. 173.

lages and a few cities were scattered across western and central Europe. But the appearance of a few cities does not denote true urbanization, by which is meant the change from a predominantly rural population to one living mostly in urban areas. Urbanization, as distinguished from the growth of cities, is measured by the percentage of the national or regional population residing in urban places. Urbanization is thus based on the relative growth of the urban and rural segments of the population; if the city and farm populations increase at the same rate, urbanization is not occurring. The first genuine urbanization occurred in northwestern Europe (England, France, and so on) in the early nineteenth century, for it was there that, for the first time, a substantial proportion of the population came to live in urban areas. During the last hundred years, most regions of the world have experienced increases both in the degree of urbanization and in the sizes and numbers of their cities.

In the 1600s, cities began to burgeon, and by 1800 not only London but also Paris had exceeded 500,000 population, and Vienna and St. Petersburg had reached 200,000. A century later, ten cities each contained more than 1 million people: London, Paris, Vienna, Moscow, St. Petersburg, Calcutta, Tokyo, Chicago, Philadelphia, and New York. In the first half of the twentieth century, urban growth was far more rapid—an estimated 875 cities throughout the world had reached 100,000 population by 1950, and nearly 100 had reached 1 million.

These larger urban agglomerations resulted from several forces: growing populations in various world regions, improved control over the natural environment resulting from technological advances in agriculture and industry, more rapid and reliable means of communication and transportation, and more sophisticated economic and political mechanisms permitting efficient exchange of goods and money between urban and rural residents. Aided by extraordinary new sources of power, factories prospered, surplus farm products flowed into the cities in increasing quantities over railroad and canal systems, businesses enlarged, and capital accumulated in these new industrial cities of the nineteenth century. In the twentieth century still more power sources were added, and, of course, the automobile arrived; together with the railroad, it practically eliminated in many regions the need to live close to one's workplace, thereby permitting city men to encroach upon the once-rural fringes of the cities. So developed the metropolitan region, with its satellite communities surrounding the central core and supplying a diurnal flow of commuters to work and pleasure.

The results of these urbanizing forces can be seen in summary. Of the world population of about 900 million in 1880, fewer than 2 per cent lived in cities of 100,000 or more, and only about 3 per cent lived in cities of 5,000 or more. By 1900, of 1.6 million people, the percentages had grown to nearly 6 and 14 respectively. And of the globe's 2.4 million population in 1950, the percentages were 13 and 30.[10] Between 1800 and 1950, the number of people living in cities of 5,000 or more was multiplied by twenty-five, and the population in cities of 100,000 grew twentyfold, whereas the total world population did not even triple. By 1950, a larger percentage of the world's people (and, of course, a far larger number of people) lived in cities having 1 million or more inhabitants than lived in places of 5,000 or more in 1800. Comparison of the mid-twentieth century with 1700 or 1600 would yield even more striking contrasts, but data are not sufficiently accurate for periods before 1800 to permit reliable quantitative comparison on a world basis.

[10] Kingsley Davis and Hilda Hertz, "The World Distribution of Urbanization," *Bulletin of the International Statistical Institute*, 37 (1954), 227–43.

THE PRE-INDUSTRIAL CITY

Gideon Sjoberg

The pre-industrial city offers a sharp contrast with the industrial centers with which we are so familiar today. Yet the contrast between pre-industrial and industrial (particularly in the areas of class structure, economic goals, political goals, and so on) may provide insight into an understanding of the changes we are currently undergoing from industrialization to automation. The problems of a dying Protestant ethic pose dilemmas equal to those undergone by society's current shifting to industrialization.

From "The Preindustrial City," *American Journal of Sociology*, LX (March 1955), pp. 438–445. Reprinted by permission of The University of Chicago Press. Copyright 1955 by The University of Chicago.

In the past few decades social scientists have been conducting field studies in a number of relatively non-Westernized cities. Their recently acquired knowledge of North Africa and various parts of Asia, combined with what was already learned, clearly indicates that these cities are not like typical cities of the United States and other highly industrialized areas but are much more like those of medieval Europe. Such communities are termed herein "preindustrial," for they have arisen without stimulus from that form of production which we associate with the European industrial revolution.

Recently Foster, in a most informative article, took cognizance of the preindustrial city.[1] His primary emphasis was upon the peasantry (which he calls "folk"); but he recognized this to be part of a broader social structure which includes the preindustrial city. He noted certain similarities between the peasantry and the city's lower class. Likewise the present author sought to analyze the total society of which the peasantry and the preindustrial city are integral parts.[2] For want of a better term this was called "feudal." Like Redfield's folk (or "primitive") society, the feudal order is highly stable and sacred; in contrast, however, it has a complex social organization. It is characterized by highly developed state and educational and/or religious institutions and by a rigid class structure.

Thus far no one has analyzed the preindustrial city per se, especially as it differs from the industrial-urban community, although Weber, Tönnies, and a few others perceived differences between the two. Yet such a survey is

needed for the understanding of urban development in so-called underdeveloped countries and, for that matter, in parts of Europe. Such is the goal of this paper. The typological analysis should also serve as a guide to future research.

ECOLOGICAL ORGANIZATION

Preindustrial cities depend for their existence upon food and raw materials obtained from without; for this reason they are marketing centers. And they serve as centers for handicraft manufacturing. In addition, they fulfil important political, religious, and educational functions. Some cities have become specialized; for example, Benares in India and Karbala in Iraq are best known as religious communities, and Peiping in China as a locus for political and educational activities.

The proportion of urbanites relative to the peasant population is small, in some societies about 10 per cent, even though a few preindustrial cities have attained populations of 100,000 or more. Growth has been by slow accretion. These characteristics are due to the non-industrial nature of the total social order. The amount of surplus food available to support an urban population has been limited by the unmechanized agriculture, transportation facilities utilizing primarily human or animal power, and inefficient methods of food preservation and storage.

The internal arrangement of the preindustrial city, in the nature of the case, is closely related to the city's economic and social structure.[3] Most streets are

---

[1] George M. Foster, "What Is Folk Culture?" *American Anthropologist*, LV (1953), 159–73.

[2] Gideon Sjoberg, "Folk and 'Feudal' Societies," *American Journal of Sociology*, LVIII (1952), 231–39.

[3] Sociologists have devoted almost no attention to the ecology of preindustrial centers. However, works of other social scientists do provide some valuable preliminary data. See, e.g., Marcel Clerget, *Le Caire: Étude de géographie urbaine et d'histoire économique* (2 vols.; Cairo: E. & R. Schindler, 1934); Robert E. Dick-

mere passageways for people and for animals used in transport. Buildings are low and crowded together. The congested conditions, combined with limited scientific knowledge, have fostered serious sanitation problems.

More significant is the rigid social segregation which typically has led to the formation of "quarters" or "wards." In some cities (e.g., Fez, Morocco, and Aleppo, Syria) these were sealed off from each other by walls, whose gates were locked at night. The quarters reflect the sharp local social divisions. Thus ethnic groups live in special sections. And the occupational groupings, some being at the same time ethnic in character, typically reside apart from one another. Often a special street or sector of the city is occupied almost exclusively by members of a particular trade; cities in such divergent cultures as medieval Europe and modern Afghanistan contain streets with names like "street of the goldsmiths." Lower-class and especially "outcaste" groups live on the city's periphery, at a distance from the primary centers of activity. Social segregation, the limited transportation facilities, the modicum of residential mobility, and the cramped living quarters have encouraged the development of well-defined neighborhoods which are almost primary groups.

_____

inson, *The West European City* (London: Routledge & Kegan Paul, 1951); Roger Le Tourneau, *Fès: Avant le protectorat* (Casablanca: Société Marocaine de Librairie et d'Édition, 1949); Edward W. Lane, *Cairo Fifty Years Ago* (London: John Murray, 1896); J. Sauvaget, *Alep* (Paris: Librairie Orientaliste Paul Geuthner, 1941); J. Weulersse, "Antioche: Essai de géographie urbaine," *Bulletin d'études orientales,* IV (1934), 27–79; Jean Kennedy, *Here Is India* (New York: Charles Scribner's Sons, 1945); and relevant articles in American geographical journals.

Despite rigid segregation the evidence suggests no real specialization of land use such as is functionally necessary in industrial-urban communities. In medieval Europe and in other areas city dwellings often serve as workshops, and religious structures are used as schools or marketing centers.[4]

Finally, the "business district" does not hold the position of dominance that it enjoys in the industrial-urban community. Thus, in the Middle East the principal mosque, or in medieval Europe the cathedral, is usually the focal point of community life. The center of Peiping is the Forbidden City.

ECONOMIC ORGANIZATION

The economy of the preindustrial city diverges sharply from that of the modern industrial center. The prime difference is the absence in the former of industrialism which may be defined as the system of production in which *inanimate* sources of power are used to multiply human effort. Preindustrial cities depend for the production of goods and services upon *animate* (human or animal) sources of energy— applied either directly or indirectly through such mechanical devices as hammers, pulleys, and wheels. The industrial-urban community, on the other hand, employs inanimate generators of power such as electricity and steam which greatly enhance the productive capacity of urbanites. This basically new form of energy production, one which requires for its development and survival a special kind of institutional complex, effects striking changes in the ecological, economic, and social organization of cities in which it has become dominant.

Other facets of the economy of the

[4] Dickinson, *op. cit.,* p. 27; O. H. K. Spate, *India and Pakistan* (London: Methuen & Co., 1954), p. 183.

preindustrial city are associated with its particular system of production. There is little fragmentation or specialization of work. The handicraftsman participates in nearly every phase of the manufacture of an article, often carrying out the work in his own home or in a small shop near by and, within the limits of certain guild and community regulations, maintaining direct control over conditions of work and methods of production.

In industrial cities, on the other hand, the complex division of labor requires a specialized managerial group, often extra-community in character, whose primary function is to direct and control others. And for the supervision and co-ordination of the activities of workers, a "factory system" has been developed, something typically lacking in preindustrial cities. (Occasionally centralized production is found in preindustrial cities—e.g., where the state organized slaves for large-scale construction projects.) Most commercial activities, also, are conducted in preindustrial cities by individuals without a highly formalized organization; for example, the craftsman has frequently been responsible for the marketing of his own products. With a few exceptions, the preindustrial community cannot support a large group of middlemen.

The various occupations are organized into what have been termed "guilds."[5]

[5] For a discussion of guilds and other facets of the preindustrial city's economy see, e.g., J. S. Burgess, *The Guilds of Peking* (New York: Columbia University Press, 1928); Edward T. Williams, *China, Yesterday and Today* (5th ed.; New York: Thomas Y. Crowell Co., 1932); T'ai-ch'u Liao, "The Apprentices in Chengtu during and after the War," *Yenching Journal of Social Studies*, IV (1948), 90–106; H. A. R. Gibb and Harold Bowen, *Islamic Society and the West* (London: Oxford University Press, 1950), Vol. I, Part I, chap. vi; Le Tour-

These strive to encompass all, except the elite, who are gainfully employed in some economic activity. Guilds have existed for merchants and handicraft workers (e.g., goldsmiths and weavers) as well as for servants, entertainers, and even beggars and thieves. Typically the guilds operate only within the local community, and there are no large-scale economic organizations such as those in industrial cities which link their members to their fellows in other communities.

Guild membership and apprenticeship are prerequisites to the practice of almost any occupation, a circumstance obviously leading to monopolization. To a degree these organizations regulate the work of their members and the price of their products and services. And the guilds recruit workers into specific occupations, typically selecting them according to such particularistic criteria as kinship rather than universalistic standards.

The guilds are integrated with still other elements of the city's social structure. They perform certain religious functions; for example, in medieval European, Chinese, and Middle Eastern cities each guild had its "patron saint" and held periodic festivals in his honor. And, by assisting members in time of trouble, the guilds serve as social security agencies.

The economic structure of the preindustrial city functions with little rationality, judged by industrial-urban standards. This is shown in the general nonstandardization of manufacturing methods as well as in the products and is even more evident in marketing. In

neau, *op. cit.*; Clerget, *op. cit.*; James W. Thompson and Edgar N. Johnson, *An Introduction to Medieval Europe* (New York: W. W. Norton Co., 1937), chap. xx; Sylvia L. Thrupp, "Medieval Guilds Reconsidered," *Journal of Economic History*, II (1942), 164–73.

preindustrial cities throughout the world a fixed price is rare; buyer and seller settle their bargain by haggling. (Of course, there are limits above which customers will not buy and below which merchants will not sell.) Often business is conducted in a leisurely manner, money not being the only desired end.

Furthermore, the sorting of goods according to size, weight, and quality is not common. Typical is the adulteration and spoilage of produce. And weights and measures are not standardized: variations exist not only between one city and the next but also within communities, for often different guilds employ their own systems. Within a single city there may be different kinds of currency, which, with the poorly developed accounting and credit systems, signalize a modicum of rationality in the whole of economic action in preindustrial cities.[6]

The economic system of the preindustrial city, based as it has been upon animate sources of power, articulates with a characteristic class structure and family, religious, educational, and governmental systems.

Of the class structure, the most striking component is a literate elite controlling and depending for its existence upon the mass of the populace, even in the traditional cities of India with their caste system. The elite is composed of individuals holding positions in the governmental, religious, and/or educational

institutions of the larger society, although at times groups such as large absentee landlords have belonged to it. At the opposite pole are the masses, comprising such groups as handicraft workers whose goods and services are produced primarily for the elite's benefit.[7] Between the elite and the lower class is a rather sharp schism, but in both groups there are gradations in rank. The members of the elite belong to the "correct" families and enjoy power, property, and certain highly valued personal attributes. Their position, moreover, is legitimized by sacred writings.

Social mobility in this city is minimal; the only real threat to the elite comes from the outside—not from the city's lower classes. And a middle class —so typical of industrial-urban communities, where it can be considered the "dominant" class—is not known in the preindustrial city. The system of production in the larger society provides goods, including food, and services in sufficient amounts to support only a small group of leisured individuals; under these conditions an urban middle class, a semileisured group, cannot arise. Nor are a middle class and extensive social mobility essential to the maintenance of the economic system.

Significant is the role of the marginal

---

[6] For an extreme example of unstandardized currency cf. Robert Coltman, Jr., *The Chinese* (Philadelphia: F. A. Davis, 1891), p. 52. In some traditional societies (e.g., China) the state has sought to standardize economic action in the city by setting up standard systems of currency and/or weights and measures; these efforts, however, generally proved ineffective. Inconsistent policies in taxation, too, hinder the development of a "rational" economy.

[7] The status of the true merchant in the preindustrial city, ideally, has been low; in medieval Europe and China many merchants were considered "outcastes." However, in some preindustrial cities a few wealthy merchants have acquired considerable power even though their role has not been highly valued. Even then most of their prestige has come through participation in religious, governmental, or educational activities, which have been highly valued (see, e.g., Ping-ti Ho, "The Salt Merchants of Yang-Shou: A Study of Commercial Capitalism in Eighteenth-Century China," *Harvard Journal of Asiatic Studies*, XVII [1954], 130–68).

or "outcaste" groups (e.g., the Eta of Japan), which are not an integral part of the dominant social system. Typically they rank lower than the urban lower class, performing tasks considered especially degrading, such as burying the dead. Slaves, beggars, and the like are outcastes in most preindustrial cities. Even such groups as professional entertainers and itinerant merchants are often viewed as outcastes, for their rovings expose them to "foreign" ideas from which the dominant social group seeks to isolate itself. Actually many outcaste groups, including some of those mentioned above, are ethnic groups, a fact which further intensifies their isolation. (A few, like the Jews in the predominantly Muslim cities of North Africa, have their own small literate religious elite which, however, enjoys no significant political power in the city as a whole.)

An assumption of many urban sociologists is that a small, unstable kinship group, notably the conjugal unit, is a necessary correlate of city life. But this premise does not hold for preindustrial cities.[8] At times sociologists and anthro-

pologists, when generalizing about various traditional societies, have imputed to peasants typically urban kinship patterns. Actually, in these societies the ideal forms of kinship and family life are most closely approximated by members of the urban literate elite, who are best able to fulfil the exacting requirements of the sacred writings. Kinship and the ability to perpetuate one's lineage are accorded marked prestige in preindustrial cities. Children, especially sons, are highly valued, and polygamy or concubinage or adoption help to assure the attainment of large families. The pre-eminence of kinship is apparent even in those preindustrial cities where divorce is permitted. Thus, among the urban Muslims or urban Chinese divorce is not an index of disorganization; here, conjugal ties are loose and distinctly subordinate to the bonds of kinship, and each member of a dissolved conjugal unit typically is absorbed by his kin group. Marriage, a prerequisite to adult status in the preindustrial city, is entered upon at an early age and is arranged between families rather than romantically by individuals.

The kinship and familial organization displays some rigid patterns of sex and age differentiation whose universality in preindustrial cities has generally been overlooked. A woman, especially of the upper class, ideally performs few significant functions outside the home. She is clearly subordinate to males, especially her father or husband. Recent evidence indicates that this is true even for such a city as Lhasa, Tibet, where women supposedly have had high status.[9] The isolation of women from public life has

[8] For materials on the kinship system and age and sex differentiation see, e.g., Le Tourneau, op. cit.; Edward W. Lane, The Manners and Customs of the Modern Egyptians (3d ed.; New York: E. P. Dutton Co., 1923); C. Snouck Hurgronje, Mekka in the Latter Part of the Nineteenth Century, trans. J. H. Monahan (London: Luzac, 1931); Horace Miner, The Primitive City of Timbuctoo (Princeton: Princeton University Press, 1953); Alice M. Bacon, Japanese Girls and Women (rev. ed.; Boston: Houghton Mifflin Co., 1902); J. S. Burgess, "Community Organization in China," Far Eastern Survey, XIV (1945), 371–73; Morton H. Fried, Fabric of Chinese Society (New York: Frederick A. Praeger, 1953); Francis L. K. Hsu, Under the Ancestors' Shadow (New York: Columbia University Press, 1948); Cornelius Osgood, The

Koreans and Their Culture (New York: Ronald Press, 1951), chap. viii; Jukichi Inouye, Home Life in Tokyo (2nd ed.; Tokyo: Tokyo Printing Co., 1911).

[9] Tsung-Lien Shen and Shen-Chi Liu, Tibet and the Tibetans (Stanford: Stanford University Press, 1953), pp. 143–44.

in some cases been extreme. In nine-teenth-century Seoul, Korea, "respec-table" women appeared on the streets only during certain hours of the night when men were supposed to stay at home.[10] Those women in preindustrial cities who evade some of the stricter re-quirements are members of certain mar-ginal groups (e.g., entertainers) or of the lower class. The role of the urban lower-class woman typically resembles that of the peasant rather than the urban upper-class woman. Industrialization, by creating demands and opportunities for their employment outside the home, is causing significant changes in the status of women as well as in the whole of the kinship system in urban areas.

A formalized system of age grading is an effective mechanism of social control in preindustrial cities. Among siblings the eldest son is privileged. And chil-dren and youth are subordinate to par-ents and other adults. This, combined with early marriage, inhibits the de-velopment of a "youth culture." On the other hand, older persons hold con-siderable power and prestige, a fact contributing to the slow pace of change.

As noted above, kinship is function-ally integrated with social class. It also reinforces and is reinforced by the eco-nomic organization: the occupations, through the guilds, select their members primarily on the basis of kinship, and much of the work is carried on in the home or immediate vicinity. Such con-ditions are not functional to the re-quirements of a highly industrialized society.

The kinship system in the preindus-trial city also articulates with a special kind of religious system, whose formal organization reaches fullest development among members of the literate elite.[11]

The city is the seat of the key religious functionaries whose actions set stand-ards for the rest of society. The urban lower class, like the peasantry, does not possess the education or the means to maintain all the exacting norms pre-scribed by the sacred writings. Yet the religious system influences the city's entire social structure. (Typically, within the preindustrial city one religion is dominant; however, certain minority groups adhere to their own beliefs.) Unlike the situation in industrial cities, religious activity is not separate from other social action but permeates fam-ily, economic, governmental, and other activities. Daily life is pervaded with religious significance. Especially impor-tant are periodic public festivals and ceremonies like Ramadan in Muslim cities. Even distinctly ethnic outcaste groups can through their own religious festivals maintain solidarity.

Magic, too, is interwoven with eco-nomic, familial, and other social activi-ties. Divination is commonly employed for determining the "correct" action on critical occasions; for example, in tradi-tional Japanese and Chinese cities, the selection of marriage partners. And non-scientific procedures are widely employed to treat illness among all elements of the population of the pre-industrial city.

Formal education typically is re-stricted to the male elite, its purpose be-ing to train individuals for positions in

[10] Osgood, *op. cit.*, p. 146.

[11] For information on various aspects of religious behavior see, e.g., Le Tourneau, *op. cit.*; Miner, *op. cit.*; Lane, *Manners and Customs*; Hurgronje, *op. cit.*; André Chouraqui, *Les Juifs d'Afrique du Nord* (Paris: Presses Universitaires de France, 1952) ; Justus Doolittle, *Social Life of the Chinese* (London: Sampson Low, 1868) ; John K. Shryock, *The Temples of Anking and Their Cults* (Paris: Privately printed, 1931) ; Derk Bodde (ed.), *Annual Cus-toms and Festivals in Peking* (Peiping: Henri Vetch, 1936) ; Edwin Benson, *Life in a Medieval City* (New York: Macmil-lan Co., 1920) ; Hsu, *op. cit.*

the governmental, educational, or religious hierarchies. The economy of pre-industrial cities does not require mass literacy, nor, in fact, does the system of production provide the leisure so necessary for the acquisition of formal education. Considerable time is needed merely to learn the written language, which often is quite different from that spoken. The teacher occupies a position of honor, primarily because of the prestige of all learning and especially of knowledge of the sacred literature, and learning is traditional and characteristically based upon sacred writings.[12] Students are expected to memorize rather than evaluate and initiate, even in institutions of higher learning.

Since preindustrial cities have no agencies of mass communication, they are relatively isolated from one another. Moreover, the masses within a city are isolated from the elite. The former must rely upon verbal communication, which is formalized in special groups such as storytellers or their counterparts. Through verse and song these transmit upper-class tradition to nonliterate individuals.

The formal government of the preindustrial city is the province of the elite and is closely integrated with the educational and religious systems. It performs two principal functions: exacting tribute from the city's masses to support the activities of the elite and maintaining law and order through a "police force" (at times a branch of the army) and a court system. The police force exists primarily for the control of "outsiders," and the courts support custom and the rule of the sacred literature, a code of

enacted legislation typically being absent.

In actual practice little reliance is placed upon formal machinery for regulating social life.[13] Much more significant are the informal controls exerted by the kinship, guild, and religious systems, and here, of course, personal standing is decisive. Status distinctions are visibly correlated with personal attributes, chiefly speech, dress, and personal mannerisms which proclaim ethnic group, occupation, age, sex, and social class. In nineteenth-century Seoul, not only did the upper-class mode of dress differ considerably from that of the masses, but speech varied according to social class, the verb forms and pronouns depending upon whether the speaker ranked higher or lower or was the equal of the person being addressed.[14] Obviously, then, escape from one's role is difficult, even in the street crowds. The individual is ever conscious of his specific rights and duties. All these things conserve the social order in the preindustrial city despite its heterogeneity.

CONCLUSIONS

Throughout this paper there is the assumption that certain structural elements are universal for all urban centers. This study's hypothesis is that their form in the preindustrial city is fundamentally distinct from that in the industrial-urban community. A considerable body of data not only from medieval

[12] Le Tourneau, op. cit., Part VI; Lane, Manners and Customs, chap. ii; Charles Bell, The People of Tibet (Oxford: Claredon Press, 1928), chap. xix; O. Olufsen, The Emir of Bokhara and His Country (London: William Heinemann, 1911), chap. ix; Doolittle, op. cit.

[13] Carleton Coon, Caravan: The Story of the Middle East (New York: Henry Holt & Co., 1951), p. 259; George W. Gilmore, Korea from Its Capital (Philadelphia: Presbyterian Board of Publication, 1892), pp. 51–52.

[14] Osgood, op. cit., chap. viii; Gilmore, op. cit., chap. iv.

Europe, which is somewhat atypical,[15] but from a variety of cultures supports this point of view. Emphasis has been upon the static features of preindustrial city life. But even those preindustrial cities which have undergone considerable change approach the ideal type. For one thing, social change is of such a nature that it is not usually perceived by the general populace.

Most cities of the preindustrial type have been located in Europe or Asia. Even though Athens and Rome and the large commercial centers of Europe prior to the industrial revolution displayed certain unique features, they fit the preindustrial type quite well.[16] And many traditional Latin-American cities are quite like it, although deviations exist, for, excluding pre-Columbian cities, these were affected to some degree by the industrial revolution soon after their establishment.

It is postulated that industrialization is a key variable accounting for the distinctions between preindustrial and industrial cities. The type of social structure required to develop and maintain a form of production utilizing inanimate sources of power is quite unlike that in the preindustrial city.[17] At the very

least, extensive industrialization requires a rational, centralized, extra-community economic organization in which recruitment is based more upon universalism than on particularism, a class system which stresses achievement rather than ascription, a small and flexible kinship system, a system of mass education which emphasizes universalistic rather than particularistic criteria, and mass communication. Modification in any one of these elements affects the others and induces changes in other systems such as those of religion and social control as well. Industrialization, moreover, not only requires a special kind of social structure within the urban community but provides the means necessary for its establishment.

Anthropologists and sociologists will in the future devote increased attention to the study of cities throughout the world. They must therefore recognize that the particular kind of social structure found in cities in the United States is not typical of all societies. Miner's recent study of Timbuctoo,[18] which contains much excellent data, points to the need for recognition of the preindustrial city. His emphasis upon the folk-urban continuum diverted him from an equally significant problem: How does Timbuctoo differ from modern industrial cities in its ecological, economic, and social structure? Society there seems even more sacred and organized than Miner admits.[19] For example, he used divorce as an index of disorganization, but in

---

[15] Henri Pirenne, in *Medieval Cities* (Princeton: Princeton University Press, 1925), and others have noted that European cities grew up in opposition to and were separate from the greater society. But this thesis has been overstated for medieval Europe. Most preindustrial cities are integral parts of broader social structures.

[16] Some of these cities made extensive use of water power, which possibly fostered deviations from the type.

[17] For a discussion of the institutional prerequisites of industrialization see, e.g., Bert F. Hoselitz, "Social Structure and Economic Growth," *Economia Internazionale*, VI (1953), 52–77, and Marion J. Levy, "Some Sources of the Vulnerability of the Structures of Relatively Non-

industrialized Societies to Those of Highly Industrialized Societies," in Bert F. Hoselitz (ed.), *The Progress of Underdeveloped Areas* (Chicago: University of Chicago Press, 1952), pp. 114 ff.

[18] *Op. cit.*

[19] This point seems to have been perceived also by Asael T. Hansen in his review of Horace Miner's "The Primitive City of Timbuctoo," *American Journal of Sociology*, LIX (1954), 501–2.

Muslim society divorce within certain rules is justified by the sacred literature. The studies of Hsu and Fried would have considerably more significance had the authors perceived the generality of their findings. And, once the general structure of the preindustrial city is understood, the specific cultural deviations become more meaningful.

Beals notes the importance of the city as a center of acculturation.[20] But an understanding of this process is impossible without some knowledge of the preindustrial city's social structure. Although industrialization is clearly advancing throughout most of the world, the social structure of preindustrial civilizations is conservative, often resisting the introduction of numerous industrial forms. Certainly many cities of Europe (e.g., in France or Spain) are not so fully industrialized as some presume; a number of preindustrial patterns remain. The persistence of pre-

[20] Ralph L. Beals, "Urbanism, Urbanization and Acculturation," *American Anthropologist*, LIII (1951), 1–10.

industrial elements is also evident in cities of North Africa and many parts of Asia; for example, in India and Japan,[21] even though great social change is currently taking place. And the Latin-American city of Merida, which Redfield studied, had many preindustrial traits.[22] A conscious awareness of the ecological, economic, and social structure of the preindustrial city should do much to further the development of comparative urban community studies.

[21] See, e.g., D. R. Gadgil, *Poona: A Socio-economic Survey* (Poona: Gokhale Institute of Politics and Economics, 1952), Part II; N. V. Sovani, *Social Survey of Kolhapur City* (Poona: Gokhale Institute of Politics and Economics, 1951), Vol. II; Noel P. Gist, "Caste Differentials in South India," *American Sociological Review*, XIX (1954), 126–37; John Campbell Pelzel, "Social Stratification in Japanese Urban Economic Life" (unpublished Ph.D. dissertation, Harvard University, Department of Social Relations, 1950).

[22] Robert Redfield, *The Folk Culture of Yucatan* (Chicago: University of Chicago Press, 1941).

THE EMERGENCE OF METROPOLIS

Charles N. Glaab and A. Theodore Brown

The development of cities is really a phenomenon of the nineteenth century with twentieth-century urban America being characterized by the growth of the metropolis. At an ever increasing rate the outer perimeters of the city are growing while the inner city population growth remains static and its racial population increasingly black. Even the most carefully planned cities have fallen under the spell of metropolitan growth with some areas (the eastern seaboard complex for example) falling under the term megalopolis. But the point here is that in order to understand urban America we must understand the most significant development in man's living patterns of the twentieth-century—the metropolis.

Informing much of the late nineteenth century examination of the problems and the prospects of the American city was the view that city and country represented distinct environments, opposed ways of life. This view would continue to influence the character of popular argument—especially in political debate —until at least the 1950's. But an occasional observer around the turn of the century recognized that the conception of city as one thing and country another —a conception which had such deep roots in western culture—could no longer be applied to American society. The city by this time had enormously extended its spatial area and its influence. There was often difficulty in physically distinguishing city from countryside, for the two often blended together in sprawling urban regions. The country no longer represented an independent community, since it was affected in hundreds of economic and social ways by the city. "The city has become the central feature in modern civilization and to an ever increasing extent the dominant one," wrote the municipal reformer Frederic C. Howe in 1906. "This rural civilization, whose making engaged mankind since the dawn of history, is passing away. The city has erased the landmarks of an earlier society. Man has entered on an urban age."

In a general way, Howe was describing an aspect of the phenomenon of "metropolitanism"—the extension of the influence of the large city over enormous hinterland regions. A few years later, the phenomenon received more explicit demographic recognition in the statistics presented in the federal census of 1910. As early as 1880, the census bureau had provided data for the metropolitan district of New York and its suburbs. Aware of the inadequacy of the customary urban classifications (populations of 8,000, 4,000, and 2,500

had all been used), demographers now applied the statistical notion of the metropolitan district to the whole nation. Twenty-five metropolitan districts were identified ranging in size from New York (including Newark) with its 616,927 acres of land and 6,474,568 people to Portland with its 43,538 acres and 215,048 residents. Through this device it was possible to indicate the unity of such urban areas as the twin cities of Minnesota, the cities on San Francisco Bay, and the two Kansas Cities along the Missouri-Kansas border. Also evident was the importance of the clusters of suburban communities around the large eastern cities of New York, Boston, and Philadelphia. Through continued growth over the next half century, these cities and their suburbs would come to constitute a kind of continuous metropolitan region which may represent a new stage in urban organization—the megalopolis.[1]

The growth of the metropolis constitutes the central theme of twentieth century American urban history. For the 1950 census, demographers devised a more sophisticated device than the metropolitan district to assess the importance of the rise of metropolitan regions. This was the Standard Metropolitan Area (renamed the Standard Metropolitan Statistical Area in 1960),

[1] The term "megalopolis" was devised by Jean Gottman and is generally applied to an urban region that contains several metropolitan centers. An alternative term "conurbation" implies an urban region formed from the fusion of several earlier cities. It has more application in Europe than in the United States; the cities along the Ruhr River in Germany and the Amsterdam-Haarlem-Leiden-The Hague-Rotterdam-Utrecht complex in the Netherlands supply examples of this kind of urban development. The term "metropolis," as is evident from Chapter One, acquired a different meaning in the twentieth century than it had historically.

which was defined as a whole county containing a central city of 50,000 or more, plus any adjacent counties that appeared to be integrated to the central city. For overall examination of twentieth century metropolitan growth, it is perhaps most convenient to use the principal S.M.A.'s (those with 100,000 or more population at a given census), which the Census Bureau has "retrojected" to past census periods. But whatever measuring scheme is employed the trends are evident.

First, there was a great increase in the number of metropolitan areas and in the total population that lived in these areas. During the period from 1900 to 1950, the total United States population increased from 76.0 million to 150.7 million, while the number of principal S.M.A.'s increased from 82 to 147 and their total population from 24.1 million to 84.3 million. This represented a percentage change in the metropolitan population from 31.9 per cent of the nation's total to 56.0 per cent.

Second, for the entire period the growth rate for the principal S.M.A.'s was substantially higher than for the country as a whole: 32.6 per cent as opposed to 21.0 per cent from 1900 to 1910, 25.2 per cent as opposed to 14.9 per cent from 1910 to 1920, 27.0 per cent as opposed to 16.1 per cent from 1920 to 1930, 8.3 per cent as opposed to 7.2 per cent from 1930 to 1940, and 21.8 per cent as opposed to 14.5 per cent from 1940 to 1950. For every decade in the period except 1900–10, when it was 15.0, the growth rate for nonmetropolitan areas of the country was substantially below ten per cent.

Third, there has been a tendency for rapid growth to take place in the outlying areas of metropolitan centers at an accelerating rate. After 1920 metropolitan "rings" grew much faster than "central cities" themselves, by the 1940–1950 decade nearly two and a half times

as fast (34.8 per cent as compared with 13.7 per cent). During the first decade of the century, metropolitan rings claimed only about one-sixth of the total United States population growth (15.7 per cent); in 1940–50 this figure had risen to nearly one half (48.6 per cent).

The metropolises of the twentieth century, whose growth constituted the most dramatic demographic development to be found in statistics of United States population, were much more than greatly enlarged traditional cities. Involved in the concept of the modern metropolis are complex changes in function and structure within the city and its suburban areas—decentralization of numerous activities, separation of areas of residence and work, and a high mobility over greatly extended spatial areas. Also involved are many relationships with other cities and areas outside the immediate limits of the urban region.[2] The sociologist R. D. McKenzie in his pioneer study of metropolitan communities in the early 1930's argued that these considerations were so striking that the huge city of the twentieth century with its surrounding suburban towns and cities and its far reaching economic relationships ought to be considered as "practically a new social and economic entity." A few years earlier N. S. B. Gras had examined the existence of

[2] The terminology relating to the metropolis is confusing. Some writers use the term "metropolitan community" to designate the area where population is integrated on a daily basis to the locale, that is, pretty much the commuting area of a metropolis; the term "metropolitan region" can then describe the larger area of more indirect influence. Employing the latter concept, it would be possible to divide the whole nation into a number of extended "metropolitan regions." But there is little consistency in the use of metropolitan nomenclature, and we have not attempted to be unduly precise here.

a world-wide metropolitan community and the intricate relationship of world cities of various sizes within that community. "We may think of metropolitan economy as an organization of people having a large city as nucleus," Gras wrote. "Or we may put it this way, metropolitan economy is the organization of producers and consumers mutually dependent for goods and services, wherein their wants are supplied by a system of exchange concentrated in a large city which is the focus of local trade and the center through which normal economic relations with the outside are established and maintained."

"Just as villages remained when town economy prevailed," Gras continued, "so do towns remain when metropolitan economy comes into existence. Towns remain, but in economic subordination to the metropolis. They continue to play a part, but as tributaries to a larger center. A closer examination of these dependent towns would show different types performing different functions, but all subordinate."

Gras' conception of "metropolitan dominance"—the control of the huge city over vast surrounding areas—influenced much of the subsequent study of the metropolis. Yet, as Gras himself recognized, "dominance" alone supplied an insufficient explanation. Not only were outlying areas of the metropolis dependent upon the city, but the city in turn was dependent upon its hinterland. In fact, the whole series of relationships within a metropolitan area was so complex that the biological term of symbiosis was often employed to indicate their nature. The twentieth century metropolis provided a new system of social and economic organization—a distinctive social configuration. As Leo F. Schnore observes, the metropolitan area cannot profitably be conceived of "as a simple two-part arrangement of center and ring, a large city

with its adjacent territory. . . . The metropolitan community must be viewed —in organizational terms throughout— as a highly specialized mosaic of sub-areas tied together into a new functional unity. Moreover, it is to be viewed as a multinucleated territorial system. Within these broad areas, the large centers are marked by functional diversity, while the smaller places, many of them formerly independent cities in their own right, tend to be narrowly specialized. At the same time, however, the main centers are specialized in the coordinating functions of administration and control."

The rise of the metropolitan region is often associated with the introduction of the automobile. Up to a point this is accurate. Statistically, if all American cities are considered together, the great jump in suburban population occurred in the 1920's when the automobile became the main device of urban transportation. Nevertheless, it is clear that the process of population decentralization—a fundamental aspect of the rise of the metropolis—had begun for some cities and in some regions of the country in the latter part of the nineteenth century. Schnore, one of the few contemporary urban sociologists to undertake detailed historical analysis of urban demography, has provided an ingenious study of decentralization of population in ninety-nine metropolitan central cities that had a population of at least 100,000 at some point in their growth. His study, which takes into account annexations and the persistence through thirty-year periods of decentralizing patterns, indicates the early tendency of a number of individual cities to grow more rapidly in their peripheral areas than at their centers. New York began decentralizing as early as 1850. Nine other cities had begun to decentralize by 1900; another thirteen cities were added to the list during the first decade of the century.

The process speeded up after 1920, of course, and fully sixty cities began to decentralize between 1920 and 1940. In short, suburbanization, although it greatly accelerated in the twentieth century, is a trend in American urban development that extends back at least a hundred years. In Philadelphia, to cite an extreme example, the population movement away from the center of the city was proportionally greater in the fifty years between 1860 and 1910 than in the half century between 1900 and 1950.

The basic economic institutions that enabled larger cities to develop highly specialized metropolitan functions within a network of varying sized towns and cities also had nineteenth century origins. The techniques of modern merchandising—with their emphasis on trade over vast regions—were fully developed by the end of the century. In the 1860's, Marshall Field's in Chicago combined the features of a number of large stores in Paris and New York—a fixed price system, large display advertisements, and numerous special departments—to establish the modern department store. The Great American Tea Company was organized in 1864 in New York; five years later it became the Great Atlantic and Pacific Tea Company. It began to establish branches throughout the country and became one of the first major chain stores. Frank W. Woolworth opened his five-and-ten at Lancaster, Pennsylvania in 1879, established branches at Harrisburg and Scranton, and within a decade owned stores in a number of localities. Modern advertising techniques, low-cost mass insurance, mail-order stores, centralized stock exchanges, and specialized banking were examples of other metropolitan activities that developed in the latter part of the century. Technological innovations in printing—new presses, linotype machines, improved halftones—

permitted city newspapers greatly to expand their circulations. This provided one of the most important means through which the influence of the metropolis was extended. In the early work of American urban sociologists, measurement of newspaper circulation provided a convenient way of estimating the range of metropolitan influence.

Another significant aspect of metropolitanism with nineteenth century origins was industrial suburbanization— the growth of "satellite cities," as Graham Taylor termed them in one of the first investigations of manufacturing communities on the outskirts of large cities. Although this aspect of decentralization has not received as much attention as the creation of the residential "dormitory" suburbs, the suburbs of employment and production have been equally important in shaping the character of the modern metropolis. In the late nineteenth century, the substitution of electric power for steam in industry and improvements in transportation made it possible for manufacturers to move away from central cities, and they were encouraged to do so by a number of factors: the need for vast amounts of cheap land to build factories incorporating all stages of large-scale complex production, lower taxes, and freedom from regulation in regard to smoke and noise. Early attempts to build industrial communities in America had been influenced by conceptions of social control. Through the establishment of small carefully planned rural manufacturing towns, it was hoped that America might escape the abuses of the European manufacturing city. But after the disastrous Pullman Strike of 1894, which stemmed in large part from the system of paternalistic control instituted in George Pullman's planned community, American manufacturers abandoned social planning in setting up their decentralized manufacturing centers. To the extent that they had to provide housing and urban facilities for workers, they did so in the simplest and most economical manner and as quickly as possible got out of the business of managing communities.

Gary, Indiana, the largest city ever built by an American manufacturer, illustrated the new approach. In 1905, the United States Steel Corporation, as part of an effort to expand and consolidate portions of its vast productive facilities, purchased eleven square miles of empty land below Lake Michigan on the Calumet River in Indiana. While new mills were being constructed at the site, the corporation, through its subsidiary Gary Land Company, constructed a system of basic utilities for a city of 200,000, platted out streets and lots on the simple, efficient gridiron design, had houses built through private contractors, and sold these to incoming workers on long-term contracts. Eugene J. Buffington, who managed the U.S. Steel operation at Gary, reflected the new outlook of American manufacturers when he stated that "the most successful attempts at industrial social betterment in our country are those farthest removed from the suspicion of domination or control by the employer. . . . Gary is nothing more than the product of effort along practical lines to secure right living conditions around a steel manufacturing plant." Gary was organized as an ordinary municipality; aside from trying to restrict the sale of alcohol, the Gary Land Company made no attempt to impose controls on workers. U.S. Steel's experiment in decentralizing manufacturing was strikingly successful. Gary was well located in relation to the railroads and the labor market of Chicago, and in a few years, a vast suburban industrial complex, "the cities of the Calumet," had developed in the region.

Occasionally in the founding of smaller twentieth century industrial communities

—such as Morgan Park, a suburb of Duluth built by U.S. Steel, or Goodyear Heights, developed by the Goodyear Rubber Company outside Akron—the utilization of techniques of planning did help provide a desirable environment for living and working. But more often than not, the industrial satellites had dismal slums right from the start. Many areas in the manufacturing complex that grew up across the Mississippi River from St. Louis—including the communities of East St. Louis, Granite City, Madison, and Venice—lacked even elemental urban services. Particularly miserable was Granite City, where 65 per cent of the 8,500 workers in a granite processing factory lived; a large densely settled slum area known as "Hungry Hollow" remained a part of Granite City for several decades. Norwood and Oakley, outside of Cincinnati; Lackawanna built in a swamp outside of Buffalo; and South Omaha were other early twentieth century industrial suburbs that demonstrated the deleterious effects of the absence of planning and control.

Even though U.S. Steel provided satisfactory urban services at the beginning, and later financed a number of recreational and educational projects, Gary, too, developed many of the problems of the large manufacturing city. The first construction workers at the site had lived in tents and various thrown-together shacks of tar paper, tin, and board. The area was allowed to remain for a time, and the structures became homes for many of the unskilled immigrant laborers in the mills. The company also built dormitories for unskilled workers; they were soon overcrowded, and the area where they were located deteriorated into a slum called "Hunkeyville." When the temporary camp area was finally cleared, many of the workers moved into a section south of Gary called "The Patch," where developers had thrown together ramshackle housing outside the control of Gary municipal officials or the company. When, as part of a clean-up attempt, the company forced the tenants out of the Hunkeyville housing, most of them also moved to The Patch. Although skilled workers were able to obtain adequate living quarters, this was not possible for the unskilled. The slum areas around Gary soon developed the customary problems of alcoholism, prostitution, and crime, although, owing primarily to a good natural water supply, they were not struck by serious epidemics.

The building of industrial towns and cities in the early part of the twentieth century reflected a general pattern of decentralization clearly indicated in statistics of manufacturing. A Census Bureau study of twelve of the thirteen largest "industrial districts" showed that from 1899 to 1904 the number of persons employed in industry in central cities increased by 14.9 per cent while in the outlying zones the number increased by 32.8 per cent. From 1904 to 1909 the increase in central cities was 22.5 per cent while in the surrounding zones it was 48.8 per cent. For the decade, the growth rate was over two times as great for the suburbs—97.7 per cent to 40.8 per cent. This trend toward industrial decentralization became even more pronounced with the general acceleration of suburbanization after 1920. In 1919 eleven central cities in the country's forty largest manufacturing counties still accounted for 85 per cent of the manufacturing workers; by 1937 this percentage had fallen to just under 60. The number of wage earners in the eleven central cities during the period declined from 2,045,789 to 1,808,692 while in the outlying areas of these cities the number increased from 365,-403 to 1,218,465. In addition to the decentralization of manufacturing, many of the commercial functions of the

nineteenth century city showed a marked tendency to decentralization, again particularly after 1920.

Cheap electric power and the telephone were important in the decentralization of economic activities. Also important was the mobility of labor permitted by the trolleys and interurban railroads. But the most significant development stimulating rapid suburbanization was the automobile, and to a lesser extent, the motorized truck. In the early 1890's, mechanics in the United States and in Europe had put together workable automobiles. But until the turn of the century they were built on individual order and were largely a toy of the rich, with only 8,000 vehicles registered by 1900. During the next decade actual manufacturing began. By 1910 the number of motor vehicles had risen to 468,500, and in 1915 to 2,490,932. Then came the tremendous post-First World War expansion of the industry: motor vehicle registration jumped from 9,239,161 in 1920 to 19,940,724 in 1925 to 26,531,-999 in 1930. In spite of the depression of the 1930's, the number of motor vehicles still increased by nearly a third during the decade reaching a total of 32,035,424 registrations in 1940; by 1950 the number had grown to 48,-566,984.

In addition to the obvious effects of increasing the mobility of workers and consumers and facilitating the movement of goods and materials in cities, the general use of motor vehicles also modified the spatial pattern of the metropolis. In the late nineteenth and early twentieth century, cities spread out along the lines of trolleys and interurban railroads. The suburbanized parts of the metropolis resembled tentacles extending from the central city in radial fashion. Highways, particularly in old and larger cities like Chicago and New York, first tended to follow the railroad lines. The new suburbs made possible by the automobile became part of the older pattern of growth. Gradually, however, as road building greatly expanded after the passage of the Federal Highway Act of 1916, the interstices of the metropoiltan area began to be filled in. Complicated lateral movements of traffic became a defining characteristic of the metropolis. Newer cities, such as Los Angeles, that experienced great growth in the twentieth century spread out along highways and did not develop the clearly defined central business districts of older cities. The transportation systems of older cities, even after the automobile came into general use, still tended to funnel traffic into the center, greatly intensifying the problem of congestion.

During the 1920's and early 1930's, engineers perfected and governments adopted the various devices that were part of a high speed system of motorized transportation—grade separation of highway from city street, traffic circle, divided dual highway, and synchronized stop lights. These techniques, along with new bridges such as the George Washington in New York and the Camden-Philadelphia, and an innovation such as the Holland Tunnel under the Hudson, permitted easier movement of automobile traffic through the huge, sprawling metropolitan region. But just as in past eras, the rush-hour, weekend, and holiday traffic jam was an all too familiar aspect of urban life.

The expanded economic opportunities created by the automobile stimulated an urban land boom that radically inflated property values in American cities. Particularly where automobile routes tended to follow older fixed forms of urban transportation, considerable expansion took place in central business districts. This expansion contributed to an optimism that caused property values to rise, and as Homer Hoyt has dryly

observed, "In each successive land boom there is a speculative exaggeration of the trend of the period." In 1920, the total value of land in American cities of over 30,000 population—only about one-fifth of one per cent of all the land in the United States—was estimated at $25 billion; by 1926 this figure had doubled to $50 billion. During the same period the value of American farm land dropped from 55 to 37 billion dollars—a figure 33 per cent less than the value of land in cities above 30,000. Real estate on Manhattan Island was assessed at over five billion dollars in 1930; this was more than the value of the farm land in 23 states in 1925. The corner of State and Madison in the heart of Chicago's loop was leased during the decade at a rate of $50,000 a front foot, a rate equivalent to $21,789,000 an acre. One small holding at 1 Wall Street in New York City sold for $100,000 a front foot, a rate of nearly $44,000,000 an acre.

Inflation of downtown land values and the post-First World War prosperity of many sections of the economy stimulated the great era of skyscraper building in American cities. For twenty-five years after Jenny's initial efforts, architects experimented with the new building form; the Woolworth Tower of New York completed in 1913 established a standard style. Chicago's group of towers along the Chicago River built in the early 1920's differed little from the new "Woolworth Gothic" skyscrapers that sprang up in New York. Cleveland, Pittsburgh, San Francisco, and Kansas City developed the jagged sky lines characteristic of the twentieth-century American city. By 1929, American cities had 377 skyscrapers of more than twenty stories in height, largely built without concern for the character of the surrounding urban space and without concern for the patterns of traffic created by the buildings. Even in the cities of the plains the skyscraper was as much demanded as on the tight plots of lower Manhattan Island. Many of the nation's tallest buildings were begun in 1928 and 1929 and only completed after the depression. The most famous skyscraper of all, the Empire State Building, was finished in 1930 and for many years was a white elephant in a city which during the depression had more than enough office space. Not until the late 1950's were the pressures of urban growth great enough to stimulate another era of skyscraper building.

Although architects criticized the skyscraper for its lack of esthetic distinction and planners criticized it for contribution to intense traffic congestion, it was through the jagged towering skylines of great cities that many observers perceived the character of the new metropolitan civilization. The German director Fritz Lang was inspired to make his classic motion picture "Metropolis" with its striking vision of the urban future after a visit to Manhattan in the mid-1920's. The French historian, Bernard Fäy, who visited New York late in the decade, echoed the sentiments of many travelers to the city in finding the mass of skyscrapers an appropriate symbol of a new order:

The very thing which I admire most in New York is its adaptation to the continent. In this sense, its architecture is intellectually reasonable, logical, and beautiful. Skyscrapers are the dwellings of the supertrusts; they are Eiffel Tower cathedrals which shelter Mr. Rockefeller, the Emperor of Petroleum, or Mr. Morgan, the Czar of Gold. . . . Some say that New York crushes them—and not without reason; the individual is overwhelmed by these great buildings. This is not an architecture for men, like the Parthenon or the châteaux of the Loire and Versailles. It is an architecture for human masses. Such buildings do not shelter or isolate men as do those of Europe. They gather and shuffle them. Often more than five thousand persons are united under one roof. . . . The New York skyscrapers are the most striking manifestation of the triumph of numbers. One cannot understand or like them without first having tasted and enjoyed the thrill of counting or adding up enormous totals and of living in a gigantic, compact, and brilliant world.

As cities went upward, they also went outward. The introduction of the automobile launched a great era of suburban building. The 1920's saw the complete emergence of modern residential suburbs and this was reflected in spectacular percentage growth rates during the decade for some of the more famous of them: Beverly Hills, 2485.0, Glendale, 363.5, Inglewood, 492.8, Huntington Park, 444.9 (suburbs of Los Angeles); Cleveland Heights, 234.4, Shaker Heights, 1000.4; Garfield Heights, 511.3 (suburbs of Cleveland); Grosse Pointe Park, 724.6, Ferndale, 689.9 (suburbs of Detroit); Webster Groves, 74.0, Maplewood, 70.3, Richmond Heights, 328.3 (suburbs of St. Louis); Elmwood Park, 716.7, Oak Park, 60.5, Park Ridge, 207.9 (suburbs of Chicago). Numerous new towns and villages appeared around large cities, as demonstrated in the incorporation statistics for the decade. Of the thirty-eight new incorporations in Illinois, twenty-six were located within the metropolitan regions of Chicago or St. Louis; of the thirty-three in Michigan, twenty-two were suburbs of Detroit, and of Ohio's fifty-five incorporations, twenty-nine were near Cleveland. Cities in the 2,500–10,000 bracket showed a rapid growth rate for the period, chiefly because so many of them were located on the fringes of metropolitan areas.

In addition to all their other effects, the urban transportation devices of the twentieth century added new dimensions to one of the oldest economic activities associated with American urbanization —town promotion. No longer could promoters create great cities in the wilderness through the winning of railroads, but they could build highly profitable suburbs on car lines and highways. Early in the century, promotion was tied to the trolley and the interurban railroad, and as in past eras, the activity occurred in all sections of the country. Before the First World War, New Orleans interests, through the able use of trolley lines, built a number of profitable suburbs along the Mississippi River and on the north shore of Lake Pontchartrain. Similar communities sprang up around Shreveport when the Shreveport Railway Company and the Gladstone Realty Company joined their operations. Another Louisiana real estate firm, the Kent Company of Alexandria, gained control of the Alexandria Electric Railway Company and used the line to develop a suburban area. The company provided a typical inducement when it promised free street car rides for three years to anyone who bought a new lot in its subdivision. . . .

In the twentieth century, expansion upward and outward modified the morphology of American cities. In addition the character of urban population and its distribution throughout the areas of the city also changed. The decade of 1900–1910 was the last in which foreign migration contributed substantially to the growth of American cities. In 1907, the high year for the decade, 1,285,349 immigrants arrived in the United States. With the outbreak of war in Europe, the number fell to 326,700 in 1915 and reached a low point of 110,618 in 1919 with European immigration constituting less than 25,000 of this total. Immigration revived in the early 1920's reaching 805,228 in 1921, but the legislation establishing a quota system passed in that year and revised in 1924 reduced

annual immigration to around 300,000 in the years from 1925 to 1929. During the depression of the 1930's it dropped even more drastically and not until 1946 did the annual figure again rise above 100,000.

With immigration from abroad sharply restricted, cities grew largely through internal migration down to the 1940's when the birth rate of urban dwellers began to rise substantially. One of the most significant aspects of this rural-urban migration was the movement of southern Negroes to the cities of the East and Midwest and on a lesser magnitude to the cities of the South. From 1820 to 1910 the urbanization of the white population of the United States had always been at a more rapid rate than that of the Negro. But failures of the cotton crop in the south in 1915 and 1916 and the demand for industrial labor caused by the war reversed this pattern in the next decade, as the percentage of native white population classified as urban increased by six while that of Negroes increased by 6.7. The trend was intensified during the next decade, with the percentage of native white population classified as urban increasing by 4.9 while that of Negroes increased by 9.7. In 1910, eighty-nine per cent of all Negroes lived south of the Mason-Dixon line; as a result of the migrations, by 1930 twenty per cent of the Negro population lived in the North East and Middle West with eighty-eight per cent of this group classified as urban. This was primarily a movement to the larger cities and it continued unabated during the years of depression. Between 1930 and 1940, for example, the Negro population of Chicago increased by more than 43,000, an increase of 18.7 per cent. During the whole period from 1900 to 1950 the percentage of Negroes outside the South increased from ten per cent to thirty-two per cent and the percentage within cities rose from seventeen to forty-eight per cent.

Urbanization of the Negro population modified the social patterns of larger cities. The older ethnic colonies had always contained a fair number of people not of the predominant group. In addition, these colonies had been relatively impermanent with one ethnic group succeeding another in a given area. The Negro colonies in northern cities were much more homogeneous, and, as time proved, much more permanent. Wards in New York and Chicago had percentages of Negro population that approached 95 by 1930. To a large extent cities within cities had been created. "Black Metropolis is the second largest Negro city in the world, only New York's Harlem exceeding it in size," wrote St. Clair Drake and Horace Cayton in their 1945 study of Negro life in Chicago. "It is a city within a city—a narrow tongue of land, seven miles in length and one and one-half miles in width where more than 300,000 Negroes are packed solidly. . . . Walk the streets of the Black Belt and you will find no difference in language to mark its people off from others in the city. Only the black and brown and olive and tan faces of Negro Americans seem to distinguish it from any other section of Midwest Metropolis. But beneath the surface are patterns of life and thought, attitudes and customs, which make Black Metropolis a unique and distinctive city within a city. Understand Chicago's Black Belt and you will understand the Black Belts of a dozen large American cities."

As Drake and Cayton's account so clearly indicated, the Negro ghetto intensified old urban problems. Racial segregation drastically limited the possibility of upward mobility by individual or group. The black metropolises of Chicago, New York, Cleveland, and Detroit were areas where few could benefit from the economic and cultural advantages of the city but where all the long-standing urban problems of crime, poverty, and disease existed in aggravated form.

The urban segregation of the Negro reflected a general tendency to increased economic and cultural segregation in the twentieth century metropolis. The wealthier and more powerful members of the community steadily moved to the outer zones of the city and to the new suburban areas. A study of over 2,000 substantial Detroit families in the early 1930's demonstrated a striking deconcentration of that city's elite. In 1910 nearly fifty-two per cent of this group still lived within a three-mile radius of the main business center of Detroit, and only 9.7 per cent outside the municipal boundaries. By 1930 these percentages were nearly reversed with only 7.5 per cent of the substantial families near the business district and fifty per cent in suburban areas. Numerous studies of economic zones within cities and of spatial zones away from the center made by the urban sociologists of the 1920's and 1930's demonstrated clearly the cultural advantages and the greater stability of the outer regions of metropolitan centers. Crime, the need for public welfare, and infant mortality decreased radically in the outer areas and usually in direct proportion to the distance of the area from the center of the city. In the past, many had resented the city because its extremes of wealth and poverty seemed a denial of American equalitarian beliefs. In the twentieth century metropolis these inequalities appeared more obvious, more rigidly confined, and more permanent.

The rise of the metropolis presented a whole new set of considerations to those concerned with ordering the urban environment. But despite the complexity of the twentieth-century super-city and its tremendous influence on society, much of the debate about the city in America was still conducted in terms of the old country-city polarity. The effort to restrict foreign immigration, the crusade for religious fundamentalism, the prohibition movement, and the election of 1928 were aspects of national history influenced by the traditional defense of the values of the country and the traditional attack on the values of the city. People could still accept at face value the famous photograph of President Calvin Coolidge seated on a hay wagon with rake in hand, his clothes spotless, while in the rear his assistants stand by an automobile waiting to whisk him back to the city. Writers of popular fiction in the twenties and thirties still employed the nineteenth-century imagery of the soulless city. To find "real values" one had to flee the city. "I have had to do many things, terrible things, things no decent man should have done," says a hero of a 1925 *Cosmopolitan* short story who finds peace in the wilderness. "Thank God that's all behind me now. Out here I can be a real person again." On a higher level, twelve southerners in their notable manifesto *I'll Take My Stand*, published in 1929, defended an idyllic rural life that probably never existed. "Back to the land," a position popularized by Ralph Borsodi who established a subsistence homestead outside New York City in 1920 and preached the virtues of the Thoreauvian way of life, became an organized movement that influenced federal policy during the depression of the thirties. Its disciples offered a classical Jeffersonian defense of the agrarian ideal. "The farms have always produced our great leaders in finance, industry and statesmanship," a witness testified before a House committee in the early 1930's. "The vast population must depart from the congested industrial centers and cities and once again become self-sus-

taining on our vast and fertile farms, pasture, and prairie lands. Herein lies the real hope for the bright destiny of America."

Despite the persistence of these old ideals, many thinkers and reformers abandoned the simple notion of country versus city and began to develop new conceptions of the social environment that emphasized the community, the neighborhood, the region. The old problems that had special urban dimensions —health, poverty, and the slum—had not disappeared, and housing the poor of the cities continued to be one of the principal concerns of urban reformers. But the complexity of the new metropolitan communities forced consideration of ways of reordering the whole urban environment. Proposals for new kinds of cities and for comprehensive plans that encompassed whole urban regions now became part of the discussion of the future of American cities. Writing in 1922, Lewis Mumford, who was to become one of the better known students of urban civilization, reflected the urgency of the new point of view: "Our metropolitan civilization is not a success. It is a different kind of wilderness . . . but the feral rather than the humane quality is dominant; it is still a wilderness. The cities of America must learn to remould our mechanical and financial regime; for if metropolitanism continues they are probably destined to fall by its weight."

As had so often been the case in the past the inspiration for new ways of dealing with urban problems came from Europe. Particularly influential was the Garden City idea of Ebenezer Howard, a London court reporter and reformer. Drawing on the nineteenth century British tradition of community planning, which had earlier influenced American experiments, Howard proposed a new kind of community that he hoped would combine the best features of town and country. The size of the Garden City would be limited to 30,000 people. A permanent greenbelt would surround it, and enough industry would be developed in carefully specified areas to ensure the community's self-sufficiency. The land on which the city was built would be owned by the community as a whole and administered by a public authority. All leases would contain specific and detailed building requirements and areas of greenery would be preserved throughout the city. The profits of growth would go to the community rather than to the speculator, since only limited dividends could be paid to the original investors in a Garden City project. This would also ensure that there would be no temptation to modify land use or increase the planned density of the city. Howard foresaw Garden Cities being founded throughout England, providing a way of checking the continued growth of the huge, congested industrial cities. The successful establishment of the first Garden City of Letchworth, England, begun in 1903, led to a world-wide Garden City movement; interest was reinforced by the start of a second community called Welwyn in 1919. Letchworth and Welwyn were the only two cities built in accord with Howard's overall plan, but his ideas influenced a number of American planners and architects. Although they seldom embodied the significant aspects of Howard's conceptions of a new kind of community, "garden villages," "garden suburbs," and "garden homes"

became the fashion of the day after about 1910.

Forest Hills Gardens on Long Island, financed by the Russell Sage Foundation and designed by Frederick Law Olmsted, Jr., was completed in 1911, and the project, though it became simply a suburb for well-to-do commuters, demonstrated the possibilities in carefully planned housing developments. Many of the conceptions that were part of Garden City and other plans for new-style towns and cities were initially applied by businessmen who were not unduly concerned with creating a good community but who foresaw large real estate profits. The term "garden city" was often used to describe any planned new community that preserved a natural setting; the Van Sweringens in promoting Shaker Heights utilized the appeal of Howard's conception. Torrance, California—one of several of the small planned suburban industrial communities developed in the early years of the century—was labelled by its founder, the industrialist Jared Sidney Torrance, as the "greatest and best of the garden cities of the world." In 1914 the limited-dividend principle, which had been a fundamental part of Howard's plan, was employed in the development of a suburban area of Boston called the "garden suburb" of Billerica. Nowhere, however, was more than a portion of Howard's plan utilized during this first period of enthusiasm; often in the 1920's, "garden city" became a description of any suburban housing project.

THE CITY IN RECENT HISTORY

Mitchell Gordon

The world's population has increased from 250 million at the time of Christ to about 3.5 billion today and may reach 6 billion by A.D. 2000. The population of the United States is now in excess of 200 million and should exceed 300 million by the year 2000. By 1980 over 90 per cent of all Americans will be living in urban areas. The surge to the cities is also taking place in other countries of the world. The diseases of urban sprawl include clogged streets, impossible public transit, blight, pollution of air and water, crime, poor education, neglect of community facilities, and inadequate governmental authority and understanding. It is easy to see that the problems will become more complex unless corrective measures are soon taken.

It took sixteen and a half centuries for the population of the world to double, from approximately 250 million at the time of Christ to an estimated 500 million when Cromwell was ascending to the rule of Britain in the mid-seventeenth century. It took only two centuries to double again; the total came to one billion in 1850. The next doubling took but eighty years; the figure was two billion by 1930. It will take half that time—some forty years—to double the 1962 figure; population prognosticators place the total at six billion around A.D. 2000.

The United States is expected to grow at about the average global rate; the 180 million people it had at the time of the 1960 census should exceed 360 million by the year 2000. Some states, of course, will surge ahead even more rapidly. California will have to make room by 1980 for as many people again as it had in 1960, though it was already the most populous state in the nation by 1963.

The population density of the thirteen former colonies in 1790 was 4.5 persons per square mile. That same territory today contains close to 700 persons per square mile.

If present population trends continue, the day will come when there is "standing room only" in America. In 800 years, an average of only one square foot of space would be available for each person in the nation.

Children born after 1956 who live out their normal life expectancies can expect to see the United States a nation of 400 million people. The country had just under 100 million people as recently as 1915.

Metropolitan New York gives birth to a city roughly the size of Norfolk, Virginia, every year. New York City and its bedroom communities in northeastern New Jersey counted 300,000 births in 1960. Norfolk, with just under 305,000 people in 1960, was the 41st largest city in the United States at the time—bigger than Miami, Omaha, or Akron.

By 1980, over 90 percent of the

Reprinted with permission of The Macmillan Company from *Sick Cities* by Mitchell Gordon, pp. 15–22. © by Mitchell Gordon, 1963.

American people will be living in urban areas. The figure in 1920 was exactly 51.2 percent. In 1962 it was just under 70 percent.

Five metropolitan areas accounted for 20 percent of the nation's total population in 1960. One out of every five Americans then lived in either greater New York, Chicago, Los Angeles, Philadelphia, or Detroit.

At the time of the first United States census, in 1790, the largest city in the land, Philadelphia, had but 44,000 persons. New York was the new nation's second largest city with 33,000 inhabitants, Boston, which ranked third, had only 18,000. Levittown, New York, which didn't exist before World War II, was nearly 50 percent larger in 1960 than the country's biggest city was in 1790. Levittown had over 65,000 inhabitants at the time of the 1960 census.

Despite the many detractors of suburban life and the massive effort to renew city cores, the nation's speediest growth is expected to continue to take place in the suburbs. The United States suburban population is expected to triple between 1960 and 1980 while the population for the nation as a whole climbs less than 50 percent. In the decade to 1960, suburban populations increased 56 percent while the nation's largest cities rose less than 5 percent. Chicago's suburban population, which was only slightly smaller than the city's in 1960, is expected to be nearly twice as great as the city's in 1990. Among the nation's three largest cities, only New York will be entering the 1970's with most of its daytime work force still resident within its city limits.

The nation's major metropolises thus are turning into urban dinosaurs. They may prove just as ungainly.

The surge to the city will be even greater in some of the world's underdeveloped countries than in the United States. Urban-growth rates in parts of

Asia in the early 1960's were running 400 percent higher than those in the West, and the movement to cities on that great land mass obviously has only just begun.

Only ten cities in the world had populations in excess of one million persons in 1900. More than 60 did in 1962.

Athens is finding congestion almost as formidable a foe as Sparta was. The Greek architect and city planner, Dr. Constantine A. Doxiadis, is an expert in that country who believes the crush of cars and population is making the city untenable as the nation's capital. A number of alternative sites have been suggested, including Pella in northern Greece, a city that served as the capital of Macedon in the time of Alexander the Great. Development of a solid city stretching the entire length of the nation's east coast, from Athens in the south to Salonika in the north, is seen within a century.

In fact, Dr. Doxiadis believes a "universal" city may be covering the entire surface of the earth not very long thereafter. "Ecumenopolis," as he calls it, may come to pass before the year 2100, says he. Sound incredible? Then consider the probable effect among Americans of George Washington's time of a prediction that within two hundred years the United States Census Bureau would be defining the entire region from southern New Hampshire to northern Virginia as a single metropolitan area. In 1960 it was doing exactly that.

*

As they burgeon, foreign cities are likely to look more and more like American cities, particularly Los Angeles. The resemblance may be caused more by the automobile as a way of life in itself than by closer communications, even with the growing influence of television, the internationalization of the cinema, and the commuter touch that jet airliners give global travel. Cities shaped by the automobile, which both requires space and makes more space accessible, are bound to look increasingly alike whether the chisel bears a Volkswagen or a Buick brand. The Germans already have a word for their sprawl: *Randgemeinden.*

*

The diseases of sprawl, similarly, are likely to grow more universal. Dr. Luther Gulick, Chairman of the Institute of Public Administration, defines them thusly:

Clogged streets

Dying public transit

Spreading blight

Increasing air and water pollution

Growing lawlessness

Diverging educational opportunities

Neglect of park space and other community facilities, such as libraries

A sorely felt lack of comprehensive governmental institutions necessary for mustering fiscal and political support for the community's "most elemental" requirements. . . .

*

Or are cities themselves the disease? Lewis Mumford, in *The Culture of Cities,* indicated a good many seemed to be. He saw the metropolis as an accumulation of people accommodating themselves "to an environment without adequate natural or cultural resources: people who do without pure air, who do without sound sleep, who do without a cheerful garden or playing space, who do without the very sight of the sky and the sunlight, who do without free

motion, spontaneous play, or a robust sexual life. The so-called blighted areas of the metropolis," says he, "are essentially '*do without*' areas. If you wish the sight of urban beauty while living in these areas, you must ride in a bus a couple of miles (nowadays a car, for many more miles); if you wish a touch of nature, you must travel in a crowded train to the outskirts of the city. Lacking the means to get out, you succumb; chronic starvation produces lack of appetite. Eventually," he warns, "you may live and die without even recognizing the loss."

*

"Men come together in cities," said Aristotle, "in order to live. They remain together in order to live the good life."

In many cities today, men come together principally to earn a living—and get out of it as quickly as they can, tortuously if necessary, in order to enjoy the pleasures that Aristotle might easily have taken for granted in his day: clean air, refuge from noise and crowds, a patch of earth and a glimpse of sky.

*

Cost of living trends, to be meaningful, are adjusted for inflationary factors. Trends in living standards, to be meaningful in an urban environment, must similarly be adjusted for "congestionary" factors. The difference between the Model T Ford and the modern automobile does not consist in physical differences alone but in their abilities to accomplish what their owners expect them to accomplish. The fact that the penalties of congestion do not readily lend themselves to computation does not make them any less real. Progress against congestion may thus be regarded in the same light as the development of a new engine with greater power and gas economy. It accomplishes the same thing and something more.

*

The *Saturday Evening Post* in an editorial in 1961 called sprawl "perhaps our cruelest misuse of land since our soil mining days. Urban sprawl," it went on to state, "is not the growth of cities. Instead, the cities are disintegrating and spreading the pieces over miles and miles of countryside."

Robert Moses, responsible for so many of Gotham's public achievements in the present century, takes the opposite point of view in an article in the *Atlantic Monthly:* "The prosperous suburbanite," says he, "is as proud of his ranch home as the owner of the most gracious villa of Tuscany. The little identical suburban boxes of average people, which differ only in color and planting, represent a measure of success unheard of by hundreds of millions on other continents."

Sprawl in itself is perhaps not the evil any more than the automobile, in itself, is.

*

In 1959, on the occasion of its twenty-fifth anniversary, the National Planning Association, a nonprofit group with a wide range of interests in business and government, mapped a program of essential urban projects it felt should be carried out over a five-year period. The cost of its program averaged $60 billion a year—considerably above the $46 billion then being spent per annum by the federal government on national security programs of all types. The N.P.A. figured $100 billion would be needed in that five-year period for slum clearance, $75 billion to alleviate traffic congestion and make roads safer, $60 billion for cleaning up and conserving the nation's water resources, $35 billion for hospital and health needs, and at least $30 billion for improving educational facilities, reducing delinquency, and a host of other purposes.

Those concerned with the idleness that global disarmament might impose have only to contemplate those figures.

*

With all but 10 percent of the nation's population headed for city living within the foreseeable future, efforts to improve the nation's urban environment become highly pertinent in the peacetime competition between the free and the Communist world. The way Americans live at home inevitably will affect the nation's prestige abroad. In addition, the nation's economic efficiency is bound up in its urban condition. Unless nuclear war brings wholesale destruction first, the city cannot help but serve as the proving ground for rival ways of life.

John Kenneth Galbraith, the brilliant Harvard economist and author who became United States Ambassador to India in the Kennedy Administration, puts it this way in his book *The Liberal Hour:* "There are three weaknesses of our society which are gravely damaging to our reputation and prestige at large and which cast a dark reflection on the quality of our society. The first of these," says he, "is the unhinged and disorderly quality of our urban society and the consequent squalor, delinquency and crime."

Senator Joseph Clark, Pennsylvania Democrat, told the United States Senate in 1960 that the cities "are our greatest source of economic strength. In many ways, our national welfare is dependent upon their continued efficiency as instruments of production in our economy."

Says Dr. Gulick in the *National Civic Review* of December, 1960: "Our strength, our culture, our self-respect, our influence in the world, can never rise above our achievements here in the United States; we cannot win in the world on the foundation of defeats at home."

WHERE ARE WE GOING IF ANYWHERE?
A LOOK AT POST-CIVILIZATION

Kenneth E. Boulding

Professor Boulding gives us a perceptive look into contemporary society by analyzing three periods of the history of man: pre-civilization, civilization, and post civilization. He warns of three possible traps into which modern man may fall and thus down himself. These three—the war trap, the population trap, and the technological trap—serve as an effective focus for a study of man today.

We are living in what I call the second great change in the state of man. The first great change is the change from pre-civilized to civilized societies. The first 500,000 years or so of man's existence on earth were relatively uneventful. Compared with his present condition he puttered along in an astonishingly stationary state. To judge by his artifacts, at least, generation succeeded generation with the sons exactly like their fathers, and the daughters exactly like their mothers. There may have been changes in language and culture which are not reflected in the artifacts, but if there were these changes are lost to us. The evidence of the artifacts, however, is conclusive. Whatever changes there were, they were almost unbelievably slow. About 10,000 years ago, we begin to perceive an acceleration in the rate of change. This becomes very noticeable 5,000 years ago with the development of the first civilization. The details of this first great change are probably beyond our recovery. However, we do know that it depended on two phenomena: the first was the development of agriculture, and the second was the development of exploitation. These two great inventions seem to have developed about the same time, perhaps independently—although we do not know this—in the Nile valley, in the lower valley of the Euphrates, and in the valley of the Indus. Agriculture, that is the domestication of crops and livestock and the planting of crops in fields, gave man a secure surplus of food from the food producer. In a hunting and fishing economy it seems to take the food producer all his time to produce enough food for himself and his family. The moment we have agriculture with its superior productivity of this form of employment of human resources means that the food producer can produce more food than he and his family can eat. But this in itself is not enough to produce civilization. In some societies in these happy conditions, the

From *Human Organization*, Vol. 21, No. 2, 1962, pp. 162–167. Copyright 1962, The Society for Applied Anthropology. Reprinted with permission of the author and publisher.

food producer has simply relaxed and indulged himself with leisure. As soon, however, as we get politics, that is exploitation, we begin to get cities and civilization. Civilization, it is clear from the origin of the word, is what happens in cities, and the city is dependent in its early stages at any rate on there being a food surplus from the food producer and on there being some organization which can take it away from him. With this food surplus, the political organization feeds kings, priests, armies, architects, and builders and the city comes into being. Political science in its earliest form is the knowledge of how to take the food surplus away from the food producer without giving him very much in return.

Now I argue that we are in the middle, perhaps not even in the middle, of the second great change in the state of man, which is as drastic and as dramatic, and certainly as large if not larger, as the change from pre-civilized to civilized society. This I call the change from civilization to post-civilization. It is a strange irony that just at the moment when civilization has almost completed the conquest of pre-civilized societies, post-civilization has been treading heavily upon its heels. The student of civilization may soon find himself in the unfortunate position of the anthropologist who studies pre-civilized societies. Both are like the student of ice on a hot day—the subject matter melts away almost before he can study it.

These great changes can be thought of as a change of gear in the evolutionary process, resulting in progressive accelerations of the rate of evolutionary change. Even before the appearance of man on the earth, we can detect earlier evolutionary gear-shiftings. The formation of life obviously represented one such transition, the movement from the water to the land represented another, the development of the vertebrates

another, and so on. Man himself represents a very large acceleration of the evolutionary process. Whether he evolved from pre-existing forms or whether he landed from a space ship and was not able to get back to where he came from, is immaterial. Once he had arrived on earth, the process of evolution could go on within the confines of the human nervous system at a greatly accelerated rate. The human mind is an enormous mutation-selection process. Instead of the mutation-selection process being confined, as it were, to the flesh, it can take place within the image and hence, very rapid changes are possible. Man seems to have been pretty slow to exploit this potentiality, but one suspects that even with primitive man, the rate of change in the biosphere was much larger than it had been before, because of the appearance of what de Chardin calls the nöosphere, or sphere of knowledge.

Civilization represents a further acceleration of the rate of change, mainly because one of the main products of civilization is history. With the food surplus from agriculture it becomes possible to feed specialized scribes. With the development of writing, man did not have to depend on the uncertain memories of the aged for its records, and a great process of accumulation of social knowledge began. The past can now communicate, at least in one direction, with the present, and this enormously increases the range and possibility of enlargements of the contents of the human mind.

Out of civilization, however, comes science, which is a superior way of organizing the evolution of knowledge. We trace the first beginnings of science, of course, almost as far back as the beginning of civilization itself. Beginning about 1650, however, we begin to see the organization of science into a community of knowledge, and this leads again to an enormous acceleration of the rate of change. The world of 1650 is more remote to us than the world of ancient Egypt or Samaria would have been to the man of 1650. Already in the United States and Western Europe, in a smaller degree in Russia and in some other parts of the world, we see the beginnings of post-civilized society —a state of man as different from civilization as civilization is from savagery. What we really mean, therefore, by the anemic term "economic development" is the second great transition in the state of man. It is the movement from civilized to post-civilized society. It is nothing short of a major revolution in the human condition, and it does not represent a mere continuance and development of the old patterns of civilization.

As a dramatic illustration of the magnitude of the change, we can contemplate Indonesia. This is a country which has about the same extent, population, and per capita income as the Roman Empire at its height. For all I know it is producing a literature and an art at least comparable to that of the Augustan age. It is, therefore, a very good example of a country of high civilization. Because of this fact, it is one of the poorest countries in the world. It is very unhappy about its present state and visualizes itself as a poor country and it is desperately anxious to break out of its present condition. Jakarta is a city about the size of ancient Rome, although perhaps a little less splendid. All this points up the fact that the Roman Empire was a desperately poor and underdeveloped society, with a civilization that existed always on a shoe-string. The Roman cities seemed to have been always within about three weeks of starvation, and even at its height it is doubtful whether the Roman empire ever had less than 75–80 percent of its population in agriculture.

Civilization, that is, a state of society in which techniques are so poor that it takes about 80 percent of the population to feed the 100 percent. But we do have about 20 percent of the people who can be spared from food producing to build Parthenons, and cathedrals, to write literature and poetry, and to fight wars. By contrast, in the United States today we are rapidly getting to the point where we can produce all our food with only 10 percent of the population and still have large agricultural surpluses. But for the blessings of agricultural policy, we might soon be able to produce all our food with 5 percent of the population. It may even be that agriculture is on its way out altogether and within another generation or so we can produce our food in a totally different way. Perhaps both fields and cows are merely relics of civilization, the vestiges of a vanishing age. This means, however, that even in our society, which is at a very early stage of post-civilization, we can now spare about 90 percent of the people to produce bath-tubs, automobiles, and H-bombs, and all the other luxuries and conveniences of life. Western Europe and Japan are coming along behind the United States very fast. The Russians, likewise are advancing towards post-civilization, although by a very different road. At the moment their ideology is a handicap to them in some places—especially in agriculture, where they still have 45 percent of the people. Even this, however, is a lot better than ancient Rome. And, if the Russians ever discovered that super-peasants are a good deal more efficient than collective farms, they may cut away some of the ideology that hangs around their neck and move even more rapidly toward post-civilized society.

I am not at all sure what post-civilization will look like and, indeed, I suspect there will be several varieties of it. But it will certainly be radically different from the civilized society which it is displacing. It will certainly be a world-wide society. Until very recently each civilized society was a little island in a sea of barbarism which constantly threatened to overwhelm it. Civilization is haunted by the spectre of decline and fall, although it is note-worthy that in spite of the rise and fall of particular civilizations, civilization itself expanded steadily in geographical coverage from its very beginnings. We must face the fact, however, that post-civilized society will be worldwide, if only because of its ease of communication and transportation. I flew last year from Idlewild to Brussels, and on glimpsing the new Brussels Airport out of the corner of my eye, I thought for a moment we had come back and landed at Idlewild again. I had for a moment a horrifying vision of a world in which we went faster and faster to places which were more and more like the places we left behind, until in the end of the process we flew at infinite speed to a place that was identical with what we left behind, and we might as well have stayed home. For the first time in history there is now a world style, at least in airports, which is a symbol of the coming post-civilization. We see this in art, in architecture, in music, in literature, and in all fields of life. What in Europe looks like Americanization, in America looks like Japanification. It is simply the creeping onset of post-civilized style.

The great problem of our age, however, is the disintegration of the institutions of civilization under the impact of advancing post-civilization. The characteristic institutions of civilization are, as we have seen, first agriculture, then the city, then war, in the sense of clash of organized armed forces, and finally, inequality, the sharp contrast between the rich and the poor, between the city and the country, between the urbane and the rustic. In classical civili-

zation both birth and death rates average about forty per thousand, the expectation of life at birth is about twenty-five years. The state is based very fundamentally on violence and exploitation, and the culture tends to be spiritually monolithic, with a single church, or spiritual power perpetuating its doctrines because of its monopoly of the educational processes of transmission of the culture.

In post-civilization all these institutions suffer radical change. Agriculture, as we have seen, diminishes until it is a small proportion of the society, the city, likewise, in the classical sense, disintegrates. Los Angeles is perhaps the first example of the post-civilization, post-urban agglomeration—under no stretch of the imagination could it be called a city. War, likewise, is an institution in process of disintegration. National defense as a social system has quite fundamentally broken down on a world scale. The ICBM and the nuclear warhead has made the nation-state as militarily obsolete as the city-state, for in no country now can the armed forces preserve an area of internal peace by pushing violence to the outskirts. Poverty and inequality, likewise, are tending to disappear, at least on their classical scale. Post-civilized society is an affluent society and it produces large quantities of goods, even though it may fall rather short on services. It is a society furthermore in which the technology almost prohibits great inequalities in consumption. In civilized societies the king or the emperor could live in a Versailles and the peasant in a hovel. In post-civilized society, the proletariat disappears, everybody becomes at least middle-class, and when the product mix of the economy consists of automobiles, mass-produced clothing, domestic appliances, and the pre-fabricated homes, it is almost impossible for the rich to consume on a scale which is more, let us say, than ten times that of the poor. There is no sense in having more than ten automobiles!

Another profound change in the passage from civilization to post-civilization is the change in the expectation of life. In civilized society, as we have seen, birth and death rates tend to be about forty per thousand and the expectation of life at birth is twenty-five years. In post-civilized society the expectation of life at birth rises at least to seventy and perhaps beyond. At the moment we do not have the knowledge or techniques for prolonging the expectation of life much beyond seventy. We do not know, however, what lies in the future. It may be that we are on the edge of a biological revolution, just as dramatic and far-reaching as the discovery of atomic energy and that we may crack the problem of aging and prolong human life much beyond its present span. Whether or not, however, we go forward to Methuselah, the mere increase of the average age of death to seventy is a startling and far-reaching change. It means, for instance, that in an equilibrium population, the birth and death rate cannot be more than about fourteen-per-thousand. This unquestionably implies some form of conscious control of births and of the number of children per family. It means also a radical change in the age distribution of population, with a much larger proportion of the population in later years.

There are, unquestionably, going to be many varieties of post-civilization and some are going to be more unpleasant than others. It is perfectly possible to paint an anti-utopia in which a post-civilized society appears as universally vulgar, or even universally dull. On the whole, however, I welcome post-civilization and I have really very little affection for civilization. In most pre-civilized societies the fact that the life of man is for the most part nasty, brut-

ish, and short, does not prevent the poets and philosophers from sentimentalizing about the noble savage. Similarly we may expect the same kind of sentimentalizing about the noble Romans and civilized survivals like Winston Churchill. On the whole, though, I will not shed any tears over the grave of civilization any more than I will over pre-civilized society. Post-civilization is a realization of man's potential. On the whole its credit balance is large. It at least gives us a chance of a modest utopia, in which slavery, poverty, exploitation, gross inequality, war, and disease—these prime costs of civilization—will fall to the vanishing point. Neither the disappearance of the classical city nor the disappearance of the peasant fill me with much sorrow. Even in post-civilized society, of course, we can have cities of a kind, if we want to. We may even find culture cities in which vehicular traffic is prohibited and in which the rich indulge in the costly luxury of walking. In the meantime the masses will live scattered about the surface of the earth, commuting occasionally to quasi-automatic factories and offices, or will snuggle down with three dimensional T.V. at the end of the day.

Modest as these visions of utopia may be, there is no guarantee that we will reach them. The second great transition may be under way, but there is no guarantee that it will be accomplished. What we have at the moment is a chance to make this transition—a chance which is probably unique in the history of this planet. If we fail, the chance will probably not be repeated in this part of the universe. Whatever experiments may be going on elsewhere, the present moment indeed is unique in the whole four billion years of the history of the planet. In my more pessimistic moments, I think the chance is a slim one, and it may be that man will be written off as an unsuccessful experiment. We must, therefore, look at the traps which lie along the path of the transition, which might prevent us from making it altogether.

The most urgent trap is, of course, the trap of war. War, as I have suggested is an institution peculiarly characteristic of civilization. Pre-civilized societies have sporadic feuding and raiding, but they do not generally have permanently organized armed forces, and they do not generally develop conquest and empire; or if they do, they soon pass into a civilized form. An armed force is essentially a mobile city designed to throw things at another mobile or stationary city with presumably evil intent. As far as I know, not more than two or three civilizations have existed without war. The Mayans and the people of Mohenjodaro seem to have lived for fairly long periods without war, but this was an accident of their monopolistic situation and they unquestionably occupied themselves with other kinds of foolishness. If pre-civilized society, however, cannot afford war, post-civilized society can afford far too much of it, and hence will be forced to get rid of the institution because it is simply inappropriate to the technological age. The breakdown in the world social system of national defense really dates from about 1949, when the United States lost its monopoly of nuclear weapons. A system of national defense is only feasible if each nation is stronger than its enemies at home, so that it can preserve a relatively large area of peace within its critical boundaries. Such a system is only possible, however, if the range of the deadly missile is short and if the armed forces of each nation lose power rapidly as they move away from home. The technological developments of the twentieth century have destroyed these foundations of national defense, and have replaced it with another social system altogether which is "deterrence." . . .

Even if we avoid the war trap, we may still fall into the population trap. Population control is an unsolved problem even for the developed areas of the world, which have moved the furthest toward post-civilization. We have not developed any social institutions which can adequately deal with the establishment of an equilibrium of population. An equilibrium of population in a stable post-civilized society may represent a fairly radical interference with ancient human institutions and freedoms. In a stable post-civilized society, as I have suggested, the birth and death rates must be of the order of fourteen per thousand, and the average number of children per family cannot much exceed two. There are many social institutions which might accomplish this end. So far, however, the only really sure-fire method of controlling population is starvation and misery. Insofar as this is true, the Malthusian spectre still broods over us.

In many parts of the world—indeed, for most of the human race for the moment—the impact of certain post-civilized techniques of civilized society has produced a crisis of growth, which may easily be fatal. In the tropics especially with DDT and a few simple public health measures it is easy to reduce the death rate to nine or ten per thousand, at the same time that the birth rate stays up at forty per thousand. This means an annual increase of population of three percent per annum, almost all of it concentrated in the lower age groups. We see this phenomenon dramatically in places like the West Indies, Ceylon, and Formosa; but thanks to the activity of the world health organization, it is taking place rapidly all over the tropical world. It is not the ultimate Malthusian equilibrium which is the problem here, but the strain which is put on the society by the very rapid growth of population, a rate of growth without precedent in history. Perhaps the most important key to the transition to post-civilization is heavy investment in human resources—that is in education. The conquest of disease and infant mortality, however, before the corresponding adjustment to the birth rate, produces enormous cohorts or children in societies which do not have the resources to educate them—especially as those in the middle-age groups, who after all must do all the work of a society, come from the much smaller cohorts of the pre-DDT era. There is an uncomfortable analogy here to 2-4-D, the hormone which kills plants by making them grow too rapidly. At the moment the human race is heading for monumental disasters in many parts of the world. The population disaster is perhaps retrievable in the sense that it may be confined to certain parts of the world and may simply delay the spread of post-civilization in these areas, without seriously threatening the transition in the already developed areas.

Even in the developed countries, however, population control presents a very serious problem. The United States, for instance, at the moment is increasing in population even more rapidly than India. The time when we thought that the mere increase in income would automatically solve the population problem has gone by. In the United States, and certain other societies, in the early stages of post-civilization, the child has become an object of conspicuous domestic consumption. The consumption patterns of the American spending unit seem to follow a certain *gestalt* in which household capital accumulates in a certain order such as the first car, the first child, the washer and dryer, the second child, the deep freeze, the third child,

the second car, the fourth child, and so on. The richer we get, the more children we can afford to have at least on current income and the more children we do have. We now seem to be able to afford an average of something like four children per family, and as in a post-civilized society, these four children all survive, the population doubles every generation. A hundred years of this and even the United States is going to find itself uncomfortably crowded. It can be argued, indeed, that from the point of view of the amenities of life we are already well beyond the optimum population. One sees this clearly in California, which was a much more agreeable place thirty years ago than it is today. When the United States gets to have a billion people, which we could easily have in less than a hundred years, its standards of life may be substantially reduced.

My only positive contribution to this problem is the suggestion that everyone should come into the world with a license to have just one child. A market can then be organized in these licenses and people who wish to be childless can sell their licenses to the philoprogenitive for a price determined by supply and demand. Nobody, I may add, has taken the suggestion very seriously up till now.

The third trap on the road to post-civilization is the technological trap. Our present technology is fundamentally suicidal. It is based on the extraction of concentrated deposits of fossil fuels and ores, which in the nature of things are exhaustible. Even at present rates of consumption they will be exhausted in a time span which is not very long, even measured against human history and which is infinitesimally small on the geological time scale. If the rest of the world advances to American standards of consumption, these resources will disappear almost overnight. Economic development, it appears is the process of bringing closer the evil day when everything will be gone—all the oil, all the coal, all the ores—and we will have to go back to primitive agriculture and scratching in the woods.

There are indications, however, that suicidal technology is not absolutely necessary and that a permanent high-level technology is possible. Beginning in the early part of the twentieth century it is possible to detect an anti-entropic movement in technology. This begins perhaps with the Haber process for the fixation of nitrogen from the air. A development of similar significance is the Dow process for the extraction of magnesium from the sea. Both these processes are anti-entropic. They take the diffuse and concentrate it, instead of taking the concentrated and diffusing it, as do most processes of mining and economic production. Sir William Crookes in the last years of the nineteenth century predicted that we would all be starving by the middle of the twentieth century because of the exhaustion of Chilean nitrates. This prediction was fortunately falsified by the Haber process. These anti-entropic processes foreshadow a technology in which we shall draw all the materials we need from the virtually inexhaustible reservoirs of the sea and the air and draw our energy from controlled fusion—either artificially produced on the earth or from the sun.

It may even be that the major consequence of space research will be the development of a more self-subsistent high technology on earth. From a strictly economic point of view I suspect space is not even for the birds. It seems to be remarkably empty of economic goods. The technology necessary to send man into space, however, may be much the same technology that will enable him to manage his own larger space ship, the good planet earth, with a true high-level husbandry. One can perhaps even visualize the almost completely self-sufficient household of the future living in a kind of grounded space-ship in which the water circulates endlessly through the kidneys and the algae, the protein and carbohydrates likewise. The power comes from solar batteries on the roof and the food from the algae tanks and man, thereby, greatly reduces the scale of the circulation in the midst of which he has to live. In this happy day everyone will live under his own vine and his own fig tree and presumably none shall make them afraid. This may be a long way off, or it may be closer than we think. It is clear, however, that a fundamental technological transition is still to be accomplished.

Beyond these three traps one sees a distant fourth trap—the trap of inanition. Man is a profoundly problem-solving animal. He reacts best to situations of challenge and difficulty. If he succeeds in solving the problems which now so thoroughly possess him, will he not in the very moment of his success die of sheer boredom? Our answers to this question must depend on our view of man's capabilities; but even here there is evidence, I think, in his religious life that he might survive even heaven. This is a problem, however, that I am prepared to let future generations take care of when they come to it. The business of our generation is more immediate. . . .

What we have to do now, however, is to develop almost a new form of learning. We have to learn from rapidly changing systems. Ordinarily we learn from stable systems. It is because the world repeats itself that we catch on to the law of repetition. Learning from changing systems is perhaps another step in the acceleration of evolution that we have to take. I have been haunted by a remark which Norman Meier, the psychologist, made in a seminar a few months ago, when he said that a cat who jumps on a hot stove never jumps on a cold one. I believe the remark may originally be attributed to Mark Twain. This seems precisely to describe the state we may be in today. We have jumped on a lot of hot stoves and now perhaps the cold stove is the only place on which to jump. In the rapidly changing system it is desperately easy to learn things which are no longer true. Perhaps the greatest task of applied social science, therefore, at the moment is to study the conditions under which we learn from rapidly changing systems. If we can answer this question, then there may still be hope for the human race.

PART I

QUESTIONS FOR DISCUSSION

1. Why did people choose to live in cities? Are these reasons valid today?
2. Contrast the pre-industrial city with today's city. What are the significant differences? How are they alike?
3. What major changes have occurred in our cities during this century?
4. What has been the historical development of your community? What principal features fostered its growth?

VOCABULARY

feudal	millennium
lineage	demographic
kinship	itinerant
division of labor	familial
heterogeneous	acculturation
agrarian	megalopolis
conjugal	agglomeration
parasitic	

THE CITY TODAY

Life in the city today is not the beautiful experience that it once was when populations were much smaller and the problems were fewer and much less complex. As the populations grew, the cities became more crowded and city life became less satisfying. Technology has played a major share in destroying the once placid community that was the city. The development of the automobile provided the means of escaping from the city environment in hopes of arranging one's life in more pleasant surroundings. The upgrading of one's economic status provided opportunity for the city dwellers to purchase a home in suburbia and commute to work in the city.

Those left behind in the city now fall into two quite distinct groups: one comfortable and possessing a full bounty of material things, the other living in abject poverty so debilitating that it destroys mind and body, leaving no hope of escape. Residents of our large cities today are faced with very difficult problems, many of which seem almost impossible to solve. Among these difficulties are the unemployed and the underemployed, crowded living conditions, structural decay, racial minorities and severe discrimination, welfare loads so large that the cities cannot handle them, heavy tax burdens, absence of aesthetic beauty, a high and ever increasing crime rate, poor transportation facilities, complete apathy on the part of many people, and even the possibility that the cities are too large and complex to be governed. In the minds of some, the question arises as to whether the cities can be saved or are even worth saving.

The city no longer retains the dominant position it once held. The large shopping complexes on the outskirts of cities now provide ample parking spaces for private automobiles and a full range of shops where all purchases can be made. Apartment complexes, hotels, and motels have followed the trend to the suburbs, thus lessening the opportunities for work in the central city.

Many of the difficulties of the city have come about because there has been, in most cases, no overall plan for proper growth. New sections have been built on the edge of cities; maybe they fitted in well with the existing city layout but probably not. It is becoming increasingly clear that the planning must be of superb quality and it must be complete if we are to end up with cities that are satisfying to man's needs and desires. Perhaps there is an upper limit to the number of people that can be included within a city and still retain those conditions that man feels are required for a satisfying environment. Our large cities may have already become oversized.

One refreshing approach has come about in the last few years—the planning and construction of complete cities from raw virgin land for the accommodation of a maximum number of inhabitants. The planning for these new cities has been done in great detail. Park Forest, Illinois; Reston, Virgina; and Columbia, Maryland are the prime examples of this bold new approach. While it is too early to give the complete answer as to the degree of success this approach will provide, it does look very promising at this time. In a later selection, the builder of Columbia describes in much detail how that city was planned from the dream-stage to completion. If this project is successful, it will provide a blueprint for the future.

The cities today are overcrowded and to jam even more into them will only further complicate the present problems. It is estimated that by the end of this century our population will be approximately 90 per cent urban. Where are we going to put the extra people? If our population is to increase by another 100 million by the year 2000 then perhaps we should plan and construct new cities, separate and distinct from existing ones, to accommodate a maximum of 100,000 each. Man is, at least, beginning to understand some of the problems he faces.

A WALK IN THE CITY

John V. Lindsay

We have two Americas—one for the middle and upper class, the other for the lower class seemingly destined to ever remain second class citizens. The challenges of our citizens are many. It really makes little difference whether you read the reports or take a stroll through the depressed areas and see for yourself—the answers are the same. Mayor Lindsay urges that you become concerned citizens and commit yourself to the eradication of this blight on our nation. There is much that you can do.

You can learn about America's cities in two ways: you can read the facts and figures that our government compiles, or you can walk in the city yourself.

You can, for example, walk through the schools of New York or any other major city, schools designed to be fortresses and built in another time to hold far fewer children than they do now; schools with peeling paint and broken windows, without the tools of education and often divorced from a child's neighborhood.

Or you can read the facts and figures: fewer than three of ten ghetto children finish high school; schools in the ghettos are almost always older, more crowded, less equipped than schools in affluent neighborhoods; reading levels between white and black have widened in the past thirty years; the longer some children are in school, the more their IQ's fall.

You can walk through Brownsville or Bedford-Stuyvesant or Harlem or Hough or Watts or West Side Chicago. You can see the men who stand on corners, without jobs or skills or hope; you can observe the children, underfed, underclothed, surrounded by nothing but the evidence of resignation; you can find whole neighborhoods in which there can be no pride and little joy.

Or you can read: unemployment and sub-employment in the ghetto are at a rate greater than the joblessness that existed during the Great Depression; more than 40 per cent of housing in these neighborhoods is substandard; the gap between white and black income is wider now than it was twenty years ago; even air pollution is higher in ghettos than outside them; and three times as many ghetto children die as do others.

You can, if you wish, walk through streets where the only signs of success are among those who are outside the law: the hustlers, the numbers runners, the pimps and gangsters. You can see districts where the only working signs of government are a welfare system that degrades, a school system that fails, and a police department that cannot possibly cope with all the failures we have permitted to breed for too long.

Or you can read the facts: the urban poor are the biggest victims of crimes; they suffer more from random violence and terror than any other part of the

From *McCall's* December 1968 issue. Reprinted with permission of the author and publisher.

population; their most urgent demand, despite all the deprivation they suffer, is for more police protection.

Whether you trust the evidence of your senses or the judgment of the studies, the verdict is the same. Whether you have walked through slums you did not believe could exist or read the Riot Commission report, you will find one grim conclusion: we have built in this country two Americas, one comfortable and materially satisfied, the other condemned to a life of persistent poverty, so pervasive that it cripples the spirit as well as the body.

There are many challenges before our cities: cleaning the air and water, bettering our transportation, controlling the chaotic, dehumanizing growth that makes city life so much more unpleasant than it need be. But nothing can match the urgency of beginning-now-effective public and private action to end the shame of the cities.

There is much that you, as a citizen, can do:

You can support public programs to bring resources to our cities; not to hand, but to help, in providing jobs and the tools to rebuild shattered communities.

You can make an effort to see whether your business or profession can make a contribution within our cities—whether by training the jobless or by providing immediate employment opportunities. Even a few jobs—if multiplied by the thousands of active businesses—could mean the beginning of hope.

You can donate the most precious commodity you have—your own time— in a personal commitment to help. Neighborhood Health Centers need people to perform routine medical functions; Day Care and Head Start Centers need people to teach and care for children; dozens of small but invaluable community-action projects need people who care to begin the hard and painful task of putting a community back together again.

You can become more than a concerned citizen; you can become a working contributor to the most critical job we have in America: to make peaceful progress the effective road to a just society. We need your help.

THE EMERGING CITY

Scott Greer

The image of the town meeting where all of the electorate took an active part in decision making is a thing of the past. Today's citizen takes little interest in local and civic matters. Rather, he turns inward to his family and, perhaps here, we find the last vestiges of democratic decision making.

Today's urban citizen has lost his sense of community belonging, and even suburbia can lay no claim to functioning in this sense. What we must find in urban America is something that a citizen can identify with, something which will establish a basis for belonging.

Reprinted with permission of The Macmillan Company from *The Emerging City* by Scott Greer, pp. 93–106. Copyright © 1962 by The Free Press of Glencoe, a Division of The Macmillan Company.

The picture that emerges is of a society in which the conjugal family is extremely powerful among all types of population. This small, primary group structure is one basic area of involvement; at the other pole is work, a massive absorber of time, but an activity that is rarely related to the family through "outside" friendship with on-the-job associates. Instead, the family, its kin, and its friendship group, is relatively free-floating, within the world of large-scale secondary associations. Burgess has pointed out that the weakening of a primary community results in the increasing relative dependence of individuals upon the conjugal family as a source of primary relationships; this same principle explains the persisting importance of extended kin and the proliferation of close friendships in urban America.[1] In the metropolis the community as a solid phalanx of friends or acquaintances does not exist; if individuals are to have a community in the older sense of *communion,* they must make it for themselves. These conditions are at an extreme in the highly urban neighborhoods, and there friendship and kinship are, relatively, most important in the average individual's social world. In other kinds of neighborhoods the family is usually identified, although weakly, with the local community; it "neighbors," but strictly within bounds. By and large, the conjugal family group keeps itself to itself; outside is the world —formal organizations, work, and the communities.

Such a picture is remarkably similar to that which Oeser and Hammond present, from their studies of Melbourne, Australia.[2] Melbourne, like the American cities studied, is a mushrooming metropolitan complex in a large-scale and highly urbanized society. Its people are mostly of middle social rank, neither poor nor wealthy. Its social order centers around the single-family dwelling unit, the conjugal family, selected kinfolk, the job, and the mass media—the latter consumed in the home. Like urban Americans, the residents of Melbourne are avid fans of the various spectator sports and "do-it-yourself" activities. Neither in Melbourne nor in American cities do we find much participation, by most people, in formal organizations or the community. The society of Australia is, if anything, less hierarchical than that of America (many of its citizens have no desire to recall their family lineage). Control is by universal ballot and all must, by law, participate in elections. Yet the family retires to its domain, as in the American cities studied, to work in the garden, listen to radio or television, care for children and read the products of the mass media.

Such findings as these are important in two respects: first, in their sharp departures from an older, conventional picture of metropolitan life, and secondly, in their consistency. The agreement among the various American studies, and between these and the Australian study, leads us to suspect that such participation patterns are a result of the powerful trends associated with increasing scale in modern Western society.

The increasing surplus and changing space-time ratio of large-scale society, and its consequent freedom from older constraints, has allowed a wide range of choice for the individual household. This is manifest in the great variation in life styles that a contemporary metropolitan population exhibits. It ranges

[1] Ernest W. Burgess and Harvey J. Locke, *The Family: From Institution to Companionship,* New York: American Book Company, 1954 (2nd ed.).

[2] O. A. Oeser and S. B. Hammond (eds.), *Social Structure and Personality* *in a City,* New York: The Macmillan Company, 1954.

from the family-centered, home-centered life at the familistic pole to an opposite pole of extreme urbanism, where one finds many single individuals and couples without children. The utility of different parts of the metropolis for different styles of life results in a concentration of similar persons with similar needs in given neighborhoods.

Thus, the galaxy of local residential areas making up a metropolis exhibit, at each level of social rank, vast differences between the highly urban neighborhoods and the familistic neighborhoods. In general, the highly urban neighborhoods lie within the central city and the familistic areas lie in the outer rings of the central city and in the suburbs. One may keep in mind the image of the urban apartment-house districts, on one hand, and the tract developments on the other. The important thing is not, however, location in geographical space, but *life style.* Typically "urban" neighborhoods occur in the suburban municipalities, "suburban" neighborhoods in the central city.

As one moves across the continuum, from the urban toward the familistic neighborhoods, community participation in the local area increases. Studies in Los Angeles, Chicago, and St. Louis, have indicated that the urbanism of an area is closely associated with the importance of the locality group—geographical space becomes social fact.

The results of the Los Angeles study of four census-tract populations at middle social rank, without segregated populations but varying from very urbane to very familistic, were summarized as follows:

In general, our findings indicate a growing importance of the local area as a social fact, as we go from the highly urbanized areas . . . to the low-urban areas. Neighboring, organizational location in the area, the residences of the members of organizations in the area, the location and composition of church congregations, all vary with urbanism and increase as urbanism decreases. Readership of the local community press also increases, as does the ability to name local leaders and intention to remain in the area indefinitely.

Thus the studies of the small community, with its local organizational structure and stratification system, may apply in the low urban areas: they are not likely to fit in the highly urban area. We may think of the urbanism dimension as having, at the low-urban pole, communities much like those studied by W. Lloyd Warner, August Hollingshead, and others. At the highly urbanized pole, we encounter the big city population of the stereotype, organized not in community terms, but in terms of the corporation, politics, the mass media and the popular culture. But predominantly, the highly urban populations associate in small, informal groups, with friends and kinfolk.[3]

Further studies, which included interviews with a cross section of the entire population of metropolitan St. Louis, Missouri, support these findings. These data are reinforced by the conclusions of Janowitz, who found, among his Chicago sample, that "Family cohesion and primary group contacts seemed more relevant for predisposing an individual toward acceptance of the community's controlling institutions and associations."

Thus, few urban subareas approach the anonymity and fragmentation of the stereotype. However, fewer still approach the kind of subcommunity envisaged in the democratic ideology. Al-

[3] See Scott Greer and Ella Kube, *Urban Worlds: A Comparative Study of Four Los Angeles Areas*, Los Angeles, Laboratory in Urban Culture, Occidental College, 1955.

though more respondents can name local leaders in the suburbs than in the highly urbanized areas (in both Los Angeles and St. Louis) only some 40 per cent can do so anywhere. And a majority cannot name even one metropolitan leader. With this qualification in mind, the differences between the polar extremes are sharp and suggestive. The great variation in life style existing in the contemporary metropolis is accompanied by great variation in the social structure of its locality groups.

IMPLICATIONS FOR THE DEMOCRATIC DOGMA

The results of this brief summary may now be compared with the empirical assumptions underlying democratic political structures. Much of that ideal pattern relies upon the belief in stable subcommunities, viable wholes through which the individual may clarify in social discourse and affect through social action the objects of his desires and grievances. Such a locality group requires sufficient communication and involvement to result in the ordering of individual behavior. It must then be important to a large part of its constituency. Our ideal example from the past is the New England township, and its image still has an overpowering importance in our thinking. It is something of a political and social archetype.

The local area today however, particularly in the metropolis, does not represent such a community. Instead, it is necessarily what Janowitz calls a "community of limited liability." The individual's investment is relatively small in the interactional network that constitutes the locality group, and if his losses are too great he can cut them by getting out—the community cannot hold him. Even among the most community-oriented, "small-town-like" areas within

the metropolis, there is great variation in the importance of the local area to the individual. The local merchants have more of a stake than the home-owning residents with children, and these have more invested than the couple without children who rent an apartment (though the latter are very rare in such neighborhoods). However, even the most deeply involved can withdraw from the local community and satisfy all needs elsewhere—and the withdrawal need not be physical.

The older definition of community posited a spatially defined social aggregate that is a powerful social group. Such groups exist only when there is functional interdependence (as the local community in the suburbs is most necessary to its merchants, least so to the childless couple who rent their dwelling). Interdependence, in turn, means commitment to the ongoing social system. Such interdependence and commitment produce intensive participation and the development of common values and norms. Constraint, in this sense, is the key to community.

If this is true, then the great degree of freedom for individual location and action in large-scale society makes the "primary community" impossible. Exceptions occur only in a few survivals, such as the Appalachian backwoods, or institutional aggregates such as the prison, monastery, and army. Aside from these atypical collectives, however, there *are* groups in which the individual must interact continuously and for a large share of his waking life. Most important is the work organization.

The functional interdependence, the flow of communication, and the consequent ordering of behavior in the place of work bulk large in the individual's life. Some theorists, of whom Mayo is the best known, imply that a primary community of work is therefore possible.[4] Certainly, economic production, a share in the surplus, and status in the general society are basic functional supports of such primary communities as the peasant village. In our society they are typically provided through membership in large-scale, extended, formal organizations. However, in a most cursory inspection of the organization of modern industry, several factors appear that make such a strong work community very unlikely. These include freedom of labor, the divorce of work and household, the conflicting functions of the work organization, and their results in the labor union on one hand and the hierarchical organization of industry on the other.[5]

Free labor, which is functional for the total economic system, allows the individual to leave a given work group and join another at will. His needs may be served as well or better—and likewise the functional demands of industry. This freedom is reinforced by the complete divorce between his household group and work group; the job is left at the factory or office, and can be changed or discarded like a suit of social clothes. However, his relations with others in the work group are conditioned by this freedom. Even work is a commitment of limited liability.

Equally important is the hierarchical organization of work in our society. The "scalar principle" is undoubtedly neces-

[4] Elton Mayo, *The Social Problems of an Industrial Civilization*, Boston: Harvard University Graduate School of Business Administration, 1945.

[5] Wilbert E. Moore, *Industrial Relations and the Social Order*, New York: The Macmillan Company, 1945. For a succinct statement by Moore see "Industrial Sociology: Status and Prospects," *American Sociological Review*, 13, 382–390, especially "The Industrial Worker and His Environment." Oeser and Hammond, *op. cit.*, make some cognate generalizations with respect to labor in Australia.

sary in large organized groups; still the net effect is that the most time-absorbing social group outside the family is ordered in a way contradictory to the assumptions of democratic process. Further, the common interest of workers and management is so channeled, through the unstable division of the social product into profits and wages, as to create a well-structured division of interest as well. This schism between the leaders of work and their followers drastically reduces the common ground of values and the effective norms. The unions have risen as a response.

Finally, the division of labor is so great as to weaken the common conscience of the different levels of workmen. Durkheim postulated a solidarity, a group *élan*, based upon teamwork. However, to the routine worker his job is frequently merely the payment of a pound of flesh. A large proportion of the membership of most work organizations is made up of routine workers, and their lack of control over their work, their competition with management for economic rewards, their organized voice, the union, and their ability to leave the job, all represent limiting conditions. It is difficult to see how strong communities could arise within such market-oriented organizations.

Thus, the major organizational segment of society that orders work is unable to supply the basis for primary community. The local area is functionally weak. The kinship system is important, but in a "privatized" manner. The remaining possible structure for individual participation is the formal voluntary organization. A brief review of the findings cited earlier, however, indicates that such organizations are relatively unimportant at the grass roots. They are arenas for intensive participation to only a small minority of their members; many urban individuals have no formal organizational membership at all.

One possible exception is the labor union. Here is an organization whose functional importance for its members is great indeed. Unlike industry it is an organization based upon the assumptions of the democratic ideology; participation in decision-making is quite easy. Finally, it is a type of organization that is extremely widespread—it is probably the most important single kind of formal organization outside the churches, as measured by size of membership. Many have noted these facts and have interpreted the union as the worker's true community. What of union participation?

Many studies indicate that the average attendance of members at a local union's routine meetings is extremely low—from less than 1 per cent to perhaps 20 per cent. Most of those who attend are the same group, over and over, and these together with the paid professional staff have undue influence upon the organizational decisions. For the average member, on the other hand, the union is almost an aspect of government. He pays his dues and, as in the national elections, frequently does not vote. His leaders, with the best will in the world, far overreach their responsibility—for there is nobody else to take responsibility. Most often the leaders "run the locals" with some restraint from the small cadre of actives and the members are, in Herberg's phrase, "a plebiscitary body."[6] Far from constituting a real community for the workers, the union is largely another service organization. It can mobilize the members to strike, but not to participate in the routine functioning where the basic grounds for strikes are considered and argued out.[7]

[6] Will Herberg, "Bureaucracy and Democracy in Trade Unions," *Antioch Review*, 2, 405–417.

[7] For an analysis of unions with respect to participation and representation, see

AN EMBARRASSMENT OF FREEDOM

It is apparent that, in a society with a democratic political structure and ideology, democratic social processes are relatively rare. Shared decision-making, control through consent, is probably most common in the kinship and friendship groups, but it is hardly transmitted through them to larger entities. The other areas where individual participation is possible, the local community and the formal organization, engage only a minority in more than token participation, and the organizations of work—most important of all in many respects—are structurally unfit for democratic processes as work is organized in our society. The following picture of participation in metropolitan society results.

There are a plethora of formal organizations, labor unions, business and professional groups, churches and church-related groups, parent-teacher associations, and the like. They exert pressure and they influence the political party—another formal organization. However, the leadership in such organizations is largely professionalized and bureaucratized, and such leaders become, in effect, oligarchs. At the same time the members participate in an extremely erratic manner, and frequently "stay away in droves" from the meetings. The organization is a holding company for the members' interests; they exercise an occasional veto right in the plebiscites.

The local area is not a community in any sense, in the highly urban parts of the city; it is a community "of limited liability" in the suburbs. Communication and participation are as apt to be

Scott Greer, *Last Man In: Racial Access to Union Power*, New York: Free Press of Glencoe, 1959.

segmental as in any formal organization that is extraterritorial. And many are utterly uninvolved, even in the strongest spatially defined communities.

Formal government is highly bureaucratized and, aside from votes in national elections and (occasionally) in local elections, the individual participates very little. Most party clubs are made up of professionals, semiprofessionals, a handful of actives, and a large majority of paper members.

The organization of work is nondemocratic in its control structure and the individual's participation is largely a matter of conforming to directions and implementing decisions made far above him in the hierarchy. This is of basic importance, for, with the rise of professional leadership in all formal organizations—from labor unions to Boy Scouts, the most intense participation in all groups is apt to be that of the official, for whom the organization is his *job* in a job hierarchy.

Thus, interpreting the participation of the average individual in the polity of metropolitan society is a somewhat bizarre experience. By and large he does not participate. Since this is true, it is difficult to make a case for the widespread importance of the democratic processes in the everyday behavior of most people except in the home and friendship circle. The democracy we inhabit is, instead, largely a democracy of substantive freedoms, or freedom from restraint. Produced by struggles among various professionally directed interest groups, largely quite undemocratic in their control processes, freedom of choice for the individual is something of a by-product. It exists through the balance of countervailing forces, in work, at the market place, and in government.

This freedom is, however, a considerable area of the average person's life space. It is manifest in the metropolitan resident's ability to choose marriage or single status, children or not, large family or small. It is also apparent in his freedom to choose his local residential area, and his degree of participation in its social structure—his life style. He may privatize his nonworking world and turn inward to his single-family dwelling unit and his conjugal family (which he does) ; he may refuse to participate in many public activities and yield only a token participation in others (and he does).

Though his commitments to the job and the family are constant and have a priority in time and energy, he exercises freedom of choice in the market, the large sphere which Riesman calls consumership.[8] He also has a freedom in the symbol spheres that has never been widespread before in any society—the variety of media and of messages are overwhelming. There are some one thousand hours of television available each week to the Los Angeles resident. His relative wealth, literacy, and privacy allow an exploration of meaning never possible before to the rank and file of any society. In his home life he experiments with leisure. The hobby industries, the do-it-yourself industries, the flood of specialized publications and programs, bear testimony to the increasing use of urbanite makes of this opportunity. He is part of the *nouveaux riches* of leisure.

His wealth is a result of the increasing social surplus, produced by advancing technologies of energy transformation and social organization. It is a surplus of material products, of time, and of symbols. His rise is also a measure of the leveling of the hierarchical orders. Their remnants persist, in the relatively higher rates of competence, participation and leadership for the upper social

[8] See David Riesman with Reuel Denney and Nathan Glazer, *The Lonely Crowd*, New Haven: Yale University Press, 1950.

ranks in most of the formal organizations. Most people, however, are the descendants, and in some respects, equivalents, of the illiterates of a hundred years ago. They have neither the vested interest in, nor the tradition of responsible participation in the life of the polity. And they have great freedom from forced participation in work. They exercise it in fashioning the typical life patterns adumbrated, in avoiding organizations, politely giving lip service to the neighbors and local community leaders, avoiding work associates off the job, orienting themselves toward evenings, week ends, and vacations. These they spend *en famille*, traveling, looking at television, gossiping and eating with friends and kin, and cultivating the garden.

The bureaucratic leadership and the plebiscitary membership, the community of limited liability and the privatized citizen, are not images most Americans hold of a proper democratic society. On the other hand, the picture is less frightening than that of the atomistic man adrift in mass society, anomic and destructive. Furthermore, the ideal picture of participation in the primary political community is a strenuous one. Perhaps a revision downward, toward effective communities of limited liability and effective plebiscites might be more congruent with the organizational structure of large-scale society.

RECENT DISTORTIONS OF CLASSICAL MODELS OF URBAN STRUCTURE

Homer Hoyt

A great change has taken place in the "classical models" of our large cities. The city of the 1920's with its central retail district and its concentration of hotels, shops, department stores, museums, theaters, and office buildings has drastically changed. By the 1960's the city's dominant position had been greatly weakened by the construction of over eight thousand planned shopping centers with ample parking space in the suburbs or the peripheries of central cities. This shift to the areas outside the city has also included motels, hotels, residential complexes, and some manufacturing. The ownership of automobiles and highway complexes, coupled with the desire of the individual for more space and ownership of property, have been the major causes for this change.

Since the general patterns of city structure were described by Burgess in 1925[1] and 1929[2] and by myself in 1939,[3] there has been a tremendous growth of urban population, not only in the United States but throughout the

[1] R. E. Park and E. W. Burgess, *The City* (Chicago, Illinois: University of Chicago Press, 1925), pp. 47–62.

[2] E. W. Burgess, "Urban Areas," in *Chicago: An Experiment in Social Science Research*, T. V. Smith and L. D. White (editors) (Chicago, Illinois: University of Chicago Press, 1929), pp. 114–123.

From *Land Economics*, XL (May 1964), 199–212. Copyright, The Regents of the University of Wisconsin. Reprinted with permission of the author and publisher.

world. To what extent has this factor of growth changed the form or shape of urban communities?

While the Burgess concentric circle theory was based on a study of Chicago —a city on a flat prairie, cut off on the east by Lake Michigan—and patterns of growth in other cities would be influenced by their unique topography, his formulation had a widespread application to American cities of 1929. Burgess made a brilliant and vivid contribution to urban sociology and urban geography which inspired the present writer as well as the sociologists and geographers who made subsequent studies of city patterns.

In the era of the Greek cities in the fifth century B.C. a city was considered an artistic creation which should maintain its static form without change. To take care of population growth, the Greeks sent out colonies, like swarms of bees, to found new cities on the ideal model. Plato said that the ideal city should not contain over 5,000 inhabitants although he himself was the product of an Athens with a 250,000 population. In the Middle Ages most continental European cities were surrounded by walls and many, like Milan, Italy, preserved an unaltered form for hundreds of years.

In the United States, however, there has been a tremendous growth of metropolitan areas since 1930. The number of large urban concentrations with a population of a million or more has increased from 10 to 22. The population in the 140 metropolitan districts was 57,602,-865 in 1930, of which 40,343,422 were in central cities and 17,259,423 were outside these cities. In 1940 in these 140

metropolitan districts the population was 62,965,773 of which 42,796,170 were in central cities and 20,169,603 were outside these cities.[4] After World War II, in the rapidly growing decade from 1950 to 1960, the population of 216 Standard Metropolitan Areas grew from 91,568,113 to 115,796,265. Most of the growth in the past census decade was in the suburbs, but central city population grew from 52,648,185 to 58,441,995, a gain of only 11 percent, while the population outside central cities increased from 38,919,928 to 57,354,270, a rise of 47.4 percent.[5] The population in the central areas of 12 of the largest American metropolitan regions actually declined in this decade from 22,694,799 to 21,843,214, a loss of 3.8 percent.[6] The population loss in the central cores of these cities was much greater, since some central cities still had room for new growth within the outer edges of their boundaries. There was also a displacement of white population by non-white population. From 1930 to 1950 the non-white population in 168 SMA's increased from 4,913,703 to 8,250,210.[7] The chief gain was in the central cities where the non-white population rose from 3,624,504 in 1930 to 6,411,158 in 1950. From 1950 to 1960 the non-white population in central cities increased to

[4] United States Census of Population 1940, Vol. I, Table 18, p. 61.

[5] United States Department of Commerce, Bureau of the Census, Standard Metropolitan Areas in the United States as defined October 18, 1963, Series P-23, No. 10, December 5, 1963. (Newark, New Jersey, is included in New York Metropolitan Area).

[6] Baltimore, Boston, Chicago, Cincinnati, Cleveland, Detroit, Minneapolis-St. Paul, New York, Philadelphia, St. Louis, San Francisco-Oakland and Washington, D.C.

[7] United States Census of Population, 1930, 1940, 1950.

[3] Homer Hoyt, *The Structure and Growth of Residential Neighborhoods in American Cities* (Washington, D.C.: Federal Housing Administration, 1939).

10,030,314. The non-white population in SMA's outside central cities was only 2,720,513 in 1960. On the other hand while 43,142,399 white persons lived in central cities of SMA's in 1960, 49,081,-533 white persons lived in SMA's outside the central cities. While the central city population in these 12 SMA's was declining, population outside the central cities rose from 13,076,711 in 1950 to 20,534,833 in 1960, a gain of 57 percent.

In 1960 the population of the areas outside the central cities in these 12 great metropolitan areas almost equalled the population in the central areas and by 1964 the population in the areas outside the central cities has certainly surpassed the number in the central city.

While the cities of 50,000 population and over have been growing at a rapid rate in the past decade, the smaller cities with less than 50,000 population have been increasing in numbers at a slower pace, or from 27.4 million in 1950 to 29.4 million in 1960.[8] The smaller cities thus would be enabled to maintain their static form with the growth element chiefly affecting the larger metropolitan areas as a result of the shift in population growth from the center to the suburbs and a change in the racial composition of many central cities.

Not merely population growth, but a rise in per capita national income from $757 in 1940 to $2,500 in 1963, with a greater proportionate increase in the middle class incomes, an increase in the number of private passenger automobiles from 22,793,000 in 1933 to 70 million in 1963, and the building of expressways connecting cities and belt highways around cities, were all dynamic factors changing the shape and form of cities since the description of

city patterns in 1925 and 1939. Let us examine the different concentric circles or zones or sectors described in the books over a quarter of a century ago and see how the principles then enunciated have been changed by the growth factors.

THE CENTRAL BUSINESS DISTRICT: FINANCIAL AND OFFICE ZONE AND THE RETAIL SHOPPING ZONE

In 1929 Burgess wrote: "Zone I: The Central Business District. At the center of the city as the focus of its commercial, social and civic life is situated in the Central Business District. The heart of this district is the downtown retail district with its department stores, its smart shops, its office buildings, its clubs, its banks, its hotels, its theatres, its museums, and its headquarters of economic, social, civic and political life."[9] Burgess thus accurately described the central business district of Chicago and most large American cities as of the date he was writing (1929), a description which would hold true in the main to the end of World War II. Since 1946, extraordinary changes in the American economy have occurred which have had a pronounced effect on the structure of the downtown business districts of American cities.

Burgess had noted in 1929 the existence of local business centers, or satellite "loops" in the zone of better residences: "The typical constellation of business and recreation areas includes a bank, one or more United Cigar stores, a drug store, a high class restaurant, an automobile display row, and a so-called 'wonder' motion picture theatre."[10] I also noted, in 1939, the extensions of

[8] Harold M. Mayer, "Economic Prospects for the Smaller City," *Public Management*, August 1963.

[9] Ernest W. Burgess, "Urban Areas," *op. cit.*

[10] *Ibid.*

stringlike commercial developments beyond the central business districts, and the rise of satellite business centers: "Again, satellite business centers have developed independently beyond the central business district, or on the city's periphery. These are usually located at or near suburban railway stations, elevated or subway stations, intersecting points between radical and crosstown street car lines, or intersecting points of main automobile highways."[11]

In 1964, the central retail district, with its large department stores still remains the largest shopping district in its metropolitan area, and all the outlying business districts at street car intersections, subway or suburban railway stations are still operating, but their dominating position has been greatly weakened by the construction, since 1946, of an estimated 8,300 planned shopping districts, with free automobile parking, in the suburbs or on the periphery of the central city mass. The tremendous growth of the suburban population, which moved to areas beyond mass transit lines, facilitated by the universal ownership of the automobile, and decline in the numbers and relative incomes of the central city population, invited and made possible this new development in retail shopping.

The regional shopping center—with major department stores, variety, apparel and local convenience stores, practically duplicating the stores in the downtown retail area and built on large tracts of land entirely away from street cars, subways, elevated or railroad stations—was virtually unknown prior to World War II. The first of these centers, Country Club Plaza in Kansas City, had been established in 1925 and there were a few others with department stores and a number of neighborhood centers on commercial streets, with parking areas

[11] Hoyt, *op. cit.* p. 20.

in front of the stores, but the wave of the future was not discerned by planners or land economists before 1946.

There are many types of these new planned centers; the regional center on 50 to 100 acres of land with at least one major department store; the community center on 20 to 30 acres of land with a junior department store as the leading tenant; and the neighborhood center with a supermarket, drug store and local convenience shops on 5 to 10 acres of land. But the type having the greatest impact on the downtown stores is the regional center which directly competes with downtown in the sale of general merchandise.

General merchandise stores, that is, department and variety stores, had long been the dominating magnets and attractions of the central retail areas. In this field the CBD stores had almost a monopoly in most cities prior to 1920 and even held a dominating position after the establishment of some outlying department stores at street car intersections or subway stations in Chicago and New York. There had been for years neighborhood grocery stores, drug stores and even small apparel and dry goods stores and some variety stores outside of the central business district but the department store sales of the CBD's were probably 90 percent or more of the total department store volume of the entire metropolitan area.

In 1958 the central general merchandise stores, chiefly department stores, in the largest cities of a million population and over, had a lower sales volume than the aggregate of the sales of department stores in all the shopping centers outside of the CBD, or $3.6 billion compared to $5.65 billion. There were 125 regional shopping centers in 1958 but many more have been completed since that date and the 1963 United States Retail Census of Shopping Districts will undoubtedly show a still greater increase in the department store sales outside of the CBD.

In 94 metropolitan areas with a population of 100,000 and over and total population of 91,937,103 in 1960, dollar sales outside the CBD's had increased by 53.8 percent, but in the CBD's only 3.4 percent. There was an actual decline in general merchandise sales from 1954 to 1958 in the CBD's of Los Angeles, Chicago, Philadelphia, Detroit, Boston, St. Louis, Washington, D.C., Cleveland, Baltimore, Milwaukee and Kansas City.

These new planned shopping districts, with their ample parking areas, cover more ground than the combined areas of the CBD's in all American cities. I have calculated that there were 30,460 acres or 47.5 square miles in the central business districts of the standard metropolitan areas in the United States in 1960, compared with 33,600 acres or 52.5 square miles in all types of new planned centers.[12] Since 1960, however, many new planned centers have been built and there are now probably 150 regional shopping centers. In 1964 the ground area occupied by these centers, as well as that of the many new discount houses with large parking areas, has considerably increased the space occupied by shopping centers as compared with 1960.

In contrast to the tremendous growth of the planned shopping districts, there has been very limited building of new retail stores in downtown areas; the notable exceptions being Midtown Plaza in Rochester, New York; the redevelopment of the business center of New Haven, Connecticut, with new department stores, offices and garages, connected by a new highway to the existing expressway; the location of new Sears Roebuck and Dayton department stores in central St. Paul; and the erection of

[12] Homer Hoyt, "Changing Patterns of Land Values," *Land Economics*, May 1960, p. 115.

garages for department stores in other cities.

Office Buildings

Office building expansion, unlike retail stores, bears no direct relation to population growth but depends entirely upon the extent to which a city becomes an international or regional office management or financial center. Generalization therefore cannot be made about office buildings which would apply to all cities since the number of square feet of office space per capita in the metropolitan area varies from 2.2 square feet in San Diego to 7.5 square feet in Chicago, 16 square feet in New York and 25 square feet in Midland, Texas.

New York City has become the outstanding headquarters center of the United States, with an estimated 171,-300,000 square feet of office space. It has had a tremendous growth since 1946, with 55 million square feet added since World War II. The trend has been uptown, away from downtown Wall Street to Park Avenue, 42nd Street and Third Avenue near Grand Central Station. The world's greatest concentration of office buildings is in the Grand Central and Plaza districts of New York City. From 1947 to 1962 inclusive, there was a total increase of 50,632,000 square feet of rentable office area in Manhattan, of which 33,839,000 square feet, or 66.8 percent, was in the Grand Central and Plaza areas. In the same period, in the lower Manhattan area, or the combined financial, city hall and insurance districts, 10,935,000 square feet or 21.6 percent of the total were constructed. A partial reversal of the uptown trend in Manhattan will result from the proposed building of the World Trade Center with 10 million square feet of office space, in twin towers 1350 feet high, on the Lower West Side. This development, by the Port of New York

Authority, will be started in 1965 and is scheduled for completion by 1970.[13]

In Washington, D.C., there is approximately 16 million square feet of office space. An estimated 11 million square feet have been built since 1946, of which 9 million square feet are in the area west of 15th Street, in the direction of the high grade residential growth.

The location of new office buildings in central city areas has been determined in part by the slum or blighted areas, with old buildings which could be cleared away, such as in the Golden Triangle of Pittsburgh or Penn Center in Philadelphia, or location in air rights over railroad tracks as the Merchandise Mart and Prudential buildings in Chicago, the Pan Am Building and other buildings on Park Avenue in New York and the Prudential Building in Boston. The ability to secure land at a relatively low cost on West Wacker Drive in Chicago caused insurance companies to build there.

Sometimes these new office districts are not at the center of transportation. In Los Angeles new office building has moved away from the central business districts toward the high grade residential areas. From 1948 to 1960 15,500,-000 square feet of office floor space was constructed in Los Angeles, of which only 1,500,000 square feet was built in the 400-acre area of the central business district, although 1,000,000 square feet were erected in the southwesterly and western fringe areas of the central business district.[14] This decentralization is in marked contrast to the concentration of offices in New York City.

There has also been a tendency for

[13] *The New York Times*, January 19, 1964.

[14] *Los Angeles Centropolis 1980, Economic Survey*, Los Angeles Central City Committee and Los Angeles City Planning Department, December 12, 1960, p. 19.

large office buildings of insurance companies, which conduct a self-sufficient operation not dependent on contact with other agencies, to locate on large tracts of land several miles from the center of the city as the Prudential regional office buildings in Houston and Minneapolis in 1951, and the Connecticut General Insurance Company in Hartford. Office centers are also developing around some of the regional shopping centers, as at Northland in Detroit, Ward Parkway in Kansas City and Lenox Square in Atlanta.

In Houston more than 6 million square feet of new office space has been added to downtown areas in the past three years, the growth proceeding westerly in the direction of the high income areas. While the main office building district of most cities is still within the confines of the central area, the office center is not fixed but is moving in the direction of high income areas, as in New York City, Washington, D.C., Los Angeles and Houston. This conforms to the statement I made in 1939.[15]

A tall office building that looms in the sky as a beacon or landmark has been built in many cities of moderate size by banks, oil companies or insurance companies for the sake of prestige, regardless of cost or rental demand. In many cities of growing population few new office buildings have been erected. Thus, generalizations can no longer be made about office building locations which will apply to all cities in the United States.

Hotels and Motels

There is a concentration of hotels near each other in large cities so that they can accommodate conventions but

[15] Hoyt, *Structure and Growth, op. cit.,* p. 108.

central hotels have declined in importance because of the new motels and motor hotels (with parking) on the periphery of the central business district or on the outskirts of the city. This rapid growth in both intown motels and those on the periphery is a use not anticipated in 1939.

Apartments in Central Areas

There is a trend to the building of new apartments in or near central business districts, such as the Marina Towers in Chicago, the apartments in redeveloped areas in Southwest Washington, D.C., and as proposed for the Bunker Hill redevelopment in downtown Los Angeles. Hence the statement by Burgess that: "Beyond the workingmen's homes lies the residential district, a zone in which the better grade of apartments and single family residences predominate" must be qualified now, as it was in 1939, when I pointed to the Gold Coast of Chicago and Park Avenue in New York City.[16]

Thus, in view of the shifting of uses in the central business districts, the overall decline in the predominance of central retail areas, the rapid growth of office centers in a few cities compared to a static situation in others, the emergence of redeveloped areas, and intown motels, the former descriptions of patterns in American cities must be revised to conform to the realities of 1964.

THE WHOLESALE AND LIGHT MANUFACTURING ZONE

Burgess described the zone next to the central business district as: "Clinging close to the skirts of the retail district lies the wholesale and light manufacturing zone. Scattered through this

[16] *Ibid.*, p. 23.

zone and surrounding it, old dilapidated buildings form the homes of the lower working classes, hoboes and disreputable characters. Here the slums are harbored. Cheap second-hand stores are numerous, and low-priced 'men only' moving picture and burlesque shows flourish."[17] This is a vivid description of West Madison Street and South State Street in Chicago in the 1920's. Since that time the wholesale function has greatly declined and with the direct sale by manufacturers to merchants the 4-million-square-foot Merchandise Mart, across the Chicago River north of the Loop, absorbed most of the functions formerly performed by wholesalers. The intermixture of slums and old dilapidated buildings with light industry is being cleared away in redevelopment projects and the West Side Industrial District in Chicago has been created immediately west of the Loop on cleared land.

Light manufacturing, in the garment industry particularly, still clings close to the retail and financial center in New York City because the garment industry depends on fashion and the entertainment of out-of-town buyers.

Other light manufacturing industries have tended to move away from the center of the city to the suburbs where they can secure ample land areas for one-story plants, storage, and parking for their employees' cars. These new modern plants, in park-like surroundings, which emit no loud noise or offensive odors, are not objectionable even in middle-class residential areas, and workers can avoid city traffic in driving to their place of employment, or they can live nearby.

[17] Ernest M. Fisher, *Advanced Principles of Real Estate Practice* (New York: The Macmillan Co., 1930), p. 126, citing R. F. Park and E. W. Burgess, *The City*, *op. cit.*, Ch. II.

THE FACTORY OR HEAVY INDUSTRIAL DISTRICT

In 1929 Burgess placed the wholesale district in Zone I, the central business district, and described Zone II as the zone in transition, which included the factory district in its inner belt as follows:

Zone II: The Zone in Transition. Surrounding the Central Business District are areas of residential deterioration caused by the encroaching of business and industry from Zone I. This may therefore be called the Zone in Transition, with a factory district for its inner belt and an outer ring of retrogressing neighborhoods, of first-settlement immigrant colonies, of rooming-house districts, of homeless-men areas, of resorts of gambling, bootlegging, sexual vice, and of breeding-places of crime. In this area of physical deterioration and social disorganization our studies show the greatest concentration of cases of poverty, bad housing, juvenile delinquency, family disintegration, physical and mental disease. As families and individuals prosper, they escape from this area into Zone III beyond, leaving behind as marooned a residuum of the defeated, leaderless, and helpless.[18]

In 1939 I pointed out tendencies of heavy industries to move away from close-in locations in the "transition zone."[19] Since that time heavy manufacturing has tended more and more to seek suburban locations or rural areas, as nearly all workers now come in their own automobiles and for the most part live in the suburban areas themselves. Factory location in slum areas is not now desired for the clerks and factory workers no longer live there. All of the reasons I cited in 1939 for industries

moving to suburban areas apply with greater force in 1964.

In regard to residential uses, this zone in transition was defined as the slum and blighted area of Chicago in 1943[20] and under the slum clearance and redevelopment laws which enabled federal authorities to acquire by condemnation properties in blighted areas, it has been extensively cleared and rebuilt with modern apartments, both private and public. The remnants of this area which have not been cleared away still retain the characteristics Burgess described in 1929, and the problems of juvenile delinquency and overcrowding have been accentuated in the last 35 years by the in-migration of low income Negro families to Chicago as well as to other northern cities.

ZONE OF WORKINGMEN'S HOMES

Encircling the zone of transition, now the slum and blighted area, is Zone III, described by Burgess as follows:

Zone III: The Zone of Independent Workingmen's Homes. This third broad urban ring in Chicago, as well as in other northern industrial cities, is largely constituted by neighborhoods of second immigrant settlement. Its residents are those who desire to live near but not too close to their work. In Chicago, it is a housing area neither of tenements, apartments, nor of single dwellings; its boundaries have been roughly determined by the plotting of the two-flat dwelling, generally of frame construction, with the owner living on the lower floor with a tenant on the other.[21]

The buildings in this zone, now 35 years older than when Burgess wrote in 1929,

---

[18] Burgess, "Urban Areas," *op. cit.*
[19] Hoyt, *op. cit.*, p. 20.

[20] Chicago Plan Commission, *Master Plan of Residential Land Use of Chicago*, Homer Hoyt, Director of Research, 1943, Fig. 89, p. 68.
[21] Burgess, "Urban Areas," *op. cit.*

were in general classified in the Master Plan of Residential Land Use of Chicago as "conservation."[22] This area is not yet a slum but next in order of priority to be cleared away. In some blocks older structures can be razed and the newer ones rehabilitated. A large proportion of its former occupants, white families with children of school age, have moved to the suburbs and it is now occupied mainly by single white persons, older white families or by Negro families in all age groups.

In some cases these older close-in residential sections may be rehabilitated and become fashionable, as in the Georgetown area of Washington, D.C., Rittenhouse Square in Philadelphia and the Near North Side of Chicago; and this is an exception to be noted to Burgess' theory.

BETTER RESIDENTIAL AREA

Zone IV: The Zone of Better Residences. Extending beyond the neighborhoods of second immigrant settlements, we come to the Zone of Better Residences in which the great middle-class of native-born Americans live, small business men, professional people, clerks, and salesmen. Once communities of single homes, they are becoming, in Chicago, apartment-house and residential-hotel areas.[23]

This zone was classified in the Master Plan of Residential Land Use of Chicago in 1943 as "stable," indicating that the residences were still of sound construction and had many remaining years of useful life. As the second immigrant settlers, now indistinguishable from the native-born population, once moved from Zone III into this area, so now many of the former residents of this area have moved mainly from this area

into the new areas near the periphery of the city, or into the suburbs. Some of the areas vacated by them are now occupied by the non-white population.

THE COMMUTERS ZONE

Burgess described the commuters zone as follows:

Zone V: The Commuters Zone. Out beyond the areas of better residence is a ring of encircling small cities, towns, and hamlets, which, taken together, constitute the Commuters Zone. These are also, in the main, dormitory suburbs, because the majority of men residing there spend the day at work in the Loop (Central Business District), returning only for the night.[24]

Burgess thus took into account in his fifth zone the existence of suburban towns. However, he refers to them as a "ring" implying that they formed a circular belt around Chicago. However, at the time Burgess wrote in 1929, there was no circle of towns around Chicago but a pattern of settlement long the railroads with six great bands of suburban settlement radiating out from the central mass of Chicago like spokes of a wheel and with large vacant areas in between.[25] Chicago's early growth had taken the form first of starfish extensions of settlement along the principal highways and street car lines.[26] By 1929 the vacant areas in the city between these prongs had been filled in with homes so that there were then in fact belts or concentric circles of settled areas within the City of Chicago. At that time, however, the suburban area of Chicago conformed to the axial pattern of growth with the highest income sector located on one of the six radial bands—the North Shore, along

[22] Chicago Plan Commission, *op. cit.*
[23] Burgess, "Urban Areas," *op. cit.*

[24] *Ibid.*
[25] Chicago Plan Commission, *op. cit.*, frontispiece, p. 2.
[26] *Ibid.*, Fig. 3, p. 22.

Lake Michigan. There were other high income areas in the other bands of growth but no continuous belt of high income areas around Chicago. Since 1929 the vacant areas between these radial extensions of settlement along suburban railroads have been filled in largely with homes of middle income residents. Many of the new planned shopping districts are now located in between these bands of original settlement along railroads, where large vacant tracts could be secured.

Beyond his five zones, Burgess later identified two additional zones lying beyond the built-up area of the city: "The sixth zone is constituted by the agricultural districts lying within the circle of commutation . . . The seventh zone is the hinterland of the metropolis."[27]

Richard M. Hurd, in his classic *Principles of City Land Values*,[28] had as early as 1903 developed the central and axial principles of city growth; yet to many persons, before Burgess formulated his theory many years later, cities appeared to be a chaotic mixture of structures with no law governing their growth. Burgess, with acute powers of observation and without all of the great body of census and planning data that has been made available since he wrote, made a remarkable formulation of principles that were governing American city growth in 1929 and he related these principles to the basic facts of human society. Since 1929, however, not only have the vast detailed city data of the United States censuses been made available for study and analysis, but dynamic changes have occurred in our economy

[27] F. W. Burgess, "The New Community and Its Future," *Annals of the American Academy of Political and Social Science*, Vol. 149, May 1930, pp. 161, 162.

[28] Richard M. Hurd, *Principles of City Land Values* (1st edition 1903, republished by *The Record and Guide*, New York, New York, 1924).

which have had a profound influence on the structure of our cities. Since 1929 over 10 million new houses have been constructed on the suburban fringes of American cities, beyond the old central mass, in areas made available for residential occupancy by the increase in the number of private passenger automobiles in the United States from 8 million in 1920 to 66 million in 1964, and the highways subsequently built to accommodate them.

Apartment buildings, once confined to locations along subways, elevated lines or near suburban railroad stations, are now springing up in the suburbs, far from mass transit. Many families without children of school age desire the convenience of an apartment, involving no work of mowing lawns, painting and repairing, and with the comforts of air-conditioning and often a community swimming pool. Complete communities are now being developed in the suburbs, with a mixture of single family homes, town houses and apartments, and with their own churches, schools, shopping centers and light industries, some even with a golf course and bridle paths, of which the 7,000-acre Reston development near the Dulles Airport in the Washington, D.C., area is an outstanding example. Thus the dynamic changes of the past quarter century make it necessary to review concepts developed from studies of American cities in 1925 and 1939.

THE SECTOR THEORY

One concept needs to be examined again—the sector theory of residential development. In 1939 I formulated the sector theory which was to the effect that the high income areas of cities were in one or more sectors of the city, and not, as Burgess seemed to imply when he said: "beyond the workingmen's homes lies the residential district, a zone in which the better grade of apartment houses and single family residences predominate."

In a study of 64 American cities, block by block, based on the federal government's Work Project Administration's basic surveys of 1934, and studies of a number of large metropolitan areas, I prepared maps showing that high rent areas were located in one or more sectors of the city, and did not form a circle completely around it. Has this changed since 1939? In a survey of the entire Washington, D.C., metropolitan area in 1954 it was found that the main concentration of high-income families was in the District area west of Rock Creek Park, continuing into the Bethesda area of Montgomery County, Maryland. There were other scattered high income clusters in the Washington area. In surveys of other metropolitan areas it was discovered that the main concentration of high income families is on the north side of Dallas, the west and southwest sides of Houston, northward along the Lake Shore of Chicago, the south side of Kansas City, in the Beverly Hills area of Los Angeles, on the south side of Tulsa, the north side of Oklahoma City, the west side of Philadelphia, and the southwest side of Minneapolis. In the New York metropolitan area there are a number of nodules of high income in Westchester County, Nassau County, Bergen and Essex Counties in New Jersey, but the predominant movement was northward and eastward.

In a trip to Latin American cities in the summer of 1963 I found that the finest single family homes and apartments in Guatemala City, Bogota, Lima, La Paz, Quito, Santiago, Buenos Aires, Montevideo, Rio de Janeiro, Sao Paulo and Caracas were located on one side of the city only.[29]

[29] "The Residential and Retail Patterns of Leading Latin American Cities," *Land Economics*, November 1963.

The automobile and the resultant belt highways encircling American cities have opened up large regions beyond existing settled areas, and future high grade residential growth will probably not be confined entirely to rigidly defined sectors. As a result of the greater flexibility in urban growth patterns resulting from these radial expressways and belt highways, some higher income communities are being developed beyond low income sectors but these communities usually do not enjoy as high a social rating as new neighborhoods located in the high income sector.

CHANGES IN POPULATION GROWTH IN METROPOLITAN AREAS OUTSIDE THE UNITED STATES

Since the rate of population growth, particularly of the great cities of one million population and over, is a most important element in changing city structure, let us examine these differential rates of growth.[30] There has, in fact, been a wide variation in the rate of population growth in the great metropolitan areas throughout the world since 1940. In England, in London and the other large metropolitan areas, the population has remained stationary; on the Continent of Europe outside of Russia, the growth rate of the great metropolitan areas has slowed down to 20 percent in the decade from 1950 to 1960. In Russia, eight of the largest older metropolitan areas increased in population only 15 percent from 1939 to 1962 but in this period many entirely new cities were built and other smaller cities grew

[30] Homer Hoyt, *World Urbanization— Expanding Population in a Shrinking World*, Urban Land Institute Technical Bulletin 43, Washington, D.C., April 1962. See also "The Growth of Cities from 1800 to 1960 and Forecasts to Year 2000," *Land Economics*, May 1963, pp. 167–173.

in size until Russia now has 176 metropolitan areas with a population of 100,-000 or more. China has had a great urban surge since . . . 1950 and reports a gain of 91 percent in the population of 18 great metropolitan areas as a result of its enforced industrialization process. This was reportedly carried too far and city dwellers had to be ordered back to the farms to raise food. Japan's five largest metropolitan area concentrations increased in numbers by 41 percent from 1951 to 1961. Fast suburban trains carry worker to and from downtown places of employment. In India, Delhi and New Delhi have more than doubled in population from 1951 to 1961 as a result of greatly expanded government and manufacturing activity. Other great Indian cities have grown rapidly, with 300,000 or more sleeping in the streets of Calcutta. In Australia, Sydney and Melbourne increased by 32 percent from 1951 to 1961. In Egypt, Cairo has gained 155 percent in numbers since 1940 as a result of being the chief headquarters of the Arab world. African cities like Nairobi and Leopoldville have gained rapidly. In Latin America, the urban population has exploded, with eight of its largest metropolitan areas gaining 166 percent from 1940 to 1962. The Sao Paulo metropolitan area, jumping from 1,380,000 to 4,374,000, gained 217 percent. Mexico City shot up from 1,754,000 to 4,666,-000, a rise of 166 percent, in the same period of time.

CHANGES IN STRUCTURE OF CITIES OUTSIDE THE UNITED STATES

While there are some similarities in the patterns of urban growth in the United States and foreign cities, as for example, in the sector theory, there are also some marked differences, as a result of the following five factors:

(1) Ownership of Automobiles

The chief factor in enabling city populations to spread out, to develop vast areas of single family homes on wide lots far from main transit facilities, to develop so many new shopping centers and so many dispersed factories, has been the almost universal ownership of the private automobile. Only the United States, New Zealand, Australia and Canada, which have developed city patterns similar to ours, had a high ratio of auto ownership to population in 1955, or from 181 per 1,000 in Canada and 183 in Australia to 339 per 1,000 in the United States.[31] Northern European nations had from 58 to 111 cars per thousand of population but most Asiatic and African nations and most of the South American countries had less than 15 cars per 1,000 population. Argentina and Uruguay had 32 cars per 1,000 population in 1955.

The number of automobiles in northwestern Europe has shown marked gains recently: in West Germany from 1955 to 1963 the rate increased from 58 to 122 per 1,000 persons; in the United Kingdom for the same period the rate increased from 92 to 120 per 1,000 persons; and for the same period in Belgium the rate increased from 60 to 106 per 1,000 persons.

Obviously, in most of the world the urban population must depend upon buses or bicycles and live in apartments which can be economically served by subways, street cars or buses. Hence the great expansion into rural areas can take place only when there are suburban railroads as in Buenos Aires, Rio de Janeiro, Delhi and Tokyo, or subways as in London, Moscow, Tokyo, Madrid, Barcelona and Paris. Poor families live in central areas on steep mountainsides

[31] Morton Ginsburg, *Atlas of Economic Development* (Chicago, Illinois: University of Chicago Press, 1961), p. 74.

in Rio de Janeiro and Caracas, in shacks built by themselves; they live in blocks of tenements in central Hong Kong; sleep on the streets in downtown Calcutta, and build mud huts in central Nairobi.

(2) *Private Ownership of Property*

The pattern of American cities is the result of private ownership of property, which cannot be taken by condemnation except for a public use or in a blighted area and for which compensation must be paid when appropriated. There is now almost universal zoning control which regulates types of use, density of use and height of buildings; but these controls, first adopted in New York in 1916, had no effect upon early city growth and they have been modified or changed thousands of times. Otherwise it would not have been possible to develop the 8,300 new shopping centers nearly all of which required zoning in depth rather than strip zoning, nor could thousands of apartment buildings have been constructed in suburban areas.

Consequently, it is impossible to preserve green areas and open spaces without paying for the right. While the public cannot prevent the private owner from building on his land, zoning ordinances in some communities requiring one to five acres of land for each house have practically limited the utilization to occupancy by wealthy families because the high cost of sewer and water lines and street pavements in such low density areas virtually prevents building of houses for middle or low-income family occupancy. Urban sprawl, or the filling in of all vacant areas, has been the bane of planners who would like to restore the early star-shaped pattern. Where the State owns all of the land, as in Russia, or controls it rigidly, as in Finland, dense apartment clusters can

be built along subway lines and the areas in between kept vacant.

(3) *Central Area Attractions*

The central retail areas of foreign cities have not deteriorated as a result of outlying shopping center competition for there are few such centers because very few people own cars. Crowds throng the shops on Florida Street in Buenos Aires and Union Street in Lima, which are closed to automobile traffic in shopping hours. Galerias, an elaborate expansion of the arcade, often extending up to five or six levels, have recently been built in downtown Santiago, Sao Paulo and Rio de Janeiro. Rotterdam has its new central retail area; Cologne its shopping street, a pedestrian thoroughfare. In these foreign cities, residents find the downtown area the chief attraction. The parks of Tokyo, London, Paris, Buenos Aires and Rio de Janeiro are downtown; so are the palaces and government offices, the great cathedrals, the museums, theatres, restaurants and night life of many foreign cities. The Forum and Colosseum in Rome, the Acropolis in Athens, Notre Dame in Paris, Westminster Abbey and the Tower of London are all in or near central areas.[32]

One change is occurring which is altering the skyline of many foreign cities—the advent of the tall office building. Formerly, cities outside the United States prized their uniform skyline broken only by the spire of a great cathedral or an Eiffel Tower. But now tall office buildings loom above London and Milan; they are planned for Paris. Caracas has its 30-story Twin Towers;

[32] Homer Hoyt, "The Structure and Growth of American Cities Contrasted With the Structure of European and Asiatic Cities," *Urban Land*, Urban Land Institute, Washington, D.C., September 1959.

Rio de Janeiro a new 35-story office building, El Centro; Mexico City its 32-story office building; and Sao Paulo has a great concentration of tall buildings in its downtown area.

(4) *Stability of the Currency*

The great building boom in the United States has been financed on money borrowed from banks and insurance companies. Despite gradual inflation, most people have confidence in the American dollar. The volume of mortgage credit for building in 1 to 4 family units increased from $17.4 billion in 1940 to $182.4 billion in December 1963. Shopping centers are financed on the basis of guaranteed leases by national chain store tenants which afford sufficient funds to construct the center. In nations like Brazil, however, where the interest rates are 3 to 5 percent a month and the cruzeiro has dropped from 384 to 1300 to the dollar in a year's time, it is impossible to secure long term loans. New buildings can be effected only by paying all cash as the work proceeds. An inflation of any

marked extent in the United States would drastically curtail the supply of mortgage funds available for new building.

(5) *Redevelopment Laws*

The federal government in 1952 was authorized by Congress to pay two-thirds of the difference between the cost of acquiring sites in blighted areas and the re-sale price for new development. This has made possible the clearing and rebuilding of central areas which could not be done without both the power of condemnation and the write-down of the difference between the acquistion cost and the re-use value.

The principles of city growth and structure, formulated on the basis of experience in cities in the United States prior to 1930, are thus subject to modification not only as a result of dynamic changes in the United States in the last few decades but these principles, originating here, are subject to further revisions when it is sought to apply them to foreign cities.

BOSTON AND THE UNITED STATES

Harvey Cox

Boston gives us an objective view of two contemporary phenomena. First, we see an attempt on the part of some to establish an independence from city life not really possible. The attempt to preserve life as it was 300 years ago is folly in our urban world.

Likewise, Boston gives clear indication that the secularization of society is upon us. While some may regard this secularization as a sign of religious weakening, Dr. Cox looks to it as signs of religious maturity in American society.

We land at Boston's Logan International Airport, not because Boston is either the political or the commercial capital of the United States, but because along the shores of Massachusetts Bay the contrast between the epochs is more pointedly evident than in any other city in America. Boston is at once the oldest city in America and the newest. It is both the historic site of the Puritan colonizers and the launching pad of the new electronic civilization. It combines in a proportion lacking in any other North American metropolis, just enough Old-World elegance and space-age streamlining to make it the most transparent American example of the emergence of the secular city.

Martin Myerson and Edward C. Bansfield, two authorities on urban problems, have called Boston "one of the few beautiful cities in America." They suggest that the reason for its special position is that it was built up largely in the pre-industrial period and therefore possesses a great many structures "with the simplicity and charm of an age which could afford nothing less." Also, Boston was governed for a long time by an aristocracy of wealth and taste. It remains true that most of the really beautiful cities of the world were laid out by such people, not by popular referendum. They were designed "by monarchs, nobles and prelates who had absolute power and who cared not a whit for the convenience or welfare of ordinary people."

But Boston, the "good gray lady," had sunk to an abysmally low ebb before her current astonishing rebirth. Picturesque streets became clogged with gasoline buggies. The frontal collision between Yankees and Irish drove many people with money and civic interests to the suburbs. As Mr. Justice Brandeis reported, at the turn of the century the wealthy citizens of Boston told their sons: "Boston holds nothing for you except heavy taxes and political misrule. When you marry, pick out a suburb to build your house in, join the Country Club, and make your life center about your club, your home and your children." The advice was taken not just by the sons of the wealthy, but by everyone with enough savings to flee to Newton or Belmont.

But urban renewal, the great political fact of the 1960s for American cities, has come to Boston in an extra large package. Under one of the most vigorous mayors in her history, aided by one of the toughest urban renewers in the business, Boston has bitten off a huge chunk of self-redevelopment. Early in the process a couple of serious errors were made. The old West End was ruthlessly demolished and its lower-class families scattered to the winds to make room for the futuristic Charles River Park, where both the apartment buildings and the rents charged soar to the upper reaches. A public-housing project on Columbia Point, land reclaimed from the harbor and accessible only over a narrow peninsula, is now also commonly conceded to be a mistake of the first magnitude. But in several other areas, renewal authorities are trying with real success to make up for a bad start. The design for the new Boston City Hall, chosen by an objective jury from 256 entries, has been acclaimed by several architects one of the boldest and most inventive plans yet devised for a civic building in America. In the so-called gray areas of the city, a program called "neighborhood conservation" has begun to replace the bulldozer as the pathway to new metropolitan life. Most significantly, however, the master plan for Boston's redevelopment envisages the preservation of the distinctive character of such sections as Beacon Hill, Back Bay, and North End. This is important. The nourishment of the local color accumulated in diverse quarters *within* a city is just as important as safeguarding variety *among* cities.

But all this activity in the "new" Boston has not simply materialized full-blown out of the brows of Boston's eager urban renewers. The economic basis for it lies mainly in the spectacular growth of a whole new technical and industrial complex in and around Boston. The city and its environs have become what *The New Yorker* has called "the center of a new world." It is the new world of the electronic computer and that peculiar brand of industry which goes along with it: research-oriented, highly skilled bands of specialists working in laboratory-factories on projects which change even faster than automobile designs. The nerve center of this renaissance is Cambridge, just across the Charles River from Boston, but its tentacles spread out for miles in every direction, especially along Route 128, the circumferential highway around Boston that has become synonymous with the electronics industry.

But technopolis in Boston is far from achieved. The tensions between the old and the new are raw and nerve-racking. Wealthy Bostonians, heeding the advice of their fathers, not only left Back Bay but resisted all Boston's efforts to annex them. The town of Brookline presents the most ludicrous anomaly of all. Almost completely surrounded by the City of Boston, it nonetheless clings to its independent status, pretending to spurn all involvement with the corruption of The Hub. Metropolitan Boston exhibits a more serious imbalance between the size of the city proper and the size of the metropolitan area than any other urban region. Suburbanites gleefully utilize the city's harbor, hospitals, and highways, to say nothing of its concerts, films, and theatres. But they retire behind zoning laws and economic ram-

parts when it comes to the urgent issues of the city itself. Consequently Bostonians groan under an oppressive property-tax burden, which still cannot seem to support an adequate school system, pay the police, or keep the streets clean.

So Boston presents not only a starkly etched contrast of old and young; it also typifies in a particularly glaring way the same crisis faced by every urban region in America—the civic abdication of the middle classes and their withdrawal into a parasitic preserve on the periphery of the city. Like every American city, but in exacerbated form, Boston is impaled on the hyphen in techno-polis. Technically and sociologically, it is a metropolitan region, interdependent in every respect. Politically it is a congeries of fiefdoms and protectorates engaged in the legalized looting of the center city, all the while groping ineffectually with the colossal problems of metropolitan living.

Part of this anarchic miasma stems from the unwillingness of substantial groups within the populace to accept the reality of the secular city. They still want to cling to town and even tribal styles of living. Within the city, clan feuds between Irish, Italian, and Yankee political war parties rage on, while in the suburbs harried escapees from the issues of the inner city deck out their modern homes with wagon wheels and fake colonial furniture. They keep the spotlight shining on the old white church on the green in an effort to convince themselves that they really do live in the simple self-sufficient village founded there three hundred years ago.

But it is all a disastrous self-delusion. Efforts to live in an eighteenth-century town or to maintain the purity and power of the tribe will eventually be exposed for the charades they are. The actual interdependence and technological unity of the urban region will eventually require a political expression.

Besides exemplifying the urban crisis exceptionally well, Boston also portrays with unusual clarity the distinctively American version of the contrast between secularization and secularism. What city better symbolizes a country where a venerable quasi-sacral Protestant culture is just now breathing its last? Its departure, though lamented by some romantics and arcadians, has been greeted by many Protestants with the same relief that European Christians accept the death of "Western Christendom." Protestants may for the first time stand free enough of their culture to be against it or for it selectively, as the guidance of the Gospel suggests. But unfortunately, just as this promising possibility has emerged, the sly temptation of a new sacral society has also appeared. It is the danger of what Martin Marty calls "American shinto." He refers to the "American religion" with three denominations, Catholic–Protestant–Jew, laid open so neatly by Will Herberg and others. It is one of the hidden pitfalls of the present ecumenical movement that we will be urged to remember, *à la* Brotherhood Week posters, that after all we are all Americans and have a common religious heritage.

As Franklin Littell has made potently clear in his book *From State Church to Pluralism,* this "religious past" is really a myth that badly needs demythologizing. People of a variety of religions (and none) came to America for a multiplicity of reasons, not all of them pious. The Protestant sacral culture was imposed on them. The secularization of American society has been a healthy development. It brought about the much-needed emancipation of Catholics, Jews, and others from an enforced Protestant cultural religion. By freeing them it also freed Protestants from important aspects of their culture bondage. It would be too bad if Catholics and Jews, having rightly pushed for the de-Protestantizing of

American society and having in effect won, should now join Protestants in reconstituting a kind of tripartite American religion with Americanized versions of Moses, Luther, and Saint Thomas sharing the haloes in its hagiography. At this point, Christians should continue to support the secularization of American society, recognizing that secularists, atheists, and agnostics do not have to be second-class citizens.

We have yet to measure the enormous contribution made by the brief administration of John F. Kennedy to the desacralizing of American society. His election itself marked the end of Protestant cultural hegemony. But in the way he fulfilled the office, in his quiet refusal to function as the high priest of the American religion, Kennedy made an indispensable contribution to the authentic and healthy secularization of our society. He was a supremely political leader. Though there can be little doubt that his Christian conscience informed many of his decisions, especially in the area of racial justice, he stalwartly declined to accept the semireligious halo that Americans, deprived of a monarch who reigns *gratia dei,* have often tried to attach to their chief executive. In thus divesting his office of any sacral significance, Kennedy did, in his place, what the Christians of Eastern Europe do when they seek to distinguish between the political or economic and the ideological claims of Communist regimes.

The secularists of America may be God's way of warning us that the era of sacred societies is over. Christians have contributed to its demise, perhaps more so than most of us realize. By separating pope from emperor and thus granting a certain provisional autonomy to the secular arm, Western Christianity introduced a process which has produced the modern open society and the ecclesiastically neutral or secular state.

But, as we have seen, the seeds of secularization go back still further: to the creation story in which man is made responsible for the care of the world; to the separation of the kingly from the prophetic office in Israel; to the New Testament injunctions to respect those in authority so long as they do not make religious claims.

The task of American Christians vis-à-vis their nonreligious fellow citizens is not to browbeat them but to make sure they stay secular. They must be helped to be true to their own premises and not to allow themselves to be perverted into a new fideism, the intolerant religion of secularism. In this respect the decision by the California State Board of Education that the schools should have no hesitance in teaching

about religion was a welcome one. The board paid its teachers a welcome compliment by suggesting they "are competent to differentiate between teaching about religion and conducting compulsory worship." Significantly, the board added that it would be just as illegal to teach a "point of view denying God" as it would be to "promote a particular religious sect."

This is a decision which points toward maturation in American society. It recognizes that the public school is no place for required prayers and hymn-singing. But it also recognizes, as so many disciples of secularism do not, that atheists and agnostics have no more right to propagandize their sectarian views through the schools than anyone else does.

NEW COMMUNITIES

Robert C. Weaver

The author uses Park Forest, Illinois; Reston, Virginia; and Columbia, Maryland as examples of broader concepts of metropolitan community development. Particularly, Reston and Columbia were planned in great detail to provide the total community. The builders had foresight, large areas of land, financial resources, and the freedom of "open space" thus minimizing interference. The author cautions that the new communities should also provide for the low-income residents. The new communities are just one part of the total need. The vast majority of our citizens will still be found in the central cities, suburbia, and the outlying towns.

Park Forest, some thirty miles from Chicago, was the first American new-community development started and finished during the immediate post-World War II period. It demonstrated that American private enterprise is capable of creating novel and advanced

patterns of urban living. And, perhaps more important, it proved that such development was economically feasible.

In the years ahead we will see a great diversity of increasingly large developments in this nation. We are already familiar with the Levittowns which,

Reprinted by permission of the publishers from Robert C. Weaver, *Dilemmas of Urban America*. Cambridge, Mass.: Harvard University Press, Copyright, 1965, by the President and Fellows of Harvard College.

though less imaginative and exciting than Park Forest, achieved economies through mass construction and land development techniques in large-scale subdivisions, including swimming pools and self-contained neighborhood facilities. Recently it has been reported that William B. Levitt has upgraded his planning, that he is emphasizing curving streets and minimizing use of the bulldozer so as to preserve trees and the other natural attributes of suburban sites. But his are not new communities in the sense that the term is used by me.

Other and broader concepts of metropolitan community development are being initiated. Reston, a new community in Fairfax County, Virginia, located near Dulles International Airport and eighteen miles from Washington, is under construction. It represents a significant achievement in large-scale land assembly. Over 40 percent of the ten square miles to be developed will remain in open space, principally parks and recreation land. With high standards of design, architectural diversity, and good site planning, this new community is expected ultimately to have 75,000 residents. It will provide single standing homes, town houses, and apartment buildings of wide varieties, yet reflecting imaginative design. Builders of individual homes, small and large builders, as well as the sponsors, will be involved in the construction program. Reston will include bridle paths, stables, golf courses, tennis courts, and artificial lakes. Many types of commercial, educational, and cultural facilities will be provided. The sponsors also hope to have government office buildings and a variety of industrial development.

The new community of Columbia in Howard County, Maryland, will contain 15,000 acres lying between Baltimore and Washington. In planning it, the sponsor is seeking new and exciting concepts for the total development of a new suburban city. According to the plan, a high level of industrial employment opportunities and commercial development will afford the variety and vitality that render urban life interesting and satisfying. A degree of ethnic and economic class diversification is also contemplated. Columbia's developer is working with new concepts in transportation, recreation, and education. Of course, he, too, is encouraging new and advanced architectural design, and he is paying special attention to land utilization.

Both Reston and Columbia will provide a new type of living, aesthetically attractive, affording economies in land use, and assuring provision of utilities and other public facilities of high quality. Both Reston and Columbia are being developed around a town center. They avoid the British defect of failing to provide adequate community facilities during the earlier stages of development. Each of these communities is conceived of as a single organized system which brings together a number of new villages, a feature which may or may not contribute to their social and economic viability.

New communities facilitate well-planned, large-scale development. Thus they represent a potential beneficial long-term investment in the utilization of our land resources. And they can exert a deflationary influence upon land values. This would follow because less reliance would be placed upon utilization of land now held for speculation. New communities are usually farther removed from urban centers than land held for speculation and thus are on cheaper land. Their greatest economic impact results from their augmenting the supply of residential land in large increments.

Private sponsors of new communities are able to achieve high standards of development, with variety and mixture in housing design, that are impossible in the incremental, haphazard development of smaller-scale subdivisions. They are also in a position to influence positively local regulations affecting land use and building methods. Thus, new communities can provide a significant laboratory for demonstrating how zoning, subdivision controls, and building codes can be improved. For instance, zoning might be used to retard rather than accelerate inflation in land costs. Similarly, building codes could be based on more realistic performance standards than now generally exist. The well-financed developer, too, has the scope to develop and implement new standards for architectural control. Indeed, there may be real design premiums incident to private finance since this type of financing "has the advantage of insuring that the design . . . is closely attuned to the needs of the public." Our better privately financed new communities will, I believe, have more architectural character and more attractively designed houses than the British new towns.

New communities can provide a setting for experimentation and innovation in many other fields. In them more efficient and effective institutions for education, recreation, communications, and transportation could be established. Instead of adjusting these activities to an existing physical environment and an established complex system of governmental restrictions (as we are forced to do to varying degrees in the existing urban areas), it will be possible to determine first what man's requirements are and then create a physical environment responsive to these needs.

THE ROLE OF NEW COMMUNITIES IN SUBURBIA

Clearly, new communities are desirable and possible in this country. In the United States we shall probably develop some new communities which are an integral part of the metropolitan areas. Most groups will frequently contain many of the desirable elements of the city. Here, as in Europe, the new communities will be large-scale developments, providing thousands of residential units. Included, in varying mixes, will often be libraries, parks, theaters, and shops. Some will have offices, factories, and industries that afford opportunities for work close at hand. Unlike the European new towns, the residents in our new communities will not generally walk or ride a bicycle to work; here the more common mode of transportation will be the automobile, as it seems to be becoming in Europe. However, in proportion as employment opportunities are nearby, the necessity for commuting will be reduced. Moreover, new communities represent orderly growth, a most favorable condition for the development and extension of mass transportation facilities linking central city, traditional suburbs, and new communities.

Of course, there will be many phony new communities in America. As the concept gains acceptance and catches the imagination of our people, there will be a tendency to identify any large subdivision as a new community. Some alleged to be new communities will be better-laid-out suburbs, but devoid of adequate community facilities, cultural and recreational institutions, and employment opportunities.

There is a role for government in the encouragement and development of new communities. It can be effected through financial assistance to local public agencies which elect to sponsor and assist in the assembly and improvement of land for such communities. But one must recognize that, at present, there are few such local public agencies able, willing, and ready to perform these functions. Thus primary reliance must be placed upon working through the increasing number of private investors and sponsors who are prepared to enter the field of well-planned, large-scale housing developments.

The new communities which will increasingly appear in this country will not solve our problems of future suburban development. As a matter of fact, most of this growth in the years immediately ahead will not occur in new communities: it will continue to be accommodated in smaller, more conventional subdivisions. We must, therefore, be concerned with the quality of these developments, encouraging conformity with a metropolitan plan, insisting that there be adequate provision of basic facilities such as water, sewers, and open spaces. In addition there must be encouragement of better land use which preserves trees and contours. Obviously, government at all its levels has a key responsibility for achieving these results.

There are signs that the home-building industry is recognizing the necessity for planning, designing, and building homes for the complete environment of the homeowner. In December 1964 the National Association of Home Builders in its annual convention issued a policy statement spelling out such an objective. "Our American society," the resolution affirmed, "is increasingly oriented to the home as the center of the American environment. The whole complex of environmental factors—cultural and physical—require intensive examination. To that end, we have commenced and intend to continue to study the relationship of the design and construction of homes to man's aesthetic, physical, and sociological environment."

Despite the concern of home-builders for better-planned and executed suburban developments, most of their efforts will be concentrated upon producing what will primarily be conventional subdivisions. And even the new communities which are now in planning and execution will not realize the full potential of this form of development. Though the hundred-odd existing and projected American new communities represent feasible examples of an extremely attractive style of life for the middle-income and upper-income family, the broad base of our economic pyramid—more than a third of the total population—is usually excluded. This is the element in our society which is necessary for the successful operation of industrial and commercial facilities, as well as for manning the multiplicity of local services, such as janitorial, domestic, and retail services, and maintenance work. For new communities which are remote from concentrations of this manpower and womanpower, the lack of such workers can be both inconvenient and uneconomic.

Our new communities, therefore, will face three alternatives: (1) to plan for the inclusion of housing for this essential component; (2) to occasion the development of unplanned shack towns nearby which will soon evolve into rural slums; or (3) to depend upon commuters to supply these labor requirements, with consequent high incidence of absenteeism and upward pressures on labor costs. The higher labor costs, in large measure, would reflect high transportation costs and inconveniences.

Although I am a firm and long-time advocate of open occupancy and economic diversification in housing and have repeatedly emphasized the importance of such patterns in suburbia, I cannot delude myself into the belief that new communities will be a principal or the exclusive means of achieving these objectives. As in other respects, they can provide demonstrations of what can be done, but the quantitative impact will be slight. For one thing, the new communities will not be numerous enough.

For another, many private sponsors of new communities are sufficiently affluent to obtain financing from conventional sources which are not subject to federal standards.

Nevertheless, everything possible should be done to encourage the new communities to choose the first of their three alternatives—that is, to include housing for low-income residents along with higher-income groups. We need direct inducements to outlying communities to welcome the less affluent; financial assistance to make it possible for private developers to build for them (with adequate safeguards written in the law); and wider coverage and effective enforcement of the Executive Order on Equal Opportunity in Housing. This order, issued by President Kennedy in November 1962, prohibits racial discrimination in certain types of publicly assisted housing.

Proponents of new towns in the United States frequently tend to exaggerate the degree of diversification in European new towns. In addition, such diversification as exists is hardly a unique attribute of those towns; rather it is due to the European tradition of including many economic classes in publicly assisted housing. Indeed, my impression is that class diversification is significantly less characteristic of European new towns than in other types of subsidized housing. The significance of new communities in this regard could, however, be much greater in the United States. For here the need is to break an entrenched suburban tradition of economic and racial homogeneity, and this can best be accomplished in a large new development.

Logically, restriction of government financial assistance in suburbia to new communities that meet certain requirements of economic diversity, planning, and open occupancy would encourage a suburban environment which would satisfy the objectives of many critics of existing suburbs. A leading proponent of such action advocates creation of new communities pursuant to regional open-space and transportation plans, and says, "These towns will also accommodate industrial workers and industries displaced [from the central cities]." They would be open to nonwhites as well as whites, thereby serving as the instrument for breaking down ethnic ghettos in suburbia.

But legislation limiting federal assistance to new communities and excluding more conventional subdivisions will not be enacted in the near future. Thus, our challenge for the present is to extract the maximum from new communities and influence, as far as possible, the nature of the other suburbs of tomorrow, at the same time that we utilize the public lands placed in urban use, making them a symbol of national policy. . . .

The suburbia which is frequently criticized today takes a form which, though not articulated in public policy, was *de facto* public policy because of federal income tax provisions and mortgage-insurance support by the Federal Housing Administration. And some of us will recall that this kind of suburbia created at least as many problems as it solved; included, of course, was encouragement of exodus from the central city. Most of those problems were unanticipated. Will not the electorate ask if similar by-products are inherent in the new-community approach? Will not overemphasis upon new communities militate against effective concern and action for better suburban development in the future?

I am concerned, not only with a decade or so ahead, but with the remainder of this decade and the years immediately following. By 1970 we shall be at a level of two million housing starts a year. It is of crucial importance that the houses we then produce and those we build in the intervening years not have septic tanks that are wet and wells that are dry. We must act now to discourage the bulldozing away of contours and trees. We should improve the flow of traffic through encouraging, revitalizing, and initiating mass transportation. We need to act now to discourage culturally sterile suburban housing developments devoid of, or deficient in, shops, theaters, libraries, and parks within easy access. Nor can we afford to countenance continuing scatteration and uneconomic utilization of urban land.

In a word, we must take immediate action to create better suburbs and to provide an urban setting which increasingly recognizes the need for metropolitan planning. But, alas, there is no magic in planning. As a process *per se* it has little significance even when it operates in the context of clearly established goals, adequate factual materials, and efficient professional guidance, unless there is widespread citizen participation, as well as local political involvement. Only then can planning provide a vehicle for achieving a rational urban environment.

Neither urban planning nor its distortion is new. Very recently, a group of archeologists discovered, in Turkey, the remains of a city believed to be over 8,000 years old. Moreover, they un-

covered evidence of a city plan, with houses and markets carefully laid out in ordered pattern. This is believed to be the oldest executed city plan in existence. But those who dwelt in the orderly arrangement it facilitated did not seem to have been concerned primarily with the good life. Instead, according to John Melleart, assistant director of the British Institute of Archaeology, they appear to have been preoccupied with fertility and death.

I do not mean to imply that such preoccupations might be supposed to provide the basis for city planning, although we are certainly much occupied by fertility, and unless we plan more carefully we are in danger of killing our chances for decent living. What I am saying is that fertility—our great growth—should not be viewed as a death sentence for our great cities or their metropolitan fringes. Rather, in my view, this growth offers unparalleled opportunity to achieve a standard and scale of living no society has yet been able to devise. It all depends on how we utilize our urban land, the degree to which we harness our technology and affluence to provide more attractive and viable communities, and the extent to which we foster the development of opportunity and choice for all.

WHAT'S RIGHT WITH CITIES

Senior Scholastic

Despite the many problems in the cities at least 70 per cent of our people live there now. The cities have many major industries and are centers of education and culture. They offer something to the many ethnic groups: they offer excitement of the bright lights and fine food; they provide escape from the hum-drum of rural life. Some of the cities are even beginning to solve some of their pressing problems such as race relations, unequal educational opportunities, smog, and urban decay. Wilmington, N.C., New Haven, Atlanta, Boston, Hartford, and Baltimore are just a few of the cities where improvements have taken place.

Name a problem—almost any one—and chances are that some American city has it. Yet, despite the difficulties and disadvantages—real or supposed—some seven out of every 10 Americans live in a city or a nearby suburb. And according to census figures, cities are growing all the time.

In 1910, for instance, the U.S. had only 50 cities of 100,000 plus population. By 1940, the figures had jumped to 92, and in 1960 it had jumped again —to 132. As of 1960 more than 51 million people were living in cities of 100,000 or more. And another rise is expected when the 1970 census is in.

Why do they come? There are as many reasons as there are city residents. But here are some:

Cities are a place of opportunity for thousands of people with varying and specialized interests, skills, and ambitions. Major industry has settled in or near cities and attracts all types of workers—from laborers to engineers, clerks to executives, trainees to specialists. Cities are the places where there is such competition in commerce that new ideas are always on the rise. It's in the cities that most new technological aids—computers, for instance—are first developed and used.

Cities, too, are centers of learning and culture. This attracts artists, sculptors, musicians, dancers, actors, writers, and experts in a wide number of fields from archaeology to zoology. City people set the styles—in clothing, in hairdos, in the latest fads and slang.

In the city, newer and older residents alike find much to their liking. Those who seek an escape from the "hum-drum" life or restrictions of the small town or farm may find a new freedom. Those coming from foreign countries to settle most often find a "colony" of people who speak their language or serve their native food in local restaurants. This ethnic diversity adds to a city's excitement and interest. Chinatown and French restaurants, for instance, are attractions in New York and San Francisco. Those who seek out persons with similar intellectual or professional interests can find a wide variety of new friends. And most cities have a host of other attractions: bright lights, theatres, museums, historic buildings, planetariums, concerts and colleges, parades and parks.

Of course, to many people the city is also the place where they were born and raised and the place they're so used to that they couldn't live anywhere else. This feeling is found even in such persons as the young ghetto resident in New York who told a reporter: "No matter what, I wouldn't want to live anywhere else. There's always something happening in this city."

This attitude extends also to the more fortunate middle-class workers who have private homes in more pleasant areas within or near a city. "I was born here," said another New Yorker. "I can see the Empire State Building from my kitchen window. I wouldn't trade it for anything else."

Beyond all this, however, there is much more "right" with cities than most of the screaming headlines or broadcasts usually tell. There are many cities, for example, that are making great strides in solving their racial problems—often quietly but steadily. One smaller city, Wilmington, N.C., was cited in a *U.S. News & World Report* article recently as being a place "where white and Negro people, more often than not, live in harmony." Other cities are making strides, too. Dozens are now experimenting with ways of rehabilitating or rebuilding slum areas. Businessmen, young people, government officials, and ghetto residents themselves are taking part in a variety of programs aimed at cleaning up rundown neighborhoods, helping new business ventures, and creating new educational or job opportunities.

In short, awareness is definitely a city dweller's "plus." And it's paid off in both big and little ways. For example, New Yorkers a few years back banded together to fight a growing litter problem—with the result that many city streets are much cleaner than many a beer-can littered country road. Or consider San Francisco, where citizens fought successfully to stop a highway project that would have obstructed the view of city residents of the colorful San Francisco Bay and its Golden Gate Bridge. Civic outcries in many cities have saved many landmarks, kept trees from being chopped down on picturesque streets, led to new zoning laws, and brought about stricter enforcement of air pollution regulations—all to keep the special flavor of city life and to make life happier for city dwellers.

What's right with cities is often dramatized by the action many city folks take to solve their city's problems. Pittsburgh, for instance, was a morass of smog, urban decay, and unsightliness only 20 years ago. But today, because of the combined action of the citizenry and the city government, it is frequently hailed as a "showcase of urban renewal."

One by one, other U.S. cities have taken the cue to replace ugliness with beauty and economic slump with local prosperity. Among those noted for such actions are Akron, Baltimore, Boston, Detroit, Hartford, New Haven, Philadelphia, San Francisco, Atlanta, and Seattle. It hasn't been easy. A lack of funds and inability to agree on what should be done—plus a number of planning mistakes along the way—have hampered or slowed such plans. But the successes are growing.

Everybody in the cities—the terribly poor, the terribly rich, and everybody in between—knows there are problems. But they also know that there are many things that are right and that problems can be solved.

WHAT'S WRONG WITH CITIES

Senior Scholastic

The larger the cities the more acute the problems. In varying degrees all of the cities face weak city governments, transportation crises, slums, pollution of air and water, high-density living, racial bias, increasing crime, high taxes, inadequate financial resources, inadequate school systems, burgeoning welfare needs, and insufficient job opportunities. Perhaps the most heartening thought is that people are beginning to understand some of the problems and desire to see real improvements made.

Just about anyone who lives in a U.S. city these days could come up with a long list of answers to our "what's wrong" query. If it isn't the traffic snarls, it's the air pollution. If it isn't the fear of being mugged, it's the reality of being burglarized. If it isn't another tax increase, it's a strike that stops another vital municipal service. If it isn't the growing burden of welfare costs on every taxpayer, it's rentals so high that even men with good jobs can't afford decent housing.

These stresses and pressures aren't so acute in the medium-sized cities of the U.S.—though these, too, have their problems. But everything grinds together in a seething urban caldron in the giant cities—the Detroits, Chicagos, Los Angeleses.

Take New York City this fall. In fact, New York's Mayor John Lindsay may very well wish someone else *would* take it for a while. For a warmup there were the "routine" crises such as high crime, miles and miles of slums, stifling air pollution, jammed airports, smelly rivers, racial antagonisms, antiquated subways, and a seemingly endless rise in the numbers of those on public welfare. Added to these "routine" crises this fall was a virtual epidemic of strikes by the men and women who work for the city.

Biggest, longest, and most disruptive was an on-again-off-again strike against the public schools. The issues—which involved community control of schools, teacher job security, and racial antagonisms—were admittedly complex. Still, the effect of the school stoppage was shattering. By early November only a small percentage of the one million students in the New York City public schools had yet attended classes on a regular basis. In addition, attitudes had hardened in many places into an ugly black-white confrontation.

While city officials and state education authorities hunted desperately for ways to defuse the situation and reopen the schools, city policemen announced their own ministrike. Each day about 20 per cent of the police force called in "sick." No parking tickets were written. With fewer traffic cops to call signals, traffic, always irritating, became downright infuriating. Then the firemen's union started its own slowdown, claiming that firemen would demand whatever hikes the police might win.

No sooner had these two unions agreed to go back to work on a full-time basis than the men who operate city incinerators started a slowdown. Through it all, city hall was alternately picketed by striking teachers, militant blacks, off-duty policemen and firemen, and angry parents.

It's been said that being mayor of New York City is the second most difficult job in the U.S. (No. 1 being the Presidency). But mayors of other major cities are quick to line up for Numbers 3, 4, and 5.

Detroit's Mayor Jerome Cavanagh, for one, says his job is impossible. The reason, he argues is that mayors have all the problems to solve and none of the resources and authority to solve them.

Most cities are desperately short of two indispensable items: money and power. Without a good portion of each, tackling even one major city ailment on a scale likely to cure it becomes a near-impossible task. With all the problems interlocked, and with money desperately short, it's a wonder anyone even applies for the mayor's job.

Some 58 million people live in the "inner cities" of the U.S., the cores of the great metropolitan areas that now include more than 140 million Americans. As the inner-city population grows, pressures on these inner cities intensify by leaps and bounds.

While the specifics may vary a little from Chicago to Baltimore, or from Los Angeles to Pittsburgh, few of the big cities could cross off even one of the following items from their own list of major problems:

DECAY   City after city is blotched with acres of deteriorated housing. Despite a boom in private building and more than a decade of federal urban renewal programs, slums remain a prominent feature of every single U.S. city. For the cities, slums are a double-edged problem. Because they harbor and foster more crime, more disease, more welfare clients, more unemployment, more drug addiction, they require proportionally more city services and more expenditures than other areas. Yet they produce far less in taxes.

Though experiments abound and some partial successes have been chalked up, no city has wiped out its slums. Federal urban renewal programs (aimed at eliminating slums) have actually destroyed more low-cost housing than they have replaced. One result: as one slum is bulldozed, bigger slums grow up in another area as the dispossessed take over new quarters.

CRIME   In every recent year, FBI crime statistics have shown a consistent rise in serious crimes. The rise is a nationwide phenomenon, but it gets the most attention in the cities. One result is a rising belief among many city dwellers that neither they nor their property is safe. This very fear helps keep many law-abiding people off the streets and behind locked doors after dark. That, too, helps make the city unsafe. Repeatedly there are stories of passersby who refused to help a person being mugged or attacked—or even refused to telephone the police. This "I-don't-want-to-get-involved" attitude seems to be an outgrowth of modern urban life. Many people just don't want to accept responsibility for the urban community they live in. It is just too big for them to identify with.

The simplest answer to the crime problem, some say, is to hire more police, pay them more, train them better. But even this partial solution runs into economic reality: it costs money to hire more men, and most cities are up against the wall financially.

CONGESTION   Getting from here to there can be the most frustrating part of living in a city. Whether you use a car, a bus, or a subway, it is likely to be a slow, utterly nerve-racking trip at rush hour—the time when most people need to go from here to there. Better build more subways, say the problem solvers. But where is the money to come from? Well then, run more buses. But buses add to air pollution and to traffic snarls. All right, so build more roads? But on whose land and through whose front yard? Won't this just encourage more traffic and lead to newer—and bigger—traffic snarls? And by the time a highway is planned, approved, and built (sometimes a 20-year process), will it be able to handle the additional traffic arising from population increases?

GARBAGE   Out in the country, you can burn your own debris, or haul it to a dump, or pay someone to take it away. In big cities, such "do-it-yourselfing" isn't feasible—or legal. Usually, the city government itself assumes the job of collecting and disposing of the millions of tons of refuse that city dwellers each day heave into their trash cans.

Just collecting it is a headache in Big Town. When will the big and noisy garbage trucks clatter down those already clogged streets? During business hours? Or perhaps at night when the natives like to sleep? Then where to put the stuff? Burning trash thickens the already gray haze that separates the sunlight from most metropolitan areas. Put it in a big hole? Many cities have already filled all the convenient big holes.

WATER AND SEWAGE   The urban household with its garbage disposals, dishwashers, and two bathrooms, uses prodigious amounts of water. That same water then drains away, full of detergents and human waste. Where to dump it without polluting the source of drinking water? The old answer was to pipe sewage to the nearest river or lake. But most of these are now so dirty that they aren't fit to supply fresh water that hasn't first undergone extensive (and costly) treatment. So why not build plants to treat the water? Fine, but such plants cost millions, and city taxpayers are already moving to suburbia because they believe their tax bills are too high.

RACE   As whites hurry to suburbia, the inner cities become blacker. For the cities, it is a social and economic upheaval of major importance. In the 10 years between the 1950 and 1960 federal censuses, only eight of the 20 largest cities gained in white population. But black population increased in all 20. By 1960, 17 per cent of the North's inner city population was black. Many of these Negroes were not city-born. In 1960 two thirds of the adult Negroes in Northern cities were born in the South.

In other words, while the inner cities have been losing middle-class whites to the surrounding suburbs, these cities have been gaining poorly educated rural Negroes who had lost their agricultural jobs in the South as machines replaced human labor. Big Town beckoned to these newcomers as a place to find a job, to make a better life. Unfortunately, many found that they lacked the education needed to crack the urban job market. In 1950 five out of every six Negroes who migrated to Northern cities found jobs. By 1960 the figure was down to four out of six. That means two in six did not find a job.

Crowded into the ghettos, unable to find meaningful work, subjected to discrimination many thought they were leaving behind, some blacks have given up all hope. Others have just become angrier. The very successes of the civil rights movement of the early 1960's fanned hopes that sometimes turned to bitter anger when the Promised Land didn't arrive for everyone. Four summers of urban riots have painted a vivid picture of how deep the anger lies.

WELFARE   Cities have traditionally beckoned to those in rural America down on their luck. In recent years, however, the kind of jobs undereducated rural people could find have been disappearing. But rural people continue to move into cities. Caught in this technological squeeze, millions have turned to public welfare. The cost to cities forced to pay a large share of the welfare bills has reached major proportions—and has spurred a major reappraisal of the entire welfare system.

As in so many of the other problems cited, the cities today are paying the bill for a situation created elsewhere and thrust on them. In one major city, a citizens' budget committee put their grievance bluntly: rural Southern areas with low levels of welfare payments have succeeded in shifting the bulk of the nation's relief load to northern urban areas.

What this shift can mean to Big Town is again vividly clear in New York City. A recent study showed that by next June one million people, or one out of every eight New Yorkers, would be fully or partially supported by public welfare. The cost? A whopping 26 per cent of the city's budget.

LACK OF POWER   With power, all the other problems might seem a little more soluble, but Big Town is just a little sister when it comes to governmental authority. "The basic local government structure in the United States was designed primarily for a rural agricultural society whose inhabitants had a basic distrust of all governments," says the National League of Cities. Most cities do not have the legal authority for a frontal assault on their problems. City boundaries are often haphazard, not really reflecting where the real city begins and ends. Special districts and authorities carve up the power to tax and make decisions.

State legislatures, which have total authority over their cities (and which are usually controlled by rural interest), have consistently been unwilling to give the cities broad and continuing power to run their own affairs or even to decide for themselves what taxes to levy on their citizens. It all adds up to a system of buck-passing when the time comes to assess the blame for urban failures.

"Nobody can tell just who is responsible for what," said a conference of city experts convened by the National League of Cities in 1966. "Schools, for example, are paid for partly by the local school district, partly by the state, a little by Washington, with the state set-

ting the standards, the local authorities picking the teachers, and the federal government decreeing the racial balance."

MONEY   At the start of this century, local governments spent more per person than did the state and federal governments combined. In 1902 local governments spent 54.8 per cent of all government monies, compared with just 34.5 per cent by the federal government.

In the following six and a half decades, local government responsibilities have multiplied, population has soared, and so has government spending at all levels. But the local government's share of the fiscal pie has dwindled. Local governments now spend about 20 per cent of all government money. Where cities once collected more than 70 per cent of all taxes, they now collect only about 15 per cent while trying to provide services for most of the population.

The one big source of local revenue is the property tax, which provides about 88 per cent of all locally raised revenue. In most places, this tax is about as high as it can go, and no other source has proved particularly workable for raising large sums.

Thus, the gap between urban financial needs and urban financial abilities keeps widening. A study prepared for the National League of Cities showed that by 1975 U.S. cities will need to spend about $150 billion a year. But their own revenue resources will produce only about $70 billion. From federal and state aid cities can expect about $30 billion. That leaves a $50 billion gap between what will be needed and what will be available.

The problems list could go on and on. Whether the cities created the problems or simply inherited them is debatable. But it seems increasingly clear that *most* of the serious domestic problems in the U.S. today are focused in the city. What is worse, many people are coming to the conclusion that the problems aren't going to be solved.

"Trust is the cornerstone of civic order, but few of us, white or black, really trust the community in which we live," wrote Max Ways, an editor of *Fortune* magazine in the January 1968 issue. "We have no reason to suppose that they will keep the air and rivers clear or that they can effectively protect our lives or our property."

It's a depressing picture—particularly for those millions who live in cities because that's where the action is and they don't want to be anywhere else. But whether by choice or by circumstance, millions of city dwellers are each day made aware that plenty is wrong in the cities and each day hope against hope that more can be made right.

CAN THE BIG CITIES EVER COME BACK?

U.S. News & World Report

There is certainly no assurance that the big cities can in fact be saved. The large number of unemployed and underemployed has had a debilitating influence on the entire environment. Major difficulties in the areas of transportation, housing, health, education, crime, sanitation, outflow of businesses with the resulting loss of jobs, and the inflow of still more Negroes without adequate readiness for city life illustrate the magnitude of the problems. Can the planners find solutions; can the economy support the fiscal requirements; and will huge appropriations be politically acceptable with those outside the cities? The task is large and the time is late.

Riots, skyrocketing crime, tax problems that multiply raise this question:

Can the big cities of this country ever stage a comeback?

Trends now accelerating do not suggest a strongly affirmative answer.

Despite all the remedies tried, all the billions spent, problems keep growing in central cities across the nation.

Migrants, mostly untrained, keep pouring in from rural areas. Middle and upper-income whites, more and more, live in suburbs.

Result: School problems mount. Relief costs keep soaring. Crime tends to get out of hand, adding to the cost of trying to police the cities.

At the same time, the tax base—income and property from which money can be drawn to pay the mounting bills —often stagnates or declines in relation to the expanding size of the problems.

Now, adding to all the difficulties, signs grow that business is becoming somewhat less interested than before in centering expansion within the central cities. Costs there are seen as growing too high, labor problems too great, uncertainties too discouraging.

LAYING PLANS   On August 24, nearly 1,000 city officials, businessmen and other community leaders met in Washington, D.C., to establish some long-range goals for the rebuilding of the nation's big cities.

Out of this meeting is expected to come a detailed study of just what it will cost to rebuild two or three specific cities as a means of finding out what can be done.

Already big-city mayors have told Congress it will take at least 1 trillion dollars—1,000 billion—to overcome problems they face.

Yet Congress, responsive to interests of suburbs, smaller cities and countryside, seems not inclined to vote the massive sums and tax increases needed to give large-scale help to big cities.

It is this situation that is giving rise to other possibilities—slowing migration of low-income people into cities, decentralizing city administration, or developing new approaches to be used by metropolitan areas.

DRAMATIC EXAMPLES   The plight of the cities, generally, is dramatized by what is happening in those that have been hit by spectacular and costly riots.

In Detroit, considered by many to be a model of racial peace and "progressive" leadership, race rioting was the worst in the nation's history.

Today, suburban real estate operators in the Detroit area forecast a renewed flow of whites from the city. And conversely, the slow trickle of whites back into the city from the suburbs has stopped, at least for the time being. One apartment-house developer said gloomily: "I don't know how long it will take for business to pick up—or even if it will."

Many of the stores in Negro areas that were destroyed or closed down during the "insurrection" are not expected to reopen. Public schools are forced to provide portable classrooms for 3,500 displaced youngsters. The superintendent said he foresaw even more difficulty than before in finding teachers for Detroit's public schools.

In Newark, N.J., scene of another big riot this summer, forecasts are that half the small businesses in Negro areas and perhaps as many as a fourth of the larger ones will not reopen. Racial tension between whites and Negroes continues to run high. Recovery in such cities, the experts say, is not likely to come soon.

Rioting in Chicago last year was not "major." Yet officials noticed a decline in business in the Negro area directly west of the Loop because businessmen cannot get insurance coverage at the normal rates. A number of stores are boarded up still, and apparently will remain that way.

In Los Angeles, where the Watts riot of 1965 took 34 lives and caused about 50 million dollars' worth of property damage over an area of 46 square miles, only three of the 40 businesses destroyed have been rebuilt. Insurance rates have gone up three to five times since the riots. One druggist said he is now paying monthly for insurance what he paid in one year before the rioting. A white grocer said:

"I wouldn't open a branch in Watts even if the Government guaranteed me a healthy net profit and posted a couple dozen armed guards around the clock. The way things are going these days, you never know when things will break wide open again."

In the riot area itself, Negro discontent persists.

OPTIMISTIC TALK, THEN—   Just after the riots, city officials were talking optimistically of upgrading the Negro neighborhoods. Mentioned were tree-shaded malls, new apartment buildings, spacious parks and new business and industry.

Today, however, a federal estimate is that one out of three persons in the riot area remains jobless or underemployed. Negro spokesmen say that median income is down, while relief rolls have gone up 34 per cent—largely because a number of organizations have been created to inform people of their "welfare rights."

Negroes who have benefited from job training are moving to better neighborhoods. Left behind, as a nucleus for future trouble are the castoffs along with new and unskilled migrants from other parts of the country.

What city planners in Los Angeles and big cities are discovering is this painful fact:

No longer can they count on a big drop in the tide of ill-prepared people from the South. Developing in that part of the nation, they find, is a virtually inexhaustible reservoir of migration for future years.

CENSUS CLUES   A few figures explain why city planners are increasingly alarmed.

The huge flow of Negroes out of the South in recent times has reduced that region's share of the Negro population in America from 77 per cent in 1940 to about 54 per cent at present.

In absolute numbers, however, the Negro population of the South has gone up, in that period of time, from 9.9 million to 11.2 million.

Furthermore, about 38 per cent of Negroes now living in the South are under 14 years of age. Another 11 per cent are aged 14 to 19. As these youngsters enter the labor force, many will be moving to cities in the North and West where jobs are more plentiful—and welfare more generous. Negro migration from the South, which amounted to 1.5

million during the 1950s, is expected by some authorities to reach 2 million during the 1960s.

Nor does the problem for cities end there.

Nonwhite children accounted for one third of the increase of children under 14 in metropolitan areas between 1960 and 1966. They are increasing at a rate three times as fast as that for whites.

Accordingly, one estimate is that 14 cities will have Negro populations of 40 per cent or more by 1970. Today, Washington and Newark, N.J., are the only big cities with Negro majorities, but population experts are saying that 20 or more cities will share that distinction by the 1980s.

If these projections turn out to be true, cities today are getting a foretaste of even bigger problems in the offing.

WELFARE, CRIME AND SCHOOLS   In city after city, welfare costs are going up. Police try to stem a rising tide of crime flowing out of Negro slums. Public schools are under pressure from courts to integrate across neighborhood boundaries—thereby spurring the exodus of middle-class taxpayers from the city.

This is what some cities are up against:

· In New York City, which has 1.25 million Negroes, welfare rolls have more than doubled since 1958. Negroes and Puerto Ricans make up more than 80 per cent of all welfare recipients.

· In Cleveland, where the Negro share of population has gone up from 28 to 35 per cent since 1960, police costs over those years have almost tripled. Murders increased from 84 in 1960 to 139 last year, forcible rapes are up from 79 to 159, and aggravated assaults up from 530 to 1,137.

· In Los Angeles, school officials have prepared a record budget of 663.5 million dollars for 1967–68. A big item in that outlay consists of special services aimed primarily at "disadvantaged" Negro and Mexican-American children. These include smaller classes in slum schools, remedial teaching—and a school for pregnant girls aged 13 to 15.

A SHATTERED HOPE   Over the years, city officials hoped, social problems spilling out from the slums would diminish as raw migrants picked up job skills and education. The growing number of Negroes entering the professions and skilled occupations each year was seen as an important solution to the social problems of the slums.

Now, evidence grows that the untutored migrant is only the beginning of those problems.

One bit of evidence: a sampling of arrested rioters in Los Angeles in 1965 found many who were not ignorant newcomers or teen-age hoodlums. Forty-one per cent were married, 32 per cent were high-school graduates, 38 per cent were in skilled and semiskilled jobs, 22 per cent earned $400 or more a month, and 75 per cent had lived in Los Angeles for at least five years.

Said Dr. Seymour Martin Lipset, professor of sociology and government at Harvard:

"What you are getting in the big cities is a situation quite similar to that in newly independent countries—where the situation of people, in this case Negroes, has not changed enough to match their expectations. Revolutions tend to come when things are getting better—but not fast enough."

REVOLUTION ASIDE—   Finding a way to stave off revolution comes at a time when cities are trying to cope with a multitude of other woes.

Streets are snarled in traffic. Air pollution becomes worse each year. Water and power shortages are becoming critical in some places.

What is making the dilemma of cities acute is a basic fact: Tax resources are lagging further and further behind skyrocketing costs.

Personal income and property values in cities declined as middle-class people moved out—followed by a large chunk of downtown business. Now industries are shifting to suburbs and small towns to find cheaper land and a labor pool of skilled workers and technicians.

Recently a congressional hearing on open housing was told that employment in U.S. manufacturing has increased by nearly 2 million jobs since 1961—but almost all of the increase has been outside areas of Negro concentration.

In New York, Leonard Yaseen, chairman of a firm specializing in industrial relocation, said: "I look for New York to lose 100,000 industrial jobs in the next three or four years—and I think this reflects what is going on in most of the big cities."

High-speed roads, once seen as making it easier for suburbanites to commute downtown, are making it easier for jobs to move to the suburbs. One engineering study predicted recently that the Capital Beltway around Washington, D.C., will lure about 10,000 jobs from the city by 1976—lopping about 9 per cent from the city's expected growth in jobs during the next nine years.

Result is that tax bases in big cities are only growing slowly or, in some cases, actually shrinking. From John Shannon, assistant director of the U.S. Advisory Commission on Intergovernmental Relations, came this summary of the problem:

In the mid-1950s, tax experts assumed that city tax bases would show a 5 per cent increase annually. Today average gains are running well below that figure.

PROPOSALS FOR COMEBACK   It is against that broad background of trouble that suggestions are made of what it will take for cities to make a comeback.

One widely publicized estimate is that it will cost at least 1 trillion dollars—30 per cent of it in public spending—over the next 12 years to renovate metropolitan areas and bring the central cities back to health.

Some proposals call for spending of 10 billion dollars a year or more to help Negro slum dwellers. Vice President Hubert H. Humphrey recently suggested the equivalent of the Marshall Plan for helping Negroes.

Being explored is the idea that perhaps it is time to discourage the flow of Negro migration to cities of the North and West. Recently Secretary of Agriculture Orville L. Freeman proposed a national policy aimed at providing more opportunities in smaller towns and cities in order to stem the flow of people out of rural areas.

On August 23, the Republican Coordinating Committee—pointing to problems raised by migration to the cities—urged a drive to locate new industries in rural regions by offering tax inducements, channeling Government contracts to such industries and stepping up aid to rural education and road building.

AN "UNDERCLASS"   Another thought comes from Daniel P. Moynihan, former Assistant Secretary of Labor and now director of the Joint Center for Urban Studies operated by Harvard University and Massachusetts Institute of Technology.

Dr. Moynihan finds the cities' social problems centering in an "urban underclass" of aimless and unstable Negroes who are the products of widespread disorganization of families in the slums.

These figures are cited:

Nationwide, 6 out of every 10 Negroes reaching the age of 18 have at some time been supported by federal aid to dependent children. Probably not more than one third of low-income Negro children reaching 18 have lived their entire lives with both parents.

Also cited is the high rate of illegitimacy among low-income Negroes—as in Detroit, where a 1965 study showed that one quarter of low-income Negro households reported children of illegitimate birth.

It is Dr. Moynihan's contention that cities can solve their central problem of Negro slums only with aid from federal programs aimed at reinforcing Negro family ties. Among them would be family allowances and federally supported jobs for the unemployed.

ONE JUDGE'S SUGGESTION   Some planners would like to disperse Negroes from central cities to the suburbs. Recently U.S. District Judge J. Skelly Wright, in a decision involving the 90 per cent Negro enrollment in public schools of Washington, D.C., suggested that school officials explore the possibility of large-scale exchange of pupils between city and suburbs on a voluntary basis.

Few suburbs, however, seem eager to take on the central city's problems— nor is it likely that Congress would countenance forced dispersal of Negroes from the central cities.

Changes in the structure of city governments to handle the broad range of their problems are also under discussion.

One such proposal is to decentralize urban government somewhat, setting up "little city halls" in neighborhoods to provide a closer relationship between officials and people. Presumably this would bring a greater measure of public support for laws and policies aimed at improving cities.

One possibility suggested recently by

Police Commissioner Howard R. Leary of New York City was that some police precinct houses should become centers where slum dwellers could get advice on health, housing and welfare problems. This, he thought, would be one way of "humanizing" the police department.

Others are suggesting that schools serve as neighborhood centers, remaining open at night for adult-education classes and neighborhood meetings.

Said Dr. Stephen K. Bailey, dean of the Maxwell Graduate School of Citizenship and Public Affairs at Syracuse University:

"We're caught in a paradox where the necessities of living together in cities impose the need for certain controls, yet those controls could cut into the fabric of our values—individual rights, equality and all the rest."

This is becoming clear:

The crisis of the big cities, coming to a head in recent years, continues without letup. And no real solution appears in the immediate future.

PART II

QUESTIONS FOR DISCUSSION

1. Select some community you are familiar with which is undergoing a loss in population and describe the factors influencing this phenomenon.
2. What features of city life seem most conducive to positive social behavior? Which seem most negative?
3. What factors have led the urban dweller to lose his sense of belonging to the community? How might this sense of belonging be regained?
4. Assume you are contemplating moving to a new community. What features would influence you to select a given community? What conditions would cause you to reject a community?
5. What geographical features influenced the development of your community? Consider water supply, transportation, topography, climate, and agricultural and economic factors.
6. What are the problems involved when a city expands over natural or political boundaries?
7. What difficulties result when a city expands too rapidly? Choose a community which has undergone this experience.
8. What advantages do you see in the planning and development of a complete new city?

VOCABULARY

primary group
epoch
mutation
antithesis
life style
annexation
demographic
topography
urban
high-density living
urban sprawl
metropolitan
mass consumption

manifestations
communal
mobility
local services
subdivision
hypotheses
commercial clutter
integral
aesthetic
primary industry
aggregation
town houses
dependent industry

URBAN ETHNIC GROUPS

True assimilation of ethnic minorities into American society has long been held as the ideal in our supposed cultural melting pot. Some minorities have been successfully assimilated but others, many others, have not. Almost anyone will supply a ready answer for this situation and perhaps some of the most obvious are the most correct.

The most obvious deterrent to assimilation is race. Traditionally Americans have frowned on mixed marriages. The rise of Chinatown and the Negro ghettos in our cities have indicated this unwillingness to assimilate. The logic, or lack of it, behind the opposition to mixed marriages generally takes the form of "What will happen to the children?" If true open entry into the mainstream of American society were possible, this would be a cause of little concern. However, children of Negro-white marriages have generally found themselves forced to live in Negro communities. Evidence of a breakdown of opposition to racially mixed marriages has not been evident on any national scale. While race explains part of the difficulty of assimilation, other factors must be present for Caucasian groups.

The Jews form the most classic example of a closely knit religious group who have tended to sustain their ethnic and religious origins. While utilizing to the maximum normal routes of assimilation in society, particularly the public schools, they have tended to retain features of ethnic diversity.

Certainly religious differences do present difficulties and the national tendency has been to avoid Christian-Jewish mixed marriages. Increasing secularism, combined with the slow breakdown of more conservative religious patterns, has not materially altered this pattern. As in race, America's respect for diversity is somewhat suspect.

However, there do appear to be signs that at least some progress is being made. One of the most hopeful, religiously, is the ecumenical movement. While it did tend to reach its fullest vigor about 1965 and subsequently die down in institutionalized religion, the sociological phenomenon of the underground church has come to supplant it. Here groups of all and no denominations come together to worship in what they feel is true fellowship. Such meetings appear to be alive and well on many of our college campuses. Similarly, or coincidentally, this coming together religiously may foster breakdowns in traditional racial barriers. The participation of many clergy in civil rights demonstrations, often in defiance of higher authority, bears out that religious action in support of racial causes can bring people together.

While backlash sentiments give clear evidence of the racist feelings in our country, there are at least signs of progress. Whether this progress will come fast enough is questionable. An open society must be the goal of all concerned people. For it is only in an open society, free of artificial barriers, that real freedom can be assured.

ETHNIC PRESSURES

Paul Jacobs

The life of the Negro ghetto dweller is one which forces the world of fantasy to often take hold when reality simply cannot be faced. It is small wonder then the slightest occurrence can trigger off deep-seated psychological needs. The desires to be someone, to be a man, to be important, to be needed, and to do something which can make these desires come true are emotions we all feel. That the ghetto dweller may choose paths socially unacceptable to attain these goals, many Americans find difficult to understand. Yet understand we must.

Thus, when the young Negro spat in my face in downtown Los Angeles, he was spitting on all of white America. I was Whitey, and he hates Whitey because he believes Whitey despises and hates him.

And he is right. The pattern of life of poor whites in America is determined by the contempt in which they are held for having failed to achieve the individual affluence which is the society's basic values. The life of poor Puerto Ricans, Mexicans, and Indians is marked by the same contempt, mixed with some fear about their odd behavior, the kind of fear that resulted in the infamous "zoot-suit" riots in Los Angeles during the war, when gangs of servicemen roamed the streets, savagely beating every teen-ager who looked like a Mexican. But the lives of the poor Negroes in American cities are marked not only by contempt and fear but by active hate. And it is hate which makes ghettoization continue and intensify.

Another characteristic of life common to all the poor but qualitatively different for minorities is their continual contact with government agencies. Most middle-class people in cities have minimal contact with government: occasionally they get a traffic ticket; once a year they write checks to the collector of internal revenue and the state treasurer; every few years an assessor from the county tax office makes an appraisal of their possessions; they vote every two years if they are public-spirited citizens; they go to PTA meetings if they are concerned about their children's education.

But the poor—white, Mexican, Puerto Rican, Indian, and Negro alike—are in continual contact with government agencies. They spend a large proportion of their time waiting for interviews in welfare offices or answering caseworkers' questions in their homes; when they are sick, they wait in the county clinic to see a doctor; they go to a state employment agency for jobs. Because their children frequently get into trouble at school, they are visited by truant officers. Their children get into more trouble outside of school, too, and they have more contact with the police, then the courts, then the jails, then the probation and parole officers, and then the police again, as the whole cycle repeats itself. They see the marshals, too, very often when they stop making payments on the TV and the credit store tries to repossess the set. Their cars are old, they have more accidents in them, and they get more traffic tickets which they cannot pay; so they end up being arrested rather than just cited. If they need psychiatric help, they must be committed to state hospitals, unlike those with higher incomes who can remain at home while undergoing treatment.

For most of the poor, then, government is seen as a network of agencies that affect their lives directly and often. These frequent and affective contacts tend to be either abrasive, rubbing raw their physical and psychic skins, or non-supportive, because their real problems are ignored or not understood. The abrasive quality of the relationships between the poor and such institutions as welfare bureaus or the police departments, which inevitably come into some degree of conflict with citizens, is carried over into poor people's relationships with schools and hospitals, which for the rest of the population are either supportive or at least neutral.

The poor, and especially the minority poor, generally tend, in their contacts with city, county, state, and federal government agencies, to be treated either punitively or in ways which reinforce their feelings of dependency, and frequently both. The help extended to the poor is grudging, tight-lipped, and censorious, for it is generally assumed that they are responsible for their own bad condition and that if they wanted to get out of it badly enough, they could do so.

It is also assumed that they are incapable of running their own lives and that therefore they need not be given the same rights as the rest of society. They are thought of as being somehow subhuman, not truly men and women. That is why the looting and the burning

and the sniping take place: a man squinting down the sights of a rifle, hidden from view behind a curtained window, feels powerful, for now he can decide on life or death. A man hurling a Molotov cocktail into a supermarket and watching it burst into flames can say, as one said to me, "That was the first time in my life I ever felt like a man." Another man, who proudly showed me a closetful of suits, said, "Those are loot suits."

And it doesn't matter if the suits don't fit, for they are important as symbols. Looting in the cities can be just as much an act of politics as it is a desire for goods. It is a way in which the poor can make a representation to the society, for they have no other kind of representation; it is a way in which the black poor can express their hate of the white world for not giving them their chance to share in the goodies. And it doesn't matter whether the store being looted is owned by a black man or a white man; *owning* a store is what white people do, not black ones.

The ideas of law and order held by the minority poor can be different from those held by the rest of society. The poor guard their possessions as best they can, but they view the theft of them as being an inevitable part of the world in which they live, rather than as an abnormal circumstance, which is how stealing is perceived outside the ghettos.

So, too, whether or not it is only Jewish men who come to the doors of the poor Negroes selling cheap, shoddy merchandise at high prices, all of them are thought of as Jews, as "Goldbergs in Their Jew Canoes," the Cadillacs in which it is believed they drive into the ghetto to collect the money of the poor. The ghetto dwellers believe it is in the natural order of things for them to be cheated by the Jewish merchants, since they believe cheating to be part of the Jewish psyche. And so, when a "selec-

tive demolition program," as the burn-
ings are described, breaks out, the
Jewish-owned stores become immediate
targets.

But Negro businessmen exploit Negroes viciously, too, and there are
Mexican-Americans fattening on the
troubles of their community. The ghettos
have their own ministers, too, who
thrive while their flocks starve (a Cadil-
lac is also called a "Baptist preacher"
in the ghetto), their cynical politicians
who exploit their ethnic or racial background but do nothing for their constituents, and their "community leaders"
seeking only to advance themselves
rather than the people they claim to
serve. As many organizational jealousies
can be found in the ghettos as outside
them, and as many groups fighting desperately for the right to speak in the
name of the whole community.

So we must learn, painfully, not to
romanticize any group and not to expect
that a group that is discriminated
against is therefore less capable of prejudice against other groups. We must
learn how complex are the problems of
the urban poor, who have fewer resources to deal with their difficulties
than any other group in society. Take
health, for example. A family with a
pregnant wife, an unemployed sick husband, and two children, one of whom
is ill, must get to four different physical
locations at four different times in order
to even try to solve their health problems: the pregnant mother goes to a
prenatal clinic, which meets only twice
a week; she takes one child to a Well
Baby clinic, which is held on a different
day, and the sick child to another clinic,
which also meets on a different day; the
unemployed father must visit the county
hospital for treatment of his illness. In
each of these places the waiting time
will be interminable; and the family
may have to pay for the treatment and
care they get.

Or consider what is required to help
one unemployed, unskilled Negro teen-
ager get a job and keep it: he will
probably need a basic education that includes learning how to read, write, and
speak intelligibly; his past arrest record
will need to be expunged or ignored;
he will need many hours of vocational
counseling; his poor health will need
repairing, some of his bad and rotting
teeth replacement; he should spend
hours with a psychiatric social worker,
and another worker may need to spend
hours or days with his family. When
all this and a good deal more has been
done to help him in his personal life,
he will probably still be living in a
ghetto from which he cannot escape and
be part of a social condition which itself
requires fundamental and radical transformation.

The brutal fact about American
society today is that a whole constellation of forces, agencies, and circumstances, whose origins are different,
whose operations are fragmented, and
whose jurisdictions are separate, have
converged in the cities. The effect of
this constellation bearing down upon us
has been disastrous.

This is not to suggest that the ghettos
are always frightening, for they are not.
Fun and games can be found in them,
and there are great sources of humor
and deep springs of strength among the
ghetto people. In the housing projects
the women come and go, laughing with
each other about the latest tricks of
their little James; on a crowded street a
young Negro teen-ager says hello to me
and asks as I walk by, "Who you bull-
shittin' today, white boy? You scarin'
the white folks again today?" And when
I laugh in answer, he continues with a
grin, "You know, white boy, you really
should be payin' me so I don't have to
go and hustle me some bread. Where
you be without me, stirrin' it up around
here? You white mother, you should be

hiring me and then I won't have to advertise for no job like I'm doin' now. See, I cut this article out of the paper, where it says I'm a black nationalist, a extremist, and I'm going to stick it up on the wall right here on the street. That way, I figure, some white mother might walk down the street, looking to hire a extremist and, like, I'm available. How about it, white boy, you know anybody wants to hire him a black extremist? Like man, I need bread."

In some important ways the ghettos even give strength and security to the people who live in them, and they are a source of great inner vitality. But this strength, security, and vitality can also be a source of weakness, for it makes the ghetto dwellers want to remain inside the ghetto rather than venture beyond its borders.

Until recently another consequence of remaining inside the ghetto has been that some of its inhabitants, especially the kids and teen-agers, always live part of their lives in a fantasy world. School dropouts, unable to face the reality of working in a car wash, talk about becoming jet pilots. They dream about the hi-fi they will buy when they become wealthy entertainers, for their psyches cannot stand the knowledge that they will be poor all their lives. In their minds the boys see themselves as sexual giants, the girls as sought-after beauty queens. Their transistor radios are turned on all the time to the Negro or Spanish stations; the radio is their fix, the music the drug that takes them out of the ugly reality into a private fantasy world. And if the talk and the radio fail

them, they can always light up a joint —for to "blow grass," smoke marijuana, helps greatly to soften the sharp outlines of their lives.

It is hard for such ghetto children to grow up, for they think they have nothing to grow up to, and few of the usual ways in which children become adults are open to them. They do not graduate from high school and then take their first steps toward adulthood and maturity in college or in a job. They have no adult occupations with which to identify, and so they remain caught in the matrix of childhood. Even when the fourteen- or fifteen-year-old becomes pregnant and gives birth, she is not really a mother; her baby is no more to her than some kind of doll, and she plays with it happily, her own mother's eyes on her, until baby begins to cry. Then the child-mother grows impatient and slaps the doll, until the thirty-three-year-old grandmother takes the infant away from her.

These people, adults by chronology but not personality, never have an opportunity to break with the patterns they have learned: to lie to and run from the agencies of government, which they see only in negative and oppressive roles. Their lives run by a clock that keeps C.P.T., Colored People's Time, which assumes that appointments made won't be kept, work promised won't be delivered, jobs found won't be gone to, since those are all part of the outside world. Like Mexican Time and the one-time J.P.T., Jewish People's Time, C.P.T. is a phrase that draws the lines of the ghetto.

BEYOND THE MELTING POT

Nathan Glazer and Daniel P. Moynihan

The idea of the United States being the melting pot of all immigrants coming to her shores is as old as the Republic. New restrictions on immigration, beginning in 1882 when the Chinese were excluded, reinforced the early ethnic stock rather than diluting it. The authors use New York City to dispel the melting pot theory as of now. The Jewish community, the Catholics, the Negroes and the Puerto Ricans have not merged into the single American society as one would have thought. The ethnic patterns have remained strong; the candidate for political office who forgets this is in serious trouble.

The idea of the melting pot is as old as the Republic. "I could point out to you a family," wrote the naturalized New Yorker, M-G. Jean de Crèvecoeur, in 1782, "whose grandfather was an Englishman, whose wife was Dutch, whose son married a French woman, and whose present four sons have now four wives of different nations. *He* is an American, who leaving behind him all his ancient prejudices and manners, receives new ones from the new mode of life he has embraced. . . . Here individuals of all nations are melted into a new race of men. . . ."[1] It was an idea close to the heart of the American self-image. But as a century passed, and the number of individuals and nations involved grew, the confidence that they could be fused together waned, and so also the conviction that it would be a good thing if they were to be. In 1882 the Chinese were excluded, and the first general immigration law was enacted.

[1] Hector St. John Crèvecoeur (Michel-Guillaume Jean de Crèvecoeur), *Letters from an American Farmer*, New York, Fox, Duffield & Co., 1904, pp. 54–55.

In a steady succession thereafter, new and more selective barriers were raised until, by the National Origins Act of 1924, the nation formally adopted the policy of using immigration to reinforce, rather than further dilute, the racial stock of the early America.

This latter process was well underway, had become in ways inexorable, when Israel Zangwill's play *The Melting Pot* was first performed in 1908. The play (quite a bad one) was an instant success. It ran for months on Broadway; its title was seized upon as a concise evocation of a profoundly significant American fact.

Behold David Quixano, the the Russian Jewish immigrant—a "pogrom orphan"—escaped to New York City, exulting in the glory of his new country:

. . . America is God's Crucible, the great Melting Pot where all the races of Europe are melting and reforming! Here you stand, good folk, think I, when I see them at Ellis Island, here you stand in your fifty groups with your fifty languages and histories, and your fifty blood hatreds and rivalries, but you won't be long like that brothers, for these are the fires of God you've come to—these are the fires of God. A fig for your feuds and vendettas! German and Frenchman, Irishman and Englishman, Jews and Russians—into the Crucible with you all! God is making the American.

. . . The real American has not yet arrived. He is only in the Crucible, I tell you—he will be the fusion of all the races, the coming superman.[2]

Yet looking back, it is possible to speculate that the response to *The Melting Pot* was as much one of relief as of affirmation: more a matter of reassurance that what had already taken place would turn out all right, rather than encouragement to carry on in the same direction.

Zangwill's hero throws himself into the amalgam process with the utmost energy; by curtainfall he has written his American symphony and won his Muscovite aristocrat: almost all concerned have been reconciled to the homogeneous future. Yet the play seems but little involved with American reality. It is a drama about Jewish separatism and Russian anti-Semitism, with a German concertmaster and an Irish maid thrown in for comic relief. Both protagonists are New Model Europeans of the time. Free thinkers and revolutionaries, it was doubtless in the power of such to merge. But neither of these doctrines was dominant among the ethnic groups of New York City in the 1900's, and in significant ways this became less so as time passed. Individuals, in very considerable numbers to be sure, broke out of their mold, but the groups remained. The experience of Zangwill's hero and heroine was *not* general. The point about the melting pot is that it did not happen.

[2] Israel Zangwill, *The Melting Pot*, New York: Macmillan, 1909, pp. 37–38.

Significantly, Zangwill was himself much involved in one of the more significant deterrents to the melting pot process. He was a Zionist. He gave more and more of his energy to this cause as time passed, and retreated from his earlier position on racial and religious mixture. Only eight years after the opening of *The Melting Pot* he was writing "It was vain for Paul to declare that there should be neither Jew nor Greek. Nature will return even if driven out with a pitchfork, still more if driven out with a dogma."[3]

We may argue whether it was "nature" that returned to frustrate continually the imminent creation of a single American nationality. The fact is that in every generation, throughout the history of the American republic, the merging of the varying streams of population differentiated from one another by origin, religion, outlook has seemed to lie just ahead—a generation, perhaps, in the future. This continual deferral of the final smelting of the different ingredients (or at least the different white ingredients) into a seamless national web as is to be found in the major national states of Europe suggests that we must search for some systematic and general causes for this American pattern of subnationalities; that it is not the temporary upsetting inflow of new and unassimilated immigrants that creates a pattern of ethnic groups within the nation, but rather some central tendency in the national ethos which structures people, whether those coming in afresh or the descendants of those who have been here for generations, into groups of different status and character.

It is striking that in 1963, almost forty years after mass immigration from Europe to this country ended, the ethnic pattern is still so strong in New York City. It is true we can point to

[3] Joseph Leftwich, *Israel Zangwill*, New York: Thomas Yoseloff, 1957, p. 255.

specific causes that have served to maintain the pattern. But we know that it was not created by the great new migrations of Southern Negroes and Puerto Ricans into the city; nor by the "new" immigration, which added the great communities of East European Jews and Italians to the city; it was not even created by the great migration of Irish and Germans in the 1840's. Even in the 1830's, while the migration from Europe was still mild, and still consisted for the most part of English-speaking groups, one still finds in the politics of New York State, and of the city, the strong impress of group differentiation. In a fascinating study of the politics of the Jacksonian period in New York State, Lee Benson concludes: "At least since the 1820's, when manhood suffrage became widespread, ethnic and religious differences have tended to be *relatively* the most widespread sources of political differences."[4]

There were ways of making distinctions among Welshmen and Englishmen, Yorkers and New Englanders, long before people speaking strange tongues and practicing strange religions came upon the scene. The group-forming characteristics of American social life— more concretely, the general expectation among those of new and old groups that group membership is significant and formative for opinion and behavior —are as old as the city. The tendency is fixed deep in American life generally; the specific pattern of ethnic differentiation, however, in every generation is created by specific events.

We can distinguish four major events or processes that have structured this pattern in New York during the past generation and whose effects will remain to maintain this pattern for some time to come—to be replaced by others

[4] Lee Benson, *The Concept of Jacksonian Democracy*, Princeton, N.J.: Princeton University Press, 1961, p. 165.

we can scarcely now discern. These four formative events are the following:

First, the shaping of the Jewish community under the impact of the Nazi persecution of the Jews in Europe and the establishment of the state of Israel; second, the parallel, if less marked, shaping of a Catholic community by the reemergence of the Catholic school controversy; third, the migration of Southern Negroes to New York following World War I and continuing through the fifties; fourth, the influx of Puerto Ricans during the fifteen years following World War II.

THE JEWS

Developments within the Jewish community have had the most immediate significance. A fourth of the city is Jewish; very much more than a fourth of its wealth, energy, talent, and style is derived from the Jews. Over the past thirty years this community has undergone profound emotional experiences, centered almost entirely on the fact of Jewishness, has been measurably strengthened by immigration, and has become involved in vast Zionist enterprises, the rationale of which is exclusively Jewish. There are two aspects of these developments as they affect melting pot tendencies, one negative, the other positive.

The negative aspect has prevented a change that might otherwise have occurred. Prior to the 1930's Jews contributed significantly to the ethnic pattern of New York politics by virtue of their radicalism. This kept them apart from the Catholic establishment in the Democratic party and the Protestant regime within the Republican party but did give them a distinct role of their own. At the time of *The Melting Pot* there were, to be sure, a great many Democratic and Republican Jewish merchants and businessmen. Most East

Side Jews probably voted the Tammany ticket. But indigenous Jewish politics, the politics of the *Jewish Daily Forward*, of the Workmen's Circle, and the needle-trade unions were predominantly socialist. The Russian Revolution, in which Russian Jews played a prominent role, had a strong attraction for a small but important number of their kinsmen in New York. It would appear, for example, that during the 1930's most Communist party members in New York City were Jewish.[5] It must be stressed that the vast majority of New York Jews had nothing whatever to do with Communism. Some of the strongest centers of anti-Communist activity were and are to be found within the New York Jewish community. Nonetheless there was an ethnic cast to this form of political radicalism in New York, as there had been to the earlier Socialist movement.

Both Socialism and Communism are now considerably diminished and both have lost almost entirely any ethnic base. But just at the moment when the last distinctly Jewish political activity might have disappeared, a transcendent Jewish political interest was created by the ghastly persecutions of the Nazis, the vast dislocations of World War II, and the establishment of the State of Israel. These were matters that no Jew or Christian could ignore. They were equally matters about which little could be done except through politics. From the beginnings of the Zionist movement a certain number of New York Jews have been involved on that account with the high politics of the nation. Since the mid-1930's, however, this involvement has reached deeper and deeper into the New York Jewish community. They are the one group in the city (apart from the white Protestant financial establishment) of which it may

[5] See Nathan Glazer, *The Social Basis of American Communism*, New York: Harcourt, Brace & World, 1961, Chap. IV.

fairly be said that among the leadership echelons there is a lively, active, and effective interest in who will be the next U.S. Secretary of State but one . . . or two, or three.

In a positive sense, events of the Nazi era and its aftermath have produced an intense group consciousness among New York Jews that binds together persons of widely disparate situations and beliefs. A pronounced religious revival has occurred. Among those without formal religious ties there is a heightened sense of the defensive importance of organized Jewish activity. Among intellectuals, the feeling of Jewishness is never far from the surface.

Now, as in the past, the Jewish community in New York is the one most actively committed to the principles of racial integration and group tolerance. But open housing is something different from the melting pot. There is no reason to think that any considerable portion of the Jewish community of New York ever subscribed to Israel Zangwill's vision of a nonreligious, intermarried, homogeneous population, but it surely does not do so today. To the contrary, much of the visible activity of the community is aimed in directions that will intensify Jewish identity: Jewish elementary and secondary schools, Jewish colleges and universities, Jewish periodicals, Jewish investments in Israel, and the like. In the meantime, Jewish politicians make more (or at least not less) of the "Jewish" vote.

This is not to say the Jewish community of New York has been *created* or *maintained* by these events of the thirties or forties: that would be too narrow a view of Jewish history, and would ignore the group-making characteristics of American civilization. But the Jewish community was *shaped* by these styles of life, many alternative courses of development were possible. Within the frame set by these large social movements, the historical drama shaped a community intensely conscious of its Jewishness. Religion plays in many ways the smallest part of the story of American Jews. In New York City in particular the religious definition of the group explains least. Here the formal religious groups are weakest, the degree of affiliation to synagogues and temples smallest. In a city with 2,000,-000 Jews, Jews need make no excuses to explain Jewishness and Jewish interests. On the one hand, there is the social and economic structure of the community; on the other, ideologies and emotions molded by the specific history of recent decades. Together they have shaped a community that itself shapes New York and will for generations to come.[6]

THE CATHOLICS

Outwardly, events since World War I have brought Catholics, notably the Irish Catholics, ever closer to the centers of power and doctrine in American life. But following a pattern common in human affairs, the process of closing the gap has heightened resentment, among some at all events, that a gap should exist. Here, as in much else concerning this general subject, it is hardly possible to isolate New York events from those of the nation generally, but because New York tends to be the center of Catholic thinking and publishing, the distinction is not crucial. The great division between the Catholic Church and the leftist and liberal groups in the city during the period from the Spanish Civil War to the era of McCarthy has been narrowed, with most elements of city politics converging

[6] For the complex interplay of religious, ideological and socioeconomic factors within the American Jewish community, see *American Judaism* by Nathan Glazer, Chicago: University of Chicago Press, 1957.

on center positions. However issues of church-state relations have become considerably more difficult, and the issue of government aid to Catholic schools has become acute.

Controversy over church-state relations is nothing new to the American Catholic Church. What is new, however, and what is increasingly avowed, is the extent to which the current controversy derives from Catholic-Jewish disagreements rather than from traditional Catholic-Protestant differences. Relations between the two latter groups have steadily improved: to the point that after three centuries of separation Catholics in the 1960's began increasingly to talk of the prospects of reestablishing Christian unity. In general (there are, of course, many individual exceptions) the dominant view within Protestant and Catholic circles is that the United States is and ought to be a Christian commonwealth, to the point at very least of proclaiming "In God We Trust" on the currency and celebrating Christmas in the public schools. However, as this *rapprochement* has proceeded, within the Jewish community a contrary view has arisen which asserts that the separation of church and state ought to be even more complete than it has been, and that the "Post-Protestant era" means Post-Christian as well, insofar as government relations with religion are concerned.

The most dramatic episode of this development was the decision of the United States Supreme Court on June 25, 1962, that the recitation of an official prayer in the New York school system was unconstitutional. The case was brought by five parents of children in the public schools of the New York City suburb of New Hyde Park. Two of the parents were Jewish, one a member of the Ethical Culture Society, one a Unitarian, and one a nonbeliever. Before it concluded, however, the principal protagonists of the Catholic-Jewish controversy in New York City were involved. The attorney for the Archdiocese of New York, for example, argued in the Supreme Court for a group of parents who supported the prayer. The response to the decision could hardly have been more diametrical. Cardinal Spellman declared, "I am shocked and frightened. . . ." The New York Board of Rabbis, on the other hand, hailed the decision: "The recitation of prayers in the public schools, which is tantamount to the teaching of prayer, is not in conformity with the spirit of the American concept of the separation of church and state. All the religious groups in this country will best advance their respective faiths by adherence to this principle." The American Jewish Committee, the American Jewish Congress, and the Anti-Defamation League of B'nai B'rith strongly supported the Court. Only among the Orthodox was there mild disagreement with the Supreme Court decision.

Although the argument could certainly be made that the American Catholic Church ought to be the first to object to the spectacle of civil servants composing government prayers, and although many Catholic commentators noted that the decision strengthened the case for private Church-sponsored schools, the general Catholic reaction was most hostile. The Jesuit publication *America*, in an editorial "To our Jewish Friends," declared that Jewish efforts to assert an ever more strict separation of church and state were painting the Jewish community into a corner, where it would be isolated from the rest of Americans.

Significantly, Proestant reaction to the decision was mixed. The Brooklyn *Tablet* took the cue, stating that the crucial question raised by the decision was "What are the Protestants going to do about it? For, although this is a national problem, it is particularly a Protestant problem, given the large Protestant enrollment in the public schools. Catholics have been fighting long—and sometimes alone—against the Church-State extremists. May we count on Protestants to supply more leadership in this case? If so, we pledge our support to joint efforts against the common enemy: secularism."[7]

The subject of aid to Catholic schools is only one aspect of the more general issue of church-state relations, and here again the ethnic composition of New York City tends to produce the same alignment of opposing groups. There are elements within the Jewish community, again the Orthodox, that favor public assistance for religious schools, but the dominant view is opposed. In 1961 the New York Republican party at the state level made a tentative move toward the Catholic position by proposing a Constitutional amendment that would have permitted state construction loans to private institutions of higher learning, sectarian as well as secular. Opposition from Jewish (as well as some Protestant) groups was pronounced, and the measure was beaten at the polls.

The situation developing in this area could soberly be termed dangerous. An element of interfaith competition has entered the controversy. As the costs of education mount, it becomes increasingly difficult to maintain the quality of the education provided by private schools deprived of public assistance. It is not uncommon to hear it stated in Catholic circles that the results of national scholarship competitions already point to the weakness of Catholic education in fields such as the physical sciences. The specter is raised that a parochial education will involve sacrifice for the students as well as for their parents.

[7] Quoted in the *New York Herald Tribune*, July 2, 1962.

There is understandably much resentment within Catholic educational circles at the relative crudity of most such observations. At the same time this resentment is often accompanied by an unmistakable withdrawal. In a thoughtful address calling for more meticulous assessment of the qualities of Catholic education, Bishop McEntegart of the Diocese of Brooklyn went on to state that "Judgment on the effectiveness of an educational system should be something more profound and more subtle than counting heads of so-called intellectuals who happen to be named in Who's Who or the 'Social Register.' "[8]

Whether the course of the controversy will lead Catholics further into separatist views of this kind is not clear. But it is abundantly evident that so long as Catholics maintain a separate education system and the rest of the community refuses to help support it by tax funds or tax relief, a basic divisive issue will exist. This will be an ethnic issue in measure that the Catholic community continues to include the bulk of the Irish, Italian, and Polish population in the city, at least the bulk of those

[8] *The Tablet*, February 17, 1962. In an address given in Washington on April 30, 1962, Very Reverend William F. Kelley, S.J. President of Marquette University, implicitly proposed a secondary role for Catholic education. As reported in *The Washington Post*, Father Kelley suggested that Catholic schools leave "research and the exploration for new knowledge" to "research institutes" like Hopkins, Harvard, and M.I.T., it being "perfectly respectable and professionally honorable" to concentrate on the transmission of the knowledge of the past:

It is an entirely sound plan to be trailing along at a respectable distance with a trained and educated citizenry competent to appreciate and consume the discovery of the successful investigator. Let us remember that if there are no followers, there can be no leader.

affiliated with organizations taking a position on the issue. If, as may very well happen, the Catholics abandon elementary and even secondary education to concentrate on their colleges and universities, the larger issue of church-state relations will no doubt subside.

But it is not the single issue of school aid, no matter how important and long-lived it is, that alone shapes the polarization between the Jewish and the emerging Catholic community. There have been other issues in the past—for example, the struggle over the legitimacy of city hospitals giving advice on birth control, which put Jews and liberal Protestants on one side and Catholics on the other. There are the recurrent disputes over government censorship of books and movies and magazines that have become freer and freer in their handling of sex and sexual perversion. This again ranges Jewish and Protestant supports of the widest possible freedom of speech against Catholics who are more anxious about the impact of such material on young people and family life. One can see emerging such issues as the rigid state laws on divorce and abortion.[9]

Many of these issues involve Catholic *religious* doctrine. But there exists here a situation that is broader than a conflict over doctrines and the degree to which government should recognize them. What is involved is the emergence of two subcultures, two value systems, shaped and defined certainly in part by religious practice and experience and organization but by now supported by the existence of two communities. If the bishops and the rabbis were to disappear tomorrow, the subcultures and subcommunities would remain. One is secular in its attitudes,

[9] See *A Tale of Ten Cities*, Albert Vorspan and Eugene Lipman, New York: *Union of American Hebrew Congregations*, 1962, pp. 175 ff.

liberal in its outlook on sexual life and divorce, positive about science and social science. The other is religious in its outlook, resists the growing liberalization in sexual mores and its reflection in cultural and family life, feels strongly the tension between moral values and modern science and technology. The conflict may be seen in many ways—not least in the fact that the new disciplines such as psychoanalysis, particularly in New York, are so largely staffed by Jews.

Thus a Jewish ethos and a Catholic ethos emerge: they are more strongly affected by a specific religious doctrine in the Catholic case than in the Jewish, but neither is purely the expression of the spirit of a religion. Each is the result of the interplay of religion, ethnic group, American setting, and specific issues. The important fact is that the differences in values and attitudes between the two groups do not, in general, become smaller with time. On the contrary: there is probably a wider gap between Jews and Catholics in New York today than in the days of Al Smith.[10]

NEGROES AND PUERTO RICANS

A close examination of Catholic-Jewish relations will reveal some of the tendency of ethnic relations in New

[10] Gerhard Lenski, *The Religious Factor*, New York: Doubleday, 1961, gives a great deal of evidence to the effect that value differences between Catholics and white Protestants and Jews (the latter two often linked, but not always) in Detroit have increased as the groups move from working-class and immigrant generation to middle-class and later generations. Parochial schooling plays some part in these differences. For an interesting evocation of the milieu in which Jewish-Catholic political cooperation flourished, see *Al Smith*, by Oscar Handlin, Boston: Little, Brown, 1958.

York to be a form of class relations as well. However, the tendency is unmistakably clear with regard to the Negroes and Puerto Ricans. Some 22 per cent of the population of the city is now Negro or Puerto Rican, and the proportion will increase. (Thirty-six per cent of the births in 1961 were Negro or Puerto Rican.) To a degree that cannot fail to startle anyone who encounters the reality for the first time, the overwhelming portion of both groups constitutes a submerged, exploited, and very possible permanent proletariat.

New York is properly regarded as the wealthiest city in the nation. Its more affluent suburbs enjoy some of the highest standards of living on earth. In the city itself white-collar wages are high, and skilled labor through aggressive trade union activity has obtained almost unprecedented standards. Bricklayers earn $5.35 an hour, plus 52¢ for pension, vacation, and insurance benefits. Electricians have a nominal twenty-five hour week and a base pay of $4.96 an hour plus fringe benefits.[11] But amidst such plenty, unbelievable squalor persists: the line of demarcation is a color line in the case of Negroes, a less definite but equally real ethnic line in the case of Puerto Ricans.

The relationships between the rise of the Negro-Puerto Rican labor supply and the decline of industrial wages is unmistakable. In 1950 there were 246,-000 Puerto Ricans in the city. By 1960 this number had increased by two and one-half times to 613,000, or 8 per cent. In 1950 the average hourly earnings of manufacturing production workers in New York City ranked tenth in the nation. By 1960 they ranked thirtieth. In the same period comparable wages in Birmingham, Alabama, rose from thirty-third to tenth. In 1959 median family income for Puerto Ricans was $3,811

[11] U.S. Bureau of Labor statistics data for October, 1962.

as against $6,091 for all the city's families (and $8,052 for suburbs of Westchester). In 1962 average weekly earnings of manufacturing production workers were 19 per cent higher in Birmingham than in New York City, 15 per cent higher in New Orleans, and almost 10 per cent higher in the nation as a whole.

These economic conditions vastly reinforce the ethnic distinctions that serve to separate the Negro community and the Puerto Rican community from the rest of the city. The Negro separation is strengthened by the fact that the colored community is on the whole Protestant, and much of its leadership comes from Protestant clergy. Thus the Negroes provide the missing element of the Protestant-Catholic-Jew triad.

Housing segregation, otherwise an intolerable offense to the persons affected, serves nonetheless to ensure the Negroes a share of seats on the City Council and in the State Legislature and Congress. This power, as well as their voting power generally, has brought Negro political leaders to positions of considerable prominence. Following the 1961 mayoralty election, Mayor Wagner appointed the talented Harlem leader, J. Raymond Jones, as a political secretary through whom he would deal with all the Democratic party organizations of the city. Puerto Ricans have only begun to make their influence felt, but they are clearly on the way to doing so.

Their fate gives them an interest in the same issues: the housing of the poor in a city of perpetual housing shortage; the raising of the wages of the poorly paid service semiskilled occupation in which most of them work; the development of new approaches to raising motivation and capacity by means of education and training in the depressed areas of the city. They live adjacent to each other in vast neighborhoods. And they cooperate on many specific issues—

for example, in fighting urban renewal programs that would displace them. But there are deeply felt differences between them. The more Americanized group is also more deeply marked by color. The furtive hope of the new group that it may move ahead as other immigrants have without the barrier of color, and the powerful links of language and culture that mark off the Puerto Ricans, suggest that, despite the fact that the two groups increasingly comprise the proletariat of the city, their history will be distinct.

Thus the cast of major characters for the next decades is complete: the Jews; the Catholics, subdivided at least into Irish and Italian components; the Negroes; the Puerto Ricans; and, of course, the white Anglo-Saxon Protestants. These latter, ranging from the Rockefeller brothers to reform district leaders in the Democratic party are, man for man, among the most influential and powerful persons in the city, and will continue to play a conspicuous and creative role in almost every aspect of the life of the metropolis.

THE ROLE OF POLITICS

The large movements of history and people which tend to reinforce the role of the ethnic groups in the city have been accompanied by new developments in political life which similarly strengthen ethnic identities. This is a complicated matter, but we can point to a number of elements. First, there is some tendency (encouraged by the development of genuine ethnic-class combinations) to substitute ethnic issues in politics for class issues. Second, there has been a decline in the vigor and creativity of politics in New York City, which seems to make New York politicians prefer to deal in terms of premelting pot verities rather than to cope with the chaotic present. Third, the development of public opinion polling would seem to have significantly strengthened the historic tendency of New York political parties to occupy the same middle ground on substantive issues, and indirectly has the effect of strengthening the ethnic component in political campaigns. As competing parties and factions use substantially the same polling techniques, they get substantially the same information about the likes and dislikes of the electorate. Hence they tend to adopt similar positions on political issues. (In much the same way, the development of marketing survey techniques in business has produced standardized commercial products such as cigarettes, automobiles, detergents, and so forth.) For the time being at least, this seems to have increased the importance of racial and ethnic distinctions that, like advertising, can still create distinctions in appearance even if little or none exist in fact. Everything we say in this field is highly speculative, but the impression that the political patterns of the city strengthen the roles of ethnic groups is overwhelming.

It is not easy to illustrate the substitution of ethnic appeals for class appeals. To the extent it occurs, those involved would hope to conceal it, always assuming the practice is deliberate. The basic fact is that for the first half of the twentieth century New York was a center of political radicalism. Faced with fierce opposition, some at least of the left wing discovered that their tactic was to couch class appeals in ethnic terms. In such manner Vito Marcantonio, a notorious fellow traveler, flourished in the United States Congress as an Italian representative of the Italians and Puerto Ricans of East Harlem. In response to such tactics, the traditional parties have themselves employed the ethnic shorthand to deal with what are essentially class problems. Thus much

was made in terms of its ethnic significance of the appointment of a Puerto Rican as a City Commissioner responsible for the relocation of families affected by urban renewal projects, but behind this significance was the more basic one that the slum-dwelling proletariat of the city was being given some control over its housing. In much the same way the balanced ticket makes it possible to offer a slate of candidates ranging across the social spectrum— rich man, poor man, beggar man, thief —but to do so in terms of the ethnic groups represented rather than the classes. In a democratic culture that has never much liked to identify individuals in terms of social classes, and does so less in the aftermath of the radical 1930's and 1940's, the ethnic shorthand is a considerable advantage.

This is of course possible only because of the splintering of traditional economic classes along ethnic lines, which tends to create class-ethnic combinations that have considerable significance at the present time in New York. The sharp division and increasing conflict between the well-paid Jewish cutters in the International Ladies' Garment Workers' Union and the low-paid Negro and Puerto Rican majority in the union have been widely publicized. One Negro cutter hailed the union before the State Commission for Human Rights and obtained a favorable decision. Similar distinctions between skilled and unskilled workers are common enough throughout the trade unions of the city. At a higher level, not dissimilar patterns can be found among the large law firms and banks, where Protestant-Catholic-Jew distinctions exist and are important, even if somewhat less so than in past times.

From time to time the most significant issues of class relations assume ethnic form. Reform movements in New York

City politics have invariably been class movements as well. Citing a study of Theodore Lowi, showing that reform in New York City has always meant a change in the class and ethnic background of top city appointees, James Q. Wilson summarized the phenomenon as follows:

The three "reform" mayors preceding Wagner favored upper-middle-class Yankee Protestants six to one over the Irish as appointees. Almost 40 per cent of the appointees of Seth Low were listed in the Social Register. Further, all four reform mayors—Low, Mitchel, La Guardia, and Wagner—have appointed a much larger percentage of Jews to their cabinets than their regular organization predecessors.

In fact, of course, the problem posed by the amateur Democrats is not simply one of ethnic succession. Militant reform leaders in Manhattan get angry when they hear this "explanation" of their motives, for they reject the idea that ethnicity or religion ought to be considered at all in politics. Although most amateur Democrats are either Jewish or Anglo-Saxon and practically none are Catholic, it is not their entry into politics so much as it is their desire to see a certain political ethic (which middle-class Jews and Yankees happen to share) implemented in local politics.[12]

The 1961 Democratic primary fight, which ended with the defeat of Carmine DeSapio and the regular Democratic organization, was a mixture of class and ethnic conflict that produced the utmost bitterness. In the mayoralty election that followed, the Democratic State Chairman, Michael H. Prendergast, in an unprecedented move, came out in support of an independent candidate, a

[12] James Q. Wilson, *The Amateur Democrat*, Chicago: University of Chicago Press, 1962, p. 304.

conservative Italian Catholic, Lawrence E. Gerosa, against Mayor Wagner, who was running for reelection with the support of the middle-class reform elements within the Democratic party. In a bitter *cri de coeur*, almost inevitably his last statement as an acknowledged political leader, Prendergast lashed out at what he regarded as a leftwing conspiracy to take over the Democratic party and merge it with the Liberal party of David Dubinsky and Alex Rose, in the process excluding the traditional Catholic leadership of the city democracy. He declared:

The New York Post lays the whole plot bare in a signed column entitled "One Big Party?" in its September 27 issue. Every Democrat should read it. "The first prerequisite of the new coalition," James A. Wechsler writes, "is that Mayor Wagner win the election." He goes on to say that the new "troops" which Messrs. Dubinsky and Rose will bring to this alliance will have to fight a "rear-guard action" on the part of "Catholics of Irish descent" who, Mr. Wechsler declares, "take their temporal guidance from Patrick Scanlan and his Brooklyn Tablet propaganda sheet. . . .

It's time to call a spade a spade. The party of Al Smith's time was big enough for Democrats of all descent. The Democratic party of today is big enough for Americans of every race, creed, color or national origin.

Although much larger issues were at stake, it was natural enough for a traditionalist in politics such as Prendergast to describe the conflict in ethnic terms. And in justice it must be said that the ethnic elements of the controversy were probably much more significant than Prendergast's opponents would likely admit.

Apart from the reform movement represented by the Committee for Democratic Voters (which has yet to wield any decisive power over city—or statewide —political nominations), the level of political creativity in New York politics has not been high over the past several decades. The almost pathetic tendency to follow established patterns has been reinforced by the growing practice of nominating sons and grandsons of prominent public persons. The cast of such men as Roosevelt, Rockefeller, Harriman, Wagner, and Morgenthau seems almost bent on recreating the gaslight era. In this context the balanced ticket and the balanced distribution of patronage along ethnic lines have assumed an almost fervid sanctity—to the point indeed of caricature, as in the 1961 mayoralty contest in which the Republican team of Lefkowitz, Gilhooley, and Fino faced Democrats Wagner, Screvane, and Beame, the latter victors in a primary contest with Levitt, Mackell, and Di Fede. It will be noted that each ticket consisted of a Jew, an Italian Catholic, and an Irish Catholic, or German-Irish Catholic in the case of Wagner.

The development of polling techniques has greatly facilitated the calculations—and perhaps also the illusions —that go into the construction of a balanced ticket. It should be noted that these techniques would apply equally well, or badly, to all manner of social and economic classifications, but that so far it is the ethnic information that has attracted the interest of the political leaders and persons of influence in politics. Here, for example, is the key passage of the poll on the basis of which Robert M. Morgenthau was nominated as the Democratic candidate for governor in 1962.

The optimum way to look at the anatomy of the New York State electorate is to take three symbolic races for Governor and two for the Senate and compare them group by group. The three

we will select for Governor are Screvane, Morgenthau, and Burke.[13] We select these because each represents a different fundamental assumption. Screvane makes sense as a candidate, if the election should be cast in terms of an extension of the Wagner-Rockefeller fight. This could have the advantage of potentially firming up a strong New York City vote, where, in fact, the election must be won by the Democrats. On the other hand, a Rockefeller-Screvane battle would make it more difficult to cast the election in national terms of Rockefeller vs. Kennedy, which, as we shall also see, is a critical dimension to pursue.

A Morgenthau-Rockefeller race is run mainly because it represents meeting the Rockefeller-Javits ticket on its own grounds of maximum strength: among Jewish and liberal-minded voters, especially in New York City. Morgenthau is the kind of name that stands with Lehman, and, as we shall see, has undoubted appeal with Jewish voters. The question of running a moderately liberal Jewish candidate for Governor is whether this would in turn lose the Democrats some conservative Catholic voters who are not enchanted with Rockefeller and Javits to begin with, but who might normally vote Republican.

The third tack that might be taken on the Governorship is to put up an outstanding Irish Catholic candidate on the assumption that with liberal Republicans Rockefeller and Javits running, the Catholic vote can be moved appreciably over to the Democratic column, especially in view of Rockefeller's divorce as a silent but powerful issue. Here, Court of Appeals Judge Adrian Burke,

[13] Paul R. Screvane, President of the City Council, an Italian Catholic; Robert M. Morgenthau, United States Attorney for the Southern District of New York, a Jew; Adrian P. Burke, Judge of the Court of Appeals, an Irish Catholic.

who far outstripped the statewide ticket in 1954 might be considered typical of this type of candidate.

Let us then look at each of these alternatives and see how the pattern of the vote varies by each. For it is certain that the key Democratic decision in 1962 must be over the candidate for Governor first, and then followed by the candidate for U.S. Senate. We also include the breakdowns by key groups for Bunche and Murrow against Javits.[14]

Here some fascinating and revealing patterns emerge which point the way sharply toward the kind of choice the Democrats can make optimally in their selection of Gubernatorial and Senatorial candidates for 1962 in New York.

—By area, it appears that the recent Democratic gains in the suburbs are quite solid, and a range of from 40 to 43 per cent of the vote seems wholly obtainable.

—By race and religion, we find equally revealing results. The Protestant vote is as low as it was for Kennedy in 1960, when the religious issue was running strong.

—By contrast, the Catholic vote remains relatively stable, with a slight play for Burke above the rest, and with Bunche and Murrow showing some weakness here. (The relative percentages, however, for a James A. Farley[15] race against Javits show Farley with 30 per cent Protestant, a relatively lower standing; 58 per cent of the Catholics, a very good showing, but with only 36 per cent of the Jewish vote, a very poor result, and 67 per cent of the Negro vote, only a fair showing).

The really volatile votes in his election clearly are going to be the Jewish and Negro votes. The Jewish vote ranges from a low of 56 per cent (for Burke); 61 per cent for Murrow (against Javits); 70 per cent for Screvane (against Rockefeller); a very good 71 per cent for Bunche (against Javits); and a thumping 82 per cent for Morgenthau (against Rockefeller). Here the conclusion is perfectly obvious: by running a Lehman type of Jewish candidate against Rockefeller, the Jewish vote can be anchored well up into the 70's and even into the 80's. By running an Irish Catholic candidate against Rockefeller, the Jewish vote comes tumbling precipitously down into the 50's. What is more, with Javits on the ticket, with strong appeal among Jews, any weakness among Jews with the Gubernatorial candidate, and the defection of the Jewish vote can be large enough to reduce the city vote to disastrously low proportions for the Democrats.

The Negro vote is only slightly less volatile. It ranges from a low of 55 per cent (for Burke, again); to 68 per cent for Morgenthau, not too good (an indication that Negroes will not automatically vote for a Jewish candidate, there being friction between the two groups); 70 per cent for Screvane (who carried over some of the strong Wagner appeal among Negroes); 74 per cent for Murrow, a good showing; and an incredibly high 93 per cent for Bunche.

Observation. The conclusion for Governor seems self-evident from these results. A candidate who would run in the Wagner image, such as Screvane, would poll a powerful New York vote, but would fade more upstate and would not pull in a full measure of the Jewish swing vote. An Irish Catholic candidate would not do appreciably better than Screvane upstate (a pattern that has been repeated throughout New York's modern political history, with Kennedy the sole exception in 1960), but

[14] Ralph J. Bunche, United Nations official, a Negro; Edward R. Murrow, Director, United States Information Agency, a white Protestant; Jacob K. Javits, United States Senator, a Jew.

[15] James A. Farley, former Postmaster General, an Irish Catholic.

KEY GROUP BREAKDOWNS†

	Democratic Candidates for Governor Pitted Against Rockefeller			Democratic Candidates for U.S. Senate Against Javits	
	Screvane	Burke	Morgenthau	Bunche	Murrow
	%	%	%	%	%
Statewide	47	43	49	47	46
BY AREA					
New York City (43%)	61	54	61	57	55
Suburbs (16%)	41	41	43	42	40
Upstate (41%)	35	35	40	40	40
BY OCCUPATION					
Business and Professional (14%)	35	22	30	57	33
White Collar (19%)	36	44	51	50	44
Sales and Service (8%)	49	49	54	42	42
Labor (34%)	56	53	57	34	52
Small Business, Shopkeeper (5%)	38	41	41	42	36
Retired and other (13%)	39	30	39	52	43
BY ETHNIC GROUPS					
White USA (29%)	35	37	36	36	40
Irish (9%)	44	49	44	48	36
English-Scotch (7%)	42	26	33	34	34
German (16%)	29	34	39	42	41
Italian (13%)	59	53	53	45	55
BY RELIGION AND RACE					
White Protestant (37%)	27	27	29	35	32
White Catholic (37%)	51	54	51	42	48
White Jewish (18%)	70	56	82	71	61
Negro (8%)	70	55	68	93	74
SEX BY AGE					
Men (49%)	47	40	48	47	43
21–34 (15%)	42	39	40	43	34
35–49 (16%)	53	39	54	43	54
50 and over (18%)	48	43	51	55	42
Women (51%)	47	48	50	47	49
21–34 (15%)	56	56	58	55	45
35–49 (18%)	50	52	59	53	58
50 and over (18%)	39	35	36	37	41
BY UNION MEMBERSHIP					
Union Member (25%)	66	61	65	49	57
Union Family (11%)	56	59	57	52	47
Nonunion (64%)	38	35	42	45	40
BY INCOME GROUPS					
Upper Middle (22%)	33	20	32	40	27
Lower Middle (64%)	47	47	52	45	48
Low (14%)	63	61	62	66	61

† Each figure gives the percentage of total vote that the proposed candidate received in the specified category. Thus, 35 per cent of the business and professional vote were recorded as saying they would vote for Screvane against Rockefeller.

with good appeal in the suburbs, yet with a disastrous showing among Jews and Negroes in New York City. A Lehman-type Jewish candidate, such as Morgenthau, by contrast, would appeal to a number of Protestants upstate (as, indeed, Lehman always did in his runs), would hold well in the suburbs, and could bring in solidly the pivotal Jewish vote in New York City.

The first choice must be a Jewish candidate for Governor of the highest caliber. (*sic.*)

There are two things to note about this poll. In the first place, the New York Jews did *not* vote solidly for Morgenthau, who lost by half a million votes. A week before the election Morgenthau headquarters received a report that a follow-up poll showed that 50 percent of New York City Jews who had voted for the Democratic candidate Averell Harriman in 1958 were undecided about voting for Morgenthau four years later. An analysis of the vote cast in predominately Jewish election districts shows that Rockefeller significantly improved his performance over 1958, when he had run against Averell Harriman, another white Protestant. In important areas such as Long Beach, Rockefeller went from 37.2 percent in 1958 to 62.7 percent in 1962, which is

sufficient evidence that a Jewish name alone does not pull many votes. It could also confirm the preelection fears of the Democrats that the notoriety of their search for a "Lehman type of Jewish candidate" had produced a strong resentment within the Jewish community. The following are returns from predominantly Jewish districts:

These returns, which are typical enough, reveal an important fact about ethnic voting. Class interests and geographical location are the dominant influences in voting behavior, whatever the ethnic group involved. In urban, Democratic Bronx, the great majority of Jews vote Democratic. In suburban, Republican Westchester, the next county, the great majority of Jews vote Republican. But within that over-all pattern a definite ethnic swing does occur. Thus Rockefeller got barely a fifth of the vote in the third Assembly district of Democratic Bronx, while he got almost three-quarters in Harrison in Republican Westchester, *but he improved his performance in both areas* despite the fact that his 1962 plurality was lower, statewide, than 1948. Similarly, Rockefeller got as little as 8.8 percent of the vote in the predominately Negro third ward of Democratic Albany, and as much as 76 percent in upper-middle-class, Republican Rye in

	Rockefeller			Javits		
	1962	1958	Dif.	1962	1956	Dif.
NEW YORK CITY						
Bronx AD 2, School 90	27.2	20.5	+6.7	41.9	19.2	+22.7
3	21.6	18.7	+2.9	44.0	17.5	+26.5
5	26.4	19.8	+6.6	39.9	21.4	+18.5
Queens AD 7 School 164	43.8	36.5	+7.3	66.5	32.0	+34.5
SUBURBS						
Jericho (part)	50.7	34.4	+16.3	60.7	36.1	+24.6
Long Beach (part)	62.7	37.2	+25.5	66.2	34.3	+31.9
Harrison (part)	71.3	69.6	+1.7	71.4	64.6	+6.8
New Rochelle Ward 4	57.8	58.8	−1.0	57.1	55.8	+1.3

Westchester, but generally speaking, Rockefeller appears to have lost Negro votes in 1962 over 1958.

A second point to note is that while the poll provided detailed information on the response to the various potential candidates classified by sex, occupational status, and similar characteristics of the persons interviewed, the candidates proposed were all essentially ethnic prototypes, and the responses analyzed in the commentary were those on the ethnic line. These are terms, howsoever misleading, which are familiar to New York politics, and with which New York politicians prefer to deal.

THE FUTURE

We have tried to show how deeply the pattern of ethnicity is impressed on the life of the city. Ethnicity is more than an influence on events; it is commonly the source of events. Social and political institutions do not merely respond to ethnic interests; a great number of institutions exist for the specific purpose of serving ethnic interests. This in turn tends to perpetuate them. In many ways, the atmosphere of New York City is hospitable to ethnic groupings: it recognizes them, and rewards them, and to that extent encourages them.

This is not to say that no individual group will disappear. This, on the contrary, is a recurring phenomenon. The disappearance of the Germans is a particularly revealing case.

In terms of size or the achievements of its members, the Germans ought certainly to be included among the principal ethnic groups of the city. If never quite as numerous as the Irish, they were indisputably the second largest group in the late nineteenth century, accounting for perhaps a third of the population and enjoying the highest reputation. But today, while German influ-

ence is to be seen in virtually every aspect of the city's life, the Germans *as a group* are vanished. No appeals are made to the German vote, there are no German politicians in the sense that there are Irish or Italian politicians, there are in fact few Germans in political life and, generally speaking, no German component in the structure of the ethnic interests of the city.

The logical explanation of this development, in terms of the presumed course of American social evolution, is simply that the Germans have been "assimilated" by the Anglo-Saxon center. To some extent this has happened. The German immigrants of the nineteenth century were certainly much closer to the old Americans than were the Irish who arrived in the same period. Many were Protestants, many were skilled workers or even members of the professions, and their level of education in general was high. Despite the language difference, they did not seem nearly so alien to the New York mercantile establishment as did the Irish. At the time of their arrival German sympathies were high in New York. (George Templeton Strong was violent in his support of doughty Prussia in its struggle with imperial, tyrannical France.) All of this greatly facilitated German assimilation.

In any event, there were obstacles to the Germans' becoming a distinct ethnic bloc. Each of the five groups we have discussed arrived with a high degree of homogeneity: in matters of education, skills, and religion the members of the group were for the most part alike. This homogeneity, as we have tried to show, invested ethnicity with meaning and importance that it would not otherwise have had. But this was not so with the Germans, who were split between Catholics and Protestants, liberals and conservatives, craftsmen and businessmen and laborers. They reflected, as it were, an entire modern society, not simply an element of one. The only thing all had in common were the outward manifestations of German culture: language for a generation or two, and after that a fondness for certain types of food and drink and a consciousness of the German fatherland. This was a powerful enough bond and would very likely be visible today, except for the impact of the World Wars. The Germanophobia of America during the First World War is, of course, notorious. It had limits in New York where, for instance, German was *not* driven from the public school curriculum, but the attraction of things German was marred. This period was followed, in hardly more than a decade, by the Nazi era, during which German fascism made its appearance in Jewish New York with what results one can imagine. The German American Bund was never a major force in the city, but it did exist. The revulsion against Nazism extended indiscriminately to things German. Thereafter, German Americans, as shocked by the Nazis as any, were disinclined to make overmuch of their national origins.

Even so, it is not clear that consciousness of German nationality has entirely ceased to exist among German-Americans in the city, or elsewhere. There is evidence that for many it has simply been submerged. In New York City, which ought logically to be producing a series of Italian and Jewish mayors, the political phenomenon of the postwar period has been Robert F. Wagner.

It is even possible that the future will see a certain resurgence of German identity in New York, although we expect it will be mild. The enemy of two world wars has become an increasingly powerful and important ally in the Cold War. Berlin has become a symbol of resistance to totalitarianism. Germany has become an integral part of the New Europe. Significantly, the German Americans of the city have recently

begun an annual Steuben Day Parade, adding for the politicians of the city yet another command performance at an ethnic outing.

Despite this mild German resurgence, it is a good general rule that except where color is involved as well the specifically *national* aspect of most ethnic groups rarely survives the third generation in any significant terms. The intermarriage which de Crèvecoeur described continues apace, so that even the strongest national traditions are steadily diluted. The groups do not disappear, however, because of their *religious* aspect which serves as the basis of a subcommunity, and a subculture. Doctrines and practices are modified to some extent to conform to an American norm, but a distinctive set of values is nurtured in the social groupings defined by religious affiliation. This is quite contrary to early expectations. It appeared to de Crèvecoeur, for example, that religious as well as national identity was being melted into one by the process of mixed neighborhoods and marriage:

. . . This mixed neighborhood will exhibit a strange religious medley, that will be neither pure Catholicism nor pure Calvinism. A very perceptible indifference even in the first generation, will become apparent; and it may happen that the daughter of the Catholic will marry the son of the seceder, and settle by themselves at a distance from their parents. What religious education will they give their children? A very imperfect one. If there happens to be in the neighborhood any place of worship, we will suppose a Quaker's meeting; rather than not shew their fine clothes, they will go to it, and some of them may attach themselves to that society. Others will remain in a perfect state of indifference; the children of these zealous parents will not be able to tell what their religious principles are, and their grandchildren still less.

Thus all sects are mixed as well as all nations; thus religious indifference is imperceptibly disseminated from one continent to the other; which is at present one of the strongest characteristics of the Americans.[16]

If this was the case in the late eighteenth century, it is no longer. Religious identities are strongly held by New Yorkers, and Americans generally, and they are for the most part transmitted by blood line from the original immigrant group. A great deal of intermarriage occurs among nationality groups of the three great religious groups, of the kind Ruby Jo Kennedy described in New Haven, Connecticut under the general term of the Triple Melting Pot,[17] but this does not weaken religious identity. When marriages occur between different religions, often one is dominant, and the result among the children is not indifference, but an increase in the numbers of one of the groups.

Religion and race seem to define the major groups into which American society is evolving as the specifically national aspect of ethnicity declines. In our large American cities, four major groups emerge: Catholics, Jews, white Protestants, and Negroes, each making up the city in different proportions. This evolution is by no means complete. And yet we can discern that the next stage of the evolution of the immigrant groups will involve a Catholic group in which the distinctions between Irish, Italian, Polish, and German Catholic are steadily reduced by intermarriage; A Jewish group, in which the line between East European, German, and Near Eastern Jews is already weak; the Negro group; and a white Protestant

[16] de Crèvecoeur, *op. cit.*, pp. 65–66.

[17] Ruby Jo Reeves Kennedy, "Single or Triple Melting Pot: Intermarriage in New Haven," *American Journal of Sociology*, Vol. 58, No. 1, July, 1952, pp. 55–66.

group, which adds to its Anglo-Saxon and Dutch old-stock elements German and Scandinavian Protestants, as well as, more typically, the white Protestant immigrants to the city from the interior.

The white Protestants are a distinct ethnic group in New York, one that has probably passed its low point and will now begin to grow in numbers and probably also in influence. It has its special occupations with the customary freemasonry. This involves the banks, corporation front offices, educational and philanthropic institutions, and the law offices who serve them. It has its own social world (epitomized by, but by no means confined to, the *Social Register*), its own churches, schools, voluntary organizations and all the varied institutions of a New York minority. These are accompanied by the characteristic styles in food, clothing, and drink, special family patterns, special psychological problems and ailments. For a long while political conservatism, as well as social aloofness, tended to keep the white Protestants out of the main stream of New York politics, much in the way that political radicalism tended to isolate the Jews in the early parts of the century. Theodore Roosevelt, when cautioned that none of his friends would touch New York politics, had a point in replying that it must follow that none of his friends were members of the governing classes.

There has been a resurgence of liberalism within the white Protestant group, in part based on its growth through vigorous young migrants from outside the city, who are conspicuous in the communications industry, law firms, and corporation offices of New York. These are the young people that supported Adlai Stevenson and helped lead and staff the Democratic reform movement. The influence of the white Protestant group on this city, it appears, must now grow as its numbers grow.

In this large array of the four major religio-racial groups, where do the Puerto Ricans stand? Ultimately perhaps they are to be absorbed into the Catholic group. But that is a long time away. The Puerto Ricans are separated from the Catholics as well as the Negroes by color and culture. One cannot even guess how this large element will ultimately relate itself to the other elements of the city; perhaps it will serve, in line with its own nature and genius, to soften the sharp lines that divide them.

Protestants will enjoy immunities in politics even in New York. When the Irish era came to an end in the Brooklyn Democratic party in 1961, Joseph T. Sharkey was succeeded by a troika (as it was called) of an Irish Catholic, a Jew, and a Negro Protestant. The last was a distinguished clergyman, who was at the same time head of the New York City Council of Protestant Churches. It would have been unlikely for a rabbi, unheard of for a priest, to hold such a position.

Religion and race define the next stage in the evolution of the American peoples. But the American nationality is still forming: its processes are mysterious, and the final form, if there is ever to be a final form, is as yet unknown.

WHO NEEDS THE NEGRO?

Sidney M. Willhelm and Edwin H. Powell

When the Negro was needed he was welcomed. When northern factories were in need of labor he was actively recruited. When our war effort needed more men he was praised. But today, our authors ask "Who needs the Negro?"

As quickly as he moves from one location to another the whites flee and turn the area over to him. Today's technological society has little place for the unskilled and uneducated. But a society which views certain segments as unnecessary presents threats for all of us, regardless of race.

A discontented, restless generation of American Negroes, anxious to abandon a history of enslavement for equal participation in our society, has abruptly ended centuries of seeming lethargy. But is their demand for "Freedom NOW" a genuine Negro revolt? Is there actually a civil rights struggle? Is the fundamental conflict between black and white?

The tendency to look upon the racial crisis as a struggle for equality between Negro and white is too narrow in scope. The crisis is caused not so much by the transition from slavery to equality as by a change from an economics of exploitation to an economics of uselessness. With the onset of automation the Negro is moving out of his historical state of oppression into uselessness. Increasingly, he is not so much economically exploited as he is irrelevant. And the Negro's economic anxiety is an anxiety that will spread to others in our society as automation proceeds.

The tremendous historical change for the Negro is taking place in these terms: he is not needed. He is not so much oppressed as unwanted; not so much unwanted as unnecessary; not so much abused as ignored. The dominant whites no longer need to exploit him. If he disappeared tomorrow he would hardly be missed. As automation proceeds, it is easier and easier to disregard him.

AFTER THEM THE TEMPEST

The Negro movement is merely the advance turbulence of a general tempest. At the moment that the Negro passes a major milestone in his struggle for full citizenship our society shifts from an industrial to an automated economy. He is like the breathless runner in the nightmare who, no matter how he strains, can only see his goal recede farther in the distance. Even if he won his demands for civil rights he could not keep up with the spreading effects of the introduction of total machine production. The "Negro Problem" therefore is not only one of civil rights but is also one of economic and human rights: How are we to re-arrange our social life in response to the rapid alterations in economic production?

On the face of it the idea of a "Negro Revolution" is absurd. The Negro is not challenging basic American values. He wants to join the white man's system, not upset it; he wants to come into the house, not bomb it. Rather than being engaged in a revolution to overthrow an oppressive system, the Negro is being disengaged by the system.

NEGRO REMOVAL

The Negro flees the South—one region to another. He abandons the country for the city. And the white's response? He flees the Negro, abandoning the city to him. The usual explanation is that the Negro leaves his rural birthplace because the city needs his labor, especially after the cutting off of European immigration. But if this is so, why is the Negro's unemployment rate in urban centers so high?

Basically, 20,000,000 Negroes are unwanted. Our values inhibit genocide —so we discard them by establishing new forms of "Indian reservations" called "Negro ghettos." We even make them somewhat economically self-sufficient through an "Indian hand-out." One out of every four Negroes in Chicago, for example, receives some form of public welfare assistance. Is it an exaggeration to suggest that the deteriorated city has now become the junk heap upon which the economically worthless are thrown?

Urban renewal is often offered as a remedy, a medication which can help check the spreading blight of slum neighborhoods and slum lives. But what in fact has urban renewal brought about? Isn't the Negro simply being shuttled around—turned over to the onward rush of economic interests as the Indian was? Reservation lands were once thought worthless—so they were given to the Indian; when this turned out to be wrong economically, they were taken away again. So with Negro slums as they become less profitable than middle-class urban renewal. The Negroes—and the slums—are being moved from one part of the city to another, while their old neighborhoods are converted into bulldozer wastelands ("Hiroshima flats" as one famous project has been nicknamed) until more prosperous tenants finally arrive. Presumably the bulldozers can then move to the "new" Negro neighborhoods, by then probably sufficiently blighted to require a new urban renewal project.

One writer comments: "Planners endeavor to improve city life by property improvement: to upgrade property values rather than human values." "Urban Renewal" becomes "Negro Removal."

Migration. In 1940, 59 percent of the Negro population lived in the South while only 22 percent lived in the North. By 1960, the share of the Negro population living in the South dropped to 40 percent while that in the North had grown to 34 percent. The border states remained constant at around 25 percent. Between 1950 and 1960 the twelve largest United States cities lost over 2 million "Anglos" and gained nearly 2 million Negro residents.

Urban Renewal. Fourteen years after the adoption of urban renewal by our federal government, only a handful of racially integrated new neighborhoods exist although many old integrated neighborhoods have been razed. "There is, if anything, more rigid housing segregation today in our cities than there was a decade ago," declares one writer. And of the people relocated by urban renewal 72 percent are non-white and of these most are Negroes—another source claims 80 percent of the families are Negroes. Moreover, one-half of the land cleared through urban renewal goes to autos as highways and parking lots, so that at most one-fourth of the land area is used for housing. *Urban renewal thus provides fewer housing units than it supplants.*

Employment. In the late 1940's, the non-white unemployment rate was about 60 percent larger than that for whites—in 1948, the unemployment rate for non-whites was 5.2 percent and for whites, 3.2 percent. By 1954, the non-white rate of unemployment was twice that of whites—8.9 percent

for non-whites compared to 4.5 percent for whites. In 1962, it was almost $2\frac{1}{2}$ times greater—11 percent against 4.5 percent. This disproportionate growth in Negro unemployment took place in spite of a narrowing difference in education. Further, three out of four non-farm Negro male workers are in unskilled or semiskilled occupations compared to one out of three for Anglos.

These items seem separate. But for the Negro they come together and spell out: *unwanted.*

For the Negro knows what is happening to him. He knows that the main problem is unemployment—and that he is being removed from economic participation in white society. He recognizes that urban renewal is Negro removal. He sees that he embarrasses even white liberals—that he contaminates what many whites consider to be conducive to pleasant urban life. He is aware of the attempt to wall him off, out of sight and out of mind. And he also knows that he cannot let this happen to him.

ARISE AND CONFORM

In one shameful sense the Negro demands *are* revolutionary. The Negro is so disadvantaged economically and socially that any real attempt to bridge the gap nationally (not to single out the South) would involve a tremendous, even "revolutionary" re-allocation of financial resources—particularly in light of the cry "Now!"

But there is no real revolution. Our basic institutions are being appealed to, not overturned. Except for a loud minority, what Negroes even actually demand the massive remedy—to which they are certainly entitled? "Freedom NOW!" is an inspirational myth. How little most Negroes demand in comparison with what many whites already have!

In 1960, the median money wage was $3,058 for Negroes compared to $5,425 for whites: 71 percent of Negro families earned less than $5,000 while only 39 percent of the white families had incomes below $5,000.

The relative gap between Negro and white family income has been increasing since the mid-fifties, indicating that Negro family income has not kept pace with whites. Since 1952 the Negro level has been faltering.

Of 280,000 new houses constructed in Chicago between 1950–1960 less than ½ of 1 percent were occupied by Negroes.

Only ½ of 1 percent of people with an income below $5,000 per year have received FHA assistance.

A Negro boy has about half the chance to complete high school as a white boy; one third as much to complete college or become a professional man; one seventh as much of earning $10,000 a year; twice as much chance of becoming unemployed. His average life expectancy is seven years shorter.

The average Negro with four years of college will earn less in his lifetime than the average white who never went beyond the eighth grade. The figures differ little between North and South.

QUEST FOR IDENTITY

As the Negro becomes an outcast he seeks to reorient himself through the civil rights struggle. The civil rights movement is a *quest for identity* by the Negro minority. Eminent Negroes participating for the first time in racial demonstrations have discovered that they can be proud to be Negroes. Through the civil rights movement the Negro announces to others, and thus to himself, his identity and worth. Without the struggle, the Negro would be left alone in an agony of isolation, in despair over his insignificance—an entity without identity.

The Negro's anguish does not rise only from brutalities of past oppression; in a system of exploitation the most humble can lay claim to an identity. The Southern Negro knew himself because he "kept his place" as required. Now there is no place to keep. The vast social changes in our society expose him to new experiences. The Negro, acutely aware of his unworthiness *to himself,* rebounds in frustration, extremely conscious of his insignificance as never before. As he becomes irrelevant to the white, he fears his relevance to himself. Martin Luther King writes in his letter from a Birmingham jail that Negroes "are forever fighting a degenerating sense of 'nobodiness'." Ralph Ellison writes of the "Invisible Man." James Baldwin declared during a television interview:

I know how my nephew feels, I know how I feel, I know how the cats in the barbershop feel. A boy last week, he was sixteen, in San Francisco told me on TV . . . He said, "I got no country. I got no flag." Now, he's only 16 years old, and I couldn't say, "You do." I don't have any evidence to prove he does.

Baldwin notes that in the rural South the whites think of the Negro constantly; but in the great Northern urban areas they seldom think of him. Of these two conditions the second may be the more terrible.

Even the flight from the South is a manifestation of irrelevance rather than exploitation or rejection. The Southern Negro was once a powerless cog in an established system of exploitation; he flees his birthplace for Northern cities with thoughts of freedom. The South responds to this exodus not as a loss but as a beneficial "drainage" of the discontented. And the Northern white reacts to the Negro's arrival by fleeing to the suburb. Black and white both share the endeavor to avoid one another rather than make attempts to resolve differences. The Southern white is mistaken in thinking that the "Negro problem" has departed with the Negro; and the Northern white is now learning his error in fleeing the city. In this geographical relocation, the Negro becomes an orphan—forsaken, ignored, denied.

There is no possibility of resubjugating the Negro or of jailing 20,000,000 Americans of varying shades of "black." Thus the real frustration of the "total society" comes from the difficulty of discarding 20,000,000 people made superfluous through automation.

Out of the anonymity of our automating society the Negro will be attracted to organizations which can endow him with identity. It is doubtful that existing moderate organizations—NAACP, CORE, Southern Christian Leadership Council, and the rest—will meet his need for identification. Moderates strive for equality in the civil rights struggle so that the Negro might assimilate into the dominant white society. Equality, however, means the loss of identity through making all people into one homogeneous group. Actually, the moderate seeks to promote the Negro's escape from insubordination by eradicating the Negro—by making him a dark white man. But the Negro cannot establish his identity by erasing himself.

The organizations most capable of elevating him as an identifiable entity will in the long run have the greatest attraction. The extreme groups do not arise, as many writers claim, solely be-

cause the moderates fail. They arise because the moderate is likely to succeed—this success is not enough. The extremes persist because—untried—they still offer a hope, a dream, and identity.

Although an immigrant to the city, the Negro is not, as liberals hopefully assume, still another wave of the same sort that left Europe for America. The differences are too great for such analogy. The Negro's past is an American experience of subordination in a system of exploitation. It is no simple matter in our society for the Negro to shed his past as the European rid himself of his alien ways. Moreover, the Negro enters an urban setting at a time when the economy operates at a national rather than a local level. Corporations have replaced community-bound business interests and demand educated skills and knowledge. Negroes cannot become like early European immigrants, a large, unskilled, and poorly paid labor force. Urban growth today demands just the opposite. The Negro is as unprepared for today's cosmopolitan and automating society as he is unnecessary for the mechanizing Southern farms he flees.

Even Keynesian economics offers little hope. The consumption strategy for economic prosperity of the Keynesian school is already provided through our vast military expenditures. The "effective demand" is generated through the "institutionalized waste" of the arms race. Indeed, it was during World Wars I and II that the Negro made his greatest strides toward racial equality precisely because his labor was deemed essential to the war effort. But the military now needs missiles, not men; scientists, not soldiers. Our society prospers without a redistribution of income in favor of the lower brackets—despite liberal slogans. In the military system we have an impersonal, omnipotent consumer of tremendous proportions that, in effect, supplants a mass purchasing power that could have been placed in the Negro's hands.

BOOMS: BABIES TO UNEMPLOYED

There is a vital point that is seldom, if ever, noticed when scanning the unemployment figures along racial lines. It is quite correct that the unemployment rate for the Negro has been twice that of the white; but whites, too, are unemployed. If civil rights were the issue, why should a white displace a white? A common cause of unemployment, apart from race, apart from civil wrongs, exists. Harold Baron, Co-Director of the Research Department of the Chicago Urban League, writes:

The decade 1960–1970 is witnessing a tremendous increase in the labor force as the progeny of the post-war baby boom enters the labor market. Twenty-six million new youths will hunt jobs, making a net addition of 15,000,000 to the total. If we make a projection based on recent rates of job increase (and even allow for a lesser loss in the number of agricultural jobs), we arrive at an increase of 3,500,-000 jobs. *This leaves a staggering addition of 11,500,000 unemployed.* And the 4,000,-000 currently unemployed, and we will have 15,500,000 persons out of work. Even assuming a return to the higher rate of job increase of the 1947 to 1957 decade, there would still be an increase of 5,000,-000. (*New University Thought, 1963*).

The civil rights myth actually perpetuates the economic status quo. As long as the issue is split along racial lines, divide and rule prevails, and we do not question the economic ideology that justifies prevailing production and consumption. If the contention can be presented as racial strife rather than economic dislocation, then the economic interests stand to gain a decided advantage: serious questioning of the merits and demerits of our production and distribution of wealth will not take place. The evil will be defined as Southern bigotry overflowing into the North rather than the economics of displacement.

In short and in summary, the historical transition for the Negro is not occurring in a civil rights context; it is instead a movement out of the Southern cotton fields into the Northern factories and then to the automated urbanity of "nobodiness." The issue becomes a question of human—not only civil—rights and involves white and Negro alike. For the Negro is merely a weathervane for the future. *His* experience will be a common one for many whites now deprived of some sort of usefulness; *his* frustrations will become those for many others the longer we hesitate to confront the meaning of human dignity in an automated society. As more of us become unnecessary— as human energy and thought themselves become increasingly unnecessary —the greater will be our social anxiety. Then perhaps we will become aware that racial strife today is not between black and white, but is instead a search for human rights in a world of machines that makes so many human beings utterly dispensable.

THORNS ON THE YELLOW ROSE OF TEXAS

Robert Coles and Harry Huge

The plight of minority groups is well known as we immediately think of job discrimination, poor housing, and inadequate education. But is it possible in America that people are suffering from severe malnutrition?

The Mexican-American is another of the exploited millions in America. Alongside the tremendous oil wealth of Texas we find the poverty and hunger so typical of their lives.

About as much cotton is grown in Texas as in India, which is the world's second largest producer. Texas sends the most beef to our markets. It offers up our chief supply of oil (about half the country's yearly supply). A huge chemical industry flourishes near Houston. Wheat production is very substantial; the same goes for corn, rice and peanuts. Texas is a large turkey-raising state; its land is grazed by thousands and thousands of sheep and goats; it yields enormous amounts of magnesium, sulphur, natural gas and bromine. In large cities like Dallas and Houston, the state has institutions that accompany all that wealth: well-run banks and insurance companies, well-known theaters and private museums, well-supported medical centers and private secondary schools, prosperous department stores whose buyers travel to London, Paris.

There's an unusual richness of social and cultural traditions as well. Counties along the Rio Grande are heavily Mexican and Catholic. The southeastern section is very much a part of the South. A quarter of the nation's rice is grown there. Near Corpus Christi millions of waterfowl from all over North America choose to winter. The people on the Gulf Coast and to the north, in the so-called "piney woods" section, are also Southern: Protestant, tied to one another the way rural people are, but also deeply divided racially. Further north and to the west, white, Anglo-Saxon Protestant fundamentalism loses whatever softening a warm and wet climate provides. The land becomes dry, the countryside more austere, and the people sternly, insistently Baptist. In Waco, right in the center of the state, 66 Baptist churches are needed by a population of about 100,000.

W. R. Poage, Chairman of the House Agriculture Committee proudly calls Waco his home. The 11-county district that he has represented in Washington since 1936 is doing just fine. His counties and dozens of others in Texas don't need a lot of new-fangled social legislation meant to feed the hungry and give them money and work. In Poage's words: "From my limited knowledge of nutrition I would assume that it was true that many Americans suffer from an improper diet, but the problem there is one of education and of personal decisions. It differs greatly from the in-

From the April 19, 1969, issue. Reprinted by permission of *The New Republic*, © 1969, Harrison-Blaine of New Jersey, Inc.

ability of citizens to secure either
through gainful employment or public
relief enough nutrients."

William Robert Poage wrote those
words in a letter to county health officers all over the nation. He asked
whether those health officers have "any
personal knowledge of any serious
hunger" in their counties, the kind of
hunger that is "occasioned by inability
of the individual to either buy food or
receive public assistance." The replies
came back from all over, and in a
chorus they said no, there isn't any
serious hunger or malnutrition among
Americans. One doctor in Texas didn't
mince words: "I am very sorry that the
poor have become a political football,
because the kicking around does them
more harm than good. I am persuaded
that it is only by learning and working
that people can better themselves. Giving them 'things' and doing things for
them can only make them weak." In
Limestone County, part of Poage's district, the health officer shunned such
long, philosophical discussions. His
reply was the shortest one received: "I
have had no cases of starvation or malnutrition reported to my office." The
health officer of Milam County, also in
Poage's district, insisted that "the general health of the people in the county
is good and that in my private practice
I have not had the opportunity to treat
any patient with any of these conditions." He had earlier said: "Not a
single death [in the county] was
ascribed [italics ours] to malnutrition
or any disease caused by any dietary
deficiency."

Recently we traveled around Poage's
district. We went to Milam County
and Limestone County and Robertson
County (which connects them). We
went to Waco, in McLennan County
and to small towns nearby or not-so-
nearby—Sunrise, Hearne. We started in
San Antonio, which is only a few hours'

drive from Mr. Poage's territory. Located midway between the Atlantic and
Pacific, San Antonio is the first large
city north of the Rio Grande, and in
1960 its some 700,000 people were
about half "anglo" and half of Mexican
descent (41.7 percent) or black (7 percent). There's an excellent system of
freeways, a fine new library, a new convention center, new office buildings and
hotels, a river that works its way
through the heart of the business district and is lined with cafes, restaurants,
stores and even an outdoor theater, all
very European in atmosphere; and not
the least, a few old and graceful buildings in the Spanish missions (San Jose,
Espada) whose arches, courtyards,
aqueducts and beautifully wrought fa-
cades remind us that not all "culture"
comes from England by way of New
England.

There is another San Antonio, much
of it on the city's West Side, which is
predominantly Mexican-American. No
outsiders like us have to come there and
make a lot of mean, wild, reckless
charges; the office of San Antonio's city
manager has bluntly and extensively
described the *barrios* in an application
to the Department of Housing and Urban development "for a grant to plan a
comprehensive city demonstration program." The city officials acknowledge
that there is a "San Antonio where 28
percent of the families have incomes of
less than $3,000 a year, and where over
6 percent of the families have annual
incomes of less than $1,000"—the latter
figure almost incredible for an urban
center. "The need for physical improvements . . . may best be described as
total," the city manager says. "The environmental deficiencies have their effect
on every aspect of the residents' lives."

What San Antonio's officials spell out
we saw: unpaved, undrained streets;
homes without water; homes with outdoor privies; homes that are nothing

but rural shacks packed together in an urban ghetto that comprises only 8 percent of San Antonio's land area but whose residents must put up with far higher percentages of suffering—32.3 percent of the city's infant deaths, 44.6 percent of its tuberculosis and well over half of its midwife deliveries. After we had gone from home to home on one street we began to realize that in almost every way thousands of people are walled off—as in the ghettos once present in Europe. The white people we met, rarely go "over there," as one lawyer put it, and the Mexican-Americans rarely leave except to seek out work, which often enough they don't find: "Yes, we came up here to San Antonio because we thought surely in a city we could find work, but we can't. My husband looks all over but finds work nowhere. He is sad, very sad, and sometimes he says life is not worth living. We would all starve to death if I didn't go wash the floors, in the bank, and thank God for my mother, that she is here to care for my children. You ask how much money we have for ourselves every week. I'm afraid not enough: sometimes it is $25, and sometimes less and sometimes up to $40, when my husband and me both can find something to do. My sister, she's here, too; and she is very sick with her lungs and can't work. If the priests didn't help her and her children, they would all starve to death. Her husband can't find work, and they told him to go home, the welfare people did, and keep looking for a job. Maybe if our men left us, we could get relief, but they won't leave. I pray every day that it will all get better, but I'll be honest and tell you, I don't believe there is much hope, no sir, not until the Next World. I've lost three of my children, and when I cry about it, I quickly remind myself that they must be happier where they are. No, a midwife helped me out, right here. I don't think I've ever seen a doctor for more than a minute. I haven't the money, and they're not around here to see; and the hospital is way away, and how can we get there; and if it's life-or-death, like with my babies it was, each time, because they were sick—well the priest, he got us there, but it was too late, and the nurse, she said we should take better care of ourselves, and go get some help someplace, though she didn't know where."

Albert Pena is one of Bexar County's four Commissioners (San Antonio is in Bexar County) and was born in those barrios and still lives there. We asked him where this woman could go for help. "There's nothing the poor here can do," he said, "except try to make their voices heard, and it's not easy by any stretch. They've gerrymandered the city so that the Mexican-Americans have one Congressman and the rest of the city shares two others. They won't let our children speak Spanish in school; instead they tell them right away, in the first grade, they have to learn English and be graded by the way they speak it —mind you, the children are six or seven and have been speaking Spanish all their lives. The children are scared and confused; soon they drop out, by the thousands they do. As for welfare and public assistance, it's almost unbelievable. Over 100,000 people in the county make below $2,000 a year, but only about 20,000 people get public assistance, and *less* than that have been allowed to take part in the Agriculture Department's food program."

We went to see Joe Bernal, the only Mexican-American in the state's senate. (There are a million and a half Mexican-Americans in Texas.) An active, outspoken, basically joyful man, he gave us a stern and somber lecture. He reminded us that Texas, unlike any other state, sets a constitutional limit on the amount of funds that can be spent for public assistance. Despite the natural population growth, despite inflationary pressures that have reduced the value of the dollar, there is no way to increase welfare payments or even hold payments to their present levels without excluding all new applicants—unless the voters agree to raise the ceiling on welfare funds, which in 1968 the voters refused to do. As a result grants to the poor are going down and will be going down further—the latest cut to go into effect May 1. Estimates of what is to come have a family of 4 or more children getting under $100 a month. Since rents are fixed and often half or more of that figure, the amount available for food is obvious. Families get no supplemental allowances—no money to travel to a hospital, no money for drugs, no clothing issues, bus tokens, shelter provisions.

Senator Bernal told us about another one of his state's laws. Section 288 of the Texas Penal Code, passed in 1933, makes it illegal for teachers, principals and superintendents to teach or conduct school business in any language except English, except when they are teaching a foreign language to English-speaking students. All textbooks must be in English. The state's two voices of enlightenment in Washington, D.C., Senator Ralph Yarborough, who authored the first bilingual education legislation introduced in the Congress, and Rep. Bob Eckhardt of Houston, recently cosponsored and helped become law the Bilingual Education Bill. It aims to help schools in, say, Texas or California teach Mexican-American children how to read and write English as well as Spanish. Next to California, the various school districts of Texas have sent in more requests for funds under this new Bilingual Education Law than districts in any other state—but all to no avail unless the state legislature acts.

Men like Commissioner Pena and Senator Bernal are intelligent, tough, and lonely. Few of their people have risen high in office; every day there is a new indignity, a new outrage to fight: the Texas Rangers, a virtual law unto themselves, and the way they intimidate and manhandle farm hands trying to follow the lead of Cesar Chavez; the absurd welfare laws; the severe unemployment among Mexican-Americans; the insulting educational practices that lead to almost unbelievable statistics— for example, 52 percent of all Mexican-Americans in Texas over 25 finished only 4 years of school, and a mere 11 percent went to high school. The city manager of San Antonio admits that 44.3 percent of the Mexican-Americans under his jurisdiction are "functionally illiterate." The 1960 census showed that 20 percent of adult Mexican-Americans in Bexar County: "have not completed any years of school at all."

Things are changing, though. We met a number of young men who intend to follow the lead of Albert Pena and Joe Bernal, who speak of *La Raza* (roughly, a prideful way to signify the Mexican-American "people") and insist upon the rights and power that must be won for some five million citizens who live mainly in the Southwest. One youth put it this way: "We've been quiet. A lot of us have been afraid to speak up. We've been content to go to church and pray, and be happy we have our family together, as bad as it is. Some people here, if you talk with them, you find they're afraid they'll be sent to Mexico, or something like that, if they start protesting like the black man has been doing. But something is happening, I can tell you. If you look into it, you'll see that our people are organizing—in Los Angeles and New Mexico and here in Texas, too. They're breaking loose from the anglos, and from our own bosses, who work with them and are just as bad as the anglos are. It won't take as long as some people think before we're really on the march."

North of San Antonio one meets up with gently rolling hills, small but full rivers, scrub oaks. Austin rises out of the prairie, but a few moments later the countryside is once again quiet, even desolate except for cows and chickens and an occasional scarecrow. We approached Congressman Poage's territory from the south and west. In Hearne we interviewed some of the Congressman's constituents: Mexican-Americans, blacks, whites. "Up here we're white, not anglo," a grocer told us. "You know why? The Mexicans are thinning out, and tne Negroes, they're getting thicker. I've been through Alabama and Mississippi, because I was stationed there during the war, in Montgomery, and I'll tell you, around here it's like there—not completely, but a lot so. To tell the truth, I prefer it like that—rather than like you find it up in New York and Philadelphia. I've also been to both of those places, and the colored there, they're fat and sassy. They think they own the world, that everything's coming to them for free. You see it on television all the time, the way they're pushing on us, pushing all the time. I'll say this about our colored folks down here, they're a lot better. They'll only do what they *have* to, of course—but at least they're not marching down our streets asking for this and that and everything."

Actually, the blacks and Mexican-Americans of Hearne have a hard enough time walking down their own streets, which are unpaved and on occasion hard to drive through, let alone march down. Near the 79 Hi Cafe we crossed the railroad tracks and entered the city's black section. The inevitable shacks were there—mounted on cement blocks, full of cracks, lucky if tin roofs covered them and if a somewhat decent privy stood nearby and if a boardwalk made the last steps into or out of the house a half-way easy job. An earlier rain had settled into muddy ditches, which were everywhere. We asked a number of people how things go for them, and from one man heard the following: "We don't have heat here, except for the stove; and no water running, not inside the house, only in the streets. Plenty runs there though—yes it does. So, I guess it's hard, but isn't it always? The first thing I remember my mother told me, it must have been 35 years ago or so, was never to expect much, just be glad if you stay alive. That's what I tell my kids. No sir, we don't have food stamps, but there's commodities, if you're good and lucky and they say it's o.k., the welfare people. I don't get welfare, and I don't want it if I can help it. I try to get by through the small jobs I get, one this week, then maybe one the next. If it's a good week I'll get $50, but most of the time, I confess, it's half that. You don't get rich that way, I guess; but there's no use complaining. There's no one to complain to, anyway. You go downtown and they'll throw you in jail fast as can be if you do that."

Downtown, the town of Hearne has railroad tracks and railroad cars and a bank called The Planters and Merchants State Bank and a movie-house which featured *Night of the Living Dead* and a black business section in which one sees Pentecostal churches and men walking the streets in overalls and cowboy hats. Not far away is the large Hearne Cotton Compress Company, which receives cotton from gins in Robertson County and presses the bales and ships them out.

It is all very interesting and educational for people like us, but not so good for thousands of people whose way-of-life does perhaps explain why Rep.

W. R. Poage of Texas and Rep. Jamie Whitten of Mississippi think and vote so much alike and become similarly enraged when those bleeding-heart liberals from the North start talking so emotionally about "hunger" and "malnutrition" and all the rest. In Robertson County, just outside Hearne, and again in Limestone County, we asked several members of the middle class who should know (because each runs a grocery store) whether children go hungry and become malnourished because their parents cannot afford the right amount and kind of food. "Well sir," replied one grocer, "I don't think they're really hungry. No, they get a lot of coke and they love Kool-Aid. They take to starches, too. I'm not sure which is the cart and which is the horse, though. The cheapest things are your soft drinks and your starches—bread and things like that. It *is* expensive to buy meat and fresh vegetables, especially in the winter time. We don't have food stamps here, just the commodities, and I'll admit, I couldn't get my family to eat that stuff day after day, all that flour and cornmeal. I think a lot of those people are just lazy, but if you ask me where they can find good jobs here, I'd have to admit it's not so easy. I know, because my kid brother came back from Vietnam and he didn't just find work ready and waiting, and he's—well, he's not a nigra and not a Mexican. I'll admit it's easier for us, but in this country if a man really wants to work, he'll go and do it. He'll sacrifice and pray hard and somehow he'll get ahead. I believe that. Of course, if a child is hungry, and he's not getting the right food, then he should be fed. But his parents owe it to him to get off their rear ends and work, and if they can't find any, they should go some place else and get a job there. My father, he came here from Louisiana. Yes sir, there wasn't work there, so he came here, that's right."

We found him kind, helpful, even generous with us. He wanted to tell us about the town, his county, even show it all to us—the rich land, the flowers just beginning to appear, the open, courteous quality of the people he brought us to meet. Meet them we did— and found them sturdy, stubborn, God-fearing, possessed of a curious and almost uncanny mixture of pride, aloofness and friendliness. They all fought as hard with themselves, with their conflicted sensibilities, as we did with the logic of their various assertions. Yes, children are innocent and need to be fed; but no, we cannot coddle people. Yes, there is plenty of misery around; but no, special "favors" (we heard that word over and over again) simply cannot be granted. Yes, some people really do need help; but no, the only help we ought to get has to come from God and our own exertions.

So we left and drove on, past signs that urge each and every driver to "Get Right with God," signs that straddle twenty centuries, like "Christ Is the Answer-Wrecking Service." In Waco and the rest of McLennan County, Congressman Poage's home county, it is the same story—prosperity and misery. ("Waco is in trouble . . . Almost 30 percent of Waco's buildings are substandard," says the city's chief official in his Model Cities application to the federal government.) Once again the blacks are found living near the railroad tracks, on unpaved Harlem Ave. Once again the effort is made to speak with reasonably prosperous white people, and once again they reach out for understanding and compassion, but suddenly stop and with a remark or two summarize this nation's ambiguities: "Why can't we get rid of our slums, here in Waco and every other place? I believe in justice, and so does everyone I know. You'd think a lot of our poor folk, they'd be doing better by now, with all the prosperity we've had since the Depression. Maybe they just don't care, don't really *want* to better themselves."

The masked lady of justice—scales in hand—stands on top of the McLennan County Court House in Waco, there to be seen for miles around. Nearby the Baptist churches fight it out with Sophia Loren, one of whose movies is in town for the weekend. Nearby, people live decently and comfortably, and live lives that eventually get to make up a bundle of dry statistics: in Limestone County almost half the population makes less than $3,000 a year, and a quarter makes less than $2,000, but only 1,681 people get public assistance and 1,947 get commodity foods—and the infant mortality rate is 42.4, double the nation's rate. In Robertson County the same figures hold. In McLennan County—because of Waco it is called 80 percent urban—nearly a third of the population makes less than $3,000 a year, 7 percent less than $1,000, but only one-sixth of those who make less than $2,000 are permitted to take part in the commodity food program.

There are, other statistics, more encouraging ones. The *Texas Almanac* declares that the same Limestone County has been found to have one of the state's major oil fields, with an estimated volume of over 100-million barrels. All that oil makes money, of course, and the

Securities and Exchange Commission has on file the earnings of some oil companies that operate in Texas. Texaco had a net income of $754,386,000 in 1967; Gulf managed to reap $578,287,-000 that year and Sinclair Oil Company a modest $95,322,000. At the same time, as of November 1968, Texas—whose large cities and industrial wealth make it comparable to Michigan and Pennsylvania—ranks 47th among states in welfare payments per recipient, ahead of only South Carolina, Alabama and Mississippi, which have no such wealth. As for Mr. Poage's Congressional district, during 1966, $244,000 in food assistance money came into the 11 counties from the Agriculture Department, but one-tenth of one percent of the people in the district—a handful of rich farmers—managed to get $5,318,-892 in various benefits from that same Agriculture Department. Still, as the grocer insisted, "oil and crops are our big, important businesses here, and you've got to support them. You can't interfere with them, because then you're down the road to socialism."

We have travelled hundreds of miles down the roads of that grocer's native state, and it turns out he has nothing to worry about. The miserable, wretched roads and the first-rate, well-paved ones cover different territory, and few people in Texas are interfering with anything very big or important.

CUBANS IN OUR MIDST

Department of Health, Education, and Welfare

The Cuban refugees for the most part are highly skilled. They arrived in the U.S. in four basic waves: the pro-Batista political elites in early 1959; the business elites in 1959–60; the upper-middle socio-economic group in 1960–61; and the

Source: Cuban Refugee Program, Welfare Administration, Department of Health, Education, and Welfare.

upper-middle, middle, and lower socio-economic groups since mid-1961. The program has been financed primarily by the Federal government with state and local governments assisting church groups and civic organizations, and just plain citizens have also given a hand. Resettlement has been coordinated primarily between a church group and a sponsor who needs a particular type of skill. There have been many problems, some large, but one must gauge the success by the results. Nearly one-quarter million Cubans have been resettled throughout the fifty states and the District of Columbia. This example shows what Americans can do to relieve deprivations when we set our minds to it.

WHO ARE THE CUBAN REFUGEES?

By and large, the Cuban refugees are a highly skilled group. About 50 percent of the refugee wage earners are professional, technical, and managerial personnel; about 25 percent clerical, sales, and skilled workers; and about 25 percent unskilled and semiskilled. These are estimates based on studies of sample groups at the Cuban Refugee Center.

Among the refugees have been, for example, some 2,000 accountants, 200 architects, 100 chemists, 300 dentists, 550 engineers, 1,800 lawyers, 500 pharmacists, 1,000 physicians, and 3,500 teachers and college professors.

The refugee stream has always included members of all Cuban socioeconomic groups. However, the proportion of each group has varied as conditions in Cuba have changed.

The first group of refugees to come out of Cuba, in 1959, were those who had been closely associated with the Batista government—political leaders, high government officials, military officers, and businessmen who had had important political connections. These were few in number—about 3,000.

In May 1959, the Cuban government enacted an agrarian reform law, and in June seized three U.S.-owned cattle ranches. Seizures of land, cattle, and farm equipment continued at intervals throughout 1959 and into 1960. (See "Chronology of Important Events in United States-Cuban Relations: 1957–1962," issued by the Department of State, 1963, mimeographed.) During this period, the refugees began to include the island's richest families, the owners of sugar mills and large cattle ranches, sugar plantations, and businesses.

An increasing number of seizures in 1960 affecting U.S.-owned hotels, oil refineries, banks, and other businesses, and other developments within Cuba, resulted in a broader social spectrum among the refugees. Members of the upper elite continued to leave Cuba. But now they were joined by professionals and technicians of all types; company directors, executives, managers, and stockholders; advertising, marketing, newspaper, radio, and television executives and medium-rank personnel; persons whose incomes derived from rents; owners of medium-sized cattle ranches and sugar plantations; insurance and finance company men; and representatives of American companies which exported to Cuba.

By the summer of 1961, the middle and lower socioeconomic groups began to be more fully represented in the refugee stream: the small merchants, office employees, skilled and semiskilled factory workers, lower-grade technicians, and unskilled workers.

These are the four major waves of refugees, insofar as they can be identified on the basis of general impressions and in the absence of precise statistical data: the pro-Batista political elite, early 1959; the business elite, 1959–60; the upper-middle socioeconomic group, 1960–61; the upper-middle, middle, and lower socioeconomic groups, since mid-1961.

The majority of the refugee wage earners are in the most productive years of their lives. Forty-six percent are between the ages of 20 and 39 and 19 percent between the ages of 40 and 49. The average family size of the refugees registered at the Refugee Center is 1.8 persons.

DEVELOPING THE PROGRAM

Throughout the Cuban Refugee Program, an attempt has been made to implement the nine points spelled out by the President. When the program was established, it was considered both necessary and desirable to utilize the services of existing agencies to the greatest possible extent: necessary because the need was urgent and no time was available to set up separate entities to deal with the problem; desirable because it seemed clear that the program was temporary in nature, that while it could not be predicted how long various operations would be needed, there would come a day when the bulk of the problems surrounding the Cuban refugees would be resolved.

The Federal staff employed on the program consists of about 100 persons. These include the small staff of the director's office in Washington, a few staff members detailed to participating units of the Department of Health, Education, and Welfare, and the staff of the Cuban Refugee Center in Miami, where most of the Federal employees are located.

Within HEW, two units of the Welfare Administration are closely associated with the program: the Bureau of Family Services, which is concerned

with the program of financial assistance for needy refugees; and the Children's Bureau, which administers the program of foster care for unaccompanied Cuban children.

Also within the Department, the Public Health Service provides overall guidance of medical and dental services for needy refugees, and the Office of Education supervises programs relating to education of refugee children in Miami, English and vocational courses for adults, and loans to needy Cuban college students.

The Employment Service of the U.S. Department of Labor has worked closely with HEW in analyzing the occupational background of refugees and in providing job opportunities through the cooperation of its affiliated State employment services.

In Florida, at the State and local levels, the Florida State Department of Public Welfare is concerned with financial assistance and surplus food distribution to needy refugee families, the Dade County Health Department with medical services, the Dade County Public Schools with education of children and adults, and the University of Miami with professional refresher courses for selected groups of refugees.

Four voluntary agencies in the Miami area have primary responsibility for the foster care program for unaccompanied Cuban children: the Catholic Welfare Bureau, the Children's Service Bureau of Dade County, the Jewish Family and Children's Service, and United HIAS Service of the Hebrew Immigrant Aid Society.

In the resettlement program, four national voluntary agencies, with offices in the Refugee Center, work under contract with HEW: Catholic Relief Services of the National Catholic Welfare Conference, Church World Service of the National Council of Churches (Protestant), United HIAS Service (Jewish), and the International Rescue Committee (nonsectarian).

Throughout the nation, cooperating agencies and institutions include: State and local welfare departments, public and voluntary children's agencies, local churches and civic groups participating in the resettlement program, colleges and universities participating in the loan program or in special training programs, and governors' and mayors' resettlement committees.

It has been estimated that as many as 40 to 50 persons may be involved in arranging for the resettlement of a single refugee. Most of these are volunteers—American citizens in a local community who are concerned about the plight of the Cubans.

RESETTLEMENT:
THE OVERALL PICTURE

Resettlement is the major objective of the Cuban Refugee Program, as it has been in other refugee programs in the United States and throughout the world. . .

Resettlement is necessary to relieve the burden on Miami; to reduce Federal expenditures for assistance; to enable the refugees to become self-supporting, contributing members of our society during their exile; to enable them to retain their skills and, if possible, to further develop their skills; and to enable them to have the experience of participating in the mainstream of American life. Resettlement is considered to be the most immediate, effective, and economical means of achieving these objectives. As in other welfare programs, the fundamental concern is with the rehabilitation of the recipients. In the case of the Cuban refugees, rehabilitation must almost always take the form of resettlement.

Most resettlements are arranged

through the four national voluntary agencies, which have offices in the Refugee Center. . .

In general, the refugees choose a resettlement agency along religious lines. This accounts for the fact that most Cubans have registered with the Catholic agency.

Resettlements are made when local affiliates of these agencies undertake to sponsor a refugee or refugee family in their community. In most cases, these are church groups, since the majority of the resettlements have been made through the Catholic and Protestant agencies. A valuable though smaller role has been played by civic organizations, such as the International Institutes affiliated with the American Council for Nationalities Service and the Jaycees, Kiwanis, Lions, and Rotary Clubs. In some communities, civic and religious organizations have participated jointly in the sponsorship of refugees. In several cities and States, resettlement has been given an overall impetus by mayors' and governors' committees.

Basically, the sponsor of a refugee is responsible for: locating a job or job opportunities; arranging for at least temporary housing, including household furnishings, the payment of a month's rent and utilities, and, usually, the provision of 2 or 3 weeks' supply of groceries; welcoming the refugee; helping the refugee and his family to become oriented to the new community, to enroll the children in school, to find the way to the supermarket, to locate English classes for adults if needed, and so on; and, finally, providing guidance and counseling on any problems that may arise.

The Federal Government pays the refugee's cost of transportation to the city of resettlement. To those who are receiving public assistance in Miami, it also provides a "transition allowance" to help the refugee get started in the new community. For a family, this allowance is $100; for a single person, $60. (The Government has also stated that it will pay the resettled refugees' transportation costs back to Miami at such time as it may become possible for them to return to Cuba.)

In the resettlement program, the sponsor chooses the refugee or family he wishes to sponsor. After a sponsor sends information to the resettlement agency on the type of job opportunities available in his community, the size of the family he can sponsor, and other relevant points, the resettlement agency generally sends him dossiers on two or more refugees who appear to meet the specific qualifications. The sponsor then makes his own selection.

PROBLEMS IN RESETTLEMENT

Resettlement is a complex operation. A successful resettlement requires bringing together a refugee, a sponsor, and a resettlement opportunity appropriate to the refugee's background and abilities. To carry out successfully a continuing resettlement program requires systematic efforts to create and maintain the interest of sponsors and potential sponsors, orient refugees to the desirability and necessity of resettlement, and develop efficient procedures for matching the refugee with the requirements of the sponsor and the job opportunity.

In addition, there are two major factors which are independent of the control of the program: one is the economic conditions and the need for workers in communities throughout the nation; the second is the ability of the refugees to meet requirements that apply to certain types of positions in the United States.

Fortunately, the majority of the refugees are highly skilled and educated persons—professional, technical, and managerial workers, office personnel, and skilled workers. Even in communities which may be suffering from unemployment of semiskilled or unskilled citizens, there is usually a demand for various types of skilled personnel which cannot be met by the local labor force.

Nevertheless, overall economic conditions do affect the resettlement program. The Federal Government itself does not send refugees anywhere on its own initiative. The relocation process is a voluntary activity initiated by a sponsoring citizen or organization, usually a church. The sponsor undertakes to assist the refugee breadwinner in finding living quarters and a job. In a few cases, the action is initiated by an employer who is unable to find local workers to fill a particular position, and arrangements are then made through one of the resettlement agencies for housing and the other aspects of sponsorship. In every case, the resettlement of a refugee is in response to an invitation from a group or individual in a local community.

A study of the geographic distribution of resettled refugees indicates that resettlement closely reflects economic conditions prevailing in various parts of the United States. There are currently some 2,500 areas with economic problems which have been designated as redevelopment areas under the Area Redevelopment Act; these areas contain about 37 million persons, or 20 percent of the U.S. population. Cuban refugees have been relocated in only 66 of these redevelopment areas. During the period from February 15, 1961, through April 20, 1963, for which detailed statistics are available, a total of 54,324 persons were resettled in 1,355 communities. Only 1,694 persons, or 3.1 percent of the total, were resettled in the 66 redevelopment areas. Two-thirds of these redevelopment areas received four persons or less. Only 11 redevelopment areas received over 18 persons.

The second factor which is largely outside the control of the refugee program, the ability of refugees to meet requirements which apply to certain types of positions in this country, relates primarily to professional persons.

One common requirement affecting employability in certain professions is U.S. citizenship or a declaration of intent to become a citizen, a requirement which cannot be met by the vast majority of the refugees because of their immigration status. Data published by the American Immigration and Citizenship Conference in its "Guide to Occupational Practice Requirements in the U.S.A. for Foreign-Trained Architects, Dentists, Engineers, Lawyers, Librarians, Musicians, Nurses, Physicians, Teachers, Veterinarians (July 1961)" show that citizenship or a declaration of intent is a requirement for licensing as follows:

Architects	24 States
Dentists	45 States and D.C.
Lawyers	most States
Professional nurses	22 States, Puerto Rico and V.I.
Practical nurses	28 States, Puerto Rico and V.I.
Physicians	41 States and Puerto Rico
Public-school teachers	most States
Veterinarians	29 States

Other requirements also affect certain professionals. Six States do not accept any foreign-trained physicians. Dental studies pursued in a foreign university received virtually no recognition in the United States. The same is true of law studies pursued in countries such as Cuba that do not base their legal system on English common law.

These problems would affect almost any refugee program, regardless of the specific origin or circumstances of the refugees.

OCCUPATION EXPERIENCE AND AGE CATEGORIES OF AIRLIFT ARRIVALS
(December 1, 1965–December 27, 1968)

Professional, semi-prof.,		Ages			
managerial	7%	0– 5	12%		
Clerical & Sales	12%	6–18	22%		
Skilled	9%	19–29	9%	Men	28%
Semi-skilled	3%	30–39	19%	Women	39%
Service occupations	3%	40–49	16%	Children	33%
Farm-fishing	2%	50–60	11%		
Children, students,		61–65	4%		
housewives	64%	over 65	7%		

CUBAN REFUGEES HAVE BEEN RESETTLED TO SELF-SUPPORT OPPORTUNITIES IN ALL 50 STATES.* THEY HAVE GONE TO MORE THAN 2,400 COMMUNITIES

States	Number of Refugees	States	Number of Refugees
Alabama	371	Montana	152
Alaska	1	Nebraska	443
Arizona	196	Nevada	1,225
Arkansas	77	New Hampshire	138
California	27,613	New Jersey	39,619
Colorado	1,291	New Mexico	426
Connecticut	2,859	New York	63,348
Delaware	321	North Carolina	744
District of Columbia	2,087	North Dakota	45
Florida	8,139	Ohio	2,135
Georgia	1,823	Oklahoma	510
Hawaii	30	Oregon	892
Idaho	7	Pennsylvania	3,246
Illinois	16,602	Rhode Island	432
Indiana	1,200	South Carolina	239
Iowa	540	South Dakota	55
Kansas	936	Tennessee	536
Kentucky	328	Texas	4,518
Louisiana	5,610	Utah	15
Maine	29	Vermont	94
Maryland	1,380	Virginia	1,800
Massachusetts	6,564	Washington	395
Michigan	2,127	West Virginia	163
Minnesota	484	Wisconsin	627
Mississippi	108	Wyoming	18
Missouri	1,161		

* Total persons resettled from January 1961 to July 31, 1969: 223,841
Source: Cuban Refugee Center, August 8, 1969.

PART III

QUESTIONS FOR DISCUSSION

1. What are likely to be the consequences of the increased concentration of minority groups in the city?
2. Why have the Cuban refugees prospered more than other ethnic groups? Particularly, contrast the Puerto Rican with the Cuban.
3. What are the problems which make difficult the communication between minority groups and public officials?
4. In what ways do the problems of the Mexican-Americans contrast with other minority groups?
5. Where are the minority groups located in your community? What are the conditions of their lives and what action is being taken to foster better social relations? What additional programs need to be implemented?

VOCABULARY

migration
birth rate
functional illiterate
pluralism
emigration
immigration

mortality rate
non-violence
militant
racial bias
ethnic diversity
environment

GOVERNING THE CITY

The pressing problems of our cities include areas such as law enforcement, health, education, welfare, economic advancement, urban planning, housing, transportation, environmental standards, and finance. These problems could be grouped by a general description that they are moral, legal, financial, and political.

They are moral in that minorities are denied satisfaction of their needs because of color, origin, or social class. They are legal in that sixteen years after the U.S. Supreme Court decision of 1954, in Brown v. Board of Education, ruled out de jure segregation as unconstitutional complete acceptance is still far from fact. De facto segregation was not a part of that decision. It is clear that segregation by any name is just that and just as degrading to those who are the victims. At this time there is still strife in our land, so vicious that it could tear our nation apart if good leadership, public compassion, and understanding are not soon available.

The problem is financial in that the cities do not now have access to the funds necessary to carry out the vitally needed programs of our cities. The cities are already carrying such a heavy tax load that businesses are fleeing to the suburbs for relief, and many of our citizens are doing the same, both for tax reasons and for escape from the problems of the innercity. Financial help must soon be made available if the cities are to solve the problems of human suffering. The crisis is also political in that solutions to all of the cities' most pressing problems rest in the political arena.

The first order of business must be more human understanding, improved management, better budgeting procedures, and a real effort to search out better political structures rendering essential decisions. The usual forms of government existing in our cities have convinced many concerned citizens that we must get away from the many small municipal governments clustering around our central cities and combine the small and the large into some form of metro government. It is suggested that the combined or metro governments will produce more efficiency and economy while providing better rule. The cities of Toronto, Nashville, and Miami are examples of such metro governments; they offer opportunities for thoughtful study. Why has the metro government been so hard to sell to the people? The minority core groups within the central city feel that they will lose their voice in a government likely to be dominated by the upper strata of suburbia. Those in suburbia feel that they will be forced to pay an undue share of the cost of improvements within the city and that they will be swallowed up by the large city. Logically, the metro government would insure improvements in area planning as the suburbs and the city grow toward each other; this would be particularly true in areas such as zoning, financial support, and area-wide development. If agreement can be reached on such joint efforts it would then logically follow that the next step should be a merging of the political structures. Metropolitan areas should not be deterred by local pride, community identification, and the sacredness of small inefficient governments.

The failure of governments to provide for the common man has led to frustrations. The little guy feels that politicians have broken faith with him, that his interests have been overlooked or forgotten, and that existing governments cannot be relied upon for solutions to his problems as he sees them. He is likely to turn to some candidate who seems to offer a way out of his dilemma. This phenomenon brings out the Wallaces, the Maddoxes, the Tony Imperiales (Newark), and the Stenvigs (Minneapolis) as they preach a return to the "old values"—values that are dead and gone, if they ever existed.

In summary it would be appropriate to list the following as essentials for improvements in government: (1) common planning to insure coordinated zoning; (2) added financial support from the state and federal governments; (3) thorough consideration of some type of metro political structure to improve the quality of government and hopefully reduce costs; (4) find ways to strengthen the status and quality of mayors so that the office can be a stepping stone to higher office for the deserving and not a dead-end as is now nearly always the case; (5) encourage the most capable citizens to participate actively by running for office; and (6) by word and deed, encourage all our citizens to think and act as Americans, not as members of an ethnic group, a minority, or a particular socio-economic class.

Certainly ways must be found if we are to have governments that are efficient, concerned with the humanitarian aspects of life, and dedicated to an environment fit for man. The solutions to our most pressing problems are in the political field—the crisis is political.

THE CRISIS IS POLITICAL

Paul Douglass

The crisis in our cities is moral and local, legal, and financial. The author believes that this financial crisis is the crisis of civilization itself. Of course, the crisis is intellectual. It is through this latter effort that man must select the leaders who will dream the dreams and be wise enough to guide the decisions through the maze that is the political arena.

When John Smith (1580–1631) was rescued from execution by Pocahontas (1595–1617), he breathed the air of the new age and exclaimed: *"These are the times for men to live.* If I had been given my choice of days to be born from the womb of Queen Bess (1588–1603) to that of a bar maid over here, I would choose today. These are the times when men spread their wings and soar like eagles."

Tomorrow is the age of cities, just as yesterday was the age of Arcadia. To build cities and live in them properly is the great business of the last quarter of this bloody and magnificent 20th century. "Man builds towns," said W. R. Lethaby, "so that towns shall build his sons." The Greeks had a proverb: "The City teaches the man."

If we may take a phrase from Frank Lloyd Wright, we are in the throes of building "the living city" which embodies the form and design of man's habitat in his pursuit of (1) work, (2) leisure, and (3) culture in this age of machines and experts.

The city as we know it is a remnant, much like the wall which once surround the mediaeval town. Today downtown is everywhere. As never before in human history we are consciously planning and shaping the architecture of our environment—and doing so with a concern for beauty and spaciousness. Frank Lloyd Wright expressed this vision when he said: "What sap and leaves are to the great oak, a healthy aesthetic is to the people."

President Lyndon Johnson expressed the idea at the White House Conference on Natural Beauty when he said: "Beauty must not be just a holiday treat, but a part of our daily life. What a citizen sees every day is his America. If it is attractive, it adds to the quality of his life. Ugliness is costly. A beautiful America will require the effort of government at every level of business, and of private groups."

Thomas Jefferson put the thought in these words: "Communities should be planned with an eye to the effect made upon the human spirit so that man is continually surrounded with a maximum of beauty."

The promise of the city is this: that the daily rounds of life may be simplified that each man will have more disposable time, money, and energy to attend to the truly significant aspects of human experience and aspiration. To-

Delivered at the 49th Animated Magazine, Rollins College, Winter Park, Florida, February 25, 1968. Reprinted from *Vital Speeches of the Day*, Vol. XXXIV, No. 12, April 1, 1968, pp. 372–374.

morrow's city is the launching pad of the mind and spirit.

Wounded and blighted cities now claim our attention. State and local governments have bonds outstanding in the amount to $105 billion dollars. The development of our cities in the megalopolis escalates this tremendous investment to umpteen billions without end. Wentworth Eldredge uses the verb *tame* —taming the megalopolis. The Congressional Record bulges with speeches on the "crisis" in our cities.

Let me begin by taking the world "crisis" in its literal meaning: a crisis is a stage in the sequence of events at which the trend of all future events— for better or for worse—is determined. The crisis in our cities is *moral, legal, financial,* and *political*.

By moral I mean judgment of behavior according to standards set by Sentence 1 of Paragraph 2 of the Declaration of Independence and the 12th verse of the 7th Chapter of Matthew.

Example: On December 4, 1965, Frank M. Otey was proposed for membership in the University Club of Winter Park. Mr. Otey was the principal of Hungerford High School in the all-Negroid Town of Eatonville. He was graduated from Tuskegee Institute in 1939 with a degree of bachelor of science. He was graduated from Florida A & M in 1953 with the degree of master of science. In 1948, 1951, and 1952 he took advanced studies in Indiana University. He served three years in the United States Army, completing his tour of duty with the rank of sergeant major. Upon the proposal of his name, the membership discussed the nomination to elect Principal Otey to the University Club for over an hour. He was declared not elected to the University of Winter Park. On January 15, 1966, the name of Principal Otey was again proposed for election. The motion for his election was tabled by a vote of 66 to 32. The motion still lies on the table. Principal Otey was Negroid. The pigmentation of his skin differs from that of the Caucasoid.

The problem of the city is moral and it is local.

In 1954 the United States Supreme Court in *Brown v. Board of Education* (347 U. S. 483) required the abandonment of practices which fostered *de jure* segregation. Most courts however felt that *de facto* segregation was not proscribed.

You will remember that Thomas Jefferson preached that popular education would furnish the means of enlightenment and the mechanics to lay the ax to the root of pseudo-aristocracy. Horace Mann saw the public school as an instrumentality of equality and brotherhood to eliminate social and class divisions inimical to democracy.

And yet the Office of Education, United States Department of Health, Education, and Welfare reports to us that more than *4 times* as many Florida 18-year old Negroid men failed the Armed Forces Qualification Test than Florida 18-year old white men.

The Civil Rights Act of 1964 and the Elementary and Secondary Education Act of 1965 authorized technical and financial assistance to schools in the process of desegregation.

Now comes the new case of *Hobson v. Hansen* (269 F. Supp. 401) requiring District of Columbia schools to take affirmative steps to alleviate racial imbalance in schools resulting primarily from de facto circumstances. The result of this decision may compel mixing students across traditional community lines. It may lead to the re-alignment of community loyalties. It may affect the political structure of our metropolitan areas. It may—and probably will—lead to the establishment on an accelerated schedule of educational parks: campus-type facilities where the city and surrounding communities will combine their funds as they congregate our children. Desegregation of our schools will lead to a new form of metropolitan redevelopment and integration. We stand on the threshold of the most massive public school building program in human history.

The crisis of the city is legal.

It is as cliché as carrying coals to Newcastle to say the crisis of the city is financial. We have only to look at our tax bills. We have only to review our public officers who are elected on the assurance that there will be no new taxes. We have only to look at the largess with which we appropriate deficits and assent to soaring bonded indebtedness.

Nevertheless in a world which during the last 5,000 years has killed one out of every four persons born in warfare, we are compelled to take note of the fact that our world is spending $120 billion annually on the current military account. Shortly before his untimely death Dag Hammarskjold under General Assembly resolution established a consultative group to report on the peaceful use of resources which could be released by disarmament. The nations of the world submitted detailed budgets to show what would happen in the scale of priorities with the curbing of the armament race. What would happen? *Adequate funds for city social investment.* What is necessary to achieve this desirable end? The clear determination of local people to demand that their government wage *peacefare.* We are at the point where we must insist locally on statesmanship in international society, just as once "the law" on historic frontiers subdued brigandage and established public order. Utopian, you say? Buckminster Fuller gives the an-

swer. Take your choice: *Utopia or oblivion.*

The crisis of the city is financial. And the financial crisis of the city is the crisis of civilization itself.

Symbols of architecture expresses the spirit of an age. In classic Athens the Parthenon commanded the defensible eminence of the Acropolis. The Gothic cathedral of Amiens with its arches, elasticity and equilibrium in variety expressive of the audacity of 13th century Christianity stands as the expression of the human spirit in still another age. The symbol of our age now is a richly fruitful pattern of a productive society coupled necessarily with mass consumption. With a relentless logic necessitating abundance, our heavily industrialized society exists as a tightly woven web of techniques residing in the functional intelligence of man in this universe. Just as the Parthenon and the Gothic cathedral were once expressive of the genius of another age, so today the architecture of our generation is a vast, real, and invisible superstructure: a functional pattern of an unseen but very real and enormously fruitful configuration of scientific concepts and theories which overarch and undergird the 21st century.

The automated machine joined with the programmed computer are at a galloping rate enfranchising man from work as we have known it. We now enter a period in which the mind and the spirit come into their own The city becomes a vibrant complex for concern for ideas and the circulation of information and knowledge. The city becomes an educational nexus of men concerned with ideas. Just as agriculture once provided the foundations of the traditional society, so now are we entering a period when the development and use of the mind is the dominant factor. The municipal housekeeping functions of yesterday's city give way now to the province of the mind. Sustained lifetime education, utilizing all the mechanics with which we are coming to be so lavishly possessed, becomes as much a part of our culture as the motor car has been in another generation. The form and design of the city is already expressing this idiom. The magnificence of the Orlando Public Library; the construction of music halls and museums; the extension of the institutions and apparatus of higher learning indicate the direction of the urban growth. Now we must embrace this idiom consciously, we must plan and build the city of the mind.

Yes, the crisis of the city is intellectual.

In the final analysis plans for the future city resolve themselves into politics. Somehow, somewhere, and by somebody, dreams must be brought down to earth for implementation. Somehow and everywhere voters must select a leader. In our cities we call that leader the mayor. The future of our cities to a very large extent depends upon the choice of mayor.

Politics is always controversy—controversy about what is best for the community to do and through whom. Thus the mayor becomes a teacher. He communicates ideas to people to act upon. His is a rigorous and demanding job. Yet politics is the unavoidable element. Through politics we forge social order. Politics develop fruitful cooperation to achieve goals. Politics is the process of comprehensive decision-making. It establishes teamwork through agreement.

It allocates values. It mobilizes resources. It administers common services to achieve societal goals.

Let the technicians dream all their grand visions. Steps toward Utopia become real in the community only through politics. In the politics of the city the mayor acts as the catalytic agent. He is the front-line educator—the comprehensive teacher of the public. He stands between public purpose and private chaos.

Since World War II Philadelphia has experienced a notable renaissance. In writing the natural history of this remarkable development, John W. Bodine has identified as a concept the influence of the *"indispensable one-hundredth of one per cent."* By this he refers to the tiny core of thoughtful and dedicated citizens who provide the goals and energy for the achievement of community goals. When Wentworth Eldredge entitled his 2-volume book *Taming Megalopolis* he added the subtitle: *"What Is and What Could Be."*

In the case of *Merritt v. Peters* Florida became the first state to rule that the protection of beauty of the community is a reasonable standard in this world of *Junkyards, Geraniums and Jurisprudence,* as the American Bar Association calls a current publication.

It was Paul Valery who said that the *mind makes higher values.* "Man's outlook," he said, "has involved him in an adventure."

The crisis of our age is political. The catalytic agent of this crisis is the mayor.

METRO'S THREE FACES

Daniel R. Grant

This selection briefly discusses the formation and operation of the metro governments in Toronto, Miami-Dade, and Nashville. The first two have the two-level approach while Nashville has the one-level government. Toronto did well for about eight years and then ran into leadership problems. Miami ran into trouble from the start, due mainly to leadership weaknesses and financial problems. Nashville seems to be doing well but not enough time has passed to provide a value judgment. Metro governments will not reduce overall costs but they can provide better planning and greater efficiencies in local government. Metro governments all need leadership, program priorities, and fiscal authority.

Comparative government is a term that once strongly connoted foreign government but, in recent years, it has increasingly come to suggest the genuinely comparative study of all governments, whether American or foreign. Still more recently, students of state and local government have begun to pioneer more rigorous efforts to study, on a comparative basis, such subjects as legislative systems, the administrative process, nonpartisanship, and community leadership and power structure. It is no accident, however, that we still have no comparative studies of metropolitan government, for the number of "metro experiments" is still pitifully small and their limited years of experience classify them all as still in early childhood.

Nevertheless, the pressures are strong for an early comparative appraisal of the experience and results of the unique metropolitan schemes adopted in Baton Rouge in 1947, Toronto in 1953, Miami in 1957 and Nashville in 1962. Influential citizens from small and medium-sized metropolitan areas continue to seek earnestly for rational solutions to

urban problems they believe to be the result of irrational local governmental structure. Their enthusiasm and drive for metropolitan reform inevitably lead them to those few cases where thoroughgoing reorganization has been adopted, and their questions tend to focus on whether or not the adoption of metropolitan government has resulted in greater efficiency and economy, reduction of taxes and expenditures, and improvement in the quality and quantity of services.

Still other people are interested in an appraisal of the experience but are asking different types of questions. Minority group leaders who have predicted that metropolitan government would dilute their strong core city political influence need to know whether this prediction has been borne out. Professional planners and others interested in planning want to know whether or not metropolitan government has facilitated areawide planning and, especially, implementation of such plans. Those social scientists who have criticized the proponents of metropolitan consolidation

From the June 1966 issue of the *National Civic Review*. Reprinted by permission of the National Municipal League.

for failure to calculate the social costs of stifling local community pride and civic participation and of hampering political access to decision-makers, need to know whether or not this prediction has been supported by actual experience. Political leaders are interested in what happens to political alignments, and political scientists are curious about how politically viable such a government will be. They are intrigued by the possibility that the concept of "metropolitan community" may be merely a figment of the imagination of census-minded chamber of commerce leaders. Finally, serious students of metropolitan government are especially interested in both the "expandability" and "exportability" of each scheme adopted in recent years.

Obviously, it would be impossible to do justice to all of these questions here; the purpose is much more modest. An attempt will be made to summarize very briefly the apparent comparative experience of three metropolitan systems— Toronto, Miami and Nashville—with respect to several of the above questions, relying almost entirely on material already published about each one. To the extent that this is a comparative appraisal of metropolitan governments, therefore, it is primarily a "library comparison" rather than one based on systematic study on the scene.

It is well known that Toronto's Metro was established as a federation of thirteen municipalities, but it may not be so well known that, while Miami's metropolitan experiment is a two-level government, it is not actually a federation of cities. An increasing percentage of the population of Dade County lives in unincorporated areas and looks to metro for many local as well as area-wide services, causing John C. Bollens and Henry J. Schmandt to call the Miami approach the "comprehensive urban county plan." Nashville's metro-

politan government involves the one-government approach, with both the city of Nashville and Davidson County being replaced by a new consolidated government. The urbanized area receives and is taxed for a larger complement of services than the nonurbanized area.

METRO AND EFFICIENCY AND ECONOMY

How has metro apparently affected taxes, expenditures and services in Toronto, Miami and Nashville, or, more specifically, has it attained the much publicized goals of efficiency and economy? Before attempting to answer this question, it is important to point out that some critics of metropolitan reorganization proposals have set up straw dummies to knock over by imputing to pro-metro forces naive claims of efficiency and economy leading to reduced taxes. Reform leaders in all three cities emphasized primarily the elimination of service bottlenecks and few, if any, predicted any reduction of over-all expenditures or taxes. Greater efficiency and economy were claimed, however, for the administration of expanded services.

It is quite clear that metropolitan government has not resulted in any over-all reduction of expenditures or taxes in Toronto, Miami or Nashville, for they have actually increased in all three cases. Furthermore, it can be argued with considerable supporting evidence that the new progressive image has, in each case, contributed to a rather costly "revolution of rising expectations" among local pressure groups, agency heads and citizens generally. Groups long frustrated in their efforts to secure new or improved services were given hope by the bright new governmental face, and strong pressures were generated that the appropriating bodies simply could not resist.

Even so, there is much evidence to

support the contention that all three systems have contributed significantly to greater efficiency and economy in local government and, in some specific cases, have produced dramatic savings. Frank Smallwood reported in his recent appraisal of Toronto, for example, "Although Metro was not established with the primary objective of saving money, in the field of capital financing it has been able to do just that."[1] He concludes that Metropolitan Toronto's handling of all capital financing for the thirteen cities originally involved has resulted in tremendous savings in interest costs on bonds—more than $50 million in ten years by a conservative estimate. The elimination of duplication has been more common in Nashville and Toronto than in Miami, but economies of scale and greater specialization and professionalization of personnel have resulted from the adoption of metropolitian government in all three areas.

One other comment should be made concerning taxes and this relates to equity rather than economy. In Nashville and, to a certain extent, Toronto and Miami, the establishment of metropolitan government has had the effect of financing local government on a more equitable basis, as judged by fiscal experts and by citizens generally. The tax resources of core city businesses were made available for suburban service needs and, conversely, suburbanites were required for the first time to share in the cost of some of the core city's areawide problems. Toronto is still wrestling with the problem of unequal tax burdens in its cities, particularly in financing schools. Miami is experiencing a crisis over the effects of 100 per cent assessment of property values, complicated by a situation in which large numbers of residential taxpayers had pre-

[1] Frank Smallwood, *Metro Toronto: A Decade Later* (Bureau of Municipal Research, Toronto, 1963), page 12.

viously paid no property taxes at all because of Florida's $5,000 homestead exemption. Dade Metro also has a problem of equity in financing urban services in the unincorporated areas from revenues collected on an areawide tax base, but this would presumably be a county problem even if metropolitan government had never been adopted.

METRO AND CORE CITY MINORITY GROUPS

A common explanation of defeats of metropolitan government proposals is the opposition of core city minority groups who fear that their relatively strong political role will be weakened by a merger with the higher income, lily-white suburbs. On the surface, this prediction seems to be logical, but one would have considerable difficulty proving it from the experience of Toronto, Miami and Nashville. In the case of the Negro minority in Nashville, where it accounted for more than a third of the core city's population, a recent study has concluded that the prediction has not been borne out by experience thus far.[2] Dade County's three major minority groups, Latin-Americans, Negroes and Jews, almost constitute a majority when added together, and this fact has many implications for metropolitan government there. Interviews in Miami indicate a belief that Negroes have better access to officials under metro than under the old county government. Perhaps the only evidence which might be interpreted as supporting this prediction is the conclusion of Eric Hardy and others that Toronto's Metro has given much greater emphasis to the

[2] Peter R. Moody, Jr., *The Effects of the Adoption of Metropolitian Government in Nashville and Davidson County, Tennessee, on Negro Political Influence* (Unpublished senior honors' thesis, Vanderbilt University, 1965).

high-visibility public works types of projects than to the lower-visibility social service functions of government. It could be argued that this is a reflection of the new suburban influence and a declining influence of core city groups interested in improved social services. Even so, there is no charge that Toronto's social service functions have been cut back but only that the "great leap forward" has been primarily in the area of public works.

FACILITATION AND IMPLEMENTATION OF METROPOLITAN PLANNING

Metropolitan area government is certainly not necessary in order to have metropolitan area planning. It is not inconceivable that an independent planning agency may have greater freedom and better financial support and produce more ambitious areawide plans than would be true if it were merely a subordinate agency within a multipurpose metropolitan government. Advocates of metropolitan government argue, however, that the implementation of plans should be much less difficult if there is a formal areawide political structure with legitimate power to carry out such plans. Indeed, some would contend that the major advantage of metropolitan government lies in being able to do something about regional plans, rather than seeing them ignored or vetoed by small, legally protected segments of the area.

Oddly enough, planning is not one of the outstanding showpieces of Toronto's Metro. Hardy and Smallwood have both repeated a weakness with respect to planning for Metropolitan Toronto, not so much on the part of the professional planning staff as by the council, which after ten years still had not adopted an official plan. Dade County has more to show because there was not even a

metropolitan planning agency prior to the adoption of metropolitan government, and many cite metropolitan planning as the greatest accomplishment of metro thus far. It is still too early to assess the effect on planning in Nashville, but some rather dramatic examples of implementation of areawide projects have already occurred with respect to acquisition of park sites, construction of branch libraries and coordination of school locations with other urban facilities. It remains to be seen, however, whether zoning practices will be changed.

THE SOCIAL COSTS OF HAVING METRO

The predictions of loss of local community pride and civic participation and the weakening of political access to community decision-makers presumably would apply more to Nashville's one-government approach than to the two-level approach of Toronto and Miami, though the charge is aimed in part at both types. Until someone gives us a good operational definition of these social costs and a method of measuring them, the best we can do is to express honest opinions about the effect of metropolitan government on them. My own opinion is that: (1) For the great majority of sub-metropolitan communities, local civic pride and community identification do not rise or fall on separate municipal status, as illustrated by the fact that some of the strongest sub-communities in Nashville (such as Madison and Donelson) and in Miami (such as Coconut Grove and Key Biscayne) are not separately incorporated; (2) the idea of widespread participation by suburbanites in the government of satellite cities is sheer mythology in the great majority of cases, for their record of voting on purely local issues is probably poorer than any other category of

voting; and (3) the social costs of metropolitan community frustration in matters such as mass transit and traffic
regulation are far greater than the
possible social costs of loss of sub-
metropolitan pride and participation.
What doth it profit suburban man fighting for satellite city autonomy if he gain
the whole world of freedom from metropolitan controls and lose his suburban
soul to federal controls from Washington? If fragmented metropolitan communities cannot find some viable decision-making locus, we can be sure that
pressures for solutions will push problems to higher, less fragmented levels
of government.

Without the benefit of empirical data,
it can only be said that the Toronto,
Miami and Nashville subcommunities
show no signs of decreased civic pride
and participation. A voter opinion survey in Nashville after the first year of
the metropolitan government's operation
revealed that, by a ratio of more than
two and a half to one, the voters agreed
that, "Under metro it is easier to know
who to call or see when you have a
problem than it was under separate city
and county government." If the essence
of democracy is the ability to fix responsibility, it may well be that metropolitan government comes out on the
plus side in any measurement of social
costs.

POLITICAL ACCEPTANCE
AND STABILITY

What has been the political survival
power of the three systems? Answering
this question is considerably easier than
attempting to explain why each has
taken a somewhat different political direction. Toronto experienced remarkable
stability and unanimity during its first
seven or eight years but, in more recent
years, has developed serious problems
of factionalism within the council. Dade

County ran into serious political opposition at the very beginning and, with the
exception of only a few brief breathing
periods, has been plagued with political
instability continuously. Two county
managers have been fired and elections
have been held almost annually since
1957 to accept or reject crippling
charter amendments. In Nashville, few
would be so bold as to claim that permanent political acceptance and stability
of the metropolitan government have
been achieved, but most would agree
that its first three years' experience has
exceeded the hopes of the most optimistic supporters in this respect. No
major political opposition has arisen,
and the only charter amendments thus
far were relatively non-controversial
ones recommended by the metropolitan
government's mayor and council and
were passed with little fanfare in a referendum in October 1965. A voter opinion survey in 1964 indicated that a
higher percentage, 71 per cent, expressed satisfaction with "the way metro
has worked in its first year of operation" than the 57 per cent that actually
voted for it in 1962.[3]

What explains these three different
patterns of political stability or instability, and to what extent is the particular type of structure adopted a key
variable? In Toronto, three factors seem
to be critical: (1) leadership, (2) program priorities and (3) the federal and
representational characteristics of the
original design. All who have studied
Toronto's experience give prominence to
the role of Chairman Frederick G.
Gardiner as forceful, vigorous, popular
leader of the new government for the
first eight years. Similarly, they point
to the political wisdom of the early emphasis on highly visible public works
projects to symbolize the results of the

[3] "Opinions Surveyed on Metro," *National Civic Review* (July 1965), page
375.

new metropolitan unity. The federal concept, along with the plan of designating the heads of the municipal governments to sit on the metropolitan council, probably contributed to political stability during the early years by calming the fears of the constituent cities. More recently, as attested to by the Royal Commission report in June 1965, the type of federation and system of representation seem to be contributing increasingly to instability.

*   *   *

The three factors which seem to have been critical in Miami almost parallel those in Toronto: (1) leadership, (2) program priorities and (3) fiscal authority. From the outset, Miami's metropolitan government has suffered from a political leadership vacuum, with almost endless debate over whether or not the professional manager should attempt to fill this vacuum himself. In addition, most writers about Miami's political troubles feel that the original priority given to rapid assumption by metro of many municipal functions permanently alienated the cities and made it impossible to have anything like the harmonious honeymoon which Toronto Metro and its cities had.[4] In some ways, an even more critical factor has been the totally inadequate fiscal authority given to the metropolitan government. Much of the political opposition might have melted away if Miami, like Toronto, could have quickly financed large popular monuments to the new system. In the hands of skillful demagogues, Miami's present financial crisis over the drastic shift in the property tax burden might become an unpopular monument.

Political stability, thus far, in Nashville is a reflection of many factors but, again, leadership heads the list, followed

[4] See Edward Sofen, *The Metropolitan Miami Experiment* (Indiana University Press, Bloomington, 1962).

by fiscal authority, court decisions and newspaper behavior. The political hard knocks to be expected from total merger of two large units of government were considerably cushioned by having as metropolitan mayor a seasoned political leader who had just been elected by a comfortable majority of the voters and who has retained the support of a dependable working majority in the metropolitan council. While the financial picture could not be called rosy, Nashville is not hampered with some of the severe restrictions placed upon Miami, and its fiscal authority has generally contributed to political stability. Also of great importance are the sympathetic court decisions upholding the metropolitan government and the sympathetic newspaper reporting of its news.

THE EXPANDABILITY OF METRO

To what extent is flexibility or adaptability to change a characteristic of the three metropolitan systems? In particular, how "expandable" is metropolitan government, both in terms of adding functions and of geographic expansion? To consider the functional aspect first, Toronto's Metro has already asked for and received, by provincial action, such additional functions as police protection, licensing and air pollution control. But it cannot expect a *carte blanche* from a rural-oriented provincial parliament. Miami's Metro already has far more authority granted in the charter than it is able financially and politically to exercise, but expansion beyond the charter authorizations to any significant degree would require amendment of the state constitution. Nashville's problems of expansion will more likely be geographic rather than functional, because it is not a two-level government and has broad urban powers.

All three systems cannot expand beyond their present geographic limits without legislative action and, perhaps more significant, without jumping certain political hurdles. Because of the historic sanctity of county boundary lines and the traditional requirement of popular approval by separate majorities, it is difficult to conceive of metropolitan Nashville or Miami ever being able to extend their boundaries but, presumably, it would not be so difficult for Toronto. Toronto's council representation scheme does complicate the problem of adding new territory, somewhat like admitting a new state to the Union. Consolidation of the thirteen municipalities in the Toronto federation into one city and five boroughs has recently been adopted, presumably allowing for minor boundary adjustments without upsetting representation.

THE EXPORTABILITY OF METRO

To what extent is each of the three systems "exportable" to other metropolitan areas? This question can properly be considered only in two parts—structural exportability and political exportability. It seems clear that the two-level structure of Toronto and Miami would be appropriate for the larger and older metropolitan areas which have a sizeable number of municipalities already operating with a full complement of urban services. The one-government structure of Nashville is more logical for the smaller and medium-sized metropolitan areas with fewer units of government and the bulk of the population in the core city and the unincorporated suburbs. Much could be learned from all three on the importance of both administrative and political expertise in the charter-drafting process. The Miami experience makes it clear that traditional county fiscal powers alone are inadequate for assuming the role of metropolitan government.

"Political exportability" is another matter, involving the actual prospects of transplanting a similar system of metropolitan government in one of the other 220 metropolitan areas. The method used to establish the Toronto scheme, by act of the provincial parliament with no referendum, seems to be out of the question for American cities. On the other hand, the long process of study, legislation, charter-drafting and referenda in the cases of both Miami and Nashville, indicates that it is not impossible to achieve metropolitan government, even when forced to follow "the American way." Even so, the Miami and Nashville systems involve only single counties, and this writer is not yet so bold as to assert that the American way permits multi-county metropolitan areas to adopt a rational governmental structure. It remains to be seen whether more urban-minded reapportioned legislatures will look with favor on this.

CONCLUSIONS

It is not possible here to discuss at length the significance of these comparisons of metropolitan government experience. A few conclusions, however, seem to stand out:

1. The record of administrative competence of all three metropolitan governments is outstanding, whether measured in terms of traditional standards of efficiency and economy or in broader terms of improvements in qualitative service performance by more specialized, professionalized public servants.

2. The twin variables of leadership and fiscal authority seem to be more critical determinants of political stability (as for Toronto and Nashville) than does the choice of a two-level approach (as for Toronto and Miami). Miami's problem of political instability seems to stem primarily from a leadership vacuum and fiscal impotence.

3. The common and basic feature of all metropolitan systems—areawide government for areawide problems—is only a structural means to a host of ends desired by supporters of such governments. Establishing metropolitan government guaranteed none of these desired ends in Toronto, Miami or Nashville; it merely removed one bottleneck and put a greater spotlight on such other factors as leadership, personnel, economic resources, and political and social traditions and forces in the community, all of which are involved in the process of governing the metropolis.

THE MAYOR AS CHIEF EXECUTIVE

Duane Lockard

This selection discusses some of the differences between the mayor-council (weak and strong) and the manager-council forms of government. In either system there is a sharing of powers between the council and the mayor/manager. Perhaps the most promising way for comparing the two types of city government is by evaluating the effects of popular election of the mayor. The votes do give the mayor strength in the running of government, but they do not gurantee a successful administration. There are too many examples of scalawags being elected to office. The author categorizes mayors as reformers, program-politicians, evaders, or stooges. He names several mayors to illustrate the four classifications.

It is sometimes said that the difference distinguishing the mayor-council from the manager-council government is that the former retains the traditional American principle of separation of powers and that the latter system has legislative supremacy. The reasoning is that the mayor stands in somewhat the same theoretical position as does a governor or the President, both of whom deal with a separate legislative body in a government where both branches have independent authority and neither is in subordination to the other. In manager-council government, however, the manager is seen as an expert administrator who is analogous to a prime minister in a parliamentary system, at least in the sense that he is subordinate to the legislative body.

But the distinction is more apparent than real. On the one hand, specialization of governmental tasks has produced in the British government a sharp separation of actual power between the executive and the legislative elements of government, the classic interpretation of the British constitution notwithstanding. By the same token, it is nonsense to talk of American government at the national or state level as if the executive and legislative branches were islands apart. As Richard Neustadt has wisely said of the federal government: "The constitutional convention of 1787 is supposed to have created a government of 'separated powers.' It did nothing of the sort. Rather it created a government of separated institutions *sharing* powers."[1] Exactly the same thing can be said of mayor-council relationships. True, they are apart in a sense, indeed often in violent conflict (although some of this is sound and fury only), but they are harnessed to the same load and must share power not only between themselves but with other governmental elements and with nongovernmental elements as they all bargain, deploy, and maneuver in the making of public policy. So, too, with managers and their councils. Managers have their separate bailiwicks to defend against council interference, and the council has its provinces and prerogatives. Cooperation, conflict, maneuver, and pressuring are as characteristic of manager-council relationships as they are of other executive-legislative relationships. The theory of absolute subordination of the manager to the council is not even good theory, for it presupposes an executive who is supine and without any notions of his own which, if it were in fact to prevail, would surely spell the defeat of the system in the long run—perhaps not a very long run, either.

Far more promising as an analytical approach to the two forms of government is an evaluation of the fact that the mayor is subject to popular election, the manager is not. Direct election involves a major source of power; yet, paradoxically, it also harbors potential weakness. Popularity is itself a reservoir of power, and a popular mayor can make much of his public endorsement. Opponents perforce respect popularity, for it can be translated into votes and into pressure for compliance with the mayor's desires. Moreover, the ethos of American democracy makes it morally

[1] Richard Neustadt, *Presidential Power* (New York: John Wiley, 1961), p. 33. Italics in original.

right and inwardly satisfying to go along with a popular leader; complementally, a mayor who has won by a good margin and who feels he has substantial support may feel morally as well as politically justified in pressing his demands because he has sanctification by way of the ballot. Under certain circumstances this can produce strong and resourceful leadership—true whether the objectives of the leadership are ignoble or grand—a debauchery of public service, or a noble program of community improvement.

It does not, however, follow that leadership inheres in the system of direct election. The system opens the way to resourceful leadership—no doubt more so than any other kind of local governmental structure yet tried in this country. But it does just open the way—it does not assure that it will be forthcoming. For in many communities the rule becomes "Risk Not, Lose Not." If the vox populi can inspire leadership, it can also encourage evasion. If those who stick their political necks out for policies that are unpopular seem invariably to get them chopped off, and those who avoid contentious issues are rewarded with reelection, the lesson for the ambitious is quickly apparent: endorse popular issues to keep in the public eye, but never promote a controversial issue. It appears that communities go through cycles of evading and avoiding until some crisis arises or until difficulties are so pressing that the need for action finally steels the nerve of some political entrepreneur who then risks bold proposals and actions. Then the cycle repeats itself. This phenomenon is by no means limited to the city with the mayor-council system of government, of course, but the difficulties of hideaway leaders do seem to stand as a countervailing possibility to the leadership potential of popular election.

Direct elections cannot help being at

least in part popularity contests. If a candidate is affable, has joined the right lodges, has been a regular communicant at his church, these are assets on election day. That such seemingly irrelevant qualifications are criteria for judging mayoral candidates distresses many observers of local government, for it seems a most inept way of choosing a man to administer a multimillion-dollar operation. And it is undeniably true that sometimes popular election does bring to office men who lack either administrative ability or essential honesty, if not both. Of course, the infallible method of selecting executives in business, government, or elsewhere has yet to be devised, but if one assumes that the essence of the mayor's task is to be an administrative overseer it seems that more propitious methods of choice could be found. In fact, the method of choosing city managers is unquestionably more orderly and more likely to produce trained administrators than is the elective process.

But does it follow that the appropriate criterion is the question of administrative expertise? It is obvious that other criteria are used. For the mayor no less than the governor is commonly conceived to be a representative. He is chosen in part because voters believe he shares their values, their aspirations, and their attitudes. They wish him to be responsive to their preferences; accordingly, candidates compete in pledging to do just that. The components of voter motivation in making choices among potential candidates are enormously complicated, and one is well advised to be chary when generalizing about them, but it does seem justified to say that voters usually do not much concern themselves with the relative managerial talents of candidates. Indeed most voters would probably be ill-equipped to do more than judge between the grossest extremes of excellence and ineptitude in

managerial capacities. What therefore may seem irrelevant criteria to one who assumes administrative ability to be the crux of mayoral qualifications may be quite relevant to the person seeking a mayor to represent him and act more or less consistently with his (the voter's) preferences. Thus the question of criteria is a question of values.

In this connection it is significant to recall a point made earlier: the larger the city, the less likely it is that a mayor will in fact involve himself in the minutiae of administrative detail. This does not mean that he has no concern with management problems—inevitably he will often be involved in administrative matters, but he will be more concerned with the broader problems of the government than with operating details. He will be attempting to convince others of the rightness of programs, promoting school-bond campaigns or urban renewal programs, seeking to get the governor's support for a state highway bypass to relieve downtown traffic, mediating between real estate developers and the city planning board about a new project, etc. These are the kinds of political problems the mayor works on, and as a result he has neither much time nor much need to involve himself in the workings of the police department or the treasurer's office. As Sayre and Kaufman sum up the problems of the New York Mayor: "It is political help (in the broadest sense of the word 'political') rather than managerial assistance that the Mayor most needs."[2] In short, mayors at least in the larger cities are, like governors, far more concerned with being policy formulators than being administrative managers.

This does not mean that ability and a reputation for intelligence and decisive-

[2] Wallace S. Sayre and Herbert Kaufman, *Governing New York City* (New York: Russell Sage Foundation, 1960), p. 668.

ness are unimportant attributes for a candidate. It is apparent that the urban community of today is no longer the city of a half-century ago, when ethnic minorities were herded to the polls by political bosses to vote in blind obedience. A new era has come to urban politics. The day of the prototype of the ethnic politician who could identify with the ethnics and could do little more is gone. James Michael Curley's formula of a touch of brogue, some recognition, a little gravy, and a patronage job no longer works—indeed, it had ceased to work for Curley himself and forced him to retire long before he wanted to. It is likely that a candidate for mayor of Boston who seemed invincible in view of his fitting the standard patterns of the Boston politician and in the formidable backing he had, lost the election of 1959 because he

. . . fitted too well the image of the Irish politician that the Irish electorate found embarrassing and wanted to repudiate. . . . It appears . . . that the nationality-minded voter prefers a candidate who has the attributes of his group but has them in association with those of the admired Anglo-Saxon model. The perfect candidate is of Irish, Polish, or Jewish extraction, but has the speech, dress, and manner and also the public virtues (honesty, impartiality, devotion to the public good) that belong in the public mind to the upper class Anglo-Saxon.[3]

It is appropriate to emphasize differences among mayors in operation, not only because there are enormous

[3] Edward C. Banfield, "The Political Implications of Metropolitan Growth," 90 *Daedalus* 61, 72 (1960). See Murray B. Levin, *The Alienated Voter* (New York: Holt, Rinehart and Winston, Inc., 1960) for a view of the 1959 election that in part confirms and in part denies Banfield's interpretation.

differences among them but because this offers a convenient way of analyzing the office. Although mayors might be classified in many ways the following categories will serve to illustrate the major variations—the reformer, the program-politician, the evaders, and (inelegantly) the stooges.

(1) THE REFORMER TYPE. Invariably dramatic and often demagogic, always courageous but inclined to moralistic tilting with windmills, the reform mayor is surely one of the more colorful breeds of American politician. The flaming political success of some reformers has led lesser imitations to talk the language of the reformer, confusing spectators about the genuine and the bogus reformer types. But the prototype of the reform mayor is unmistakable and genuine—he rides to power against sin, promising to clean the Augean stables promptly and dramatically. Flamboyance aside, the successful reformer is a competent politician; his success depends upon his ability to weld together a following—both a wide following in the community and a narrower set of devotees who carry out the operations of the reform administration.

The conditions of urban politics at the turn of the century offered more than ample grounds for the reformer's art. All across the nation reform movements—both lasting and fleeting—sprang up and challenged entrenched political machines. The number one requisite for these movements was a colorful and resourceful leader as the focus for attention, someone to provide leadership and to take office as mayor once the dragon was slain. Thus "Golden Rule" Jones of Toledo, Ohio, and his friend Tom Johnson of Cleveland were dramatic and successful leaders who inspired devoted followings and passionate opposition as well, but their popularity made them unbeatable at the polls. Jones acquired his nickname from his simple belief in the New Testament principle; his sympathy and love for the downtrodden immigrants and his relentless efforts to improve their lot made him unchallengeable politically. Johnson, a wealthy owner of transit franchises, gave up his monopolistic operations to go into politics after being converted to Henry George's single-tax ideas. Lincoln Steffens, while making his muckraking tour of American cities, called Johnson the best mayor in the United States. Brand Whitlock, a disciple of Jones and close friend of Johnson, succeeded Jones as the mayor of Toledo and continued to win public support with reformist ideas. Significantly, none of these reformers was a doctrinaire supporter of nostrums for "solution" of municipal problems.[4]

No other reformer—past, present, or even, one is tempted to say, in the probable future can quite match Fiorello La Guardia of New York. Flamboyant egoist, demagogue, driving political master, and chief flagellant of the party leaders of New York City, La Guardia stands alone.

It must be admitted that in exploiting racial and religious prejudices La Guardia

could run circles around the bosses he despised and derided. When it came to raking ashes of Old World hates, warming ancient grudges, waving the bloody shirt, tuning the ear to ancestral voices, he could easily outdemagogue the demagogues. And for what purpose? To redress old wrongs abroad? To combat foreign levy or malice domestic? . . . Not on your tintype. Fiorello La Guardia knew better. He knew that the aim of the rabble rousers is simply to shoo into office for entirely extraneous, illogical and even silly reasons the municipal officials who clean city streets, teach in schools, protect, house and keep healthy, strong and happy millions of people crowded together here.[5]

La Guardia attracted not only a popular following among voters (he was mayor from 1934 to 1945) but devoted and unusually able lieutenants. As Rexford Tugwell points out, La Guardia had to depend upon these people who in many respects knew more about the government of the city than he did—but none of them could be elected mayor. It took the personal qualities that this man possessed to make a personal organization and a personal movement to hold power and to do things for the city. As Tugwell also says:

It is hard to estimate even roughly how many words La Guardia devoted to telling New Yorkers about their city and its operation. There must have been millions about the budget alone, and anyone who thinks it easy to talk about finances and hold the attention of voters is innocent indeed. And

[4] Whitlock's fascinating autobiography stands beside Steffens' as required reading for those who want a view of the conditions of municipal government and politics fifty years ago: *Forty Years of It* (New York: Appleton-Century-Crofts, Inc., 1914). Whitlock's discussion of Jones (pp. 112–50) and of Johnson (pp. 151–75) are particularly recommended; on his own mayoralty, see pp. 180ff. He says at one point: *I shall not attempt in these pages a treatise on municipal government. . . . Nonpartisanship in municipal elections, municipal ownership, home rule for cities —who is interested in these? . . . One cannot discover a panacea, some sort of sociological patent medicine to be administered to the community, like Social-*

ism, or Prohibition, or absolute law enforcement, or the commission form of government (p. 215).

[5] Robert Moses, *La Guardia, A Salute and A Memoir* (New York: Simon and Schuster, 1957), p. 18. Reprinted from an article in *The New York Times Magazine*, September 8, 1957.

especially if budgets are not your own best subject.[6]

There are other reform mayors, of course, some of them currently operating or only recently departed for other activities. Richardson Dilworth in Philadelphia carried on the reform mayor role that Joseph Clark relinquished when he went to the United States Senate. Neither Clark nor Dilworth has the flamboyant qualities of a La Guardia, but both came to and held power because of their crusade against a corrupt Republican organization that had long dominated Philadelphia politics. Both demonstrated that an upper-class Yankee Protestant is not disqualified from political leadership in the large cities of the East.[7] DeLesseps Morrison, until recently a reform mayor of New Orleans, demonstrates that ability and upper-class status are no disqualification even in the rough and demagogic politics of Louisiana's largest city. The decline of the old-fashioned machine has reduced the reformer's opportunities to ride the white charger against bona fide bosses, for an essential precondition to effective reform mayor operations is a sufficiently deteriorated political climate to make the public receptive to the reformer's charms.

(2) THE PROGRAM-POLITICIAN TYPE. It is not quite accurate, perhaps, to say

there is a stereotype of incompetence associated with the mayoralty, but something close to that seems to prevail in many minds. The maledictions pronounced on urban government in its truly unholy past still cling and are applied today as if no change had occurred in the intervening years. Thus, Robert S. Allen in the introduction to his book *Our Fair City*, asserts that there had been no essential change in American local government in the forty-three years since Lincoln Steffens had pronounced the American city "corrupt and content." "There is not a major city in the country," said Allen, "that does not possess . . . a dismal record. Nauseous misrule, fleeting, and often inept, reform, and then back to the old garbage cans. Still 'corrupt and content' is distinctly the underlying motif of municipal rule in our country."[8]

Writing off contemporary urban government as misrule and mayors as incompetents is not justified, however. Admittedly there are many American cities run by less than Periclean standards, but the picture of universal misrule is inaccurate. Seymour Freedgood, writing in *Fortune* in 1957, expressed a view remarkably unlike Allen's. Observing that the large cities (those over half a million population) are hard pressed by suburbanization, financial problems, state limitations, and so on, Freedgood says they need "top notch leadership," and adds:

They have it. Since the 1930's, and at an accelerating rate after the second world war, the electorate in city after city has put into office as competent, hard-driving, and skillful a chief executive as ever sat in the high-backed chair behind the broad mahogany desk. At the same

---

[6] *The Art of Politics, As Practiced by Three Great Americans: Franklin Delano Roosevelt, Luis Muñoz Marin, and Fiorello H. La Guardia* (Garden City, N.Y.: Doubleday & Company, 1958), p. 131. See Chaps. 12–15 particularly for an analysis of what made La Guardia the phenomenal and intriguing figure that he was.

[7] On Clark and Dilworth, see James Reichley, *The Art of Government: Reform and Organization Politics in Philadelphia* (New York: Fund for the Republic, 1959).

[8] *Our Fair City* (New York: Vanguard Press, 1947), p. 15. If Allen would not still in the 1960's defend such a position, there are others who would.

time they have strengthened the power of the office.

This has not been a victory for "good government." To most people, good government is primarily honest and efficient administration, and they believe that the sure way for the city to get it is to tighten civil service, eliminate patronage, and accept all the other artifacts of "scientific" government, including the council-city-manager plan. But today's big city mayor is not a good-government man, at least in these terms, and if he ever was, he got over it a long time ago. He is a tough-minded, soft-spoken politician who often outrages good-government people, or, as the politicians have called them, the Goo-Goos.[9]

The tough-minded, soft-spoken, hard-driving politician has turned up, not only in the big city, but in not a few smaller communities in the last decade. The office of mayor seems to have intrinsic challenge and is as well an inviting stepping stone to higher political rewards. Candidates accordingly have included some able aspirants. Program-oriented in order to attract support, ready to work with a political organization and to use patronage and other traditional tools to get and hold office but unready to depend upon these alone, the program-politician type of mayor is a leader and a promoter. Freegood describes tellingly the characteristic traits of the breed:

The profile of today's big-city mayor—with one difference—is quite similar to that of the chief executive of a large corporation. Typically, the mayor is a college graduate, usually with a legal or business background and is now in his late fifties. He puts in hard, grinding hours at his desk, sometimes six or seven days a week, and his wife suffers as much as his golf game. The difference is in salary: he usually makes $20,000 to $25,000. . . .

"Public relations" take a big chunk of his time. He is aggressively press-conscious, holds frequent news conferences, often appears on TV-radio with his "Report to the People"; and from his office flows a flood of releases on civic improvements. About five nights a week there are civic receptions, banquets, policy meetings, and visits with neighborhood civic groups. In between he may serve as a labor negotiator, or a member of the Civil Defense Board. . . .

Despite the fact that His Honor is likely to be a Democrat, he gets along well with the businessmen, though he is apt to feel that they have a lot to learn about political decision-making. . . .

Above all the mayor is a politician. True, he may have risen to the office on the back of a reform movement. But he is not, as happened too often in the past, a "non-political" civic leader who rallies the do-gooders, drives the rascals out of City Hall, serves for an undistinguished term or two, and then withdraws—or gets driven out—leaving the city to another cycle of corruption. Instead, he fits the qualifications of the mayors whom Lincoln Steffens called on the public to elect: "politicians working for the reform of the city with the methods of politics." His main interest is in government, not abstract virtue, and he knows that the art of government is politics.[10]

It would be easy to cite a long list of competent program-politician type mayors. Mayor William B. Hartsfield,

[9] "New Strength in City Hall," 56 *Fortune* 156 (November, 1957), and reprinted in *The Exploding Metropolis* (Garden City, N.Y.: Doubleday & Company, 1958), p. 63. Quoted by courtesy of *Fortune* Magazine. © 1957, Time, Inc. All rights reserved.

[10] *Ibid.*, pp. 67–68. Quoted by courtesy of *Fortune* Magazine. © 1957, Time, Inc. All rights reserved.

twenty-four years the mayor of Atlanta, is a good example; he led Atlanta into the ranks of the metropolitan cities, giving it improved management and budgeting procedures providing leadership for urban renewal, recreational, cultural, highway and other projects. "An unabashed ham," wrote a *New York Times* reporter on the occasion of Hartsfield's announcement of his retirement. "He often put [that quality] to use when it seemed in the city's interest."[11]

A comparable mixture of ham, determination, hard work, and resourceful leadership make Richard C. Lee of New Haven, Connecticut, one of the more remarkable mayors of recent years. Urban renewal has been the cornerstone of Lee's political career, and so successful has he been in promoting renewal in New Haven that he has acquired for the city more federal aid per capita than any other city in the land and he has also parlayed the remaking of the downtown core of the city into a political bonanza. Hard-headed bankers and businessmen, not usually accustomed to giving campaign backing to liberal Democrats, have backed him financially and otherwise in his four successive re-election campaigns between 1955 and 1961. (He first won the office in 1953, having lost twice in earlier bids—once by a heartbreaking two votes.) Predecessors had been satisfied to muddle along, allowing a slow deterioration of city assets, offering little leadership. Lee reversed this process, asserting strong leadership and beginning to reconstruct the city—doing so, moreover, without raising tax rates.[12]

One could cite others: Mayor Raymond Tucker of St. Louis, an erstwhile professor of engineering; Murray Seasongood and Charles Taft, the only outstanding mayors that come to mind who served in manager cities; or Frank P. Zeidler or Daniel Webster Hoan of Milwaukee. Even though it was apparently not expected by many observers, the current mayor of Chicago has turned out to be an effective executive leader. As Freedgood has said, "When he was elected many people believed he would sell City Hall to Cicero [meaning the gangsters] without a qualm. Instead, Daley went along to a remarkable extent in putting into effect reform legislation that tightened and improved the structure of Chicago's city government."[13] He may not be elegant in speech (he is reported to have said at a "town-and-gown" dinner at the University of Chicago that "We will go on to a new high platitude of success"), but his control over the political organization of the city and his determination to achieve improvements in the city appear to be getting results.

There are others, leaders distinguished by the common drive to move the city ahead, or at least in some direction that it was not going in before. In this sense they might be labeled liberal or progressive in outlook and program. But the driving, tough leadership mantle does not belong solely to the progressive. Mayor J. Bracken Lee of Salt Lake City, for instance, is a professed and active conservative. As strong and resourceful a mayor as any of the progressive types, he won the office over a liberal Democrat in 1959, having campaigned against heavy spending in government, a goal he has

---

[11] *The New York Times*, June 11, 1961.
[12] See the profiles by Joe Alex Morris, "He Is Saving a 'Dead City'," 230 *Saturday Evening Post* 31 (April 19, 1958), and Jeanne R. Lowe, "Lee of New Haven and His Political Jackpot," 215 *Harper's*

Magazine 36 (October, 1957). See also the forthcoming work (from Yale University Press) by Raymond Wolfinger, *The Politics of Progress.*
[13] Freedgood, *op. cit.*, p. 74.

vigorously pursued ever since. In his first budget he cut a quarter of a million from the requests, and got into a row with a popular chief of police and fired him over the prospective budget cuts in the police department. This and some other maneuvers have stirred up hornets' nests of opposition, but have won him support at the same time.[14]

(3) THE EVADER TYPE   It is difficult to compose a list of well-known evader types; their careers do not commend them to national audiences. Indeed, it is the capacity to *not* attract notoriety or excessive publicity as pushers of anything notable that is their major stock in trade. To assure their tenure they avoid commitments, seek zealously to placate disputes, and follow the lead set by councilmen or other actors. Of course, all mayors use the evader routine on some issues; the conditions of political competition demand it occasionally. But there is a difference between being evasive occasionally and being evasive permanently.

The evasive stance is most common in smaller communities that are not growing or that have not developed serious problems of slums, finances, traffic bottlenecks, transit failures, or the like. But the larger cities have nurtured the type also, however serious their problems. New York City has had such mayors. Vincent R. Impellitteri, who ran in 1950 as an Independent against candidates from the divided and discredited Democratic organization and a Republican, won the election. He seemed not to know what to do with his prize. He "retreated into his self-described role as presiding officer of the Board of Estimate, sharing initia-

tive and responsibility with any who would ease his burdens of accountability."[15]

The weak-mayor system seems at times to discourage mayors from even attempting leadership, since their resources for backing up their initiatives are limited, but weak-mayor system or strong there is also involved a matter of basic attitude and a calculation of the probable consequences of risking leadership resources. It is claimed that P. Kenneth Petersen, until recently mayor of Minneapolis, one of the few large cities with what approximates a classic form of weak-mayor government, zealously avoided commitment on issues. Alan Altshuler in a study of Minneapolis politics attributes the following strategy to Petersen:

He does not actively sponsor anything. He waits for private groups to agree on a project. If he likes it, he endorses it. Since he has no formal power with which to pressure the Council himself, he feels that the private groups must take the responsibility for getting their plan accepted. He never attempts to coerce aldermen. Instead, he calls them into his office to reason with them. . . . The Mayor has let citizens' groups use the facilities of his office to work out solutions to certain pressing and highly controversial problems. Such solutions are often then seized upon by him and by the Council and adopted without amendment.[16]

Others claim that Petersen did not even employ the resources at hand such as press conferences to embarrass the council when it was vulnerable.

[14] See the typically *Time*titled article, "Nettled Nickle-Nipper," 75 *Time*, 14–15 (April 4, 1960), on Lee's successes and problems.

[15] Sayre and Kaufman, *op. cit.*, p. 697.
[16] *A Report on Politics in Minneapolis* (Cambridge, Mass.: Joint Center for Urban Studies of M.I.T. and Harvard University, 1959), pp. II, 14–15 (mimeographed).

Some mayors ride into office as reformers but end up as evasive, long-term tenants at city hall. Such was the long career of Jasper McLevy of Bridgeport, Connecticut. Running as a Socialist candidate in 1933, he won the office because he was neither a Democrat nor a Republican in a city where a corrupt dual machine had discredited both major parties. He held the office for the next twenty-four years. Notwithstanding his Socialist label, his tenure was marked by penuriousness that would have done credit to the arch-conservative J. Bracken Lee, by the creation of a well-oiled local organization to support his biennial candidacy, and by a gradual decline of conditions in the city until another reformer displaced the reformer-turned-evader.

One final example may serve to illustrate another variation in the pattern. Mayors of Chicago, according to Meyerson and Banfield in their study of a Chicago public housing controversy, were traditionally eager to make the most of public housing projects: "Back in 1915 Mayor William Hale [Big Bill, the Builder] Thompson had demostrated a formula for winning elections which had proved itself time and again; it called for (among other things) assiduous cultivation of the Negro vote and an energetic appeal to the booster spirit which glorified in vast public works. Politicians of both parties had not forgotten this time-tested formula, and public housing seemingly fitted the formula perfectly since it was presumed to appeal both to Negroes and to boosters."[17] But Mayor Martin H. Kennelly fooled those who predicted he would behave as his predecessors had. In time the promoters of

[17] Martin Meyerson and Edward C. Banfield, *Politics, Planning and the Public Interest* (New York: The Free Press of Glencoe, Inc., 1955), p. 61.

public housing realized he was not going to be mayor in the same sense that his predecessors had been, "or, indeed, in any sense at all. Until 1948 it was reasonable for them to suppose that the Mayor was the person with whom a general understanding would have to be reached. But when it became evident that the city government was to be run by the 'Big Boys' of the Council, it would not have been easy for the heads of the [Housing] Authority, even if they had tried, to reach an understanding with them."[18] Bereft of the focused leadership of the mayor's office, the program drifted, and in good measure so did the city itself.

(4) THE STOOGE TYPE Happily, contemporary politics affords few examples of this species. It took the old-fashioned machine to pull off the election of a pliant, controlled candidate to the office of mayor. Once chosen, the proxy mayor would be careful to do the bidding of the boss who called the signals from the background. The old Philadelphia organization and that of Edward Crump in Memphis, Tennessee, hand-picked minions for the front office to respond puppet-like to the bidding of the real political power source. Not only party organizations and factional groups managed to get pliant mayors to do their bidding—it has often been claimed with considerable truth that business groups achieved the same sort of dominance over "their" mayors, and apparently the underworld on rare occasions achieved similar control.

No doubt the practical relationships of the "subordinated" mayor with his masters were not entirely one-sided; the possession of the formal authority of office counted for something, at least, and there was always the possibility of

[18] *Ibid.*, p. 258.

a break with the masters and an attempt to strike out independently. Many mayors tried to get out from under such domination—some were successful for brief periods, but the odds were against it. The reason is simple: if the political conditions of a community are such that an organization has strong enough control over access to office to choose a compliant stooge, then it is likely that the power can be used to squash a rebel.

How widespread this phenomenon is today, it is difficult to say. Probably there are communities where in essence this does prevail, although it is difficult to believe that any political organization today can muster the quasi-totalitarian sweep of powers that sustained the old-fashioned proxy mayor and backstage boss relationship. Doubtless the relationship where it exists today is a modified one, best described perhaps as a cooperative relationship with dominance of the mayor on most but not all questions.

A BIG CITY MAYOR SPEAKS OUT

U.S. Senate Subcommittee on Executive Reorganization

Mayor Yorty in a testimony before a Senate Subcommittee is roundly criticized for doing nothing for the needy people, as lacking in leadership, and, along with his constituents, as being in need of some soul-searching. The Mayor in reply emphasized his lack of authority—the government's weak-mayor strong-council structure. Further, he explains that the city is not responsible for schools, welfare, hiring, health, and housing—these are the responsibilities of the county, state, or elected school boards. The city is left with the ceremonial functions, police, firemen, and sanitation. Whatever the merits of Mayor Yorty may be, he certainly heads a government in which he has little authority and responsibility—a situation not conducive to providing for the needs of the people.

Mayor Yorty. Thank you, Senator. First of all, I want to thank you for inviting me here and inviting the mayors to express our opinions directly to this committee about some of the Federal programs, and what we foresee as being needed in the future.

I would like to start by saying I think it is very important that it be recognized here at the Federal level that the cities, while maybe from the vantage point of Washington they all look about the same, with population figures differing, the structure of the cities are very different, and therefore the programs need to be tailored, I think, more to the individual cities than they have sometimes in the past. I might

Reprinted from *Federal Role in Urban Affairs*, Part 3, pp. 671–672; 766–768; 770–771; 774–779. Hearings before the Subcommittee on Executive Reorganization of the Committee on Government Operations, U.S. Senate, 89th Congress, 2d Session, August 22–23, 1966.

say, for instance, that in Los Angeles, of the larger cities of the Nation, it is the only really large city that has a non-partisan city government.

GOVERNMENTAL STRUCTURE OF LOS ANGELES

Also, we have a different structure from the other cities. The mayor of Los Angeles has nothing to do, for instance, with the school system. We have an independently elected school board, with their own taxing power and they make up their own budget.

Also, the mayor of Los Angeles has nothing to do with the welfare program. This is handled by the county for the State. So I am not involved as mayor in any of those programs either. We don't have a department of employment in the city. This is another State function, the State department of employment which is entirely separate and I have no jurisdiction over that.

The health department is part of the county structure. Our effort to build a rapid transit system is through State agency, with the members originally appointed by the Governor, but now with some local appointments, but still the transit district is much larger than the city.

Our housing authority, while it is called a city housing authority, is nevertheless a State agency, and it is presently at our request being operated by the Federal Government.

Also, another difference that we have from some other cities is that we have not only what we call a weak mayor-strong council type of government, but we have a commission form of government. The major departments of the city of Los Angeles are actually headed by commissioners who are dollar-a-year type people, receive no real compensation for the work that they do, coming in usually once a week and heading a department.

MINORITY GROUP REPRESENTATION IN CITY GOVERNMENT

When I became mayor in 1961 I completely integrated these commissions for the first time in the history of the city. Before that, there was sort of a token representation for minorities on these commissions, and my first exhibit there is a talk that I made to a U.S. conference of mayors shortly after I became mayor, suggesting that in all cities that minorities should be given more of a voice in the government, and it was my intention at that time to try and make Los Angeles a model city as far as race relations were concerned, and this was the first step within my jurisdiction to do something about these commissions.

MAJOR PROBLEM IN LOS ANGELES IS UNEMPLOYMENT

What would you say is the major problem that you have to face now, Mr. Mayor, in connection with the city of Los Angeles?

Mayor Yorty. It depends on what field you mean, but I would say primarily in the field of where we have human relations. It still gets back to taking the people who are unskilled and unemployed, and if they had skills they would have jobs because there are jobs available, as you know, but only for skilled people.

I think, No. 1, these people must be provided with the opportunity to work, and as I said before, I think Dr. King must have been wrestling with this problem a lot, because he said the other day that our problem is primarily economic, and I think we should have a guaranteed annual income for everyone. So I can see what he is thinking is that if you cannot get them a job, he thinks they should at least have an income, but basically I think we must realize that they cannot compete in a capitalistic competitive system, and so we modify it as to them and supply them with some kind of work and try and make it meaningful work. But if it cannot be so meaningful, at least it should be some kind of work that they can do and draw income. I think if they did this, this would solve a lot of other problems.

Senator Kennedy. How would you go about doing that?

Mayor Yorty. Well, I think it can only be done by some kind of an effort under OEO probably. The kind of work that we supply them with I do not know. I would hope that maybe we could work in cooperation with the private sector, so that what benefit they could get for their services they would pay for, and there is some of this being done.

Senator Kennedy. Have you worked out yourself the kind of a program you would like to see?

Mayor Yorty. We have worked it out with this opportunities industrialization center, which we hope, of course, will not just hire them after they get out of a job, but we hope are going to fit them for jobs that are available.

We feel that a good job was done in Philadelphia by Reverend Sullivan, and I hope that it is going to work in our community.

The Ford Foundation did make a grant, a great cross section of the people are involved in the program.

Senator Kennedy. What specifically would you do now?

What do you specifically recommend

be done in the Watts area or the curfew area or however you wish to describe it?

YORTY HOUSING RESTORATION PLAN

Mayor Yorty. We have a rehabilitation program going in there. We have one that we are planning that we are going to call code enforcement and rehabilitation. We were hoping through this to put together a package for one area at a time, whereby in addition to code enforcement, I mean building and safety, that we would try to tie the various Federal programs together, to get the grants for the people who need that where they are eligible up to the $1,500 to rehabilitate their property, and loans at a low interest rate, if they need more, and to see if we cannot also provide that the employment must come primarily from the area.

Now, this will cause some problems, particularly right now, because the construction industry is in very bad shape, and we have tremendous unemployment in the construction industry, but this is a plan which we hope to put together.

I think it is 16 districts, is it not, that we are laying out in the city, with the idea of just really bringing them up to high standards and putting together all the grants that we can, whether they be local, State, or Federal.

Senator Kennedy. Do you have one individual under your direction that handles all requests for Federal grants?

Mayor Yorty. By and large, Mr. Goe here is the clearinghouse for most of those grants, although some go direct, like the airport department and harbor department.

Senator Kennedy. What is the cost of the kind of program which you describe?

Mayor Yorty. We figured about $15

million Federal and about $6 million that we would match.

Senator Kennedy. So it is $22 million?

Mayor Yorty. Yes, we think about 16 districts.

Senator Kennedy. It is $22 million for each of the 16 districts?

Mayor Yorty. Roughly, yes.

Senator Kennedy. Per year?

Mayor Yorty. No. This would be more or less of a permanent bringing them up to standards. Once they are up to standard it would last a long time.

Senator Kennedy. How long would the program last?

Mayor Yorty. Three years on each one.

Senator Kennedy. And how many people would be involved?

Mayor Yorty. I do not know yet. Have we got any estimate?

Mr. Goe. We could only guess at this time, Senator, if I may answer this. Our "guesstimate" is, based on information from the building industry, that we could very probably, if this were universally applied over all of the obsolescent areas of the city, employ most of the unemployed who could be brought up to a median skill level on a permanent basis.

Senator Kennedy. How many people would that be? How many unemployed do you have in Los Angeles, to get back to my figure?

Mr. Goe. I do not know the figure, Senator. I can give you a pretty good "guesstimate" about the south-central area.

HOW MANY WILL BE INVOLVED IN HOUSING PROPOSAL?

Senator Kennedy. What I do not understand is how you can develop a program that is going to bring everybody up to median skills and you are going to give them employment if you do not know how many people there are.

Mr. Goe. The criteria of the program pretty well limits it in making guesses. First of all, there is no such program in existence now. The Housing Act as amended provides for loans and grants for rehabilitation, as you know; it also provides for two-thirds/one-third matching fund with city capital projects money allocations. No one has yet put this together as an employment package, and we are attempting to do this.

So each area—for example, one area has a boundary, or within the boundary there are 1,400 homes and commercial enterprises. We now look back into the census tracts and pull out all the figures about who these people are and what their employment status is, and then we will match that to that particular area of 1,400 units, so it would be impossible to say at this point how many people there are in that specific area who are, first, unemployed, and who, second, could benefit from an MDTA-type training program and bring their skill level up so they could carry on the rehabilitation.

WHAT SHOULD BE DONE TO IMPROVE RACE RELATIONS IN UNITED STATES?

Mr. Mayor, what is your feeling about how you would work toward improving the relationship that exists between the races, not only in Los Angeles but across the country?

What are your ideas about that? Would you say that is a problem?

Mayor Yorty. It is one of the great problems of course, and as I pointed out before, one of the problems I have with the city and that all the mayors have is that we are the head of law enforcement, and when the politicians run around and make a lot of promises that are not kept and some that cannot be kept, and get people agitated, expecting more than is going to be made available to them, and then they reach out illegally to get it, it is the policeman who has to stop them, and it has created an intolerable situation for the police departments. And of course I think Los Angeles, as proven by the record, has basically good race relations. Certainly the Negroes have proved by the Urban League and others to be better off in Los Angeles than any large city in the Nation. We are pretty proud of that record and we hope to improve it.

Senator Kennedy. Would you say with the unemployment rate in Watts of 35 per cent that the Negro is better off?

Mayor Yorty. No, I did not say that. I said that based on a study of all the cities, that the Negroes in Los Angeles have a higher average income, better housing and are better off than in the New York or say Chicago or Detroit or some of the rest. They have better standards. But that as Sam Rayburn used to say, all of this does not mean anything to the guy that is out of a job, because if everybody else is working, as Mr. Sam used to say, that man is in a depression.

Senator Kennedy. That is right.

Mayor Yorty. And so we want to take care of all those people just as much as anybody else does certainly, and I would like to get jobs for all of them. We will do everything we can to stimulate projects at our level to make jobs, but we have to do it within our means and within our jurisdiction. We have to rely on other jurisdictions, and Federal jurisdiction too, for some of the funds and for some of the help with the projects.

NOT POLITICIANS' PROMISES, BUT THE PROMISE OF AMERICA, LEADS PEOPLE TO EXPECT A BETTER LIFE

Senator Kennedy. May I just say, it seems to me that it is not just a question for the individuals. It is not just a question of the politician and going around and making a great number of promises. I expect somebody reading the Declaration of Independence and the Constitution of the United States and our major State documents would feel that he was entitled to move ahead in society and that his children should have an opportunity to obtain employment and his children should have an opportunity to go to decent schools and have good teachers, so that he can move ahead so that the next generation can live even a better life.

Mayor Yorty. One of the problems there——

Senator Kennedy. One of the problems is, if I may say so, Mr. Mayor, is not just a question of people going around, politicians whether in Los Angeles or elsewhere, promising Negroes or the poor all kinds of things as far as the future is concerned, but the fact that these people expect to have as much of a chance as you and I have had.

Mayor Yorty. Well, certainly they will not have the chance you have had, but I hope they have the one that I have had. But I might say that one of the problems I found from one of my Negro staff members which rather surprised me and surprised Mr. Shriver was the fact that a lot of these people thought that they were going to be given money. They heard about the war on poverty ending poverty, and they got the impression that when you are poor, the way not to be poor is for somebody to give you money, and they were waiting for this money and this money did not come.

UNEMPLOYED PEOPLE WANT A JOB

Senator Kennedy. Of course I think, if I may say so, I suppose it is just a basic difference in one's philosophy. I do not think—I am sure there are some who are like that but I think there are an awful lot of people who would just like to find employment.

Mayor Yorty. Oh——

Senator Kennedy. Wait a minute.

Mayor Yorty. Obviously.

Senator Kennedy. I think there are an awful lot of people who would just like to find a job. When I asked you the question how we can improve race relations, you begin the answer to the question about the police and go into the fact that politicians make promises to them, as if it is sort of a group of people that we just do not want to get too close to.

MAYOR LACKS AUTHORITY OVER VITAL URBAN FUNCTIONS

Senator Ribicoff. As I listened to your testimony, Mayor Yorty, I made some notes. This morning you have really waived authority and responsibility in the following areas: schools, welfare, transportation, employment, health, and housing, which leaves you as the head of the city basically with a ceremonial function, police and recreation.

Mayor Yorty. That is right, and fire.

Senator Ribicoff. And fire.

Mayor Yorty. Yes.

Senator Ribicoff. Collecting sewage?

Mayor Yorty. Sanitation; this is right.

Senator Ribicoff. In other words, basically you lack jurisdiction, author-ity, responsibility for what makes a city move?

Mayor Yorty. That is exactly it.

Senator Ribicoff. What makes a city go around.

MAYOR HAS TRIED TO OBTAIN AUTHORITY OVER THESE FUNCTIONS

Mayor Yorty. That is exactly right, Senator, and, of course, for 5 years I have been trying to get charter amendments. Some of the cities of the country have modernized their city government, and we badly need to do it but, unfortunately, under our form of government the city council has all the power. It is, I think, the only one in the nation that meets every day the year round, and charter amendments have to be put on the ballot by them. Any reform would strengthen the mayor, and to some extent at the hands of the council. So they do not want to put those things on the ballot.

Then, on the other hand, even if the city charter were better and the mayor was stronger, this still would not give the mayor jurisdiction over these areas that we are talking about. This is one reason that I gave up the health department and consolidated it—agreed to a consolidation with the country—so as to get one place at least in the country where all the health problems could be worked out.

LOS ANGELES DOES NOT STAND FOR A DAMN THING

Senator Ribicoff. I would think the people of Los Angeles have an awful lot of soul searching to do of their own. They brag all over the country what a great city they are and how big they are and what they achieve and what they stand for.

I would say that the city of Los Angeles right now, from your testimony, does not stand for a damn thing.

Mayor Yorty. Well, it stands for a lot. We are a great city.

Senator Ribicoff. Oh, yes; you are a great city.

Mayor Yorty. In many of the areas.

Senator Ribicoff. But you do not have any jusisdiction over the basic throb of life of a city from early morning until late at night.

Senator Kennedy. I think, Mr. Chairman, if I may say so, your statement was based on the testimony of the mayor, not what you personally feel.

Mayor Yorty. Also, you see, there is another——

Senator Kennedy. I want you to be able to get in and out of Los Angeles.

LOS ANGELES GOVERNMENT SHOULD BE ORGANIZED ON COUNTY BASIS

Mayor Yorty. There is another factor in this, that is the problems that you are talking about there, they are under a jurisdiction, though not under mine, and I think, as I said at the start, I think in the East sometimes they tend to look at cities as all the same, and they forget that structures of the cities may be entirely different and the jurisdictions different.

Now in many ways, for instance welfare, it is better that the county handles it, because the county can handle it countywide, and this includes over 75 cities, and it is much more efficient to do it that way. Probably in time we will consolidate more city services with the county.

The late Chief Parker felt that we should have one law enforcement agency for the whole county, and I would agree with him on that, if we could work it out. But in this way we could achieve the kind of unity and jurisdiction that you already have in the East, where a large area, with all the problems will be under the city, where we have this big county structure.

LOS ANGELES NEEDS BETTER ORGANIZATION TO TAKE ADVANTAGE OF FEDERAL PROGRAMS

Senator Ribicoff. But I would predict that we are going to move toward doing something about the cties of America. I think that there is a realization that the future of our country depends upon solving the crisis of the American city.

I believe that there will be Federal programs that will be initiated in the next 2 years and that will really put America on the road to start doing something about the cities of America.

That means the cities are going to have to be in position to take advantage of these programs. I would say, as I have listened to you, and if it is the charter it is no reflection on you personally, that the one city that won't be able to take advantage of any of these programs will be Los Angeles, because you are not organized to do so.

Mayor Yorty. The only way we can organize is the way we did with as I explained to you about the Youth Opportunities Board, and the way we are working with our present OEO Board. We do it by a joint powers agreement with the other jurisdictions that are involved, so at that point we can work together. When you get to solving the problems of the cities, in our community we probably have to work countywide.

Senator Ribicoff. I understand that Mr. Shriver has been trying to get a new poverty director in Los Angeles for some time, but is having difficulty in getting one, because no one will be assured that if a poverty man has to take on some controversial programs, that he has anybody in Los Angeles that will back him up in the tough decisions.

Now, we know this. That if these programs are going to work, you have to have someone in authority, if he is the mayor, or whoever, to really stand back of a man to make some really unpopular, tough decisions. Now, in Los Angeles apparently there is nobody to back a man up who wants to make a tough decision.

Mayor Yorty. Well, I don't think that is a correct statement, as I have backed the war on poverty since the very start.

Senator Ribicoff. In other words, you are getting——

Mayor Yorty. Well, we have more poverty funds than anybody in the Nation, according to Mr. Shriver.

Senator Ribicoff. That is the trouble. Next to New York you have——

Mayor Yorty. We have more than New York, he said.

POVERTY FUNDS ARE NOT HELPING THOSE IN NEED IN LOS ANGELES

Senator Ribicoff. $33 million, but basically I think what is happening as I listen to this testimony, and the questioning of Senator Kennedy, instead of that $33 million really helping the people in Watts, and the Mexican-Americans, the Negroes, and the poor white—there must be plenty of white poor in Los Angeles—that money is being used basically to prop up your school system because the people in Los Angeles and the State of California are unwilling to pay the bill to educate their kids.

Now if they are not using their money to educate their kids, I think it is unfair to use the general tax funds of

this country through the poverty program for the educational system of Los Angeles. I am willing to do it with our eyes wide open on Federal educational programs.

Mayor Yorty. But, Senator, you have to take into consideration the fact that we have one of the best educational systems in the Nation and we are supporting it, including free higher education.

Senator Ribicoff. That is absolutely correct. In other words, this is a great thing for the middle class, and it is. I think that the higher education system in California is the most far reaching, I think it is the best in the entire United States. There is no question about this. I noticed this when I was Secretary and I have said it publicly. I think the middle class get a very good education financed free. But as I listened to you today, you are giving short shrift and you are short-changing a few generations by doing absolutely nothing for the disadvantaged groups, the people on the bottom of the ladder, the group of people that the McCone report says something should be done for.

With $250 a year being spent for these youngsters in smaller classes and, illiteracies, to bring them up, and here you are in the Los Angeles area doing absolutely nothing for the people who need it the most.

PROGRAMS AND PROJECTS MUST BE TRANSLATED INTO EFFECTIVE ASSISTANCE TO PEOPLE

Mayor Yorty. Have you looked at this list of projects that we have going and what we are doing?

Senator Ribicoff. I am very unimpressed with a list of projects if they are not translated into doing something for the people.

Mayor Yorty. There are all kinds of things being done for these people through all these projects.

Senator Ribicoff. And yet the Mc-Cone report——

Mayor Yorty. By your own director more than any in the Nation. I would like to see one of your cities dissected as McCone did ours, and point out the faults.

Senator Ribicoff. Well, I will tell you this. All right.

Mayor Yorty. We will do the same.

Senator Ribicoff. The mayor of New Haven will be here on Thursday. Of course, he is a friend of mine so I won't dissect him, but will you do that, Senator Kennedy?

Senator Kennedy. He is a very good friend of mine.

Mayor Yorty. He is a very good mayor. It is a very unfair statement to say that nothing is being done in our city.

Senator Kennedy. The mayor of Los Angeles I would like to have stay here through all of these hearings, and I think he could safely do so, because as I understand from your testimony you have nothing to get back to.

Mayor Yorty. That is sort of a ridiculous statement but I think——

Senator Kennedy. That is what you have to gather from the testimony you have given to this committee.

Mayor Yorty. I think that I have explained, and I said when I came back here that I thought in the East they tend to look at the whole Nation, look at the cities and think they are all the same. They are all different, and they have to be handled differently, and ours certainly has to be handled in a different way, because of the various jurisdictions that are involved in the various problems.

Senator Ribicoff. I bring this up not because it happens to refer to my own

State of Connecticut, but the McCone report states, and this gets to another phase.

Moreover, unlike such as New Haven, Connecticut, private groups have not taken full advantage of the numerous federally supported programs designed to assist the construction of low-cost housing.

In other words, you have a rich city. You have a powerful city, with people and industries who parade themselves across the world as standing for something positive. Now there is much that can be done in the private sector. Someone has to bring them together. I think that, really, the people of Los Angeles, both official and private, have an awful lot of soul searching to do. They can wring their hands and view with alarm what happened in Watts, and then go home and pray that it doesn't happen again. But it would seem to me that the people of Los Angeles aren't doing very much to prevent another Watts by helping themselves. They are closing their eyes to the grave problems of public and personal responsibility that I think a city like Los Angeles, if it is to be worthy of its name, should undertake.

Mayor Yorty. I don't think that that is a fair conclusion. As a matter of fact, if you look at the housing in Los Angeles, you can hardly compare it with some of the cities you are talking about. Our public housing at the moment we have vacancies in it. Mainly we lack the larger units that we could use, but we like the rent supplement program, and we are one of the cities using that, and we hope that it can be expanded, but there isn't enough money to do the whole job now.

Again you get back to this matter. I could sit here and blame the Federal Government as many are doing for not appropriating enough, if I wanted to, but I just don't believe in that.

McCONE REPORT POINTS THE WAY TO IMPROVEMENT OF CONDITIONS

Senator Kennedy. Mr. Chairman, could I just add a qualification to what you just said? I think it has to be impressed on the rest of the country the fact that John McCone, Warren Christopher, and others made this kind of study. The initial report—I know there is a great deal of controversy about it, but in my judgment it was a major step forward and highlighted some of the needs not only in Watts but elsewhere across the country, and the fact that this was supplemented by this second report.

Also, I think that the effort that has been made by the newspapers and particularly the Los Angeles Times in pointing out some of the matters that need to have attention has been also extremely impressive. Budd Schulberg, who has established, made an effort in Watts and, there have been a number of others. I went there a year or so ago, but I was terribly impressed by the fact that there were a number of people in private companies and corporations, private individuals who went into Watts and went into the more deprived areas to try to help the people, and I am sure it could be improved and could be expanded, but I think that in a lot of other places of the country even that much hasn't been done.

Mayor Yorty. Well, there is lots being done in that area.

LOS ANGELES NEEDS LEADERSHIP TO GIVE DIRECTION

Senator Kennedy. I think what is lacking, if I may say so, Mr. Mayor, is just one authority who speaks out and gives some direction and says, "This is what we have to do and this is what we have to face up to."

I think the impression that you have, we had Mayor Cavanagh earlier, Mayor Lindsay yesterday, who is a different political affiliation from me, but at least saying "This is what we are going to try to do and this is the direction I would like to have my city move in" instead of always saying "This is a problem I really haven't got the background on, I don't really have the jurisdiction to do anything about it."

Mayor Yorty. No, I think it is only fair to say when I don't have the jurisdiction, so I can only tell the others what I think they should do and what they ought to do, and we do. But if you try to tell them too much, then they think you are demagoging on them. They say "We can't do it," and so forth. So I tried to explain to you what we are up against, and how we try to work together with the other jurisdictions, and we can work with them and we are. But one of the best projects we had going was broken up, the Youth Opportunities Board, with a good structure, by I think the failure at the Federal level to understand that our area was different, when they tried to give us the same criteria for the OEO Board as for everybody else.

MAYOR'S ACTIONS DURING RIOT

Senator Kennedy. Mr. Mayor, is it true or correct that you left the city the night that they began to have the riots in Watts?

Mayor Yorty. That is not true.

Senator Kennedy. Were you in the city all the time?

Mayor Yorty. I was in the city all but 2 hours; yes.

Senator Kennedy. Did you leave the city at all during that time?

Mayor Yorty. Yes; for 2 hours.

Senator Kennedy. Is that when you went to make a speech?

Mayor Yorty. I went to make a pre-scheduled speech, but the riot had stopped. This was a very peculiar stop-and-start riot. The chief of police thought that it would not start again, and there were 700 people waiting an hour away in San Francisco at the Commonwealth Club, and I had to decide whether I could keep that commitment, although I would only be a minute away by telephone, or not and so I went up and made it and came right back. Later that night it started again.

Senator Kennedy. Were there disorders while you were away?

Mayor Yorty. No. During that time —the chief and I decided that morning on the big decision that was made before I left that we would call out the National Guard just in case. But Chief Parker was of the opinion that it wouldn't start again. But this riot would——

Senator Kennedy. Were there any disorders while you were away?

Mayor Yorty. Well, some, but not a big problem. What would happen is that this thing would be late into the night and then it would stop, and you couldn't tell which night it was going to end. But, then, of course, we had a long delay in getting out the Guard. They didn't get in until late at night with the disorders raging.

Besides that, the first night the police department made a mistake in their tactics, which we frankly admit.

LINDSAY AND ROCKEFELLER AT ODDS

Walter Lippmann

Mr. Lippmann poses the question as to whether we can remain a free society and still provide the essential services to the great urban masses. He suggests that the problems of metropolis are not really soluble, only manageable at best. The garbage strike in New York City serves to illustrate the difficulties faced by Mayor Lindsay as he sought a solution. On the other hand, Governor Rockefeller, seeing the futility of the Mayor's position, forced the end of the strike by meeting the main points of the striker's demands. Our society will not survive unless the many minorities learn to adjust to the needs of the urban society.

Living in a big city like New York fits G. K. Chesterton's description of modern civilization. We are, he said, like men at the bottom of the ocean. They get their air and everything else they need through tubes that can easily become tangled and fouled up.

Robinson Crusoe, the self-sufficient man, could not have lived in New York City. These last few weeks the garbage piled up in the streets, and if the snow-storm that was threatened had come, the traffic would have been impossible. In recent months we have nearly had a standstill of transportation, both horizontal and vertical. The schools have been closed by a teachers' strike, and there have been threats by the police and the firemen.

New York is a dramatic and conspicuous example of the vulnerability of urban living. Certain services are indispensable to city dwellers. In the past they have been more or less taken for granted. But in our time such services as collecting garbage and operating subways and buses are performed by men who have learned to organize. These men read that this is an affluent society. They hear about the goods and services of affluent people. They realize that by striking they can come nearer to a glittering, affluent good life. They know they have power, and they have not yet tested the limits of that power.

MANAGEABLE PROBLEM   Two of the best men in public life, Mayor Lindsay and Governor Rockefeller, are struggling with this problem. It is, I believe, inherently insoluble. Under prevailing standards the problem cannot be solved if it is reduced to an issue of abstract principle. The problem can only be *managed.* Thus it is quite true that there ought to be no such thing as a strike against the public security and welfare. But in fact there are such strikes and if garbage men organize and strike, there is no clearly accepted method of preventing them from doing it.

This was the dilemma which Mayor Lindsay found himself facing when, having come to the end of his own resources, he asked the governor of the state to call out the National Guard. This was not a solution. The National Guard cannot collect the garbage and operate the subways and teach school. If the National Guard had tried to break the garbage strike by collecting the garbage, there would probably have been something like a general strike by city employees.

The city has been caught between the

intolerable and the impossible. It has had to choose between letting the garbage pile up and trying to make the militia collect it. This abstract issue was unrealistic. The issue could not be resolved by a showdown on principle. Governor Rockefeller took the unheroic and unpopular but realistic view of the situation. He by-passed the legal principle at issue and tried to manage the problem by buying his way out of an illegal but most effective strike.

FATEFUL QUESTION   What he did was not according to the law. It was not noble and it was not heroic. But the fact of the matter is that a great modern city has no means of enforcing a law against powerful unions. There is no way of evading the fact that in a city as big as New York only the garbage men can collect the garbage. This is their power. The individual citizen does not have his own incinerator. The police and the firemen cannot collect garbage. The courts cannot put in jail or levy fines on thousands of garbage men.

This ultimate defenselessness of modern cities is ominous. If the unions keep on exploiting it there will certainly be a reaction, and the reaction will be some American variant of Fascism, that is to say a counter-revolution of the victims, themselves for the most part poor and unprivileged, against organized minorities. We already have such a reaction against militant Negroes. It is called the white backlash. But there is developing also a blacklash against the insecurity of modern living brought on by other minorities.

Modern living is dangerous. We are confronted with a fateful question—can we remain a free society and still provide the great urban masses with the vital services they must have?

We must remind ourselves that it is not written in any book or enshrined in any law that American democracy will master the problem of modern living. The American way of life was formed in a simple environment when the mass of the people had not yet become dependent, as they are today, upon the restraint and the goodwill and cooperation of the people of their communities.

The future is in doubt. For it is not certain that the indispensable virtues of a free life are now being generated in sufficient force and quantity amidst the violence and nihilism of the modern age.

IN POLITICS IT'S THE NEW POPULISM

Newsweek

What we are seeing now is the far-ranging, fast-spreading revolt of the little man as he looks for new champions from within his own ranks—for example, Barry Goldwater was able to gain temporary hold of the GOP; Ronald Reagan was elected Governor of California; Governors Wallace and Maddox ranted and raved against bureaucrats in their drive for political office; and Tony Imperiale is using his Newark vigilantes to build his chances for the governor's chair. Part of the appeal is emotional and there is some bigotry present. But the little man also feels a sense of being deserted by the government. There is a feeling of alienation from the political system. New populism is a quest for recognition. The little man feels a wide gap between himself and the intellectual, between the governed and the governor, and between the rich and the poor. The workers are on the battleline between blacks and whites and they resent advice from the "outside." They are searching for "old values," values and a style of life long disappeared from our land. This is the new populism and it seems too early to tell what direction it will take.

In Minneapolis, a policeman named Charles Stenvig becomes mayor by rolling up an astounding 62 per cent of the vote against the experienced president of the City Council. In New York, Mayor John Lindsay and former Mayor Robert Wagner, both liberals of national stature, bow to obscure interlopers in their parties' mayoral primaries, In Boston, grandmotherly Louise Day Hicks, whose crusade for the "forgotten man" and against school busing carried her within an inch of City Hall two years ago, leads a big field in the up-

coming City Council elections. And in Newark, a onetime construction worker named Anthony Imperiale, master of karate, the bowie knife and a fleet of 72 radio cars that regularly patrol the city's white neighborhoods, confidently maps his campaign to win next year's race for mayor and "get rid of every quisling" in sight.

This is the year of the New Populism, a far-ranging, fast-spreading revolt of the little man against the Establishment at the nation's polls. Middle America, long counted upon to supply the pluralities on Election Day, is beginning to supply eye-opening victories from coast to coast. The over-all political cast of the country remains mixed, to be sure. The freshman crop of U.S. senators elected just last year, for example, includes a significant share of conventional liberals and moderates. Only a fortnight ago, a Negro candidate topped the field in the Detroit mayoral primary, and progressive Lindsay may yet eke out a victory in New York next month. But—especially in close-to-home city politics—the frustrated middle-class majority has increasingly been turning to newfound champions drawn from its own ranks.

The seeds of popular rebellion have been long implanted beneath the surface of liberal hegemony. Even as John Kennedy and Lyndon Johnson held sway in Washington, Barry Goldwater astounded the political pros with his temporary seizure of the GOP, Ronald Reagan carried the banner of the "citizen politician" from the movie lots to the California Statehouse, and George Wallace and Lester Maddox found that fulminations against "those bureaucrats" was a sure path to popularity both in the South and, to some extent, in the rest of the nation.

But this was the year that the phenomenon finally broke the surface with a series of municipal victories impossible to dismiss as regional aberrations. And this was the year that the New Populism began to be seen more clearly for what it really is.

It is not, most politicians now agree, simply a burst of racist backlash. Though sheer bigotry has certainly played a part in fueling the little man's revolt, part of his resentment of the black man is traceable to his sense of desertion by a government that appears preoccupied with Negroes' needs and inattentive to his own. Liberals who have shouted "racism!" at white response to the black revolution are now beginning to realize that this oversimplifies the impulses involved and bolsters Middle America's mounting impression that liberals neither understand nor sympathize with lower-middle-class whites.

And it is not simply a swing to the political right. Though the New Populists have unquestionably turned conservative on law enforcement, they show few signs of wanting to scrap the social reforms—medicare, aid to education, and social security improvements—wrought by the liberal left. "It's a swing against anarchy," says liberal Congressman Allard Lowenstein, and indeed the disgruntlement with the progressives seems to stem far more from their permissiveness than from their programs.

Perhaps, most of all, the New Populism is a quest for recognition. "People felt that nobody was representing them and nobody was listening," says Minneapolis's Charlie Stenvig. "They felt alienated from the political system, and they'd had it up to their Adam's apples on just about everything. So they took a guy like me—four kids, an average home, a working man they could associate themselves with. They just said, 'Lookit, we're sick of you politicians.'"

Stenvig was, indeed, a paragon of Middle America: the son of a telephone company employee, a Methodist of Norwegian stock, a graduate of a local high school and a local college (Augsburg), and an up-through-the-ranks detective on the police force. His opponent, by contrast, was almost pure Establishment: the son of an investment banker, a graduate of Stanford and Harvard Law, and a resident of the fashionable Kenwood suburb.

In his campaign, Stenvig pounded away at the privileged bastions of suburbia—he pledged to "bring government back to the citizens of Minneapolis and away from the influence of the golden West out there in Wayzata"—a privileged enclave on the city's fringes. To low-income whites, the suburbs are where the liberals live. "The liberal preaches from his lily-white suburb," explains United Auto Workers official Paul Schrade, "while the worker usually lives on the borderline of the ghetto. The workers are on the front lines of the black-white conflict and resent the advice of rear-echelon generals."

Minneapolis's workers relished Stenvig's assault on the suburbs—"He told those rich guys to go suck a lemon," chortles one local auto mechanic—and as mayor he has kept up the attack. He has protested the financing plan for a new hospital on the ground that the suburbs would not pay enough of the tab, and he has staffed city jobs with what he calls "just average working people."

A few of these appointments have aroused the only controversy in what most people in Minneapolis agree has been an extremely hard-working, well-intentioned municipal administration. Antonio G. Felicetta, vice president of the regional joint council of the Teamsters union, created a citywide sensation recently when he delivered some pungent remarks in his new role as a member of the city Commission on Human Relations. "I'm not going to take bulls---," he announced to a local journalist. "If there are any grievances, I sure as hell would want to see them taken care of. But I sure as hell wouldn't want to give 'em [welfare recipients] half my goddam paycheck when I'm working and they're sitting on their asses." Felicetta was promptly denounced as a "card-carrying bigot" by a group of Minneapolis blacks, but he also received a torrent of phone calls saying "That's the way, Tony, sock it to 'em."

Middle America's radical right has always delighted in such tough words—and deeds. Newark's Tony Imperiale became an instant folk hero in these circles when he organized a band of white vigilantes in the wake of the disastrous summer riots in 1967. And last week, as he looked ahead to the day when he becomes mayor, he made plain that official investiture will not change his tune. "If any militant comes into my office, puts his ass on my desk and tells me what I have to do," he vowed, "I'll throw his ass off the wall and throw him out the door."

There is little question that Tony—38 years old, 5 feet 6¾ inches high and 260 pounds thick—is capable of doing just that. As he drove his volunteer ambulance—part of his vigilante patrol—past the corner of Mt. Prospect Street and Bloomfield Avenue in Newark's rugged North Ward one evening recently, he recalled an example of the sort of direct action he favors: "We came down here one night with eight guys and kicked the crap outa 22 junkies. Each time we came back to slap them around they lessened in ranks and finally took the hint." Imperiale keeps an arsenal of about 40 serviceable guns in his house, including a 14-inch-barrel scatter-gun stowed behind the couch (there have already been two attempts on his life).

Imperiale is a bit too rough-and-ready for the taste of most other politicians of the New Populism. And outside the South, most of them would disclaim any ideological kinship with Dixie's two most prominent contributions to the movement, former Alabama Gov. George Wallace and incumbent Georgia Gov. Lester Maddox. But Wallace, whose Presidential campaigns of 1964 and 1968 featured attacks on "pointy-headed intellectuals" and "briefcase-toting bureaucrats" that gave his appeal a dimension beyond sheer racism, claims paternity for much of the movement. "My vote was only the tip of the iceberg," he says. "There's others I'm responsible for: Stenvig, Mayor Yorty of Los Angeles, two mayoral candidates in New York. They were making Alabama speeches with a Minneapolis, Los Angeles and New York accent. The only thing they omitted was the drawl."

One of the things that draws the Populists together is their common wistfulness for the "old values," for traditional verities and styles of life that somehow seem to have gone awry. Lester Maddox, for example, likes to think of himself as part of "the mainstream of the thinking of the American people: the achievers, the success-makers, the builders, the individuals who like to set their own goals and accept the challenges." A number of Middle America's politicians also like to brandish the crusader's cross. "God is going to be my principal adviser," declares Charlie Stenvig, and Mary Beck, a 61-year-old Detroit councilwoman who placed a strong third in last month's mayoral primary, dedicated her campaign newspaper "to the laws of God and man."

When Populists brood on the agonies of contemporary society, a certain nostalgia for a simpler life is never far from the surface. "I was born in a little town of 6,000 people," recalls Democrat Mario Procaccino, who appears to be leading Lindsay and a conservative Republican in the New York mayor's race. "We respected our parents, our teachers, and our priest or man of the cloth. We had respect for men in public office. We looked up to them . . ."

Procaccino frequently exhibits another characteristic of this new political breed: emotionalism. He wept when he announced his candidacy. Occasionally he takes his wife, Marie, and his daughter, Marierose, for an evening visit to the top of the Empire State Building. "I look out over the city and say to myself, 'What's the matter with these people? Why can't they get together?'" Many middle-class voters seem to warm to these displays of feeling, perhaps because they themselves are so upset, perhaps because they sense that their government has been run recently by soulless technocrats spouting bureaucratic jargon or politial cant. "I like him because he's so emotional," beamed one housewife to her neighbor as Procaccino campaigned through Queens last week. "Any tears he sheds, you know he has heart. He doesn't fear to shed them and they bring the people closer to him."

Mayor Sam Yorty of Los Angeles is another extremely warm-blooded politician, endowed with a coloratura stumping style that ranges between acid vituperation and passionate enthusiasm. Ever since the Watts riots of 1965, he has concentrated the former on militants and the latter on guardians of law and order. This approach proved immensely popular in last spring's mayoral election, when he won an upset victory over Negro challenger Thomas Bradley. "Personally, I like the way Yorty shoots off his mouth too much," said one white-haired old man at Los Angeles's recent 188th birthday party at the Hollywood Bowl. "He'll do a better job for me than the other guy keeping down crime and taxes."

Yorty is an interesting case history in the shifting course of Middle America's mainstream. During the 1930s, he was a New Deal liberal, espousing such progressive programs as a 30-hour workweek. In the 40s, he took up the cause of zealous anti-Communism, and now he is sounding the alarms of law and order. He is no political newcomer —he has been running for office ever since 1936—but today's disgruntled voters seem willing to reward the old pros provided they step to the new beat.

More often, however, Middle America is turning to new political faces, even when they don't look exactly like the one in the mirror. Its latest champion, S. I. Hayakawa, the feisty little professor of English who is now president of San Francisco State College, is not by nature a man of the people. "I've been, all my life, the kind of intellectual highbrow I disapprove of," he admits. But his uncompromising suppression of radical disruption at San Francisco State last fall suddenly vaulted him into political prominence: he began being mentioned as a possible opponent next year of Republican Sen. George Murphy, he started a statewide round of speech-making, and a recent Field Poll gave him a higher popularity rating than either San Francisco Mayor Joseph Alioto or California's former Democratic Assembly Speaker Jesse Unruh.

The yawning gap between the intellectual and the common man, between the governors and the governed, lies at the heart of the New Populism, and one of the first to discern it was Louise Day Hicks of Boston. A 50-year-old attorney from the predominantly Irish wards of South Boston, she pitched her 1967 mayoral campaign toward "the forgotten man," stressed the school-busing issue—and very nearly won. "I represented the alienated voter," she said last week in the midst of her new City Council campaign, "and that's who I'm representing now, except that the number has grown." Busing is no longer her main issue—some of her liberal opponents, in fact, now agree with her that the state busing law is unworkable. Now she concentrates her fire on higher taxes, declining municipal services and a government that, she contends, "is only concerned about the rich and the poor" and not about the man in the middle who pays the bills.

"The only thing saving this country," Mrs. Hicks says, "is the affluence that the middle class is feeling. But they don't realize the purchasing power is gone. When they do realize that, we're in for real trouble. There'll be a revolt —not violence, because the American people won't resort to violence, but they are going to speak up in a way to be heard."

In fact, they are aleady speaking up, and there is no reason to believe that November's elections will show a muting of their voices. "These people today are in revolt," warns Chicago Congressman Roman Pucinski. What's more, the middle class has become keenly aware of its political muscle and how to apply it. "The public is so much smarter than when I first started in politics," marvels Ken O'Donnell, JFK's special assistant who is running for the 1970 Democratic nomination for governor of Massachusetts. "Then it was no issues: just vote Democratic, vote Republican, and how to help your friends. What Gene McCarthy did was open the eyes of the people that they are the country. Before, it had been assumed that you couldn't bring a President down, that you couldn't fight the system. The McCarthy movement showed that you could do it after all."

The New Populism, as a matter of fact, seems to some analysts part of the same phenomenon as the New Politics. Eugene McCarthy and Robert Kennedy were trying to achieve on a national scale essentially the same goal that Charlie Stenvig and Louise Day Hicks have set on the municipal level: to bring new faces and new forces into play in the political arena, to mobilize the amateurs against the political pros, to return power to people whose interests and whose voices, they believed, had been too long ignored. Of course, the McCarthy-Kennedy movement was headed in a liberal direction, while the

New Populism is exhibiting a rightward bent. And the fact is that several of its new champions seem to be helping to foment, not just reflect, the public's bitterness. Still, the two movements share some common impulses, which may explain the startling number of voters who felt a kinship with both Bobby Kennedy and George Wallace during last year's campaign.

It is still much too soon to say how long the New Populism may last or what direction it may take. It has cast itself loose from the traditional political parties, neither one of which seems to hold its favor, and it has lost faith in the programs and pieties of traditional liberalism. As George Wallace puts it, "The great pointy heads who knew best how to run everybody's life have had their day." Frustrated, fearful and confused, Middle America is stirring itself to seek out new pathways, and the nation has already begun to reverberate with the commotion of its search.

THE FEDERAL ROLE IN URBAN AFFAIRS

Abraham Ribicoff

Senator Ribicoff states quite correctly that "the fate of the city and the future of our country are one and the same thing." Spiraling costs of city governments and a decreasing tax base have brought progress to a screeching halt. Even though the federal government has pumped over $100 billion into the states and cities in the last dozen years, our problems seem to increase. There is conflict in some of the federal programs in that they sometimes are working at cross-purposes. The problem of determining urban needs is complicated; there is much disagreement from the experts in the field as to the most viable programs. The search for the answers goes on and the answers must be found.

This is a year of national unrest.

Violence has erupted from north to south, from west to east, and across the Nation women and children fear for their safety in our city streets.

Why is this so?

Why do our cities seethe with dissatisfaction?

Why, when the massive resources of our Government have been poured into the cities for the past 20 years, when many dedicated people have worked with such resolve, do we have an urban crisis of such proportions?

This is what we propose to determine in these hearings.

For the crisis of our cities is the crisis of the modern United States. Seventy percent of all Americans now live in or close to cities. The number grows each year. So the fate of the city and the future of our country are one and the same thing.

As Richard Hofstadter put it: "America was born in the country and grew up in the city." As Americans have flocked to the cities, the tapestry of our national life has changed dra-

Hearings of the Subcommittee on Executive Reorganization, August 15, 1966, pp. 1–4.

matically. Hope has been the magnet, a very American hope of bettering yourself, and improving the lot of your children. Into the cities have flocked the poor, and underskilled, the undereducated, the deprived. They have come for reasons of race or lack of opportunity —or both. Into the cities, too, have come those who simply wish to savor the full urban life. Too often too many do not find what they seek.

PROBLEMS OF THE CITIES

For as the central city grows, so do its problems. Out moves the middle class into the suburbs. Out, too, moves industry—source of jobs. Into the older houses move more people than they were built to hold; family and community patterns of social organization are lost. Up go costs—costs of schooling, crime control, and public welfare. Tax revenues decline; educated and concerned leaders move elsewhere; sometimes slums are razed but in their place rise shining buildings—with modern lobbies and swimming pools— which the poor cannot afford.

Our cities are in trouble. But we discovered long ago that our Nation is indivisible; that the interests of one are the interests of all. Omaha, Nebr., may be 1,200 miles from Harlem, but Harlem's riots affect the resident of Omaha as surely as the family in Scarsdale.

If the crisis is a national concern— and it is—then it is a concern to the Congress of the United States, and to this committee, whose duty it is to assure that the Federal Government is best organized to meet modern needs.

HOW MUCH DOES FEDERAL GOVERNMENT SPEND IN THE CITIES

How much has our Federal Government been spending in our cities? $20 billion? $25 billion? We are not even certain—but we intend to find out. We have tried to find out for a few weeks from every agency of the Federal Government as to how much is being spent on an annual basis directly or indirectly for the cities. No one has the answer.

We hope during the next few weeks someone will know. We do know that through some 15 Federal agencies administering some 70 programs we have invested $96 billion over the past decade in city and State aid, and this does not include social security payments or FHA and VA mortgage insurance.

Some programs have undoubtedly prevented starvation and brought new hope and opportunity to countless among the poor. And President Johnson has proposed other new programs to upgrade the quality of life in our cities. The President's demonstration cites program, especially, is a significant new departure deserving our unqualified support. I was pleased to serve on the President's HUD task force which first proposed this landmark legislation, and I trust it will pass the Senate this week.

But this program itself, and the larger job ahead, shows the awesome dilemmas of public choice that confront a nation about to embark on a meaningful urban policy. We must learn from past experience. We must ask ourselves some probing questions.

IMPORTANT QUESTIONS OF FEDERAL POLICY

For example, have urban aid programs been too diffused and uncoordinated to guide the process of urban development?

Are the techniques of our city aid programs obsolete and limited? Do they reflect the needs and conditions of national life a generation ago, and not the needs of modern America?

Is the effectiveness of the programs that do exist hurt by division of authority among many agencies, and many levels of government?

Most serious of all, do the goals of major Federal programs conflict—some working to revitalize the central city, some encouraging new urban clusters, some causing regional sprawl?

In short, do we have a clear, constructive national strategy geared toward the improvement of our cities? If not, what steps must we take to obtain it?

History shows us that civilization has been based on cities. Some have vanished—some have flourished almost from antiquity. Now we cannot expect to find the answers to the problems of our cities in the United States in a month—or even a year. I expect that these hearings will continue a long time, as long as needed.

Since the problem of the cities is the problem of all Americans, we will hear from many besides responsible Federal officials. The Federal Government must assume the duties with which it is charged, but our system of government is not based on the concept that the Federal Government is the sole source of wisdom and skill.

We shall hear testimony from mayors—from men and women and young people working and living in the city slums—from sociologists and psychologists and other experts who have studied the problems of our cities, and gained insight and understanding.

We shall hear testimony from experts in many fields—for no one phrase—and no one area of concern can characterize the problems of our cities.

AREAS OF INQUIRY

We shall explore the problems of police protection, health, justice, welfare, education, employment, economic development, finance, community organization, urban planning, housing, renewal and rehabilitation, transportation, environmental pollution, legal services, and more.

We shall explore, and try to find the answers to the problems of the woman in Watts who has no hospital to go to; the mother holding her sick baby in the crowded clinic waiting room; the listless child, locked in a Harlem slum, in a crowded schoolroom with shattered windows; the high school dropout. Such problems illustrate the magnitude of the crisis facing our Nation. Building a constructive and realistic national urban policy will not be easy.

The questions are difficult—the answers will be complicated.

GOAL OF HEARINGS

But there is nothing complicated about what we want. All of us want a society in which a woman is not afraid to stay home alone at night. All of us want a society where children are schooled to the uppermost limits of their ability, live in decent housing, and get three square meals a day. We want jobs and opportunity for all our citizens. No child in the United States should fear rat bites in his bed. All Americans should feel that justice and equal opportunity can be realized without resort to violence and looting.

We undertake these hearings thoughtfully and without preconceived solutions to all the problems. We will strive to get the pertinent facts, the sound ideas, and to look at people and their problems with understanding.

Our mission will be to come up with the understanding necessary to insure that our efforts are organized in the most efficient, effective, and coordinated manner. If what exists is good, we will recommend keeping it. But where we have failed, we must weed out our errors, and try new ways.

We must find how the huge complex of modern government can better deliver help to our cities, and assure that our money and energies are wisely used. This effort must be made. Answers to the problems of the cities must be found.

The bell is tolling for all of us. The Nation is summoning this Congress and succeeding ones to action.

PART IV

QUESTIONS FOR DISCUSSION

1. Compare the weak-mayor, strong-council form of city government with that of the strong-mayor, weak-council. Which seems to be more efficient in administering affairs?
2. Why has the "law and order" issue become so prominent in city politics today? Where is this likely to lead?
3. In view of recent national publicity in the big-city mayoral elections one would answer that the big-city mayor occupies an important position in national politics. In reality what are his chances for higher offices?
4. The hope of overcoming city problems rests in the political area. Why is this so?

VOCABULARY

nonpartisanship
exportability
elite
industrialized
legitimize
crisis
viable
propensity

expandability
cohesive
salient
central government
electorate
mandate
controversy
comparative government

POVERTY AND WELFARE

•

Poverty is a relative thing. Many conservative people accuse welfare and poverty programs of aiding the best fed and best dressed poor in the world. Whether these statements are true or not is not really the central issue. To be sure, we do not have the human misery of an India or China, but might it not be possible that our poor suffer degradation of an even more debilitating nature? The reasons for this are not totally physical, but are also deeply psychological.

One of the major factors accounting for this psychological pressure is the mass media. Today even the poorest often have a television set—very likely over priced and over financed. Into the homes of these poor come the images of middle class America, the great American mass. They see cars, clothes, food, and the almost endless pressure to consume them. The implications of the advertising are clear. If you do not possess these commodities, you are participating somewhat less than you should in the American dream.

Often critics of the poor are quick to accuse these people of buying Cadillacs and feeding their children grits. Is it any wonder that after seeing what they conceive to be the meaning of the term middle class—that is, the new car—that they rush out to buy one as soon as enough money (the required down payment) is available?

You may think that no sensible salesman, certainly no salesman with any genuine concern, would sell to these people. Quite the contrary is true. There are both firms and people who make their sole living out of exploiting the misery and desires of the poor. Exorbitant prices combined with scalpers' interest rates insure that the poor stay poor.

In addition to the problems surrounding the purchase of merchandise such as television sets and automobiles, comes the fact that even the basic essentials of life such as food and medicine are likely to cost the poor more. Ghetto prices have been found to be higher in food and drug stores. Likewise the rural poor, often in need of credit until the crop comes in, find themselves having to buy food from some local merchant, who, of course, finances the credit through higher prices. Lastly, company towns and large southern land owners have traditionally operated their own stores with high prices but always friendly credit.

Poverty also breeds a sense of despair that tears down the human spirit. Equally tragic are our programs designed to deal with the problem. Recent proposals include a federal minimum income, and economists are seriously considering the negative income tax. Certainly a minimum level of income needs to be established. However, programs which serve to make the recipient feel indebted to the giver, programs which destroy human self-respect and pride cannot continue. On the same front, programs must be established to reach all the poor of our country. Particularly acute is the problem of the migrant who finds residency requirements and local pressure particularly acute. Similarly, the urban citizen often finds it necessary to deceive welfare workers because of certain laws.

The cry has traditionally been work, more jobs. Recently bumper stickers have begun to appear saying "I fight poverty, I work." How simple this solution is. However, with the demand for unskilled labor dropping every year in both percentage and number needed, no work may actually exist. Perhaps the time has come when we may need to refine the definition of work. Welfare destroys initiative; a man engaged in production feels pride. As automation increases, some of the poverty fighters mentioned above may find themselves in the straits of unemployment. The Protestant Ethic may well need revision if we are to realistically come to grips with problems of poverty and alter the conditions imposed by our present welfare system.

THREE POVERTIES

Michael Harrington

The author gives a vivid description of three categories of the poor. The first is the intellectual, bohemian, or beat group who choose their lot. They suffer the same conditions of the other poor but they do not really enter into the subculture. They achieve progress or go back to their middle class. The alcoholic is the second type and represents one of the major and little understood problems of our society. He is the misfit of all social classes; he is the epitome of physical and moral desolation as he lives out his existence on cheap wine, whiskey, beer, or canned heat. The third group is made up of the hillbillies, the Oakies, and the rural Negro from the South. He has few possessions, no roots, and no home; he has little chance of escaping. Collectively, these three groups of poor are the responsibility and shame of all America.

I

Most of the poor people described in this book come from the large, established cultures of poverty. They are the classic poor.

There is another kind of poverty. It exists in the interstices of the society in some cases, or else its specific quality is new. There have not been congressional investigations into the plight of these people. There are few statistics on what it means for them to be poor. Here, one learns from novels, from psychologists, from the records of Night Court, or from a walk through the streets.

There is one subculture of poverty in the United States that at times is spirited, ebullient, enthusiastic. It is the only humorous part of the other America. Here live the poor who are intellectuals, bohemians, beats. They strive or pose; they achieve or go back to the middle class from whence they usually come. But their lives are lived in the midst of physical deprivation and, often enough, of hunger.

There is a poverty that, in some ways, is the most terrible and destructive to be found in the other America. The city dweller meets it when the drifter from skid row asks for a handout. These are the alcoholic poor. They have long been defined as a major problem in our society, but they have not been understood as a problem of poverty, and that is an important fact about them.

And there is a new poverty that is becoming more and more important, a consequence of the revolution taking place in American agriculture. In Detroit, Cincinnati, St. Louis, Oakland, and other cities of the United States, one finds the rural poor in the urban slums, the hill folks, the Oakies who failed, the war workers from the forties who never went back home.

I have known the rural poor in the city and the alcoholics. I have been

Reprinted with permission of The Macmillan Company from *The Other America* by Michael Harrington, pp. 82–100. © Michael Harrington, 1962.

both participant and spectator in the intellectual slums of Chicago and New York. These are some impressions.

To the newspaper reader of the late fifties, the intellectuals who are poor appeared under the rather romantic guise of the Beat Generation. Bearded and eccentric, they suddenly became good copy for *Time* magazine, and that made them a phenomenon. Their aura, as the slick magazine writers described it, was compounded of Whitmanesque search, phoniness, eroticism, and perverse ingratitude. To most people, it must have seemed that they were leading an easy, indolent life. Few realized that, in addition to all the other myths and legends about them, these people were poor. In most cases, they were willfully and even joyously impoverished; but they were poor nevertheless.

The Beats are only the newest expression of an old phenomenon. There are the graduate-student poor who cluster around the great universities. There is the older tradition of Bohemia, with its more political and conscious theory of *épater les bourgeois*. All these groups have in common the experience of a curious kind of poverty. Outside religious orders, these are the only citizens of the affluent society to have chosen to be poor.

To begin with, the Beat and the Bohemian are a slum phenomenon.

The Venice West of the Beats in Los Angeles is an old real-estate scheme that went bad. Originally, it was supposed to be a new Venice, complete with picturesque canals and bridges. The plan went awry; the bridges are cracked, and there are oil riggings all over the area. The inhabitants are low-paid workers, drifters, outcasts of one kind or another, and the rebellious young people. In New York the Bohemian scene is no longer really centered in Greenwich Village, for luxury apartments are inexorably destroying the low-rent character of the area. The intellectual poor, or most of them, have moved east, to the tenements and lofts of the Lower East Side. Paradoxically, they are threatened constantly by low-income housing projects and health and safety regulations. They do not have the qualifications or the desire to move into public housing. Their freedom depends, in part, upon the culture of poverty.

Since they live in slum areas, the intellectual poor are often involved in a town-gown conflict. The Italian-Americans of the South Village in New York are regularly disturbed by the antics of the strangers in the midst. The fact that Bohemia (or the Beats, or whatever one calls it) is interracial, and often aggressively so, is a source of deep tension. In Chicago, before urban renewal destroyed one of the most extensive university slums on the South Side, the problem came from another direction. Negroes were moving into the area, and the indigenous white community was resisting. The students, whatever their views on racial equality, were white, and that was always a possible source of trouble.

I remember the strange feeling of walking down a tense street at night in the late forties. I knew myself as completely sympathetic to the Negro attempt to break through the walls of the ghetto, and I would have welcomed an integrated neighborhood. (The whites, the city planners, the forces of law and authority effectively destroyed that possibility.) At the same time, I knew that the color of my skin could give rise to violence. It was an uncomfortable irony.

But even if the intellectual poor are aliens in the slum world (or perhaps "visitors" would be a better term), they share its physical misery. The housing of Bohemia is often simply appalling. Rooms or apartments are in the cheapest, most run-down tenements, or in industrial lofts that are illegal for living purposes. The spirit may be that of *la vie de bohème:* the bugs, rats, the littered streets and the hall bathrooms are genuinely part of the culture of poverty. It is a paradox that a child of the middle class will actively seek out a damp basement room, or what might have been the servants' quarters in an old mansion.

Sometimes there is plain hunger. I remember a friend who subsisted for a while on a surplus Government ration that had been sent to starving refugees after World War II. My own discovery, realized in a rooming house in the Chelsea section of Manhattan, was that a can of corned-beef hash would make two meals. The regular dietary tricks of the born poor, the lumpy, pasty menus that give the illusion of a satisfied stomach, are quickly learned by the middle-class rebel.

But then, even hunger can be amusing in an exceptional case or two. One friend of mine whose family had stopped sending him funds by an oversight was left with a charge account in a fancy store that specialized in cocktail delicacies. As a result, he lived for some time on nuts, rattlesnake meat, turtle soup, and other exotic foods of the rich. Eventually, he developed a near allergy to all the foods of the upper class while living on a few dollars a week.

The jobs of the intellectual poor have one main requirement: they cannot really be stable. There are forays into the working world, but not careers. Some ferret out the drifters' section of the economic underworld: the dishwashing and luncheonette work of the minorities and the alcoholics. At 80 Warren Street in Manhattan, the building in New York described in the chapter on the rejects, one can regularly see an offspring of the middle class reading a book of philosophic analysis or

poetry in the midst of a crowd of crushed and beaten men waiting to make a few dollars.

Then there is unemployment compensation. It comes to those who stay on a covered job long enough to qualify (and the work patterns of the intellectual poor are sometimes ruled by the state regulations). It is a sort of state subsidy for the practice and study of the arts. Indeed, some, legislators might be appalled to discover how many novels had been written on these funds.

And yet, even though the intellectual poor share the tenements, the diets, the jobs of the born poor, they do not really enter into the culture of poverty. They have chosen a way of life instead of being victimized by it. They are passing through, either moving back toward the larger society or achieving a place in literature or the arts. They do not participate in the atmosphere of defeatism and pessimism that permeates the lives of the truly poor. In the contrast, one can begin to understand the importance of the spirit, the subjectivity, of poverty in the other America.

This difference can be seen most easily in the apartments of the intellectual poor. A loft or a tenement apartment will be transformed by middle-class education and ingenuity. (One friend of mine discovered that a telephone booth is a perfectly prefabricated shower.) The walls will be scraped to reveal the original bricks. A few cheap prints of good paintings will bring color and life into the room. The bathroom in the hall will still be terribly cold in the winter, the heat may come from an open oven, and baths may be taken in tubs set in the middle of the kitchen, but the physical dilapidation and privation are not destructive.

For that matter, there is a most curious irony among the intellectual poor. They come to the slums of the other America, to the physical life of impoverishment, because they are fleeing a spiritual poverty in the Affluent Society. Allen Ginsberg wrote of the Beats in *Howl, and Other Poems*, "I saw the best minds of my generation destroyed by madness." His claim is exaggerated, yet it contains a certain truth. Though many of these people have the talent and the education to win commercial success in the great society, they choose to live in the slums because they have found simple, material well-being hollow.

The interracialism of the intellectual poor is a good index of the seriousness of their rebellion. Like most of the educated middle class in America outside the South, they share the rhetoric of equality. But, unlike most people, their life has led them to an interracial world. Here, in the strange subculture of voluntary poverty, the Negro can find a social integration unknown to the rest of the society.

And yet, the prosperity of the middle class in the past decade and a half has had its impact upon the intellectual poor. In the older Bohemias, the refusal to obey social conventions was justified in terms of political radicalism or dedication to the artistic *avant-garde*. But in the fifties there were no vast social movements to identify with apart from the civil-rights organizations, and *avant-garde* had lost much of its vitality. As a result, protest among these people became more individual and personal, and the voice of Zen was heard.

Some of these people are, to be sure, enjoying a brief pose before taking up their position in the world of middle-class America. They accept the poverty because it provides them a certain freedom. As one writer brilliantly described them, they reject the working world because it does not give them time. They spend their entire life making time, until that is all there is, and still they do not produce. At best, they return

sheepishly to the conventional world from whence they came; at worst, they simply vegetate.

There are tragedies, too. The slums of the intellectual poor are at the bottom of society, and, often enough, they are neighbor to the underworld. As a result, there are biographies that end in suicide, at the mental hospital, or in the police station. There is no point in romanticizing this, yet it is another sign of the failure of the great society that drives these people to hunger for value and belief rather than for food, and sometimes pushes them beyond the limits of their control.

Perhaps the most tragic group among the intellectual poor is the small minority who become narcotics addicts. There is a "junkie poverty" that is terrible. All of the turmoil and commotion and pain becomes reduced to a desire for a fix of heroin. There is a literal disintegration of the physical surroundings, and if the addict is not reduced to crime to satisfy the craving, the most complete impoverishment results.

The poseurs and the addicts make good tabloid reading, and they are the ones most people think of when they imagine the life of these middle-class rebels. Yet, perhaps it is more significant to remember that our affluent society contains those of talent and insight who are driven to prefer poverty, to choose it, rather than to submit to the desolation of an empty abundance. It is a strange part of the other America that one finds in the intellectual slums.

II

Perhaps the bitterest, most physical and obvious poverty that can be seen in an American city exists in skid row among the alcoholics.

During 1951 and 1952, I lived on Chrystie Street, one block from the

Bowery in New York. I was a member of the Catholic Worker group that had a house there. Beds were given out on a "first come, first served" basis; we had a bread line in the early morning that provided coffee and rich brown bread, and a soup line at noon; and hand-me-down clothes that readers of the newspaper sent in were distributed. Those of us who came to live at the Worker house accepted a philosophy of voluntary poverty. We had no money and received no pay. We shared the living conditions of the people whom we were helping: alcoholics and the mentally ill. We did not participate in the living hell of that area, for we were not tortured by alcoholism and we had chosen our lot. But we were close, very close, to that world. We could see its horror every day.

The Bowery today does not look as it did then. The elevated tracks of the Third Avenue El have been dismantled, and in time skid row may be driven to some other part of the city, particularly if the Third Avenue property values keep going up. Thus, some of the places I describe no longer exist. Yet that is mere detail, for the essential world of these impressions is still very much with us.

The Third Avenue El gave the Bowery a sort of surrealist character. A dirty, hulking structure, it was as derelict as the men who acted out their misery beneath it. Along both sides of the street were flophouses where a man could get a bed for a night. Each morning, someone had to go through, checking to see if anyone had died during the night. The liquor stores were there, of course, specializing in cheap wine.

The men and women of the Bowery usually drank wine, or sometimes beer or shots of cheap whisky. For those in the direst straits, obsessed by the need for alcohol, there was always canned heat. It is liquid alcohol, and it can be drunk after it is strained through a handkerchief or a stale piece of bread. It has the reputation of knocking a man out before doing serious damage to his nervous system. It is, I am told, tasteless, a method of reaching oblivion and not much else.

There were other businesses around. The secondhand stores were there so that the men could sell whatever they could scavenge or steal (sometimes from one another). They preyed on the misery of the place, and they were indispensable to it. There were a couple of restaurants where at night the derelicts fought to keep their eyes open so that they would not be thrown out; these were most depressing, garishly lighted places. And there were missions, called by some "Three Sixteens" because they so often had the scriptural quotation from John 3:16 over the door: "For God so loved the world that He sent His only begotten son . . ." In warm weather the "Sallies"—Salvation Army lassies and men—would be out on the avenue.

Over the whole place there hung the smell of urine. The men lived out of doors when they didn't have money for a flop. Sometimes, in the winter, they passed out in the snow or crawled into a doorway. In the summer the stench from some of the favorite haunts was all but overpowering.

There is an almost typical face of the Bowery, or so it seemed to me. The men are dirty, and often their faces are caked with blood after a particularly terrible drunk. They wake up without knowing how they were hurt. Their clothes are ragged, ill-fitting, incongruous. Their trousers stink of the streets and of dried urine. And the human look is usually weak and afraid of direct and full contact with someone else's eyes.

In the summer the Bowery is at its best, if one can use such a word to describe a place of incredible physical and moral desolation. The men sit together and talk, or lounge along the walk in groups. They are capable of stripping the clothes from another alcoholic when he is passed out, yet their drinking is hardly ever solitary. If one of them is lucky enough to panhandle his way to a bottle, he will seek out friends and share his good fortune.

Indeed, this is primarily a male society. There are a few women here, but the overwhelming impression is of standing, waiting, drunken men. Some psychologists have argued that there may be a link between homosexual tendencies and alcoholism. At the Catholic Worker, we occasionally ran into trouble in the house on this score. Whatever the eventual conclusions from scientific research, the Bowery has a locker-room camaraderie among some of the most broken and hurt of the society.

Active sex hardly matters here. This is a place whose inhabitants are drunk, or on their way to being drunk, twenty-four hours a day. As a result, there is a literal impotence that is joined to the personality impotence of defeated and self-destructive outcasts.

Winter is a catastrophe. Life on skid row is lived out of doors, and the cold and the snow bring with them intense suffering. The men often get drunk enough to lie in the streets in the midst of a storm. The first time one sees a body covered with a light blanket of snow, stretched out on the sidewalk, the sight comes as a shock and a dilemma. Is the man dead or just drunk? Or worse, the habitués are so obsessed and driven that stealing goes on in the dead of winter, and a man who needs a drink will take the shoes of a fellow alcoholic in the middle of January.

The result, of course, is disease. There is a sort of war between the Bowery and the city hospitals. The ambulance drivers and attendants become cynical and inured to the sufferings of those who seem to seek their own hurt so desperately. The administrative staffs must worry about someone from skid row who wants a bed for a couple of nights and who tries to stimulate delirium tremens. The officials become angry when these men sell their blood in order to get enough money to drink—and then turn up in the hospital and need blood transfusions.

The end of the line for the Bowery is the hospital and potter's field. Indeed, the Emergency Room of a public hospital like Bellevue could be a study in itself. I remember a not untypical scene when I was up there with one of the men from the Catholic Worker. There were the alcoholics, the dazed old people, a Negro woman whose lip was hanging by a thread, the little children. One cannot blame the doctors or the administrators for the sickening, depressing atmosphere. That responsibility belongs to the city, whose charity is inadequately financed, maddening in its slowness, and bureaucratically inexplicable to the uneducated poor.

Who are the men and women of the Bowery?

They are different from almost all the other poor people, for they come from every social class, every educational background to be found in the United States. At the Catholic Worker I met newspapermen, a dentist, priests, along with factory workers and drifters from the countryside. This is the one place in the other America where the poor are actually the sum total of misfits from all of the social classes.

Yet there are some strange factors at work in producing the subculture of alcoholism. One met quite a few men of Irish-American extraction (a clear majority, it seemed to me), some Polish-Americans, some Negroes (skid row is not ideologically integrated, but it is usually too drunk to care about race), a few Italians. In the two years that I spent on the Bowery, meeting some hundreds of men and women, I don't think I ran into a single Jew.

When they "dried out," the alcoholics from the middle class used to talk about themselves much as the amateur, college-educated psychologist would speak. They understood their condition as having deep roots in their personal problems and attitudes. But the ones who came from working-class or farm backgrounds were, like the mentally disturbed poor generally, mystified by what had happened to them. If they were religious—and a good many we met at the Worker were Catholic—this meant that sobering up usually involved frantic self-accusation.

I remember talking to an elderly man whom I got to know at the Worker. He was neat, hard-working, and with a great deal of self-respect whenever he was sober. He would stay off alcohol for long periods, sometimes up to three months. During that time he would lead an orderly life marked by careful religious observances. Then, suddenly, he would go on a drinking bout for two or three weeks. Sometimes we would hear about him when he had been taken into a hospital. He would come back then, and the whole process would begin anew.

I was talking to him one evening about alcoholism. I tried to say that it was not something a man chose, that it was related to deep problems, and that it could not be banished by a mere act of the will, no matter how courageous an individual was. He was frantic in his disagreement with me. "We are this way because we want to be," he said. "We are committing a mortal sin by doing it, and we are going to Hell because of it."

Sometimes this self-hatred turned toward others. One day a man stumbled in off the street. He was a physical mess: there was caked blood on his face, his clothes stank, and he wore the semi-human, possessed look that comes at the end of a long, terrible drunk. He lurched in, and I went to help him. We got him bathed and shaved and DDT'd. (The battle against lice and bedbugs was never won at the Worker, but we tried.) In a couple of days, with sleep and regular food and some new hand-me-down clothes, he was in pretty good shape.

Two or three evenings after he came in, he was standing next to me, waiting to go in for dinner. A man came in from the street, his double of two or three days earlier. There were the same blood and clothes and obsessed face. When I went to help the newcomer, the first man said to me, "Why give a hand to that bum?" In his voice there was the passion of genuine self-hatred. When the Bowery sobers up for a day or two, it promises, it sobs, it recriminates against itself. And so it goes, on and on.

Sometimes all this repressed emotion breaks out into a fist fight on the Bowery. If they were not so tragic, they might be funny. The violence is a ballet of mistakes, of drunken, sweeping, impossible punches. The men cannot really hurt each other with any calculation. The real danger is that a man will throw himself off balance when one of his round-house blows miscarries. The weakness and ineffectualness of the Bowery are summed up in these fights.

But then there come periods when the endless nights and days of drinking stop for a while. The sobering up is almost as horrible as the drunkenness itself. Sometimes at the Catholic Worker a man would wake with the shakes. His whole body would be trembling uncontrollably, and his face would be crumpled as if on the verge of tears. He would plead for one shot of whisky, just one, to get over the morning. It was a random risk, completely unpredictable, to answer his plea. There was no way of knowing when that one shot would actually work to tranquilize and make a day of sobriety possible, or when it would drive him out onto the street, and send him back to the world of drunkenness he had begun to flee.

Sometimes, the drying-out process would last for a week. I remember a woman who had been drunk, more or less continuously, for about three months. When she stopped and made it across the line of trembling and shaking, she was still like a caged tiger. She could not bear to sit still for more than a moment. She roamed the house for days on end.

Once they come back to the world of sobriety, the alcoholic poor face the problem of eating. Until then, their obsession is drink, and only drink. They subsist in the period of drunkenness off anything they can scavenge, including the waste in garbage cans, on food from missions, or from the cheap fare in one of the grimy restaurants of the neighborhood. When they become sober, there is a world to face, at least until the next drunk.

For the ones from middle-class families, there is the possibility of money from relatives or even of returning to a job. One of the men at the Catholic Worker when I was there is a successful magazine writer; I have seen his byline over the years in some of the better publications. But for most of them, their drinking lives. They exist as a source of cheap labor for the dirty, casual jobs in the economic underworld.

"He went to the mountains" was one of the standard refrains on the Bowery. It meant that a man had taken a job as a dishwasher or janitor in one of the Catskill resorts. Employment agencies, quick to market human desperation, always had openings for such

work. Usually, the job would last a couple of weeks, perhaps for a summer. Sometimes a man would stay off the bottle for the whole time. But he would find his way back to the Bowery with a pocketful of money and he would buy drinks for his cronies for a couple of days. And then he would be exactly where he started.

One of the most tragic of these stories was told to me by the late brilliant cameraman who filmed *On the Bowery*. One of the "stars" of that picture was a Bowery habitué who had been around the Catholic Worker when I was there. During the filming of the movie he stayed off alcohol. Finally, when it was over, he had to be paid. The people who produced the film knew what might happen when he got the money—and they also knew that a doctor had told the man that one more serious binge and he would probably die. Yet he had worked, and they had no choice but to pay him. He took the money, drank, and died.

Though all this takes place in the middle of New York City, it is hardly noticed. It is a form of poverty, of social disintegration, that does not attract sympathy. People get moral when they talk about alcoholics, and the very language is loaded against such unfortunates. (I have not used the word "bum" since I went to the Catholic Worker; it is part of the vocabulary of not caring.) And since alcoholic poverty is so immediately and deeply a matter of personality, dealing with it requires a most massive effort. One hardly knows where to begin.

But, of course, nothing is being done, really. For sheer callousness and cynicism, I have never seen anything to rival the attitudes of the tourists and the police. Just below Houston on the Bowery was a place called Sammy's Bowery Follies (I don't know if it is still there; I hope not). It has been

written up in magazines, and it is designed for tourists. The gimmick is that
it is an old-fashioned Bowery Bar with
Nineties bartenders and laughing,
painted women who are fixtures of the
place. Of an evening, well-dressed tourists would arrive there, walking through
a couple of rows of human misery,
sometimes responding to a panhandler's
plea with *noblesse oblige*. They were
within a few feet of desperation and
degradation, yet they seemed to find it
"interesting" and "quaint." This is a
small, if radical, case of the invisibility
of the poor.

But even more vicious was the police
pickup.

I never understood how the exact
number to be arrested was computed,
but there must have been some method
to this social madness. The paddy
wagon would arrive on the Bowery; the
police would arrest the first men they
came to, at random; and that was that.
At night, in the drama of dereliction
and indifference called Night Court in
New York, the alcoholics would be
lined up. Sometimes they were still
drunk. The magistrate would tell them
of their legal rights; they would usually
plead guilty, and they would be sen-
tenced. Some of the older men would
have been through this time and time
again. It was a social ritual, having no
apparent effect on anything. It furnished, I suppose, statistics to prove
that the authorities were doing their
duty, that they were coping with the
problem.

These alcoholics will probably be left
to themselves for a long while. Though
their spiritual torment is well known by
most Americans, what is not understood
is the grim, terrible, physically debilitating life of the alcoholic: the fact that
these people are poor.

Let me end this description with a
sad incident, for that is the proper note
for an impression such as this.

About six months after I had left the
Catholic Worker, I had come back one
evening to see some friends and to talk.
I had a job, and had begun to build up
the wardrobe that had been stolen from
me when I first came to Chrystie
Street. (The voluntary poverty of the
Worker is made real by the fact that if
you stay for six months, all your property will be taken anyway.) I had on a
fairly decent suit, and I was standing
in the back yard with a couple of men I
knew from the Bowery. One of them
said to me, while the other nodded
agreement: "We wondered when you
would wise up, Mike. Hanging around
here, helping us, that's nothing. Only
nuts would do it. It's good you're wised
up and going someplace." They were
happy that I had left. They couldn't
understand why anyone would want to
care for them.

III

Part of the culture of poverty in the
United States is made up of urban
hillbillies.

Properly speaking, only part of this
group actually comes from the Appalachian hills to the big city. The others
are Arkansas cotton pickers, people
from southeast Missouri ("Swamp East
Missouri," they call it), Oakies on
the West Coast who never recovered
from the migration of the thirties. Yet
they share common problems—the fact
that the backwoods has completely un-
fitted them for urban life—a common
poverty, and they often like the same
"country" music.

A few of them are still in the backwoods, but near the big cities. Just outside Grafton, New York, a few miles
from Albany, is a settlement that is literally in the woods. None of the towns-
people had talked to them (this has
resulted in some marvelous myth making), and all I could do was to drive

past some of the lean-tos and glimpse
a few people in the distance. The legislators at the state capital nearby are
discussing various modern welfare programs; these hill folks are living as if
they were in the eighteenth century.

But the really important group is not
out in the woods on the fringe of the
cities. They are in the slums. They came
up from the Appalachians to Detroit
for war jobs, and stayed on; they have
drifted into Chicago, where they form
a sizable community with their own
churches and neighborhoods and ways
of life; they work in the factories of
Oakland, California, at the dirtiest and
most menial jobs. They can be identified by their ninth-generation Anglo-
Saxon faces, by their accents, and by
the ubiquity of country music.

In Oakland, California, for instance,
one can walk into a bar a few miles
from the Pacific Ocean and be trans-
ported into the hills or the dustbowl
of Oklahoma. The singing group has
been affected by radio—the guitars are
electric—but the music and the patrons
are country. The atmosphere is not
picturesque, however; it is tough, in-
cipient with violence, and there are
brawling and prostitution. The bouncer
is a uniformed officer from a private
protection agency. He wears handcuffs
on his belt and carries a billy.

I met some of these people about ten
years ago in St. Louis, Missouri. I was
working for the Board of Education as
a social worker. Attached to the Madison School, I went out and visited the
homes of every student who missed
school more than two or three times in
a row or who had been in trouble. My
job was not that of a truant officer (although that was its origin). The Pupil
Welfare Department was intelligent,
capable, and sincere. It rejected a
theory of evil, malevolent children, and
sought to deal with problems of truancy
by tracing their roots in the home, the

neighborhood, or the personality of the
child. Time has passed since then, and
perhaps the neighborhood has changed.
But these are still the conditions under
which the country folk live, and suffer,
in the cities of the other America.

These people were, for the most part,
Arkansas sharecroppers and cotton
pickers. They came to St. Louis when
times were bad, or during the slack season. They had an intricate web of kinfolk relationships, and there was always
a relative sending word from St. Louis
about work in the city or calling them
back to the fields. Their lives were almost completely mercurial. An entire
family would literally pack up and leave
on a moment's notice. They had few
possessions, no roots, no homes.

They lived in one of the worst urban
slums for white people that I have ever
seen. This was old St. Louis, down by
the river, and some of the houses had
probably been the homes of aristocrats
of an earlier day. There were slim windows, archways, courtyards. But this
architectural charm was vestigial. The
houses had been cut into rooms, and
the families were packed into them. For
the most part, there were no bathrooms
working inside these places. There were
outhouses in the back yard, and sometimes the common pump was there, too.
Then the place became a quagmire.
Sometimes the way to the outhouse led
through somebody's room. (That occurred, I suppose, when what was formerly a kitchen was converted into an
"apartment.") When that happened,
people would be passing through all
night long.

As often happens in the culture of
poverty, marriage was somewhat irregular among these folk. The women were
not promiscuous—they lived with one
man at a time, and for considerable
periods. But, after some years and a
child or two, the marriage would break
up. It was not uncommon to meet two

or three sets of half-brothers and half-sisters living under the same roof.

The children were forced to go to school under state law, but it was a battle to keep them there. As soon as they could get a work permit, they would do so in order to pick up pin money. Their world of home was dirty and often violent, and they had no motivation to change. In the eighth grade the average age was around sixteen, and for a good percentage of the pupils that was the end of education. Predictably, the IQ's were lower than those of children in middle-class schools.

I remember at one time having to investigate a serious charge made by one student against another. The family of one girl claimed that a boy had tried to rape their daughter. I talked to all sides, and my impression was strange. There were passions and clan hatreds involved, but there was also a casualness, almost a listlessness about the whole business. In the end, it was impossible to come up with a substantial conclusion one way or the other, but no one was really pressing the matter. There was an acceptance of violence and rape; it was part of life.

The school itself had a magnificent faculty. All those who wanted an easier time could get transfers after the first year or so. Those who stayed were volunteers, and they were, for the most part, competent and dedicated people. That was what made their frustrations so difficult to bear. The school had the children nine months a year, six hours or so a day. The home and the neighborhood possessed them the rest of the time. It was an unequal battle, and it was further complicated by the fact that one never knew when a family was going to pick up and leave.

There were, for example, compulsory showers. We would check a student's hair for lice as a matter of course, for bugs can spread like an epidemic in a school. The old-fashioned steel combs that one uses to get the nits out of the hair was an ordinary part of the nurses' equipment. But it was a holding action at best to work for cleanliness and hygiene. The homes were dirty and rat-infested and bug-ridden. We could do a little for a short while, but that was not much.

And yet this grim description, like the account of a Negro ghetto, misses the quality of life. As one walked along the streets in the late summer, the air was filled with hillbilly music from a hundred radios. There was a sort of loose, defeated gaiety about the place, the casualness of a people who expected little. These were poor Southern whites. In some ways, they resembled the stereotype of the happy-go-lucky Negro, and the truth in the description is about the same for both.

But their humor and easy ways were contained in an environment of misery. I remember families who could not send their children to school because there were not enough shoes for all. One family passed the shoes from child to child, so that at least a couple of them would be in school each day. The Public Welfare Department made valiant efforts to fill this minimal need, but it took time, and while the search was going on nothing could really be done.

But perhaps the saddest group of all were the students in the special class. They had IQ's so low that any attempt to bring them a standard education would inevitably fail. An extremely competent and dedicated young woman tried to teach them the rudiments of living in a modern society: basic things like learning to understand traffic lights, to distinguish money, and the like. Such children can appear in any social class. The particular tragedy here was that no one really understood what was happening to them. The folk traditions about people being "touched" were about as deep as anyone got, and if they received pity it was coloured by toughness and taunts. (This lack of understanding of mental illness and retardation, so basic to the culture of poverty, will be discussed in greater detail in a later chapter.)

I remember vividly one instance of such callousness. There was a child who had an extremely serious chronic condition. Though he had periods of apparent health, the doctors said he was headed toward an early death. The disease had left him "strange," and his fellow students often delighted in tormenting him. Their values, their experiences, had not prepared them for sympathy or pity.

The whole neighborhood lived close enough to crime to make it a danger and a possibility. Only, even here the people were impoverished. The crime was, for the most part, violent, petty, and paltry. It could wreck lives and end in prison sentences or reform schools, but it could never really pay off. The world of the organized rackets, of modern rationalized crime, was as distant from this backwoods city slum as big business.

Indeed, one of the most frustrating things about social work in this neighborhood is that one could read the fates written on some of the children's faces. It was relatively easy to guess which boys might end in a penitentiary, which girls would become pregnant before they were out of grade school. But there was nothing legally or humanly that could be done, short of the abolition of the neighborhood and the culture it contained.

All of this might be dramatized by a report from Chicago. In that city, according to an article in *Harper's*, police and merchants were becoming even more hostile toward the country folk than they were toward Negroes. The people were so rootless, so mercurial, that this racially explosive metropolis had altered some of the values of its hatred.

These settlements will continue to grow. More and more poor farmers and agricultural laborers are being pushed off the land. In the late fifties and early sixties, they came to the city in a time of recession and automation. The cards, in short, are stacked against them as never before. And there will be more of these music-filled, miserable country neighborhoods springing up in the cities of the other America.

THE AMERICAN POOR

Office of Economic Opportunity

Poverty does not strike with equal force throughout our country. Those who are black, poorly educated, over sixty-five, and living in urban areas dominate the group. Of particular concern for the urban theorist is the concern generated by the fact that today's urban centers are becoming increasingly populated by the above

Reprinted from Office of Economic Opportunity, *Selected Readings about the President's War on Poverty Program,* Program Support Division, Community Action Program, Office of Economic Opportunity, Washington, D.C., 1965.

group. Means must be found to break the cycle of poverty predicted for these people and provide for their integration into the mainstream of American abundance.

Prosperity has been kind to most Americans. Despite higher price levels, real income—the buying power of aggregate dollars available to most of us —has risen sharply. A cursory look at our cities, suburbs, highways and countryside reveals a land almost of conspicuous consumption.

A closer look, both at the countryside and our inner cities, would show clearly that prosperity has passed millions of us by. Rural and urban poverty afflict these millions who view the affluent society from the outside.

The poor live in a world unrecognizable to the majority of the nation. That world has been eloquently described by authors and newspapermen who have dared to enter it—if only for a close-up glance. They have found a land where the inhabitants are isolated from the mainstream of American economic, political and social life. It is a world where the major concern is survival for today, where even a minor illness can become a major tragedy, where privacy is almost unknown, where the American dream is hollow and unreal, where the poverty of the father is visited upon the next generation.

Americans are not poor in the way that poverty afflicts millions of the world's underdeveloped nations. But domestic poverty is possibly more cruel since it coexists with abundance. As author Michael Harrington has pointed out, "tens of millions of Americans are, at this very moment, maimed in body and spirit, existing at levels beneath those necessary for human decency. If these people are not starving, they are hungry, and sometimes fat with hunger, for that is what cheap foods do. They are without adequate housing and education and medical care."

Significant progress has been made in reducing poverty in the United States. Between 1947 and 1956, unemployment rates were low and incomes grew at a relatively rapid rate. The number of poor families declined from 11.9 to 9.9 million at a time of rapid population growth. In 1947, the poor accounted for 32 per cent of American families. By 1956, some 23 per cent remained in poverty.

Between 1957 and 1962, the rate of decline slowed significantly. Economic growth slowed and the unemployment rate rose and remained high. The number of families remaining in poverty declined only from 9.9 to 9.3 million, about a fifth of the 47 million family units in the nation.

Arbitrary income cutoff points cannot be used to delimit poverty, since a family of eight with $4,000 annually may suffer greater want than an aged couple with $2,500. But poverty and affluence are still best determined with an income measuring stick.

In 1962, the Social Security Administration defined a low-cost budget for a nonfarm family of four, and put the income requirement at $3,955. It also defined an "economy-plan" budget which it reported would cost $3,165. On balance, it has been determined that a family of four must have at least $3,000 a year to burst the bonds of poverty.

Low income family budgets assume that a third of family income will go for food, about $20 per week for a family of four. Of the $2,000 remaining to a family at the poverty line, about $800 would be allowed for housing. The remaining $1,200—less than $25 weekly—would go for clothing, transportation, medical care, education, recreation, insurance, personal care, and so on.

The 9.3 million families with incomes below $3,000 comprise 30 million persons. Of these, 11 million—about one-sixth of America's young—are children. Condemned to deprivation, inadequate educational opportunity and cultural alienation, far too many of these children will inherit poverty for their entire lives and, in turn, pass it on to their children.

More than 5.4 million of the nation's impoverished families have incomes below $2,000 a year. More than a million children of very large families—six or more in the family unit—live in these circumstances.

A minimum income of $1,500 annually—less than $30 a week—has been found necessary to support an unattached individual above the poverty line. Some 45 per cent of all unattached individuals—a total of five million—lived below the poverty level in 1962. Of these, more than three million had incomes of a thousand dollars or less.

Hard-core poverty can be eliminated in the foreseeable future only through an active program striking at the roots of want and deprivation. Should present trends continue, about 13 per cent of all families would still be poor in 1980. In view of the nature of today's poverty, there is reason to believe that even reduction to this level would not be achieved if nothing were done about the problem.

Poverty exacts a frightening social and economic cost. Just by lifting our impoverished families to the $3,000 mark, $11 billion annually would be added to the wealth of the nation. The costs in needless ignorance, crime delinquency, health deterioration, unemployment, and wasted lives is incalcu-

lable. Since abuse and misuse of human resources represents tragic social and economic waste, America will never reach her full potential while massive poverty is tolerated.

Of all nations, America can most readily afford the costs of combatting poverty. Present programs, stressing education, training and social services, seek to break the poverty cycle. They represent an important beginning in the only war this nation seeks—the war against needless want.

The report of the House Committee on Education and Labor has pointed out that the nation "cannot leave the further wearing away of poverty solely to the general progress of the economy." It stated that a faster reduction of "poverty will require that the lowest fifth of our families be able to earn a larger share of the national income."

Today, the lowest fifth receives only 5 per cent of national income while the highest fifth, by contrast, receives 43 per cent. There is no good economic reason that improved distribution cannot be achieved without impairment to any sector of the U.S. economy.

ETHNIC COMPOSITION

About 45 per cent of nonwhite families had incomes under $3,000 annually in 1962, compared with 17 per cent of white families. And while the incomes of both white and nonwhite families have risen in the post-war period, the relative position of the nonwhite has not improved. Data of the Census Bureau, on the contrary, suggests that the relative position of nonwhite families may have deteriorated.

Nearly half of Negro families—49 per cent—had incomes below $3,000 annually (in 1962) dollars) in 1960 and 54 per cent of American Indian families were in the poverty category. But only 11 per cent of Japanese and 16 per cent of Chinese families had low incomes. About 35 per cent of persons with Spanish surnames—Mexican-Americans—in the Southwest were poor, and 32 per cent of Puerto Rican families were in this category.

Of the two million Negro poor families in the United States (incomes below $3,000 in 1959), nearly three-fourths lived in the South. About 23 per cent lived in the North, but only 4 per cent in the West.

Of the 1.4 million poor Negro families living in the South, 53 per cent were found to reside in urban areas, 32 per cent were rural nonfarm and 15 per cent were on the farm. Nearly all of the Negro poor in the North and West—about 95 per cent—lived in urban areas.

Of the 700,000 families with Spanish surnames living in the Southwest, 240,000 were poor. About 57 per cent of the poor lived in Texas, 24 per cent in California and the remainder in Arizona, Colorado and New Mexico.

Nearly all of the 200,000 Puerto Rican families in continental United States lived in urban areas in 1960. About 73 per cent of these lived in the New York metropolitan area. About 76 per cent of the 80,000 impoverished Puerto Rican families lived in the New York area.

White poverty is less concentrated by geography. About two-fifths of the nation's poor white families are in the South and another 29 per cent are in the North Central area.

Among white families, there is a direct relationship between poverty and age. A third of poor white families are headed by persons over age 65. Among nonwhites, only 17 per cent of impoverished families are headed by elderly persons.

Lack of education is a deeply rooted cause of poverty which respects no racial boundaries. About 70 per cent of nonwhite poor families and 60 per cent of white poor families are headed by persons with less than a grade school education.

Many more of nonwhite poor families are headed by wage workers than is the case with whites. About 36 per cent of nonwhite family heads are employed in the services or as laborers, a proportion three times as great as among white families. Proportionately, on the other hand, twice as many of the white poor are farmers (12 per cent against 6).

Nonwhite poor families have more and younger children; 67 per cent of the former families include at least one child under 18 while only 45 per cent of whites are so characterized. About 43 per cent of nonwhite poor families include children under six, as compared with 23 per cent of whites. Nearly a fourth of the nonwhite poor have four or more children but only 8 per cent of whites were so situated.

Nonwhite poor families are much larger than white families in similar economic circumstances. Over half of white families of low income are two person units, compared with only a third of nonwhites.

URBAN POOR NEIGHBORHOODS

The poor are a minority in most urban complexes, but the greatest concentrations of poverty lie within these centers. Over half of all poor families —4.9 million—live in cities of a quarter of a million or more. Nonwhite low income families are highly concentrated in these big cities which house half of all poor white families and 63 per cent of the nonwhite poor.

New York City's poor make up an eighth of its total population. This meant that the central city housed 371,000 families with incomes below the $3,000 level in 1960.

Certain Chicago areas illustrate the deterioration of poor neighborhoods. Changes in Chicago over recent years appear to be typical of those in other major urban concentrations. The population of the inner city decreased by 2 per cent during the fifties. In the same decade, Negro population increased by 65 per cent. As the sixties began, Negroes accounted for 23 per cent of Chicago's total population.

In the Chicago neighborhoods cited here, at least one-fourth of all families had incomes below $3,000 annually in 1959. Unemployment rates were far higher than the national average; the population suffered serious educational deficiencies; slum housing was common or predominant; median family income was significantly lower than that of the metropolitan area. The neighborhoods now are predominantly Negro, but they are not the sum total of Negro neighborhoods in the city.

East Garfield Park, in Central Chicago, is bounded by industrial areas and railroad tracks. Almost 30 per cent of the housing is substandard and there has been little residential construction since the early thirties. As the fifties began, the neighborhood was predominantly white. Today, it is about three-fifths Negro. During the fifties total population declined by 5 per cent, but Negro population increased by 250 per cent. Nearly 80 per cent of today's East Garfield housing is multiple dwelling and there is almost no individual home ownership.

The Near West Side has long housed waves of new immigrants, and since 1930 has been predominantly populated by persons of Italian extraction. Beginning with 1930, Mexican migrants began to move in and were soon joined by Southern Negroes seeking employment in the big city. Together, the Mexican and Negro population now is the second largest group to inhabit the Near West Side. As the newcomers came, older groups—Germans, Irish, Russian-Jews, and Poles—moved out. Newcomers included Puerto Ricans who, in 1960, numbered 19 per cent of all Puerto Ricans in the city.

An increasing part of the Near West Side is becoming industrial. Industry is located on the borders of the neighborhood, close to the railroad tracks and in the northeastern section. The eastern portion of the area is marked by light industry and wholesale houses. Madison Street, in the heart of the area, has become a big city "skid row," complete with cheap saloons and flophouses.

The Near West Side is a multiple-housing community where, in 1960, 30 per cent of the dwellings contained 10 or more rental units and 46 per cent more contained three to nine units. Large single-home units on Ashland Avenue, long ago occupied by the wealthy and near-wealthy, today house cheap boarding-houses and small businesses. Only 10 per cent of the area's housing is owner occupied.

An influx of Negro population in the forties reversed a population decline in the Near South Side but outflow exceeded intake again in the fifties. Negroes now make up about 77 per cent of the area's population. While the percentage of Negroes increased during the fifties, there was only a small absolute increase in numbers. The higher percentage of Negroes was chiefly attributable to an outflow of whites.

New housing construction in the Near South Side was virtually nonexistent until 1955 when the Chicago Housing Authority completed the Harold L. Ickes Homes with 803 units.

Industrial and commercial development has increased and less land is being used for residential purposes. Substandard conditions and overcrowding prevail in deteriorating housing generally sandwiched in between industrial and commercial establishments. Warehousing and industrial uses predominate in the area west of the Illinois Central tracks. Wholesale establishments and auto agencies dominate along Michigan Boulevard.

Negroes started to move into the Kenwood area in the middle forties, and by 1960 the neighborhood was 84 per cent Negro. The remaining whites in Kenwood are concentrated in new high rise apartment houses in the southeastern corner of the area. Most whites are of the German and Russian-Jewish stock who once were the preponderant majority. The Japanese population of the area has dwindled.

The southern half of Kenwood has been included in the Hyde Park-Kenwood conservation area established by the Chicago Community Conservation Board in 1956. In 1962, ground was broken for 1,949 residential units. In the same year, work was begun by the Chicago Dwellings Association on a nine-story structure which will contain 103 rental units for elderly middle-income families.

HOW THE POOR LIVE

Nowhere does poverty manifest itself with greater impact than in housing. Housing for the poor often lacks adequate plumbing and heating facilities, is in woeful disrepair, is vermin infested and constitutes a threat to the health and safety of the occupants.

More than any other group, the poor live in rental housing. About half of the poor are renters, while in the over $6,000 group 74 per cent are home owners.

Nearly half of the 8.5 million housing units found dilapidated or lacking some or all plumbing in the census report of 1960 was occupied by households with incomes below $2,000 a year, and 1.3 million more units were occupied by families with incomes between $2,000 and $3,000.

Large families with six, seven or eight children are poor even when incomes are significantly above $3,000. It is not surprising, therefore, to find such families living in substandard housing even when incomes are in the $4,000—$5,000 range.

While poor housing is usually a hallmark of poverty, good or relatively good housing may hide want and privation. The 1960 census found that five million families with incomes under $2,000 and another three million with incomes between $2,000 and $3,000 lived in adequate housing. Good housing occupied by owners tends to be more common than that occupied by renters among the poor.

Relatively good housing among the poor is accounted for by such factors as acquisition before retirement, inheritance and periods of relative affluence. The incidence of elderly couples with low incomes among the better housed poor explains why there is considerably less crowding among households with annual incomes below $3,000 than at any other point on the income scale. With children gone, these couples often have a whole house to themselves, although it was originally intended for families of three, four or more.

Overcrowding often afflicts the urban poor families who are renters. The worst condition prevails in the $2,000 to $3,000 income group where one in five renters have an average density of more than one person to a room. While there is less overcrowding in rural areas, a significant amount prevails, especially in the dilapidated shacks that dot depressed areas.

The statistics show poor homeowners are less mobile than those of higher income groups. Some 60 per cent of these families with less than $2,000, and more than half those with incomes between $2,000 and $3,000, had been living in the same unit since 1949 at the time of the 1960 census. In contrast, only 30 per cent of owners with incomes of $6,000 or more had remained in the same house.

This is not the case with renters. Only 20 per cent of those with incomes below $2,000 had not moved since 1949.

The 11 million children living in poverty stricken families are most victimized by squalid housing. Large families are especially handicapped by lack of adequate housing. Large units are often in short supply and are almost always expensive.

The drab existence forced upon the children of the poor by inadequate housing, "often in the worst slums and frequently completely lacking in play areas and open space, cannot help but exert a stultifying influence upon them. . . . It is small wonder that there is such a high correlation between the incidence of substandard housing and such things as juvenile delinquency, school dropouts, and health problems . . ." the House report stressed.

Almost 70 per cent of family heads over age 65 were homeowners, although poverty afflicts about half the households of senior citizens. A fifth of all housing units occupied by families headed by senior citizens, or in which senior citizens live, are substandard. These units, whether owner occupied, or rental, have been classified as dilapidated or lacking in essential plumbing facilities.

While there is relatively little crowding in households headed by poor persons over age 65, this often is not the case where the elderly live in a family headed by a person under age 60. Overcrowding in households of this type reflect the moving in of parents with children in city or suburban

homes not built to accommodate extra persons.

The condition of housing among the nonwhite poor is worse than among the impoverished whites. Only 38 per cent of nonwhite own their own homes. About half the nonwhite renters and two-fifths of homeowners live in substandard housing. Housing for nonwhites is worst in the South. For renters it is best in the West. For owners, it is best in the North.

Racial bias, as well as poverty, contributes to substandard minority housing. Among non-white families with incomes of $5,000 or more, 16 per cent lived in substandard housing in 1960. Among whites, the figure was 4.9 per cent.

Overcrowding is three times greater among nonwhite than among whites, with conditions poorest in the South. Nonwhites live in older buildings and generally are forced to take the leavings of the housing market. This is particularly true among the nonwhite poor.

Three major Federal housing programs are concerned with low income families. The major program is that of the Public Housing Administration which administers loans and grants assisting local housing authorities. A total of 550,000 public housing units have been constructed, but the great majority of the poor have not been affected. Public housing, particularly the huge high-rise buildings of our cities, has been criticized for creating a new kind of ghetto in which the poor lose neighborhood roots and become further alienated. The general view, however, is that despite its faults, public housing creates better living than the housing it has replaced.

An FHA program conducted under Sec. 221 of the Housing Act has made it possible to produce some housing within the reach of low income families. Under this program, interest rates below the going market rate are charged. Some 35,000 rental units have been constructed since the program began in 1961.

Urban renewal programs have eliminated more than a quarter of a million substandard housing units occupied for the most part by the poor. Three-fourths of those displaced by these programs are reported to have been relocated—or will be relocated—in decent housing.

Three special senior citizen programs involving public housing, mortgage insurance and long term direct loans had resulted in the construction of 46,000 units by the end of 1963. At that time, another 87,000 units were reported to be under construction.

Housing remains one of the pressing unmet needs of the poor despite current and anticipated government programs. Millions of housing units are substandard and other millions are deteriorating. Housing is a legitimate area of concern for Community Action Programs. Much can be done through proper enforcement of local building codes.

CHILDREN OF THE POOR

The children pay hardest for the impoverishment of the parents. Ill-housed, poorly-fed, ill-educated and neglected, an alarming number of the children of poverty will become parents of another generation of the dispossessed.

There were, in 1960, some 66 million children under 18 years of age in 27.5 million families. Families with one child had a median income of $5,904, while those with six children had a median income of $4,475. Generally speaking, income tends to decline with family size.

About 87 per cent of children below 18 lived with both parents; 10 per cent with one parent and the remaining

three lived in foster homes, institutions or with relatives. Far more than white children, nonwhites were to be found in non-normal family situations—economically or otherwise. One of every three nonwhite children was in a one-parent family in 1960, against a one to ten ratio for whites. Nonwhite mothers were three times as prone to have broken marriages—more by separation or desertion than by divorce.

Formal divorces resulted in far more support arrangements than separations by other means. Only a third of husbandless nonwhite mothers were divorced, against three-fifths of white mothers in similar circumstances. Only 2 per cent of white mothers said they had never been married, but 12 per cent of nonwhite mothers so acknowledged.

Broken homes headed by mothers have far lower incomes than homes with normal parent relationships. In March of 1962, such homes represented 8.5 per cent of the total. Young mothers without husbands tended to have more children than those living with husbands. This was true for both whites and nonwhites, although in greater degree with the latter.

Wife-husband families with children had median incomes of $6,510 and 2.4 children in 1962. Mother-child families had 2.1 children, but incomes of only $2,675. Nonwhite couples had incomes of $3,895 and three children. Nonwhite mothers heading families had 2.8 children and $1,655. Only one in 13 husband-wife families lived on farms and 3 per cent of mother-child families were so situated. The 2.2 million non-farm families headed by mothers only had five million children. Half subsisted on incomes below $2,340 and a fourth had less than $2,000. The larger the family, the lower was the level of income, and those with four or more children had median incomes of $1,860.

Information on the more than half
million mother-child families living
with parents or other relatives is lacking but data from 1956 would indicate
that these "subfamilies" have only
about half the income of mother-child
families living as independent units.

Some 2.5 million widows and children receive payments under the social
security laws—the Old Age and Survivors Insurance. While amounts are
not large, they are significantly higher
than payments under public assistance
programs in many states. A widowed
mother and two children receive between $180 and $190 monthly under the
program.

Society generally does not frown
upon payments to widows and children
under OASI. But those who receive
other forms of public assistance tend
to be regarded as "charity" cases at
best, or as ne'er-do-well.

Aid to Dependent Children payments
generally go to indigent families who
have no father in the house—whether
because of separation, divorce or because the father and mother never
married. While it is dependent upon
federal support, ADC operates under
state rules. The District of Columbia,
for example, has a "man-in-the-house"
rule under which assistance is denied if
an able-bodied male is found in the
home—regardless of his employment
status. The rule has led to real and
faked desertions so that needy families
may survive.

The report of the House Select Committee noted that at the end of 1961,
(ADC) payments were going to 625,000
families with no father in the home—
less than half the total estimated to be
in need, and possibly not more than
four in ten. To the extent that eligibility
for participation in surplus food distribution or food stamp programs is related to eligibility for public assistance,

many of the needy mother-child families
who receive no assistance may be
barred from these also.

Half of all ADC payments go to families of four or more, but only 29 per
cent of all ADC recipients draw $150
or more monthly. Many states have
limits on ADC payments, and nine pay
no more than $155 regardless of need.
Average payment was only $112 a
month according to a 1961 study.

Husband-wife families, the House
report noted, "can look to even less
help from public programs than broken
families can. It is perhaps the inability
of the man to earn—particularly among
nonwhites—that is conducive to marriage disruption or the failure ever to
undertake legal marriage that leaves so
many mothers to bring up children
without a father. . . ."

LEGACY OF POVERTY

"There seems to be a sufficient basis,
however, for adopting as a working
hypothesis that perhaps the single me-
dium most conducive to the growth
of poverty is poverty itself," the House
report stressed. It added that while
adequate family income alone will not
guarantee a child freedom from poverty as adults, such income is usually
a necessary condition.

A study of ADC families completed
in 1961 showed that more than 40 per
cent of mothers and/or fathers were
raised in homes that had received assistance at one time or another. ADC
parents had low educational attainment
in twice the measure of the general
population.

Despite recent advances, a third of
today's children will not complete high
school and at least a quarter of a
million annually will drop out before
completing elementary school. Subject
to low skill jobs and chronic unem-

ployment, these youth may well become the fathers and mothers of a new poverty generation.

The nonwhite poor are particularly condemned to repeat the poverty cycle. For these, patterns of discrimination combine with inherited poverty to cut off opportunity for jobs and self-development.

"The Negro baby born in America today—regardless of the section or State in which he is born—has about one-half as much chance of completing high school as a white baby born in the same place on the same day, one-third as much chance of becoming a professional man, twice as much chance of becoming unemployed, about a seventh as much chance of earning $10,000 a year, a life expectancy which is seven years less, and the prospects of earning only half as much," President John F. Kennedy pointed out in his civil rights message of February 1963.

THE MERCHANT AND THE LOW-INCOME CONSUMER

David Caplovitz

The urban poor are trained in a society that convinces them that they want the "good things of life." It matters little that they have no means to attain them. Their small income, small savings, job insecurity, and little expertise in quality goods or cost of credit makes them ripe for "plucking" by the unscrupulous merchant of the slum area. The quality of the consumables is poor, the markup is at least 100 per cent and often much more, and the rates of interest are excessive (merchants get around the law by including interest in the cost of the goods). The shopping habits of the poor insure their continued indebtedness with little hope of upgrading their place in society.

The visitor to East Harlem cannot fail to notice the sixty or so furniture and appliance stores that mark the area, mostly around Third Avenue and 125th Street. At first this may seem surprising. After all, this is obviously a low-income area. Many of the residents are on relief. Many are employed in seasonal work and in marginal industries, such as the garment industry, which are the first to feel the effects of a recession in the economy. On the face of it, residents of the area would seem unable to afford the merchandise offered for sale in these stores.

That merchants nevertheless find it profitable to locate in these areas attests to a commonly overlooked fact: low-income families, like those of higher income, are consumers of many major durables. The popular image of the American as striving for the material possessions which bestow upon him both comfort and prestige in the eyes

Reprinted with permission of The Macmillan Company from *The Poor Pay More* by David Caplovitz, pp. 12–30. © by The Free Press of Glencoe, a Division of The Macmillan Company, 1963.

of his fellows does not hold only for the ever-increasing middle class. The cultural pressures to buy major durables reach low- as well as middle-income families. In some ways, consumption may take on even more significance for low-income families than for those in higher classes. Since many have small prospect of greatly improving their low social standing through occupational mobility, they are apt to turn to consumption as at least one sphere in which they can make some progress toward the American dream of success. If the upper strata that were observed by Veblen engaged in conspicuous consumption to symbolize their social superiority, it might be said that the lower classes today are apt to engage in *compensatory consumption*. Appliances, automobiles, and the dream of a home of their own can become compensations for blocked social mobility.[1]

Fascinated by a rising standard of living offered them on every hand on the installment plan, they [the working class] do not readily segregate themselves from the rest of the city. They want what Middletown wants, so long as it gives them their great symbol of advancement—an automobile. Car ownership stands to them for a large share of the "American dream"; they cling to it as they cling to self respect, and it was not unusual to see a family drive up to the relief commissary in 1935 to stand in line for its four or five dollar weekly food dole. [The Lynds go on to quote

[1] I am indebted to Robert K. Merton for suggesting the apt phrase, "compensatory consumption." The idea expressed by this term figures prominently in the writings of Robert S. Lynd. Observing the workers in Middletown, Lynd noted that their declining opportunities for occupational advancement and even the depression did not make them class-conscious. Instead, their aspirations shifted to the realm of consumption.

a union official:] It's easy to see why our workers don't think much about joining unions. So long as they have a car and can borrow or steal a gallon of gas, they'll ride around and pay no attention to labor organization. . . . [Robert S. Lynd and Helen Merrill Lynd, *Middletown in Transition* (New York: Harcourt, Brace and Co., 1937), p. 26. See also pp. 447–448.]

It should be noted that the Lynds identify the installment plan as the mechanism through which workers are able to realize their consumption aspirations. Similar observations are to be found in *Knowledge for What?* (Princeton University Press: 1939), pp. 91, 198. Lynd's student, Eli Chinoy, also makes use of the idea of compensatory consumption in his study of automobile workers. He found that when confronted with the impossibility of rising to the ranks of management, workers shifted their aspirations from the occupational to the consumption sphere. "With their wants constantly stimulated by high powered advertising, they measure their success by what they are able to buy." Eli Chinoy, "Aspirations of Automobile Workers," *American Journal of Sociology*, 57 (1952), 453–459. For further discussion of the political implications of this process, see Daniel Bell, "Work and its Discontents" in *The End of Ideology* (New York: The Free Press of Glencoe, 1960), pp. 246 ff.

The dilemma of the low-income consumer lies in these facts. He is trained by society (and his position in it) to want the symbols and appurtenances of the "good life" at the same time that he lacks the means needed to fulfill these socially induced wants. People with small incomes lack not only the ready cash for consuming major durables but are also poorly qualified for that growing substitute for available cash—credit. Their low income, their negligible savings, their job insecurity all contribute to their being poor credit risks. Moreover, many low-income families in New York City are fairly recent migrants from the South or from Puerto Rico and so do not have other requisites of good credit, such as long-term residence at the same address and friends who meet the credit requirements and are willing to vouch for them.[2]

Not having enough cash and credit would seem to create a sufficient problem for low-income consumers. But they have other limitations as well. They tend to lack the information and training needed to be effective consumers in a bureaucratic society. Partly because of their limited education and partly because as migrants from more traditional societies they are unfamiliar with urban culture, they are not apt to follow the announcements of sales in the newspapers, to engage in comparative shopping, to know their way around the major department stores and bargain centers, to know how to evaluate the advice of salesmen—practices necessary for some degree of sophistication in the realm of consumption. The institution of credit introduces special complex requirements for intelligent consumption. Because of the diverse and frequently misleading ways in which charges for credit are stated, even the highly-educated consumer has difficulty knowing which set of terms is most economical.[3]

These characteristics of the low-income consumer—his socially supported want for major durables, his small funds, his poor credit position, his lack of shopping sophistication—constitute the conditions under which durables are marketed in low-income areas. To understand the paradox set by the many stores selling high-cost durables in these areas it is necessary to know how the merchants adapt to these conditions. Clearly the normal marketing arrangements, based on a model of the "adequate" consumer (the consumer with funds, credit, and shopping sophistication), cannot prevail if these merchants are to stay in business.

On the basis of interviews with fourteen of these merchants, the broad outlines of this marketing system can be described. This picture, in turn, provides a backdrop for the more detailed examination in later chapters of the marketing relationship from the viewpoint of the consumer.

MERCHANDISING IN A LOW-INCOME AREA

The key to the marketing system in low-income areas lies in special adaptations of the institution of credit. The

---

[2] A frequent practice in extending credit to poor risks is to have cosigners who will make good the debt should the original borrower default. The new arrivals are apt to be disadvantaged by their greater difficulty in finding cosigners.

[3] Professor Samuel S. Myers of Morgan State College has studied the credit terms of major department stores and appliance outlets in Baltimore. Visiting the ten most popular stores, he priced the same model of TV set and gathered information on down-payments and credit terms. He found that the cash price was practically the same in the various stores, but that there were wide variations in the credit

terms leading to sizeable differences in the final cost to the consumer. (Based on personal communication with Professor Myers.)

In his statement to the Douglas Committee considering the "Truth in Interest" bill, George Katona presented findings from the consumer surveys carried out by the Survey Research Center of the University of Michigan. These studies show that people with high income and substantial education are no better informed about the costs of credit than people of low income and little education. See *Consumer Credit Labeling Bill, op. cit.*, p. 806.

many merchants who locate in these areas and find it profitable to do so are prepared to offer credit in spite of the high risks involved. Moreover, their credit is tailored to the particular needs of the low-income consumer. All kinds of durable goods can be obtained in this market at terms not too different from the slogan, "a dollar down, a dollar a week." The consumer can buy furniture, a TV set, a stereophonic phonograph, or, if he is so minded, a combination phonograph-TV set, if not for a dollar a week then for only a few dollars a week. In practically every one of these stores, the availability of "easy credit" is announced to the customer in both English and Spanish by large signs in the windows and sometimes by neon signs over the doorways. Of the fourteen merchants interviewed, twelve claimed that from 75 to 90 per cent of their business consisted of credit and the other two said that credit made up half their business. That these merchants extend credit to their customers does not, of course explain how they stay in business. They still face the problem of dealing with their risks.

The Markup and Quality of Goods

It might at first seem that the merchant would solve his problem by charging high rates of interest on the credit he extends. But the law in New York State now regulates the amount that can be charged for credit, and most of these merchants claim they use installment contracts which conform to the law. The fact is that they do not always use these contracts. Some merchants will give customers only a card on which payments are noted. In these transactions the cost of credit and the cash price are not specified as the law requires. The customer peddlers, whom we shall soon meet, seldom use

installment contracts. In all these cases the consumer has no idea of how much he is paying for credit, for the cost of credit is not differentiated from the cost of the product.

Although credit charges are now regulated by law, no law regulates the merchant's markup on his goods. East Harlem is known to the merchants of furniture and appliances in New York City as the area in which pricing is done by "numbers." We first heard of the "number" system from a woman who had been employed as a bookkeeper in such a store. She illustrated a "one number" item by writing down a hypothetical wholesale price and then adding the same figure to it, a 100 per cent markup. Her frequent references to "two number" and "three number" prices indicated that prices are never less than "one number," and are often more.

The system of pricing in the low-income market differs from that in the bureaucratic market of the downtown stores in another respect: In East Harlem there are hardly any "one price" stores. In keeping with a multi-price policy, price tags are conspicuously absent from the merchandise. The customer has to ask, "how much?," and the answer he gets will depend on several things. If the merchant considers him a poor risk, if he thinks the customer is naive, or if the customer was referred to him by another merchant or a peddler to whom he must pay a commission, the price will be higher. The fact that prices can be affected by "referrals" calls attention to another peculiarity of the low-income market, what the merchants call the "T.O." system.

Anyone closely familiar with sales practices in a large retailing establishment probably understands the meaning of "T.O." When a salesman is confronted with a customer who is not responding to the "sales pitch," he will call over another salesman, signal the nature of the situation by whispering, "this is a T.O.," and then introduce him to the customer as the "assistant manager."[4] In East Harlem, as the interviewers learned, T.O.s extend beyond the store. When a merchant finds himself with a customer who seems to be a greater risk than he is prepared to accept, he does not send the customer away. Instead, he will tell the customer that he happens to be out of the item he wants, but that it can be obtained at the store of his "friend" or "cousin," just a few blocks away. The merchant will then take the customer to a storekeeper with a less conservative credit policy.[5] The second merchant fully understands that his colleague expects a commission and takes this into account in fixing the price.[6] As a result, the

customer who happens to walk into the "wrong" store ends up paying more. In essence, he is being charged for the service of having his credit potential matched with the risk policy of a merchant.

As for the merchandise sold in these stores, the interviewers noticed that the furniture on display was of obviously poor quality. Most of all, they were struck by the absence of well-known brands of appliances in most of the stores. To find out about the sales of better-known brands, they initially asked about the volume of sales of "high-*price* lines." But this question had little meaning for the merchants, because high prices were being charged for the low-quality goods in evidence. The question had to be rephrased in terms of "high *quality*" merchandise or, as the merchants themselves refer to such goods, "custom lines." To quote from the report of these interviews:

> It became apparent that the question raised a problem of communication. We were familiar with the prices generally charged for high quality lines and began to notice that the same prices were charged for much lower quality merchandise. The markup was obviously quite different from that in other areas. The local merchants said that the sale of "custom" merchandise was limited by a slow turnover. In fact, a comparable markup on the higher quality lines would make the final price so prohibitively high that they could not be moved at all. A lower markup would be inconsistent with the risk and would result in such small profits that the business could not be continued.

The high markup on low-quality goods is thus a major device used by

---

[4] The initials stand for "turn over." The "assistant manager" is ready to make a small concession to the customer, who is usually so flattered by this gesture that he offers no further resistance to the sale. For further descriptions of the "T.O.," see Cecil L. French, "Correlates of Success in Retail Selling," *American Journal of Sociology*, 66 (September, 1960), 128–134; and Erving Goffman, *Presentation of Self in Everyday Life* (New York: Doubleday, Anchor Books, 1959), pp. 178–180.

[5] The interviewers found that the stores closer to the main shopping area of 125th Street generally had more conservative credit policies than those somewhat farther away. This was indicated by the percentage of credit sales the merchants reported as defaults. The higher-rental stores near 125th Street reported default rates of 5 and 6 per cent, those six or seven blocks away, as high as 20 per cent.

[6] The referring merchant does not receive his commission right away. Whether he gets it at all depends upon the customer's payment record. He will keep a record of his referrals and check on them after several months. When the merchant who has made the sale has received a certain percentage of the payments, he will give the referring merchant his commission.

the merchants to protect themselves against the risks of their credit business. This policy represents a marked departure from the "normal" marketing situation. In the "normal" market, competition between merchants results in a pricing policy roughly commensurate with the quality of the goods. It is apparent, then, that these merchants do not see themselves competing with stores outside the neighborhood. This results in the irony that the people who can least afford the goods they buy are required to pay high prices relative to quality, thus receiving a comparatively low return for their consumer dollar.

In large part, these merchants have a "captive" market because their customers do not meet the economic requirements of consumers in the larger, bureaucratic marketplace. But also, they can sell inferior goods at high prices because, in their own words, the customers are not "price and quality conscious." Interviews found that the merchants perceive their customers as unsophisticated shoppers. One merchant rather cynically explained that the amount of goods sold a customer depends not on the customer but on the merchant's willingness to extend him credit. If the merchant is willing to accept great risk, he can sell the customer almost as much as he cares to. Another merchant, commenting on the buying habits of the customer, said, "People do not shop in this area. Each person who comes into the store wants to buy something and is a potential customer. It is just up to who catches him."

The notion of "who catches him" is rather important in this economy. Merchants compete not so much in price or quality, but in getting customers to the store on other grounds. (Some of these gathering techniques will shortly be described.)

Another merchant commented rather

grudgingly that the Negroes were beginning to show signs of greater sophistication by "shopping around." Presumably this practice is not followed by the newer migrants to the area.

But although the merchants are ready to exploit the naivete of their traditionalistic customers, it is important to point out that they also cater to the customer's traditionalism. As a result of the heavy influex of Puerto Ricans into the area, many of these stores now employ Puerto Rican salesmen. The customers who enter these stores need not be concerned about possible embarrassment because of their broken English or their poor dress. On the contrary, these merchants are adept at making the customer feel at ease, as a personal experience will testify.

Visiting the area and stopping occasionally to read the ads in the windows, I happened to pause before an appliance store. A salesman promptly emerged and said, "I know, I bet you're looking for a nice TV set. Come inside. We've got lots of nice ones." Finding myself thrust into the role of customer, I followed him into the store and listened to his sales pitch. Part way through his talk, he asked my name. I hesitated a moment and then provided him with a fictitious last name, at which point he said, "No, no—no last names. What's your first name? . . . Ah, Dave; I'm Irv. We only care about first names here." When I was ready to leave after making some excuse about having to think things over, he handed me his card. Like most business cards of employees, this one had the name and address of the enterprise in large type and in small type the name of the salesman. But instead of his full name, there appeared only the amiable, "Irv."

As this episode indicates, the merchants in this low-income area are ready to personalize their services. To consumers from a more traditional society, unaccustomed to the impersonality of the bureaucratic market, this may be no small matter.

So far, we reviewed the elements of the system of exchange that comprise the low-income market. For the consumer, these are the availability of merchandise, the "easy" installments, and the reassurance of dealing with merchants who make them feel at home. In return, the merchant reserves for himself the right to sell low-quality merchandise at exorbitant prices.

But the high markup on goods does not insure that the business will be profitable. No matter what he charges, the merchant can remain in business only if customers actually pay. In this market, the customer's intention and ability to pay—the assumptions underlying any credit system—cannot be taken for granted. Techniques for insuring continuity of payments are a fundamental part of this distinctive economy.

Formal Controls

When the merchant uses an installment contract, he has recourse to legal controls over his customers. But as we shall see, legal controls are not sufficient to cope with the merchant's problem and they are seldom used.

REPOSSESSION The merchant who offers credit can always repossess his merchandise should the customer default on payments. But repossession, according to the merchants, is rare. They claim that the merchandise receives such heavy use as to become practically worthless in a short time. And no doubt the shoddy merchandise will not stand much use, heavy or light. One merchant said that he will occasionally repossess an item, not to regain his equity, but to punish a customer he feels is trying to cheat him.

LIENS AGAINST PROPERTY AND WAGES The merchant can, of course, sue the defaulting customer. By winning a court judgment, he can have the customers' property attached. Should this fail to satisfy the debt, he can take the further step of having the customer's salary garnisheed.[7] But these devices are not fully adequate for several reasons. Not all customers have property of value or regular jobs. Furthermore, their employers will not hesitate to fire them rather than submit to the nuisance of a garnishment. But since the customer knows he may lose his job if he is garnisheed, the mere threat of garnishment is sometimes enough to insure regularity of payments.[8] The main limitation with legal controls, however, is that the merchant who uses them repeatedly runs the risk of forfeiting good will in the neighborhood.

DISCOUNTING PAPER The concern with good will places a limitation on the use of another legal practice open to merchants for minimizing their risk: the sale of their contracts to a credit agency at a discount. By selling his contracts to one of the licensed finance companies, the merchant can realize an immediate return on his investment. The problem with this technique is that

[7] It is of some interest that the low-income families we interviewed were all familiar with the word "garnishee." This may well be one word in the language that the poorly educated are more likely to know than the better educated.

[8] Welfare families cannot, of course, be garnisheed, and more than half the merchants reported that they sell to them. But the merchants can threaten to disclose the credit purchase to the welfare authorities. Since recipients of welfare funds are not supposed to buy on credit, this threat exerts powerful pressure on the family.

the merchant loses control over his customer. As an impersonal, bureaucratic organization, the credit agency has recourse only to legal controls. Should the customer miss a payment, the credit agency will take the matter to court. But in the customer's mind, his contract exists with the merchant, not with the credit agency. Consequently, the legal actions taken against him reflect upon the merchant, and so good will is not preserved after all.

For this reason, the merchant is reluctant to "sell his paper," particularly if he has reason to believe that the customer will miss some payments. When he does sell some of his contracts at a discount, his motive is not to reduce risk, but rather to obtain working capital. Since so much of his capital is tied up in credit transactions, he frequently finds it necessary to make such sales. Oddly enough, he is apt to sell his better "paper," that is, the contracts of customers who pay regularly, for he wants to avoid incurring the ill will of customers. This practice also has its drawbacks for the merchant. Competitors can find out from the credit agencies which customers pay regularly and then try to lure them away from the original merchant. Some merchants reported that in order to retain control over their customers, they will buy back contracts from credit agencies they suspect are giving information to competitors.[9]

[9] Not all merchants are particularly concerned with good will. A few specialize in extending credit to the worst risks, customers turned away by most other merchants. These men will try to collect as much as they can on their accounts during the year and then will sell all their outstanding accounts to a finance company. As a result, the most inadequate consumers are apt to meet with the bureaucratic controls employed by the finance company. For a description of how

CREDIT ASSOCIATION RATINGS All credit merchants report their bad debtors to the credit association to which they belong. The merchants interviewed said that they always consult the "skip lists" of their association before extending credit to a new customer.[10] In this way they can avoid at least the customers known to be bad risks. This form of control tends to be effective in the long run because the customers find that they are unable to obtain credit until they have made good on their past debts. During the interviews with them, some customers mentioned this need to restore their credit rating as the reason why they were paying off debts in spite of their belief that they had been cheated.

But these various formal techniques of control are not sufficient to cope with the merchant's problem of risk. He also depends heavily on informal and personal techniques of control.

Informal Controls

The merchant starts from the premise that most of his customers are honest people who intend to pay but have difficulty managing their money. Missed payments are seen as more often due to poor management and to emergencies than to dishonesty. The merchants anticipate that their customers will miss some payments and they rely on informal controls to insure that payments are eventually made.

All the merchants described their credit business as operating on a "fifteen-month year." This means that

bill collectors operate, See Hillel Black, *Buy Now, Pay Later* (New York: William Morrow and Co., 1961), chap. 4.

[10] See *Ibid.*, chap. 3, for a description of the world's largest credit association, the one serving most of the stores in the New York City area.

they expect the customer to miss about one of every four payments and they compute the markup accordingly. Unlike the credit companies, which insist upon regular payments and add service charges for late payments, the neighborhood merchant is prepared to extend "flexible" credit. Should the customer miss an occasional payment or should he be short on another, the merchant considers this a normal part of his business.

To insure the close personal control necessary for this system of credit, the merchant frequently draws up a contract calling for weekly payments which the customer usually brings to the store. This serves several functions for the merchant. To begin with, the sum of money represented by a weekly payment is relatively small and so helps to create the illusion of "easy credit." Customers are apt to think more of the size of the payments than of the cost of the item or the length of the contract.

More importantly, the frequent contact of a weekly-payment system enables the merchant to get to know his customer. He learns when the customer receives his pay check, when his rent is due, who his friends are, when job layoffs, illnesses, and other emergencies occur—in short, all sorts of information which allow him to interpret the reason for a missed payment. Some merchants reported that when they know the customer has missed a payment for a legitimate reason such as illness or a job layoff, they will send a sympathetic note and offer the customer a gift (an inexpensive lamp or wall picture) when payments are resumed. This procedure, they say, frequently brings the customer back with his missed payments.

The short interval between payments also functions to give the merchant an early warning when something is amiss. His chances of locating the delinquent customer are that much greater. Furthermore, the merchant can keep tabs on a delinquent customer through his knowledge of the latter's friends, relatives, neighbors, and associates, who are also apt to be customers of his. In this way, still another informal device, the existing network of social relations, is utilized by the neighborhood merchant in conducting his business.[11]

The weekly-payment system also provides the merchant with the opportunity to sell other items to the customer. When the first purchase is almost paid for, the merchant will try to persuade the customer to make another. Having the customer in the store, where he can look at the merchandise, makes the next sale that much easier. This system of successive sales is, of course, an ideal arrangement— for the merchant. As a result, the customer remains continuously in debt to him. The pattern is somewhat reminiscent of the Southern sharecropper's relation to the company store. And since a number of customers grew up in more traditional environments with just such economies, they may find the arrangement acceptable. The practice of buying from peddlers, found to be common in these low-income areas, also involves the principle of continuous indebtedness. The urban low-income economy, then, is in some respects like the sharecropper system; it might almost be called an "urban sharecropper system."[12]

[11] The merchant's access to these networks of social relations is not entirely independent of economic considerations. Just as merchants who refer customers receive commissions, so customers who recommend others are often given commissions. Frequently, this is why a customer will urge his friends to deal with a particular merchant.

[12] The local merchants are not the only ones promoting continuous debt. The

THE CUSTOMER PEDDLERS

Characteristic of the comparatively traditional and personal form of the low-income economy is the important role played in it by the door-to-door credit salesman, the customer peddler. The study of merchants found that these peddlers are not necessarily competitors of the store-owners. Almost all merchants make use of peddlers in the great competition for customers. The merchants tend to regard peddlers as necessary evils who add greatly to the final cost of purchases. But they need them because in their view, customers are too ignorant, frightened, or lazy to come to the stores themselves. Thus, the merchants' apparent contempt for peddlers does not bar them from employing outdoor salesmen (or "canvassers," as they describe the peddlers who work for one store or another). Even the merchants who are themselves reluctant to hire canvassers find they must do so in order to meet the competition. The peddler's main function for the merchant, then, is getting the customer to the store, and if he will not come, getting the store to the customer. But this is not his only function.

Much more than the storekeeper, the peddler operates on the basis of a personal relationship with the customer. By going to the customer's home, he gets to know the entire family; he sees the condition of the home and he comes to know the family's habits and wants.

_____

coupon books issued by banks and finance companies which underwrite installment contracts contain notices in the middle announcing that the consumer can, if he wishes, refinance the loan. The consumer is told, in effect, that he is a good risk because presumably he has regularly paid half the installments and that he need not wait until he has made the last payment before borrowing more money.

From this vantage point he is better able than the merchant to evaluate the customer as a credit risk. Since many of the merchant's potential customers lack the standard credentials of credit, such as having a permanent job, the merchant needs some other basis for discriminating between good and bad risks. If the peddler, who has come to know the family, is ready to vouch for the customer, the merchant will be ready to make the transaction. In short, the peddler acts as a fiduciary agent, a Dun and Bradstreet for the poor, telling the merchant which family is likely to meet its obligations and which is not.

Not all peddlers are employed by stores. Many are independent enterprisers (who may have started as canvassers for stores).[13] A number of the independent peddlers have accumulated enough capital to supply their customers with major durables. These are the elite peddlers, known as "dealers," why buy appliances and furniture from local merchants at a "wholesale" price, and then sell them on credit to their customers. In these transactions, the peddler either takes the customer to the store or sends the customer to the store with his card on which he has written some such message as "Please give Mr. Jones a TV set."[14] The mer-

_____

[13] A systematic study of local merchants and peddlers would probably find that a typical pattern is to start as a canvasser, become a self-employed peddler, and finally a storekeeper.

[14] According to a former customer peddler, now in the furniture business, the peddlers' message will either read "Please _give_ Mr. Jones . . ." or "Please let Mr. Jones _pick out_ . . ." In the former case, the customer is given the merchandise right away; in the latter, it is set aside for him until the peddler says that it is all right to let the customer have it. The peddler uses the second form when his customer is already heavily in debt to him

chant then sells the customer the TV set at a price much higher than he would ordinarily charge. The "dealer" is generally given two months to pay the merchant the "wholesale" price, and meanwhile he takes over the responsibility of collecting from his customer. Some "dealers" are so successful that they employ canvassers in their own right.[15] And some merchants do so much business with "dealers" that they come to think of themselves as "wholesalers" even though they are fully prepared to do their own retail business.

Independent peddlers without much capital also have economic relations with local merchants. They act as brokers, directing their customers to neighborhood stores that will extend them credit. And for this service they of course receive a commission. In these transactions, it is the merchant who accepts the risks and assumes the responsibility for collecting payments. The peddler who acts as a broker performs the same function as the merchant in the T.O. system. He knows which merchants will accept great risk and which will not, and directs his customers accordingly.

There are, then, three kinds of customer peddlers operating in these low-income neighborhoods who cooperate with local merchants: the canvassers who are employed directly by the stores; the small entrepreneurs who act as brokers; and the more successful entrepreneurs who operate as "dealers." A fourth type of peddler consists of salesmen representing large companies not necessarily located in the neighborhood. These men are, for the most part, canvassers for firms specializing in a particular commodity, e.g., encyclopedias, vacuum cleaners, or pots and pans. They differ from the other peddlers by specializing in what they sell and by depending more on contracts and legal controls. They are also less interested in developing continuous relationships with their customers.

Peddlers thus aid the local merchants by finding customers, evaluating them as credit risks, and helping in the collection of payments. And as the merchants themselves point out, these services add greatly to the cost of the goods. One storekeeper said that peddlers are apt to charge five and six times the amount the store charges for relatively inexpensive purchases. Pointing to a religious picture which he sells for $5, he maintained that peddlers sell it for as much as $30. And he estimated that the peddler adds 30 to 50 per cent to the final sales price of appliances and furniture.

UNETHICAL AND ILLEGAL PRACTICES

The interviewers uncovered some evidence that some local merchants engage in the illegal practice of selling reconditioned furniture and appliances as new. Of course, no merchant would admit that he did this himself, but five of them hinted that their competitors engaged in this practice.[16] As we shall

---

and he wants to be certain that the customer will agree to the higher weekly payments that will be necessary.

[15] One tiny store in the area, with little merchandise in evidence, is reported to employ over a hundred canvassers. The owner would not consent to an interview, but the student-observers did notice that this apparently small merchant kept some four or five bookkeepers at work in a back room. The owner is obviously a "dealer" whose store is his office. As a "dealer," he has no interest in maintaining stock and displays for street trade.

[16] Events are sometimes more telling than words. During an interview with a merchant, the interviewer volunteered to

see, several of the consumers we interviewed were quite certain that they had
been victimized in this way.

One unethical, if not illegal, activity
widely practiced by stores is "bait"
advertising with its concomitant, the
"switch sale." In the competition for
customers, merchants depend heavily
upon advertising displays in their windows which announce furniture or
appliances at unusually low prices. The
customer may enter the store assuming
that the low offer in the window signi-
fies a reasonably low price line. Under
severe pressure, the storekeeper may
even be prepared to sell the merchandise at the advertised price, for not to
do so would be against the law. What
most often happens, however, is that
the unsuspecting customer is convinced
by the salesman that he doesn't really
want the goods advertised in the window and is then persuaded to buy a
smaller amount of more expensive
goods. Generally, not much persuasion
is necessary. The most popular "bait
ad" is the announcement of three rooms
of furniture for "only $149" or "only
$199." The customer who inquires
about this bargain is shown a bedroom
set consisting of two cheap and (sometimes deliberately) chipped bureaus
and one bed frame. He learns that the
spring and mattress are not included
in the advertised price, but can be had
for another $75 or $100. The living-
room set in these "specials" consists of
a fragile-looking sofa and one unmatch-
ing chair.[17]

The frequent success of this kind of
exploitation, known in the trade as the

help several men who were carrying bed
frames into the store. The owner ex-
citedly told him not to help because he
might get paint on his hands.

[17] In one store in which I inspected this
special offer, I was told by the salesman
that he would find a chair that was a
"fairly close match."

"switch sale," is reflected in this comment by one merchant: "I don't know
how they do it. They advertise three
rooms of furniture for $149 and the
customers swarm in. *They end up buying a $400 bedroom set for $600 and
none of us can believe how easy it is to
make these sales.*"

In sum, a fairly intricate system of
sales-and-credit has evolved in response to the distinctive situation of
the low-income consumer and the local
merchant. It is a system heavily slanted
in the direction of a traditional economy in which informal, personal ties
play a major part in the transaction. At
the same time it is connected to impersonal bureaucratic agencies through
the instrument of the installment contract. Should the informal system break
down, credit companies, courts of law,
and agencies of law enforcement come
to play a part.

The system is not only different from
the larger, more formal economy; in
some respects it is a *deviant* system in
which practices that violate prevailing
moral standards are commonplace. As
Merton has pointed out in his analysis
of the political machine, the persistence
of deviant social structures can only be
understood when their social functions
(as well as dysfunctions) are taken into
account.[18] The basic function of the
low-income marketing system is to provide consumer goods to people who
fail to meet the requirements of the
more legitimate, bureaucratic market, or
who choose to exclude themselves from
the larger market because they do not
feel comfortable in it. As we have seen,
the system is extraordinarily flexible.
Almost no one—however great a risk
—is turned away. Various mechanisms
sift and sort customers according to
their credit risk and match them with

[18] Robert K. Merton, *Social Theory and
Social Structure*, rev. ed. (New York: The
Free Press of Glencoe, 1957), pp. 71–82.

merchants ready to sell them the goods they want. Even the family on welfare is permitted to maintain its self-respect by consuming in much the same way as do its social peers who happen not to be on welfare. Whether the system, with its patently exploitative features, can be seriously altered without the emergence of more legitimate institutions to perform its functions, is a question to be considered at length in the concluding chapter of this book.

WELFARE PROBLEMS OF THE CITIES

Arthur J. Naparstek and George T. Martin

One of the most recent proposals made by President Nixon is a reform of our nation's welfare system. Implementation of many of his plans (universal minimum level, incentives to work) still face stern opposition. Cries of "welfare state" and "too little, too late" are heard in response.

We must come to grips with a program that does little more than tear down the spirit of those who receive welfare. A welfare reform will not solve the problems of the cities but it is an essential step in any program designed to uplift both the physical condition and the spirit of the poor.

In recent years, the plight of the American cities—particularly the inner city—has been labelled a "crisis." The rhetoric used to describe this crisis includes frequent references to anarchy, radical change, crime in the streets, and breakdowns in law and order. However, although it is true that violence has occurred with increasing frequency in the slums of many American cities, the conditions in the inner city have existed for a long time. The rhetoric of crisis is, principally, a response to the current problems in black-white relations, and not necessarily to significant urban problems. More specifically, this rhetoric is a result of a feeling of some members of the white majority that they are threatened by a black minority. The rhetoric of crisis was not propagated around critical urban problems such as air and water pollution, trans-

portation, taxation, and education. The term "crisis" reflects a fear of black violence.

The mood of crisis has elicited a series of rather hysterical responses in the nation's cities, including massive police and military actions, repressive laws, and the initiation of quickly-conceived crash programs in the areas of employment, housing, and public welfare. Most of these programs have been aimed at cooling off the so-called crisis; many have been ineffective, if not irrelevant. Some of these programs, directed towards alleviating or even curing the problems, have actually created further frustrations.

The nation's present urban "crisis" can be more accurately described and treated as an endemic problem—a chronic disease. This is not simply a problem in semantics, for the manner

From *Current History*, December 1968. Reprinted by permission of the publisher.

in which the nation responds to the situation is based, in large measure, on how it is perceived and in what rhetoric it is expressed.

It is clear that there are serious difficulties structured into our urban society, including housing segregation and social discrimination leading to ghetto formation and breakdowns in the educational system, the employment market, and in political structures. Both as a cause and a result, the bitter facts of urban poverty underlie and pervade all these difficulties. As far as the general public is concerned, this poverty has only recently been "rediscovered."

One of the major problems confronting American urban centers, then, is poverty. For the black poor in the ghettos, of course, poverty is bred and nurtured by institutionalized racism. For both the black and the white poor, however, poverty leads to powerlessness. Poverty is not new to American cities—historically, it has been a chronic condition. In fact, even black poverty is not new to the American city. What is relatively new is violence on the part of the black poor and society's resulting realization of the grim facts of urban poverty.

For the past six years, the nation has been committed to a struggle against this poverty. The current strategy is to develop more jobs and to train the poor the fill them. Efforts to increase the number of jobs and to improve the employability of potential workers have resulted in a bewildering array of programs. Federally-funded programs stemming from area redevelopment projects, from the Manpower Development and Training Act, from community work and training programs for public assistance recipients under the Social Security Act, from the Office of Economic Opportunity, and from the Department of Labor's education, training, and human reclamation projects

have all been initiated within the past six years. However, there is a serious question as to whether these employment and self-help programs are relevant to the majority of the nation's poor.[1]

Data from the Bureau of the Census for the year 1963 show that, of a total of about 35 million people in the nation who live in poverty, almost one-half (15 million) are age 18 or younger, and over one-seventh (5.2 million) are age 65 or older. Also, of the some 7 million families who comprise the poverty group, over 1.5 million are headed by a female with at least one child age 18 or younger. Moreover, more than one-fourth of these poor families are headed by a fulltime worker.[2] Thus, of those people who live in poverty, most are either too old or too young to work, and many others are already fully employed. As a consequence, government programs with an employment and training focus are irrelevant to the majority of the nation's poor.

Indeed, a careful analysis of the so-called war on poverty clearly reveals that the large bulk of the poor remain untouched by programs with this emphasis. One of the major difficulties is that self-help, bootstrap-type programs, while perhaps desirable in themselves, have been superimposed on a welfare system designed to deal with the economic and social problems of the 1930's and totally inadequate for contemporary needs.

As a matter of fact, the net effect of this unholy matrimony has been largely negative. In its discussion of public

[1] Eveline M. Burns, "Where Welfare Falls Short," *The Public Interest*, Fall 1965.

[2] Mollie Orshansky, "Counting the Poor: Another Look at the Poverty Profile," *Social Security Bulletin*, January 1965.

assistance, the Report of the National Advisory Commission on Civil Disorders indicated that the present welfare system contributes materially to the tensions and the social disorganizations which have contributed to urban riots.[3] Of the reasons which can be offered for this seeming paradox, two stand out: (1) the government programs do not basically reduce the powerlessness of their recipients, as they are most often controlled by the nonpoor; (2) the programs have often raised aspiration levels without materially raising actual levels of living. It is this latter factor—the sense of relative deprivation—which may explain how many of the government programs created to remedy the nation's urban problems have actually helped to perpetuate them by increasing the frustration and feeling of lack of hope among the urban poor.

For example, some of the employment programs have resulted in a process referred to as "creaming." In "creaming," only the most talented and skilled of the urban poor are recruited for programs, while the poor masses are left relatively untouched. Two consequences of this are significant: (1) actual and potential leadership in the ghettos is virtually eliminated; (2) the masses of the poor who are left unaffected by the programs are even further frustrated.

PUBLIC WELFARE AND POVERTY

The major thrust of the government's programs has been to deal with the symptoms of poverty, not with its causes. Programs have not been designed to alter significantly the social, political, and economic systems which sustain poverty in the world's most affluent nation.

[3] *Report of the National Advisory Commission on Civil Disorders* (New York: Bantam Books, 1968), p. 457.

The nation's current public assistance system was a product of the New Deal. It was initiated in 1935 by the Committee on Economic Security and was intended to be residual in nature. In other words, it was assumed that the economic and social system was basically sound. Unemployment compensation would take care of any unemployment that rose out of temporary economic readjustments. Old-age assistance and aid-to-dependent-children would gradually be replaced by social security programs—primarily old age and survivors' insurance. Finally, locally-financed programs—known as general assistance programs—would cover those few not included in these programs. The public welfare programs remain residual in the 1960's still unable to reduce national poverty on a systematic basis. At present, less than 10 million of the nation's some 35 million poor people receive any income maintenance payments under public assistance.[4] In spite of this fact, the system is still overloaded.[5]

Since 1935, the composition of the public assistance recipient groups has changed substantially. The Aid to Families with Dependent Children (AFDC) programs is a prime example. In 1935, the typical recipient in the program was a white widow with one or two children; today, the typical recipient is a black woman with three or four children who, moreover, lives in a central city ghetto.[6]

Among all the current national welfare programs, AFDC and AFDC-UP (Aid to Families with Dependent Children-with Unemployed Parents) clearly

[4] Orshansky, *op. cit.*

[5] For a discussion of this point, see Eveline M. Burns, "Social Security in Evolution: Toward What?" *Social Service Review*, June 1965.

[6] Burns, "Where Welfare Falls Short," *op. cit.*

have the greatest impact upon family life in the central cities and perhaps contribute to the chronically bad conditions there. States and local governments contribute an average of about 45 per cent of the cost of these programs. However, each state sets grant levels for its residents; consequently, monthly payments vary widely. The range is from $9.30 monthly for each AFDC recipient in Mississippi to $62.55 in New York.[7] Not only are payments pitifully inadequate, they are often accompanied by the degrading indignities of the means test and by unconscionable delays. It is not surprising that life on AFDC in the ghetto has been described as a treadmill to nowhere.

In his message to Congress on the welfare of children on February 8, 1967, President Lyndon Johnson pointed out that in 1966: (1) 12 million children in families living below the poverty line received no AFDC benefits (only 3.2 million children received any benefits in 1966), (2) 33 states do not even meet their own minimum standards for subsistence in their payments, (3) a number of states discourage parents from working by arbitrarily reducing welfare payments when parents earn their first dollar.[8] This fact emphasizes the confiscatory nature of present regulations and their negative effect upon the motivation to work of all family members, including adolescents.

It is clear that the present system excludes a great number of persons who are in need and provides only minimum assistance to those who are included. But perhaps the most serious indictment of the present system is that, for the relatively few poor who are reached,

restrictions which encourage dependency and undermine self-respect are the rule. It is in this sense that current public assistance programs, particularly AFDC, have contributed substantially to the sense of powerlessness felt by the urban poor.[9]

Although public assistance laws are inadequate and punitive, administrative practices often are far worse. Broad discretion in doling out benefits is given to administrators—largely because there is little consensus at the legislative level concerning the programs' conceptual goals. State statutes are often vague, and the task of interpreting the law falls upon the welfare bureaucracies, so that political struggles are shifted from legislative to administrative arenas.[10] Indeed, it has been asserted that the present climate of public welfare administration in the nation is based upon insidious, paranoid, and primitive preoccupations stemming from the poor-law heritage of "keeping the town books clean."[11]

STRATEGIES FOR CHANGE

Critics of the current public welfare system have advanced several strategies aimed at reform or elimination of the present program. These strategies focus on active protest against the welfare bureaucracies and on legal redress of grievances by recipients through the

[7] *Report of the National Advisory Commission on Civil Disorders*, p. 457.

[8] Lyndon B. Johnson, Message to Congress on the Welfare of Children, Washington, D.C., February 8, 1967.

[9] See *Report of the National Advisory Commission on Civil Disorders, Chapter III*, "The Welfare System," pp. 457–461, for further discussion of how the welfare system contributes to the powerlessness of the poor.

[10] Richard A. Cloward and Richard M. Elman, "Poverty, Injustice and the Welfare State," *The Nation*, February 28 and March 7, 1966.

[11] Alan D. Wade, "The Guaranteed Minimum Income: Social Work's Challenge and Opportunity," *Social Work*, January 1967, p. 98.

nation's courts. In addition, several alternative approaches to income maintenance have recently been much discussed.

The strategy of active protest centers upon the organization of welfare recipient groups across the nation. The general focus of these groups has been to demand from the present system the maximum it can legally give and to confront the system with its own inequities.[12] A more strategic goal of the welfare protest movement is the effective destruction of the present system and its replacement by a totally new approach to income maintenance, perhaps, in the form of a guaranteed income. As some protesters plan it, the collapse of the system would come through overloading it—that is, efforts would be made to register the millions of people currently deemed eligible but not receiving assistance. The assumption is that an already overloaded public welfare bureaucracy can tolerate little addition to its rolls—that a breakdown would occur; any change would be for the better.[13]

Such organization of welfare recipients into a protest movement serves the direct purpose of reducing the feeling—as well as the fact—of powerlessness. One recent study of AFDC mothers has shown that members of a welfare client organization were more likely to have feelings of mastery and control than non-members.[14]

The strategy of legal change of the present system has focused upon the constitutional rights of the welfare recipient.[15] Recent decisions by state courts have overturned such punitive public assistance regulations as the man-in-the-house rule and residency requirements. The decision overturning the man-in-the-house rule has been upheld by the Supreme Court;[16] the residency requirement ruling is currently on its docket. Two types of legal action are required: one designed to achieve basic changes in the structure of social welfare laws (usually through the application of constitutional principles to the present laws), and the other designed to insure that present laws are implemented equitably at the administrative level.[17]

Other approaches to change are being tentatively developed through experiments by such agencies as the Office of Economic Opportunity and by Model Cities. For example, the Model Cities program is considering the funding of local experiments with the family allowance scheme.[18] This past summer the Office of Economic Opportunity awarded a community action program grant to the national coordinating organization of welfare rights groups "for a program to train welfare recipients on welfare rights, education and information."

Prominent among the possible alternatives to the nation's present income

[12] For example, only a minority of the states actually live up to their own minimum standards of subsistence in welfare payments. Protest in several states has focused on this fact.

[13] For an exposition of this strategy, see Richard A. Cloward and Frances Fox Piven, "A Strategy to End Poverty," *The Nation*, May 2, 1966.

[14] Helene Levens, "Organizational Affiliation and Powerlessness: A Case Study of the Welfare Poor," *Social Problems*, Summer 1968.

[15] See, for example, Charles A. Reich, "Individual Rights and Social Welfare: The Emerging Legal Issues," *Yale Law Journal*, June 1965.

[16] See *Current History*, August 1968, p. 127.

[17] Cloward and Elman, "Poverty, Injustice and the Welfare State," *op. cit.*

[18] The Office of Economic Opportunity has already funded an experimental project concerning the negative income tax. The research is under the overall direction of the Institute of Research on Poverty at the University of Wisconsin.

maintenance system which have been discussed in recent years are the negative income tax, the demogrant (a government grant of money to categories of individuals, either universal or partial), and a combination of basic reforms in both the public welfare and Social Security programs. All of these alternatives have been loosely referred to under the rubric of the "guaranteed income" when, in fact, only the universal demogrant would result in a guaranteed income for all citizens.

The negative income tax proposal, recently popularized by conservative economist Milton Friedman, has taken various forms and has been presented for differing reasons.[19] All the proposals, however, would use the nation's tax structure in some fashion. The basic idea is to define minimum income for all citizens—perhaps adjusted regionally—and to supplement the income of those citizens which does not reach the minimum. Friedman would make the negative income tax replace all current income maintenance programs; the basic goal is to save money through the elimination of complicated administrative structures. Others would make the program an important supplement to current income maintenance programs.

The partial demogrant would allot funds to certain categories of the nation's population, such as children, regardless of their income. Some form of the children's or family allowance already exists in some 60 nations in the world, including almost all of the industrialized nations.[20] All children of

a specified age category receive a set allowance, paid to their parents. The universal demogrant, on the other hand, would allot funds to all persons. Each citizen would receive a specified amount of money.[21] Utilization of the universal demogrant would probably be the best and most direct method of reducing the powerlessness of the poor. It could be used to redistribute the greatest amount of money to the poor with the fewest conditions attached.[22] The great problem with this scheme is, of course, its very high initial cost, although taxes could recover the bulk of funds granted the non-poor.

Reforms in both the present public welfare and Social Security programs would be the least revolutionary of all the alternatives discussed. One important thrust of this approach is aimed at the creation of federal legislation which would be directed at establishing national minimum standards, uniform and applicable in all 50 states, for public assistance payments.[23]

The public welfare system is only one example of an overworked and outdated governmental system which attempts to serve the nation's cities. Although reform of public welfare is not

Eveline M. Burns (ed.), *Children's Allowances and the Economic Welfare of Children: The Report of a Conference* (New York: Citizens' Committee for Children, Inc., 1968).

[21] See, for example, Burns, "Social Security in Evolution: Toward What?" *op. cit.*

[22] The assumption is, of course, that money is a significant source of power.

[23] See, for example, "Having the Power, We Have the Duty," Report of the Advisory Council on Public Welfare (Washington, D.C.: U.S. Government Printing Office, 1966); George E. Rohrilich, "Guaranteed-Minimum-Income Proposals and the Unfinished Business of Social Security," *Social Service Review*, June 1967.

[19] See, for example, Milton Friedman, *Capitalism and Freedom* (Chicago: University of Chicago Press, 1962); Edward E. Schwartz, "A Way to End the Means Test," *Social Work*, July 1964.

[20] See, for example, James C. Vadakin, *Children, Poverty, and Family Allowances* (New York: Basic Books, 1968);

a panacea for the urban "crisis," it is a prerequisite to the success of a wide range of programs. Programs to eliminate bad housing and racial discrimination and upgrade public education and improve city services have little chance of widespread success if the nation does not come to grips with the critical deficiencies of its public welfare system.

Indeed, the most pressing issue confronting American cities is the powerlessness of those who are poor. Only through the difficult task of restructuring the nation's economic system in such a way as to provide each citizen with an adequate and secure income can this problem be resolved. Although there are many fronts upon which to attack the urban "crisis," the problems of public welfare, poverty, and the powerlessness of the poor deserve priority in both policy and action.

THE GREAT RAT DEBATE

Congressional Record

It is a fairly common event to read of a dog biting a child, but when we read of rats attacking children we all become upset. A proposal was brought before the United States House of Representatives in 1967 to finance a rat extermination program. The comments you will read give you a clear look at the varying personal philosophies of our congressmen regarding the poor. While some of their remarks are humorous, the human misery brought about by these vermin is scarcely cause for laughter in our congressional halls.

RAT EXTERMINATION ACT
OF 1967

Mr. Matsunaga. Mr. Speaker, by direction of the Committee on Rules, I call up House Resolution 749, and ask for its immediate consideration.

H. Res. 749

Resolved, That upon the adoption of this resolution it shall be in order to move that the House resolve itself into the Committee of the Whole House on the State of the Union for the consideration of the bill (H.R. 11000) to provide Federal financial assistance to help cities and communities of the Nation develop and carry out intensive local programs of rat control and extermination. . . .

The Speaker. The gentleman from Hawaii is recognized for 1 hour . . .

Mr. Speaker, I believe we can have a lot of fun with this bill. I am sure there will be humor injected into the matter throughout the debate. Some may call it the second "antiriot" bill. Others may call it the civil rats bill. Still others may insist that we should make this applicable to two-legged rats as well as four-legged ones. And there may be those who claim that this is throwing money

Source: *Congressional Record,* July 20, 1967, pp. 19548–19555.

down a rathole. But, Mr. Speaker, in the final analysis there is a serious side to this proposed legislation.

The need for this legislation is clearly evident in the fact that last year, in seven cities alone in the United States there were approximately 1,000 reported cases of ratbite. There is reason to believe that the actual statistics are much higher because many persons are reluctant to report ratbite incidents, and many units of local and State government do not require such reports. Only 2 days ago, it was reported by the news media that an 8-month-old boy was bitten to death by rats right here in our Nation's Capital. What a shame that we should allow such a thing to happen in any of our cities or towns in the world's most affluent nation.

In addition to the disease-carrying threat which these pesky animals pose, they, in fact, cause enormous damage to both food and property. It has been estimated that there are at least 90 million rats in the United States and that each causes an average of $10 damage per year. This means a national loss of $900 million to the rats every year, unless we do something about it. . . .

H.R. 11000 would authorize Federal assistance to cover two-thirds of the cost of 3-year local programs for rat extermination and control. The grants would be made to local governments, and the bill requires that the community have an approved workable program in order to be eligible for such aid. The Secretary of Housing and Urban Development, who would make the grants, would be required to cooperate and consult with other departments which have responsibilities related to the problem of rat control. Appropriations of $20 million would be authorized for each of the fiscal years 1968 and 1969 to make these grants. In view of the savings in property damages and the

relief in human misery, which are sure to result, this legislation may be properly considered as a worthwhile investment.

Mr. Speaker, I urge the adoption of House Resolution 749 in order that H.R. 11000 may be considered.

Mr. Gross. Mr. Speaker, will the gentleman yield?

Mr. Matsunaga. I yield to the gentleman from Iowa.

Mr. Gross. I thank the gentleman for yielding. I believe the gentleman said that there are some 90 million rats in the United States of the four-legged variety. I do not know how many others there may be.

Is that correct; 90 million rats?

Mr. Matsunaga. It has been estimated by three experts in the area of rat control that there are approximately 90 million rats, or a minimum of that many. The Department of the Interior estimated it to be about 100 million, and the World Health Organization has estimated that there is a rat for every person in the world. The gentleman can take his choice.

Mr. Gross. Does the gentleman imply that with the passage of this $40 million bill we are then going to embark upon rat killing around the world?

Mr. Matsunaga. Not around the world. This bill would be confined to the United States, to cities, townships, and communities within our own country.

Mr. Gross. I have read the hearings fairly carefully. I do not know whether the gentleman has or not. Nowhere do I find any evidence as to who took the rat census in the United States, much less in the world.

Mr. Matsunaga. The experts in this area did. . . .

Mr. Gross. Mr. Speaker, will the gentleman yield further?

Mr. Matsunaga. I yield further to the gentleman from Iowa.

Mr. Gross. The gentleman spoke of city rats. What about country rats?

Mr. Matsunaga. The country rats are being taken care of under existing programs. . . .

Mr. Haley. Mr. Speaker, will the gentleman yield?

Mr. Matsunaga. I yield to the gentleman from Florida.

Mr. Haley. Mr. Speaker, I wonder sometime if some of our distinguished committees that bring before us a monstrosity such as this, would just take into consideration the fact that we have a lot of cat lovers in the Nation, and why not just buy some cats and turn them loose on the rats and thereby we could take care of this situation, without any $25 million from the Treasury of the United States.

Mr. Matsunaga. I would support such a program, if the gentleman from Florida will introduce such a bill. . . .

Mr. Latta. Mr. Speaker, I yield myself such time as I may consume.

Mr. Speaker, I agree with my colleague, the gentleman from Hawaii [Mr. Matsunaga], that this matter does have a serious side, and I hasten to point out that the serious side of this piece of legislation is the sum of $20 million for fiscal year 1968 and for fiscal year 1969, another $20 million, and Lord knows how much thereafter, because this program does not terminate after 2 years. This is the beginning of an all-new program.

Mr. Speaker, every person with experience in this Congress well knows that when these programs start, future years bring greater and greater appropriations. This will be only the beginning.

I say to my colleagues, in view of the fiscal situation facing this country today, this is one program we can do without. . . .

Mr. Speaker, it seems to me that here is a request for $20 million for 1968

and $20 million for 1969, that we can refuse.

Mr. Speaker, there is still some local responsibility remaining in this country and the killing of rats is one of them. This is not a national matter.

There is also some responsibility on the part of individual citizens. Certainly the Federal Government cannot, and should not, fulfill every need or wish of every one of its citizens. Our tax structure cannot stand it. The matter of putting out a little bit of rat poison should not be requested of the Federal Government. . . .

The rat bill before us came to this Congress in a Presidential recommendation, if you please.

It seems to me, my colleagues, that here is a matter, that could be laid aside until the fiscal situation in this country has brightened. Certainly when we are expending the billions of dollars that we are in Vietnam, we can lay this proposal aside. If there is any local responsibility on the part of local government remaining, this proposal can be laid aside. If the individual has any responsibility remaining, we can lay this matter aside. The individual does not want to pay for a new rat control program at this time with all of the costly new Federal employees to be employed to put out rat poison that the individual citizen could put out for himself.

Mr. Speaker, this bill is extremely broad and the sky is the limit. I call your attention to the bill itself.

On page 2 line 10, it says:

(2) the elimination or modification of physical surroundings and conditions (including rat harborages and food supplies) which encourage or tend to encourage persistent rat habitation and increases in their numbers; and

It reads, "the elimination or modification of physical surroundings." This, if you please, can mean a building. They could move in and tear down a building under this legislation.

Oh, it might be denied that they have that intent and purpose, but I have been around here long enough to know that if you give the bureaucrats the general language, they are going to interpret it and use it any way they see fit. . . .

Mr. Broyhill of Virginia. Mr. Speaker will the gentleman yield?

Mr. Latta. I yield to the gentleman from Virginia.

Mr. Broyhill of Virginia. Mr. Speaker, the gentleman made a very clear statement on how this rat bill discriminates against a lot of rats in this country. The committee report also shows that the bill discriminates against 97½ percent of the rats.

But I think the most profound statement the gentleman made is the fact that it does set up a new bureau and sets up possibly a commissioner on rats or an administrator of rats and a bunch of new bureaucrats on rats. There is no question but that there will be a great demand for a lot of rat patronage. I think by the time we get through taking care of all of the bureaucrats in this new rat bureau along with the waste and empire building, none of the $40 million will be left to take care of the 2½ percent of the rats who were supposed to be covered in the bill.

Mr. Speaker, I think the "rat smart thing" for us to do is to vote down this rat bill "rat now."

Mr. Latta. I may say to the gentleman that when he raises the question of discriminating between city and country rats, it also discriminates against persons suffering from bites from other animals.

Forgetting about the rodents for a moment, it was mentioned by the gentleman from Hawaii that we have over 1,000 rat bite cases in the United States in a year's time.

How about the snake bite cases?

If we are going to start eradicating all the rats—how about snakes in the West? How about bugs? You can go into homes and apartment buildings here in the city of Washington and find bugs galore. What are you going to do about the bugs? Are we to forget about the people bitten by bugs? Should we start a bug corps? . . .

Mr. Gross. Mr. Speaker, will the gentleman yield?

Mr. Latta. I yield to the gentleman from Iowa.

Mr. Gross. On the matter of rat bites, it would be interesting to know, how many children are bitten by squirrels that they feed and try to handle. On the basis of that does anyone suggest a program to exterminate squirrels?

Mr. Latta. The gentleman raises a question which indicates that the bill has a lot of possibilities for amendment.

Mr. Speaker, I yield 5 minutes to the gentleman from Iowa [Mr. Gross].

Mr. Gross. Mr. Speaker, this bill is so ludicrous that we should not even entertain the rule. We should vote down the rule on this bill, and it is my hope the House will do just that. . . .

I am constrained to believe the program is devised to take care of some more broken down political hacks. . . .

Mr. Gross. Who is going to run it, there is not going to be a high commissioner or administrator of the rat corps?

Mr. Ashley. Mr. Speaker, we are talking about a very modest program.

Mr. Gross. I am sure the gentleman is—at $40 million. I have heard that before. . . .

Mr. Patman. Mr. Speaker, will the gentleman yield?

Mr. Gross. I yield very briefly to the gentleman from Texas.

Mr. Patman. Mr. Speaker, this is a bill to prevent infant mortality, unnecessary infant mortality, and for the health and protection of the people.

Mr. Gross. The gentleman can make that speech if he wants to on his own time.

I am trying to get information as to who is responsible for this monstrosity. I noticed in the paper last night that there is a Peace Corps contingent from Argentina in this country. We are the underdeveloped, the underprivileged country now. The Argentines have invaded us with a Peace Corps, and they apparently are going to hold forth in two of the most underdeveloped and underprivileged areas of the country, in Los Angeles, Calif., and in Boston, Mass.

I would like to suggest that whoever is running the Argentine Peace Corps in the United States—and we are financing it in this country—should assign the members to clean out the rats in Boston and Los Angeles. . . .

Mr. Matsunaga. Mr. Speaker, I yield 5 minutes to the gentlewoman from Michigan [Mrs. Griffiths].

Mrs. Griffiths. Mr. Speaker, I thank the chairman.

Before this bill becomes too funny, I would like to say a few words for it. I am in support of this bill, Mr. Speaker. When I first came to this Congress I asked the Library of Congress how much money this Nation had spent on defense in its history. They put some Ph. D.'s to work on the subject, and after 3 months replied that at that time —13 years ago—we had spent more than $1 trillion on defense. I observed the other day, when we had the Defense appropriation bill—which as I recall was for more than $75 billion—there was only one person who voted "No."

I would like to point out to those who may not be aware of it or to those who may have forgotten it, that rats are Johnny-come-latelys to recorded history. They were unknown in the ancient cities of the world. They came in out of the Arabian deserts about the 12th century, and from that day to this they have killed more human beings than all of the generals in the world combined. They have made Genghis Khan, Hitler, and all the other men look like pikers. Man has attempted to kill them and he has won a few battles, but he has lost the war.

The only enemy that has ever really killed rats is other rats.

For the benefit of those who may not know it, the average rat lives 3 years. It has a rootless tooth that grows 29½ inches in those 3 years. They have been known to cut through 4 feet of reinforced concrete.

All of the methods that one could possibly use cannot conceivably kill off more than 98 percent of the rats in one block. If there are left two males and 10 females, there will be 3,000 rats in 1 year to replace those that have been killed. . . .

Rats are a living cargo of death. Their tails swish through sewers and over that food we eat. Their stomachs are filled with tularemia, amebic dysentery. They carry the most deadly diseases, and some think it is funny. Some do not want to spend $40 million.

Mr. Speaker, if we are going to spend $79 billion to try to kill off a few Vietcong, believe me I would spend $40 million to kill off the most devastating enemy man has ever had.

Mr. Latta. Mr. Speaker, I have no further requests for time.

Mr. Matsunaga. Mr. Speaker, I yield such time as he may consume to the gentleman from Ohio [Mr. Feighan].

Mr. Feighan. Mr. Speaker, H.R. 11000, a bill to provide $20 million of Federal financial assistance to help cities and communities develop and carry out rat control programs, represents a most significant legislative attempt to meet the challenge of an unbelievable problem in our modern industrial age. . . .

Cleveland averages well over 50 rat bites a year. This figure is low because many persons are reluctant to report such incidents and also because many doctors, totally unfamiliar with the rat bite, do not recognize it. Obviously, rats pose an ominous disease-carrying threat. Were an epidemic to arise, it would quickly spread throughout the city. The great number of rats present also cause great property damage. In 1962, the damage in Cleveland was estimated to be approximately $2,000,-000. This figure has risen to $3,000,000 annually. These destructive rodents chew up doors, walls, floors, woodwork, undermine foundations both interior and exterior, and undermine sidewalks and streets.

Finally, rat infestation has a tremendous demoralizing effect on the populace in these areas. They are reluctant to admit that rats exist and, thus, frequently do not cooperate with the Federal and State authorities in eliminating the menace. They are reluctant to repair or improve their property, for they know all too well that the rats will destroy it again. When the slightly above poverty level or average income neighborhoods become infested, the inhabitants move further out of the central city, thus accelerating the cancerous spread of deteriorated housing.

Under the auspices of Mr. Stephen Chorvat, chief of the bureau of neighborhood conservation, the public health service in Cleveland has been working diligently to contain and eliminate the rats. However, the present lack of manpower and facilities has made the task insurmountable. Cleveland has seven neighborhood sanitarians and 14 sanitarian aides fighting the city's millions of rats. They estimate a need for 25 sanitarians and 100 aides, as well as much additional equipment to exterminate these rodents. . . .

Mr. Devine. The committee report claims "many children" are attacked, "maimed and even killed by rats, as an everyday occurrence." Come, now, let us have some supporting information. I am sure if rats were killing children every day, all of us would have heard something about it. The report goes on to say Philadelphia, St. Louis, and Cleveland have all recently averaged over 50 ratbites per year. Golly, almost one a week—so, spend $40 million.

Inquiry through local dealers indicates rattraps—not mousetraps—sell for $3.30 per dozen or about 28 cents each. A pretty fair brand of cheese costs 49 cents per pound and would bait 35 traps. So, for an extremely small personal investment, nearly every citizen could cooperate and eliminate this problem, and at the same time, save their Government $40 million. Would not this seem to be a wise step, particularly when the President and his advisers are calling on all Americans for more taxes to pay for the costs of Government?

Finally, one of our respected colleagues tells me he has about 23 cats in and around his barns, all of which he will make available to HUD, without charge. These feline ratcatchers are most effective, particularly since they are led by a highly respected tomcat called Cotton that has earned a most enviable reputation in the ratcatching department.

Seriously, here is an excellent opportunity for the President, the administration, the Congress, to do more than pay lipservice to reducing Federal spending, and I urge my colleagues to vote against this bill known as H.R. 11000. . . .

Mr. Barrett. Mr. Speaker, the bill before us today, H.R. 11000, the Rat Extermination Act of 1967, is one of the most humane and compassionate bills ever to be considered by this body. The rat menace which afflicts our urban areas is a shocking disgrace to our Nation, whose affluence is the wonder of the modern world. . . .

We must act and act now to rid our cities of this ghastly threat to decent and safe living. And we must provide substantial Federal aid to get the job done because, as everyone knows, our cities do not have the financial resources and the tax sources to even carry on their present level of municipal activities.

Mr. Speaker, I have noticed an unfortunate tendency among a number of people when this bill is discussed to indulge in jesting remarks, puns, and supposedly comical cliches. Let me assure my colleagues, Mr. Speaker, that in many of the areas of our cities this is no laughing or joking matter. It is a matter of the utmost seriousness and gravity. Believe me, Mr. Speaker, there is nothing funny about rats and rat bites. . . .

Mr. Grover. Mr. Speaker, I have requested information on annual bites from the health department in Nassau County, N.Y., a part of which county I represent.

The following bites are documented and I list them for the interest of the opponents and proponents of the legislation before us.

Bites by	
Dogs	5,779
Cats	323
Hamsters	123
Squirrels	73
Rabbits	51
Monkeys	19
Horses	18
Mice	39
Raccoon	7
Gerbils (desert rodent)	5
Possum	4
Chipmunk	4
Guinea pig	4
Bear	1
Mole	1
Chinchilla	1
Woodchuck	1

There were no wild rat bites and 16 bites by experiment-test rats.

In 1963 there was noted one llama bite.

Mr. Bray. Mr. Speaker, the American people, of a certainty, are against rats; but this bill, which makes control of rats a Federal responsibility, reaches the height of absurdity. . . .

I am well aware that the liberal left, who would have the Government care for everyone and also have the Government dominate everyone's lives, will accuse those of us who do not want the Government in the rat control business of being for rats. I certainly want to eliminate rats but a Federal bureau certainly is not the answer. Now, I do not believe the Federal Government should pay for haircuts but this does not mean I am for beatniks. Neither do I believe the Government should buy soap for everyone, but this does not indicate I am against bathing. . . .

We who vote against this bill are well aware that we will be accused of being for rats, and against people. However, most of us were willing to face that baseless charge, in order to keep our Government from being financially ruined to the point where it cannot carry out its true responsibilities. I trust that the bureaucrats who are so eager to do everything for us will leave us a few pleasures and duties to perform for ourselves. . . .

Mr. Fino. Mr. Speaker, I rise in support of this bill with some misgivings. This legislation, although a mere drop in the bucket, constitutes a real breakthrough for the Department of Housing and Urban Development. . . .

However, I do want to praise HUD for recommending this bill because it is the first HUD bill which is not a payoff to the big builders or a gravy train for ivory tower social planners.

This rat bill is a bold step forward for HUD policy. Many of these rats HUD wants to exterminate have grown fat on liberal benevolence. Many of these same rats were born in slums financed by welfare handouts and perpetuated by pro-slumlord Democratic Federal tax policies. . . .

For too many years, local city Democratic administrations have been giving tax breaks to slumlords. These same rats that HUD now wants to kill off spent their underprivileged childhoods nourishing themselves on garbage left uncollected by local city Democratic administrations. These same rats hid in darkness perpetuated by payola-ridden Democratic building departments.

For these reasons, I am sure America's rats are going to be bitterly resentful that this administration has turned on them after all these many years. . . .

Mr. Ryan. Mr. Speaker, H.R. 11000, the Rat Extermination Act of 1967, is important.

Although the rat extermination bill will only be really adequate if it is enacted in conjunction with a massive legislative attack aimed at eliminating the slums, its purposes are nonetheless in the interest of all Americans to whom rats are a recurrent problem. The rat is not just a symbol of poverty. It is one of the cruelest manifestations of the urban slum. For the mother who has to leave her young children alone in her house, the rat is a danger that the mother thinks about in dread. For the family on welfare, the food which the rat seems to so readily devour cuts deeply into their small allowance. For the 14,000 people who were bitten by

rats last year, the rat is a cause of great pain. For over 5,000 people who were inflicted with plague, typhus, leptospirosis, and other rat-associated diseases, the rat has caused incomparable hardships. For the Nation that suffers over a billion dollars worth of damages in a year directly because of rats, they are a great economic loss. . . .

In Detroit an extensive effort to exterminate rats has had encouraging results. The four-point program to starve the rat, demolish his home, protect buildings from rat infestation, and kill the rat, involved improved garbage collection, home improvements, various means of rat extermination, and citizen participation. As a result the incidence of ratbites has decreased to under 20 reported cases per year.

It is a sad commentary that so few communities have even started to use the program that Detroit employed. . . .

This bill does recognize that the problem of rat control is related to the conditions of the urban slums. It has a citizen education component which will train people in the community on basic standards of health and see that sanitary and healthful conditions are maintained after the rats are eradicated. . . .

Mr. Moorhead. Mr. Speaker, I rise in support of the Rat Extermination Act of 1967. . . .

The No. 1 environmental health problem in Pittsburgh is reported to be slum housing, and we all know this to be the habitat of the rat.

Therefore, Mr. Speaker, I deem it urgent to adopt H.R. 11000 to provide a comprehensive, sophisticated approach toward eliminating this No. 1 public health nuisance—who is certainly no laughing matter—Brother Rat.

Mr. Matsunaga. Mr. Speaker, I have no further requests for time. I move the previous question.

The previous question was ordered.

The Speaker pro tempore (Mr.

Rooney of New York). The question is on the resolution.

Mr. Rhodes of Arizona. Mr. Speaker, on that I demand the yeas and nays.

The yeas and nays were ordered.

The question was taken; and there were—yeas 176, nays 207, not voting 49. . . .

POVERTY PURIFIES SOCIETY

Herbert Spencer

This article, written in 1880, presents the viewpoint that society is wrong in its efforts to prevent misery among us. The author believes that man should be "constantly excreting its unhealthy, imbecile, slow, vacillating, and faithless members" —much in the same manner as the animals of the wild kingdom. What a difference from the views of the thinking and concerned man of today?

The well-being of existing humanity, and the unfolding of it into this ultimate perfection, are both secured by that same beneficent, though severe discipline, to which the animate creation at large is subject: a discipline which is pitiless in the working out of good: a felicity-pursuing law which never swerves for the avoidance of partial and temporary suffering. The poverty of the incapable, the distresses that come upon the imprudent, the starvation of the idle, and those shoulderings aside of the weak by the strong, which leave so many "in shallows and in miseries," are the decrees of a large, far-seeing benevolence. It seems hard that an unskilfulness which with all his efforts he cannot overcome, should entail hunger upon the artisan. It seems hard that a labourer incapacitated by sickness from competing with his stronger fellows, should have to bear the resulting privations. It seems hard that widows and orphans should be left to struggle for life or death. Nevertheless, when regarded not separately, but in connection with the interests of universal humanity, these harsh fatalities are seen to be full of the highest beneficence—the same beneficence which brings to early graves the children of diseased parents, and singles out the low-spirited, the intemperate, and the debilitated as the victims of an epidemic.

There are many very amiable people —people over whom in so far as their feelings are concerned we may fitly rejoice—who have not the nerve to look this matter fairly in the face. Disabled as they are by their sympathies with present suffering, from duly regarding ultimate consequences, they pursue a course which is very injudicious, and in the end even cruel. We do not consider it true kindness in a mother to gratify her child with sweetmeats that are certain to make it ill. We should think it a very foolish sort of benevolence which led a surgeon to let his patient's disease progress to a fatal issue, rather than inflict pain by an

From *Social Statics* by Herbert Spencer (New York: A. Appleton and Company, 1880; 1st pub., 1850), pp. 353–356.

operation. Similarly, we must call those spurious philanthropists, who, to prevent present misery, would entail greater misery upon future generations. All defenders of a poor-law must, however, be classed amongst such. That rigorous necessity which, when allowed to act on them, becomes so sharp a spur to the lazy, and so strong a bridle to the random, these paupers friends would repeal, because of the wailings it here and there produces. Blind to the fact, that under the natural order of things society is constantly excreting its unhealthy, imbecile, slow, vacillating, faithless members, these unthinking, though well-meaning, men advocate an interference which not only stops the purifying process, but even increases the vitiation—absolutely encourages the multiplication of the reckless and incompetent by offering them an unfailing provision, and *dis*courages the multiplication of the competent and provident by heightening the prospective difficulty of maintaining a family. And thus, in their eagerness to prevent the really salutary sufferings that surround us, these sigh-wise and groan-foolish people bequeath to posterity a continually increasing curse.

Returning again to the highest point of view, we find that there is a second and still more injurious mode in which law-enforced charity checks the process of adaptation. To become fit for the social state, man has not only to lose his savageness, but he has to acquire the capacities needful for civilized life. Power of application must be developed; such modification of the intellect as shall qualify it for its new tasks must take place; and, above all, there must be gained the ability to sacrifice a small immediate gratification for a future great one. The state of transition will of course be an unhappy state. Misery inevitably results from incongruity between constitution and conditions. All these evils, which afflict us, and seem to the uninitiated the obvious consequences of this or that removable cause, are unavoidable attendants on the adaptation now in progress. Humanity is being pressed against the inexorable necessities of its new position—is being moulded into harmony with them, and has to bear the resulting unhappiness as best it can. The process *must* be undergone, and the sufferings *must* be endured. No power on earth, no cunningly-devised laws of statesmen, no world-rectifying schemes of the humane, no communist panaceas, no reforms that men ever did broach or ever will broach, can diminish them one jot. Intensified they may be, and are; and in preventing their intensification, the philanthropic will find ample scope for exertion. But there is bound up with the change a *normal* amount of suffering, which cannot be lessened without altering the very laws of life. Every attempt at mitigation of this eventuates in exacerbation of it. All that a poor-law, or any kindred institution can do, is to partially suspend the transition—to take off for awhile, from certain members of society, the painful pressure which is effecting their transformation. At best this is merely to postpone what must ultimately be borne. But it is more than this; it is to undo what has already been done. For the circumstances to which adaptation is taking place cannot be superseded without causing a retrogression—a partial loss of the adaptation previously effected; and as the whole process must some time or other be passed through, the lost ground must be gone over again, and the attendant pain borne afresh. Thus, besides retarding the adaptation, a poor-law adds to the distresses inevitably attending it.

PART V

QUESTIONS FOR DISCUSSION

RESEARCH

1. ~~Describe~~ some of the unscrupulous business practices which work to the detriment of the ghetto dweller.
2. What knowledge of consumer economics do you feel is essential for the ghetto dweller?
3. What is likely to be the background of a recently arrived ghetto dweller in terms of his economic background and sophistication?
4. Is there evidence that any of the three poverties described by Harrington are present in your community? What is your community doing to deal with these problems and what additional programs would you recommend?
5. What are the welfare problems of the cities?. Do you feel the welfare system in your community is adequate?

VOCABULARY

AFDC
alcoholic
aliens
bait advertising
"bum"
callousness
compensatory consumption
cynicism
discounting paper
flexible credit
indifference

informal controls
intellectual
marginal industries
migrants
lien
occupational mobility
seasonal work
subculture
switch sales
recession
urban culture

RESEARCH THE ADEQUACY OF THE WELFARE SYSTEMS IN THE URBAN SETTING.

RESEARCH THE RELATIONSHIP BETWEEN EDUCATION AND UNEMPLOYMENT

PART VI

EDUCATION AND UNEMPLOYMENT

The urban scene, traditionally the center of great universities, provides us with immediate problems in the field of education. For most of the ghetto children, the dream of a university education is "the impossible dream." Their entire life pattern, from birth and even from the prenatal stage, is one of constant deprivation.

Research has presented us with some facts of the early childhood of the ghetto dweller which show how much of a poor start he receives. We know, for example, that permanent brain damage can result even while the child is still in the mother's womb. Improper prenatal care, such as lack of appropriate food and failure to receive medical checkups, can all contribute to this poor start.

Of even greater concern is the important role played by the first three years of life. We now know that up to 80 per cent of the brain cells are formed by this age, and failure to receive an appropriate diet can inhibit their development. Likewise, a lack of necessary affection and emotional responses can foster negative feelings in the child. All of the above data are characteristics of urban life. Combine with these the sterile, harsh life of the inner city, a life of restricted experiences, and all the necessary ingredients are present for a poor start in life.

The typical inner-city child starts school with a handicap of almost one grade in contrast with his middle class counterpart. Typically his school will be staffed with middle class teachers who find the ghetto world beyond their comprehension. They are often the most inexperienced, sent to the ghetto because of their lack of seniority. Defeated almost before they begin their first day on the job, they adopt attitudes toward the children which only serve to reinforce views the children already hold for themselves.

Looking at the school's curriculum, the child is expected to read material so foreign to his world that he seems to be reading about another country. The world of the middle class, where a child has his own room, where mother is home all day to take care of the one-family home, where the yard is spacious and tree

235

shaded, and where he romps with his pets, is something the ghetto child has never seen and certainly never experienced. Reading becomes a real hardship, and he continues to fall behind, often losing as much as a grade in normal development for every two grades he advances. Lacking this all-important skill of reading, school work becomes more and more demanding and the likelihood of increased failure begins.

Nothing succeeds like success, and nothing so strikes down the human spirit as these failures. The pattern of failure reinforces one basic concept: he is a failure. As he enters the junior high years, he is nearing the age of dropping out. Anyone with a basic understanding of self concept knows that the child who finds the school a place of negative reinforcement will take the first opportunity to break away from the hostile environment. The junior high school student, ill prepared to leave school and enter the world of work, nevertheless, feels he must do so to restore some type of positive self image.

What type of student drops out? According to research findings, he is likely to be black and male. When you combine the characteristics of being a black, male, adolescent dropout, the opportunities for unemployment are almost guaranteed. And nationwide studies show that the age group of seventeen through twenty-one has the highest unemployment rate. The problem, however, cannot and should not be measured in terms of simply how much outlay will be made for unemployment compensation. Rather the loss in positive production and potential human resources must be the concern. Even more frightening is that a new cycle of poverty has begun. Michael Harrington in *The Other America* focuses sharply on this new cycle of poverty. It must be broken somehow.

Various government and private programs have begun which attempt to deal with disadvantaged children at the age when something can still be done. One of the most publicized has been Operation Head Start. Designed to deal with the preschool child, its purpose is to provide these children with a multitude of experiences. Recently this program was under heavy criticism. It seems that the children make initial gains but begin to regress to former patterns of learning by about the third grade. Three possible areas of weakness in the program are: (1) the program may start too late and permanent damage may have already been done, (2) upon entering elementary school the parental involvement characteristic of Head Start programs is ended and, (3) the elementary schools may not know how to build upon the experiences provided by Head Start. Most likely the answer lies in a combination of all of these.

At the Junior High School level, Higher Horizons has received significant attention. Combining guidance, remedial work, parental involvement, and cultural enrichment, this program has had significant success in altering the dropout patterns so characteristic of this age group.

Job Corps, a program of the Great Society, has had some notable success. Recently cut back by the Nixon administration, Job Corps has had admitted successes and failures. However, if all programs were scrapped on the basis of some inefficiencies, one must wonder how many would still be functioning.

What is needed is a reorientation of national priorities. As long as programs designed to break the awful cycle of deprivation in learning are relegated to minor roles in national goals, the awful spectre of our disadvantaged children will be a cause for national shame.

THE SOCIAL WORLD OF THE URBAN SLUM CHILD

Suzanne Keller

The family life of the urban slum child is likely to be one of unfounded optimism and certain deprivation. Parents are likely to be poorly educated, have insecure jobs, and have distorted perceptions of their world. Transferring these traits into domestic patterns, we find the child's world limited in terms of educational experiences. The effect on intellectual development is clearly spelled out as IQ scores drop as the child moves ahead in school.

Perhaps most disheartening is the parents' set view for the likelihood of a change of social status and their participation in upward social mobility. The outlook for such social mobility on their part is extremely bleak.

The children studied are forty-six first- and fifth-grade children currently living and attending public school in the poorer sections of New York City. Both colored and white children are included, though in view of the incompleteness of the larger study from which they are drawn, they are not equally represented. By means of an Index of Social Class developed at the Institute, based on occupational and educational level of the main support of the family and on a Crowding Index, these children were all classified as Level IV on a ten-level stratification continuum, which might be considered as somewhere at the top of the lower-lower class stratum or at the bottom of the upper-lower class stratum. The children were seen in the schools for several hours, during which they took a number of tests tapping their verbal, intellectual and conceptual abilities. Their parents received questionnaires by mail and the children themselves gave accounts of their typical week-end activities and their life at home. It must be pointed out that the major purpose of the larger study was to compare test performances on various measures, and not to obtain full and comprehensive information on socioeconomic backgrounds. The background measures, in fact, permit at best only a rough classification of the socioeconomic levels of the children. But, although these measures are gross, they do depict some aspects of life in the slums of Harlem and in some of the poorer white sections in the changing neighborhoods of Brooklyn and Manhattan. One-fifth of the families were interviewed in their own homes.

The following summary is divided into two parts: an over-all comparison, and a comparison of Negroes and whites separately. Four areas are discussed: (1) social and economic characteristics of the families, such as size, available space, regional origins of the parents and educational and occupational attainments; (2) the children's

From Suzanne Keller, "The Social World of the Urban Slum Child," *American Journal of Orthopsychiatry*, XXXIII, 5, Oct. 1963, 823–831. Copyright © 1963, the American Orthopsychiatric Association, Inc. Reproduced by permission.

after-school and weekend activities; (3) the children's self-perceptions; and (4) parental aspirations for the children.

SOCIAL AND
ECONOMIC BACKGROUNDS

The children were selected so as to be roughly comparable in the educational and occupational attainments of the main support of the family and a Crowding Index. On all three of these they fell on the lower end of a socioeconomic continuum, although gross measures such as these hardly tap more than a fraction of the characteristics associated with lower-class life. The breadwinners in these families were employed as porters, short-order cooks, unskilled and semiskilled factory workers and maintenance and service workers. A few were bus or taxi drivers, clerks and self-employed. The somewhat higher occupational positions of the self-employed were offset by overcrowded living conditions and conspicuously low educational attainments. One out of six of the breadwinners was unemployed at the time of the study and these families were receiving welfare assistance. On the average, the parents of these children had not gone beyond the first year of high school, and the mothers had somewhat more schooling than the fathers.

Family size, nativity and family composition showed some important variations within the group. Less than three-fifths of these families conformed to the modal American type of two parents with between two and three children; more than two-fifths were large families with six to ten members. The average number of persons per room in the household was 1.2; this went as high as 1.5 persons per room for the larger families.

These families are not by and large the poor immigrant of half a century

ago. These poor are Americanized, the majority born and raised on native ground. They also have been poor for a long time—two thirds have held their current low-level jobs for six years or more, one third for as long as ten years or more. Nor have they experienced extensive job mobility—one half have had no other job during the past ten years, and none more than three jobs during that time. If either rapid horizontal or vertical mobility is characteristic of workers at higher levels and at the lowest levels, it does not, apparently, characterize these.

These, then, are among the poorest elements of the population, they hold low-level jobs, they have had such jobs for a number of years, and they typically have not finished high school. Their actual chances for upward mobility are therefore objectively low. Thus their own subjective appraisals for such mobility are interesting. When asked to classify themselves in one of three groups, those going up, those going down in the world, and those doing neither, fully two thirds felt they were going up in the world, three tenths felt they were at a standstill, and only 2 per cent stated that they were going downhill: The ethic of success is very much in evidence.

LIFE OUTSIDE OF SCHOOL

All forty-six children live in homes that contain both radio and television sets and all utilize both media regularly and frequently. Three fourths had spent at least two hours (a sizable proportion as many as five) before their television sets the previous day watching a variety of entertainment programs—cartoons, the fights, Westerns, a few adult shows such as "I Love Lucy" and "Hitchcock Presents," and some of the better known comedians. The larger society seems to come to these children via entertainment and escapist stories on television. The children are familiar, even in the first grade, with the names of programs and of leading characters —a fact which might be used in school instruction.

This emphasis on peer-group entertainment also runs through their accounts of typical weekend activities. These children are between the ages of five and thirteen, years crucial for the acquisition of skills and information and the development of any talents they may possess. Life is not yet as serious as it will one day be, responsibilities are at a minimum, and the mind is receptive to new experiences and to the exploration of the natural and the social world. Yet hardly any of these children mention using their time to prepare themselves for something—they play, they watch television, they see films and they listen to music on the radio. Sometimes they visit relatives and go to Church on Sundays. They do not read, they do not study, they do not take lessons, they do not get instruction in any of the things that interest many children at these ages.

There is clearly a lack of sustained interaction with adult members of their families—a fact corroborating the findings of studies by Esther Milner, Walter B. Miller and others. Only about one half, for example, regularly eat one meal with one or both parents, the rest either eat alone or with brothers and sisters only. This robs them of one of the important socializing and intellectually stimulating experiences of childhood. According to Bossard and Boll,[1] the family meal is a focus for a number of important emotional, cultural and educational experiences. Participation and interaction with significant others in an organized way helps shape the

[1] J. H. S. Bossard and E. S. Boll, *The Sociology of Child Development*, New York: Harper, 1960, Chap. 13.

personality and sensitizes the participants to each other's needs and inclinations. Organized conversation helps shape vocabulary, influences the development of verbal facility and subtlety and determines a whole set of complex attitudes and feelings about the use of language. The family meal also serves as an acculturating agency, for, in their interaction, the members teach each other and develop a way of seeing themselves and the world in which they live. The family meal has been described as a forum, as a clearing house for information, as a school for life and as an opportunity to act out deeper personality needs. Such experiences were absent in the lives of at least one-half of the lower-class children here discussed.

SELF-PERCEPTIONS

Compared to middle-class children these children are evidently handicapped, both in their objective living conditions and in their opportunities for learning outside of school, either from their parents and other family members through sustained relationships and contacts, or through organized activities other than play or passive response to the mass media. Presumably, this will affect their self-perceptions and their school performance.

The Self-Concept and Motivation Test of the Institute contains ten incompleted sentences, each relating to some with judgment or evaluation of the child. One in particular seems to tap the self-image of the child by comparison with other children: "When I look at other boys and girls, and then look at myself, I feel. . ." In all, 28 of 46 responses (or 60 per cent) were unfavorable to the child, and only 14 of the 46 (30 per cent) were favorable. The favorable responses read: "I feel good, happy, the same." The unfavorable ones read: "I feel ashamed, sad, heartbroken." The proportion of unfavorable self-references, moreover, increases from 55 per cent in the first grade to 65 per cent in the fifth. These children, then, typically express a low self-esteem, drawing unfavorable comparisons between themselves and their school mates. If such self-deprecation is representative of the feelings of most young children from lower socioeconomic backgrounds, it suggests one potential source for early school failure.

PARENTAL ASPIRATIONS FOR THEIR CHILDREN

A number of studies have shown that parents may abandon their hopes for conspicuous achievements only to project them the more intensely onto their children.[2] These parents, too, conform to this pattern. When they were asked to indicate a first and a second choice of possible future occupations, although they could have nothing but vague hopes and expectations about the occupational future of their young children, their replies provide some insight into their ambitions and hopes. In their choices for the boys, fully two thirds of the parents currently engaged in unskilled and semiskilled labor or unemployed hoped that their sons would become professional men such as doctors, lawyers, engineers or business executives. Parents of girls most frequently mentioned such traditional feminine callings as nursing and teaching.

[2] E. Chinoy, *Automobile Workers and the American Dream*, New York: Random House, 1955.

S. M. Lipset and R. Bendix, *Social Mobility in Industrial Society*, Berkeley and Los Angeles: University of California Press, 1962, Chap. IX.

F. Zweig, *The Worker in an Affluent Society*, New York: The Free Press, 1961, p. 21.

As to the amount of schooling they would like their children to obtain, here again, aspirations were high. Eight tenths of the parents wish their children to acquire a college degree. Only one tenth would be satisfied with a high school diploma.

These responses compare interestingly with those given in private interviews in the homes of the ten families who had not answered the mail questionnaire. When asked what they considered the best sort of job to have, security and steady work, rather than prestige, power or riches, received greatest emphasis. Ideally, then, on the fantasy level perhaps, these parents would like to see their sons get to the top. More realistically, they will be satisfied if their children manage to do what they themselves have failed to do —get a steady and secure job.

In sum, the children described in this paper come from large families living in relatively crowded quarters in the midst or on the edge of poverty. Only two out of three are being supported solely by their fathers' earnings in low-level jobs, and one out of six are currently exposed to the stings of their parents' unemployment and the mixed blessings of public assistance. The majority of the parents, most of whom are native born, have been in this relatively deprived status for a long time—two thirds for more than six years, one third for more then ten. Nor has there been the sort of rapid job mobility one has come to expect from the official statistics on national trends, for, most of these people had held at most two other jobs at similar levels during the previous ten years.

All of this might lead to a pervasive sense of discouragement among them— and well it may, for we have no data to tap these feelings directly. Such discouragement is not, however, translated into resignation or indifference toward upward mobility. For, fully two thirds of the group believe that they are on the way up in the world and a bare 2 per cent feel that things are going downhill. These great expectations are further reflected in the high hopes they have for their children, whom they would like to see graduating from college and entering one of the professions. Whether these desires reflect concrete plans or unrealistic fantasies about the future cannot be assessed.

What else do we know about these children, most of whom do poorly in school about which they care very little? Television seems to be a rather persistent influence. They like to play and they have friends. But they have little sustained contact with adults, they have few organized conversations with other adults the way middle-class children do, and few participate in shared family activities. Even at meal times, one half of these children are alone or in the company of their brothers and sisters. It is interesting that, although these children are poor, they are not starving—the foods typically eaten at breakfast and dinner include a considerable variety of nutritionally adequate foods although amounts were not indicated. Poverty, today, probably extends more to housing, to lack of spending money, to lack of comforts and to a constricted milieu for learning and exploring the world. A city, especially a metropolis, would seem to be a fascinating place in which to grow up, but one would not believe this from these accounts of restricted movement and the monotonous repetitiveness of activities—TV and more TV, play with other children, movies and, as the single organized activity besides school, Church on Sunday for one-half of the group. Their world seems to be small and monotonous, though not necessarily unhappy.

This constriction of experience and the poverty of spirit it engenders may account for the below normal IQ scores of this group of poor children by the time of the fifth grade (mean IQ is 88.57 on Lorge Thorndike nonverbal IQ test; in first grade, Lorge Thorndike IQ mean scores were 96.56), confirming countless other studies that have shown a similar scholastic and verbal inferiority for children from underprivileged environments. It may also account for the high degree of negative self-evaluations already discussed.

In recent years there has been talk of the existence of a lower-class culture that performs much the same function for its members as any culture does: It defines the world, structures perceptions and habitual reactions, sets goals and standards and permits people to evaluate and approve each other's conduct. This means that lower-class culture patterns, while substantially different from middle-class patterns, nevertheless provide a web of shared meanings for those subject to its rewards and penalties. Still, cultural relativism ignores the fact that schools and industry are middle-class in organization and outlook. If lower-class children conform to the "focal concerns"[3] of their milieu they will typically be misfits in the schools they attend. Short of adapting the public school to the cultural milieu of different groups, the children of this background will be at a disadvantage.

Clearly these children have a profound initial handicap in the scholastic competition with middle-class children. This initial disadvantage rarely turns to later advantage—instead, they become negativistic or bored and fail to learn the rudiments of the verbal and intellectual skills expected of adults in an industrial society.

[3] W. B. Miller, "Lower Class Culture as a Generating Milieu of Gang Delinquency," *Journal of Social Issues,* 14: 5–19 (1958).

The discrepancy in preschool orientation by social class is duplicated within the lower class by race. Using the same index of socioeconomic status, we find that even when gross socioeconomic factors are controlled, Negroes and whites do not live in comparable social environments.

For one thing, lower-class Negro (Level IV on the Index) children come from larger families than white children (nearly one half as compared to one third among the white children have at least three brothers or sisters). Thus an already low income must stretch farther for one group than for the other. More significantly, only one half the Negro children were supported solely by the earnings of their fathers, whereas fully nine tenths of the white children had fathers who could assume the traditional male role of chief breadwinner. In addition, three times as many Negro as white children at the same socioeconomic level live in families where the adults are currently unemployed and receiving welfare and other types of aid for the indigent. In educational attainment, too, the white families were somewhat at an advantage, the fathers of the white children having on the average one more year of schooling than the Negro fathers, and the white mothers having one half a year more. In each group, however, the mothers were somewhat better educated than the fathers.

One of the striking differences occurs with regard to place of birth. Three fourths of the Negro parents were geographically mobile, two thirds having been born in the South and one tenth outside the United States. None of the white children came from mobile families—all had parents both of whom had been born in the North.

As regards occupational mobility, however, Negro families were more likely to have held their present low-level jobs for a long time. In fact, whereas more than half the white families were at this low level for less than six years, more than half the Negro families had been there for six years or more. Thus, whereas Negro families at this level were more mobile geographically, they were less mobile occupationally. This does not, apparently, diminish their belief in their own success. Fully three fourths of the Negro families, as against only one third of the white families, felt that they were going up in the world. Only one fifth of the Negro families felt that they were at a standstill, but three fifths of the white felt this way. Negro lower-class children are thus raised in objectively inferior homes in which subjective appraisals of life's chances are much higher than among a comparable group of white families. Without more extensive data it is impossible to account for this discrepancy, although two possibilities suggest themselves. One relates to the differential geographical mobility of Negro families, which may lead them to expect other types of mobility as well. That is, they may have migrated to New York in the hope of improving their standing. The other relates to the relative standing of two equally low-level socioeconomic groups in the larger world. Level IV has been described as somewhere at the top of the lowest and most underprivileged stratum, or at the bottom of the upper-lower stratum. But, while the two groups were objectively at the same socioeconomic level, their status relative to most others of their rate is quite different. The majority of white persons in this country are above the lower-class level but the same does not hold true for Negroes. This means, then, that the top of the lower-lower class is an exceedingly low status for most of the white families but perhaps a relatively high one for the Negro families. In other words, the white families may feel relatively deprived by comparison with others, whereas the Negro families may feel relatively favored. Further exploration on a larger sample should clarify this. It would be interesting, for example, to see whether this expressed optimism is also characteristic of the very lowest socioeconomic group among Negroes.

The most striking finding regarding the children themselves concerns the self-perceptions of the fifth graders. Negro children definitely exhibit more negative self-evaluations than do white children; 30 per cent of the white children but fully 80 per cent of the Negro children draw unfavorable self-other comparisons, paralleling findings from a number of other studies.[4]

These fifth-grade Negro children had also been evaluated by their teachers and some of their observations are relevant. More than half were judged to have little motivation for school work, to be typically sad or preoccupied, and

[4] For a summary of such studies, see R. M. Drager and K. S. Miller, "Comparative Psychological Studies of Negroes and Whites in the United States," *Psycholog. Bull.*, 57 (5) : 382–383 (1960).

to be working below capacity in school. The interplay between self-perception and school achievement must be explored further, particularly in view of the fact that the parents of the Negro children were very much concerned about their children's work, for, whereas nearly all the white families were satisfied with their children's school work, only one half of the Negro families were. This may be yet another indication of the greater ambitiousness of the Negro families already noted.

These preliminary results reveal rather striking differences between Negro and white school children at the same socioeconomic level in their objective living conditions, parental aspirations, and their self-evaluations. Similarly, by inference, lower-class children, irrespective of race, differ sharply in their preparation for school from the ideal middle-class children with whom they must compete. Presumably, in both instances, this will exert a negative effect on intellectual interests and ambitions and may thus help account for the long-demonstrated correlation between socioeconomic deprivation and school failure.

THE FIRST SEMESTER IN A SLUM SCHOOL

Marjorie B. Smiley and Harry L. Miller

Totally out of touch with the world of the slum child, the inner-city teacher finds herself completely bewildered. Material which has no relationship with the life of the disadvantaged child is taught and the response is inevitable. Discipline problems reign supreme and the wonder is that the children come to school at all. The

From Leonard Kornberg, ed., "Bridges to Slum-Ghetto Children: Case Studies in Learning to Become a Teacher" (Flushing, New York, Bridge Project, Department of Education, Queens College, 1962).

material, written by the middle class, written for the middle class, and taught by the middle class is meaningless in the slum setting. New ways of enrichment must be found if urban education is to become a genuine learning experience.

I am interested in Ernest and he is really the only real problem in my class, out of the ordinary as a problem. I have mentioned him, I think, on every recording. He is a child who just does not pay attention. I don't know what it is, I don't know if he is just bored, and I feel that he must be, since he is a holdover. This is his second year in the third grade. I know he must be bored with much of the curriculum, and I can't change it drastically just for him. But I don't know what the nature of his problem is completely. In many of the subject areas he is interested because he does well in these. For instance, he does math pretty well, and he is interested and volunteers and occasionally, not as often as he might, though, not as often as he is able to. When I call on him he never gives me an answer. He just stands there and he seems not to get confused. It's not a willful refusal to answer. He just doesn't seem—well, maybe it's more a confusion. Whatever he is thinking about just sort of slipped away from him. On many occasions it's because, of course, he's not paying attention and he didn't even hear my question. But in many of the areas he does do pretty well, because in social studies he seems to have a very good interest. Reading is his problem. He just doesn't pay attention when we're reading. He just can't seem to be interested. And I get a very strong feeling that he considers all of this very much beneath him. The stories which we read—although the readers have been changed as I mentioned, and the new reader is much better in terms of interest. It has much higher interest levels than the other one did. I think

that Ernest was getting very tired of Sally and Puff, and he really seemed to be very much annoyed with them. The new reader introduces a whole new town, with a name which the other series never had, and children with last names which the other series didn't have. It just seems to be a lot more realistic. The stories are more appealing, I think. Also, to children. But in terms of their realism and in terms of situations which are much more frequent than just sitting around in the yard all day —the reader should appeal to him more than the other one did but it doesn't seem to be doing this. I still get the impression, he doesn't know of course that he is reading a first-grade reader, and if he did I think that he would completely give up altogether, but he still thinks that he's reading a third-grade reader. He's much bigger and taller than any of the other children in the class and much more physically mature, and I get the feeling that he just feels out of his element. I have been thinking about what to do about his problem. I did some very brief individual work with him. I really haven't had the time to devote to him. I have been thinking about it very seriously this week, and it really has been troubling me because I really don't know what to do about him and I'm really very concerned.

In our unit on food we had just finished the study of dairy foods last week and this week I had planned to begin them with the study of bread. This is another subtopic within the topic of food which they are concerned with. The social-studies book is a little bit inadequate on this particular topic and although I had no other materials to rely on for the lesson, actually what happened was that the story from the book which I had to read to them, since as I had mentioned before, they are not able to read their social-studies book by themselves. The reading level is quite difficult for them. The story which I read to them, as I was saying, was one which described actually the whole process of bread, the whole process of how the wheat is grown; it described the whole thing from the time the seed is planted to the time the flour goes to the factory to be made into bread, and somehow I think it was a little bit too much in one lesson, although I didn't see any way really to break it up. Perhaps I could have, just reading one or two paragraphs and then discussing it with them and asking them questions about it, but I hadn't done this, and I went through the whole story which meant by the time we got to the end, many of them had forgotten what had . . . what the first steps were in the process. We wrote an experience chart after the reading of it. Well, we had discussed it, of course, stopping here and there along the way to discuss certain things. One of the boys in the class had been to visit his relatives on a farm the previous summer, and he had seen a combine and a tractor and some of the machines which we were discussing, so he was able to tell us a little about these, but most of the children were unfamiliar with this type of machinery, but they could understand, of course, most of the things, most of the events which go into the whole process of growing the wheat and cutting the grain and storing it and the grain elevator, but it seemed to be just a little bit too much to cover in one lesson. However, I had read it, so we did the experience chart and some of the children did remember some of the events, so that we finally were able

to talk again about all of the steps in this process, and one of the difficulties I think in the lesson was that I didn't seem to be able to make a clear distinction between wheat and grain and flour, some of the terms were used, I don't think they quite saw the difference. For example, between the wheat growing in the field and the flour. In other words, what exactly happens to it, to make this change and then understanding again at the end of the story that when the flour is ready, then it has to go to a bread factory where it is made into bread. However, insofar as their reaction to the lesson, they didn't seem to be very interested at all in the lesson. Perhaps because the story, not only being on a reading level a little bit above them, but in terms which were used that they did not understand, and I think since we are not finished with the story of bread by any means we will have to still do some work on what happens at the factory where the bread is made, etc. Perhaps we'll have a chance to go over some of this and to clear up some of these things in their minds and to try to make a more successful impression about the whole topic.

I brought in my own victrola and a record, a Mitch Miller record, which I had used during student teaching, Mitch Miller Sing Along Folk Songs. Many of the songs the children would know, "Pop Goes the Weasel," at least know some of the words, the tune to "Clementine." I used this, took out the victrola and actually, because we had quite a bit of singing previously, I thought that the children perhaps would be ready for this and I didn't spend too much time preparing them for the use of a new term for the class, which, of course, was victrola. This was the main reason why it was a bit of a failure. I took out the victrola and of course the children were very excited. I had them turn around because the victrola was in the back of the room. I told them to sit with their backs of their chairs against their desks and, at listening time, we always say, what kind of a time is it? We point to our ears. It's listening time. It's a time to look and listen but it's not a time to use, and we point to our mouths. It's not the time to use our mouths. I started using it, and of course the tunes are very catchy —songs like "When Johnny Comes Marching Home." Well, within about three minutes the rhythm had just gotten the children and this I should have been aware of. I was aware subconsciously, but I guess I didn't consider the fact that these children, because of their hyperactivity, at least for many of them, it was just impossible for them just to sit and listen to music. They had to be a part of it. Well, of course, people started popping up all over the place, and tried to express themselves to this music and because I had not planned for it, well, we'll listen once and we'll think what we are going to do, then we'll stand up and we'll do it, because I hadn't specifically told the children exactly step by step what we were going to do, mild chaos broke out in the room. There was no fighting or anything of that sort, but while one person was dancing around, another person clapping hands, so that there was no unity in the music at all. We tried to sing the songs but it was more of a movement type music rather than . . . the children didn't exactly want to sing, particularly to "Johnny Comes Marching Home." It was marching music and they wanted to march. The children did sing "Pop Goes the Weasel" every time we came to the line "Pop Goes the Weasel," but of course at this point the children would pop out of their chairs. We tried to organize this a bit but at this point the children were full of activity so I felt, since it

was near recess time, that perhaps the best thing would be to discontinue the use of the record but to continue the activity in the basement through games the children weren't really gaining anything from the classroom except through unorganized participation in music and I hope, I feel, I did learn one thing, that the children do respond to music. . . .

One of my least successful lessons during the week was a science music lesson. I had acquired a record from the music department at P.S. 109 about Creepy, the Crawly Caterpillar. The story was mostly a narration with musical background to express various feelings, the feeling of children who were playing, or birds who were singing, or activity of a creepy crawly caterpillar. And then the story went into the fact that the caterpillar had a secret and the only way we could find out what it is is by making believe that we are caterpillars. And the story goes on that the caterpillar crawls up into a tree and to his warm and woolly cocoon bed and when he comes out he's a butterfly, and that's the secert. I think one reason why the lesson was not successful was that the record player that was being used in my room did not have sufficient volume, so that the entire class could not listen without having to strain to hear, so that I had to stop the recording once we got started and send for another victrola. Luckily the teacher next door had one that I could use, and had much louder volume for the children, so that we had to interrupt once, and several of the children whose attention span is quite short were lost at that point and became quite restless. Some did continue to listen, but of course there was this undercurrent of whispering or trying to do something else, and the children were reminded of what they were supposed to be doing, how to listen, and our rules for listening. I think that perhaps there was not a realization that a caterpillar does turn into a butterfly. We tried to discuss this after the record but there should probably have been some lead-up discussion to the playing of this record and things to look for. I failed to realize that the children haven't developed their listening abilities to any great extent, so they have to constantly be given things that they have to especially find out.

Every morning they ask: are we going to gym today? And I finally got them to a point where they stop asking because I tell them the more they ask, the less time I'll have to take them to gym, but they are impossible at times in the classroom. How can I reward their behavior? Their bad behavior? By taking them to gym, something they look forward to and enjoy. I don't see how that is possible. If I can't contain them while they are in the classroom, but am I going to contain them walking down three flights of stairs, going through the lunchroom, going through the corridors, walking up the three flights to get to the gym, first of all, and it's just a pathetic situation where the administration tells us we must, must, must, and the individual teachers feel that we can't, and here is another place where we feel we are banging our heads against the stone wall, and I definitely feel that if the class as a whole is all discipline during the day, particularly in the morning because our gym period is in the afternoon right after lunch, it's just ridiculous to begin with, that they should not be taken to gym as a form of punishment, but obviously the administration disagrees with me and since I'm a new teacher, I have no right to voice my opinion, as I have already been told.

As far as my lessons I can say that I did very little teaching this week. I just found it was impossible to do a lesson. Last week we had a spelling meeting and I had received a spelling inventory test and I gave it on Monday and I could not go on with the rest of it. I could not allow them to study in class. They had to take the stuff home, the words home to study at home. It was just impossible, an impossible week. The children were highstrung. You should look at them in the wrong way and they were very upset, and Michael did not add anything to it at all. There was no lesson I feel that I had taught last week that was successful, and I just can't differentiate between my poor lessons and my least successful lesson because all of them were just the same. They were interrupted; every time I started something they were interrupted by another child in the class or by a group of children in the class who just would not sit and listen. It was just an impossible situation.

I met him right before I was having lunch, and he said to me—how did the rehearsal go? And I said it was terrible. And he said why? And I said because my children may be mature enough to write a play and do a beautiful job on a play—but I said I have some children in my class who are not mature enough to be in kindergarten as far as their behavior is concerned. And I told him that I think it's very unfair of you to require us to put on a play with children who really can't be controlled. I said I can't have my eyes in thirty-four places at once. He tried to calm me down. Then he said you're doing a good job anyway, I'm sure, and would you mind if I observed a rehearsal? I'd like to see it. He said—when is your next rehearsal? And I said Monday. And he said, would you please write me a note. I'd very much like to see a rehearsal. So as not to argue with him again, I said I would do it, and I intend to do it. I want him to see exactly what happens during rehearsal. He has no conception of what goes on. Many of these children do want to put on this play for their class and many of them are capable of doing it. Of working. They have marvelous suggestions, and there are just those few of them who cannot be trusted when your back is turned and get into all sorts of mischief and I told Dr. F_____ I said to him, I don't think this play is worth having three accidents per rehearsal, and he said why, and I said for the simple reason that these are animals sometimes. They just cannot be trusted alone. I felt terrible for saying it, but that was exactly how I felt. And as far as rehearsal is concerned, I will have my children bring their books and they will be doing work and one boy already told me, Jimmy, that he refuses to be in this play. So I said, alright, Jimmy, if that's your choice—it's all right with me and I said you'll be doing so much work that you won't believe it. So I wrote out on the report card that he refuses to cooperate in the class performance of a play of Benjamin Franklin.

Miss G. asked Lydia, she must have asked Lydia to read her composition and Lydia did, and when she came up, she told me that Miss G. had asked her why she was sad, and she said she was sad yesterday when Miss D. started to cry, because on Thursday I went into a minor hysteria when we were having our rehearsals and it was horrible, so I turned around and started writing on the board so the kids wouldn't see me, but they did see me, and then I got a note from Miss G., who said that she read the compositions and they were lovely, and if I please come down to see her on Monday. So this woman is quite a lovely person. I mean, after hearing about the wild escapade in my classroom, of the teacher crying in front of all the kids, she sends up this little note to reassure me that my work is going well because the compositions weren't really great at all, but they were

something, and I feel embarrassed, you know, to go down and have to see her and have her know about what happened on Thursday, and I just wonder what's going to happen. And little Lydia told me this so innocently. She told Miss G. about me crying and I wanted to hit her over the head at this very moment and that afternoon, I was about ready to walk down into Miss G.'s office and tell her that it was all over. We had had the fire drill. The kids were acting up, making a lot of noise in the hallway. I saw Miss P. with them and all the crazy things that they were doing when she was in the room and how if you single them out, there were like a hundred in five minutes, not a hundred, that's a little bit of an exaggeration, maybe ninety-nine, in the five minutes she was there, many, many wild things were going on like people calling out and raising hands, kids falling over, teetering over in their chairs and falling over and I thought, this goes on all the time except that I didn't correct it, and it was just a wild afternoon. So I got very upset that afternoon and I was about ready to walk down into Miss G.'s office and tell her that I was ready to leave and that I didn't know how to control the children and that I had not wanted to control, so I walked in to Norma and said, Norma, I don't have control in that room, and it was just the talking, to get it out of my system and she told, who knows what she told me because I really wasn't listening, but she was quite sweet. She stayed until 3:30 and then I came in on Friday and everything was just superb, why I had control, and on Friday it amazed me. You know, if I said stop something they'd stop and if I'd, I did a lot of, what do you call those things, finger plays, I think you call them finger plays, but I just stand in front of the room and start acting like a moron and the kids do whatever I do like if I put my hand on my head, I would put my hands on my shoulders and then stretch them out and when I did this, the kids all did it with me which amazed me because half the time, like Thursday, I was standing there and I was sure that as many times during the day, as a matter of fact, we had certain things like, I would just want to see if how many kids were with me and I would say put your finger on your nose, put your finger on your toes, and maybe two kids would do it and those were the two that I had. But Friday, when I do these crazy things, everybody was there. It was very very good. Now I have to find out what I did on Friday that made these kids act like they did because whatever it was, I want to keep it up, and that's the funny thing about it. I can't put my finger on what it is. I know that maybe I was with them more. You're going to wonder what that means. On Thursday, after I saw their behavior in the hallway and how the other children were behaving, of the other two classes, I felt very discouraged and so when I came in, I saw Norma there. I had gone to the ladies' room. Norma was with the class for five minutes, and I saw them doing all the things that I mentioned before and I sort of got very disgusted with them and so I sort of threw myself out halfway in the situation, like, what could I do? I became very negative and after that I had started to cry when we started to rehearse because they were completely wild and on Friday, practically every moment I was there with them. No matter what the activity was, I never got so disgusted that I removed myself even mentally, because I think I did that Thursday, like, just then, I can't stand it, I can't stand it, and I don't care what they do. So I would let things go by, but Friday I was with them all the way and that might be one of the reasons.

I really can't single out one or two other children who gave me a lot of trouble this week. Of course it was the boys. I have eleven boys and except for one or two they can be really impossible. This week they were all obnoxious. They started with spitballs and I just couldn't stop them. I gave them extra homework, and I told them they weren't going to the puppet show on Thursday. I said if this keeps up you won't go to the Christmas party. I had them standing, I had them sitting with their hands folded. I tried everything but wherever my eyes are there's a spitball in the other direction. And them pushing on line. They line up in the yard before lunch and pretty soon the whole line is down on the floor. I tell them to straighten themselves up, so one leans back a little bit and pushes the whole line down, and it's very hard to see which particular individual it is. Of course, I know one of the boys is very sneaky and inclined to do this, and this is Robert, and the others of course are no better once they start. Monkey see, Monkey do. As far as general confusion this week, Ricky seems to be regressing again, and especially in that he didn't behave and he was given extra homework, and he did not do it. And as I said, I want to catch this now, and I'm going to send for his mother now, so that he will understand that if he doesn't behave, he must suffer the consequences, and take his punishment. So on the whole, I don't know why, but this week except for Wednesday and Friday, the kids were pretty crazy and wild and I don't know what got into them. Right after Thanksgiving, right before Christmas, change of barometer, I don't know, but the girls weren't too bad. The boys were really crazy. Some of the children I've had the least difficulty with during the past week are maybe all the girls, except for Elena, who has been a little chatty this week.

And maybe one boy, Jose, who is very quiet and very well behaved, does his work well, conscientiously, good worker, studies well, does well on tests, and behaves nicely too. He is the only boy who really knows how to behave in the class. One boy out of eleven. Their behavior is different from some of the others in that they just sit quietly and do their work and they can concentrate, work independently without my being with them every minute, they can copy say, a social-studies story, off the blackboard for fifteen minutes without getting up and walking out of their seats or throwing a spitball or something. They have a longer attention span. They know how to behave and work independently by themselves. And they don't get out of their seats for any reason. They don't talk to their neighbors, they do this occasionally in a whisper so they don't disturb everyone else. If you tell them to do something, if you give them extra homework, they do it. They know they did something wrong, and they do it. In general these girls and this one boy know how to behave. Their parents have taught them how, I guess, and they know that if they are punished they accept their punishment and the next time they do it they just won't repeat the behavior that was punished. These children, I have many of them, really, most of them are girls, and they are a pleasure to have. If I could have a class with just my girls with Jose without the other ten boys I would be very happy.

As for the social studies, I am still having trouble making that meaningful and interesting to them, and it is possible that the words in the lesson are as meaningless to them as their conversation is to me, but the whole thing would be probably in establishing some sort of a background, but I am trying to establish the background and this is what they are not interested in. I am going to start taking trips with them in December, and I hope that this will give them some visual background besides what they get in the textbooks and the bulletin boards that I have in school. And maybe give them some actual experience in knowing what the history of New York was all about. And seeing what it was all about. We are going to the New York Historical Society some Friday in December and the Museum of the City of New York in May. I tried to get a trip to that much earlier but they said they were all booked up until May. I am really at my wits' end what to do. I know it's not meaningful, and still it's something that has to be taught and some of them do learn it and are interested and I am not going to drop social studies for the sake of those who cannot get interested in it, so I guess I will just have to go on coping with the discipline problem, and being rewarded by the fact that some of them are learning and are interested, so I will just have to go on like that, and I am going to see if I can get some film strips that will further motivate them to be interested. There are times, such as when we discuss Indian life, that they are interested.

I mimeographed a sheet of all the words in the pre-primers, a total of all the words that he should be knowing and I brought him up to my desk while the other children were having a writing period of something and I went through the list with him and I said, how many words do you know and I found out that of the whole list (there were about sixty words on it) he knew about four. So of course I said to myself, this child should not even be in this reading class, and since I have only the one reading group and I can't put it up to two groups, he has to drag along with the rest of them. Even if I wanted to, I don't have another book to give him to read. So I sent home a list with a note to his mother and I said, Please help Andre with these words. These are the words that are to be studied. I will see how much progress he has made next week. I did not indicate to the parent that the child is weak in reading because I feel that's not the thing the parent wants to hear in a letter. However, if she does come up to school to see me, or if I feel it's necessary to send for her, I will discuss the matter with her then. Now, Julio is a boy who was thrown out of Catholic school in the area. The reason he was thrown out of the school was because he beat up another boy and had a serious fight and the nuns just wouldn't keep him. So you know, that when a child is thrown out of a Catholic school like that, he's dead. So like I said, he talks constantly, and constantly is a sneak. If I look at him he would sit up straight. He didn't know that I could hear him. Now, I heard him and know it was him because he's a Spanish boy and I could detect his accent. I'd say to him, were you talking? He'd look me straight in the eye and say, no. And I don't want to ram a lie down a child's throat . . . I never want to say, you are lying. I don't feel that's right. So I just took Julio away from the table he was sitting at and put him at a desk, in an individual desk. In my room, most of the children sit four at a table, two at each table, two tables together. Now, I have about five individual desks which I had pushed together to make another table. However, I separated these desks and I put Julio at one and since I did that and since I keep severe discipline on him, I am constantly at him, telling him he's not getting away with anything. I don't want him to open up his mouth because he is a bright child and if he would pay attention, I'm sure he would progress lovely, but he's too busy causing trouble, talking, and telling me what other people did when he really did it him-

self, so I have him sitting now by himself and I find that, I sat him by himself Thursday, and the rest of Thursday and Friday I didn't have any trouble with him except for yesterday afternoon when he came into school and told me he got beat up, but that didn't happen in my classroom so I didn't concern myself with it.

I do think that in teaching them, I will have to oversimplify a lot of materials that I have to present to them. I can't take anything for granted with my class. I know that if the material is presented clearly enough and accurately enough, they will grasp this, but I cannot assume that the class knows this or the class knows that. I have to find out what the class knows and what the class doesn't know, and I can't assume because they knew it on Monday that they are going to know it on Wednesday. If they knew it on Monday, they may very well have forgotten it by Wednesday. Now I didn't think that I would have to be so cautious in the classroom and so keen and observant as to what the children know and what the children don't know. I thought that well, this is the second grade. They should know how to count to twenty, they should know the number story, they should be able to read all the words in this book. I can't believe that I have to be so on guard to find out exactly what they don't know. I must realize that in presenting my material to them I always have to ask them, do you understand? Are you sure that you know this? Who could tell me why such and such a thing happens? Why do we have a fire drill? Because my children don't know that, and ordinarily you would assume that being in the school and having gone through fire drills, they would know the importance of fire drills, but you make no assumptions. You walk into the classroom and you see what the children know and then you go from there, and this is a big problem. Every single day you have to keep watching and watching and watching to see what they know and what they don't know, because if you assume something and you go on the basis of that you are going to have a very big problem because naturally you're going to go on and on and the children will not raise their hands and say, I don't know what you're doing. You have to ask them.

Well, coming back after being out on Monday, the children were wild. First thing, naturally, they ran to tell me how the sub told them how terrible they were and that she would never come back to teach them again. I looked at my anecdotal record book and I saw what she had written. I figured why. The three of them, Michael, Lans, Sammy, and this girl, Dolores, were behaving just terribly and giving a difficult time and it was hard to calm them down when I came back at the end of the week. Once again, this was a week of disciplining the children. When I came back on Wednesday, they were very very noisy and gave me all kinds of compliments. My hair looked beautiful and they were beginning to behave accordingly. Lans was in his glory then, still getting out of his seat; Michael running all over the room; and Sammy running all over the place, and it was just a wild week. In fact, on Thursday they had me so upset that I went home crying and I started to cry in the classroom. They just got me. Usually I would say I'm not going to let it bother me and this and that, and it's just gotten to the point this week that all I had to do was if they did just one more thing I would just have sat down and started to cry. It was all I could do and I was so mad that I slammed the door and I just came out with the statement that if one person got out of his seat I would walk right out of the room and I got my coat on and my boots in that

rain and they were sitting with their coats on. I had just gotten to the point that I could leave them in the classroom to walk out and I knew they wouldn't kill the room or something like that. I would just walk out. That's how mad they got me and actually again with all that discipline I naturally had not gotten beyond anything but the basic lesson, reading and arithmetic— we didn't do any art work this week— nothing. I'll show you why I never got to anything else. On Thursday morning we spent a half an hour beginning at about ten to nine—Wednesday I started the reading lesson about five to nine or nine o'clock, and it went along smoothly. It was not so bad, but in the afternoon they were wild. Thursday when I said what book did you read— one would take out the book, one is writing in a notebook, one is doing everything else. Everyone closes their book, and they opened and closed their books until they could all do it at the same time. Not ten minutes later when I start the lesson and I call on a person, they don't have their book out. And this was the type that was Thursday and Friday, and whatever I would say they would stand, one would stand, three were standing, they were going downstairs. This was the end of it. As they progressed they were getting worse. They forgot everything I had taught at the beginning. This never happened—this getting out of seats. I couldn't open the windows. They were stuck. So I would open the door for a few minutes, just to get the room cooled through. The door was opened. Three of them are out of their seats, hanging out the door looking. You can't open the door to the room, you can't leave chalk on the blackboard. They are out of their seats touching everything. I am new to the system and I don't know all the tricks to the trade, as if I was an experienced teacher. One teacher once told me, I don't remember the exact words, but in essence you say the children are bad because the weather is bad if it rains, or they are bad because it is too sunny and warm and they want to go out. In other words, you can never predict how they are going to behave and this is the answer she gives me, and when I ask for help and stand there and say please help me, this is the answer that you get. You don't know what to do. B_____ is more helpful. He came down and told me that he sees our problems and that they are quite a bunch, and when they hang over my desk they just want to be near me. They want love and if I ever put my arms around them or something they just loved it. I can't go around hugging twenty-eight children every minute of the day. It's impossible every two minutes to go over and hug someone or put your arms around them and tell them how great they are if they are going to behave. It goes around in a circle and you never get any help. They probably sense that you are young—if I threaten these children they'll behave for about twenty minutes or so. Threatening threatening, threatening is the only thing that penetrates. Would you like me to send a note home? Would you like me to do this? I found out that I am constantly threatening children, and you can't have a sensible lesson. It took me Friday afternoon to do a math lesson. One page took me an hour. Why? Because they don't know how to open their books, they don't know how to do the lesson. They have just become impossible. They talk all day long, and while I'm yelling at them telling them and explaining to them why they mustn't talk, they talk right in front of me unless I go over and pull on their arm or yell, and if I turn around they do it again, and honestly, you just don't know what to do after a while. You

can't hit them. And you just don't know what to do with them.

Well, once again comes Lavinia, and I just don't know what to say, really. You must be getting sick and tired of hearing her name; I know I am and everyone is. I am constantly reprimanding her, no matter where or when, or what we are doing. She is always doing the wrong thing, and I just have the feeling and know that it is conscious on her part. She knows exactly what she's doing, and it must be the wrong thing. I guess I'm beginning to put some psychology into it and I think she's just looking for attention. She's doing it by this negative way. I guess the only thing is my problem about handling her. I have tried punishment, in several ways, and punishment doesn't work, and I just can't get myself to do anything else. I praise her when she deserves it for what she does, and she is pretty bright, and she reads nicely, and she generally knows what is going on but I find myself just not—you know—I really feel absolutely at a loss!

On Friday she was again acting up and I said to myself, "I just can't be bothered." I just don't know what to do and I just don't want to keep saying, "Lavinia, Lavinia," when the other kids have something to work with. So I took her and I put her in Miss G_____'s room and I said right in front of her in class, "What a bad girl Lavinia is, and she can't have fun with the rest of us." Well, she went in and I made her stand in the corner there, not even sit. And later on Miss G_____ came in and she said she felt terrible. Her class was all playing and Lavinia was just standing there. So I said, "Bring her back," and I guess I was getting a little soft. Not that it mattered to Lavinia, I don't think. It might, but I don't know.

Anyway, she came back and she apologized for not behaving and with that she was quite all right for the rest of the day, which wasn't too long, about twenty minutes.

One thing she did this week also, Friday, was quite puzzling to me and I believe that something must be wrong with her, I just don't know. She came up to me at 12:00 o'clock when we came into the classroom after she hung up her coat and she handed me a nickel. I said, "Lavinia, what is the nickel for?" She didn't answer. I said, "I don't want the nickel." She said, "Here, you take it." She did not say a word. She just kept pushing the nickel towards me. I made her stand next to me, and I said, "Lavinia, why are you giving me the nickel?" She did not answer. I said, "Go sit down and take your nickel." This went on and on and everyone was looking and she just stood there with this smirk on her face handing me the nickel. I asked her if she found it on the floor and if she was giving it to me and she said no. She didn't say no, she shook her head. Finally I took it and I put it in her little pocket. She took it out and handed it to me again. I said, "Lavinia, if the nickel is yours, you take it," and finally she said to me. "No. I want you to buy candy." I said, "Lavinia, I don't need candy. Thank you very, very much but you take the nickel and you buy candy," and with that she walked away laughing. It was very funny. So I can't figure her out.

I am planning to speak to Mrs. J_____ about the problem with Daniel. It's a problem that I really can't cope with. Any routine or discipline I have established in the class is virtually at the point of complete breakdown because of him. It seems that he just completely sets the other children off their equilibrium. He's someone—I hate to use the word—vicious, but that's certainly what he is. I know—on Friday—it's really a horrible thing—the guidance counsellor had wanted to see him because—well, he's been in other classrooms before this one, and the teachers have been having quite a bit of problems with him and she wanted to meet him. She has more or less stayed away from him because he was under the care of Northside center. She didn't want to more or less overstep her limit, but she did call for him, and she spoke to him, and she sent back a note that he would try his best and would try more in class and do better in class. When she finally came back to me after he had spoken to her, she was quite despondent and told me the fire was burning low, and this is quite unusual for her, because she really has to be agitated to a very extreme degree to sound like that, and as soon as I saw Vernon was upset, I knew that whatever Daniel did was really pretty wretched, but I just told him to take his seat and sit down, and he got very indignant, and he refused to take the book out. He took his coat out of the closet and ran out of the room and was running up and down the halls.

Then I sent a note into Miss G_____ to see if she could coerce him into the room because I had tried and was quite unsuccessful with it, and she said that she had gotten him into her room and she was talking to him and a few minutes later I had a note saying Daniel ran out and she thinks he's left the building but fortunately or unfortunately he hadn't, and when I took my class down before lunch to go to the bathroom, they were lined up quietly. There was no hubbub; they were fine. And all of a sudden Daniel was there and spitting and kicking and hitting, and he had half of them on the floor, and the children just couldn't take it any more, and what ensued after that I have never never seen in my class, but I calmed them down, and Daniel was crying because Moses or one of the other boys had given him a few good punches. And then he left, but before he left he said he was going to bring back a knife on Tuesday and kill Moses and Lewis and one or two others, and my children really, really, as far as I can see even though there has been some discipline problems—these things are to be expected—I have more or less managed to cope with them either through parental cooperation or sitting down and talking to the child. Sometimes there hasn't been a permanent improvement, but with a reminder or two their behavior has once again improved. But with Daniel there is—I just can't cope with him.

I've tried to get him individually, sent him to the guidance counsellor to see what she can do, and I feel he is . . . I don't know what it is, really. I can't put my finger on what the problem is, and I know the children are really out to get him more or less, because they don't want to be punched and smacked and sat upon, and I know neither do I, so I am going to have to speak to Mrs. J———— about this and see what can be done.

I had absolutely no arithmetic supplies. Every time I need a bead board I send across the hall. She's gotten so disgusted with me—not disgusted, really—she's let me keep it already because I guess she doesn't want the interruptions, and I can't blame her. There are still quite a few arithmetic supplies that I still could use. There are quite a few art supplies that I could use and I don't know, it's gotten to the point, since the beginning of the year I've been asking for the alphabet cards to put in front of my room for the children—these are not only penmanship cards, but to see the ABC sequence and the alphabetizing and things like that but I still haven't

received it. I requested 9 × 6 yellow lined paper because my supply, my one package, has run out—I still haven't gotten that. So that I really make do with what I have, but in many cases this is pretty difficult. Crayons, things like that that I have asked for time and again haven't been forthcoming, and there's always an excuse for not getting it. It will be here soon. But perhaps by June, May, perhaps even, these things will be coming. So where the lack is I've been forced to borrow—to bring my own—to buy my own and just make do with what I have, and I feel that the problem can be enriched far more than it has been had the needed supplies been forthcoming. But since they haven't, I've had to gear myself down more or less.

I know that a lesson that I wanted to do on the thermometer—as far as my math and science go I wanted to show why we use the thermometer—have the three beakers, one with ice water—one with room-temperature water, one with hot water. Your children go out of the room and then they put their hands in either the ice water and then into the room temperature . . . How does it feel? It feels warm—and then from the hot water to the cold water. How does it feel? It feels cold. Well, really, it's a constant thing. How can we tell how cold or warm it really is? I wanted all this by using a thermometer but, of course, I had no thermometer, no beakers to do the experiment with. The beakers I had brought from home in hopes that I would get a thermometer from somewhere but no such luck. So I had to cast that lesson aside.

I mean, there are so many things that I can get on my own. I, too, am limited, so that eventually, after I've been teaching for about two or three years, all these materials will be mine. I have gotten some art supplies; I've gotten envelopes, folders that I requested to keep the children's work in. So maybe slowly but surely these things will be coming in.

Another thing that I requested were enough rulers for the whole class, and when they were delivered to me there was a grand total of twelve. So the work that I had hoped to do with measurements had to be cast aside. But we'll just have to do the best with what we have for the time being and see what evolves.

SCHOOL DROPOUTS

John Norton

The school dropout provides a key in the solution of our unemployment problems. In areas of the greatest dropout rate, there also exists high unemployment. Moreover, traditional curriculum appropriate for the middle class of suburbia provides no incentive for the troubled inner-city child. Unless immediate steps are taken to alter the educational and employment opportunities of the inner-city young, the phrase "social dynamite" coined by James Conant will become social reality.

The amount of schooling of different individuals varies enormously. Some children do not continue in school even to the fifth grade. In succeeding grades, the attrition is higher than most people realize.

According to the U.S. Office of Education, the high school graduating class of 1954 contained only 553 of each 1,000 pupils who had reached the fifth grade seven years earlier.

Just how long each child should continue in school is a matter of opinion. There is wide agreement, however, that the many pupils who drop out of school at 16, or at whatever earlier age the law or circumstances permit, constitute a major problem. One study concludes that school dropouts create an explosive situation and are a serious threat to our society.

School Dropout Rate

For example, the number of high-school graduates in 1962, as a per cent of eighth-grade enrollment in 1957–58, varied from 92.3 per cent in Wisconsin to 51.8 per cent in Georgia. The median for 50 states and the District of Columbia was 70.6 per cent. (See table for data on all states.) The average dropout rate between eighth-grade and high-school graduation is approximately 32 per cent.

It should not be assumed that these 32 per cent who quit school in the ninth, tenth, eleventh, or twelfth grades

Norton, John K., *Changing Demands on Education and Their Fiscal Implications,* Washington, D.C.: National Committee for Support of the Public Schools, 1963, pp. 53–63.

1962 HIGH-SCHOOL GRADUATES AS PER CENT OF 1957–58 EIGHTH-GRADE ENROLLMENT

1.	92.3%	Wisconsin	18.	74.1%	New York	35.	62.9%	Florida
2.	88.2	Minnesota	19.	73.3	Montana	36.	62.2	New Mexico
3.	86.4	California	20.	73.3	Rhode Island	37.	61.0	Maine
4.	84.8	Nebraska	21.	73.1	Connecticut	38.	60.6	Texas
5.	84.5	Illinois	22.	73.1	Wyoming	39.	57.8	Arkansas
6.	84.2	Washington	23.	73.0	Missouri	40.	57.8	Louisiana
7.	80.6	Hawaii	24.	72.9	Colorado	41.	57.8	Mississippi
8.	78.8	New Jersey	25.	72.5	Idaho	42.	57.4	North Carolina
9.	78.6	Iowa	26.	72.4	Ohio	43.	56.4	Vermont
10.	78.4	Michigan	27.	72.0	Delaware	44.	55.5	West Virginia
11.	78.1	Kansas	28.	71.1	Arizona	45.	55.1	Tennessee
12.	78.1	South Dakota	29.	70.1	Alaska	46.	55.0	Alabama
13.	78.0	Pennsylvania	30.	69.3	New Hampshire	47.	54.2	South Carolina
14.	77.9	Oregon	31.	68.2	Massachusetts	48.	52.6	Kentucky
15.	77.2	Utah	32.	67.9	Oklahoma	49.	51.9	Virginia
16.	76.8	North Dakota	33.	67.5	Maryland	50.	51.8	Georgia
17.	74.1	Indiana	34.	63.7	Nevada		70.6	50 states and D.C.

Source: National Education Association, Research Division. *Rankings of the States*, 1963. Research Report 1963-R1. Washington, D.C.: The Association, 1963. Table 47.

are incapable of learning. Many are victims of inadequate schooling in one form or another.

Age of School Dropouts

The greatest percentage of withdrawal occurs at about the age when attendance is no longer compulsory, which is sixteen years in most states. In October of 1959, 929,000, or 17.1 per cent of youths aged sixteen and seventeen years were not enrolled in schools.

Grade Reached by School Dropouts

Less than 60 per cent of the boys and girls who reach the fifth grade stay in school through high school. Out of every three reaching the ninth grade, one fails to get a high-school diploma.

The first major drop occurs between the ninth and tenth grades when many pupils are making the transition from junior to senior high school. . . . Another signifi-

cant drop occurs between the tenth and eleventh grades. Many of these pupils have obviously tried the secondary school and found it wanting for their needs.

Current trends indicate that about 7.5 million of the young people entering the labor force during the 1960's will not have completed high school, and that 2.5 million will not have completed even eighth grade.

Reasons for Dropping Out of School

According to the U.S. Department of Labor, Bureau of Labor Statistics,

Pupils who drop out from the eighth, ninth, and tenth grades most often do so for reasons closely related to their school experiences, such as grade retardation, academic difficulties, and failure to participate in pupil activities. Dropouts from the later grades, however, are chiefly accounted for by other well-defined reasons such as marriage, or the need to work.

Lack of guidance counselors and courses of study to meet the widely varying capacities and goals of high-school pupils today are among the major factors causing pupils to quit school. Parental and community attitudes are also influential. After visiting public schools in "two totally different neighborhoods," Conant concludes:

One lesson to be drawn from visiting and contrasting a well-to-do suburb and a slum is all important for understanding American public education. This lesson is that to a considerable degree what a school should do and can do is determined by the status and ambitions of the families being served.

Children of Migrant Workers

It is estimated that 400,000 migrant workers, accompanied by more than 100,000 children, travel from community to community and from state to state each year in search of agricultural employment.

Educationally, these children are the most deprived group in the nation. Frequent moves force them to fall further and further behind in their studies. When they drop out of school for good, their average achievement is below the fourth-grade level. A few states are attempting to deal with this problem, but it is an extremely difficult one.

CHARACTERISTICS OF SCHOOL DROPOUTS

The National Education Association Project on School Dropouts is studying intensively the characteristics of school dropouts. The following are some of the findings:

1. The average dropout is not uneducable. He does tend to score lower on IQ tests than his in-school counter-part, but a nation-wide study conducted by the U.S. Department of Labor showed that 70 per cent of the dropouts surveyed had registered IQ scores above 90, clearly in the educable group. An intensive six-year study in the State of New York revealed that 13 per cent of the dropouts had IQ scores above 110. This rating should permit high-school graduation and some post-high-school training.

2. The average dropout is at least two years retarded in reading ability by the time he quits school. Reading remains the fundamental educational skill; without it no student can perform adequately in school. The consequences of retardation in reading are obvious: dropouts fail three times as many courses as "stay-ins," and nine of every ten dropouts have been retained in some grade at least one extra year.

3. The majority of dropouts are from lower socioeconomic families. They often come from families where the father is missing, where cultural background and horizons are limited, where education is viewed with indifference, distrust, or open resentment. Any redemptive or preventive effort of the school will have to take account of the student's total environment and will depend heavily on the school's staff of guidance counselors and school-community coordinators.

4. There is a high percentage of dropouts among minority groups. This fact was detailed as follows at the 1961 Conference on Unemployed, Out-of-School Youth in Urban Areas:

Estimates of the number of Mexican-American youth who leave school before getting to high school range as high as 50 per cent in the major cities.

Today, two thirds of all Negroes live in urban areas, one third in urban areas outside the South.

In a slum section composed almost entirely of Negroes in one of our largest cities the following situation was found. A total of 59 per cent of the male youth between the ages of sixteen and twenty-one were out of school and unemployed. They were roaming the streets. Of the boys who graduated from high school, 48 per cent were unemployed in contrast to 63 per cent of the boys who had dropped out of school.

An even worse state of affairs was found in another special study in a different city. In a slum area of 125,000 people, mostly Negro, a sampling of the youth population shows that roughly 70 per cent of the boys and girls ages sixteen to twenty-one are out-of-school and unemployed.

The problem of unemployed youth in the large cities is in no small part a Negro problem. We do not facilitate its solution by trying to find phrases to hide this fact.

5. Dropouts are not entirely from minority groups. Of the four special surveys made for the Conference on Unemployed, Out-of-School Youth in Urban Areas, two dealt with racially mixed urban school districts where the majority of the dropouts interviewed were white. Like the minority group dropouts, however, most of these white boys and girls belonged to lower income families who had recently arrived in the city. Theirs were families who had left subsistence farms, families said to be among the nation's least educated, with a lack of motivation no less deadening than that of darker-skinned families from depressed areas. But the problem of school dropouts is not confined to the big cities. It exists in small towns. It is particularly acute in rural areas, and the problems of the rural areas and the big cities are closely related.

State-Wide Study of Dropouts

A state-wide study of dropouts by the Illinois Office of Public Instruction revealed the following:

Approximately 54 per cent of the students who took more than eight years to finish elementary school became high-school dropouts.

Only 2 per cent of the students who took college preparatory courses became dropouts, while 38 per cent of those who studied general curriculum left high school before graduating.

About 60 per cent of the students who were absent more than 25 days out of the normal 185-day school year became dropouts.

Over 30 per cent of the dropouts occurred before the end of the freshman year; another 30 per cent occurred during the sophomore year.

High-school graduates held more part-time jobs than dropouts held.

Dropouts had more frequent access to family cars and owned more cars than did those who graduated.

Students who finished high school engaged in more extracurricular activities than did dropouts.

A large percentage of dropouts came from broken homes.

WHAT HAPPENS TO SCHOOL DROPOUTS?

A number of studies have been made to discover what happens to young people who drop out of school. Among the more important findings are these:

1. A large percentage is unemployed. The U.S. Department of Labor in October 1960 surveyed the employment status of June, 1960 graduates and pregraduation dropouts. The survey found that

about three fourths of the male dropouts, but almost nine tenths of the high-school graduates (those not enrolled in college), were working. About two thirds of the unmarried female dropouts, but three fourths of the graduates, were working. Furthermore, the unemployed dropouts had been unemployed for longer periods than the unemployed graduates.

Conant stated that

in the slums of the largest cities . . . the great need is for reduction of unemployment of male youth under twenty-one.

The present (1960) unemployment rate nationwide is roughly 7 per cent for all age brackets, but unemployment among youth under twenty years of age is about 20 per cent, or nearly three times greater than the nationwide rate for all workers.

A survey made in New York City in the summer of 1962 showed that 45,000 youths needed work but were unable to find it. Many of these were Puerto Ricans and Negroes, the groups which have the most difficulty in finding jobs. Many are school dropouts, and their lack of education and training further hampers them.

Ewan Clague, Director of the Bureau of Labor Statistics, stated at the Conference on Unemployed, Out-of-School Youth in Urban Areas that 300,000 boys and 115,000 girls between the ages sixteen and twenty reported themselves out of school looking for work in October 1960.

2. Most school dropouts when employed work at unskilled jobs. Unskilled and immature, the dropout finds himself abandoned in a labor market where he has little to offer.

Casual jobs and work requiring little in the ways of skills training typify the employment activity of most fourteen- to seventeen-year-olds. Job opportunities for youth in this age group are concentrated mainly in the trade and service industries and in agriculture.

The jobs available to school dropouts are usually of the lowest order. Frequently they offer irregular employment and are the least open to advancement. Also, employers are loath to employ and to provide on-the-job training to youths in the sixteen to twenty-one age group, since they may be subject to call for military service.

Two thirds of the nation's force of service workers and operatives and laborers are former dropouts. Two thirds of the unemployed men and women in the United States possess less than a high-school education.

3. Dropouts face keen competition. Because of the rapid rise in births in the 1940's and 1950's, the population reaching age eighteen will shortly increase especially fast—from 2.6 million in 1960 to 3.8 million in 1965, up nearly 50 per cent in only five years. The 1965 rate will continue through 1970. Because of this increase, the number of new workers entering the labor force will mount steadily. Altogether 26 million young people will enter the labor force during the 1960's, almost 40 per cent more than during the 1950's.

The estimated 7.5 million youths who, according to recent experience, will drop out of school during the 1960's may glut the labor market already overcrowded with unskilled workers at a time when the number of unskilled occupations is declining.

4. The life earnings of school dropouts are low. During his lifetime, the average boy who drops out of school before high-school graduation will earn much less than the average high-school

graduate. "The typical male high school graduate can be expected to earn over his lifetime (from age twenty-five to death) $72,000 more than the typical male elementary-school graduate."

School Dropouts and Delinquency

Exact numbers and percents of school dropouts who become delinquent are not known. It is claimed that they are relatively large. Out-of-school, unemployed youth are more apt to become delinquent. A youngster out of school and out of work is a potential source of trouble to himself and to the community. A youth who drops out of school and cannot find a job, which gives him a sense of belonging to the community and of purpose in life, is apt to feel at odds with society and is more likely to become delinquent.

Careful studies of juvenile delinquency show that this problem is not confined to communities and families of low socioeconomic status. It occurs in favored communities and families, although at a lower rate of incidence. Nor is juvenile delinquency a peculiar problem of the United States. It is world-wide. These facts call for fundamental study of this disturbing problem and incisive action by responsible agencies, including the schools.

CONCLUSIONS

1. Today, for most youths under eighteen, work should be secondary to getting education and training appropriate to their abilities and needs.

2. Lack of basic education seriously complicates the retraining of the long-term unemployed.

3. A substantial percentage on relief rolls are those who lose their jobs and lack the training for other employment.

4. Out-of-school, unemployed youths commit a disproportionately high percentage of juvenile crimes.

5. Full development of each youth's talents and abilities is the key to meeting future manpower needs. To assure such development, youths must have protection and guidance, jobs that provide productive experience, and, perhaps most important, the kind of education needed in our modern complex and technically oriented economy.

[These] conclusions raise many questions about the adequacy of today's public elementary and secondary schools. Is the guidance program adequate? Is the curriculum or program of studies broad enough to meet the present needs of America's children and youth? Are adequate provisions made for the children of "disadvantaged Americans"—parents with low socio-economic status, language handicaps, lack of vocational skills with resulting unemployment, and little interest in having their children continue in school? Are the quality of teachers and their training and teaching equal to the demands of a rapidly changing society?

The powerful impacts of our dynamic economy upon all Americans hold fundamental implications for public schools.

THE REJECTS

Michael Harrington

Pervasive unemployment takes its toll in a man's pride. Men accustomed to work and proud of their ability to hold a job often find themselves suddenly cut off by a shut down, a layoff, or automation. The cause is not nearly as significant as the fact that these conditions leave a man bereft of this all important pride.

An even sadder commentary in our society lies in the knowledge that certain groups or industries will attempt to exploit this misery for profit. Crooked unionism and sweatshops are often stripping away any remaining sense of dignity. Mr. Harrington provides an inciteful look into the world of these rejects.

In New York City, some of my friends call 80 Warren Street "the "slave market."

It is a big building in downtown Manhattan. Its corridors have the littered, trampled air of a courthouse. They are lined with employment-agency offices. Some of these places list good-paying and highly skilled jobs. But many of them provide the work force for the economic underworld in the big city: the dishwashers and day workers, the fly-by-night jobs.

Early every morning, there is a great press of human beings in 80 Warren Street. It is made up of Puerto Ricans and Negroes, alcoholics, drifters, and disturbed people. Some of them will pay a flat fee (usually around 10 per cent) for a day's work. They pay $0.50 for a $5.00 job and they are given the address of a luncheonette. If all goes well, they will make their wage. If not, they have a legal right to come back and get their half-dollar. But many of them don't know that, for they are people that are not familiar with laws and rights.

But perhaps the most depressing time at 80 Warren Street is in the afternoon. The jobs have all been handed out, yet the people still mill around. Some of them sit on benches in the larger offices. There is no real point to their waiting, yet they have nothing else to do. For some, it is probably a point of pride to be there, a feeling that they are somehow still looking for a job even if they know that there is no chance to get one until early in the morning.

Most of the people at 80 Warren Street were born poor. (The alcoholics are an exception.) They are incompetent as far as American society is concerned, lacking the education and the skills to get decent work. If they find steady employment, it will be in a sweatshop or a kitchen.

In a Chicago factory, another group of people are working. A year or so ago, they were in a union shop making good wages, with sick leave, pension rights, and vacations. Now they are making artificial Christmas trees at less than half the pay they had been receiving. They have no contract rights, and the foreman is absolute monarch. Permission is required if a worker wants to go to the bathroom. A few are fired every day for insubordination.

These are people who have become poor. They possess skills, and they once moved upward with the rest of the society. But now their jobs have been destroyed, and their skills have been rendered useless. In the process, they have been pushed down toward the poverty from whence they came. This particular group is Negro, and the chances of ever breaking through, of returning to the old conditions, are very slim. Yet their plight is not exclusively racial, for it is shared by all the semi-skilled and unskilled workers who are the victims of technological unemployment in the mass-production industries. They are involved in an interracial misery.

These people are the rejects of the affluent society. They never had the right skills in the first place, or they lost them when the rest of the economy advanced. They are the ones who make up a huge portion of the culture of poverty in the cities of America. They are to be counted in the millions.

I

Each big city in the United States has an economic underworld. And often enough this phrase is a literal description: it refers to the kitchens and furnace rooms that are under the city; it tells of the place where tens of thousands of hidden people labor at impossible wages. Like the underworld of crime, the economic underworld is out of sight, clandestine.

The workers in the economic underworld are concentrated among the urban section of the more than 16,000,000 Americans denied coverage by the Minimum-Wage Law of 1961. They are domestic workers, hotel employees,

bus boys, and dishwashers, and some of the people working in small retail stores. In the most recent Government figures, for example, hotel workers averaged $47.44 a week, laundry workers $46.45, general-merchandise employees $48.37, and workers in factories making work clothing $45.58.

This sector of the American economy has proved itself immune to progress. And one of the main reasons is that it is almost impossible to organize the workers of the economic underworld in their self-defense. They are at the mercy of unscrupulous employers (and, in the case of hospital workers, management might well be a board composed of the "best" people of the city who, in pursuing a charitable bent, participate in a conspiracy to exploit the most helpless citizens). They are cheated by crooked unions; they are used by racketeers.

In the late fifties I talked to some hospital workers in Chicago. They were walking a picket line, seeking union recognition. (They lost.) Most of them made about $30 a week and were the main support of their families. The hospital deducted several dollars a week for food that they ate on the job. But then, they had no choice in this matter. If they didn't take the food, they had to pay for it anyway.

When the union came, it found a work force at the point of desperation. A majority of them had signed up as soon as they had the chance. But, like most of the workers in the economic underworld, these women were hard to keep organized. Their dues were minuscule, and in effect they were being subsidized by the better-paid workers in the union. Their skills were so low that supervisory personnel could take over many of their functions during a strike. It required an enormous effort to reach them and to help them, and in this case it failed.

An extreme instance of this institutional poverty took place in Atlanta, Georgia, among hospital workers in mid-1960. Men who worked the dishwashing machines received $0.68 an hour; women kitchen helpers got $0.56; and the maids $0.55 an hour. If these people all put in the regular two thousand hours of work a year, they would receive just over $1,000 for their services.

The restaurants of the economic underworld are somewhat like the hospitals. The "hidden help" in the kitchen are an unstable group. They shift jobs rapidly. As a result, a union will sign up all the employees in a place, but before a union certification election can occur half of those who had joined will have moved on to other work. This means that it is extremely expensive for the labor movement to try to organize these workers: they are dispersed in small groups; they cannot pay for themselves; and they require constant servicing checking, and rechecking to be sure that the new workers are brought into the union structure.

The fact that the economic underworld is so hard to organize makes it a perfect place for two types of racketeers to operate: labor racketeers and their constant companions the management racketeers. In the mid-fifties, some of the locals of the Hotel and Restaurant Employees Union in Chicago were under racket domination. (The crooks have since been cleaned out.) The deal was very simple. The dishonest union man would demand a payoff from the dishonest restaurateur. Sometimes it was figured as a percentage tax on the number of place settings in an establishment. In return for this money, the "unionist" would allow management to pay well below the prevailing union wage. This meant that waitresses were brought into the economic underworld along with the kitchen help.

In New York, a city that specializes in sweatshops, this crooked unionism was even more blatant. There are Puerto Ricans who are "members" of unions they never even heard of. Their rights in these labor organizations are confined to the payment of dues. The businessman, who is so essential to racketeering unionism, makes his payment to the union leader. In return he gets immunity from organization and the right to pay starvation wages. The contracts that come out of these deals are "black and white." All the standard provisions of an honest union contract providing for wage rates, fringe benefits, and the protection of working conditions in the shop are x'ed out. The only agreement is that the place is unionized, which is to say that it is protected from honest unionism.

Indeed, one of the paradoxical consequences of the AFL-CIO "No Raiding" agreement is that it helps to keep some of these lowest-paid workers in the grip of labor racketeers. As long as the racket local manages to keep a charter in a recognized international (and, in the late fifties, this was becoming more difficult, but not impossible), then the honest unions are stopped from going in and decertifying the crooks. Many unionists who see the positive value in the No Raiding procedure have argued for an amendment: "Raiding" will be permitted if an honest union can show that the local in a given situation is a racket outfit creating substandard conditions.

Finally, the economic underworld is made up of small shops, of handfuls of workers, but that does not mean that its total population is insignificant. When the hotels, the restaurants, the hospitals, and the sweatshops are added up, one confronts a section of the economy that employs millions and millions of workers. In retailing alone, there are 6,000,000 or 7,000,000 employees who are unorganized, and many of them are not covered by minimum wage. For instance, in 1961 the general-merchandise stores (with an average weekly wage of $48.37) counted over 1,250,000 employees. Those who made work clothes, averaging just over $45.00 a week, totaled some 300,000 citizens, most of them living in the other America of the poor.

Thus, in the society of abundance and high standards of living there is an economically backward sector which is incredibly capable of being exploited; it is unorganized, and in many cases without the protection of Federal law. It is in this area that the disabled, the retarded, and the minorities toil. In Los Angeles they might be Mexican-Americans, in the runaway shops of West Virginia or Pennsylvania, white Anglo-Saxon Protestants. All of them are poor; regardless of race, creed, or color, all of them are victims.

In the spring of 1961, American society faced up to the problem of the economic underworld. It decided that it was not worth solving. Since these workers cannot organize to help themselves, their only real hope for aid must be directed toward the intervention of the Federal Government. After the election of President Kennedy, this issue was joined in terms of a minimum-wage bill. The AFL-CIO proposal that minimum-wage coverage should be extended to about 6,500,000 new workers; the Administration proposed new coverage for a little better than 3,000,000 workers; the conservatives of the Dixiecrat-Republican coalition wanted to hold the figure down to about 1,000,000.

There was tremendous logrolling in Congress over the issue. In order to win support for the Administration approach, concessions were made. It does not take much political acumen to guess which human beings were conceded: the poor. The laundry workers (there

are over 300,000 of them, and according to the most recent Bureau of Labor statistics figures they averaged $47.72 a week) and the hospital workers were dropped from the extension of coverage. The papers announced that over 3,000,000 new workers had been granted coverage—but they failed to note that a good number of them were already in well-paid industries and didn't need help.

In power politics, organized strength tells. So it was that America turned its back on the rejects in the economic underworld. As one reporter put it, "We've got the people who make $26 a day safely covered; it's the people making $26 a week who are left out." Once again, there is the irony that the welfare state benefits least those who need help most.

II

The men and women in the economic underworld were, for the most part, born poor. But there is another, and perhaps more tragic, type of industrial poverty: the experience of those who become poor.

This is what happens to them.

On a cold evening in Chicago (winter is a most bitter enemy of the poor) I talked to a group of Negro workers. Until a short time before our meeting, they had worked in the meat-packing industry and were members of the Packinghouse Workers Union. They had been making around $2.25 an hour, with fringe benefits and various guarantees for sick leave, vacation, and the like. More than that, they had found a certain dignity for themselves in that they belonged to one of the most integrated unions in the United States. (The industry had traditionally employed many Negroes; one factor was that much of the work was regarded as "dirty," that is, Negro, tasks.)

A number of these people had found jobs in a plant making artificial Christmas trees. They received $1 an hour and no fringe benefits. The shop was, of course, nonunion. Several workers were fired every day, and crowds gathered on Monday morning to compete for their places.

The $1 an hour was bad enough, but there was an even more important aspect to this impoverishment. When they worked at Armour, these employees knew a certain job security; they had rights in the shop because of the union. It was not only that their wages had been cut by more than half when the plant closed; it was also that they had been humiliated. This was particularly true of these Negroes. As members of a minority group, they had been fortunate to get such good jobs and to belong to a union that took civil rights seriously. Now that they had been thrust into the economic underworld, that racial gain was wiped out. The Christmas-tree shop hired Negroes only. That was because they were available cheap; that was because they could be "kept in their place."

One of the workers I talked to was a woman in her thirties. When she spoke, the bitterness was not so much directed against the low pay: what concerned her most was the "slavery" of her working conditions. She had to ask the supervisor's permission to go to the bathroom. At any moment she could be fired for insubordination, and there was no grievance procedure or arbitration to protect her rights. She was vivacious and articulate, a born leader. So she tried to organize the shop. A majority of the workers had signed cards asking for a union election, but the National Labor Relations Board had postponed the date. The election will never take place. The Christmas-tree season is over, and these people are out on the streets again.

Yet the workers in the sweatshop considered themselves lucky. They were making $1 an hour, which was something. Two men I talked to were in a different classification: they had passed the line of human obsolescence in this industrial society. They were over forty years of age. They had been laid off at Armour in the summer of 1959. Eighteen months later, neither of them had found a steady job of any kind. "When I come to the hiring window," one of them said, "the man just looks at me; he doesn't even ask questions; he says, 'You're too old.'"

Other men talked of how racial discrimination worked against them when the plant closed. One technique is simplicity itself. A job is rated by a plant well over its actual skill level. Training and educational qualifications are specified in great detail. When the white worker applies, these criteria are waived. When the Negro worker shows up in the hiring line, the letter of the law is enforced. Technically, there has been no discrimination. The Negro was turned down for lack of skill, not because of race. But that, of course, is the most obvious and palpable evasion.

What happens to the man who goes eighteen months without a steady job? The men told me. First, the "luxuries" go: the car, the house, everything that has been purchased on installment but not yet paid for. Then comes doubling up with relatives (and one of the persistent problems in becoming poor is that marriages are often wrecked in the process). Finally—and this is particularly true of the "older" worker—there is relief, formal admission into the other America.

The Armour workers who became poor were, to a considerable extent, Negro. In attitudes toward poverty, there is a curious double standard. America more or less expects the Negro to be poor (and is convinced that things are getting better, a point to be dealt with in a later chapter). There is no emotional shock when people hear of the experience of these human beings in Chicago. The mind and the feelings, even of good-willed individuals, are so suffused with an unconscious racism that misery is overlooked.

But what happened at Armour is not primarily racial, even though the situation is compounded and intensified by the fact that Negroes are involved. The same basic process is at work in Pennsylvania and in Detroit.

In a brilliant report, Harvey Swados wrote of his first impression of Saint Michael, Pennsylvania: "It is a strange thing to come to a town and find it full of grown men. They stroll the narrow, shabby streets, chat at the corners, lean against the peeling pillars of the town saloon, the St. Michael Hotel & Restaurant, and they look more like movie actors than real human beings, because something is wrong."

That "something" happened on April 24, 1958, when Maryland Shaft Number 1 closed down. Since then some of the miners have been able to get jobs elsewhere. But for most of them, there are idleness and a profound change in the way of life. What, after all, do you do with a man who is a skilled coal miner? When the mine closes down, what industry do you put him into? He is physically strong; he has lived his life in a tight community of coal miners; and he has intense loyalties to his fellow workers and to his little town in the mountains. But he has a skill that is hardly transferable.

Some of the men from Maryland Shaft Number 1 got jobs in the steel industry, but they have already been hit by layoffs there. The automation process that destroyed the work in coal is spreading to steel: their problem is following after them. Others are working, for a fraction of their previous wage, as orderlies in hospitals and institutions, as janitors and stockmen in big stores.

But, again, the most humiliating part of this experience maims the spirit. As Swados puts it, "It is truly ironic that a substantial portion of these men, who pride themselves on their ability to live with danger, to work hard, fight hard, drink hard, love hard, are now learning housework and taking over the woman's role in the family."

For the miners have always been an almost legendary section of the work force. Their towns are as isolated as ships, and they have had the pride of métier, the élan of seamen. Their union battles were long and bloody, sometimes approaching the dimensions of civil war, as in the fabled Harlan County struggles. They had a tough life, but part of the compensation was the knowledge that they were equal to it. Now the job has been taken away, and the pride with it.

In many of these mining areas, there are small garment shops that are running away from union labor in New York and other established centers. Their pay is miserable, and they look for the wives of the unemployed. So the miners do the housework and hang around the saloon, and the wife has become the breadwinner.

In Detroit one can see still another part of this process: it is not minority poverty as with the Armour workers, nor is it depressed-area poverty as in the case of the coal miners. It is the slide backward, the becoming poor, that takes place in the midst of a huge American industrial city.

In 1956 Packard closed out a Detroit factory and destroyed some 4,000 jobs. What happened to the men and women involved has been carefully described in a special study of the Senate Committee on Unemployement Problems. The report is entitled "Too Old to Work, Too Young to Retire."

When the Packard plant closed, the world fell in on some of the men. There were those who cried. They had worked in the shop for years, and they had developed a personal identification with the car they built. Some of them were particularly bitter because they felt the company had blundered by lowering standards and turning out an inferior product. They were laid off in 1956, but many of them had still not found regular work when the recession hit in 1958 and again in 1960.

The workers in the best position were those who were both young and skilled. Their unemployment averaged "only" a little better than five and a half months. The young and semiskilled were out on the street for an average of seven and a half months; the old, skilled workers for eight and a half months. Finally, the "old" semiskilled workers (say, machine operators over forty-five) averaged better than a year of unemployment. The old and unskilled were out for fourteen months.

For almost every one of these human beings, there was a horrible sinking experience. Of those who were able to find jobs, almost 40 per cent took a position inferior to the one they had held. Skilled workers took semiskilled or even common-laborer jobs. Most of these did not become poor. They were humiliated and downgraded, but not dragged below the subsistence level. But some of the old, the unskilled, and the Negroes entered the other America in the late fifties. They came from a well-organized and relatively high-paying industry. They ended by becoming impoverished.

So it was in Detroit, Michigan, and the story is substantially the same as in Saint Michael, Pennsylvania or Chicago,

Illinois. In the fifties and early sixties, a society with an enormous technology and the ability to provide a standard of living for every citizen saw millions of people move back. Some of them retrogressed all the way, and ended where they had been before the gains of the welfare state were made. Many of them slid back but did not become impoverished.

In the next section there will be a more precise description of the dimension of this development in American industry. At this point, however, the main data are not statistical, but personal and individual. Psychological deprivation is one of the chief components of poverty, as we noted in the opening chapter. And the terrible thing that is happening to these people is that suddenly they feel themselves to be rejects, outcasts. At that moment the affluent society ceases to be a reality or even a hope; it becomes a taunt.

III

The human rejects who have become poor are a particular, and striking, case of the invisibility of poverty in the other America.

In the thirties, as noted before, unemployment was a general problem of the society. A quarter of the work force was in the streets, and everyone was affected. Big business was hit by the stock crash; small business failed because of the general climate; white-collar workers were laid off like everyone else. From out of this experience, there came a definition of "good times": if the statistics announced that more people were working than ever before, that was prosperity; if there was a dip in employment, with 4,000,000 to 6,000,000 temporarily laid off, that was a recession.

But the definitions of the thirties

blind us to a new reality. It is now possible (or rather it is the reality) to have an increase in the number of employed, an expansion of consumption, a boom in production and, at the same time, localized depressions. In the midst of general prosperity, there will be types of jobs, entire areas, and huge industries in which misery is on the increase. The familiar America of high living standards moves upward; the other America of poverty continues to move downward.

Professor John Dunlop, of Harvard, has made an illuminating distinction to describe this process. In the thirties, he notes, there was mass unemployment; in the postwar period there has been class unemployment. Special groups will be singled out by the working of the economy to suffer, while all others will experience prosperity.

When class unemployment takes place, the peculiar law that it is better to be miserable when everyone else is miserable goes into effect. It is possible for conservatives and other opponents of Federal action to point to figures showing production and total unemployment at record highs. The average citizen assumes that this means that good times are general; the class hit by depression condition is forgotten or ignored.

In the fifties and early sixties, the people who were downgraded and even impoverished came primarily from the mass-production industries. In 1929, according to the Bureal of Labor Statistics, 59 per cent of the work force was blue collar, 41 per cent white collar. By 1957 the blue-collar percentage had declined to 47 per cent; the service industries and professions had risen to 53 per cent. These figures chart the decline of industrial jobs in a period when the economy as a whole was moving upward.

For many people this development was a sign that America was becoming a classless, economically democratic society. The nation, they argued, was becoming more and more white collar, and non-manual. Yet what this thesis misses is that at least part of this shift is downward, that when a worker moves from a unionized industrial job to a nonunionized service job he loses pay, working conditions, and pride. Here again there is a social problem of the eyes. Class becomes somewhat less obvious—there are fewer blue shirts and lunch boxes—but the disabilities of class remain and, in some cases, are intensified.

So it was that the Government announced in 1960 that during a period of high employment in the fifties, one-fifth of those out of work came from chronically depressed areas and industries. At such a time the unemployment rate for blue-collar workers was almost three times that of white-collar workers. In the depressed areas fully a quarter of the jobless had been out of work for better than half a year. A high percentage of them were family men with dependent children. And unemployment for Negroes was two and a half to three times higher than for whites.

George Meany, president of the AFL-CIO, focused on the class nature of this unemployment with a few simple figures: between 1953 and 1959, 1,500,000 blue-collar jobs, 11 per cent of the total, were eliminated from the economy; at the same time the number of clerical and professional workers increased by some 600,000.

During this period the amount of unemployment considered "normal" was constantly on the rise. After the 1949 recession, an unemployment rate of 3.1 per cent existed inside prosperity; after the 1954 recession the figure had gone up to 4.3 per cent; and after the business recovery from the downturn of 1958, 5.1 per cent of the work force was still idle. (The 1961 "recovery" began with almost 7 per cent unemployed.) In a matter of a decade, the "normal" unemployment of 1958 was equal to the recession unemployment of 1949.

But—and this is important for the culture of poverty in America—it must be emphasized that these figures contain an increase in long-term joblessness. It is bad enough for a worker to be laid off for a matter of weeks. When this becomes months, or even years, it is not simply a setback. It is a basic threat to fundamental living standards, a menace of impoverishment. Put in the dry but accurate words of the Bureau of Labor Statistics: "All of the moderate increase in the rate of total unemployment was accounted for by the proportionately much greater rise in the continuing unemployed."

Once depression hits an area, its very life seems to leave. The tax base narrows; public services decline; a sort of civic disintegration takes over. Low-paying industry may come in, but that is an exploitation of the problem, not a solution. Or else nothing happens. And then the vicious circle begins to work. Because a place is poor and dispirited, manufacturers don't want to locate there; because of this, the area becomes even poorer. To quote the Bureau of Labor Statistics again: "However, the very fact of being an area of high unemployment as against being a prosperous area, in turn, has an influence on the kinds of industries that might be attracted." More simply: no one, particularly corporations, is attracted by the smell of defeat.

In 1961 the Congress addressed itself to this problem. Its response was as inadequate for those becoming poor as it was for those who had been living in the economic underworld all along. A pathetically small amount of money was set aside for retraining individuals. The main emphasis was on loans that would help the depressed areas to bring in industry. The money appropriated was not enough, according to the analysis of the Administration that proposed the law. But more than that, there was no real provision for regional planning, for a massive assault on the institutions of pessimism and incompetence that develop in a depressed area.

As of this writing, the new rejects face a future as bleak as that of the old rejects: the Federal Government, the one force strong enough to act, has been unable to come up with an effective program. The result, if this situation continues, will be an expansion of the other America, a new recruitment of the poor.

But then, there are those who have an easy answer, who can tell a man how to avoid becoming poor. Their advice is summed up in a single word: Move! Here again, however, a familiar irony is at work. The poor generally are those who cannot help themselves. And those most hurt by class unemployment are precisely the ones who can't move.

Unemployment in the depressed area hits the married man with children. It strikes the older worker who has been a model citizen and who has saved up to buy a house. ("Owning a home is perhaps the most formidable barrier to moving out of a labor-surplus area," the statisticians note.) It involves the semiskilled and the unskilled who will not be able to find decent jobs even if they do move.

The upside-down effect is also at work: what was intended as an advantage becomes a disability. In the post-war period many people hailed the negotiation of "fringe" benefits by unions. They believed that this was providing a stability for the wage worker that would eventually bring him the security of an annual salary. And, to be sure, significant gains were made. But one of the side effects of this process comes into play when an area or an industry becomes depressed. Because of these benefits, and particularly because of the pension system, there has been a decline in the number of workers who quit their jobs. Arthur M. Ross, of the University of California, has spoken of our "industrial feudalism," a system that binds the worker to his plant.

Take the mines as a case in point. The United Mine Workers contracts provide that a man must have worked for twenty years out of the last thirty if he is to be eligible for a pension of $100 a month at the age of sixty. Seniority under this system cannot be transferred from one company to another, or even from one company mine to another, unless there happens to be a shortage of miners. (And, in the fifties, the number of miners declined by better than half: from 441,631 to 218,600.)

The mine closes. A man who needs only a year or two to complete his eligibility stays around, hoping against hope that something will happen, that he can get enough work to secure his pension. If a worker has already put in his twenty years, there is a tendency to wait it out at home until the pension comes. For both types, there is increasing penury, idleness, the grim, debilitating experience of doing nothing.

Progress in this case has, as it so often does in the other America, become upside-down. The pension plan, negotiated to give security and a decent life to the worker, becomes a fetter on his mobility. It ties him into the fate of the company, the industry, the area. It keeps him from moving—if that would do any good.

And finally, there are some simple human reasons why people don't move. Perhaps they have children in school and don't want to take them away from their friends; perhaps, like the miners, they are part of a work clan or an ethnic group and can't imagine life apart from the familiar ways. Riding through the coal and steel towns of Pennsylvania and West Virginia, it is hard for the outsider to imagine people developing affection for these gouged and scarred hills. The fact is that they do.

In short, the simple prescription of the comfortable middle-class citizen, "I can't see why those people don't just move, but I guess they're lazy," is spoken out of profound ignorance. There are many reasons why they can't move; and in many cases it wouldn't make any difference if they did. These are not people that are subject to a temporary, cyclical kind of joblessness. They are more often the ones who have had their very function in the economy obliterated.

Yet, aren't there cushions that have been built up by the welfare state and the unions to handle these problems?

The answer is Yes. These workers are better off than they were before the New Deal and the rise of mass industrial unionism. But the Yes must be qualified in the usual way: those who need protection and cushions most have them the least. It is precisely the worker who is in danger of tumbling over the abyss and into the other America who gets the least support from society.

In the industrial states where organized labor has political strength, the unemployment-compensation rates are usually higher. In the backward states, where the most grinding poverty exists, they are low. Even then, Professor Seymour Harris, of Harvard, has pointed out that unemployment compensation in the fifties was less of a percentage of the working wage than it had been in the late thirties. At any rate, there has been a real advance: the roof does not fall in all at once.

During the fifties, about half of the unemployed shared in these welfare benefits. But the other half were not covered. (Their occupations were excluded from the law; they were involved in shifting, menial jobs, and didn't work long enough over a year to qualify.) Those who had salable skills could use this money for the transition to a new job. The others had a respite before they had to face plain poverty.

The conservative image would have those facing impoverishment racing to the relief office. The fact is that they do not. Those who are becoming poor were in the middle third that struggled and accomplished in the thirties and forties. They have a pride, a spirit, and the last thing they want to do is to go to welfare. The Senate study on the Packard shutdown revealed that even the workers who had been out on the streets for over a year shied away from applying for the relief rolls. They would take low-paying jobs, they would downgrade their skills, and they would accept humiliation rather than go on the public dole.

And those who finally are forced on relief face a special degradation if they had been hard-working and virtuous in the days of their prosperity. To receive public assistance, they may be required to give the state a lien on their house and a claim on their estate when they die. The American dream of saving so as to pass on opportunities to children is shattered in the bureaucratic maze.

If this process of turning the clock back, of rejecting those who had once made advances, goes on, then the other America will grow during the 1960's.

IV

These statistics can be made personal and summary, the ironies can be gathered together, by looking at what happened when the Armour plant in Oklahoma City closed in June, 1960.

When the plant closed, there were 325 people still working. There had been progressive layoffs, so the final work force was "old" (76 per cent were over forty). Their first big problem was that they had participated in the credit boom of the fifties. That magic means of expanding consumption broke down the instant the closing was announced. The Credit Union, for instance, understood that these people would be out a long time (and in other packing-house closings other creditors got the point). Debts were subtracted from severance pay.

Almost all of the 325 workers were in debt. For 265 of them, the average liability was over $900. In good times this would have provided copy for celebrations of the strength of the economy. But not now. The unemployment-compensation system ruled that waiting period for eligibility would be computed on the basis of the total severance pay. With the debts taken out, however, the actual payment was often less than half of this theoretical figure. (The plants with a younger and more heavily indebted work force have an even more intense problem.)

These particular workers were part of the famous "middle class" work force. Well over a hundred of them owned houses, some of them mortgage free. Many of them had made recent purchases because Armour had announced, shortly before the closing, that it was going to expand. For those with houses and debts, the problem of moving on was extremely complicated.

Still, about half of the workers were

surveyed and found ready to pick up stakes and move. As it happened, no one could find guarantees of work in the industry in nearby states, since the reduction in jobs was hitting many plants. (In the three years between 1956 and 1959, the industry had permanently destroyed around 30,000 jobs.) Therefore moving was no real answer, even for those who could.

Most of these Oklahoma City people will not work regularly again. In East St. Louis in a similar situation, 50 per cent of the workers were without regular employment eight months after the closing; in Fargo, a third of the workers were still on the streets after a year; and in Chicago, less than half had found regular work after sixteen months.

These are the new rejects; penalized by pensions, penalized by credit, penalized by home-owning, penalized by steadiness and by saving, they are the rightfully proud ones who will provide some of the new recruits to the other America.

The old poor of the economic underworld, the new poor of the depressed areas and industries—these are a major component of urban poverty in the United States.

So far, these groups have proved to be immune from the welfare state. If they manage to survive, if they advance,

it is not because of help from the Federal Government. And the majority have no real hope of advancing. They are, like most of the population of the other America, unable to help themselves through no fault of their own.

In the early sixties the United States carefully documented the plight of these rejects. Congressional hearings and Government statistics establishd and defined their misery beyond doubt. Yet, having made an official effort to see these people, having demonstrated the kind of help they need, the society turned its back upon them. It passed an inadequate minimum-wage bill that excluded some of the most desperate rejects of the economic underworld; it produced a depressed-area law that by its own standards could hardly begin to deal with the problem.

As a result, the urban poverty of the rejects was given a new lease on life. And long after this book is published, the old and obsolete workers who are over forty, the married and family men at the wrong place in the economy, the ones with no skill or the wrong skill, and the people born into the backward industry or the inferior school system will be living in the midst of the affluent society.

If something is not done, the other America may grow even larger.

THE COSTS OF UNEMPLOYMENT

U.S. Senate Special Committee on Unemployment Problems

When people become unemployed, the entire community suffers. Unemployment may well result in a loss of family solidarity, a lack of necessary physical care, and a loss in personal pride. Adequate education can provide some measure of hope

From the 1960 report of the U.S. Senate Special Committee on Unemployment Problems; Senator Eugene McCarthy, Chairman.

but it takes time, and our nation cannot long afford this continual loss of human resources. As this reading suggests, only the cooperative efforts of all segments of society, including business, labor, education, and civic leadership can effectively deal with this problem.

THE ECONOMIC AND SOCIAL COSTS OF UNEMPLOYMENT

Whether measured by economic and material loss or by human suffering and wasted skills, the cost of unemployment is high. Unused natural resources remain to be used in the future. But work, the creative activity of man, once wasted can never be recovered; what might have been produced is lost. The damage to individuals and to society from unemployment often cannot be repaired.

The Economic Costs of Unemployment

The clearest measure of economic loss resulting from business recession is the estimated decrease in gross national product (GNP). During the depression of 1929–32, GNP dropped by approximately $46 billion, a decline of nearly 44 percent measured in current dollars and almost 29 percent in constant dollars. The three recessions since World War II have been short compared with the depression of the 1930's, but they have nonetheless been costly.

It is possible to calculate the difference between the value of goods and services actually produced in the whole economy in a given period, and the value of goods and services which would have been produced had there been full employment and full production. There will, however, be differences of opinion in estimating the latter figure. The difference depends upon the estimated annual rate of growth, measured in terms of gross national product, which could have been expected under conditions of sustained full employment and full production.

The labor force has increased every year by about 1 percent a year during the fifties. The rate will be higher in the next decade. The average productivity of each man-hour of work also tends to grow as a result of technological advance and other forces, but at a rate which fluctuates considerably from year to year, depending in large part upon the general level of economic activity. The rate of productivity advance which would be experienced under sustained full employment, combined with the rate of increase in the labor force, gives the potential rate of growth in the economy.

The average rate of productivity advance per man-hour worked was 3.5 percent per year for the period 1947 through 1959. Many economists have said that an average rate of growth of 5 percent is necessary to maintain full employment. The Rockefeller Brothers Fund report, "The Challenge to America," stated that a 5-percent growth rate was not only possible but essential. The report asserted that without a 5-percent rate, "we shall have to hold back otherwise desirable expenditures in the Government field and keep the growth of private expenditures below a level commensurate with our aspirations," if we are to meet the national defense programs necessary for survival.[1]

Other economists have suggested that a growth rate of 4 percent per year is about what we can expect. The Joint

[1] Rockefeller Bros. Fund, Inc.: "The Challenge to America." Garden City, N.Y., Doubleday & Co., 1958, p. 73.

Economic Committee has recommended a 4.5 percent rate of growth. Gov. Nelson Rockefeller of New York, on the other hand, recently suggested a 6-percent growth rate as the goal for which we should aim. . . .

The Economic Cost to the Individual and His Family

Nine out of ten workers in the United States are members of families with responsibility for the support of other members. Nearly half of the 44 million families in the United States in 1957 were supported by the efforts of one wage earner; 45 percent had two or more wage earners; 5 percent had income exclusively from pensions, investments, or social welfare assistance.

The financial problems of the families of the unemployed have never been fully or accurately studied, but a number of State unemployment bureaus have made intensive studies of spending patterns before and during unemployment. A sampling of unemployment compensation beneficiaries in Oregon in 1958 showed that 37 percent of the beneficiaries interviewed were heads of families for whom unemployment benefits were the only reported regular family income. Another 17 percent lived alone and were totally dependent upon unemployment compensation. Twenty-one percent were normally the chief wage earners in families which had, however, other wage earners.[2]

Many families in the United States are dependent upon the earnings of two or more members or have adjusted their standards of living to the earnings of two or more members. Loss of job by any member contributing to the income of the family forces economic and

[2] U.S. Department of Labor, "The Labor Market and Employment Security," August 1959, p. 13.

social adjustment for everyone; in some cases it may even endanger family welfare.

Loss of jobs by the many individuals who do not qualify for unemployment insurance benefits usually means a complete loss of income, but even those who are eligible for benefits suffer a drastic reduction in income. In 1959, for example, unemployment insurance benefits averaged about $30 a week; very few of the unemployed who received unemployment benefits received more than half of their previous income.

Unemployment benefits for many are quickly exhausted. During the 1958 business downturn about two-thirds of the unemployed received benefits, but in the last part of 1959 fewer than half the unemployed collected benefits. Family incomes during these periods must, of course, be supplemented from other sources. Other members of the family may be able to get jobs, small family-farm production may be increased, or tenants may be taken into the family home.

Social security payments are particularly important as a source of income for older workers who become unemployed. Persons between 65 and 72 years old cannot collect these pensions if they continue to work, except at relatively low pay, but if they lose their jobs they become eligible at once. Old age and survivors' insurance is important as a source of family income only if the recipient is a member of a family. Since many pension recipients live with their children or other relatives, some pensions do help support unemployed relatives.

Family investments and savings, including insurance policies, are another source of income during times of stress. According to a Michigan study introduced into the record during the committee hearings in Detroit—

About 44 percent of the unemployed heads of families reported that they had some savings which they used in the emergency. Although the extent of the savings drawn is not known, reliance upon savings was by far the most important measure taken. . . . This fact indicates the extent to which thrift and self-responsibility are relied upon to meet unemployment emergencies.[3]

Measures taken to adjust to loss of income, according to the same study, were, in the order of importance: use of savings, reductions in buying, getting help from relatives, piling up bills, and borrowing money. Some families moved to cheaper quarters, were able to have another member of the family go to work, or sought relief from a public welfare agency. The average family took two of these measures. The major areas for economizing were clothing, recreational and community activities, food, insurance, living quarters, and postponement of medical or dental care.

The effects of unemployment are felt long after the unemployed person has gone back to work. Accumulated debts have to be repaid, neglected health problems attended to, and depleted savings replenished. In most cases it takes a family a long time to regain the financial position it held before unemployment.

The Social Effects of Unemployment

Many serious social problems follow directly from unemployment. In some areas of chronic unemployment these problems are as bad now as they were during the depression of the 1930's. The social effects of unemployment vary considerably according to the age, length of unemployment, the economic

[3] Committee hearings, pt. 3, p. 1205.

level of the unemployed, and other factors, but there is a common pattern of unfortunate consequences.

Unemployment is, of course, the greatest hazard for people in the lowest social and income groups, whose members often hold short-term jobs and are subject to layoffs. The family's normal standard of living is low, and family life is often disorganized and unstable. Children generally leave school at an early age and the delinquency rate is high. One witness before the committee observed:

Except in those cases where there is obvious personal disability in either or both parents, the social scientist is reluctant to accept this as a normal situation. The cultural environment that is often the result of the unemployment situation also becomes a cause of unemployment as the employer sifts through the applications for the "right kind" of employee. This is obviously a vicious circle. This acts as a barricade to the normal aspirations of American people to move up into the broad middle class. The basic sociological question is whether we must necessarily and always have a residual category of people at the bottom of the social structure.

Unemployment also has serious effects upon citizens who consider themselves members of the middle class. For them unemployment carries a suggestion of failure, even though it may be the result of forces beyond the control of anyone in the family. Persons responsible for support of the family suffer loss of prestige and status. Members of the family are inclined to withdraw from participation in community and neighborhood activities, unions, lodges, and similar groups. One witness in Evansville, Ind., described the reaction in his own words:

I know all morning you have heard quite a bit about the financial status of the unemployed, but I would like to say a few words about the emotional status. . . . There is a social aspect to unemployment that arises from the ties and bonds of group relations and friends and neighbors and so on. Everybody wants to be recognized socially, and while I was unemployed, emotional problems did arise; for instance, with my friends, they knew I was unemployed and knew I could not afford to entertain, they didn't think I could afford it, and rather than ask us to go places with them, they wanted to save us the embarrassment and that leaves quite a problem of being under the pressure that we were under. I say "we"—my whole family was involved. It made us wonder if we were actually forsaken by our friends or if this was true friendship to ignore us. The children—naturally, the family was under tension and worried all the time.[4]

The effect on the children of the unemployed is most distressing. Their health, security, educational opportunities, and entire future are endangered. In one county in West Virginia the school superintendent reported that one out of three pupils in a school enrollment of 22,347 came from a family in which the person who normally supported the family was unemployed; in the month of October 1959 24.8 percent of the school lunches were free or sold at a reduced price. The superintendent in another county said:

We know of many, many cases where the only meal that those children have during the entire day is that balanced meal at noon.[5]

In another survey of 11 schools, the family head of 39 percent of the children was unemployed. Children in one school were weighed in November and again at the start of their Christmas vacation to measure the effect of the school's hot lunch program. The net gain of between 3 and 5 pounds per pupil was completely wiped out during the Christmas vacation when the children had to eat at home.

A witness in Pennsylvania said:

Thousands of women are working and thousands of men are at home. . . . A man looks for a job and finds none. His unemployment compensation expires. His wife goes to work and he stays home and looks after the children. . . . What happens to that home?[6]

An unemployed mine worker summarized his life and future this way:

The biggest majority of us never had an opportunity to get an education, so then we had to go into the mines at an early age—15, 16 years old. The biggest part of us are married, and if we should leave here now and go to the city, what confronts us? If you're over 35 you can't get a job. And if a man's got a family and he goes to the city, what job can he get if he doesn't have any skill?

The director of the welfare department of St. Louis County in Minnesota reported:

In all too many families the stress of unemployment tends to separate rather than to mold the family into a smoother functioning unit. . . . The most important reaction is that there seems to be an increase in the hostile reaction toward one another and also toward society . . . the wife blames the husband for being out of work. . . . In many instances the roles become reversed. In many of these situations,

4 Committee hearings, pt. 7, p. 2794.
5 Committee hearings, pt. 6, p. 2424.

6 Committee hearings, pt. 2, pp. 549, 550.

the family is never able fully to recover, to the detriment of themselves and the community.[7]

A Kentucky witness described his problem:

I have been unemployed now since the last of February 1958, and I am just picking up odd jobs. I drawed one claim of unemployment, that is all I ever had in my life. I have always tried to find work. I have been off hunting for work, and I can't find any. And I have got four kids going to school. And that hurts.[8]

During fiscal year 1959, the Federal Government donated 700 million pounds of surplus foods to needy persons; in September 1959, more than 4 million persons in family units received donated commodities.

The problems of the underemployed are similar to those of the unemployed. In 1958, one-fourth of the 44 million families in the United States had annual cash incomes of less than $3,000; nearly one-fifth had incomes of less than $2,500.

Unemployment affects communities as well as families. If plants are closed, wages in other industries may be cut, retail sales drop, and plans to improve businesses and community facilities are often canceled. Property values generally decline and tax rates rise.

Many communities have made great efforts to solve their own problems. The adversity of unemployment often creates a common understanding and a community willingness to work together. This determination to rehabilitate a community was manifested strongly in the cooperative efforts of business, labor, and civic leaders in communities such as Evansville, Ind., and Scranton, Pa. In spite of the best efforts, however, the obstacles in most cases are too great for the community to overcome alone. One community leader in Pennsylvania expressed both the spirit of his community and the nature of the problem in these words:

It is an amazing thing that the unemployment, bad as it is, has not sapped or destroyed the spirit of the people in a community like this. . . . They are fighting and fighting very hard. . . . There is a great resource here in spirit and pride. There are institutions already built up, and I don't think we can today just casually walk away from them and abandon them and say we can put a steel mill or a factory in a field some place and the community will build up around it. . . . What sort of community will that be? . . . Which is easier to do, to build a community or to build an industry? . . . And which are the things that have the roots, the industrial plants or the people? . . . And these communities had their days when they were raw young communities without traditions . . . and now they are mature and can make a tremendous contribution to stability and to decency and to the morality of citizens, and do things for family life that a settled community can do, it is a shame if we just abandon them. . . . You probably will have to change a great deal of thinking, but I think we should not rule out some subsidies on a Government level to industries which will come into a place like this.[9]

The economic and social costs of unemployment deserve far greater attention than they have received. Present measures to deal with unemployment and its consequences at the local, State, and Federal governmental levels are seriously inadequate.

[7] Committee hearings, pt. 4, p. 1511.
[8] Committee hearings, pt. 5, p. 1999.

[9] Committee hearings, pt. 2, p. 512.

PART VI

QUESTIONS FOR DISCUSSION

1. What are the debilitating factors resulting from automation? What have these done to the urban poor?
2. Why is high school education no longer adequate in our technological society?
3. What accounts for the high drop-out rate in our inner city schools? Is there a correlation between unemployment patterns and evidence of a lack of educational opportunity?
4. What are apt to be the shortcomings existing in a ghetto school system? What behavior is evidenced when these ghetto children are placed in an integrated advantaged school setting? What does research indicate concerning the advantages and disadvantages of bussing to achieve an equal educational opportunity?

VOCABULARY

union shop
welfare state
referendum
white-collar jobs
subsistence farms
socioeconomic
AFL-CIO
patriarch
neighborhood school
blue-collar jobs
extracurricular

curriculum
attrition
recession
de facto segregation
remedial
IQ
norms
marketable skills
enrichment
minimum wage

URBAN TAX TANGLE

On all sides we are hearing that the fiscal problems of the cities are of such magnitude that they cannot be solved without massive assistance from sources outside their control. TEMPO, the General Electric Company's Center for Advanced Studies, estimates that the cities will need about $150 billion annually by 1975, and of this amount, they can raise a maximum of $70 billion. Under the present policies the cities can expect to receive another $30 billion from federal and state governments, leaving an annual deficit of $50 billion. Raising city taxes still further will only accelerate the flight from the cities of those taxpayers most able to pay.

Property taxes continue to be the main source of revenue for both city and local governments. Property taxes are levied on property owned by corporations and individuals. Normally included in this category are land and buildings, and in some states, furniture, appliances, jewelry, and so forth are also taxed as tangibles. Many states also have an intangible tax on financial holdings such as stocks, bonds, mortgages, and the like. The property tax is the easiest to collect. It involves assessing the value of the property, determining the tax rate, and the collection process. A failure to pay this tax results in confiscation of the property by the taxing authority.

It is now clear that property taxes have reached their upper limits and are in several ways a very unfair tax. Even if it were a good tax it still would not provide the funds required to operate the cities. It can logically be argued that the property tax is unfair in that the assessment values are not necessarily related to real values, and there exists the opportunity for the assessor to give preferential treatment to his friends. These taxes are not related to ability to pay; they do not respond to growth in the economy as in the case of other taxes. The property tax is particularly unfair to those citizens who are living on small fixed incomes in that they can be forced to give up a home because of inability to pay.

Local governments have had to resort to other types of taxes such as sales (general and selective), fees, and charges of various types. The main criticism of the sales tax is similar to some of the objections of property taxes—it is not related to ability to pay. The family on low income pays the same rate as our more affluent families. Use taxes and charges are considered fairer in that the family pays for what it uses, thereby discouraging waste. One of the newest sources of revenue to the city is the municipal income tax which is levied at a percentage rate against earnings within the city. This can cause some to be taxed twice on the same earnings, once in the city where he works and again in the city where he lives.

The cities are in a real financial bind as the various taxing sources available to them are far from sufficient to provide all the services now needed. State assistance to the cities has grown but the states have about reached their upper limits of ability to aid. It is becoming increasingly recognized that more aid must be provided from the federal government. The Heller Plan recommends that the federal government return a percentage of federal revenues to the states and local governments. The plan would provide that the program be of permanent nature and thus federal aid to states and cities would grow along with the increased revenues of the federal government. The distribution would be on a per capita basis with allowances made for those states with low incomes or heavy pockets of poverty. Provisions would insure that the local governments would not be left at the mercy of state legislatures as the funds pass through the state. The Heller Plan sees a continuing need for the categorical and general purpose grants.

The hope for our nation's future lies in the cities. We cannot exist without our cities, and if they are to be able to provide an acceptable environment for man, then massive help from the federal government must be provided soon and on a continuing basis. From every corner of our land, the mayors are saying "We just can't make it anymore."

LOCAL TAXATION PROBLEMS

Leonard Goodall

For years, city revenues and expenses have been rising faster than those of the federal government. Property taxes continue to be the primary source of their revenue. The author comments on the various types of taxes and points out that property taxes do not respond to growth as do other taxes; further, the tax assessor is usually elected and often has had little formal training for his job. Generally speaking, property taxes have been roundly criticized by students of taxation. Perhaps the strongest argument against this tax is that it is not related to ability to pay. Sales taxes are open to the same criticisms. Once again, the only feasible solution for state and local governments is some form of federal refund to them, based on a percentage of federal income taxes with certain assurances for protection of local governments and allowances provided for those states with low-income, low-tax status.

By any measure city government is big business. In 1965 city governments in the United States received revenues of over twenty billion dollars, double their budgets of just a decade earlier. City revenues and expenditures for years have been rising faster in percentage terms than those of the national government although they still trail school districts, which have the dubious honor of recording the most rapid rise in revenues and expenditures of all governmental units. In most parts of the country private and secondary education is administered and financed by independent school districts, so most of the rising cost in this area is not directly reflected in city budgets. Even without this cost, however, increasing population with its accompanying social and economic problems as well as the constant demand for more and better services has placed a strain on the financial resources of the cities.

CITY REVENUES

The Traditional Sources

Historically the property tax has been the primary revenue source for local governments, especially so since the depression of the early 30's when many states abandoned this tax as a source of state revenue and left it to the counties, municipalities, and school districts. As revenue needs have increased, the cities have supplemented this source with other revenues, including general and selective sales taxes, special fees and charges, and intergovernmental revenues.

THE PROPERTY TAX   The property tax is theoretically a tax levied against all property. In reality it usually reaches mainly land and buildings, with tangible property (furniture, appliances, jewelry, etc.) and intangible personal property (stocks, bonds, mortgages, etc.) either going untaxed or being taxed in an unsystematic and "catch as catch can" way in many states. The administration of the tax involves three steps: assessment, establishment of the tax rate, and collection.

Assessment, i.e. placing a value on property for tax purposes, is the responsibility of a city or county assessor who is usually elected and often has little formal training in the job of property assessment. In addition to the problem of lack of training, the office of assessor is especially susceptible to pressure and attempts at corruption since the decisions made there affect the amount of taxes people pay. Consequently the office of assessor has had a stormy history and has come in for much criticism by students of government, economics, and taxation.

The tax rate is set by the legislative body of the taxing unit (the city council in the case of cities). To illustrate, if the assessed valuation of property in a city were one million dollars and the council determined that it needed to raise twenty thousand dollars from the property tax, the tax rate would be set at two dollars on each one hundred dollars of assessed valuation. The owner of property assessed at five thousand dollars would then have to pay a property tax of one hundred dollars. After the tax rate is established, collection is usually the responsibility of a city or county collector. Since a piece of property will often be taxed by several different governmental units—county, city, school district, etc.—it is the practice in many states for a single agency, often the county collector or county treasurer, to collect all the tax and then distribute it to the various governments. This way the taxpayer pays his total amount at one time instead of having to pay separate amounts to each individual government.

The property tax has long been the largest single source of revenue for local governments. As Table 1 indicates it produced three billion seven hundred sixty-seven million dollars in 1955 and six billion five hundred thirty-seven million dollars in 1965. Although the dollar amounts are increasing, the percentage of total city revenues coming from the tax is gradually decreasing. One reason for this is that cities have reached out for new taxes in an attempt to meet their needs. Another is that property tax revenues do not respond to growth of the economy as rapidly as other taxes, such as general and selective sales taxes and the income tax.

The property tax has been the target of much criticism by students of taxation. They have pointed out that assessed values often have little relation to real values; that assessors are usually elected and thus may be guided by political considerations in setting assessments; that property assessment is a complex task for which many assessors are not trained; and that the tax usually discriminates against those whose wealth is in the form of real rather than personal property. It is also true that today the property tax is not closely related to ability to pay, and, in many cases, it is probably actually regressive. Although these criticisms are certainly justified in many cases, the property tax appears destined to remain an important source of revenue for municipalities. There are several reasons for this. First, even though the percentage of local revenue coming from this tax is declining, it continues to be a major source of revenue for local governments, and it is unlikely that a substitute source capable of providing equal amounts could be found. Second, it is one tax that can be levied and collected with relative efficiency at the local level. Finally, the force of inertia will probably help to retain the tax since it now

TABLE 1   CITY REVENUE SOURCES* (DOLLAR AMOUNTS IN MILLIONS)

	1965		1955	
Total Revenues	$20,318	100.00%	$10,227	100.00%
General Revenues	15,884	78.18%	7,824	76.50%
Intergov'tal Revenues	3,534	17.39%	1,438	14.06%
From State	2,745	13.51%	1,236	12.09%
From Federal	557	2.74%	NA	NA
From other Local	232	1.14%	NA	NA
Taxes	9,289	45.72%	5,100	49.87%
Property	6,537	32.17%	3,767	36.83%
General Sales	1,184	5.83%	433	4.23%
Selective Sales	611	3.01%	295	2.88%
Other	957	4.71%	606	5.93%
Charges & Misc.	3,061	15.07%	1,285	12.56%
Utility Revenue	3,760	18.51%	2,080	20.34%
Liquor Stores	92	.45%	57	.56%
Insurance Trust	582	2.86%	267	2.61%

* Figures may not add because of rounding.
Source: U.S. Bureau of the Census, *City Government Finances in 1955.*
U.S. Bureau of the Census, *City Government Finances in 1965.*

exists, and, in the minds of many, "any old tax is a good tax and any new tax is a bad tax."

THE SALES TAX   The sales tax is ordinarily a tax levied on retail sales and collected by the retailer. This has been a very important revenue producer for state governments since the 1930's, but municipalities in some states are also beginning to levy a retail sales tax. In states where municipalities are authorized to levy a general sales tax, the state will commonly levy a tax of two or three cents on the dollar and the municipality will levy a tax of one-half or one per cent on top of that. In some states, like Illinois and California, the state will collect the municipal sales tax along with its own, making it simpler for the retail merchant to pay the tax as well as provide a service to the municipalities. The state collecting agency then distributes the funds to the cities in which they were collected.

Sales taxes may be either general or selective. A general sales tax applies to nearly all retail sales. A selective sales tax applies to only certain items. A tax of so many cents per gallon on gas or per carton on cigarettes would be examples of the latter. Sales taxes are attractive because they are good revenue producers, and they arouse little resistance from the public since people do not seem to protest a tax of a few cents here and a few cents there. On the other hand, the total sales tax load has now reached five per cent in a few states, and there is surely some point at which there will be a public reaction. A few cents here and there is one thing; a nickle or a dime here and there is another. Sales taxes have become one of the main sources of city revenues, with general and selective sales taxes providing almost nine per cent of all city revenues in 1965.

A criticism often heard of the sales tax is that it is regressive. Because those in low income categories must spend most of their earnings on necessities such as food, clothing, and shelter, they are the ones who are hardest hit by a sales tax. A low sales tax that is part of an overall progressive tax system may not be too vulnerable to this charge, but the higher the sales tax rises the more valid the criticism becomes.

One criticism of the municipal sales tax, especially in metropolitan areas is that it may tend to "drive business out of town." If one city has a sales tax and nearby cities do not, people may trade in the neighboring cities to avoid the tax. This will not happen on small purchases because the potential saving is too small, but it may occur on larger purchases such as automobiles or major appliances. In metropolitan areas where some municipalities have a sales tax and some do not, this can lead to marketing battles among merchants, where some will advertise, "Buy your new car in Village Meadows and avoid the sales tax." An approach to eliminating this problem is the enactment of a use tax, usually set at the same level as the sales tax and levied against items bought outside the city but brought into the city for use. A use tax is almost impossible for a city to enforce on purchases of appliances or smaller items, but it can be enforced on auto purchases because the purchaser ordinarily must give his address in applying for a car license. This assumes that the state auto license agency will cooperate with cities in enforcement.

FEES AND CHARGES   Certain services provided by municipalities lend themselves well to financing on a fee basis. Water, sewers, municipal golf courses, toll bridges, parking lots, and city owned utilities commonly fall into this category. Fees are much like taxes if the citizen has no choice about paying them. This is often the case, as when he must pay a monthly amount for garbage collection or sewage disposal and does not have the option of not using the service. On the other hand, there are

many instances where the amount paid depends on how much the individual chooses to use a given service. One's water bill will be affected by whether he chooses to water his lawn every day or once a week, and he also decides for himself whether he wants to use the municipal golf course.

Fees and charges have the advantage of placing the costs of services on the users and thus removing them from the shoulders of the general taxpayer. They also have the advantage of linking costs and benefits, something which cannot be done where services are financed out of general tax revenues. This makes it possible for officials to determine whether a particular service is carrying its own weight financially and adjust fees accordingly. Of course there may be times when officials want to set fees below cost in order to encourage use of a service. The costs of public subway or bus transportation, for example, may intentionally be kept low if officials believe that it costs less to subsidize a loss on public transportation than it would cost to build the streets and freeways necessary if those people decided to drive to work.

The use of fees also discourages waste on the part of the user. It would be possible to finance water costs out of general tax revenues or by levying a flat rate fee (in fact, some cities do it this way), but where this is the case there is no incentive to remember to turn off the water sprinkler or get the leaky faucet fixed. The use of a fee based on amount used encourages the consumer to use the service efficiently and to save where possible.

In summary, the use of fees is advantageous where they can be efficiently collected, where the benefits accrue solely or primarily to those who pay the fees, and where the service might be wasted if a charge were not made. This method of financing is generally popular with the taxpayer since it is based on the principal that those who use a service pay for it. In 1965 over fifteen per cent of city revenues came from general fees and charges, and another eighteen per cent came from fees charged by municipally owned utilities. In both cases most of this money is not available for general use but goes directly to finance the service producing the revenue.

INTERGOVERNMENTAL REVENUES An increasingly important factor in city financing is the money received from state and national governments. At the national level the grant-in-aid system discussed in the preceding chapter is the most important means for providing financial assistance to local governments. As mentioned previously, the fact that the national government seems to have access to more taxable resources, the necessity of equalizing resources and needs, and the desire to provide incentive to local governments motivated the national program of grants-in-aid. The figures in Table 1 do not indicate the full impact of national funds on local finances since such funds are sometimes channeled through the state, and many times national aid to states equals or surpasses the amount of state aid to local governments, thus influencing state ability to provide local aid.

An alternative to providing assistance through grants-in-aid is the use of shared revenues, a technique employed by many states. Many states return a certain percentage of the income tax, sales tax, gas tax, or other taxes to local governments. This varies from the grant-in-aid system in that shared revenues are usually returned to their point of origin without reference to matching funds or other requirements; in addition, they are not tied to specific projects and thus may be spent as desired.

An exception to this is shared gas tax revenues which are often earmarked for use on streets and highways.

Shared taxes are economical to administer since the entire process is handled by the state. They give municipalities the advantage of access to a tax source that they might not have otherwise, and there is the added benefit for city officials of receiving revenues without the usual accompanying political burden of having to levy taxes. Shared taxes are levied by the state, and the formula determining the amount to be returned to municipalities is set by the state. This can occasionally be hazardous for municipalities because it means that in times of economic crisis, just when they need funds the most, the state may choose to cut the cities out and retain the entire amount for state functions. Especially significant is the fact that the shared revenue approach is usually used with taxes that are highly responsive to economic expansion and are therefore good revenue producers.

Closely related to shared revenues is the principle of state collection of local taxes mentioned above. The main difference is that with the latter the decision about levying the tax remains with the municipality and the state acts merely as the collecting agency.

The Newer Sources

The greatest amount of city revenue comes from the sources discussed above, but two other sources should be given some attention. One is the municipal income tax, already in use in many cities. The other is the Heller plan, not yet a reality but under discussion in Congress.

MUNICIPAL INCOME TAX Beginning with Philadelphia in 1940 and Toledo in 1946, about five hundred cities have enacted municipal income taxes up to the present time. The tax is often called an earnings tax because it is usually a tax on corporate and personal earnings rather than on income. Unearned income in the form of rents, interest, dividends, and capital gains is usually excluded.

Several characteristics are common to municipal income taxes: (1) as mentioned, they are levied against earnings rather than total income; (2) there are ordinarily no exemptions, exclusions, or deductions such as are found in state and national income taxes; (3) it is usually a flat rate tax of one-half or one per cent; (4) it is levied on all earnings within the city limits regardless of where the recipient lives and also on the income of residents earned outside the city.

These facts make it obvious that the tax is meant to be simply a revenue producer and not an instrument for such social policies as income redistribution. Because of this these taxes have usually faced the opposition of organized labor and other groups with a similar point of view, making it difficult to secure passage in those cities where adoption is dependent on a general referendum. On the other hand, the main selling point of the tax is that the suburban dwellers will help pay it. Because it is levied on income earned in the city without regard to the residence of the earner, a large portion of it will be paid by those who live in the suburbs and drive into the city to work.

Some suburban communities have retaliated by levying earnings taxes of their own. This creates the possibility of an individual being taxed twice, by the city in which he works and by the city in which he lives. To avoid this danger over half of the cities levying the tax have reciprocity agreements with other nearby cities that also levy it. The city of Toledo, for example, has an agreement with neighboring cities whereby the tax is paid only once, and the amount is then shared equally by the city of residence and the city of employment.

Because cities may levy an income tax only when authorized by the state, nearly all the cities are located in a few states, mainly Pennsylvania and Ohio. Besides Philadelphia and Toledo, other larger cities with a tax of this nature are Detroit, Louisville, St. Louis, and Kansas City. The tax has only two primary advantages: it is a good revenue producer and it enables the central city to tax the suburbanite. These two facts make the tax sufficiently attractive that we may expect to see it spread gradually to other cities. One thing which might change the picture would be enactment by the national government of the Heller plan, which could alter the form in which cities would receive revenue from taxes on income. Let us turn now to a discussion of this plan.

THE HELLER PLAN   The Heller plan is essentially an attempt to apply the shared revenues principle at the national level. Professor Walter W. Heller, professor of economics at the University of Minnesota and former chairman of the President's Council of Economic Advisors under Kennedy and Johnson, has proposed that some portion of the national income tax revenue, perhaps one per cent, be returned to the states for use as they see fit. Details have not been worked out, but there seems to be some general agreement among those discussing the idea on these points: (1) each year the national government would place in a special trust fund a certain percentage of income tax revenues for distribution to the states; (2) the funds would be returned to the states with no or few limitations. Some have suggested limits which would prevent use of the funds for highway construction and certain other functions that already receive large amounts of federal aid. Other suggested limitations are that a stated minimum amount must be spent on education or that a certain minimum amount must be redistributed by states to the municipalities and school districts; (3) most of the funds would be distributed on some basis such as population or point of origin, but some portion, perhaps twenty or twenty-five per cent, would be distributed on a formula based on need.

This proposal has evoked mixed reactions. Advocates like the fact that this plan would make available to state and local governments funds from what most people agree to be the most progressive and fairest tax in the federal tax system. By attaching few requirements the plan would strengthen the decision-making process at the state and local level and widen the flexibility and latitude of these governments. At the same time critics question whether this is good or bad. They believe that the past record of state governments and state legislatures has not shown that they are capable of spending wisely this large new source of funds. They prefer to channel any new revenues into the traditional system of grants for specific programs in which standards and regulations can be imposed.

In discussing city revenues it should be pointed out that enactment of the Heller plan would not necessarily make new funds available for cities. This would depend entirely on the form in which the plan is adopted. If a requirement were written in that a certain amount must be redistributed by the states to municipalities this would assure them of help. Otherwise the extent of help received would depend on the attitudes of the legislature in each state. Various forms of the plan have been introduced in Congress, but no action has yet been taken.

A variation of the Heller plan has been recommended by Mayor Schmied of Louisville. He suggests that cities be allowed to levy a small gross income tax of one or two per cent to be paid directly to the city. The tax would then be deductible from the amount of federal income tax which the individual owes. This would leave administration of the tax at the local level and would allow each city to decide whether it wanted the tax. It is safe to say that nearly all cities would want it, but there would probably be a few that would not.

CITY EXPENDITURES

The figures for city expenditures in 1955 and 1965 are shown in Table 2. Although the table shows cities spending somewhat over twelve per cent of their expenditures for education, this is misleading. In the first place most cities spend little or nothing on education because the function is the responsibility of an independent school district whose budget is separate from that of the city. Second, the few cities that do operate school systems spend far more than twelve per cent of their budgets on education. In 1965 New York City used twenty-six per cent of its total expenditures to operate its schools, and in Washington, D.C., the figure was about twenty-two per cent.

The most interesting point revealed by the data in Table 2 is how little the proportionate amounts have changed in the ten year period. With the exception of the "other" category, the share of the total allotted to each function was within one percentage point of the share allotted to that function a decade earlier. This may indicate the extent to which inflexibility is built into city budgets through state restrictions, earmarked revenues and the like. It may also reflect the fact that department heads come to

TABLE 2.   CITY EXPENDITURES
(DOLLAR AMOUNTS IN MILLIONS)

	1965		1955	
Total Expenditures	$20,680	100.00%	$8,363	100.00%
General Expenditures	16,012	77.43%	6,524	78.01%
Education	2,489	12.04%	1,103	13.19%
Highways	1,807	8.74%	720	8.60%
Public Welfare	927	4.48%	470	5.62%
Hospitals	1,115	5.39%	546	6.53%
Health				
Police Protection	1,739	8.41%	681	8.14%
Fire Protection	1,146	5.54%	495	5.92%
Sewerage & Sanitation	1,774	8.58%	731	8.74%
Parks & Recreation	775	3.75%	323	3.86%
Housing & Urban Ren.	686	3.32%	205	2.45%
Airports	182	.88%	60	.72%
Water Tran. & Term	73	.35%	40	.48%
Parking	94	.45%	42	.50%
Libraries	267	1.29%	102	1.22%
Gen. Govt.	1,088	5.26%	392	4.69%
Interest	603	2.92%	209	2.50%
Other	1,247	6.03%	404	4.83%
Utilities	3,966	19.18%	1,541	18.43%
Water	1,820	8.80%	689	8.24%
Electric	1,291	6.24%	366	4.38%
Transit	622	3.20%	444	5.31%
Gas	192	.93%	43	.51%
Liquor Store Exp's	78	.38%	11	.13%
Insurance Trust	624	3.02%	288	3.44%

Source: U.S. Bureau of the Census, *City Government Finances in 1955.*
U.S. Bureau of the Census, *City Government Finances in 1965.*

think in terms of their "rightful share of the pie," and it thus becomes very hard to make meaningful changes in the budget. In any case, it is obvious that all of the talk about new emphasis in local government, such as the shift in interest from physical and engineering problems to human problems, is not reflected in the expenditures of city dollars up to 1965.

INCREASING FEDERAL AID TO STATES AND CITIES

Walter W. Heller and Joseph A. Peckman

In view of largely unmet needs of the states and cities and in the absence of adequate taxing possibilities, revenue sharing with the states and cities by the federal government is essential. The authors recommend that the federal government distribute a fixed percentage of federal income taxes. The distribution would be on a per-capita basis. Allowances could be made to vary the distribution to compensate for those low-income, low-tax states. They also suggest that the distribution be done with minimum constraints. The Congress would probably have to require that states submit plans for the use of the funds to insure the availability of funds to local units; otherwise states might reserve an undue share for state projects. Although revenue sharing is still somewhat controversial, the states and cities are in urgent need of financial help.

We were very pleased to receive this invitation to present our views on revenue sharing to this committee. First broached in 1964, the idea that the Federal Government should share some of its revenues with State-local government with few strings attached has an unusual degree of support from elected public officials and legislators in both political parties, scholars, businessmen, and other opinion leaders. It also has evoked a great deal of criticism from similar groups. The compendium which this committee has assembled and these hearings will perform an extremely valuable service in identifying the major issues and in evaluating alternative solutions.

Like everything else in politics, there seem to be about as many different versions of the revenue sharing plan as there are supporters. In this statement, we should like to outline in the form of questions and answers the major elements of our plan, to explain its rationale, and to evaluate some of the more important suggestions for modifying it.

Q What are the major purposes of revenue sharing?

A Revenue sharing is intended to allocate to the States and local governments, *on a permanent basis,* a portion of the very productive and highly "growth-elastic" receipts of the Federal Government. The bulk of Federal revenues is derived from income taxes, which rise at a faster rate than income as income grows. By contrast, State-local revenues barely keep pace with income. State-local needs have outstripped the potentialities of their revenue system at constant tax rates, with the result that tax rates have been pushed steadily upward throughout the postwar period and many new taxes have been added. Since State-local taxes are on balance regressive, the higher State-local taxes impose unnecessarily harsh burdens on low-income recipi-

Reprinted from *Revenue Sharing and Its Alternatives: What Future for Fiscal Federalism?* pp. 111–117. Hearings before the Subcommittee on Fiscal Policy of the Joint Economic Committee of the United States. July 31, August 1–3, 1967.

ents. In addition, essential public services are not adequately supported in many, if not most, communities because they do not have the means to finance them.

Although there is no room for revenue sharing in the Federal budget this year, it is not too soon to plan for using the Nation's fiscal resources productively once Vietnam relaxes its fiscal grip. In view of their large unmet needs, the States and local governments should receive a generous share of the huge Federal revenue potential in the post-Vietnam economy. Revenue sharing clearly deserves to be considered among the major competing alternatives, certainly before tax reduction is carried too far.

Q What are the essential features of the revenue-sharing plan?

A The core of the revenue-sharing plan is the regular distribution of a specified portion of the Federal individual income tax to the States primarily on the basis of population and with few strings attached. This distribution would be over and above existing and future conditional grants. The essential features of the plan are as follows:

A Percentage Set-Aside. The Federal Government would each year set aside and distribute to the States an eventual 2 percent of the Federal individual income tax base (the amount reported as net taxable income by all individuals). This would mean that, under the existing rate schedule, the Federal Government would collect 2 percentage points in each bracket for the States and 12 to 68 percentage points for itself.

Use of a Trust Fund. The sums collected for the States would be placed in a trust fund from which periodic distributions would be made. The trust fund would be the natural vehicle for handling such earmarked funds, just as it is in the case of payroll taxes for

social security purposes and motor vehicle and gasoline taxes for the highway program. It would underscore the fact that the States receive the funds as a matter of right, free from the uncertainties and hazards of the annual appropriation process.

The Federal commitment to share income tax revenues with the States would be a contractual one in the sense of being payable—at whatever percentage Congress provided—through thick and thin, through surplus and deficit in the Federal budget. The plan could hardly have its claimed advantages of stiffening and strengthening State and local governments if they were always fearful that Federal deficits would deprive them of their share of the Federal income tax.

Per Capita Distribution. The States would share the income tax proceeds on the basis of population. Per capita sharing would transfer some funds from States with high incomes—and therefore high per capita income tax liabilities—to low-income, low-tax States. If the modest equalization implicit in per capita sharing were deemed too limited, a small portion of the fund could be set aside for supplements to States with low per capita income or with a high incidence of poverty and dependency.

Pass-Through. Whether to leave the fiscal claims of the localities to the mercies of the political process and the institutional realities of each State or to require a pass-through to them is not an easy question. Previously, we have left this question open, but we now conclude that the legitimate—and pressing —claims of local government require explicit recognition in the basic formula of revenue sharing.

Few Strings. Constraints on the use of the funds would be much less detailed than those applying to conditional grants. However, the funds would not be available for highway construction, since there is a special Federal trust fund with its own earmarked revenue sources for this purpose. An audit of the actual use of the funds would be required, as well as certification by the appropriate State and local officials that all applicable Federal laws, such as the Civil Rights Act, have been complied with in the activities financed by the grants.

Revenue Impact. The Federal individual income tax base will reach the $300 billion mark in 1967. Accordingly, each percent of the base would provide the States with $3 billion a year. If 2 percent of the income tax base were being distributed in 1967, the grant would be $6 billion, or roughly $30 per capita. Without taking account of special equalization features, this would mean, for example, grants of about $60 million for Arkansas, $560 million for California, $60 million for Colorado, $320 million for Illinois, $180 million for Massachusetts, $110 million each for Louisiana and Minnesota, $120 million for Missouri, $20 million for Montana, $560 million for New York, $150 million for North Carolina, $360 million for Pennsylvania, $30 million for Utah, $130 million for Virginia, and $120 million for Wisconsin.

The income tax base, to which the allotments are keyed, has grown from $65 billion in 1946 to $128 billion in 1955, $210 billion in 1963, and the estimated $300 billion in 1967—and has risen from 31 percent of GNP in 1946 to an estimated 38 percent in 1967. By 1972, the base should grow to $425 billion (assuming a 6-percent annual growth in money GNP, and the base growing 20 percent faster than GNP). On this base, the 2-percent to be set aside for the states would reach $8.5 billion by 1972. Truly, a share in the Federal income tax would be a share in U.S. economic growth.

The competing claims of Federal tax cuts and expenditure increases would probably require that the plan start modestly (perhaps at one half of 1 percent or 1 percent) and build up gradually to 2 percent over three or four years. This gradual build-up would moderate the impact of the new plan on the Federal budget during the first few years after its adoption and enable the States to program their fiscal affairs more efficiently.

Q Why is the per capita method used to distribute funds? Why not return the money where it came from?

A The per capita method of distributing the grants among the States was chosen because it is the best available index of both fiscal capacity and need. It allocates more money to the relatively populous States; at the same time, it automatically distributes relatively more to a poor State than to a rich State. For example, a $25 per capita distribution would amount to 10 percent of the budget of a State that can afford to spend $250 per capita and only 5 percent of the budget of a State that can afford to spend $500 per capita.

As we have already indicated, more equalization could easily be provided if desired. We favor using a small part of the fund—say, 10 percent—for the poorest third of the States. This additional allotment—though a small part of the aggregate grants—would raise the average per capita grant in the ten poorest States by over 50 percent.

Tax effort might also be given some weight in the formula to give the States an incentive to maintain or increase tax collections out of their own sources. Such a spur could be built in by weighting the per capita grants to each State by the ratio of that State's tax effort to the average tax effort in the country— tax effort being defined as the ratio of State-local revenues to personal income. An interesting and rather mixed set of above- and below-par States emerges by this standard. For example, in 1964:

Louisiana, New Mexico, and North Dakota would have had effort indexes of 120 or above.

Nine States would have had an index of 85 or less: Connecticut, Delaware, Illinois, Maryland, Missouri, New Jersey, Ohio, Pennsylvania, and Virginia.

On the other hand, it would be totally inappropriate to allocate the funds in proportion to the amounts collected from each State. This would give disproportionately larger shares to the wealthiest States, and would widen rather than narrow differentials in State fiscal capacities.

Q What happens during a recession? Aren't you worried that the States and local governments would be in trouble if the revenue sharing funds declined?

A The tax base has declined only twice since the end of World War II—by 4 percent in 1949 and by less than one-tenth of 1 percent in 1958. These are within the range of fluctuations that State and local governments have become accustomed to in their own tax sources. Nevertheless, in a deep recession, there would be no problem. In such circumstances, the Congress could easily add to the normal amounts going into the revenue sharing reserve fund to prevent financial distress at the State-local level. Few anti-recession measures would be as efficient from both the efficiency and stabilization standpoints.

Q The Federal Government already has a well-developed system of categorical grants. Why do we need general-purpose grants?

A Categorical and general-purpose grants have very different functions and these cannot be satisfied if the Federal system were limited to one or the other.

In distributing future fiscal dividends, the Federal Government can and should give high priority to categorical aid. Their dramatic growth will doubtless continue. They tripled in the 1950's reaching $7 billion by 1960. They are well on the way to tripling again by 1970, as is reflected in the President's request of $17.5 billion in categorical aids for fiscal 1968.

In appraising the relative role of conditional or unconditional grants, one must be clear on the distinction between the defects or flaws in the administration of the existing grant-in-aid system—those which can presumably be overcome by improvements in it—and those which are intrinsic to the conditional grant-in-aid instrument.

Keen awareness of the limitations in practice was expressed in testimony before the Senate Subcommittee on Intergovernmental Relations last year by the Director of the Bureau of the Budget. He identified the problems as:

Proliferation of programs to a total of 162 by early-1966, under 399 separate authorizations.

Excessive categorization of grants which, together with direct negotiations between individual bureaus and their counterparts in State-local governments, have led to bypassing of governors and mayors and weakening of their control over their own administrations.

The difficulties in coordination and broad policy planning by Federal, State, and local governments that result from the fragmentation of grants and appropriations.[1]

These problems suggest that there are limits, in terms of efficiency in practical application, to increased re-

[1] Charles L. Schultze, Hearings before the Subcommittee on Intergovernmental Relations of the Committee on Government Operations, U.S. Senate, 89th Cong., 2d sess.; Part I: The Federal Level, pp. 390–391.

liance on central direction of resources through conditional Federal grants. They obviously call for reforms internal to the grant-in-aid system. To conclude that the categorical grant-in-aid system needs to be scuttled not only goes too far, but misses the point.

Categorical grants are needed because the benefits of many public services "spill over" from the community in which they are performed to other communities. Expenditures for such services would be too low if financed entirely by State-local sources, because each State or community would tend to pay only for the benefits likely to accrue to its own citizens. States have a well-developed system of categorical grants to local governments for this reason. Unless the Federal Government steps in to represent the national interest in the benefits derived from State-local services, the latter will be badly undernourished. So categorical grants-in-aid must continue to be our *major* reliance in transferring Federal funds to the States.

General purpose or block grants are justified on substantially different grounds. In the first place, all States do not have equal capacity to pay for local services. Even though the poorer States make a larger relative revenue effort, they are unable to match the revenue-raising ability of the richest States. Second, Federal use of the best tax sources leaves a substantial gap between State-local need and State-local fiscal capacity. Moreover, no State can push its rates much higher than the rates in neighboring States for fear of placing its citizens and business enterprises at a disadvantage. This justifies some Federal assistance even for purely State-local activities, with the poorer States needing relatively more help because of their low fiscal capacity.

The categorical grant system cannot perform these functions. Though they admirably serve the national purpose, they often put State-local finance at cross-purposes. In drawing on a limited supply of resources to finance and staff particular activities, the matching grant may siphon resources away from nonaided programs. The poorer the State, the greater the tax effort that must be made to achieve any given amount of matching, and hence the less that is left over for purely State-local functions. To some extent, then, the State-local government trades fiscal freedom for fiscal strength.

In contrast, general-purpose grants would combine flexibility with strength. On the one hand, the funds would not be tied to specified national interests, bound by detailed controls, forced into particular channels and subject to annual Federal decisions. On the other, it would not have to be wrung out of a reluctant State-local tax base at great political risk to innovative governors and legislators. In short, revenue sharing would provide a dependable flow of Federal funds in a form that would enlarge, not restrict, the options of the State and local decision-makers.

For these reasons, the general-purpose grants are needed to supplement the categorical grants, but not to replace them. Considering the large unmet needs throughout the country for public programs with large spillover effects, the adoption of revenue sharing should not be the occasion for reducing categorical grants. It is a well-known axiom of logic that two objectives cannot be satisfied by using only one instrument.

Q We have been told that the major domestic problem is the plight of our cities. How can you make sure that the cities will get a fair share of the revenue sharing funds?

A Per capita revenue sharing would miss its mark if it failed to relieve some of the intense fiscal pressures on local, and particularly urban, governments. Indeed, it is in and through the metropolitan area that most of our aspirations for a greater society will be achieved or thwarted. Revenue sharing cannot be expected to break the bottlenecks of tradition and vested interest that stand in our path. But it can be expected to provide some of the financial resources needed for that battle, always bearing in mind that it will be a supplement to Federal programs for model cities, for urban redevelopment, for community action against poverty, and the like.

The question is not *whether* revenue sharing should put funds at the disposal of local governments, but *how*. Can one count on relief coming automatically from a general grant made to the States, or should a specific part of the State shares be specifically reserved for the local units?

All States give aid to local units and most give significant amounts. As a matter of fact, the State grant-in-aid system for local governments is much more highly developed than the Federal grant system. In the aggregate, transfers from State to local governments account for more than a third of State expenditures and about 30 percent of local general revenues. By contrast, Federal grants amount to only 17 percent of State-local revenues. Thus, even without any specific requirements, we would expect the local governments to receive at least a third of any general funds the States might receive from the Federal Government.

Nevertheless, in the light of urgent local needs and the observed tendency of State capitals to shortchange their major central cities, we have been persuaded that an explicit "pass-through" rule may be desirable to recognize the legitimate claims of local government. This can be done in one of three ways:

1. *State Plans*. The most flexible method of handling the problem is to require the governors to prepare plans for the use of the funds. As guidance for the development of these plans, the Congress might indicate the general areas which it regarded as most urgent, including the need for making funds available to local governments. To be sure that the plan represented a broad spectrum of opinion in the State, the governor might be directed to consult with local officials and representatives of local citizens associations before incorporating the plan in his budget. The development of such plans would provide the occasion for a complete review and possibly a revamping of State-local relations throughout the country.

2. *Minimum Pass-Through*. The legislation might provide a minimum percentage pass-through for all States. In view of recent trends, the minimum should be at least 40 percent and might even be as high as 50 percent. This would prevent any State from short-changing its local governments (although it might be difficult to detect offsetting reductions in existing grants if the State legislature was of a mind to do so). The disadvantage of a fixed percentage is that the extent to which the States delegate responsibilities to, and share revenues with, local governments varies greatly. In some States, the appropriate percentage may well exceed the 50 percent mark, and in others it may be below it. The danger is that any minimum percentage is likely to become a maximum, so that stipulating the percentage may do more harm than good in some States.

3. *Minimum Pass-Through Plus Guaranteed Share for Cities*. Providing a minimum pass-through percentage does not insure a fair allocation to the large central cities, most of which are in dire financial straits and need relatively more help than other communities because of their heavy public welfare loads and disappearing bases as

the middle-class continues its exodus to the suburbs. A minimum per capita outlay from the revenue sharing grant to these central cities would solve the problem, but it is virtually impossible to settle on a simple cutoff rule for such cities. For example, if all cities with population above 50,000 were included in this special proviso, no city in Alaska, Idaho, North Dakota, Vermont, or Wyoming would be protected for the minimum. In other States, the counties are major operational units and should be eligible for special treatment if this approach is taken. Moreover, the existing distribution of State-local responsibilities for education, health, welfare, and highways differ greatly and it would be impossible, as well as unwise, to set a given figure that would be equitable in all States.

It is, nevertheless, true that the problem should not be insuperable, since there are only 50 States to deal with and our senators and congressmen are very familiar with their State-local patterns and problems. An objective review of these problems on a State-by-State basis by the congressional committees, or the Advisory Commission on Intergovernmental Relations, or an ad hoc commission that might be set up for this explicit purpose should be able to come up with acceptable solutions. Any formulas or set of formulas that would be included in any revenue sharing plan could be made subject to periodic review. Furthermore, the legislation could provide escape clauses from the statutory minima in the event that the governor and mayors of the principal local governments make an official request to the trustee of the revenue sharing funds.

These approaches suggest the range of alternatives. Although the problem is complicated by the large number and variety of local government units and the varying State-local relationships throughout the country, it should be possible to arrive at an equitable solution—provided the problem is approached sympathetically and in a constructive attitude by the major decision makers at all levels of government.

Q You argue that the States and local governments need financial assistance. Don't most of the current projections show that they will be accumulating large surpluses in the next few years?

A In spite of dramatic postwar growth in categorical aids as well as State-local tax revenues, there has been no let-up in the intense fiscal pressures on States and localities. Some recent projections seem to suggest that prosperity in State-local finance is just around the corner, that spending pressures will relent while revenues grow. But these projections are vulnerable on two counts:

First, they rely too heavily on projections of demographic factors, which tend to show that the pressure for government services at the State-local level will not build up as fast during the next decade as it did during the last. But these projections not only under-emphasize current deficiencies in State-local services, but tend to underestimate the demand for increased *quality* of these services, which—because of the slow growth in productivity in these sectors—must reflect itself in increased expenditures. Virtually all projections of State-local financial needs have in the past underestimated the great surge in State-local expenditures for this reason.

Second, the projections show relatively small net surpluses on balance for all State and local governments. This aggregation process tends to obscure the sharp pressures for higher expenditures and taxes, because they lump together States where pressures will be heavy with those where pressures will be lighter. In those circumstances where surpluses will be developing, expenditures will tend to rise to eliminate them, since there will be urgent unmet needs in such States. In all the others, it will be necessary to raise taxes to keep going.

Recent and current tax activity among the States testify to the unrelenting pressures for more funds. Between 1959 and 1967, every State but one raised rates or adopted a new major tax; there were 230 rate increases and 19 new tax adoptions in this period. This year, the governors asked their legislatures for $3 billion in additional revenues, and many of these proposed have already been enacted. In the first six months of 1967:

Michigan enacted new personal and corporate income taxes.

Nebraska added new personal and corporate income taxes and a sales tax.

West Virginia adopted a corporate income tax.

Minnesota added a sales tax.

Increases in sales tax rates were enacted in Illinois, Iowa, Nevada, North Dakota, Rhode Island, Washington, Wyoming.

Individual income tax rates were increased in California, Iowa, Maryland, Montana, Vermont.

Corporation income tax rates were raised in California, Iowa, Maryland, Minnesota, Montana, Tennessee.

In addition to these actions already taken, other State legislatures are still considering proposals by their governors. The California revisions, which increased State taxes by more than 20 percent, were approved by the Governor on July 29. Only two States—Kansas and North Carolina—lowered taxes to some extent, and both were cases of tax reductions concentrated at the lower income levels.

All this activity does not warrant the complacent conclusion that State and local governments can meet future needs with their present resources. The projections which were made as recently as last year are already out of date, and will become increasingly so with the passage of time.

Q Many people have recommended a Federal income tax credit for State income taxes as a substitute for revenue sharing. Wouldn't the credit do the trick?

A Federal income tax crediting for State income taxes is an attractive device, particularly if it could be coupled with tax sharing or general assistance. But, if a choice has to be made, the balance of advantages favors the revenue sharing plan:

First, because of its contributions to interstate equalization, which the income tax credit can't possibly duplicate.

Second, because its entire proceeds would flow into State and local treasuries while a good part of the benefits of the tax credit would initially accrue directly to the taxpayers rather than to their governments.

Third, because the tax credit would have to overcome the barriers involved in inducing 15 States to adopt a tax they have not chosen to adopt on their own.

Having said this, however, we wish to add that adoption of an income tax credit would be a major advance in Federal-State fiscal relations, a very good second best to the revenue sharing approach.

Q Why give any money at all to the State governments? Aren't they obsolete?

A We believe that the States are an essential feature of our Federal system of government. A local government is an efficient form of government for some things, but not for many others. In taxation, for example, large local differentials in tax rates on income or sales tend to encourage people to move to other communities or to purchase elsewhere to avoid the tax. As for expenditures, only a few very large cities have the financial means to support higher education and even these few are having troubles. As a matter of fact, with the growth of population, the State governments are rapidly becoming metropolitan governments in the true sense of the word. Thus, for reasons of efficiency, the State governments cannot be permitted to wither away.

No doubt, one can find examples to fit almost any charge, but a fair appraisal of the situation is that most States have been doing a good job in recent years. The State governments have actually used most of their scarce resources for urgently needed State and local programs.

Between 1955 and 1965, general expenditures of State governments rose steeply by $23 billion, to around $40 billion. Of this increase, about 60 percent went for education, health, welfare, and housing; more than two thirds of this amount went to education—most of it through grants to local governments. This evidence suggests that, if the States were to receive unencumbered funds from the Federal Government, they would spend them on urgently needed services whether the particular service were stipulated or not. To be specific, if the Federal Government allocated $6 billion for revenue sharing, there is little doubt that about $3 billion of this money would be spent on teachers' salaries, school buildings, and other educational needs.

There is little doubt that the quality of State governments varies widely, but most observers agree that most State governors are competent and dedicated public officials. Many of them have surrounded themselves with excellent staffs, and are shaking up the old State bureaucracies and introducing new programs and policies that are sometimes ahead of thinking in Washington. As the effects of reapportionment are felt, conditions will improve even in those States where many of us have despaired of making progress in improving administration. Furthermore, there is no point in denying urgent fiscal aid to the "good" States merely because there are some "bad" States ("good" and "bad" in their attitude toward public services). As the last election demonstrated, States change complexion rapidly under the impetus of new administrations. It should also be added that the State governments do not have a monopoly on incompetence—some of the Federal agencies administering grants are something less than models of efficiency.

In conclusion, revenue sharing expresses the traditional faith most of us have in pluralism and decentralization, diversity, innovation, and experimentation. For those who lack that faith— for dyed-in-the-wool Hamiltonians and those who want the States to wither away—there can be little attraction in revenue-sharing or other instruments relying heavily on State-local discretion and decision. Yet, apart from the philosophic virtues of federalism, all of us have a direct stake in the financial health of State-local governments for the simple reason that they perform the bulk of essential civilian services in the country. Revenue sharing would help them do their jobs better:

By providing new financial elbow-room, free of fatal political penalties for innovative and expansive-minded State-local officials (i.e., by serving our federalist interest in vitality and independence at the State-local level).

By nourishing the purely local services and building up the staff and structure needed to carry out effectively the national-interest or spill-over type of services financed by categorical aid (i.e., by serving the universal interest in competence and efficiency).

By enabling the economically weaker States to provide the same scope and quality of services as their wealthier brethren without putting crushingly heavier burdens on their citizens (i.e., by serving the national interest in reducing interstate disparities in levels of services associated with any given tax effort).

THE FEDERAL GOVERNMENT AND STATE-LOCAL FINANCES

Harvey E. Brazer

Federal aid to states and local governments began in the late 18th century and became of major importance during the depression years of the 1930's. Whereas in 1934 federal grants amounted to $1 billion, they grew to $17.4 billion in 1968 and no end appears in sight. The necessity for such increases stems directly from the inability of states and local goverments to tax at a rate to meet their current needs. The author discusses the "pros" and "cons" of tax sharing, income tax credits, conditional grant-in-aid, and block grants. It is now apparent that both major political parties recognize the needs of states and their local subdivisions and intend to take major steps to assist these governments in meeting their obligations.

Financing government under federalism in the United States, with its Federal Government, the fifty states, and more than 90,000 local jurisdictions, is a highly complex, cooperative venture. The responsibility for such major governmental functions as education, welfare, highways, and health is shared by all three levels of government; in the broadest sense they all draw on the common base of national income and wealth for revenue; and several major taxes are employed by two and sometimes even three levels of government. In the President's budget estimates for the fiscal year 1968, $17.4 billion is ear-marked for aid to state and local governments, about 10 percent of total Federal cash payments to the public.

This sum, in turn, will amount to more than one-sixth of the total general revenues of the recipient governmental units. And in recent years the states have been distributing approximately 35 per cent of their revenues to their local subdivisions. In 1965 state aid to local governments, in the amount of $14 billion, represented 30 per cent of local general revenue and 40 per cent more than the states received from the Federal Government. Direct grants from the Federal Government to local jurisdictions amounted to more than $1 billion.[1]

[1] U.S. Department of Commerce, Bureau of the Census, *Governmental Finances in 1964–65* (Washington, D.C.: U.S. Government Printing Office, 1966), p. 20.

Reprinted by permission from the *National Tax Journal*, XX, June 1967, pp. 155–164.

The history of Federal aid to state and local governments goes back to the 1790's, but it was not until the Great Depression of the 1930's that it became a major element in the receipts of states and local governments or in the budget of the Federal Government. In 1934 it amounted to $1 billion and it remained at about this level until after World War II. But in the past 20 years Federal aid has been growing at an accelerating rate. In the ten years to 1956 it doubled to $3.7 billion, doubled again in the next four years to 1960, and between 1960 and the budget for 1968, only eight years, it has gone from $7 billion to $17.4 billion, an increase of almost 150 per cent.[2] Moreover, President Johnson has recently suggested that Federal aid may soar to $60 billion in the next five years.[3]

Almost all of the budgeted Federal aid is in the form of conditional grants-in-aid. As of January, 1966, there were 162 identifiable major programs under which these grants-in-aid were distributed and 399 separate Congressional authorizations were required to support them.[4] Under each of these programs and authorizations the funds are specifically earmarked to selected functions and sub-functions and the recipient

state-local jurisdictions are required to comply with detailed conditions in order to qualify for the funds. Most programs also require that the grantee jurisdiction match Federal funds in varying proportions. Some programs were initiated in order to assist state and local governments to finance activities already being carried on, whereas others were designed to induce them to enter into new activities.

NEW DIRECTIONS IN FEDERAL AID

Given the very rapid rise in the contribution of the Federal Government to the support of state-local finances, one may well wonder why there has recently developed so widespread and strong an interest in a new departure in Federal aid that involves large additional Federal distributions to state and local governments, with few or no strings attached.[5] This interest appears to have originated in the Federal Administration early in 1964. It arose, at least in part, out of the issues surrounding the 15-month debate in Congress, in the news media, and among the public at large, on the unprecedentedly large tax cut contained in the Revenue Act of 1964, as passed in March of that year.

One of the major arguments in favor of the tax cut was that the Federal tax structure tends to exert a "fiscal drag" on the economy, making it increasingly difficult to attain full employment and to sustain it once it has been achieved. This fiscal drag was held to arise from

[2] U.S. Department of Commerce, Bureau of the Census, *Census of Governments, 1962, Historical Statistics on Governmental Finances and Employment*, Vol. VI, No. 4 (Washington, D.C.: U.S. Government Printing Office, 1964), p. 48, and Bureau of the Budget, *Special Analyses, Budget of the United States, Fiscal Year 1968* (Washington, D.C.: U.S. Government Printing Office, 1967), p. 148.

[3] In an address to the Governors' Conference, as reported in *The Boston Herald*, March 19, 1967, p. 1.

[4] I. M. Labovitz, *Number of Authorizations for Federal Assistance to State and Local Governments Under Laws in Force at Selected Dates During 1964–66* (Washington, D.C.: Library of Congress, 1966).

[5] The history of recent proposals for Federal tax sharing is concisely outlined in Maureen McBreen, *Federal Tax Sharing: Historical Development and Arguments For and Against Recent Proposals* (Washington, D.C.: The Library of Congress Legislative Reference Service, January 13, 1967).

the fact that with the economy growing at the target rate of about 6 per cent per year in current dollar terms Federal revenues would rise at the rate of about 8 per cent per year or more than $7 billion. At the same time, barring a major defense build-up, it was expected that expenditures would increase by no more than about $3 billion per year. The result, if tax rates were not sharply cut, would be an increasingly large "full employment surplus," but one that might never be realized because the budgetary drag would be so strong as to prevent the attainment of full employment. The tax cut of more than $10 billion was designed to remove this fiscal drag. But it was recognized by those who were looking ahead that under reasonable assumptions about the rate of growth in GNP and expansion of budgetary expenditures, within two or three years after enactment of the tax cut revenues would be growing by about $8 billion a year, or more than the rate of growth in absolute dollar terms prior to the tax reduction of 1964. Thus it appeared that substantial sums would become available periodically in amounts exceeding budgetary requirements and growing cumulatively by $4 billion per year or more.

Clearly, if we were to avoid the difficulties imposed by a growing potential budgetary surplus, appropriate means had to be found for distributing what came to be called in some circles a "fiscal dividend." One obvious means of doing so would be through repeated periodic reductions in tax rates. But once the excise taxes were repealed, as most of them were in 1965, to absorb approximately one year's excess growth in Federal revenues, Federal tax reducduction would necessarily mean major cuts in income taxes. Viewed in isolation the prospect of continued reduction in income tax rates is attractive indeed, but in the context of the overall fiscal picture that encompasses state and local finances it is not quite so attractive.

Far from experiencing actual or potential surpluses, state and local governments have been extremely hard pressed to find the revenues with which to finance burgeoning expenditures. These expenditures have been rising steadily at a rate of 10.6 per cent per year through the past twenty years. They have gone from $11 billion in 1946 to $74.5 billion in 1965. Revenues have risen apace, from $11.7 billion to $74 billion, but, unlike expenditures, at constant tax rates they tend to increase, at best, only proportionately or less than in proportion to increases in GNP. Thus these jurisdictions have been forced to seek new sources of revenue through the imposition of new taxes and to raise rates under existing taxes. At the state level the Advisory Commission on Intergovernmental Relations has counted "well over 200 rate hikes and 15 new taxes since 1959."[6]

Included in new taxes has been the adoption of a sales tax by nine states since 1959, to bring the number levying this tax to 43. In addition, there have been 25 increases in sales rates, and whereas in 1959 the most common sales tax rate was 2 per cent and only one state levied a rate in excess of 3 per cent, there are now ten states in which the sales tax rate exceeds 3 per cent and only eight that retain a rate of less than 3 per cent. Income tax rates have been increased with about the same frequency and the list of states imposing personal income taxes has been increased by three. Currently only New Hampshire taxes neither retail sales nor personal income and 28 states, accounting for well over half of the United States population, impose both sales and income taxes.

[6] Press Release, Advisory Commission on Intergovernmental Relations, Washington, D.C.: December 20, 1966.

At the local level effective property tax rates continued to push upward and in several states, most notably California, Colorado, Illinois, Kentucky, Michigan, New York, Ohio and Pennsylvania, local governments are resorting increasingly to sales and income taxes.

Plaguing the states and their local subdivisions is the ever-present threat, both real and imagined, of competition from low-tax jurisdictions for industry, trade and wealth. This factor, and limitations on taxing powers—local property tax rate limits, constitutional barriers to income taxation in such states as Illinois, Pennsylvania and Washington, and the denial of non-property taxes to local governments in many states—point up the sharp contrast between the Federal Government's ability to raise revenue and that of state and local governments.

Despite rapidly growing expenditures and continuing efforts on the tax front, in virtually every state and urban community in the nation large gaps prevail between clearly defined and obvious needs and performance in the public sphere. Recent optimistic projections of state and local revenues and expenditures by the Tax Foundation[7] are impossible to reconcile with the facts of fiscal life in the states and among local jurisdictions. For that matter, the Tax Foundation itself, in its *Tax Review* for February, 1967, notes that "At least 33 of the 47 state legislatures meeting in 1967 will hear proposals for new or increased taxes. . . . If all measures were approved, state taxes would rise by almost $3 billion annually, a 10 per cent increase over 1966 collections. Although this year's volume of proposed tax increases does not set a new record, it matches the previous high in 1965."[8] The Foundation goes on to note that

nineteen new taxes are being seriously considered in fifteen states and that proposals for increasing rates under existing taxes number seventy in twenty-eight states.

Under these circumstances, once the war in Vietnam has been brought to an end or defense expenditures stabilize and the threat of fiscal drag or the promise of fiscal dividends become imminent prospects, periodic substantial reductions in Federal income tax rates become only one of several possible alternative means of disposing of the potential Treasury surplus. We may well contemplate Federal tax reductions, but the demands of state and local finance strongly suggest that various possible forms of additional Federal aid may deserve at least as high a priority.

At least four possible means of increasing Federal aid have been proposed in recent years. They include sharing of the personal income tax with the states or with local governmental units, a credit against Federal income tax liability for state and local income taxes paid, expansion and revision of the traditional grants-in-aid, and block grants or unconditional subsidies in amounts calculated as a percentage of the Federal income tax base or income tax receipts and distributed on a per capita or modified per capita basis.

Before discussing each of these types of proposals I should note that, even if one assumes that they would have the effect merely of permitting state and local governments to reduce their taxes rather than increase their expenditures, they still have much appeal as substitutes for at least part of possible Federal income tax reductions. In contrast to the progressive Federal tax structure,

---

[7] *Fiscal Outlook for State and Local Government to 1975* (New York: Tax Foundation, Inc., 1966).

[8] Tax Foundation, Inc., "State Tax Prospects, 1967," *Tax Review*, Vol. XXVIII, No. 2, February, 1967, p. 5.

state and local taxation, dominated by property and sales taxes, is highly regressive. It follows, therefore, that substitution of Federal for state-local taxes is virtually certain to increase progression or reduce regression in the overall tax system. This substitution is also likely to bring about greater equality in the expenditure benefit to tax burden ratio experienced by people of similar income and wealth living in different parts of the country. In addition, the greater responsiveness of Federal taxes to changes in the level of economic activity means that the substitution of Federal for even a small proportion of state-local taxes will improve the built-in flexibility or automatic stabilizing influence of the total tax system.

It is, of course, a matter of value judgment as to whether these gains are offset, or more than offset, by the accompanying reduction in local "fiscal responsibility." But state and local officials and legislative bodies are accountable for the efficient use of public funds irrespective of their source, and a dollar of Federal money wasted is just as costly to a state as any other dollar. The frequently voiced opposition to Federal aid that rests on the argument that it is wasteful because of the "costs" of sending the money to Washington and then returning it is not to be taken seriously, at least in the present context. The fact is that Federal tax collection costs are typically far lower than similar costs incurred by state and local governments. In my own judgment, therefore, the gains exceed any likely losses by a comfortable margin.

TAX SHARING

Tax or revenue sharing is a term that has been loosely used to describe a wide variety of plans that would return funds to the states and local governments, with or without strings attached, in amounts calculated as a proportion of a Federal tax base or receipts from a specified tax. I prefer to use a narrower definition of this term under which it refers only to the distribution by the Federal Government of a portion of the receipts from a tax to the state or other jurisdiction from which it was collected, with no restrictions as to the uses to which the state or local share may be put. Illustrative of this "pure" form of tax sharing is a bill[9] introduced in the House of Representatives by Congressman Berry in August of 1966. Under the terms of Mr. Berry's bill 4 per cent of the Federal income taxes collected within each state would be returned to that state. A number of other bills, differing only in the proportion of the taxes to be returned and requiring that the proceeds be used only for educational purposes, were introduced in the same session of Congress.

Tax sharing, in this form, simply involves the use of the Federal Government as a tax collecting agency in behalf of the states. It has much appeal in terms of its efficiency from the point of view of both government and the taxpayer. Its appeal to state and local executives and legislators lies, of course, in its capacity to provide substantial amounts of money without requiring them to assume the political responsibility or the political risks of increasing taxes. It also has the merit, as opposed to locally imposed taxes, of avoiding possible losses to low-tax states or local communities under interjurisdictional competition for industry and wealth.

There are at least three objections to tax sharing, particularly sharing of the Federal income tax. The first, and most damaging, is the fact that income tax sharing would provide most assist-

[9] H. R. 16903.

ance to the richest states and least to the poorest, which may be presumed to need it most. It would tend, because of the progressive distribution of the income tax, to intensify inequality among the states in income distribution. A second, and far less important objection, may be found in the instability of income tax receipts and the difficulties involved in estimating receipts in advance. Finally, income tax sharing might well seriously inhibit the Federal Government in its willingness and ability to employ variations in tax rates as a tool of counter-cyclical fiscal policy.

INCOME TAX CREDITS

Another frequently advocated proposal is the allowance of a credit against Federal income taxes for state or local taxes paid.[10] This device would help only the taxpayer immediately, but it would enable the states to impose additional income taxes in the amount of the credits allowed without adding to the net tax liabilities of most taxpayers. As long as the credit is less than 70 per cent of the amount of state or local tax paid those taxpayers whose marginal Federal income tax rate exceeds the rate of the credit would not be affected by it, because they would find it to their advantage to continue to take state and local taxes as a deduction. Thus those taxpayers whose high Federal tax rates are often cited as the reason for the failure of the states to use income taxes as a major source of revenue might be the only ones paying

[10] A credit in the suggested range of 25 to 50 per cent of state or local income taxes paid was recommended by the Advisory Commission on Intergovernmental Relations in 1965. See its report entitled *Federal-State Coordination of Personal Income Taxes* (Washington, D.C.: Advisory Commission on Intergovernmental Relations, 1965), pp. 18–19.

higher state income taxes if the Federal credit were accompanied by increases in state rates.

Because the amount of sales tax paid by any one taxpayer is extremely difficult to ascertain, and because of the likelihood that renters as well as owners bear property taxes, the only attractive prospect for the credit is the income tax. But seventeen states do not impose general individual income taxes, and some of them are constitutionally prohibited from doing so. In addition, the tax credit device, like income tax sharing, would aid the richest states most and the poorest states least. And, in this sense at least, it would appear to entail an inefficient use of Federal funds.

CONDITIONAL GRANTS-IN-AID

Federal aid thus far has been almost exclusively in the form of matching conditional grants-in-aid. These grants ordinarily require that the states or other recipient units spend at least some funds of their own in order to qualify to receive Federal money. But since the matching funds may be financed either by increasing state and local taxes or reducing expenditures on other functions, the matched-grant approach does not ensure that Federal aid is not substituted for local taxes.

Conditional grants-in-aid permit the Federal Government to ensure (or attempt to ensure) minimum levels of service and minimum standards of administrative performance with respect to the aided functions. Where there is a major national interest in the attainment of such service levels, this is an important advantage of this form of aid. But it also may have the effect of forcing the states to divert funds from non-aided services, where the need may, in fact, be greater. Budgetary discretion is therefore constrained, and efficiency, in terms of using public funds to meet the most urgent needs, may suffer. Diversity in tastes among residents of different states and local communities and differences in resources undoubtedly lead to wide differences in priority orderings within the public sectors of these jurisdictions. Additional grants-in-aid tend, however, to require conformity to a uniform standard, a conformity that is inconsistent with meaningful consumer sovereignty as the determining force in decisions about the allocation of resources in the public sector and between the private and public sectors of the economy.

It is often argued that Federal grants-in-aid do release state and local funds for financing unaided services. But this is true only in those areas that would have provided the level of services required by the Federal Government in the absence of those requirements. The outcome in practice, therefore, is almost inevitably one in which the budget-distorting influence of additional grants-in-aid varies inversely with the economic well-being and directly with the fiscal needs of the state.

Present complexities are such that states and eligible local jurisdictions are finding it increasingly difficult to keep properly informed about the grants for which they may qualify, let alone find the professional talent and expertise that they must have in order to file applications and comply with the detailed provisions of the grants. Evidence of this is found in the fact that many jurisdictions now find it necessary to maintain offices in Washington whose sole function it is to keep the state capitol or city hall informed as to funds to which they may make claim; substantial sums intended for the states go begging for inordinately long periods of time because of the mass of

bureaucratic red tape frequently involved; and a new profession has developed whose members are finding it highly lucrative to sell their services as experts in the technique of filing successful applications for Federal grants. Recent legislation particularly in the fields of health and education points the way to reform. It involves the grant-in-aid for broad functional categories of expenditure, such as primary and secondary education, as opposed to grants for narrowly specified purposes.

BLOCK GRANTS

This brings us to one of the most widely discussed proposals for increasing Federal financial assistance to the states—the so-called "Heller Plan," named for Walter W. Heller, Former Chairman of the Council of Economic Advisers under Presidents Kennedy and Johnson.[11] One of the most attractive features of the plan is its basic simplicity. The Federal Government would distribute to the states each year an amount equal to a specified percentage of the Federal individual income tax base—taxable income reported by all individuals. One variant of the plan would simply divide the total distributable sum among the states according to population. At current levels of taxable income, 2 per cent, for example, would provide $6 billion, or approximately $30 per capita. Some of its advocates would attach no strings whatsoever to state use of the funds, while others would require that they be spent on a rather wide range of functions, or that they not be spent for such generously aided ones as high-

[11] For Professor Heller's views on the proposal see Chapter 3 of his recently published *New Dimensions of Political Economy* (Cambridge, Massachusetts: Harvard University Press, 1966).

ways, and that the provisions of the Civil Rights Act be applied.

The plan has several major merits. Unlike conditional grants-in-aid, its budget-distorting influences would either be offsetting or nonexistent. That is, they might serve to offset the distortions created by grants-in-aid or would involve no biases toward specific uses of the funds. The amount to be distributed would grow at least as rapidly as the economy as a whole, probably considerably faster. Thus it would provide a source of revenue that is more likely to keep pace with rising state-local expenditures than existing sources. And a minimum, perhaps equal to the prior year's amount, could be built in to insure against cyclical down-swings. The equal per capita form of this unconditional Federal grant would have some equalizing influence among the states because, for example, $30 is a larger proportion of per capita income in Alabama or Mississippi, say, than it is in Connecticut or Delaware.

The block grant, in the form in which I have presented it thus far, is a flexible plan which can be modified easily to meet most objections. Clearly, for example, if $6 billion per year (growing at about 7 to 8 percent annually) is thought inadequate, the 2 per cent of Federal taxable individual income figure can readily be raised to 3, or 4, or any other per cent that is consistent with the desired fiscal position of the Federal Government, its objectives of economic growth and stability, and the needs of state-local governments. Similarly, it would involve only a modest increase in complexity to provide a built-in penalty against those states putting forth relatively little fiscal effort or which reacted to the receipt of the block grant by reducing their fiscal effort, and to provide more interstate equalization of

fiscal capacity than would be achieved through equal per capita grants.

Fiscal effort could be taken into account by multiplying the basic per capita figure by the ratio of state-local tax collections in each state as a percentage of income received in the state to the same percentage for the United States as a whole. High tax-effort states would be rewarded with larger grants and a state which responded to the receipt of the Federal subsidy by cutting its taxes would be penalized by having that subsidy reduced. Similarly, fiscal capacity, as measured by income received in the state, could be built into the formula.

Its critics have raised two main objections against the Heller Plan. Professor Musgrave, for example, argues that "There should be some assurance that funds, which originate at the national level, will be spent according to national priorities. Lacking this relationship, the revenue transfer may well result in a Balkanization of our expenditure structure, at the very time when a comprehensive national approach to public service programs is most needed."[12] He prefers, apparently, to leave the states and their local subdivisions to their own resources except insofar as the tastes or preferences of the people living in those jurisdictions, as reflected in the policies of their legislative representatives, may coincide with the preferences of the nation as a whole as expressed in the policies that the national administration and the Congress choose to pursue.

The second major objection stems from the view that the most urgent needs in the public sector are to be found in our urban communities and that the states cannot be trusted to take

[12] R. A. Musgrave, "National Taxes and Local Needs," *The Nation*, January 16, 1967, p. 80.

proper cognizance of these needs. Thus many of those who support the general principles of the Heller Plan would insist that the funds be used solely to support education or that the states be required to distribute a minimum proportion of the amounts received to local jurisdictions.[13] It seems to me, however, that distribution to cities or a uniform proportion required to be distributed to local governments involves serious and perhaps insuperable difficulties.

The states vary widely in the distribution of functional responsibilities between the state and its local subdivisions. In 1965, in the United States as a whole, the states accounted for 35 per cent of total state-local direct general expenditure for all functions, but this proportion ranged from 22 and 24 per cent in New York and New Jersey to between 60 and 75 per cent in West Virginia, Vermont, Alaska, and Hawaii.[14] Thus a requirement that, say, 50 per cent of a Federal block grant be distributed to local jurisdictions within each state would be excessively generous for those jurisdictions in the latter group of states, whereas it would fall far below the proportion of expenditure obligations now carried by local jurisdictions in New York and New Jersey, as well as many other states. Obviously any uniform proportion would suffer from the same kind of disability. It is only within each of the states taken as a whole that all state-local functions are more less uniformly assumed. It follows, therefore, that block grants or unconditional subsidies

should be distributed to the states for further distribution, as they may choose, to their local subdivisions.

It is undeniable that state legislatures have, in the past, been dominated by rural interests, leading to the neglect of urban problems and urban needs. But the reapportionment decision of the Supreme Court in 1962 has already corrected this condition in two-thirds of the states and the process can be expected to have been completed very soon. With reapportionment the voices of the cities and their suburbs should be adequately heard by the time the Congress has moved favorably on block grants to the states.

One need only look at the contrasts to be found among cities in the responsibilities they assume to recognize that Federal block grants to these jurisdictions would be impossible to devise in a manner that would do reasonable justice to even a substantial portion of them. New York City, for example, is a very different creature from Chicago. In 1965 New York City spent $432 per capita, the City of Chicago, $113.[15] New York finances all or part of some of the most costly functions of government which in Chicago are financed through the state, the county, the school district, and several special districts. Thus any given amounts in a block grant that would be meaningful in magnitude to New York would be an excessively generous bonanza to Chicago. Needless to say, most cities in the United States would fall somewhere in between these two extremes. The vast diversity in their circumstances and in responsibilities assumed by cities within states, let alone among the several states, is so great as to defy any at-

[13] One or other of these requirements was a feature of several bills providing for block grants or revenue sharing introduced in the 1966 session of Congress. See, for example, S. 2619 (Senator Javits), and S. 3405 (Senator Miller).

[14] *Governmental Finances in 1964–65*, pp. 34–38.

[15] U.S. Department of Commerce, Bureau of the Census, *City Government Finances, 1964–65* (Washington, D.C.: U.S. Government Printing Office, 1966), pp. 21 and 38.

tempt by the Congress to design a uniform, reasonable system of block grants to these jurisdictions.

CONCLUSION

The needs of the states and their local subdivisions have now been widely recognized in Washington by both major national parties. In bills that they have introduced in the Congress and in statements of party policy, both Democrats and Republicans have made it clear that they intend to take major steps toward assisting state-local governments to meet their obligations more adequately. As soon as the Federal budget is relieved of the burden of rapidly increasing defense expenditures there seems no doubt but that the Congress will act. The major question that remains concerns the kind of action that should be taken. It seems to me that the most promising approaches lie in a combination of grants-in-aid and block grants to the states. While in an important sense they may be viewed as alternatives, because even Federal dollars are limited in amount, I would prefer to regard them as complementary, recognizing that they are really designed to serve different purposes.

The grant-in-aid is clearly most useful to the extent that the Congress wishes to ensure the more adequate financing of, and the achievement of national goals in, the supply of services in which there is an overwhelming national interest. On the other hand, the block grant is best suited to the objectives of increasing and equalizing fiscal capacity among the states and substituting the far more equitable and efficient Federal taxes for the regressive, horizontally inequitable, and frequently repressive state-local taxes.

A recent econometric study of the state-local sector of the economy finds that each dollar of block grants received by state-local governments would tend to increase expenditures by $.564, as opposed to $1.120 per dollar of grants-in-aid.[16] If our objective were to maximize total spending, clearly the grant-in-aid would emerge as superior to the block-grant. But if we are primarily concerned with the quality of the overall tax structure and equalization and expansion of state-local fiscal resources, this finding does not damage the case for block grants.

Both the block grant and the grant-in-aid warrant a far higher priority than tax sharing or tax credits in the Federal government's plans for further assisting state and local governments in the financing of their rapidly growing obligations. But whether or not grants-in-aid are expanded, reduction in complexity and improved budgetary efficiency demand their re-structuring. The number of programs and appropriations is now much larger than anyone could want, let alone fully comprehend, and the role of the Federal bureaucracy, in many areas, has become oppressive. The Congress should move immediately and aggressively toward the achievement of a simplified structure of grants-in-aid, one which specifies national goals in broad terms and permits reasonable scope for diversity in local tastes and needs.

The block grant, along lines suggested by the "Heller Plan," is a most promising device, long effectively used in other major federations, for improving the general fiscal capacity of the states, for equalizing that capacity, and for reducing the disparity among the states in the tax load imposed on similarly circumstanced residents per dollar

[16] Edward M. Gramlich, "State and Local Governments and Their Budget Constraint" (an unpublished paper that is part of an econometric model-building project sponsored by the Federal Reserve Board, dated February, 1967), p. 23.

of public expenditures. Direct Federal grants to urban jurisdictions are not, however, a plausible solution for the fiscal problems of the cities. Their fiscal salvation must be found in the state capitols and in the imaginative and vigorous exploitation of their own resources.

IS THE BIG-CITY PROBLEM HOPELESS?

U.S. News & World Report

For cities to continue the increases of property taxes, general sales taxes, and income taxes, nontax fees and charges will insure an increased out-flow of middle and upper incomes and businesses to the suburbs. Their places will be taken by the influx of low-income, low-skill inhabitants, thus reducing the ability of the cities to finance the ever-increasing demands made upon them. The mayors of cities across our nation are saying they can no longer "make it" alone. Massive federal assistance appears to be the only hope of salvation.

In more and more of this nation's big cities, officials are finding that the harder they try, the more money they spend, the larger the State and federal aid they get, the greater the troubles seem to become.

Is the problem posed by the big city in America today a hopeless one? Is there a solution in higher and higher taxes, or ever-increasing aid? Must there be a resort to dispersal in the way that the London metropolis is trying to cope with bigness?

Faced with the big-city problem, an official of the National League of Cities is making the following points:

In central cities, people who bear the main share of the tax burden are not the ones who benefit the most from the spending which is financed by their tax dollars. The heaviest spending of tax money in the cities is for social-welfare programs and rehabilitation projects to help nontaxpayers.

Property taxes, major source of city revenues, have just about reached the saturation point. Pushing them higher will serve only to accelerate the flight from the cities by taxpayers.

The idea of combining cities and suburbs into one taxing jurisdiction is not a workable answer, for this reason: Suburbs, growing rapidly, need more schools, hospitals, police and fire protection, and other services. Thus the suburbs would balk at paying for the remaking of big-city ghettos and underwriting welfare programs for the big-city poor on top of the tax money they must put up for their own needs.

Political redistricting on the basis of "one person, one vote" has not helped cities. Under the old system, there was a concentration of power in legislative representation of cities. Now, representation is often split in such a way that many legislators from metropolitan areas come out of the suburbs. This makes for factionalism, with the interests of separate sections represented, not the interests of the metropolis as a whole.

Some Government policies are encouraging the outflow of taxpaying employers and employes from cities.

For example, the presidential commission which investigated last summer's race riots noted that the 7 per cent tax-credit incentive granted by the Federal Government had sparked 50 billion dollars in new plant and equipment expenditures between 1962 and 1965—two thirds of it outside the cities.

PROBLEMS OF 1975

An in-depth study of the money troubles of municipal governments was prepared for the National League of Cities by TEMPO, the General Electric Company's Center for Advanced Studies. This examination found that city revenues are falling far behind the need for bigger and bigger spending.

By 1975, the TEMPO report said, U.S. cities will need to spend an annual total of 150 billion dollars. They can count, however, on only 70 billion dollars from their own revenue sources. Based on present trends and programs, the best that cities can get in State and federal aid by 1975 is 30 billion a year —leaving a 50-billion-dollar gap.

The TEMPO study estimated that, for the 1966–75 period, cities of the U.S. face an accumulated revenue gap of 262 billion dollars.

Where is the money to come from?

Property taxes account for 88 per cent of locally raised revenues, according to the TEMPO report, but the study warns that increasing these taxes would

be a self-defeating move. The warning is put this way:

"To the extent that revenues raised by increased property taxes are used to solve today's most pressing urban problems—renewal of slums and improvements of the condition and abilities of slum dwellers—the net effect will be to impel out-movements of middle and upper-income families and business enterprises, and in-movements of low-income groups with little capital or skills and a wide range of problems."

The report goes on:

"It is a demonstrated fact that this is precisely what has happened and continues to happen in many cities, especially core-cities, throughout the nation. It has occurred in Baltimore, Birmingham, Boston, Buffalo, Chicago, Cincinnati, Cleveland, Detroit, Kansas City, Los Angeles, Minneapolis, New York, Newark, Oakland, Philadelphia, Pittsburgh, San Francisco, and Washington, D.C., and also in Youngstown, Worcester, Toledo, Little Rock and others.

"Also, because the size of the revenue gap differs from city to city, raising local property tax rates inevitably makes the cities with the gravest problems the ones with the highest taxes. The average age of buildings in these cities increases as new commercial and residential construction is drawn irresistibly to relatively low-tax cities. Accompanying this gradual aging of buildings in the higher-tax cities is a gradual deterioration of working and living conditions, creating all manner of community problems ranging from increased sanitation problems to increased fire potential and a steady depreciation of their tax bases. Thus, high-tax cities are becoming increasingly powerless to finance their own expenditure requirements and simultaneously they are confronted by growing socio-economic problems requiring public action."

THE SEARCH FOR REVENUE

Stated in the report are these conclusions on sources of new revenue for cities:

1. General sales taxes, excise taxes and personal and business income taxes account for only 6 per cent of the revenue total and are costly to administer. Also, pushing sales and income taxes too high would be a further spur to the exodus of individual taxpayers and businesses.

2. Nontax fees and charges—for utilities, sewers, franchises, recreation-park admissions, hospital services and the like—produce 23 per cent of total revenues. These fees and charges could be boosted to provide about 25 billion dollars of the 262 billion needed to close the gap.

3. An additional 63 billion dollars might be raised by increasing the net bonded debt of cities, if barriers placed by States in the path of local issues of general obligation bonds are removed.

4. State aid, which accounts for from 8 to 17 per cent revenues, might be increased by 50 per cent over the rest of the decade, contributing some 49 billion dollars.

With all this, 125 billions still must be found. Where? From the Federal Government, the TEMPO study says. The reasoning goes this way:

Assuming no major rise in defense spending, the Federal Government might raise all or part of the money needed by the cities without being forced to boost taxes beyond rates now contemplated.

The assumption is based on continued prosperity and a 4 per cent annual rise in the gross national product, with revenues from federal income taxes increasing by 365 billion dollars—enough to justify increased appropriations to close the money gap for troubled cities.

Some urbanologists point out, how-ever, that this is based on assumption and theory—and, they emphasize, the proliferating problems of cities are real, not theoretical.

What can be done to save the cities?

Nothing tried so far seems to work. Now being urged are bolder, longer-range programs.

Some cost estimates are staggering. One estimate—by the Swedish economist and sociologist Gunnar Myrdal—is that it will take "a trillion dollars and a generation" to resolve the dilemma.

One trend of thought puts emphasis on steps to draw people away from huge centers of population.

City planners point out that as additional money is poured into central cities, and as relief payments become more generous, still more poor people crowd in.

An internationally recognized planner, Dr. Constantinos Doxiadis, says that the root cause of the urban crisis may lie "in the very fact that we are pouring resources into the cities." He adds: "The solution may lie in exactly the opposite direction, that of using resources outside the cities . . . in creating new settlements to relieve those suffering from pressures."

Once the pressures are relieved, Dr. Doxiadis says, older cities can be remodeled "in a reasonable way."

THE EISENHOWER PLAN   Relocation of big-city slum dwellers to new communities built on space now occupied by abandoned military installations or on other neglected open areas is suggested by former President Dwight D. Eisenhower.

Writing in the May, 1968, issue of "Reader's Digest," General Eisenhower says:

"To begin the physical rehabilitation of our slums, we must provide room to breathe in the inner cities. Thus, the first essential of any realistic housing plan is to reduce the density of population by encouraging large numbers of people to relocate in new, more wholesome communities. These new towns would have their own schools, shops, clinics and hospitals, their own light industry and recreational facilities."

The Eisenhower plan is a considerable enlargement on a federal program, just getting under way, to build some 50 new "cities within cities" on surplus Government property.

Ground was broken late in May for the first such federal project, in Atlanta, Ga., where the land being used—about 4 miles from the center of the city— formerly belonged to the U.S. penitentiary. Housing for some 900 families is to be privately financed.

Another approach, to provide cheaper and better transportation for New York City's "hard to employ" slum dwellers, chiefly Negroes and Puerto Ricans, to jobs in the suburbs where new industrial plants are springing up, is urged in a Columbia University study.

The study also called for relocation of numbers of the hard-core poor to areas outside the city, with federal legislation making it easier for them to achieve home ownership.

"EXPORTING" CITIZENS   The Columbia report maintains that one of the fastest ways to ease pressure on New York City—where nearly one person out of every eight is getting welfare payments—is to "export some of those at the bottom."

A report by a research team at New York University's graduate school of business administration makes this recommendation: "All antipoverty services should be paid for by the Federal Government."

The report, prepared for the Regional Plan Association of New York, points out that "poverty is a national problem. . . . Many of the poverty-stricken began life far from cities in which they now reside."

Around the country, city officials discussed their problems and the seeming hopelessness of their plight.

In St. Louis, Mayor A. J. Cervantes gave this blunt assessment of the city's plight:

"We just can't make it any more. We are in financial trouble. Everybody on the city payroll wants a raise, but we don't have money for raises. Services are going to have to be cut back.

"Our dilemma becomes more severe with higher police costs, higher wages, greater social problems, as the affluent leave our city and the unskilled and untrained come in from rural areas, bringing nothing but problems."

"A NATIONAL PROBLEM"   Mayor Cervantes says the only solution may lie in a massive "Marshall Plan" of federal aid to cities in housing, education and other needs. He adds:

"The U.S. used 1.5 per cent of the gross national product to rebuild cities of Europe after World War II.

"The same commitment should be made to American cities. It is a national problem."

In Kansas City, Mo., Robert L. Brown, assistant city manager, says that the city must lay policemen off at a time—just after major racial disturbances—when it should be adding men to the force. Mr. Brown complained that State laws block channels through which the city might raise new revenue. He said: "We've just got our hands tied. We find ourselves strapped in."

In Los Angeles, despite booming construction of skyscraper office buildings, large sections—predominantly Negro and Mexican-American—are decaying. Says an expert on urban affairs, Dr.

Fred E. Case of the University of California at Los Angeles:

"The whole heart of Los Angeles County is becoming a giant slum. Los Angeles is losing, in its decayed area, more and more of its tax base.

"We have seen the cost of government go up, property taxes approach the confiscation level, freeways become monumental traffic jams.

"Citizens are beginning to wonder whether they want or can afford the kind of city they're getting. You just can't be optimistic."

Dr. Case sees the central city as doomed if matters continue as they are.

But Mayor Samuel Yorty of Los Angeles says that "we cannot at this time pass the buck to the State or the Federal Government with any hope of inducing either of them to solve our revenue problems."

In Detroit, Mayor Jerome P. Cavanagh describes the city's present financial situation as "precarious," the outlook as "bleak." Threat of a strike by 10,000 city employes demanding more money added a disturbing note as Detroit, hit by a disastrous race riot last year, braced itself for another tense summer.

Bernard Klein, Detroit city controller, said that the answer to the city's problems is "billions of dollars, in block grants, from State and federal sources."

The immediate prospect for Detroiters is for higher taxes and fewer services.

From an official report on municipal finances in New Orleans:

"How severe is the city's fiscal crisis? Very severe must be the answer. How long will it continue? Indefinitely, and in rapidly worsening degree unless the city can both find new revenue and use its present revenues more productively."

In Chicago, it is the school system that is hit by a money crisis. The Chicago board of education operates independently of the city government.

Chicago's public-school machinery, according to one top educator, is "at the point of breaking down" because of inadequate funds. Insufficient State aid is blamed.

"DEFICIENT IN SKILLS"   One major aspect of the problem of cities was brought out in recent testimony before a congressional committee by Louis Danzig, head of the Newark, N.J., housing authority. Mr. Danzig estimated that, since 1950, some 200,000 whites have moved out of Newark while 85,000 Negroes moved in. He said:

"The majority of Negroes now are in-migrants. Often these in-migrants are deficient in education and in job skills. Some of them must be supported by public welfare. Many do not know how to live in cities. . . . Obviously, dialogue and communications are difficult."

The influx of the unskilled, Mr. Danzig said, "has occurred during a period when all municipal costs are continuing to rise and the need for increased public services is expanding."

Some Congressmen said that the plight of U.S. cities was summed up by Mr. Danzig, when, referring to the troubles of his own community, he said:

"The city is caught in a vicious circle of increasing needs and diminishing resources."

Across the country, there is widespread agreement that more-drastic measures than any yet attempted must be applied if the troubled cities of the U.S. are to be revitalized.

PART VII

QUESTIONS FOR DISCUSSION

1. Explain what is meant by the "financial plight of the cities." What is the financial situation of your community when related to obvious needs?
2. What is the tax situation of your community? Do you view this as fair or do you have meaningful suggestions for change?
3. Explain why property and sales taxes are generally viewed as the unfairest of all taxes. What taxes would you substitute for them?
4. In what form (if any) should the federal government provide assistance to the states and cities?

VOCABULARY

Gross National Product (GNP)
per capita
categorical aid
budgetary surplus
direct federal expenditure
block or unconditional grants
assessment
general sales tax
median
intangible property
regressive taxation
general purpose grants
full employment
tax credits

selected sales tax
grants-in-aid
mean
mode
income tax
progressive taxation
tangible property
revenue sharing
nontax fees
tax sharing
assessor
private sector
tax rate

DEVIANCE, CRIME, AND THE POLICE

Crime is more prevalent in large cities than in small ones, more in small cities than in rural areas, and more in poor neighborhoods than in affluent ones. The vast majority of crimes are committed by males, mostly by boys and young men —male, urban, and youthful. This strongly points to the need for increased efforts and understanding by the police department, the prosecutor's office, the courts, the jails, and the entire juvenile process from arrest to probation and release. The court dockets and rehabilitation facilities are so crowded that insufficient attention and humanitarian concern is shown at all points in the proceedings. Is it any wonder that the percentage of youthful offenders returned to a full and useful life is so small? Our total system guarantees that they have little chance to succeed.

One of the more perplexing problems in the law enforcement field is the widely varying perspectives of the policeman, the suspect, and the citizenry at large. The majority of the whites see the policeman as having a difficult job to do and believe that he does so without discrimination; with few exceptions, they believe that brutality is rarely inflicted. The average citizen views brutality in the physical sense. The Negro and other minorities view brutality as physical, verbal, harassment, and intimidation. The policeman usually sees crime as the product of the ghetto and therefore the Negro, the Mexican-American, and the Puerto Rican are always suspect, particularly so if they have long hair, wear beards, and assemble on street corners. The adult whites see field interrogations in which police stop and question individuals who appear "suspicious" as necessary and legitimate; the minorities see this action as unnecessary and humiliating. White youths see the situation in somewhat the same light as do the minorities. As riots and other disturbances occur, the whites' views are hardened, and they want the riots and rioters put down. Over-reaction by the police hardens the belief that police are unnecessarily harsh with the ghetto residents—animosity tends to increase.

There is a large segment of our population who express the feeling that the police force needs to be increased, the court system needs updating to reduce the time between arrest and sentencing, and that more concern should be shown for the rights of the victim rather than the accused. The Federal Bureau of Investigation's report for 1969 shows that all categories of major crime increased in our cities over that of 1968. In fact, the crime rate has been rising dramatically year by year.

The President's Commission on Civil Disorders emphasized the enormous distrust and hostility existing between the police and the citizens of our ghetto neighborhoods. Perhaps the most important need at this time is the provision of trained people and facilities to help young delinquents and potential delinquents grow into worthwhile citizens rather than hardened and habitual criminals. The distrust and hostility cannot be allowed to continue its growth. We must understand that force has a place but it is not the total answer; unnecessary use of force must never be condoned. The Riot Commission's recommendations should be given careful consideration by officials at every level of government. Our citizens must be made to understand that changes will be made. Our entire judicial system's future and efficiency depend upon the trust and respect of all our people. A nation without this trust and respect will not long endure.

CRIME AND SOCIAL CONDITIONS

Robert Rice

The combination of youth, unsatisfactory living conditions, racial strife, and perceptions of police as corrupt or corruptible can only serve to foster one end, that of crime. Our cities are the scene of increasing crime problems and the media forcefully bring home the message of the upward spiral of our crime rate.

No domestic issue commands more attention than crime. Political battles at the local, state, and national level are fought over methods of crime control. Yet the plight of the overworked policeman and the demands for a decent life on the part of the ghetto dweller go unanswered. Stop-gap measures do nothing more than further aggravate conditions. The need for long-range planning is paramount.

As far as its bearing on crime goes, probably the most significant contemporary social change is what is happening in and to American cities. Crime always has been more prevalent in cities than in the country, in big cities than in small ones, in poor city neighborhoods than in well-to-do ones, among groups of city dwellers whose members could not take a full part in community life than among groups whose members could.

In the cities of America during the last two decades, every condition likely to encourage crime has been reinforced. A greater proportion of Americans than ever live in cities. Many cities have grown greatly in size. The composition of the population of many cities, especially the biggest ones, has changed greatly: millions of middle-class families have fled to the suburbs before a tide of impoverished displaced agricultural, and other rural, people from the deep south, Appalachia, and Puerto Rico.

Entire neighborhoods that used to be quiet and comfortable have become dilapidated and overcrowded slums, whose residents are sequestered from the increasing prosperity of most Americans.

Moreover, the flight to the suburbs (inspired to some extent by a desire to escape "crime in the streets") has begun to create in many suburban communities citylike conditions that foster crime—in the streets and out of them. The rate of suburban crime, though much lower than the city rate, has been rising faster in recent years. From crime, as from nuclear weapons, there evidently is "no place to hide."

The following chart illustrates how much of an urban phenomenon crime is.

A second social change that has had much to do with the increase of crime has been a change in the age composition of the population. Just as most crimes, by whomever they are committed, are committed in cities, most crimes, wherever they are committed, are committed by boys and young men.

Reprinted from *The Challenge of Crime*, Public Affairs Pamphlet No. 425. Reprinted by permission of Public Affairs Committee, Inc., © 1968.

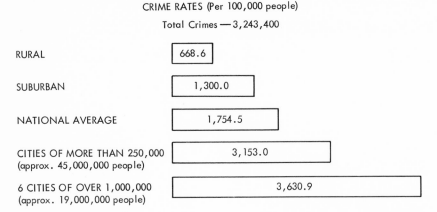

CRIME RATES (Per 100,000 people)

Total Crimes — 3,243,400

RURAL	668.6
SUBURBAN	1,300.0
NATIONAL AVERAGE	1,754.5
CITIES OF MORE THAN 250,000 (approx. 45,000,000 people)	3,153.0
6 CITIES OF OVER 1,000,000 (approx. 19,000,000 people)	3,630.9

(Of the persons of all ages arrested in 1966, 88 per cent were males.) As a result of the postwar "baby boom," the 15-to-25 age group has been the fastest growing one in the country for the last six years, and will continue to be for at least ten years more. Moreover, young people have become not only more numerous but (as every parent or teacher or newspaper reader knows) more independent, more experimental, more mobile, more impatient with traditional standards of morality, more discontented with the disparity between American professions and American performance, more resistant to all authority.

The UCR's arrest figures are the main source of information about who offenders are. For several reasons arrest figures, admittedly, do not give an accurate picture of criminals. They include the many people who are arrested mistakenly and omit the many more people who commit crimes that are not solved. They may include (no one can tell for sure) a disproportionate number of rash or incompetent or casual— and therefore presumably young— offenders, and omit a disproportionate number of prudent, experienced, professional—and therefore presumably older —ones.

However, even if full weight is given to these imperfections in arrest figures, they still give overwhelming evidence that it is mostly boys and young men who commit crimes.

The fact that crime is predominantly urban and youthful has a number of implications. The most obvious is that the agencies that need immediate shoring up with manpower, with equipment, with modern management methods, with procedural innovations, and with community concern and assistance are city police departments, city prosecutors' offices, city courts, city jails and the entire system of juvenile justice from intake offices through detention homes and courts and training schools to the probation and parole machinery. The volume of the work these agencies have to do has become so great that the criminal process, as they administer it, in many instances has become a hurly-burly that compromises both the effectiveness of law enforcement and the quality of justice.

When a prosecutor dismisses charges because he has neither the time nor the means to uncover evidence, or because there are not enough judges or courtrooms for his cases; when the average length of a lower court arraignment is less than four minutes; when a grand jury hands up more than 100 indictments in a single day; when a juvenile

ARRESTS BY AGE FOR INDEX* OFFENSES

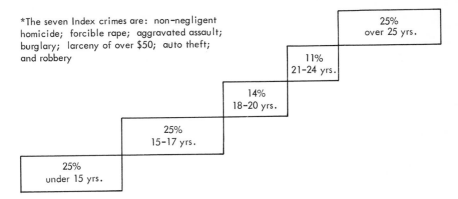

*The seven Index crimes are: non-negligent homicide; forcible rape; aggravated assault; burglary; larceny of over $50; auto theft; and robbery

25%
over 25 yrs.

11%
21-24 yrs.

14%
18-20 yrs.

25%
15-17 yrs.

25%
under 15 yrs.

More 15-year-olds than people of any other age were arrested for burglary, larceny, and auto theft. More 18-year-olds than people of any other age were arrested for robbery, murder, rape and aggravated assault. For all those offenses combined, 15-year-olds, of whom 81,160 were arrested, narrowly led 16-year-olds, with 78,583. By contrast, in the five-year group of 25-29, only about 66,000 persons were arrested for those serious offenses, and the figures continue to decline sharply as the ages of the arrestees increase. Only some 4,500 persons over 65 were arrested for Index offenses.

detention home is crowded to double its capacity, mostly with idle boys or girls waiting for training-school beds to become available; when a parole officer has 75 or 80 cases to take care of, the community is not protected against crime as it should be, nor are the persons accused of, or convicted of, crime treated as fairly as they should be.

A second implication of crime's urban and youthful character is that the quality of the everyday relationships between slum-dwellers and young people on the one hand, and the criminal justice system (most particularly the police) on the other, is of critical importance. The National Crime Commission, and recently in much stronger language the President's Commission on Civil Disorders (Riot Commission), have reported that an enormous amount of mutual distrust and hostility exists between the police and the inhabitants of city ghettoes—just those neighbor-

hoods where crime rates are highest and where police protection is most important. Moreover, both commissions are sure that the police bear the responsibility for taking the initiative to alter those relationships.

A third implication of crime's urban and youthful character—and in the long run this may be the heart of the problem, the nation's best hope for controlling crime—is that there must be greatly increased effort to help young delinquents and potential delinquents grow into constructive citizens instead of hardened and habitual criminals. Not only do most criminal careers start at an early age and with relatively small offenses, but it is much easier to influence a young offender to change his way of life than to influence an older one. Of all the National Crime Commission's recommendations, the one that probably would have the most far-reaching effect if it were fully followed is:

Communities should establish youth-serv-ing agencies—Youth Service Bureaus—located if possible in comprehensive neigh-borhood community centers and receiving juveniles (delinquent and nondelinquent) referred by the police, the juvenile court, parents, schools, and other sources.

The big deficiency in America's deal-ings with young people who get in trouble, or appear likely to get in trouble, is that, generally speaking, there is no way of giving them the help so many of them could use short of locking them up. Even though a juve-nile training school is usually a far more rehabilitative institution than an adult penitentiary, being under physical constraint, being removed from daily contact with family and friends and community life, associating almost ex-clusively with other delinquents and their supervisors, are conditions that are too severe for a great many young offenders. It, in fact, confirms some of them in their delinquent ways.

Indeed, the police and the juvenile courts recognize this problem and do not take such punitive action in many instances when they could. But this usually means virtually unrestricted freedom, even when a period of proba-tion is imposed. Most probation officers have caseloads that are too heavy to permit them to give all their clients the supervision that is necessary, and in any case no probation department has the expert manpower and facilities that a Youth Services Bureau such as the Commission envisions would have. Be-sides, there are many young people who can not legally be committed to a train-ing school, but who need help as badly as those who have broken the law. With such young people, the most the juvenile justice system can do is advise them or warn them or threaten them, and then dismiss them until they com-mit an actionable offense.

THE POLICE

Behind a majority of the Crime Com-mission's recommendations for improv-ing the performance of the police is a pervasive fact that the public seems to be largely unaware of: Every policeman necessarily exercises a very great amount of personal discretion about how he does his work. To begin with, the physical conditions of the job re-quire it. Policemen customarily work alone or in pairs, more or less removed from their supervisors, and in any case the situations they face often do not allow them time to seek advice or, for that matter, even to consider for more than a split second what action to take.

Also, every policeman meets many fewer self-evident instances of crime than he does ambiguous instances of human behavior (or misbehavior). As the Commission report says, "A crim-inal code, in practice, is not a set of specific instructions to policemen but a more or less rough map of the territory in which policemen work." When does a marital quarrel reach the point of being an assault? How much noise and profanity constitute disorderly con-duct? When is it appropriate to order a bunch of boys in front of a candy store to "break it up" and "move along"? What makes a person "sus-picious" enough to be stopped and questioned? Is it more reasonable to take a boy caught throwing rocks at a school window home and ask his parents to keep him in order, or to arrest him? Almost every policeman on almost every tour of duty must answer ques-tions of this kind.

Finally, answering such questions is no mere academic test of intelligence or judgment. Any seemingly trivial de-cision by a policeman can have pro-found effect not only on the lives of individuals but also upon the peace and safety of the community. An arrest, which starts the machinery of the criminal justice system in motion, can permanently affect the life of the person arrested, and of his family as well. A failure to make an arrest can endanger a whole neighborhood. The connection between minor, routine police actions and the outbreak of civil disorders is too well known to require elaboration. Each time a court makes a ruling that permanently limits the activities of all policemen, it is responding to what one policeman or group of policemen did in a specific situation. And because policemen carry weapons, a policeman's decision is sometimes a decision about life or death.

Recommendations

The Commission's recommendations approach the goal of improving the quality of police decisions from several directions. Some are designed to transfer as much as possible of the responsibility for decision-making from the patrolman on the beat to the department on a whole. Installing up-to-date communications and data-storage-and-retrieval systems would help in this respect by making it easier than it now is for policemen to secure rapidly the information, advice, or assistance they need. The Commission particularly recommended the development of a cigarette-package-sized two-way radio for patrolmen, so that they could always be in touch with their superiors no matter how far away from their car radios their duties took them.

But by far the most important recommendation in this area is not technological, but administrative. It is for police departments to recognize, as few of them do, that informally and inexplicitly they make law-enforcement policies every day, and to put those policies into formal and explicit form

for the benefit both of working policemen and of the public, the courts, and state and municipal legislative and executive officials. Then policemen would have direct guidance about delicate matters like dealing with demonstrations, marital disputes, street-corner gatherings, misbehaving children, drunks, and a dozen other kinds of everyday problems that they now handle *ad hoc* or by rule of thumb. The public would have a notion of what the police were doing, and an opportunity to suggest realistic changes. The courts would have a sort of manual of the day-by-day exigencies of law enforcement, and would be able to rule about police practices more knowledgeably than they often do now. Legislatures and city councils would be in a better position than they are to enact useful laws. And mayors and city managers would be better able than they are to exercise supervision.

Another group of recommendations addresses itself directly to the abuse of discretion: corruption, brutality, discriminatory enforcement, offensive personal attitudes and behavior toward minority groups. The Commission reported that, although corruption and brutality are nowhere near as prevalent today as they were in the graft-and-rubber-hose days of Prohibition, there is enough, especially in ghetto neighborhoods, to demand that most departments strengthen their internal investigation units.

The report is considerably more concerned with, and thorough in discussing, the problem that is usually—and somewhat evasively—described as police-community relations: the mutual hostility that exists in almost every big city between the police and members of minority groups, especially boys and young men. A survey of public attitudes toward the police, conducted at the Commission's request by the National

Survey Research Center, shows how extensive this hostility is.

Twenty-three per cent of whites polled thought the police were "doing an excellent job"; 15 per cent of non-whites thought so. Seven per cent of whites thought the police were "doing a poor job"; 16 per cent of non-whites thought so. Sixty-three per cent of whites thought the police were "almost all honest"; 30 per cent of non-whites thought so. One per cent of whites thought the police were "almost all corrupt"; 10 per cent of non-whites thought so. Moreover, Commission observers in several cities reported that there were grounds for these public attitudes, that policemen in ghetto neighborhoods often were abusive, or at least rude and peremptory, to the citizens, and that there was a certain amount of discriminatory enforcement of minor ordinances like those against loitering or drinking in public, evidently for the purpose of harassment.

The package of recommendations the Commission put together to meet this situation is comprehensive, but not particularly novel: more active and imaginative recruitment of Negro officers; scrupulously fair deployment and promotion policies for Negroes; selection and probation procedures designed to screen out prejudiced recruits; an increase in the race-relations content of police training courses; giving community relations specialists a voice in decisions about selection, training, promotion, and field operations; giving community relations performance the same weight in an officer's record as law-enforcement performance; and, finally, setting up high-status community-relations units in police headquarters, directly under the chief, and in each precinct, so that formal and regular relations between the police and community representatives can be maintained both citywide and in the neighborhoods.

It is fair to say that the details of these recommendations are less important than the message that is implicit in them: that there is much *racism*—to use the Riot Commission's word—in the police, and that the need to root it out in whatever way possible is urgent and immediate.

The Need for Better Manpower

Finally, the report points out, the basic—and obvious—way to make sure that policemen exercise discretion wisely and fairly is to improve the quality of policemen. In view of the emphasis that is commonly put on the need for *more* police manpower, it is noteworthy that the Commission strongly emphasized the nationwide need for *better* police manpower. To achieve this end, the report offers a number of rather technical recommendations about selection, training, probation, promotion, pay, and so forth. The details of most of these recommendations make tedious reading for laymen, and in any case are less important than the chief themes they sound.

One theme is that the increasing complexity and delicacy of police work demand that today's policemen be men of considerable learning and breadth of view, and therefore the police should concentrate on seeking recruits on college campuses. In fact, the report advocates that every department's long-range goal—which, it concedes, will take many years to reach—should be that a baccalaureate degree be a minimum entry requirement for every recruit, and an advanced degree in some such subject as law, sociology, or business administration be a minimum standard for every high-ranking official. Pursuing this theme, the report discusses at some length the many major revisions that will have to be made in pay scales, training programs, entrance standards, and promotion policies and procedures if the police are to attract and retain college graduates.

The most novel and imaginative expedient that the report suggests is that there be three levels of entry into large and medium-sized departments: police agent, police officer, and community service officer. The *police agent* would be a college man who would, presumably, be qualified for difficult and responsible duty immediately upon entry, without having to serve several years pounding a beat. The *police officer* would be in the same position a recruit is in today. The *community service officer* would be a sort of apprentice, perhaps under 21, perhaps without a high-school diploma (which is an entry requirement in almost all departments), almost certainly without full law-enforcement powers. He would perform neighborhood service duties, and help officers and agents when needed, while qualifying himself, with the department's help, for promotion to officer or agent. One justification for the CSO concept—though by no means the only one—is that there is a considerable contradiction between raising educational standards for entering policemen and attracting minority-group policemen, who are needed as badly as college-trained policemen are. Another justification is that many officers spend much of their time on service duties that are necessary and important, but can be performed without extensive (and expensive) training in law enforcement.

A second theme is "lateral entry"—permitting skilled and experienced policemen to move from department to department without having to start over

again on a beat, and without losing seniority or pension rights, and permitting qualified civilians to enter a department at a supervisory level. This, of course, would be no more than granting policemen the same right that almost all other professional men have to seek employment where they are most needed and wanted, and granting police departments the opportunity to seek the best qualified men for important and responsible jobs.

A third theme is that managing the affairs of a big-city police department is every bit as complicated as managing those of a large corporation. It requires administrators and experts of a kind and a quality that are not likely to be produced in large numbers by the ordinary police career—patrolman to detective to sergeant to lieutenant, etc. The report urges the police to avail themselves much more widely than they do, of civilian specialists of all kinds, from sociologists to financial managers, from lawyers to systems analysts.

One Big Difficulty

Finally, the police have one big difficulty that has nothing to do with discretion or decision making. This difficulty is built into America's political pattern, and it makes life hard not just for the police, but for transportation planners and pollution control experts and all sorts of other metropolitan functionaries. The difficulty is that America is becoming a nation of metropolitan areas with large common problems, but it remains a mosaic of small independent local governments.

There are some 40,000 separate law-enforcement agencies in America. Many of these are one-, two-, or three-man rural departments, but in the country's 212 Standard Metropolitan Statistical Areas, where two-thirds of Americans live and four-fifths of crimes occur, there are 313 counties and 4,144 cities, each with its own police force. Where this hurts the most is in the suburbs. Around almost every big city, especially in the East and Middle West, are dozens or even hundreds of communities with police forces too small to be very effective and too jealous of their independence to cooperate much with neighboring forces. One result of this is that it is relatively easy for organized burglary and car-theft rings and gambling and narcotics conspiracies to flourish in a metropolitan area, simply by spreading themselves across a number of jurisdictions—or by picking a jurisdiction with an inefficient or corruptible department as a headquarters. And even in the case of less elaborate criminal operations, the investigatory facilities and skills of small departments are often inadequate.

The Commission concluded that the solution to this problem was for all the departments in an area to contrive ways in which they can pool their facilities and coordinate their activities.

POLICE AND THE COMMUNITY

The President's Commission on Law Enforcement
and Administration of Justice

It is common knowledge that our perceptions play an important role in the way we carry out our lives. This selection explores the different views held by the middle-class white and black community in their perceptions of the police. The findings give credence to the growing problems encountered by police in dealing with the black community.

It seems apparent that the police must first become aware of the way the black community sees them if they are to become effective law enforcers. A real effort must be made to change these negative perceptions into more positive directions.

WHITE VIEWPOINTS

Police Discrimination

Members of the white community express their belief that the San Diego police practice discrimination. Four types of discrimination are apparent from their comments: race; age; income; and appearance. The discrimination, it is thought, is not necessarily conscious on the part of the police, but it is often interpreted as prejudice by the people who experience it. One social action agency official speaks of it in these terms:

. . . it is a statistical kind of thing, rather than being a prejudicial kind of thing. The statistics have come in that Negroes out of the ghetto at night are a source of problems, and they'll stop them. Generally, and I've seen a lot of policemen operate, the San Diego policemen have been very courteous. . . .

Source: Field Surveys IV, Volume 1. A Report of a Research Study Submitted to The President's Commission on Law Enforcement and Administration of Justice. 1967.

A poverty program official states that the police tend to see the principal crime problem in terms of the Negro community, and they, therefore, associate crime with Negroes, thus giving the police a racist overtone, whether or not it is warranted. An attorney recalls a case in which a seventeen-year-old youth escaped from Juvenile Hall. After a long chase he was shot and killed by a pursuing officer as he was trying to crawl under a barbed wire fence. The attorney does not believe that the officer intended to kill the youth, but he thinks the action does indicate how easily the policeman lost his patience with this particular Negro youth. He states that it reflects a lack of respect for the Negro's life and it is "symptomatic or at least symbolic of the attitude of the police toward Negroes generally." In discussing another case in which a Negro boy had been falsely arrested and held in Juvenile Hall missing three days of school, the attorney believes that if the boy had been Caucasian, the police would have ensured that he was not absent from school. The field interrogation procedure is thought by a large segment of the community to be utilized much more often in certain areas of the city than in others—infrequently in upper-middle-class and upper-class neighborhoods, but frequently in lower-class areas.

Another attorney comments that riots elsewhere in the nation tend to reinforce the belief held by minorities—particularly Negroes—that they are discriminated against by the police:

I think that as riots occur, it hardens people's reserve, or resolution, that the riots should be put down. As these riots are put down, it hardens the feeling of what was referred to as a ghetto here, that they are being treated differently from other people.

Appearance, as indicated by type of clothing and hairstyle, is considered by many to be an important factor in whether a person is stopped by the police. A college professor comments:

Yeah, there are police everytime you get a bevy of young men with beards and long hair . . . they'll be closely watched by the police.

Constant interrogation on the basis of appearance is deeply resented.

Well, you know, somebody stops you, and you are not doing anything. If you are sitting on a bus stop, wearing a beard, minding your own business, talking to a friend, and a police car comes up and stops and asks you for identification, this certainly can be harassment. . . . I think they [the police] are cautioned to be more aware of nodules of atypical young men.

Police Brutality

The white middle-class community does not think that physical police brutality exists in San Diego, and a few of the Caucasians interviewed believe that the police use excessive force. Most of them define police brutality as solely physical brutality. As a social action agency official defines it, police brutality is: ". . . when a policeman physically manhandles a suspect when he doesn't need to be, when he himself is not in danger." A few do interpret police brutality more broadly—to include verbal abuse, harassment, and intimidation—but most of the Caucasians do not.

A bailbondsman states that he has heard many complaints of police brutality but he has never found them valid. They are usually dropped by the complainant shortly after the person is released from the jail cell. A judge indicates that in his court he has not had any instance of police misconduct brought out. He knows of no police brutality or any kind of evasion of the *Dorado* ruling or of other Supreme Court decisions. Many Caucasians think that minority and ethnic groups unfairly charge police brutality. In their opinion, Negroes "are crying 'Wolf!' illegitimately."

Field Interrogation

The white middle-class community generally approves of field interrogations in which police stop and question persons who appear "suspicious." Most see field interrogation as a "legitimate," "progressive," "innovative" police measure for combatting crime, but they express certain reservations about the techniques. Some of the persons interviewed state that of the complaints they have heard, most concern bad language and aggressive behavior on the part of the police rather than an absence of justification for the interrogations. Police demeanor and language are seen as *key* factors which can and do erode the support for the police of those interrogated. An ambivalence in the white community regarding whether priority should be placed on preventing crime or protecting individual rights is evident in the following statement by a lawyer.

In answering specifically to the question of field interrogation, I think it has to continue in order to have effective law enforcement. . . . To me, if a police officer asks questions in an insulting manner, automatically you have a bad field interrogation. But I believe the opposite side of the coin, too. I think that the emphasis has now so far shifted that the optimum officer in a racially tense area cannot go in and ask with all courtesy and so forth, and get an answer, either from a man who, from his Southern background, re-

sents any police officer or because of this polarization that's taken place, gives answers which I wouldn't want the officer to take or expect or receive in any other section of the city, and I don't think there should be a delineation. . . .

The above statement reflects a belief that field interrogations are a necessary police procedure and that they are unfairly criticized by minority communities. One lawyer summarized his view of field interrogations as follows:

I'm in favor of the constitutional protection as you are. By the same token . . . isn't [it] merely the counterpoint of the fact that we are living in a pretty complex society? Since we don't have the cop . . . on the beat any longer, we make an attempt to achieve . . . a reasonable degree of familiarity with the neighborhood. . . . When there is somebody unfamiliar in the neighborhood, find out what he's doing there.

Another segment of the white community thinks that repeatedly stopping people on the street harms police-community relations. A social action agency executive comments that youth dislike being subjected to field interrogations and that "F.I.'s" undo the good of the preventive work which the police do in the classrooms. Several persons interviewed reveal that they know of people who have been stopped repeatedly and, although each time it was by different policemen, the cumulative effect is that of harassment. One case in which a Caucasian professor, tweedy and disheveled, had been interrogated by the police, apparently because he "looked out of place" and suspicious, resulted in his deep resentment. The person relating the incident suggests that if this can happen to a white college professor, harassment is probably "even more prevalent" in the Negro community. . . .

Another lawyer indicates the belief held by several of the persons interviewed that field interrogation is used by the police as a means of harassing people who look different and whom the police hypothesize to be law violators:

I've got a case right in my office right now that came in when it was thrown out the other day. A police officer stopped a Negro who was six foot four, and he was wearing a beard. He was driving his car down to the laundromat to do his laundry after he got off work. The officers stopped him; he asked them what for. One said, "Well, I wanted to see how long your beard was. Let's see your driver's license." There was no traffic offense, no mechanical violation. The policeman looks at his driver's license, and says, "I'm going to call in and see if there is anything out for you." He calls in and there is a warrant with the same name, a traffic warrant . . . failure to appear. They go to the Marshal's office, this guy is begging them to check the license number on that other citation, check the description. He has to go to the Marshal's office where this information is kept, refuses to check it, takes him in, makes him bail out. Comes to court, they find out that they were looking for a five foot six, 140 pound, blond, blue-eyed Caucasian.

White Middle-Class Youth

As an example of strict enforcement, a youth comments about police contacts with motorcyclists:

When you have a bike, they just pull over for no reason. So many little things . . . you have to have a horn, you have to have a baffle, and your handlebars have to be so high and no higher. . . .

Another youth volunteers:

Me and this other guy, we were playing baseball down there [in a park], just hitting the ball, for about thirty yards, and this guy almost got thrown in jail three times for it, but then the minute somebody who is older, about thirty or forty years old, plays there, it's okay. But if kids play there, with nobody on the whole lot, you can get thrown in jail for it. And here it is, a city park, and there is not one person on the lot, and the guy hits a few ground balls, and they catch him and you can go to jail for it.

The field interrogation . . . is viewed as "harassment" by some youths:

Well, I've noticed that they've been pretty petty, picayunish. A prime example—I was hitchhiking to work at 7:15 in the morning, which isn't unreasonable, and I was down in Pacific Beach, and I was standing there hitchhiking and was dressed neatly to go to work, and a policeman came on over, wants to know what I'm doing. And naturally I told him I'm hitchhiking to work, and I got twenty minutes to make it all the way down to San Diego. And I'd appreciate it if he could just, you know, go along and take care of somebody else, because I'm not breaking any laws and I want to get to work. He says, "No, I can't do that; I've got to know everybody that's on my beat." And so he proceeded to check my identification, where I lived and what not, what I did for an occupation. And this took ten or fifteen minutes. Finally I persuaded him that . . . to take off so I could get to work, and he says, "Well, I'm sorry to keep you delayed all this time. I've got to know who is in my area, district, and what to look out for," and all this. And I didn't appreciate it, because I ended up being about twenty minutes late for work, and my employer didn't appreciate it.

Some middle-class youths have a strong dislike for the police. As one mentions, "I hate cops more than I hate anything in the whole world." Another views the police as "repulsive and petty." He justifies his opinion:

. . . because of some of the nasty things that I've been through. Thinks like curfew. I was once stopped and questioned by a police officer from 9:30 until ten minutes after ten. Ten o'clock curfew, ten minutes after ten, after talking to me for forty minutes. And I had no chance to leave him, and ten o'clock came around; he knew I couldn't get home in time, so he took me in.

The youths say that they are aware of physical police brutality in San Diego. The police beat people, "like they did with one guy, Kevin, one night; they worked him over pretty bad before they took him into the police station." One of the other youths gives another example of brutality:

A friend of mine was up to this dance, and he was giving these guys some trouble . . . a woman's . . . at the YMCA, civic, so they took him over in the corner, and they bashed him over the head with their flashlights and they had to take him to the hospital afterwards to get his head sewn up.

MINORITY VIEWPOINTS

Police Discrimination

Negroes and Mexican-Americans in Southeast San Diego, and Mexican-Americans in the San Ysidro area just north of the international border, think —almost without exception—that they are the victims of differential treatment. A middle-class resident pleads: "When are they going to start treating people on the streets in our area the way they treat people in other areas?" A respected clergyman remarks:

You can't straighten them [the police] out by running them through the Police

Academy and exposing them to a few hours of lectures on human relations and the equality and dignity of the races. You know that all his life he [the policeman] has been taught that equality and dignity of the individual has primary reference to the white individual, and that the individual of the minority group is not really part of humanity in the broad sense. He [the minority person] is sub-human, in a sub-culture.

Others question whether a police officer could, in fact, ever become professional to the extent of suppressing his prejudices while on duty.

The existence of differential standards of enforcement is a source of constant irritation in the minority group communities. An attorney recalls a case in which a Negro client had been convicted for "gambling." The police, as he describes it, entered the client's house and arrested him and others present, while they were playing a "friendly poker game. . . ."

He sees the case as only one example of a situation in which conduct that is condoned in the white neighborhoods is not condoned or permitted in the Negro neighborhoods. The main problem, as seen by another attorney, is that there are "two standards of police conduct"—one for the white and one for the Negro communities.

A youth worker also holds the opinion that low income is at the root of police discrimination. "Dope peddling" and moon-shining will always be present in a poverty community, and poor people are constantly going to have contact with the police. He adds that it is not just a matter of the people hating the law, for the reciprocal is also true, that is, the law hates the people.

A dominant belief in the minority communities is that the Police Department is an agency devised to "protect the white population from Negroes and

Mexican-Americans." They are convinced that there is inequity in the services to the community. A minister comments that "law enforcement means a white man, even though the Negro is dispensing it."

A majority of the residents of Southeast San Diego felt that their community is used as a "training post" for the Police Department. They indicate that the "strange young faces of rookie 'cops' are much in evidence." Many add that the rookie officer can practice in this area because his mistakes will not affect people with influence in City Hall. Others believe that the ghetto is being used as a place to discipline officers banished from other areas. "They come to serve their exile here," many remark. Another group of ghetto residents is sure that there are "headbusters" in the Department who enjoy working in the Southeast because "this is where the action is."

Police Brutality

In its broadest sense . . . police brutality *is* considered by ethnic minorities to be a problem in the San Diego area. It should be made clear, however, that there are limited allegations of physical violence or brutality leveled at the San Diego Police Department. In spite of the belief among minority group persons that the Department relies too much upon "force," this does not include the opinion that the Department practices "man-to-man" brutality. Furthermore, minority group persons spontaneously volunteer the information that "brutality" in San Diego does not necessarily include physical violence.

Concerning other types of brutality, however, the dominant opinion of minority groups is that police officers are guilty of these practices. Language, gesture, attitude, approach—these constitute much of the characterization of

brutality in San Diego. Many persons complain of the fact that Negro youths are often called "nigger" by policemen. The very manner in which Negroes are approached by policemen is considered to be a manifestation of the brutality "syndrome." Some persons complain that they have often seen policemen with their hands already on the butts of their revolvers as they approach Negroes in the city.

Furthermore, the tactical deployment of policemen in the Logan Heights area is considered by many to be an implicit sign of police hostility and brutality directed toward minority group persons. Complaint after complaint is voiced about the "over-saturation" of Logan Heights with patrolmen, and it is often joined with references to the Police Department's obvious reliance upon a "show of force." As expressed by one active resident:

Don't you think, really, that this is part of a fear, a complex, on the part of the police community? The reason they use a lot of force, I think, in minority communities is because they know there is a lot of justification in a minority community to, you know, for being resentful; and if . . . you keep badgering someone and keep him oppressed and so forth . . . then, when he does something and you move in to try to correct him, you would be a little fearful, because this guy . . . you know in your mind, if they ever retaliate to the point that you would almost expect them to, that you are in trouble. This is the same thing we get when Negroes have meetings, you know. There is a reaction in the white community when the Negroes meet, because there is what I think is a kind of hidden, almost subconscious, inner feeling that, "Man, if these guys get together against me," which you almost expect them to do because you've been against them all these years, "Now if they ever get together, if these Negroes ever get together on us white people, there's no telling what they might do." And I think that's the fear. . . .

Negro Youth

Many lower-class Negro youths believe that the police discriminate against them. One youth, who has been in jail about fourteen times—once for twenty-three days—but has never been convicted of any crime, states that:

. . . they [the police] don't handle themselves well when they arrest the Negro race, and the way they stop them on the street and take them to jail just for suspicion.

There is a feeling among some of the youth that the police are "out to get" them. As one states:

. . . like if a police pass you, and he be starin' at you, and you stare back, that's what gives way for them to say that, you know, you give them a dirty look. But this happen to me all the time, that maybe standin' like I'm up to something, so I stare back, they turn on the light in the back, drive their cars around, drive over there, "C'mere. Stand up here. What you got on you?" Pattin' you all down—for what, I don't know. I've "looked suspicious," you know, the way I've walked, swing my arms, stuff like that.

A similar view is expressed by another young Negro:

I mean, they will stop you for hardly nothin', you know. Like last night some cats broke a few windows down here, and I was walkin', I just came from my broad's, there, walkin' down that way, and they smashed me all up against the wall, and they, you know, tell me, "Why you bust them windows?" and I say, "I

had nothing to do with it; I didn't even know they were busted 'til I walked by." And he tell me, "You a damn liar. I ought to throw your ass in jail." I say, "Wait a minute, I can't stand to go to jail; I just got out, man, not too long ago." And he say, "I don't give a damn, I'll throw your ass back in there." I mean, they gonna try to bust you for any reason at all, you know. They had a beef or somethin'; but if they get me again, it gonna be for somethin' . . . I know, 'cause there ain't no sense in goin' to jail, spendin', oh, two-three years time for somethin' you ain't had nothin' to do with, you know.

The youth, however, do not think they can "win" ultimately:

No . . . we could fight back, but . . . we ain't goin' to win. Because, look what they have—I mean, they have the whole United States on their side, you know; they could call in the Army, National Guard, anything they want to call on, you know; they could call them there and have them down here in a matter of hours, like, you know, up in L.A. But before they get down here, yeah, we might win the battle but we won't win the victory, you know what I mean?

Two youths agree that greater respect for the Negro residents of Watts resulted from the riot:

Well, everybody else gettin' it—can't see why we shouldn't. I mean, if we pulled the same thing that Watts pulled, well, these police down here goin' to start takin' it easy on people, you know. I mean, they ain't goin' to be comin' up there, you know, and every time they see you, callin' you "black boy," and "niggers," and all this. They goin' to walk up to you like you *somebody*, you know. . . .

One view of the cause of Negro hostility, which is supported (elsewhere) by segments of the white community, is the Negroes' reaction to the civil rights situation in the South:

Well, like when people [Negroes] get shot and hung and all that, back in Mississippi, you know, things like that, well, yeah, people do get pretty high when they see you [the police] . . . when they see you, they probably throw bottles. Some man'll jump on them [the white community], beat them up, somethin' like that. But, you know, they think they takin' revenge, you know, out on them hoakies [whites] back there by jumpin' on these out here.

Young police officers are thought by some to be offensive and to cause poor police-community relations.

Long time ago, they didn't call you that many "niggers," but since these little rookies comin' on, you know, they listen to these dudes [their training officers], they gonna hear all these wild fairy tales, they come down here with that, "We'll go down there and whip them black boys there," and all this bit, you know. Then they come down here. . . .

The police are viewed as overly suspicious of a Negro in a white neighborhood. A youth who worked in a white area explains:

I mean, like when I had my other job at the hospital, I went to pick up my check one Friday 'cause I'm workin' on Friday night at this job. So I had to pick up a check, was walkin' back down to check the bus . . . the police see me crossing the street and me tryin' to get across, and he pull over to the side, and he told me, "Come here, show me some I.D." He wanted to know the hours I work out here, you know, when I come to work, how

many I work, when I get off, what time my bus come about; he want to know all that.

Some youths are disillusioned by the talk of improved police-community relations.

And these people are talkin' about doin' this thing, and gettin' this thing over here, and "better relationship with the police," and all . . . I mean, there ain't no sense in all that if everytime you go down to try to do something for them they just think you just gettin' scared with them and they'll just stop and mess with you more, you know. . . . You go in and have complaints, "Okay, we'll do something about this," you know, write it down like they . . . man, like they really goin' to do somethin', you know. "What's their badge number?" they write that down; "What's their car number?" you write that down, "What's their name?"—and then you see them still ridin' around, smilin' at you, laughin' at you. You know, that ain't no kind of business, you know.

A social separation from the lower-class Negro resulting from parental training is recognized:

Well, the problem starts in the relationship between policeman and the people; it starts in the home. Unless the home-life attitude changes, the attitude of the kids won't. But it depends, but most of the time, most of my friends, their parents aren't ignorant people, they teach their kids to respect people, and police is people, so respect him, too, and that's his job. But then, I know that people who come out of these welfare homes, some of them who are very smart, they'll break away from their parent's way of thinking. Their parents think, "Oh, he's a cop—he's no good. . . ."

Well, they have asked for it themselves in their younger years. They got out and they're at the liquor store most of the time, instead of with their kids, and kids from a family like that, that's all they've heard. But that's most of it, in this area —the welfare cases, the poverty area. In this area it's in the family, and you have to break that shell first.

As it is more likely that middle-class Negro and white youths will relate socially, the middle-class Negro youths are particularly sensitive to police reaction. Perhaps as a token of acknowledgement for understanding and support of the police, the middle-class Negro youth desires to be viewed as possessing greater social responsibility. However, in their opinion, the police do not differentiate among Negroes in the area of field interrogation, which is a particular irritant to some middle-class youths. One youth resents being stopped and he recalls an incident in which an officer requested information about a man running down the street. Then, without reason, the boy says the policeman became suspicious of him, "patted him down," and questioned him. Another youth, in discussing field interrogations, states that he dislikes the shakedown part of it most: "Man, I just don't dig this pulling up your shirt to see what's under there, tapping you up and down the sleeves and legs and arms. . . ."

Related to the matter of police attitude is the belief, even among middle-class Negro youth that the police do harass interracial couples. From one case, youth is able to generalize about police attitude. The story is told of the light-skinned Negro girl who was dating a dark-skinned Negro boy. The couple was stopped by the police, and during the course of the interrogation, the policeman asked the girl confidentially, "What is a nice girl like you doing going around with a Negro?" Although none of the middle-class Negro youth interviewed had been involved in such a situation, they were willing to believe that the incident actually took place.

While the middle-class Negro youth believes he has the support and security of his family and some positive communication with society in general, many lower-class Negro youths feel they have no one to turn to—that nobody with power and influence is listening to what they view as legitimate grievances.

. . . to tell you the truth, right around here, you know, the Negro guys don't have no leaders. I mean, like you keep on talkin' about, you know, dig them Negro leaders, and all this, like this dude up here . . . well, no, they ain't no leaders in. . . . Man, they ain't nobody here to talk to, you know, because . . . nobody can understand you anyway. Like, your parents—you try to talk to them, well, you know, "Whup your ass, stay off the streets!" You know, "Don't do that," and you go on anyway. You know. I mean, you, can't talk to nobody.

The unwillingness or inability of the police to establish satisfactory channels of communication with Negro youth is viewed as hostility. The Negro youth is prepared to reciprocate in kind and to accept the consequences.

STUDY OF THE SICKNESS CALLED APATHY

A. M. Rosenthal

As our cities become larger and our nation becomes increasingly urban, the search for value dimensions becomes acute in the lives of all of us. The rural society bred a sort of quiet strength and togetherness which the impersonalness of our urban centers can never repeat. Yet we must find a bond of some kind which can serve to unite us if we are to survive in the urban world. The apathy and non-involvement discussed in this reading must not become a way of life for the city dweller.

It happens from time to time in New York that the life of the city is frozen by an instant of shock. In that instant the people of the city are seized by the paralyzing realization that they are one, that each man is in some way a mirror of every other man. They stare at each other—or, really, into themselves—and a look quite like a flush of embarrassment passes over the face of the city. Then the instant passes and the beat resumes and the people turn away and try to explain what they have seen, or try to deny it.

The last 35 minutes of the young life of Miss Catherine Genovese became such a shock in the life of the city. But at the time she died, stabbed again and again by a marauder in her quiet, dark but entirely respectable, street in Kew Gardens, New York hardly took note.

It was not until two weeks later that Catherine Genovese, known as Kitty, returned in death to cry the city awake. Even then it was not her life or her dying that froze the city, but the witnessing of her murder—the choking fact that 38 of her neighbors had seen her stabbed or heard her cries, and that not one of them, during that hideous half-hour, had lifted the telephone from the safety of his own apartment to call the police and try to save her life. When it was over and Miss Genovese was dead and the murderer gone, one man did call—not from his own apartment but from the neighbor's, and only after he had called a friend and asked her what to do.

The day that the story of the witnessing of the death of Miss Genovese appeared in this newspaper became that frozen instant. "Thirty-eight!" people said over and over. "Thirty-eight!"

It was as if the number itself had some special meaning, and in a way, of course, it did. One person or two or even three or four witnessing a murder passively would have been the unnoticed symptom of the disease in the city's body and again would have passed unnoticed. But 38—it was like a man with a running low fever suddenly beginning to cough blood; his friends could no longer ignore his illness, nor could he turn away from himself.

At first there was, briefly, the reaction of shared guilt. Even people who were sure that they certainly would have acted differently felt it somehow.

"Dear God, what have we come to?" a woman said that day. "We," not "they."

For in that instant of shock, the mirror showed quite clearly what was wrong, that the face of mankind was spotted with the disease of apathy—all mankind. But this was too frightening a thought to live with and soon the beholders began to set boundaries for the illness, to search frantically for causes that were external and to look for the carrier.

There was a rash of metropolitan masochism. "What the devil do you expect in a town, a jungle, like this?" Sociologists and psychiatrists reached for the warm comfort of jargon— "alienation of the individual from the group," "megalopolitan societies," "the disaster syndrome."

People who came from small towns said it could never happen back home. New Yorkers, ashamed, agreed. Nobody seemed to stop to ask whether there were not perhaps various forms of apathy and that some that exist in villages and towns do not exist in great cities.

Guilt turned into masochism, and masochism, as it often does, became a sadistic search for a target. Quite soon, the target became the police.

There is no doubt whatsoever that the police in New York have failed, to put it politely, to instill a feeling of total confidence in the population. There are great areas in this city—fine parks as well as slums—where no person in his right mind would wander of an evening or an early morning. There is no central emergency point to receive calls for help. And a small river of letters from citizens to this newspaper testifies to the fact that patrols are often late in answering calls and that policemen on desk duty often give the bitter edge of their tongues to citizens calling for succor.

There is no doubt of these things.

But to blame the police for apathy is a bit like blaming the sea wall for springing leaks. The police of this city are more efficient, more restrained and more responsive to public demands than any others the writer has encountered in a decade of traveling the world. Their faults are either mechanical or a reflection of a city where almost every act of police self-protection is assumed to be an act of police brutality, and where a night-club comedian can, as one did the other night, stand on a stage for an hour and a half and vilify the police as brutes, thieves, homosexuals, illiterates and "Gestapo agents" while the audience howls in laughter as it drinks Scotch from bootleg bottles hidden under the tables.

There are two tragedies in the story of Catherine Genovese. One is the fact that her life was taken from her, that she died in pain and horror at the age of 28. The other is that in dying she gave every human being—not just species New Yorker—an opportunity to examine some truths about the nature of apathy and that this has not been done.

Austin Street, where Catherine Genovese lived, is in a section of Queens known as Kew Gardens. There are two apartment buildings and the rest of the street consists of one-family homes— red-brick, stucco or wood-frame. There are Jews, Catholics and Protestants, a scattering of foreign accents, middle-class incomes.

On the night of March 13, about 3 A.M., Catherine Genovese was returning to her home. She worked late as manager of a bar in Hollis, another part of Queens. She parked her car (a red Fiat) and started to walk to her death.

Lurking near the parking lot was a man. Miss Genovese saw him in the shadows, turned and walked toward a police call box. The man pursued her, stabbed her. She screamed, "Oh, my

God, he stabbed me! Please help me! Please help me!"

Somebody threw open a window and a man called out: "Let that girl alone!" Other lights turned on, other windows were raised. The attacker got into a car and drove away. A bus passed.

The attacker drove back, got out, searched out Miss Genovese in the back of an apartment building where she had crawled for safety, stabbed her again, drove away again.

The first attack came at 3:15. The first call to the police came at 3:50. Police arrived within two minutes, they say. Miss Genovese was dead.

That night and the next morning the police combed the neighborhood looking for witnesses. They found them, 38.

Two weeks later, when this newspaper heard of the story, a reporter went knocking, door to door, asking why, why?

Through half-opened doors, they told him. Most of them were neither defiant nor terribly embarrassed nor particularly ashamed. The underlying attitude, or explanation, seemed to be fear of involvement—any kind of involvement.

"I didn't want my husband to get involved," a housewife said.

"We thought it was a lovers' quarrel," said another woman. "I went back to bed."

"I was tired," said a man.

"I don't know," said another man.

"I don't know," said still another.

"I don't know," said others.

On March 19, police arrested a 29-year-old business-machine operator named Winston Moseley and charged him with the murder of Catherine Genovese. He has confessed to killing two other women, for one of whose murders police say they have a confession from another man.

Not much is said or heard or thought in the city about Winston Moseley. In this drama, as far as the city is con-cerned, he appeared briefly, acted his piece, exited into the wings.

A week after the first story appeared, a reporter went back to Austin Street. Now the witnesses no longer wanted to talk. They were harried, annoyed; they thought they should keep their mouths shut. "I've done enough talking," one witness said. "Oh, it's you again," said a woman witness and slammed the door.

The neighbors of the witnesses are willing to talk. Their sympathy is for the silent witnesses and the embarrassment in which they now live.

Max Heilbrunn, who runs a coffee house on Austin Street, talked about all the newspaper publicity and said his neighbors felt they were being picked on. "It isn't a bad neighborhood," he said.

And this from Frank Facciola, the owner of the neighborhood barber shop: "I resent the way these newspaper and television people have hurt us. We have wonderful people here. What happened could have happened any place. There is no question in my mind that people here now would rush out to help anyone being attacked on the street."

Then he said: "The same thing [failure to call the police] happens in other sections every day. Why make such a fuss when it happens in Kew Gardens? We are trying to forget it happened here."

A Frenchwoman in the neighborhood said: "Let's forget the whole thing. It is a quiet neighborhood, good to live in. What happened, happened."

Each individual, obviously, approaches the story of Catherine Genovese, reacts to it and veers away from it against the background of his own life and experience, and his own fears and shortcomings and rationalizations.

It seems to this writer that what happened in the apartments and houses on Austin Street was a symptom of a ter-

rible reality in the human condition—
that only under certain situations and
only in response to certain reflexes or
certain beliefs will a man step out of
his shell toward his brother.

To say this is not to excuse, but to
try to understand and in so doing perhaps eventually to extend the reflexes
and beliefs and situations to include
more people. To ignore it is to perpetuate myths that lead nowhere. Of
these the two most futile philosophically
are that apathy is a response to official
ineptitude ("The cops never come on
time anyway"), or that apathy is a condition only of metropolitan life.

Certainly police procedures must be
improved—although in the story of
Miss Genovese all indications were that,
once called into action, the police machine behaved perfectly.

As far as is known, not one witness
has said that he remained silent because
he had had any unpleasant experience
with the police. It is a pointless point;
there are men who will jump into a
river to rescue a drowner; there are
others who will tell themselves that a
police launch will be cruising by or
that, if it doesn't, it should.

Nobody can say why the 38 did not
lift the phone while Miss Genovese was
being attacked, since they cannot say
themselves. It can be assumed, however,
that their apathy was indeed of a big-
city variety. It is almost a matter of
psychological survival, if one is surrounded and pressed by millions of
people, to prevent them from constantly
impinging on you and the only way to
do this is to ignore them as often as
possible. Indifference to one's neighbor
and his troubles is a conditioned reflex
of life in New York as it is in other big
cities. In every major city in which I
have lived—in Tokyo and Warsaw,
Vienna and Bombay—I have seen, over
and over again, people walk away from

accident victims. I have walked away
myself.

Out-of-towners, and sometimes New
Yorkers themselves, like to think that
there is something special about New
York metropolitan apathy. It is special
in that there are more people here than
any place else in the country—and
therefore more people to turn away from
each other.

For decades, New York turned away
from the truth that is Harlem or Bedford-Stuyvesant in Brooklyn. Everybody
knew that, in the Negro ghettoes, men,
women and children lived in filth and
degradation. But the city, as a city,
turned away with the metropolitan
brand of apathy. This, more simply,
consists of drowning the person-to-
person responsibility in a wave of impersonal social action.

Committees were organized, speeches
made, budgets passed to "do something"
about Harlem or Bedford-Stuyvesant—
to do something about the communities. This dulled the reality, and still
does, that the communities consist of
individual people who ache and suffer
in the loss of their individual prides.
Housewives who contributed to the
N.A.A.C.P. saw nothing wrong in going
down to the daily shape-up of domestic
workers in the Bronx and selecting a
maid for the day after looking over the
coffle to see which "girl" among the
Negro matrons present looked huskiest.

Now there is an acute awareness of
the problems of the Negroes in New
York. But, again, it is an impersonal
awareness, and more and more, it is
tinged with irritation at the thought
that the integration movement will im-
pinge on the daily personal life of the
city.

Nor are the Negroes in the city immune from apathy—toward one another
or toward whites. They are apathetic
toward one another's right to believe

and act as they please, one man's concept of proper action is labeled with the group epithet "Uncle Tom." And, until the recent upsurge of the integration movement, there was less action taken within the Negro community to improve conditions in Harlem than there was in the all-white sections of the East Side. It has become fashionable to sneer at "white liberals"—fashionable even among Negroes who for years did nothing for brothers even of their own color.

In their own sense of being wronged, some Negroes of New York have become totally apathetic to the sensitivities of all other groups. In a night club in Harlem the other night, an aspiring Negro politician, a most decent man, talked of how the Jewish shopkeepers exploited the Negroes, how he wished Negroes could "save a dollar like the Jews," totally apathetic toward the fact that Jews at the table might be as hurt as he would be if they talked in clichés of the happy-go-lucky Stepin Fetchit Negro. When a Jew protested, the Negro was stunned—because he was convinced he hated anti-Semitism. He did, in the abstract.

Since the Genovese case, New Yorkers have sought explanations of their apathy toward individuals. Fear, some say—fear of involvement, fear of reprisal from goons, fear of becoming "mixed-up" with the police. This, it seems to this writer, is simply rationalization.

The self-protective shells in which we live are determined not only by the difference between big cities and small. They are determined by economics and social class, by caste and by color, and by religion, and by politics.

If I were to see a beggar starving to death in rags on the streets of Paris or New York or London I would be moved to take some kind of action. But many times I have seen starving men lying like broken dolls in the streets of Calcutta or Madras and have done nothing.

I think I would have called the police to save Miss Genovese but I know that I did not save a beggar in Calcutta. Was my failing really so much smaller than that of the people who watched from their windows on Austin Street? And what was the apathy of the people of Austin Street compared, let's say, with the apathy of non-Nazi Germans toward Jews?

Geography is a factor of apathy. Indians reacted to Portuguese imprisoning Goans, but not to Russians killing Hungarians.

Color is a factor. Ghanaians reacted toward Frenchmen killing Algerians, not toward Congolese killing white missionaries.

Strangeness is a factor. Americans react to the extermination of Jews but not to the extermination of Watusis.

There are national as well as individual apathies, all inhibiting the ability to react. The "mind-your-own business" attitude is despised among individuals, and clucked at by sociologists, but glorified as pragmatic national policy among nations.

Only in scattered moments, and then in halting embarrassment, does the United States, the most involved nation in the world, get down to hard cases about the nature of governments with which it deals, and how they treat their subject citizens. People who believe that a free government should react to oppression of people in the mass by other governments are regarded as fanatics or romantics by the same diplomats who would react in horror to the oppression of one single individual in Washington. Between apathy, regarded as a moral disease, and national policy, the line is often hard to find.

There are, it seems to me, only two logical ways to look at the story of the murder of Catherine Genovese. One is the way of the neighbor on Austin Street—"Let's forget the whole thing." The other is to recognize that the bell tolls even on each man's individual island, to recognize that every man must fear the witness in himself who whispers to close the window.

IN NEW YORK IT PAYS

William F. Buckley, Jr.

Mr. Buckley deplores the continuing rise in crime in New York City. He places the blame on the concentrations of the idle and demoralized segments of our society, inadequate police protection, and a court system which delays justice while overly protecting the "rights" of the accused. Criticism is heaped on the Mallory, Mapp, and Escabedo cases. Eight proposals for improvement are presented. He is perhaps speaking for the "silent majority" when he recommends clarification of the rights of the public against those of the defendant.

The first mark of the civilized community is the ability to control its criminal element. By this standard New York City has lapsed into barbarism. Last year, 1761 major crimes were committed for every 100,000 of the city's population. During the first three months of this year the rate of crime increased 6.6 per cent over the same period of 1964. Such conditions, to be sure, constitute a "scandal"; but simply to repeat that cliché is scandalously to understate and depersonalize a very real outrage daily perpetrated on the peace of mind and body of every law-abiding New Yorker.

The basic cause of increased crime is, of course, the increasing moral and social disorder that mark contemporary society, and is thus less a problem for civil magistrates than for our churchmen and educators. (It is ironic, under the circumstances, that it has been judged by our highest civil magistrates a crime against the Court of the United States to mention the name of God in the public classrooms.) But the problem has been greatly aggravated by factors over which the city government does have control, or influence:

The city's law-enforcement facilities are inadequate. The police force is too small to cope with burgeoning crime. Current proposals (Lindsay's) to abolish two-men patrol cars, moreover, would make matters worse by diluting the effectiveness of the present force, and by jeopardizing police security. More policemen are needed.

The present Administration is doing nothing to resist the derogation of the law enforcement agencies. The disparagements of the police have created a crisis in morale and a swaggering disrespect for the policeman as the symbol of the public order. Yet far from resisting such assaults, the Wagner Administration has taken the course of appeasement: the proposed Civilian Review Board is nothing less than an agreement to elevate the campaign to discredit the police to official city policy.

Current welfare and housing policies have resulted in an undue concentration in New York City of idle and demoralized persons in an environment which breeds crime and criminals. No program to restore law and order to the city can be effective without coming to grips with New York's grave social problems.

Above all, crime has been encouraged in the city, as elsewhere, by the policies and practices of the courts. Too many judges appear to have forgotten that the primary purpose of courts of justice is to assert the demands of the public order—by meting out convincing punishment to those who transgress against it. This purpose is consistently frustrated in New York by fastidious procedural requirements that impede convictions of the guilty, and by lax sentencing policies that fail to provide an effective deterrent to crime.

To be sure, much of the trouble in bringing criminals to justice can be traced to decisions of the United States Supreme Court—for instance, the *Mallory*, *Mapp*, and *Escobedo* cases— which, if they indeed extend the implicit rights of the accused as guaranteed by the Constitution, raise the question, to which our judges have not addressed themselves, whether the Bill of Rights, as presently interpreted, sufficiently provides for the effective maintenance of law and order. Former Police Commissioner Michael J. Murphy has put it this way: "We are forced to fight by Marquess of Queensberry rules, while the *criminals* are permitted to gouge and bite."

But some of the courts of New York City have gone far beyond the specifications of the Supreme Court. They have institutionalized what commentators have taken to designating as "turnstyle justice." They have applied the rules of search and seizure, and other evidentiary and procedural requirements, with an extravagant, often ludicrous technicality. As one newspaper has observed, "the law itself has created so many escape hatches for criminals that nine postponements and a half-dozen separate hearings to suppress evidence or controvert a search warrant are not unusual before a case is ready for trial." The result is that our judicial system blinds its eyes on countless occasions to demonstrable guilt, and turns loose upon our streets the drug pusher, the sex offender, the mugger, the thief. The fact is that crime in New York City, both juvenile and adult, does pay. It pays, in large part, because the city's judicial system had defaulted on its primary duty to protect the public, in favor of an obsessive solicitude for those individuals who are responsible for breaking the peace of the city.

Proposals

1. Additional policemen should be hired. Many of them could be hired from among retired policemen, to relieve younger men currently desk-bound. To assure the police force a maximum efficiency, it should be provided with the most advanced technological tools now available, so that its equipment is at least as sophisticated as that now routinely employed by the criminal.

2. The new Administration should oppose the establishment of a Civilian Review Board, and should encourage the police to do their duty, and back them up when they do it.

3. The new Mayor and other city officials should bring vigorous pressure to

bear on local judges to abandon criminal-coddling policies, and resume the administration of justice. The Bar Associations and other civic groups should be urged, with the support of the communications media, to mobilize an irresistible public demand that the courts of law join New York City's fight against crime.

4. Parole and probation procedures should be tightened to assure the confinement or surveillance of convicted criminals for long enough periods to guard the public safety. Studies should be conducted to determine whether enough parole officers are employed by the city to do an effective job and whether civil service regulations should be revised so as to ensure that officers not qualified or not disposed to administer the law strictly can be replaced.

5. The special treatment now accorded to juvenile criminals should be re-examined in all its ramifications. Specifically existing legislation should be revised to permit severer punishment of juveniles who commit serious crimes. Youth must cease to be an excuse for vicious attacks on fellow citizens.

6. As a further deterrent to juvenile delinquency, legislation should be enacted requiring the publication of the names and addresses of juvenile offenders guilty of serious offenses, and of their parents. This practice was recently adopted by Judge Lester H. Lobel in Helena, Montana. Subsequently, juvenile crime decreased by fifty per cent. While a community like New York can hardly expect such startling results, improvement would almost surely result. "The parents," Judge Lobel observed, "can't stand the heat. I have today about a thousand parents who are about the best probation officers any court can have."

7. As the protection of the individual from acts of lawlessness is a first re-sponsibility of government, to the extent that the law-abiding citizen is victimized by the criminal, the government has failed in its duty to him. Legislation should, therefore, be enacted providing for the indemnification of victims of personal assaults and other crimes of violence.

8. Legislation should be enacted to provide (a) enticing bounties for informers who furnish information leading to criminal convictions, and (b) financial compensation for witnesses in criminal trials.

These measures are necessary inducements for wider citizen participation in the defense of the city.

Of all the crises now gripping New York, the emergence of Crime Triumphant is the gravest. The challenge to a new Administration could not be plainer: it is to make New York habitable.

There were a few scattered comments to the effect that I desired to modify the Bill of Rights—which, as a matter of fact, are half correct—and I herewith decline to terminate this sentence where logically it should be terminated, in order to make it just a little harder for the above few words to be excerpted out of the context—the current movement to fanaticize certain provisions of the Bill of Rights has of course the effect of diminishing certain other provisions of the Bill of Rights. This law of the projection of rights to the point of irreconcilability, an ancient intuition, has been brilliantly demonstrated by Professor Sidney Hook in his little book on *The Paradoxes of Freedom.* You cannot, Professor Hook maintains, extend any two freedoms indefinitely because there is a point at which they are likely to collide with each other. He gives many examples, among them: (a) the freedom of the press on one hand, and on the other, (b) the right to a fair trial; the conflict of interest between the two, at a certain point, being manifest. Another obvious example is the right to practice religion and the right to protection from religious indoctrination.

The position paper on crime sought to identify a crystallizing dilemma. The series of recent decisions by the Supreme Court reifying derivative rights of defendants that trace to the Bill of Rights are highly defensible extrapolations. For instance, if one has the "right" to counsel as of the moment one becomes *de facto* the accused, then it would appear that the right exists irrespective of whether the suspect knows of its existence; hence the Supreme Court—in its *Escobedo* decision, for example—and the Third District Court in its *Russo* decision correctly develop the Sixth Amendment. The question, however, should collaterally arise: what corresponding rights exist for the public prosecutor whose duty it is to affirm the rights of the aggrieved? The rights of the party of the first part are increasingly developed, while those of the party of the second part are relatively neglected. In England, Sir Hartley Shawcross has been waging a passionate campaign attempting to rectify the imbalance, his startling contention being that the day is past when the court is most usefully engaged as mere umpire between defendant and prosecutor, that radical revisions of the old rules are in order, revisions that aim at conscripting all parties concerned to the ascertainment of the truth. The truth is, after all, what is desired—*did* John in fact kill Jane?—and he boldly asks whether the adversary system is the most productive form of jurisprudential epistemology. For the hell of it, I spun out these considerations to a fidgety deputation from the Citizens Union of New York, a nonpartisan gathering of right-, or better, good-minded persons whose function was to ascertain, and

then to report to the people, whom, in the higher interests of New York, they should vote for. The four lawyer-interrogators who—frankness requires me to confess—were clearly there to interview me only so that they could report that they had been there to interview me, and thus document their formal open-mindedness, nodded in more or less excited confusion—agreed, yes, that radical analysis was probably in order, yes—but quickly and with evident relief guided the discussion back to the fashionable sociological platitudes of the day and never again lost their hold of the conversational leash. So that the discussion, which had begun on the theme of law enforcement, turned to crime and the bearing on it of (a) unemployment, (b) insufficient housing, (c) race relations, etc.—all of which have much to do with the causes of criminals and nothing whatever to do with their apprehension or conviction.

It is conceivable that dilemmas of the kind I felt like talking about tend to occur last to lawyers, whose training commits them to the old precepts; and that may be a reason why the legal profession, of which John Lindsay is a member, has done so little reformist thinking on the subject. It is rather the philosopher Sidney Hook who comes through with the definitive destruction of the same Hugo Black whom Lindsay venerates. On the other hand, Shawcross (who was Attorney General of England in the postwar Labor government) and Mr. C. Dickerman Williams, who almost singlehandedly stopped the establishment of the emerging doctrine that no adverse inferences of any sort are to be drawn from the use of the Fifth Amendment, are lawyers; but an organization like the Citizens Union depends, for its prestige, on its respectability; and respectability in New York, as in most other parts of the country, tends to be confined within the limits of tolerability set by, e.g., *The New York Times.*

In the days ahead the dilemma is bound to harden. Either the Supreme Court will, as unfortunately has been its recent wont, more or less laze up to different specific cases in different ways, leaving the question of what are and what aren't the rights of parties in dispute, in boundless incertitude; or else basic laws will have to be rewritten, perhaps even a Constitutional Amendment or two, aimed at clarifying the rights of the public against those of the defendant. A lot can be done about law enforcement in New York City—as I indicated in the Position Paper—under existing arrangements; but, I fear, there is a lot that can't be done.

LOTS OF LAW, LITTLE ORDER

Newsweek

Police brutality is a cry heard in almost every community. Many doubt the validity of these claims. Yet in one glaring, national moment, the meaning of police brutality came home to all Americans. Many refused to accept it. Perhaps this was simply the media distorting another issue. Yet the on-the-spot shots were difficult to refute. Regardless of one's viewpoint, however, the Chicago 1968 Democratic Convention was a time of national concern and the question of police brutality would not soon be laid to rest.

The city was primed for violence— and violence came to Chicago last week. Into the convention city straggled a motley collection of hippies, yippies and other dissidents bent on demonstrating against the Democratic Administration's conduct of the Vietnam war. They were met by Mayor Richard J. Daley's finest—backed up by an overkill array of 6,000 National Guardsmen and 7,500 riot-trained Regular Army troops. Bound and determined to enforce the mayor's concept of law and order, the police massively overreacted to provocations ranging from mischievousness to acts of defiance— and themselves became the prime source of violence.

The ugly spectacle of savage mass beatings—first acted out in the dark shadows of a Chicago park—eventually erupted under floodlights and the shocked gaze of millions of television viewers. The sight of policemen laying about with their billy clubs against a ghostly backdrop of tear gas did more than color the whole context of the nominating process in the convention hall. It left a scar on the city of Chicago that may become as indelible a part of its violent history as the Haymarket Riot and the St. Valentine's Day Massacre.

Throughout the week, a task force of eight Newsweek reporters covered the shifting battle scene as the police tactics mounted in intensity to a climatic bloody clash on nominating eve in front of the Conrad Hilton headquarters of the visiting Democratic Party. Their report:

The youthful protesters began wandering into Chicago two weeks ago. They were, on the whole, a disorganized bunch—barefooted hippies, tongue-in-cheek yippies (Youth International Party members), McCarthy buttoned students. A handful were clearly militant, set on provoking violence, but most seemed content simply to be where the action was. "It just looked like a great time," said a 26-year-old Chicago secretary who had donned old clothes to join the swelling group.

Their numbers eventually reached somewhere between 8,000 and 10,000 but were always far fewer than advance estimates. As the convention itself approached, it seemed that Mayor Daley's stern security measures plus his unyielding refusal to let the youths demonstrate near the convention, or to sleep in any city parks, had indeed been effective in discouraging many youngsters from showing up. But if Daley's measures to insure law and order turned some away, they provided a built-in challenge for those who did show up, and on the eve of the convention the demonstrators threw down the gauntlet. North of Chicago's Loop lies Lincoln Park and there, alongside Lake Michigan, the invading forces decided to make their stand by defying an 11 P.M. park curfew. They announced they would attempt to stay overnight.

The stand was an instant and total flop. The Chicago cops easily drove the uncertain youngsters out of the park shortly after the curfew hour. But several hundred of the refugees milled around at a nearby intersection causing a massive, horn-honking traffic jam. The cops barked out orders for the kids to move on and they began to disperse. Not

fast enough for some police. Billy sticks began to fly. Gangs of police rushed on foot from one group to another, and in their wake left the first of the week's bleeding heads and the sting of Mace.

Next night, the dissident youths, their ranks now grown to some 3,000, built a fragile barricade of picnic tables and trash cans in Lincoln Park and again threatened to defy the 11 P.M. curfew. For nearly two hours past the curfew time, they shouted taunts at the police who stood off at a distance awaiting orders. Finally, a squad car was surrounded near the barricade and bombarded by a hail of rocks and bottles. The police car escaped by driving through the protesters' ranks, its siren whining, its blue light flashing. "He's hitting 'em" an officer screamed. "Hit those ——— ———! Kill 'em!"

Now the waiting police were eager to move. Some youths fled from the park. Most stayed. The police then lobbed canisters of tear gas into the barricade. Coughing, gagging and stumbling, the demonstrators broke and ran, some throwing stones as they retreated. Members of the Chicago police's elite Task Force Unit raced after the kids, and in the darkness of the park, ran scores of them to the ground like cowboys bulldogging cattle. The sound of night sticks smashing into skulls resounded through the park, mixed with shrieks and screams. "Oh, no!" "Oh, my God!" "No, no, no!" A teen-aged girl lay on the ground as two policemen bent over her and beat her on the head until her screams faded into a sobbing moan.

TOLL   Another girl jumped into a walled park pond with six other youths as the cops charged down upon them. A policeman leaned over and delivered a stunning blow to her head. She toppled back, submerged and nearly drowned. The evening's toll: 100 injured, including seventeen newsmen; 130 arrests.

Angry and defiant, the youths returned again the following night to Lincoln Park, and again were driven out—this time by stinging yellow clouds of tear gas from a specially equipped dump truck. Instead of dispersing, however, many of the youths moved downtown to Grant Park, in front of the Conrad Hilton. And it was there, soon after delegates had returned from the Amphitheater, that National Guardsmen rumbled in and took up the police vigil against the youngsters. The spectacle of Army troops aligned against a college-age crowd, highlighted by the television lights and captured by television cameras set up in front of the Hilton, was a perceived reality that some observers could not bear. "You just had to do it, didn't you?" screamed an almost hysterical woman at a policeman. "You just had to do it." Then she broke down and cried. "My God," said another woman, "they're proving everything those kids have been saying."

The kids themselves relaxed, however, under assurances that the soldiers were not planning to drive them out of the park. Peter Yarrow and Mary Trask (two-thirds of the Peter, Paul and Mary folk trio) soothed the crowd by singing folk songs, and later the demonstration became an old-time revival meeting of sorts as individual demonstrators, joined for the first time by some delegates, stood on a makeshift podium and delivered testimonials of their faith in dissent over an electronic megaphone. One speaker urged observers in their hotel rooms across the street to "blink your lights if you're with us." At least fifteen lights in the Conrad Hilton flicked on and off. The kids cheered.

MARCH   Eventually, most of the demonstrators drifted off, and by morning only 80 were left—along with 800 troops. But by midafternoon, the dem-

onstrators' ranks in Grant Park had swelled again as the time approached for the movement of their avowed objective in Chicago—a march on the Amphitheater at the time of the Presidential balloting.

The march never got started. Police and Guardsmen blocked all efforts to head south to the convention hall, but in their milling attempts to move on, the demonstrators had spilled out into the streets in front of the Hilton, only some 40 yards from the hotel's heavily guarded entranceway. Nervous police moved in several more platoons as the mass in front of the Hilton continued to grow, and then the cops began a slow sweep to clear Michigan Avenue. Spectators, television cameramen, everyone in the street and on the sidewalks was swept up until the crowd was backed up into a solid mass at the south end of the Hilton. "Pigs, pigs, pigs," the contemptuous youths began yelling. "Oink, oink, oink." Then, without warning, 150 angry cops surged into the terrified crowd, and it didn't matter who was who. "We'll kill all you bastards," screamed a policeman as he kicked into the howling, terrified mob. He grabbed a youngster by his long brown hair, turned him around and jabbed a billy club into his groin. The youth, crying, fell to his knees, as another cop kicked him in the stomach. A plate-glass window in the hotel's drugstore gave way under the pressure of bodies. On the street, panicky youths trampled each other trying to get away. A jumble of bodies curled on the ground as police mercilessly pounded them to the pavement with their clubs. A young girl in a serape was sprawled on her back looking up at the onrushing police, begging them to stop hitting her. The police stepped on her stomach to get to the panicked crowds beyond her.

Finally, the police re-formed their lines, the scattered demonstrators regrouped and chanted, louder and louder, "Pigs, pigs, pigs." And for a while there was a standoff. But only for a while. The cops again charged into the crowd. "If they'd gotten beaten like this when they were kids," growled one policeman, "they wouldn't be out here starting riots."

EMBRACE   Many delegates to the convention, some of whom even then were damning the police in the Amphitheater, did not quite see things that way. Later that night, in a poignant act of sympathy, 500 McCarthy delegates marched up Michigan Avenue in a candlelight procession to Grant Park, where the kids had once again regrouped. The youths greeted the marchers, in a moving embrace between an old and a new politics, by singing "We Shall Overcome," and invited the delegates into the park. The flickering candles added an eerily religious glow to the meeting.

The demonstrators were back in Grant Park the next afternoon, their numbers larger than ever. This time the defeated hero of many of them, Sen. Eugene McCarthy, visited their ranks from his suite across the street. "If we must make a mistake, let's make it on the side of trust," he said, "instead of the side of distrust." Later that evening, when the youths tried once again to march south toward the convention, following comedian Dick Gregory, they were gassed by National Guardsmen. Gregory and a number of delegates who defied guard orders to halt were arrested. "I didn't believe it could happen here," said a golf-jacketed bystander, who described himself as an ultraconservative. "I am shocked."

There was one more major shock to come. Early the next morning police,

complaining that they had been pelted with hotel crockery as well as cans of urine and bags of fecal matter from hotel windows, invaded rooms occupied by McCarthy's campaign organization on the fifteenth floor of the Hilton and started clubbing McCarthy volunteers. "One officer proceeded to beat a boy randomly and without provocation," reported Neal Gillen, an aide to Vice President Humphrey who was visiting the McCarthy ranks at the time. Gillen's wife severely criticized another patrolman during the incident. "Is that against the law, Mrs. Bubble-Eyes?" the cop answered.

The rampaging brutality of Chicago's police was roundly and widely condemned. "It sickens me to write this because I am on the police's side," said Jack Mabley, a columnist for Chicago's American, following his description of cops clubbing a clergyman and a cripple caught up in a police assault. New York Post columnist Jimmy Breslin, after recounting the story of a Chicago policeman clubbing a doctor who was trying to help a wounded man, wrote: "In twenty years of being with the police, having police in the family, riding with police in cars, drinking with them, watching them work in demonstrations and crowds in cities all over the world, the performance of the police of Chicago . . . last night was the worst act I ever have seen perpetrated by policemen."

Were these the police who only one year ago under Superintendent Orlando Wilson were praised as being among the best in the land? Harvard economist John Kenneth Galbraith answered as he addressed young demonstrators in Grant Park: "The police are probably pretty much the same all over. Only the people in charge should incur our animosity." The most certain thing about the Chicago police force since

Wilson's time is that he is no longer in charge; Mayor Daley is the boss.

LEEWAY   And Daley's philosophy of police power was evidently set forth last April, following Chicago's West Side ghetto riots, when he ordered police to "shoot to kill" in encounters with arsonists. Daley also denounced protesters at Chicago's Civic Center as "hoodlums and Communists"—terms similar to those the mayor applied to last week's demonstrators. Under the circumstances, the Chicago police felt they had plenty of leeway in dealing with the aggravating events and annoying persons of Lincoln Park and Michigan Avenue. Given the volatile atmosphere of the ghettos and the open threats of insurrection made before the convention by extremist leaders of the demonstrations, Daley felt more than justified in mounting a massive show of force.

Though Daley himself later admitted that his police might have "overreacted" on occasion, he defended them like a Bulldog in the face of the widespread disgust and condemnation last week. "You don't know the abuse they take," he insisted. "How would you like to stand around all night and be called names not even used in a brothel house?" Seconding his motion was Hubert Humphrey who mused, "Is it any wonder the police had to take action?" There were those, however, who suggested that was precisely the sort of thing professional policemen should be able to take. Among the angriest critics was a top-level officer in the Chicago police force itself. "Everything you told me the other night was true," he told a newsman who had earlier described the succession of attacks on the press near Lincoln Park. "I'm heartbroken. Everything we've tried to do has gone down the drain."

PART VIII

QUESTIONS FOR DISCUSSION:

1. What is the pattern of crime in your community? What local programs are currently in effect to deter crime?
2. What are the factors in ghetto life which foster an increase in crime? How would you distinguish between crime as it is normally viewed and riots such as have occurred in many of our major cities?
3. How would you rationalize to a ghetto dweller that crime does not pay?
4. Describe the relationship between juveniles and police in your community. What would you recommend to improve this relationship?

VOCABULARY

Uniform Crime Reports
assimilation
mobility
arraignment
Encounter Group
alienation
white backlash

accommodation
anomaly
pathology
appeasement
apathy
racism

THE URBAN GHETTO

Recently, students in a small southern community were asked if any ghetto were present in their local community. The immediate response was that there were none. To a student, the ghetto was considered a strictly metropolitan problem. They were quick to mention Harlem, Chicago's South Side, and Watts. However, after some thought they realized that the concept of ghetto, apart from the physical scene the word symbolizes, is one which has meaning for the small town as well as the large urban centers.

As they grappled with the word, ideas such as ghetto mentality began to emerge. Likewise they began to see ghetto not as a walled structure keeping two societies apart but rather as a state of mind keeping two segments of America apart. They thought of the Catholic Church as historically symbolic of that state of mind. The discussion turned to the ecumenical movement and how Pope John XXIII threw open the windows of Catholicism to let in the fresh air of change. They became aware of the fact that change is something not easily accepted and that many people refuse to accept it.

Brought back to the central issue by the discussion leader, the students were asked to draw an analogy between their understanding of the Catholic Church's ecumenical movement and the ghetto in American life. Their perceptions were quite accurate as they brought up such words as white backlash, open housing, bussing, slums, housing patterns, unemployment, and economic exploitation. The students soon realized that if these conditions were the essential factors in making up ghetto life, then the meaning of ghetto and the realities of ghetto life were "in their own backyard."

Today ghetto means not a physical boundary, such as a wall separating black from white, poor from rich, but, perhaps more devastating, a world cut off from the mainstream of American life. Symptomatic of the nation's feelings on this matter was the recent California referendum which struck down certain features of open housing legislation. While constitutionally illegal, unwritten agreements and unscrupulous real estate practices serve to keep the ghetto dweller in his place. Adding fuel to the fire of bigotry is the practice of block busting in which certain realtors, appealing to basic fears, find some way of having a Negro family move into a white neighborhood. Through fright phone calls and high pressure tactics, these realtors get the remainder of the neighborhood to sell for low prices under the premise that property values will drop. Equally cruel are the prices the Negroes must pay to buy into the area. Often finding themselves unable to meet the payments, they will invite another family to move in to help share expenses and soon the residences are overcrowded and the beginning of the end is in sight for the neighborhood.

Politicians have characteristically ignored the ghetto dweller as a force in elections. Only recently, as characterized by the elections of Mayor Stokes of Cleveland and Mayor Lindsay of New York, have politicians recognized them in their political campaigns. These people are beginning to find means of reducing their characteristic political impotence.

Economically, the resident of the ghetto finds job opportunities declining. Industry is fleeing the city and moving to industrial parks located in suburbia. Only recently, Senator Ribicoff called for industry to provide housing for employees in the suburbs so that employees who previously lived in the ghetto could make the move to suburbia. Obviously this would also contribute to new housing patterns and perhaps speed integration. Whether Senator Ribicoff's call to fairness will be heeded is another matter.

The key feature in all of this is the high sense of frustration fostered by ghetto life. The cycle of the cities, that is, their increasing poverty and blackness, is fostering the clear development of two societies. Restricted from moving out of the city together with job opportunities vanishing and education becoming even more discriminatory, the black ghetto dwellers find their only power coming from armed revolt—people will listen then. National news coverage makes the plight of the blacks known.

But one wonders, does the plight really become known? Does the white, suburban, middle class American really understand? Do they feel empathy for the condition of the urban Negro? Or, instead, do they advocate greater police crackdowns and a return to law and order? Perhaps even worse, in a few weeks, they forget. To be hated is at least a sign of concern; to be forgotten is the cruelest fate of all.

WATTS: THE REVOLT AND AFTER

William McCord, John Howard

The term "long hot summer" appears yearly in our domestic vocabulary as the country waits to see where the riots will be this year. Where they will occur is hard to predict. That they will occur with deadly regularity seems to have become almost a way of life. Programs and more programs are established and yet nothing is done. Frustration builds until some new event, totally without consequence in isolation, starts the whole process over again and "burn, baby, burn" becomes the order of the day.

Watts was the prelude to Newark and Detroit, and within Watts there were preludes to the riot of August 1965. Let us review the gradual buildup.

Since 1961 there have been ugly clashes between the police and Negroes that should have been recognized by the white citizens of Los Angeles as symptoms of the anger festering in the ghetto. On Memorial Day in 1961 there was a racial incident in Griffith Park that caused resentment in the black community, and in April 1962 a group of Black Muslims exchanged gunfire with the police when a burglary suspect was searched outside a Muslim temple.

The incidents became more intense. In 1964 alone there were small-scale riots at Jefferson High School, at the Central Receiving Hospital, and on Avalon Boulevard (later a scene of mass destruction). In 1964, after having issued an earlier prediction, the Los Angeles County Human Relations Commission stated:

About two years ago, this Commission stated that a situation was developing in the community in which police-minority group conflicts were becoming almost a "self-fulfilling prophecy." We feel that the same situation again exists. A significant and ever-growing number of minority-group persons are being led to feel that in any contact they have with the police officers, they are going to be treated roughly. On the other hand, a growing number of law-enforcement officers feel that in any contact they have with members of minority groups they are likely to meet with resistance. These "expectations" on the part of both groups are likely to produce what each expects. . . . We believe that the climate has deteriorated in the past several weeks between law-enforcement agencies and minority-group communities.

Again, in May 1964, Assistant Attorney General Howard H. Jewel explicitly warned that demonstrations in Los Angeles could well be joined by the entire Negro community. Jewel wrote:

In Los Angeles if demonstrators are joined by the Negro community at large the policing will no longer be done by the Los Angeles Police Department, but by the State Militia. If violence erupts millions in property damage may ensue, untold lives may be lost and California will have received an unsurpassed injury to her reputation.

Mayor Sam Yorty, Chief of Police William Parker, and Governor Edmund Brown ignored these repeated predictions. When the riots broke out in 1965, Yorty flew to San Francisco, apparently believing that police could handle the situation. And Governor Brown expressed both his shock and his naïveté when, after viewing the effects of the Watts riot, he commented, "Here in California, we have a wonderful working relationship between whites and Negroes. We got along fine until this happened. . . ."

Later almost all responsible officials recognized that they had failed to understand the scope of the problem. "We just did not communicate with the right people," said Mrs. Ethel Bryan, a Negro executive assistant to Mayor Yorty. "We only talked to middle-class 'leaders' when, really, Watts had no leaders at all." Similarly, in 1967, a police inspector admitted the same problem: "Soon, I hope, we will have a conference between officers and the true leaders down there . . . but we will all check our guns outside."

For anyone who talked with the people of Watts during the tragic days of August 1965 the true feelings of the Negro community soon became apparent. However inchoately expressed, the rioters again and again said that they had rebelled for three reasons: to protest against "police brutality," to get all the material goods that "whitey" had, and to demonstrate their manhood and dignity. To understand this reasoning is a first step in comprehending why Watts exploded.

"POLICE BRUTALITY"   "Never again," said Marquette Frye, whose arrest triggered the riot, "never again in this neighborhood will any young man, like my brother and me, stand by and take abuse from an officer." Rightly or wrongly, almost every Negro who participated in the riot echoed this sentiment. "Police brutality is like when they arrest you where it can't be seen and whip you," a twenty-two-year-old Negro explained to reporters Jerry Cohen and William Murphey. "They grab you when you walk down the street. They pull you over and beat on you. That ain't right. Man, I was born in California—in Long Beach. But I'm a Negro, so I been arrested."

I[*] found no evidence of the kind of true brutality I saw in Mississippi where, at first hand, I witnessed police terrorism, but my evaluation must be tempered by two qualifications.

First, the Los Angeles police admittedly participated in sweeps of "duck ponds"—areas of high criminality—before the riots of 1965. During these raids, police randomly selected people on the street, interrogated them, and checked, for example, to see if they had failed to pay a traffic penalty. These "field investigations" were conducted regularly in Watts but never in the rich suburbs of Los Angeles. At the minimum, therefore, the Los Angeles police submitted the people of Watts to a continuing surveillance which most Negro citizens considered an insult to their dignity.

Second, during the riot itself, individual policemen may well have acted in a brutal fashion. There is conflicting testimony on this issue, so no final conclusion may be drawn. In the midst of flames and snipers, however, it is certain that some officers reacted with a

[*] The "I" in this case is William McCord.

fear and hatred that normally they would have controlled.

The story of Laurence Jacques, which was contradicted by the testimony of the police officers involved, typifies what many Negroes—with or without valid reason—believed happened during the riots.

Jacques witnessed the shooting of one looter and the arrest of another. He, too, was then arrested, although he claimed he had done nothing, and was forced to lie on the ground with another Negro. Jacques said later that one policeman had asked another, "How many did you kill?"

The second man, supposedly answered, "I killed two niggers. Why don't you kill those two lying on the ground?"

According to Jacques, the first man replied, "They won't run."

"One officer came up to me and put a shotgun at the back of my head," said Jacques. " 'Nigger, how fast can you run the fifty-yard dash?' "

"I said, 'I can't run it at all.' He kicked me in the side two times, and the other officer put his foot on the back of my head."

No officers were convicted for their behavior during the riot.

Yet stories such as Jacques's—even if they might have been complete fabrications—undeniably added fuel to the riot's flames.

"GET WHAT WHITEY HAS"   Looting of liquor, appliance, grocery, and furniture stores cost their owners millions of dollars. Most of the looters had never before been known as criminals (75 per cent of the adult rioters did have criminal records, but the typical adolescent looter had never been arrested before).

One unemployed man on welfare explained the motivation of some of the rioters: "They wanted everything the whites had, including color TV. They

saw the stores were open. If you are hungry and don't have no money, you want anything and everything. Having no job isn't no fun. With store windows broken and the police doin' other things, what would you do?"

Objective social conditions prompted this desire to "get what whitey has." Not only did Watts have a generally high rate of unemployment, but joblessness was especially acute among young males. In the age group of seventeen to twenty-five—the element most likely to riot—about 41 per cent had not been able to find jobs.

Repeated promises in 1964 and 1965 that War on Poverty funds would soon be forthcoming were not fulfilled. The federal Office of Economic Opportunity stipulated that representatives from poor areas should participate in handling poverty funds, but city officials refused to change the composition of the responsible boards.

The looters, in other words, saw tempting items spread before them along 103rd Street, but they had no money to purchase them. Not unnaturally in a climate of anarchy, they took what they wanted.†

THE SEARCH FOR DIGNITY   An intangible but pervasive impulse guided many of the rioters: a simple desire to prove their manhood. Many men viewed the riot as an insurrection against the white establishment, as a way of bringing attention to them and to their area neglected so long.

Joe, a jobless young Negro interviewed by reporters after the riot, articulated this sentiment. He believed that white policemen were always stopping him during the so-called field investigations:

† Thousands of guns were stolen during the riot. Of these, only some 700 have been recovered by the police—a bad omen for Watts, if rioting occurs again.

It seemed like they always were trying to see if they could make me break, make me do something that would save them time. It seemed like they figured they'd eventually have me in jail and they wanted to save time.

He recalled an incident that had happened long before the riot:

One night . . . a cop stopped me and said: "I've seen you before. You've been in jail. I'm gonna check on you, punk."

That night I really wanted to do something—something to that white face. But I kept thinking about my mother, how she always had told me to stay out of trouble. I figured I'd gone this far without trouble, so I held back.

When the riot began, Joe interpreted the looting in this fashion:

I didn't realize what they were doing when the looting began. I didn't understand the object of the looting. At first it just began with people breaking windows and taking nothing. Then I realized the object of the looting: it was to move all the whites out of Watts. We don't want white people in Watts.

Asked if another explosion might occur in Watts, Joe replied:

Would I riot again? I just don't know. But I know the slightest thing could touch me off.

If it comes again? I guess I will be there. Everybody has to be willing to sacrifice something for what he believes in. I'd be out of place, wouldn't I, if my race was out there fighting and I wasn't?

We really don't live alike, the whites and the Negroes. As long as the whites keep trying to brutalize my people, I'll have to be out there trying to stop them.

Another Negro, a college graduate, summarized the search for dignity in this way:

You can stand on 103rd Street, on the edge of Will Rogers Park, and look up and see the big silver and gray jetliners pass overhead. Watts is on one of the approach routes to Los Angeles International Airport. If you fly over and look down you cannot tell Watts is there. It does not look any different from any other part of the city. The things that make it Watts are invisible.

Watts is a state of mind as well as a place. Part of what it is is symbolized by the low, sweeping passage of planes overhead. Standing in the heart of Watts, you can look up and see the big world, the expensive and expansive world, but the people in that world cannot see you. Your existence is not visible to them. You can see them but they cannot see you. You can never reach them. You can shout but they won't hear you. Waving or running or jumping will not make them see you.

There was only one time when the people up in the sky saw the people down on the ground. . . .

That was when the flames of Watts riots leaped and spiraled into the air, lighting up the approach route to Los Angeles International Airport.

The importance of these motives as instigating elements in the riot can be illustrated by a comparison between Watts and Compton. The city of Compton directly borders on the riot area and 50 per cent of its population is Negro, yet it largely escaped the Watts conflagration. There were attempts to spread the riot to Compton, and over 150 people were arrested there, but about half of them came from outside the city. Nonetheless, the "fire next time" did not really ignite the Compton area.

Many explanations can be offered

for this anomaly. In 1965 Compton was still an integrated area. While the Negro proportion of the population rose rapidly from 4 per cent in 1950 to 50 per cent in 1960, the persuasive work of Compton's Human Relations Commission had largely stemmed the outflow of whites by the time of the riot. Even in the most densely concentrated Negro census tract in Compton, living conditions were better than those in Watts: median income ($5,523) was higher, people had achieved more education (a median of 10.2 years), and fewer houses were considered to be "deteriorated and dilapidated" (about 8 per cent).

Compton had developed a Negro middle class, a group with deep economic stakes in the community that was on relatively amicable terms with the white "establishment" and with the police. Clearly, a different spirit prevailed in Compton: a feeling of close cooperation between Negroes and police, a sense of integration, and a belief that the economic gains achieved by Negroes should be defended by Negroes themselves against "hoodlums."

"I think it would be naïve to say that problems are all solved—they're not all solved," a white Compton policeman, Captain Harold Lindemulder, commented after the riot.

People still have prejudices—they're not wiped out overnight, and it will take a long time before all of people's prejudices are gone. We have problems in Compton but I think the community as a whole is trying to face up to them and solve them. I'm sure that with everyone working together and continuing as they have been, in the years ahead we'll see an easing of these problems.

THE AFTERMATH

Since 1965 many agencies have launched serious efforts to transform Watts into a community like Compton.† Federal aid, in the form of antipoverty funds, has poured into the area. New programs—credit unions, "Head Start" training, even an art festival—have been created. Proposition 14, the measure designed to imbed segregation legally in California, has been declared unconstitutional. The mayor has appointed a city Human Relations Commission and ordered fuller integration among City Hall employees. And the American Civil Liberties Union has established complaint bureaus where citizens may voice their grievances and receive legal counsel.

Within Watts itself, numerous indigenous organizations have sprung up. Groups such as "SLANT" and "US" adhere to a black-power ideology or emphasize the African cultural heritage of American Negroes.

"The Sons of Watts," composed in part of former rioters, attempts to build community spirit by, among other things, distributing litter cans to help clean up the debris of Watts. And, in 1966, during the "Watts Festival," this group policed a large parade (regular officers stayed out of the area) so effectively that Mayor Sam Yorty rode in

† Some of these attempts have been well-meaning but naïve. The Los Angeles County Commission on Human Relations, for example, issued a series of recommendations in 1965, one of which was to establish an "Adult Advisor Corps" to act as "big brothers" to deprived children: "The youngsters to be served come from homes and environments that often prevent their being exposed to such cultural, educational pursuits as attendance at enriching exposures to Music Center offerings, trips to the Art Museum, associations with persons from communities other than their own—*i.e.*, Thanksgiving meals with the aforementioned." Thanksgiving meals will hardly cure such problems at the extraordinarily high rate of unemployment.

an open car and the parade was un-
marred by any incidents.

Another group, the "Citizen's Alert
Patrol" armed itself with tape recorders
and cameras and followed police to the
scene of every arrest as a guard against
"police brutality."

Still another organization, which cannot be named, claims to have infiltrated
all of the others in the hope of guiding
black-power energies into constructive
channels. Its young leader believes that
the proliferating organizations in Watts
can be brought together in a union
which will become a base for Negro
economic independence and Negro
political power.

All these movements may have
wrought a psychological change in
Watts. Indeed, former rioters themselves make up a majority of their
membership. In 1967 one detected
more hope, more dignity, and a greater
sense of importance in Watts than before the riot.

But, without denigrating this possible
change in spiritual climate of the central district, it must be recognized that
the basic problems of Watts remain
unsolved.**

One barometer of potential trouble
is the attitude of the younger, unskilled
males. The 120 men interviewed in
1967 as part of our random sample of
the Watts population voiced considerable anger about their situation. Fifty
per cent believed that the riot had

** The abortive riot of March 1966 indicates that there is still a potential for
violence. Triggered by conflict between
Negro and Mexican-American gangs, mobs
once again took to the streets of Watts.
This time the rioters were well armed.
Two men, both innocent bystanders, were
killed. Police mobilized quickly and a
sobered adult Negro community cooper-
ated in quieting the youths. Nevertheless,
East 103rd Street, the heart of the Watts
business community, was a scene of destruction and looted stores.

helped Watts; only 20 per cent believed
that it had hurt. Eighty-one per cent
favored the use of violence in defense
of civil rights; only 19 per cent definitely opposed it. Fifty per cent said
the police were abusive toward them;
only 3 per cent thought the police ad-
hered to "fair" standards of treatment.
A very high proportion (78 per cent)
admired the concept of black power;
only 6 per cent opposed it.

Objective measures of the socioeconomic situation in Watts confirmed
that little has changed since 1965:

Unemployment apparently has not
been reduced. While conflicting reports
exist, the weight of evidence indicates
that joblessness has stayed at about the
same level as before the 1965 riot. The
Chamber of Commerce attempted a
crash program to produce more jobs
but, according to the County Human
Relations Commission, came up with
perhaps 200 to 300 jobs and job-training opportunities when at least 5,000
were needed to make a serious impact
upon the Watts problem.

Further, a phenomenal high of
$5,500,000 in welfare aid went into the
riot area each month in 1966—a rather
sure indication that the conditions of
unemployment had not been alleviated.
Roughly 60 per cent of Watts residents
were on relief that year.

Despite these disillusioning facts,
some 2,000 Negroes continue to arrive
in Los Angeles each month, still lured
by the promise of a better life. Almost
all of them settle in the central district,
and few have the technical qualifications demanded by Los Angeles industry.

The fact of Watts has changed little
since 1965. The rubble has been cleared
and littered parking lots have replaced
the burned-out stores. Few businessmen
have re-established their enterprises,
often because they are unable to secure
insurance for their premises. The busi-

nesses which have been rebuilt resemble fortresses: massive, windowless, concrete structures.

There are no signs in most of the central district, as there are in Compton, of the emergence of a Negro business class to replace whites. Some groups, such as Westminster House (a Presbyterian organization), encourage Negro "industry," but the products produced by untrained handicraft workers —ashtrays made from discarded Coke bottles, papier-mâché bracelets—could hardly bring prosperity to the region.

Despite the repeal of Proposition 14, the housing pattern of Los Angeles has showed no evidence of greater integration. The Negro population has been growing at a rate about four times that of the white, and, as we have noted, almost all Negro families are congregated in the central district.

The ultimate effect of this trend has been prophesized for Los Angeles by urban expert Victor Palmieri: "This . . . is the city of the future—the very near future. A black island spreading like a giant ink blot over the heart of a metropolis which is bankrupt financially and paralyzed politically."

Palmieri reasons that three established factors—the rate of population growth of Negroes, the increasing mobility of whites, and the resulting "domino effect" upon schools—guarantees that the core of Los Angeles will be all black by 1980.

He points out that Los Angeles in 1967 can hardly handle her financial problems, since the property tax rate approaches $10 per $100, a level regarded as one of "negative return" by most economists because of its hindrance to local economic growth.

Beyond this, Palmieri argues that Los Angeles County will not manage her political problems. The region is split into more than seventy autonomous cities (and even more independent school districts) which cannot reach a consensus on such issues as urban renewal, open-housing laws, or police-review boards.

Although more optimistic in its conclusions, the McCone Commission considered a similar possibility: a complete breach between whites and blacks which could result only in further violence. The Commission concluded: "So serious and so explosive is the situation that, unless it is checked, the August [1965] riots may seem by comparison to be only a curtain raiser for what could blow up one day in the future."

Yet Los Angeles has still not looked deeply into its future. Although the McCone Commission put forward some constructive ideas, it failed to recommend drastic changes in existing white institutions or to suggest ways of linking the values of the Negro subculture with those of the large society.

Unless there are radical changes, such objective observers as sociologists Robert Blauner and Victor Palmieri foresee a crippled, festering Los Angeles, increasingly populated with frustrated Negroes. The rioters expressed their unwillingness to continue to accept indignities; until the white community realizes this, Los Angeles can look forward to more holocausts.

THE INVISIBLE WALL

Kenneth B. Clark

The ghetto provides both security and degradation for the Negro. While some Negroes talk openly of wanting to break out, others view the ghetto as a place where they know who they are and what to expect. The price that must be paid by anyone wishing to leave the ghetto is the price of uncertainty in a world which clearly would prefer that he stayed in his place.

The ghetto also provides a state of mind, a place of withdrawâl from participation in the larger society. Yet total escape from this society is impossible as the mass media infiltrate the lives of even the most destitute. The transition from the ghetto is a deeply personal experience for the Negro. It takes a different form in the life of every Negro. Yet this transition must be made if true assimilation of the Negro into our total way of life is ever to be a reality.

"Ghetto" was the name for the Jewish quarter in sixteenth-century Venice. Later, it came to mean any section of a city to which Jews were confined. America has contributed to the concept of the ghetto the restriction of persons to a special area and the limiting of their freedom of choice on the basis of skin color. The dark ghetto's invisible walls have been erected by the white society, by those who have power, both to confine those who have *no* power and to perpetuate their powerlessness. The dark ghettos are social, political, educational, and—above all—economic colonies. Their inhabitants are subject peoples, victims of the greed, cruelty, insensitivity, guilt, and fear of their masters.

The objective dimensions of the American urban ghettos are overcrowded and deteriorated housing, high infant mortality, crime, and disease. The subjective dimensions are resentment, hostility, despair, apathy, self-deprecia-tion, and its iron companion, compensatory grandiose behavior.

The ghetto is ferment, paradox, conflict, and dilemma. Yet within its pervasive pathology exists a surprising human resilience. The ghetto is hope, it is despair, it is churches and bars. It is aspiration for change and it is apathy. It is vibrancy, it is stagnation. It is courage, and it is defeatism. It is cooperation and concern, and it is suspicion, competitiveness, and rejection. It is the surge toward assimilation, and it is alienation and withdrawal within the protective walls of the ghetto.

The pathologies of the ghetto community perpetuate themselves through cumulative ugliness, deterioration, and isolation and strengthen the Negro's sense of worthlessness, giving testimony to his impotence. Yet the ghetto is not totally isolated. The mass media—radio, television, moving pictures, magazines, and the press—penetrate, indeed, invade the ghetto in continuous and inevitable communication, largely one-way, and project the values and aspirations, the manners and the style of the larger white-dominated society. Those who are required to live in congested and rat infested homes are aware that others are not so dehumanized. Young people in the ghetto are aware that other young people have been taught to read, that they have been prepared for college, and can compete successfully for white-collar, managerial, and executive jobs. Whatever accommodations they themselves must make to the negative realities which dominate their own lives, they know consciously or unconsciously that their fate is not the common fate of mankind. They tend to regard their predicament as a consequence of personal disability or as an inherent and imposed powerlessness which all Negroes share.

The privileged white community is at great pains to blind itself to conditions of the ghetto, but the residents of the ghetto are not themselves blind to life as it is outside of the ghetto. They observe that others enjoy a better life, and this knowledge brings a conglomerate of hostility, despair, and hope. If the ghetto could be contained totally, the chances of social revolt would be decreased, if not eliminated, but it cannot be contained and the outside world intrudes. The Negro lives in part in the world of television and motion pictures, bombarded by the myths of the American middle class, often believing as literal truth their pictures of luxury and happiness, and yet at the same time confronted by a harsh world of reality where the dreams do not come true or change into nightmares. The discrepancy between the reality and the dream burns into their consciousness. The oppressed can never be sure whether their failures reflect personal inferiority or the fact of color. This persistent and agonizing conflict dominates their lives.

The young people in Harlem, in the Negro ghettos of Chicago, Washington, Cleveland, Detroit, Los Angeles, and other cities, who persist, in spite of obstacles, in seeking an education, who insist upon going to night school and then the day session of a municipal college, whose parents, friends, or teachers encourage and support them demonstrate that a positive resolution of the ghetto's nuclear conflict is possible. But many resolve the conflict negatively—in either a passive or defiant way. Those within the ghetto who are defeated—those who accept the "evidence" of their personal inferiority and impotence, those who express a pervasive sense of personal failure through stagnation and despair, who drop out of school, who depend on marijuana and narcotics—demonstrate a passively negative and self-destructive solution.

The overt delinquent, the acting-out rebel, on the other hand, seeks his salvation in defiant, aggressive, and in the end self-destructive forms. Because the larger society has clearly rejected him, he rejects—or appears to reject—the values, the aspirations, and techniques of that society. His conscious or unconscious argument is that he cannot hope to win meaningful self-esteem through the avenues ordinarily available to more privileged individuals. These avenues have been blocked for him through inadequate education, through job discrimination, and through a system of social and political power which is not responsive to his needs. When a warlord of one of the last of Harlem's active fighting gangs was asked why he did not "go downtown and get a job," he laughed and replied:

Oh come on. Get off that crap. I make $40 or $50 a day selling marijuana. You want me to go down to the garment district and push one of those trucks through the street and at the end of the week take home $40 or $50 if I'm lucky? They don't have animals doing what you want me to do. There would be some society to protect animals if anybody had them pushing them damn trucks around. I'm better than an animal, but nobody protects me. Go away, mister. I got to look out for myself.

Such rebels are scornful of what they consider the hypocrisy and the dishonesty of the larger society. They point to corruption and criminal behavior among respected middle-class whites. Almost every delinquent or marginal adolescent in a Negro urban ghetto claims to know where and how the corrupt policeman accepts graft from the numbers runners and the pimps and the prostitutes. The close association, collaboration, and at times identity, of criminals and the police is the pattern of day-to-day life in the ghetto as these young people come to know and accept it. Not only do they not respect the police, but they see the police as part of their own total predicament.

Large numbers of other ghetto youth, however, are caught in the paradox of the ghetto unable to resolve their personal conflicts either in positive and socially acceptable forms of adjustment or in direct and assertive antisocial behavior. They are aware of the values and standards of the larger society, but they know that they are not personally equipped to meet its demands. They have neither succumbed totally to pathology nor have they been able to emerge from it. As adults they live out lives they feel helpless to change, in a kind of unstable equilibrium, aware of their plight and yet accepting it. They are the ones who listen to Malcolm X but do not join; who vote Democratic if they bother to register but recognize at the same time that City Hall will do little for them. They are momentarily stimulated by the verbal militance of certain Negro newspaper editors and

soapbox orators; they gain vicarious satisfaction through temporary identification with the flamboyance and antiwhite verbal extremisms of charismatic Negro politicians. They send their children to bad public schools reluctantly because they do not have the money for private schools. They are the great potential who could engage in constructive social action or who could become the pawns of the demagogues. They have no inner-determined direction. Whoever develops any movement toward power in the ghetto finally does so through winning the allegiance of this group— the largest in the ghetto—not of the semicriminal and certainly not of the elite and comfortable.

The ferment within Negro communities throughout the nation—hitherto more obvious in certain Southern communities, but beginning to express itself with increasing intensity and even spasmodic ferocity in such Northern urban communities as Chicago, Boston, Philadelphia, Rochester, and New York —suggests that the past cycle, in which personal and community powerlessness reinforce each other, is being supplanted by a more forceful pattern of personal and community action. This is proof that the reservoir of energy was there, ready to be stirred by hope, for effective or even sporadic protest could never have emerged out of total stagnation.

Although the civil rights movement gives Negroes more leverage, enabling many to channel their energies into constructive protest, there is a possibility that these energies could also be diluted into meaningless catharsis. Demonstrations that do not lead to results may become only one more safety valve— as the church has long been for Negroes —releasing Negro energies without the transformation of society, without any actual change in their relative status.

If mobilized community power and

protest do succeed in winning concrete positive changes, Negro self-confidence and pride will grow, and a new cycle of greater personal and community effectiveness should emerge. But it would not be realistic for the white community to expect protest to subside in the face of gains, for the closer the Negro community gets to the attainment of its goals—the removal of the causes and effects of racial exploitation and powerlessness—the more impatient will Negroes become for total equality. In the complex turbulence of the Negro ghetto, and consistent with the affirmative dynamics of the civil rights thrust, success feeds hope and provides the strength and the motivation for further activity. This, in turn, makes existing barriers even more intolerable. Accelerated impatience and the lowering of the threshold of frustration toward remaining inequities, paradoxically increase the chances of racial tensions and ferment and conflict. Failure would reinforce the sense of stagnation and despair and establish as fact the sense of personal and group powerlessness. A truly hopeless group makes no demands and certainly does not insist upon stark social confrontations.

The summer of 1964 brought violent protests to the ghettos of America's cities, not in mobilization of effective power, but as an outpouring of unplanned revolt. The revolts in Harlem were not led by a mob, for a mob is an uncontrolled social force bent on irrational destruction. The revolts in Harlem were, rather, a weird social defiance. Those involved in them were, in general, not the lowest class of Harlem residents—not primarily looters and semicriminals—but marginal Negroes who were upwardly mobile, demanding a higher status than their families had. This was not a race riot in the sense that mobs of whites were assaulting mobs of Negroes or vice versa, yet the fact of race was pervasive. The 1964 Harlem riot was indeed in many respects more frightening than a race riot and the participants' deliberate mockery more threatening than a mob. Small groups of young people seemed to take delight in taunting the police, whose white faces were accentuated by their white helmets: "Here's a nigger, kill me." Even those Negroes who threw bottles and bricks from the roofs were not in the grip of a wild abandon, but seemed deliberately to be prodding the police to behave openly as the barbarians that the Negroes felt they actually were. You cannot hear conversations of a mob, but during the disturbance in Harlem, groups of young people discussed their plans: "I'll go home and come back tomorrow. Whitey will still be here." "I don't want to be killed tonight; tomorrow will be all right." There was an eerie, surrealistic quality, a silence within the din, punctuated by gunfire and sporadic shattering of glass, a calm within the chaos, a deliberateness within the hysteria. The Negro seemed to feel nothing could happen to him that had not happened already; he behaved as if he had nothing to lose. His was an oddly controlled rage that seemed to say, during those days of social despair, "We have had enough. The only weapon you have is bullets. The only thing you can do is to kill us." Paradoxically, his apparent lawlessness was a protest against lawlessness directed against *him*. His acts were a desperate assertion of his desire to be treated as a man. He was affirmative up to the point of inviting death; he insisted upon being visible and understood. If this was the only way to relate to society at large, he would die rather than be ignored.

At times of overt social unrest, many white persons who claim to be in favor of civil rights and assert that they are "friends" of the Negro will admonish the Negro not to engage in disruptive and lawless demonstrations lest he incite racism and reverse the progress made in his behalf. These often well-meaning requests may reflect the unconscious condescension of benign prejudices. They demonstrate mistaken assumptions concerning the nature and dynamics of Negro protest. It is argued, for example, that Negroes should "choose" only those techniques, tactics, and demonstrations which do not inconvenience the dominant white society; the oppressed are urged to be concerned about the comfort and sensitivities of those they regard as their oppressors. The implication is that if they do not, middle-class whites will use their own power to retaliate against all Negroes. Negroes are increasingly reminded of the sting of the "white backlash." Many middle-class Negroes as well as whites accept these arguments and behave accordingly. Yet the threat is not new. The struggle of those with power to deny power to those who have none is age-old, and accommodation and appeasement have not resolved it. The "white backlash" is a new name for an old phenomenon, white resistance to the acceptance of the Negro as a human being. As the Negro demands such status—as he develops more and more effective techniques to obtain it, and as these techniques come closer to success —the resistance to his demands rises in intensity and alarm. The forms it takes vary from the overt and barbaric murders and bombings to the more subtle innuendo of irritation and disparagement.

Many whites also assume that a governing group of Negro leaders choose tactics for the Negro masses. Yet leaders of the stature and responsibility of Roy Wilkins and Whitney M. Young, Jr., James Farmer or Martin Luther King cannot impose tactics upon the masses of marginal Negroes, who are

not disciplined members of any group. And the masses of Negroes do not "choose" tactics at all. They respond to the pressures of their lives and react spontaneously to incidents which trigger explosions or demonstrations. When a bewildered white liberal asks why, in the face of the passage of the Civil Rights Bill of 1964, "they" still revolt— and not in the dignified, respectable nonviolent way of the earlier student sitins—he betrays his own alienation from the Negroes whose cause he espouses. The Civil Rights Act was so long in coming it served merely to remind many Negroes of their continued rejected and second-class status. Even well-meaning whites continue to see and talk of Negroes as "they," clearly differentiated from "we," the "outgroup" from the "ingroup." As long as this alienation remains, the masses of whites will be irritated and inconvenienced by any meaningful activity by Negroes to change their status. No real revolt can be convenient for the privileged; no real revolt can be contained within comfortable bounds or be made respectable.

In the face of the growing unrest, careful, thoughtful, and realistic planning becomes starkly imperative. Some whites would react to renewed protest by warning Negroes not to go too far too fast, not to alienate the white liberals who have, even if often timidly, supported them. To others, less well-intentioned, Negro unrest is but confirmation of their own prejudice: Negroes are, after all, behaving as the uncivilized do. But unrest *is* a characteristic of civilization, and to fight against oppression—even unwisely—is a sign that men have begun to hope. As studies on social disasters have demonstrated, people who feel there is no escape submit to their fate; it is those who see an exit sign and an open door who struggle to reach it.

Furthermore, energies devoted to a

struggle for constructive social change are clearly not simultaneously available for antisocial and self-destructive patterns of behavior. In those communities such as Montgomery, Alabama, where Negroes mobilized themselves for sustained protest against prevailing racial injustice, *the incidence of antisocial behavior and delinquency decreased almost to a vanishing point during the period of protest.*

The Negro cannot any longer feel, if he ever did, that he should have to prove himself "worthy" in order to gain his full freedom—the rights guaranteed to all other American citizens, including those most recently naturalized. The Negro cannot be asked to prove that he "deserves" the rights and responsibilities of democracy, nor can he be told that others must first be persuaded "in heart and mind" to accept him. Such tests and trials by fire are not applied to others. To impose them on the Negro is racist condescension. It is to assume that the Negro is a special type of human being who must pass a special test before admission to a tenuous status worthy of governmental protection. It is to place upon the Negro a peculiar burden reflecting and exploiting his powerlessness, and it is, paradoxically, to deny him the essential human rights of frailty and imperfection. The experience of inferior racial status has not transformed the Negro into a super human being. To demand that he demonstrate virtues not ordinarily found in more privileged people, before he may enjoy the benefits of democracy, is not only irrational and inconsistent but gratuitously cruel. And above all it is evidence that the invisible wall is opaque from outside in.

No one ought to expect the transition from a system of injustice to a system of social justice to occur without personal and social trauma for the Negro as well as the white. The intensification of conflict and resistance inherent in the immediacy of the Negro's demands, and the dramatic methods which he is now using to attain his goals, understandably obscure some of the more profound human problems involved in progressing from a racially segregated to a non-segregated society. But, when the cries of anguish of the segregationists have subsided, as they will eventually, the Negro will be confronted with his own inner anxieties, conflicts, and challenges as he dares to move into a society of open competition. It will then be clear that though the problems of adjusting to change are difficult for whites, in even more insidious ways they are quite painful for Negroes. The invisible walls of a segregated society are not only damaging but protective in a debilitating way. There is considerable psychological safety in the ghetto; there one lives among one's own and does not risk rejection among strangers. One first becomes aware of the psychological damage of such "safety" when the walls of the ghetto are breached and the Negro ventures out into the repressive, frightening white world. Some Negroes prefer to stay in the ghetto, particularly those who have developed seemingly effective defenses to protect themselves against hurt, those who fear for their children, and those who have profited from the less competitive segregated society. Other Negroes, particularly the young, are militant in their efforts to crash the remaining barriers of race. But even among this group it is not always easy to tell who is totally committed and willing to assume the risks and who is only talking militance. Most Negroes take the first steps into an integrated society tentatively and torn with conflict. To be the first Negro who is offered a job in a company brings a sense of triumph but also the dread of failure. To be the "show" Negro, the symbol of a new-found policy of racial democracy in an educational institution, private industry, or governmental agency, imposes demands for personal restraint, balance, and stability of character rare among any group of mere human beings. For a Negro to be offered friendship and to find himself unable to accept it fully, to find that he is himself in the grip of hitherto unrealized racial prejudice—or, more precisely racial anger—is to look into the hidden recesses of his own mind. A person—or a race—who has been forced to be ashamed of his identity cannot easily accept himself simply as a human being and surrender either the supportive group identification or hostility toward those who have rejected him.

The newly emerging Negro—the assertive, militant, defiant, self-affirming Negro seeking his identity—will probably at first seem a caricature, a person who wears the mask of race with its fixed artificial expression. No more than the white bigot who succumbs to his passion of hatred and fear, or the white "liberal" who struggles to reconcile his affirmation of racial justice with his visceral racism, has the Negro escaped domination of his own individuality by the role of race. Only when the need to play such a role is no longer urgent will the individual Negro and white feel free to be merely themselves, without defenses.

ONE SOCIETY OR TWO

President's Commission on Civil Disorders

Increasingly we find our nation forming into what appears to be two armed camps. As the whites flee the cities, these same cities become Negro strongholds. Likewise, suburban communities become entrenchments for the white middle class.

The Kerner Commission foresaw the coming of two societies and presented us with this challenge. We must reverse this trend and begin the process of immediate integration at all levels of life. Housing, employment, and education patterns must all be altered and our nation must become one if we are to avoid another civil war between two alienated societies.

THE KEY TRENDS

Negro Population Growth

The size of the Negro population in central cities is closely related to total national Negro population growth. In the past 16 years, about 98 percent of this growth has occurred within metropolitan areas, and 86 percent in the central cities of those areas.

CENTRAL CITIES   Further Negro population growth in central cities depends upon two key factors: in-migration from

From the President's Commission on Civil Disorders, *Report of the National Advisory Commission on Civil Disorders,* March 1, 1968.

outside metropolitan areas, and patterns of Negro settlement within metropolitan areas.

From 1960 to 1966, the Negro population of all central cities rose 2.4 million, 88.9 percent of total national Negro population growth. We estimate that natural growth accounted for 1.4 million, or 58 percent of this increase, and in-migration accounted for one million, or 42 percent.

As of 1966, the Negro population in all central cities totaled 12.1 million. By 1985, we have estimated that it will rise 68 percent to 20.3 million. We believe that natural growth will account for 5.2 million of this increase and in-migration for 3.0 million.

Growth projected on the basis of natural increase and in-migration would raise the proportion of Negroes to whites in central cities by 1985 from the present 20.7 percent to between an estimated 31 and 34.7 percent.

LARGEST CENTRAL CITIES These, however, are national figures. Much faster increases will occur in the largest central cities where Negro growth has been concentrated in the past two decades. Washington, D.C., Gary, and Newark are already over half Negro. A continuation of recent trends would cause the following 10 major cities to become over 50 percent Negro by the indicated dates:

New Orleans	1971
Richmond	1971
Baltimore	1972
Jacksonville	1972
Cleveland	1975
St. Louis	1978
Detroit	1979
Philadelphia	1981
Oakland	1983
Chicago	1984

These cities, plus Washington, D.C. (now over 66 percent Negro) and Newark, contained 12.6 million people

in 1960, or 22 percent of the total population of all 224 American central cities. All 13 cities undoubtedly will have Negro majorities by 1985, and the suburbs ringing them will remain largely all white, unless there are major changes in Negro fertility rates,[1] in-migration, settlement patterns, or public policy.

If present trends continue, many cities in addition to those listed above will have Negro school majorities by 1985, probably including:

Dallas	Louisville
Pittsburgh	Indianapolis
Buffalo	Kansas City, Mo.
Cincinnati	Hartford
Harrisburg	New Haven

Thus, continued concentration of future Negro population growth in large central cities will produce significant changes in those cities over the next 20 years. Unless there are sharp changes in the factors influencing Negro settlement patterns within metropolitan areas, there is little doubt that the trend toward Negro majorities will continue. Even a complete cessation of net Negro in-migration to central cities would merely postpone this result for a few years.

Growth of the Young Negro Population

We estimate that the Nation's white population will grow 16.6 million, or 9.6 percent, from 1966 to 1975, and the Negro population 3.8 million, or 17.7 percent, in the same period. The Negro age group from 15 to 24 years of age, however, will grow much faster than either the Negro population as a whole, or the white population in the same age group.

This rapid increase in the young

[1] The fertility rate is the number of live births each year per 1,000 women aged 15 to 44.

Negro population has important implications for the country. This group has the highest unemployment rate in the Nation, commits a relatively high proportion of all crimes and plays the most significant role in civil disorders. By the same token, it is a great reservoir of underused human resources which are vital to the Nation. . . .

The Location of New Jobs

Providing employment for the swelling Negro ghetto population will require society to link these potential workers more closely with job locations. This can be done in three ways: By developing incentives to industry to create new employment centers near Negro residential areas; by opening suburban residential areas to Negroes and encouraging them to move closer to industrial centers; or by creating better transportation between ghetto neighborhoods and new job locations.

All three involve large public outlays.

The first method—creating new industries in or near the ghetto—is not likely to occur without Government subsidies on a scale which convinces private firms that it will pay them to face the problems involved.

The second method—opening up suburban areas to Negro occupancy—obviously requires effective fair housing laws. It will also require an extensive program of federally aided, low-cost housing in many suburban areas.

The third approach—improved transportation linking ghettos and suburbs—has received little attention from city planners and municipal officials. A few demonstration projects show promise, but carrying them out on a large scale will be very costly.

Although a high proportion of new jobs will be located in suburbs, there are still millions of jobs in central cities. Turnover in those jobs alone can open up a great many potential positions for Negro central-city residents— if employers cease racial discrimination in their hiring and promotion practices. . . .

CHOICES FOR THE FUTURE

The complexity of American society offers many choices for the future of relations between central cities and suburbs and patterns of white and Negro settlement in metropolitan areas. For practical purposes, however, we see two fundamental questions:

Should future Negro population growth be concentrated in central cities, as in the past 20 years, thereby forcing Negro and white populations to become even more residentially segregated?

Should society provide greatly increased special assistance to Negroes and other relatively disadvantaged population groups?

For purposes of analysis, the Commission has defined three basic choices for the future embodying specific answers to these questions:

The Present Policies Choice

Under this course, the Nation would maintain approximately the share of resources now being allocated to programs of assistance for the poor, unemployed and disadvantaged. These programs are likely to grow, given continuing economic growth and rising Federal revenues, but they will not grow fast enough to stop, let alone reverse, the already deteriorating quality of life in central-city ghettos.

This choice carries the ultimate price, as we will point out.

The Enrichment Choice

Under this course, the Nation would seek to offset the effects of continued Negro segregation and deprivation in large city ghettos. The enrichment choice would aim at creating dramatic improvements in the quality of life in disadvantaged central-city neighborhoods—both white and Negro. It would require marked increases in Federal spending for education, housing, employment, job training, and social services.

The enrichment choice would seek to lift poor Negroes and whites above poverty status and thereby give them the capacity to enter the mainstream of American life. But it would not, at least for many years, appreciably affect either the increasing concentration of Negroes in the ghetto or racial segregation in residential areas outside the ghetto.

The Integration Choice

This choice would be aimed at reversing the movement of the country toward two societies, separate and unequal.

The integration choice—like the enrichment choice—would call for large-scale improvement in the quality of ghetto life. But it would also involve both creating strong incentives for Negro movement out of central-city ghettos and enlarging freedom of choice concerning housing, employment, and schools.

The result would fall considerably short of full integration. The experience of other ethnic groups indicates that some Negro households would be scattered in largely white residential areas. Others—probably a larger number—would voluntarily cluster together in largely Negro neighborhoods. The integration choice would thus produce both integration and segregation. But the segregation would be voluntary.

Articulating these three choices plainly oversimplifies the possibilities open to the country. We believe, however, that they encompass the basic issues—issues which the American public must face if it is serious in its concern not only about civil disorder, but the future of our democratic society.

THE PRESENT POLICIES CHOICE

Powerful forces of social and political inertia are moving the country steadily along the course of existing policies toward a divided country.

This course may well involve changes in many social and economic programs—but not enough to produce fundamental alterations in the key factors of Negro concentration, racial segregation, and the lack of sufficient enrichment to arrest the decay of deprived neighborhoods.

Some movement toward enrichment can be found in efforts to encourage industries to locate plants in central cities, in increased Federal expenditures for education, in the important concepts embodied in the "War on Poverty," and in the Model Cities Program. But Congressional appropriations for even present Federal programs have been so small that they fall short of effective enrichment.

As for challenging concentration and segregation, a national commitment to this purpose has yet to develop.

Of the three future courses we have defined, the present policies choice—the choice we are now making—is the course with the most ominous consequences for our society.

The Probability of Future Civil Disorders

We believe that the present policies choice would lead to a larger number of violent incidents of the kind that have stimulated recent major disorders.

First, it does nothing to raise the hopes, absorb the energies, or constructively challenge the talents of the rapidly growing number of young Negro men in central cities. The proportion of unemployed or underemployed among them will remain very high. These young men have contributed disproportionately to crime and violence in cities in the past, and there is danger, obviously, that they will continue to do so.

Second, under these conditions, a rising proportion of Negroes in disadvantaged city areas might come to look upon the deprivation and segregation they suffer as proper justification for violent protest or for extending support to now isolated extremists who advocate civil disruption by guerrilla tactics.

More incidents would not necessarily mean more or worse riots. For the near future, there is substantial likelihood that even an increased number of incidents could be controlled before becoming major disorders, if society undertakes to improve police and National Guard forces so that they can respond to potential disorders with more prompt and disciplined use of force.

In fact, the likelihood of incidents mushrooming into major disorders would be only slightly higher in the near future under the present policies choice than under the other two possible choices. For no new policies or programs could possibly alter basic ghetto conditions immediately. And the announcement of new programs under the other choices would immediately generate new expectations. Expectations inevitably increase faster than performance. In the short run, they might even increase the level of frustration.

In the long run, however, the present policies choice risks a seriously greater probability of major disorders, worse,

possibly, than those already experienced.

If the Negro population as a whole developed even stronger feelings of being wrongly "penned in" and discriminated against, many of its members might come to support not only riots, but the rebellion now being preached by only a handful. Large-scale violence, followed by white retaliation, could follow. This spiral could quite conceivably lead to a kind of urban *apartheid* with semimartial law in many major cities, enforced residence of Negroes in segregated areas, and a drastic reduction in personal freedom for all Americans, particularly Negroes.

The same distinction is applicable to the cost of the present policies choice. In the short run, its costs—at least its direct cash outlays—would be far less than for the other choices.

Social and economic programs likely to have significant lasting effect would require very substantial annual appropriations for many years. Their cost would far exceed the direct losses sustained in recent civil disorders. Property damage in all the disorders we investigated, including Detroit and Newark, totaled less than $100 million.

But it would be a tragic mistake to view the present policies choice as cheap. Damage figures measure only a small part of the costs of civil disorder. They cannot measure the costs in terms of the lives lost, injuries suffered, minds and attitudes closed and frozen in prejudice, or the hidden costs of the profound disruption of entire cities.

Ultimately, moreover, the economic and social costs of the present policies choice will far surpass the cost of the alternatives. The rising concentration of impoverished Negroes and other minorities within the urban ghettos will constantly expand public expenditures for welfare, law enforcement, unemployment, and other existing programs without arresting the decay of older city neighborhoods and the breeding of frustration and discontent. But the most significant item on the balance of accounts will remain largely invisible and incalculable—the toll in human values taken by continued poverty, segregation, and inequality of opportunity.

Polarization

Another and equally serious consequence is the fact that this course would lead to the permanent establishment of two societies: one predominantly white and located in the suburbs, in smaller cities, and in outlying areas, and one largely Negro located in central cities.

We are well on the way to just such a divided nation.

This division is veiled by the fact that Negroes do not now dominate many central cities. But they soon will, as we have shown, and the new Negro mayors will be facing even more difficult conditions than now exist.

As Negroes succeed whites in our largest cities, the proportion of low-income residents in those cities will probably increase. This is likely even if both white and Negro incomes continue to rise at recent rates, since Negroes have much lower incomes than whites. Moreover, many of the ills of large central cities spring from their age, their location, and their obsolete physical structures. The deterioration and economic decay stemming from these factors have been proceeding for decades and will continue to plague older cities regardless of who resides in them.

These facts underlie the fourfold dilemma of the American city:

Fewer tax dollars come in, as large numbers of middle-income taxpayers move out of central cities and property values and business decline.

More tax dollars are required to provide essential public services and facilities, and to meet the needs of expanding lower income groups.

Each tax dollar buys less, because of increasing costs.

Citizen dissatisfaction with municipal services grows as needs, expectations and standards of living increase throughout the community.

These are the conditions that would greet the Negro-dominated municipal governments that will gradually come to power in many of our major cities. The Negro electorates in those cities probably would demand basic changes in present policies. Like the present white electorates there, they would have to look for assistance to two basic sources: the private sector and the Federal Government.

With respect to the private sector, major private capital investment in those cities might have ceased almost altogether if white-dominated firms and industries decided the risks and costs were too great. The withdrawal of private capital is already far advanced in most all-Negro areas of our large cities. . . .

It is probable, however, that Congress will be more heavily influenced by representatives of the suburban and outlying city electorate. These areas will comprise 40 percent of our total population by 1985, compared with 31 percent in 1960; and central cities will decline from 32 percent to 27 percent.[2]

Since even the suburbs will be feeling the squeeze of higher local government costs, Congress might resist providing the extensive assistance which central cities will desperately need.

Thus the present policies choice, if pursued for any length of time, might

[2] Based on Census Bureau series D projections.

force simultaneously political and economic polarization in many of our largest metropolitan areas. Such polarization would involve large central cities—mainly Negro, with many poor, and nearly bankrupt—on the one hand and most suburbs—mainly white, generally affluent, but heavily taxed—on the other hand.

Some areas might avoid political confrontation by shifting to some form of metropolitan government designed to offer regional solutions for pressing urban problems such as property taxation, air and water pollution, refuse disposal, and commuter transport. Yet this would hardly eliminate the basic segregation and relative poverty of the urban Negro population. It might even increase the Negro's sense of frustration and alienation if it operated to prevent Negro political control of central cities.

The acquisition of power by Negro-dominated governments in central cities is surely a legitimate and desirable exercise of political power by a minority group. It is in an American political tradition exemplified by the achievements of the Irish in New York and Boston.

But such Negro political development would also involve virtually complete racial segregation and virtually complete spatial separation. By 1985, the separate Negro society in our central cities would contain almost 21 million citizens. That is almost 68 percent larger than the present Negro population of central cities. It is also larger than the current population of every Negro nation in Africa except Nigeria.

If developing a racially integrated society is extraordinarily difficult today when 12.1 million Negroes live in central cities, then it is quite clearly going to be virtually impossible in 1985 when almost 21 million Negroes—still much poorer and less educated than most whites—will be living there.

Can Present Policies Avoid Extreme Polarization?

There are at least two possible developments under the present policies choice which might avert such polarization. The first is a faster increase of incomes among Negroes than has occurred in the recent past. This might prevent central cities from becoming even deeper "poverty traps" than they now are. It suggests the importance of effective job programs and higher levels of welfare payments for dependent families.

The second possible development is migration of a growing Negro middle class out of the central city. This would not prevent competition for Federal funds between central cities and outlying areas, but it might diminish the racial undertones of that competition. There is, however, no evidence that a continuation of present policies would be accompanied by any such movement.

The present policies choice plainly would involve continuation of efforts like Model Cities, manpower programs, and the War on Poverty. These are in fact enrichment programs, designed to improve the quality of life in the ghetto.

Because of their limited scope and funds, however, they constitute only very modest steps toward enrichment—and would continue to do so even if these programs were somewhat enlarged or supplemented.

The premise of the enrichment choice is performance. To adopt this choice would require a substantially greater share of national resources—sufficient to make a dramatic, visible impact on life in the urban Negro ghetto.

The Effect of Enrichment on Civil Disorders

Effective enrichment policies probably would have three immediate effects on civil disorders.

First, announcement of specific large-scale programs and the demonstration of a strong intent to carry them out might persuade ghetto residents that genuine remedies for their problems were forthcoming, thereby allaying tensions.

Second, such announcements would strongly stimulate the aspirations and hopes of members of these communities—possibly well beyond the capabilities of society to deliver and to do so promptly. This might increase frustration and discontent, to some extent canceling the first effect.

Third, if there could be immediate action on meaningful job training and the creation of productive jobs for large numbers of unemployed young people, they would become much less likely to engage in civil disorders.

Such action is difficult now, when there are about 585,000 young Negro men aged 14 to 24 in the civilian labor force in central cities—of whom 81,000 or 13.8 percent, are unemployed and probably two or three times as many are underemployed. It will not become easier in the future. By 1975, this age group will have grown to approximately 700,000.

Given the size of the present problem, plus the large growth of this age group, creation of sufficient meaningful jobs will require extensive programs, begun rapidly. Even if the Nation is willing to embark on such programs, there is no certainty that they can be made effective soon enough. . . .

The Negro Middle Class

It can be argued that a rapidly enlarging Negro middle class would also promote Negro out-migration and that the enrichment choice would thus open up an escape hatch from the ghetto. This argument, however, has two weaknesses.

The first is experience. Central cities already have sizable and growing numbers of middle-class Negro families. Yet only a few have migrated from the central city. The past pattern of white ethnic groups gradually moving out of central-city areas to middle-class suburbs has not applied to Negroes. Effective open-housing laws will help make this possible, but it is probable that other more extensive changes in policies and attitudes will be required—and these would extend beyond the enrichment choice.

The second weakness in the argument is time. Even if enlargement of the Negro middle class succeeded in encouraging movement out of the central city, it could not do so fast enough to offset the rapid growth of the ghetto. . . .

Separate but Equal Societies?

The enrichment choice by no means seeks to perpetuate racial segregation. In the end, however, its premise is that disadvantaged Negroes can achieve equality of opportunity with whites while continuing in conditions of nearly complete separation. . . .

The economy of the United States and particularly the sources of employment are preponderantly white. In this circumstance, a policy of separate but equal employment could only relegate Negroes permanently to inferior incomes and economic status.

The best evidence regarding education is contained in recent reports of the Office of Education and Civil Rights Commission which suggest that both racial and economic integration are essential to educational equality for Negroes. . . .

Whether or not enrichment in ghetto areas will really work is not yet known, but the enrichment choice is based on the yet-unproven premise that it will. Certainly, enrichment programs could significantly improve existing ghetto schools if they impelled major innovations. But "separate but equal" ghetto education cannot meet the long-run fundamental educational needs of the central-city Negro population.

The three basic educational choices are: Providing Negro children with quality education in integrated schools; providing them with quality education by enriching ghetto schools; or continuing to provide many Negro children with inferior education in racially segregated school systems, severely limiting their lifetime opportunities.

Consciously or not, it is the third choice that the Nation is now making, and this choice the Commission rejects totally.

In the field of housing, it is obvious that "separate but equal" does not mean really equal. The enrichment choice could greatly improve the quantity, variety, and environment of decent housing available to the ghetto population. It could not provide Negroes with the same freedom and range of choice as whites with equal incomes. . . .

If enrichment programs were effective, they could greatly narrow the gap in income, education, housing, jobs, and other qualities of life between the ghetto and the mainstream. Hence the chances of harsh polarization—or of disorder—in the next 20 years would be greatly reduced. . . .

THE INTEGRATION CHOICE

We believe there are four important reasons why American society must give this course the most serious consideration. First, future jobs are being created primarily in the suburbs, while the chronically unemployed population is increasingly concentrated in the ghetto. This separation will make it more and more difficult for Negroes to achieve anything like full employment in decent jobs. But if, over time, these residents began to find housing outside central cities, they would be exposed to more knowledge of job opportunities, would have much shorter trips to reach jobs, and would have a far better chance of securing employment on a self-sustaining basis.

Second, in the judgment of this Commission, racial and social-class integration is the most effective way of improving the education of ghetto children.

Third, developing an adequate housing supply for low-income and middle-income families and true freedom of choice in housing for Negroes of all income levels will require substantial out-movement. We do not believe that such an out-movement will occur spontaneously merely as a result of increasing prosperity among Negroes in central cities. A national fair housing law is essential to begin such movement. In many suburban areas, a program combining positive incentives with the building of new housing will be necessary to carry it out.

Fourth, and by far the most important, integration is the only course which explicitly seeks to achieve a single nation rather than accepting the present movement toward a duel society. This choice would enable us at least to begin reversing the profoundly divisive trend already so evident in our metropolitan areas—before it becomes irreversible.

CONCLUSIONS

Three critical conclusions emerge from this analysis:

1. The nation is rapidly moving toward two increasingly separate Americas.

Within two decades, this division could be so deep that it would be almost impossible to unite:

a white society principally located in suburbs, in smaller central cities, and in the peripheral parts of large central cities; and

a Negro society largely concentrated within large central cities.

The Negro society will be permanently relegated to its current status, possibly even if we expend great amounts of money and effort in trying to "gild" the ghetto.

2. In the long run, continuation and expansion of such a permanent division threatens us with two perils.

The first is the danger of sustained violence in our cities. The timing, scale, nature, and repercussions of such violence cannot be foreseen. But if it occurred, it would further destroy our ability to achieve the basic American promises of liberty, justice, and equality.

The second is the danger of a conclusive repudiation of the traditional American ideals of individual dignity, freedom, and equality of opportunity. We will not be able to espouse these ideals meaningfully to the rest of the world, to ourselves, to our children. They may still recite the Pledge of Allegiance and say "one nation . . . indivisible." But they will be learning cynicism not patriotism.

3. We cannot escape responsibility for choosing the future of our metropolitan areas and the human relations which develop within them. It is a responsibility so critical that even an unconscious choice to continue present policies has the gravest implications.

That we have delayed in choosing or, by delaying may be making the wrong choice, does not sentence us either to separatism or despair. But we must choose. We will choose. Indeed, we are now choosing.

PART IX

QUESTIONS FOR DISCUSSION

1. What psychological pressures influence the personality of the ghetto dweller?
2. In your view what constitutes acceptable housing for a family? Describe conditions you consider essential to normal, healthy family growth.
3. What are the features of urban life that result in the breakdown of traditional values?

VOCABULARY

Model Cities Program
diversity
block busting
Public Domain
density
barriers
frustration
expectations

slum clearance
slums
ghetto
inertia
polarization
deterioration
renovation
anonymity

UNIQUE URBAN PROBLEMS

Perhaps one of the most perplexing problems of our cities today is our lack of an efficient mass transportation system. Very little progress has been made in up-dating the system to move efficiently the increased masses of humanity. The bus routes in many of our cities have not changed appreciably even though the patterns of cities have changed greatly. Half of our Negro citizens and half of our senior citizens do not own automobiles. Public transportation at reasonable cost is urgently needed to move these people to their jobs, hospital or health centers, and shopping facilities. The federal government is now looking at several proposals for new and improved modes of travel. The Dashaveyor (small electric-powered units), the Gravitrain (high-speed, below ground), express bus (not really suited to many of our major cities), and the air-cushion vehicle are all being studied. The congestion at the cities' airports, both on the ground and in the air, presents dangers to our people and reduces many of the inherent advantages of air travel. The costs to provide efficient transportation at reasonable fares are going to be so large that local, state, and federal governments will have to foot the bill for the capital investment.

Violence is another of the major problems in our cities; it gets worse by the day. It would be fair to say that violence is in a major sense the result of frustrations on the part of many of our citizens. It is more prevalent in our urban neigh-borhoods and overwhelmingly a lower-class phenomenon. A family in Atlanta earning $3,000 per year has a crime rate eight times higher than one earning $9,000. The socially alienated man sees violence as an outlet, as a way of obtaining what he believes he rightly deserves. Anarchical slogans such as "Burn, baby, burn!" are expressions of beliefs that through these actions minorities can gain goals which have long been denied them through normal channels. Violence is a language, crude and dangerous to those who use it, but in the main, a revolution against authentic grievances.

The environment of our cities is bad and getting worse day by day. The exhausts from the internal combustion engine; the pollution from hard detergents, jet aircraft, oil and sewage; and the defacing of our landscape are contributing factors. The ghetto, the educational system, lack of employment, the need for and the inadequacies of welfare, and the noise all contribute to the feeling of not belonging. They are physical and they are psychological in their affect on the human environment. The environment of city life is also affected by mass strikes or slowdowns by public employees in the fields of sanitation (garbage removal), transportation (rail, buses, and subways), law enforcement, fire fighting, and education. The large unions have the power to put the cities in a literal "deep-freeze." A city's health and well-being can be brought to a complete standstill by the determined efforts of strong union leaders. Garbage piled high on the streets is not only unsightly but is a dire threat to our health. Transportation strikes prevent food and other necessities from coming into our cities; they also prevent workers from commuting to and from their work. Strikes or slowdowns by the police or firemen are threats to our safety and our form of government. Strikes by teachers are a threat to our education, a threat not only to our society but to that of future generations—an area where we need to do much more, not less. When are we going to come to the inevitable conclusion that compulsive and binding arbitration must be the answer to these disputes?

Elimination, or at least a reduction, of our many problems of the cities is going to require (1) a dedication to do what has to be done; (2) a monumental planning effort to ensure that we are working toward an environment suitable for a wholesome and worthwhile human habitat; and (3) that funds be provided to get the job accomplished within a reasonable time period. Some of the experts estimate the cost of saving our cities at one trillion dollars. The National Planning Association predicts that it will take slightly over two trillion, spent over the next twenty years.

We have been talking about city problems for many years now. The simple truth of the matter is that we have not done much about them as yet. The future of our nation rests in the cities, and if we do not soon start the reclamation we all know must be done, there is little hope of saving our society. For the most part, we know what has to be done; we need to stop talking and start moving. The time is SHORT!

HOW TO CURE TRAFFIC JAMS

U.S. News & World Report
Interview with John A. Volpe, Secretary of Transportation

As population and private automobiles become more numerous, the human inability to move becomes more frustrating. The average speed in Manhattan has decreased from 11 mph to 7 mph over the last half century. The traffic jams are in our streets, highways, airways, and airports. We no longer have the ability to move large masses of people with efficiency. The federal government has been spending $4.5 to $5 billion per year on the interstate highway system and only about 4 per cent of that figure in other transportation areas. Some efforts are now being made to improve rail facilities. There is an urgent need for major efforts in improving all modes of transportation. The cost will be high but unavoidable.

Q Mr. Secretary, what do you consider the No. 1 problem in transportation in this country?

A Before I came to Washington, I knew about the number of near misses that occur in the air. I felt that air-traffic safety probably would be my No. 1 problem, because I want our people to be safe.

But in the time I have been on the job, I've sat in on a number of meetings of the Council for Urban Affairs, and I've become convinced that our biggest problem is to provide public transportation—mass transportation—particularly in our metropolitan centers.

I prefer to call this "public" rather than "mass" transportation because some people think this problem exists only in the large metropolitan centers where you move people primarily through mass transit. The fact is that traffic congestion is starting to be a problem in medium-size and smaller cities where the bus system has come to the point that it can't afford any longer to stay in business.

Transportation will play a giant part in solving the urban crisis in this nation.

Q Is progress being made in public transportation?

A Progress has been very, very slow indeed. There's a complete imbalance —with the amount of attention and money that has been put into highways.

You know, I was the first Federal Highway Administrator for this huge program of interstate freeways that was launched by President Eisenhower. But we have concentrated on highways almost to the exclusion of other public transportation. The Federal Government is now spending about 4.5 or 5 billion dollars a year on highways and only about 140 million dollars a year on public transit.

Q How is this transit money being used?

A About a third has been used for research and demonstration, about two thirds for grants to local authorities for new buses, rail cars and other facilities. We are putting about 130 million dol-

Reprinted from *U.S. News & World Report*, June 9, 1969. Copyright 1969 U.S. News & World Report, Inc.

lars into the Bay Area Rapid Transit system in and around San Francisco because it is the first really brand-new system in the nation.

An interesting thing about the BART line is the way the State highway department and the transit authority are co-operating. You hear about the great dispute and rages between highway interests and transit interests, but there you have an example of co-operation such as I have never seen before.

The rail line will use a common corridor—10 miles long—with the highway department. And the highway department has not only worked with the transit people in selecting and buying the corridor for joint use, but is actually taking the bids and supervising the construction work on basic elements of the rail system—stations, steel structures and so on.

Q Are rail systems the answer to mass-transit needs?

A You cannot say that any particular system will fit every city and town. In many cases, express-bus lanes could be of considerable help and might be the only thing required. In other cases, express-bus lanes would be useful but would never do the total job.

We are looking at a number of avenues open to use in the field of rapid mass transportation. I don't like the term "transit" because that connotes the same system we've had for 50 or 60 years. What President Nixon wants us to do is to look ahead 5, 10, 15 years.

We have three or four options, and I'm trying to narrow them down: First, there is the tracked air-cushion vehicle that could glide along a track at 250 or more miles per hour. A prototype has been tested in France for about two years, and the French are now going to construct a full-scale system on a seven-mile track. If all goes well, this will eventually be part of a 60-mile line from Paris to Orleans.

We have two firms—Grumman Aircraft Engineering and General Electric —working on tracked air-cushion vehicles for us. We also have a contract with a British firm that has been working on this system.

Q How soon could a radically new system of this kind be put into service?

A Well, I can't wait until the year 2000 to solve our problems. Cities right now are practically choked from traffic volumes such that the average American spends 13 per cent of his working day behind another automobile— breathing in exhaust fumes. Within two or three years unless we do something, congestion is going to bring traffic in our metropolitan areas almost to a standstill.

In New York City, 52 years ago the average speed in the center of Manhattan was 11 miles an hour with a horse and buggy. Today, after 52 years of technological progress—with men orbiting the moon—we now travel at seven miles an hour in the center of Manhattan.

With situations of this kind at hand, how can anybody say we have to wait for another 10 years to carry on research on new methods of coping with congestion?

We could start building a tracked air-cushion system probably within a year—an actual full-sized system in some location where it is badly needed.

Q How would this type of equipment be powered?

A At first, with turbofan engines of the sort that are used in airliners. However, we can be testing linear-induction motors that would completely eliminate air pollution from this type of train. When we get the new motors, we would merely substitute them for the ones installed initially.

Q That's one system. What's the second?
A The "Dashaveyor." A 5½-mile system has been constructed for use in a mine. The maximum speed for this is 80 miles an hour, and some people say that 80 miles an hour in a city is probably as fast as you want to go.
Q What is the Dashaveyor to be like?
A They would be electric-powered, self-propelled units, relatively small—say, six to 24 passengers. Units would operate automatically over a fixed guideway, either individually or in trains of variable length. Terrain would be no problem. The units can climb steep grades—vertically if necessary, like an elevator. With wheels above and below the rails, units would be nonderailable. Guideways would be lightweight, attractive and unobtrusive.
Q Is it like the "Skybus" that is operating in South Park, near Pittsburgh?
A To a degree, yes.
Q It runs on rails and is automatically controlled—
A Yes.

Now, a third proposal that I have looked into that intrigues me is the "Gravitrain." Some of the people in the Department pooh-pooh it, but I am going to take a closer look. There are many people who feel that the problems inherent in this idea can be worked out. The inventor, Lawrence K. Edwards, and others have invested about half a million dollars of their own money in this device and would like us now to put some federal money into it.

The Gravitrain would require no right-of-way on the surface of the earth and cause no air pollution whatsoever. It would have speeds of up to 250 miles an hour and would operate mainly 1,000 to 1,500 feet underground.

You would drill a tube that would dip down to those depths between stations and then back up again, sort of like the arc of a pendulum. The train would operate by gravity and pneumatic pressure. What you do is compress air behind the train as it is going downhill and then use the pent-up energy to push the train uphill to the next station.
Q How far apart would the stations be?
A They could be as far apart as 20 miles.

While I was in San Francisco recently, I flew by helicopter to the test site. Mr. Edwards said he can build this system from Dulles Airport into the city of Washington with three stops. He claims he could move people over that distance—about 26 miles—in 7 or 8 minutes.
Q Could the Gravitrain be used in a city such as New York where you count on having subway stops every few blocks?
A Probably not, although you could have a stop every mile or two. You couldn't use it in the most congested areas, but it has tremendous possibilities for moving people from airport to city.

Look at what it would do here in the Washington area, with National Airport as crowded as it is and Dulles being used at only about 20 or 25 per cent of capacity. A tremendous number of people would be taken off the roads—because rich man, poor man will use a system that is clean, that operates without bumps.
Q Would you get a smooth ride from a train that was always diving down or swooping upward?
A The inventor took an ordinary piece of white chalk and stood it on end on a little car on a model of the Gravitrain. It went downhill and up to the next station, and that piece of chalk remained upright. Then he took the chalk—a round piece of chalk—and

laid it flat, and I said, "If it doesn't fall off when the car is going down, it certainly will fall off as it goes up the hill." But that piece of chalk stayed right there—never moved!

Another thing that impressed me about the Gravitrain is that the operational costs are claimed to be considerably less than the typical rapid-transit system of today.

Q How about construction costs?

A They maintain that construction, even with today's tunneling costs, would run about 15 million dollars a mile, which is no more than the Bay Area Rapid Transit District is spending. If the laser method of tunneling is developed fully, costs would be lower.

Remember, you don't have to tear down houses or move families out. You don't run into utility lines. I suppose you do have to go to the homeowner and say, "Look, I'd like to drill a little tube 1,000 feet below your house. You'll never know it's happening. We'll give you a bond that there won't be any cracks in your house, and we'll give you something for permission to do this."

Q How would you get people in and out of the stations?

A The line would be about 125 to 150 feet below ground at the stations. You'd have escalators to take people up to ground level. They have escalators for the BART line in San Francisco.

WHERE EXPRESS BUSES HELP

Q You mentioned four methods of transporting people. What is the fourth one?

A Express-bus service. This is what some people would like to feel could do the job in many cases.

In areas where the climate is attractive, such as Los Angeles, the express-bus lane added to the present freeway lanes could be very helpful. I predict that this wouldn't work in Boston because—let's face it—there are times in winter when it could take you four hours to get into the city by bus.

However, the express-bus lanes could be used where you need mobility —in expanding areas. You can adapt a bus operation a great deal more easily than rail rapid transit. Once you build a rail lane, you fix yourself.

Mayor [Carl B.] Stokes of Cleveland came in to see us about a month ago. The bus routes presently being utilized in Cleveland are not too different from what they were 25 or 30 years ago. Yet the patterns of the city have changed. Industry has moved and so forth, but the bus network hasn't changed.

So the city has asked us for a grant to make a complete survey of their present system and to make recommendations as to how it can be revised to do a great deal better job of moving people from the "ghetto" to where the jobs are.

I was fascinated to learn how much of a part transportation plays in any solution of the urban problem, because the citizen in the "ghetto" area who wants to work—and a great many want to work—in many cases can't get to a job because he doesn't have an automobile.

Half of the Negroes in this country don't own an automobile. Half of the people over 65 years old don't own an automobile. Some 67 per cent of the families in this country that earn $2,000 or less don't own an automobile.

These are people we have to try to do something for if we're going to eliminate racial violence, poverty and so forth. I think we can fight the poverty battle a great deal better by providing public transportation.

What good is it to say there's a job

12 miles away if a person can't get to it, or perhaps it takes him an hour and a half and costs him $1.50? We've also got to enable that person to get to a health center or hospital that maybe isn't in the "ghetto," or to a school of higher learning.

PROBLEMS WITH UNIONS

Q Are you running into problems with the unions in trying to work out special bus services for people in the slum areas to get them to jobs in the suburbs?

A Under terms of some of the federal grants, unions have insisted that we clear with the Labor Department if the money is to be used to buy up a line or establish a line.

In Boston, we actually had to buy out the Eastern Massachusetts Street Railway Company—to protect the rights of all the employes—before the Federal Government would consummate the grant. The employes of the Eastern Massachusetts line became employes of the Massachusetts Bay Transportation Authority and got the same wages as the MBTA, which were higher than those being paid by the private company.

Q Will the Government own these new transportation systems you're working on?

A No. The Government must take the leadership in the research and development to determine which of these new systems is most useful, which ones involve the least controversy as far as right-of-way is concerned, which ones cause the least pollution and so forth—in other words, the system that, in particular areas, would best serve the public interest.

We have to develop systems to the point where we can say to San Francisco or Pittsburgh or Atlanta: "We

feel *this* system now has been sufficiently tested so that we can recommend it to you, if you want to use it."

Then, depending on what Congress does with the public mass-transportation bill that will be submitted to it, we would give the community or the local transit authority—whoever would run the system—a federal grant.

Q How large a grant?

A At the present it is two thirds of the capital investment. Whether it should remain at two thirds or be changed—perhaps to 90 per cent as in the Interstate Highway program—remains to be seen.

Our present thinking is that the Federal Government should not be involved in paying operating subsidies—money to cover deficits that might accrue as a result of the operation of a transit system.

Q Do you believe that these systems can be self-supporting, apart from the capital investment needed to set them up?

A I am convinced that if you give the people clean, fast, efficient service, they are going to utilize mass transit and high-speed trains, because people are being frustrated more and more every day as the crunch of automobiles gets heavier and heavier.

Q What evidence is there that you can get people to leave their cars at home and use public transportation instead?

A Look at the success of the high-speed "Metroliner" [train] between Washington and New York. I predict that if we improve the track and do some other things that will cut the express time down to two hours or two hours and fifteen minutes, we will relieve a tremendous amount of the pressure on the New York area airports, which are now saturated.

Q Are you encouraged by the other

experiments that have been made with local transit programs?

A Yes.

Q Could improved transit systems pay their own way at the fare box?

A I believe so, if you don't take the principal and interest into consideration. The community, the State, the Federal Government are going to have to provide for capital costs. And the systems are going to have to give the public clean, comfortable, fast service. We've simply got to get more than just the poor people to ride the trains and buses.

Look at what we've done in Boston —beautiful art work in some of the stations. Look at the Montreal subway stations. That service is being used.

The Metroliner is being used. The railroad has had excellent response. Yesterday afternoon I was shown a list of things that can be done: One shaves off two minutes, another shaves off three minutes, another 10 minutes. You add them all up, and you can take off anywhere from 15 to 25 minutes on the Washington-to-New York run, and probably in excess of 45 minutes on the New York-to-Boston run.

If you can go from New York to Washington in two hours or two hours and a quarter without having to fight traffic at airports, without having to worry about spending half an hour or more in taxis, I think you're going to get a lot more people to use this fast rail service.

Q Will that hurt the airlines?

A You're not going to reduce the passengers on the airlines so badly that they are going to go out of business— far from it.

What I have tried to say to all modes of transportation is that all of them—trains, buses, airliners, ships— are going to have to do an excellent job in the next decade to meet the demand

arising from the increase in the American economy and American population.

EASING AIRPORT CONGESTION

Q What can you do to get airports which are already jammed ready for the bigger planes that are about to come into use?

A We have prepared an airways-airport program which some people say has been rejected by the White House. That is not so. One or two agencies had reservations about some of the items in the package, and we're in the process of reviewing those. Preparing legislation isn't a one-shot job. Some people don't like trust funds. So we have a selling job to do.

Q What are the ingredients in this airways package of yours?

A First, we have tried to develop some short-range things that can be done. Some of them are already being done—a minor amount of automation.

In Jacksonville, we are speeding up the process of automation so that by September we will eliminate a great deal of the handiwork that the controllers do.

You know, I was in one of our control centers, and I thought, "My goodness, this is 1969 and here we have these fellows at a bench writing out little things that one controller passes on to another. And at the same time, we have the BART line being built for San Francisco and Oakland, where you just press a couple of buttons and all kinds of things happen."

It seems to me that there's no reason why we can't have the kind of control at airports that will eliminate a great deal of the talk that now has to go on between the pilot and the control tower.

All of the necessary equipment isn't available at this time. So, on a short-range basis, we are having to limit the number of flights at some of our busiest airports and take some other measures.

But for the long pull, we believe aviation has to assume its rightful share of the cost of the service the Federal Government will provide.

HIGHER TAXES AHEAD

Q How much are you going to have to spend?

A The budget of the Federal Aviation Administration will be about a billion dollars in the fiscal year that begins July 1, and we may have to spend from 2 to 3 billion dollars a year by the end of the next 10 years.

We believe strongly that we are going to have to develop some user charges to cover this bill, and the general-aviation community—the users of sport planes, business jets and so forth —has, in the past, fought user charges. We've had discussions with several of the associations that represent general aviation, and I would say we've made some progress. Some of them at least agree that, after all, it takes just as much of the time of the controller at the airport to bring in a little plane with two people in it as it does to monitor an airliner with 80 or 90 passengers.

We think we will need a user charge on general aviation, increases in the taxes paid by the airlines, possibly a head tax on the international traveler as he leaves the country. With these and one or two other measures, we can develop enough revenue to take care of the airways—that is, the runways, control towers, radio beacons and other navigation aids.

Q What about terminal buildings?

A Some people say the Federal Government shouldn't get involved in paying for terminals. I'm not so sure.

At any rate, we believe that, over a 10-year period, the user charges would grow enough to cover all of the present billion-dollar outlay and then some. The fund might grow to 2 or 3 billion dollars a year and be self-supporting.

Remember that the number of passenger miles has doubled in the last four years and will triple again in the next 10 years—to say nothing about air freight, which is growing by leaps and bounds.

All this will mean automatic increases in the amount of revenue brought in by the user charges.

Q If you have to have more airports to take care of this increase in traffic, where are you going to put them? Won't they be farther and farther from the cities and hence more and more inconvenient?

A General Eisenhower told me, in a 45-minute talk I had with him at Walter Reed Hospital the Friday before the [Nixon] inauguration: "John, 12 or 15 years ago I felt—and I feel just as strongly about it today—the airport that is going to take care of the large air carrier is going to have to be 25— possibly as much as 35—miles from the core city."

You are going to have to take the traveler into the city by means of the helicopter, the V/STOL [vertical short takeoff and landing] plane, Gravitrain or some such method.

The V/STOL plane may be a partial answer in New York. It will enable you to fly from the center of one city— Boston, for example—in the Northeast corridor to the center of New York, or from New York to the center of Washington, or even Boston to Washington. You might be able to take off from the top of a building a thousand feet long and land on another building.

The speed will be less than the jets,

but consider the amount of time you now spend on the ground. This kind of plane service would still be way ahead of the game, and it would relieve a lot of the congestion at the Kennedy International Airport and also eliminate the rubber-tire traffic that is now involved in getting from the airport to the city.

RAIL SERVICE STILL NEEDED

Q If you have that kind of air service from the heart of the cities, will you still need some kind of rapid rail service to the major airports outside the cities?

A Yes—otherwise you still won't be able to take care of the increasing number of long-haul passengers. The V/STOL's are not likely to be used over distances of 1,000 miles or more.

Now, in Florida there is a large airport being developed about 40 or 45 miles outside of Miami. We have already made a grant for a study into the feasibility of constructing a tracked air-cushion system from that airport to Miami and also to the west coast of Florida. This could be a logical place to try out this system.

Q Wouldn't a line of that kind interfere with wildlife and the flow of water in the Everglades?

A This airport is not in the Everglades National Park. It is all State-owned land. There are certainly some good arguments to be made for not disrupting wildlife, but sometimes you have to weigh the balance—what you lose against what you gain. The effect on the underground water flow is one of the things that will be considered in the study we are paying for.

Q Many of the transit improvements you are talking about are going to take a lot of time. How are you going to convince cities to get started on them?

A We have announced a special pilot program involving five cities: Seattle, Denver, Atlanta, Pittsburgh and Dallas. A joint venture—or what Washington, with its fancy language, calls a "consortium"—headed by Arthur D. Little, Inc., will try to develop systems that can command public support.

Remember, the voters defeated a bond issue for a rapid-transit system in Los Angeles last year, though there probably is no city in America that needs public transportation more than that city.

I think that if you develop a plan for a co-ordinated, balanced transportation system, and don't just tackle rapid transit alone or highways alone or train service alone, you can sell it to the public. A lot of the leadership is going to have to come from within the community, and we have this contracted with Urban America, Inc., to help develop this kind of leadership across the country. They will hold public hearings in various places.

You know, it is going to take a year and a half, under the best circumstances, to develop public support for a program. You're really talking about two or two and a half years before you actually start construction. By that time we will, I think, have some new systems ready to go—particularly the tracked air-cushion vehicle and maybe the Gravitrain.

Then, if a city doesn't do what is necessary, we will be in a position of saying, "You don't want mass transportation? O.K., then there simply are places in this city that you can't get into at all—no automobiles in maybe an area a mile by two miles." Or the city may be faced with having to lay down a rule that if you want to come into that congested section, it will cost you 50 cents to go there by car.

In other words, if we don't have mass transportation, the center of many of these cities is simply not going to be accessible to all the people who want to go there.

Q You spoke earlier of using a trust fund built up with user charges to solve some aviation problems. How would you pay for the federal share of the cost of mass transit?

A If you try to finance mass transit entirely with user charges, you will be defeating the purpose. We are trying to get people to use this kind of transportation—in many cases our poorer people —and it has been proven in almost every city that the minute you increase the transit fare by a nickel or a dime, passenger volume goes down.

Q What financing do you favor?

A There are various taxes that are now going into that Treasury's general fund. We hope that, with the termination of the Vietnam war, we could take one of these tax sources and dedicate a portion of it to a trust fund for mass transportation.

Q Is the 7 per cent automobile excise tax a candidate?

A That is a possibility. The trouble is that some of the automobile manufacturers hope that the tax will be eliminated in about three years. On the other hand, there are some enlightened people in the gasoline industry and the auto industry who realize that you're going to come to a point where the sale of automobiles and gasoline may be curtailed because you just won't be able to move the cars for all the traffic.

One refiner, the Jenney Manufacturing Company in Boston, has taken out full-page advertisements in the newspapers advocating expansion of our mass-transit systems because they believe that if people could drive out to visit a brother or a married daughter in an hour instead of fighting traffic for two hours, they would probably do it more often.

Enlightened vision may permit us to tap the automobile excise tax. Perhaps 25 per cent of the revenue from it could go into a dedicated fund.

BILLIONS FOR MASS TRANSIT

Q How much do you think you will need for the mass-transit program?

A Our plans envision starting on a moderate scale with something like 300 or 400 million dollars a year, reaching possibly a billion dollars in the fourth year and leveling off at that point.

Q What about your Interstate Highway program? When will this be completed?

A Around 1974 or 1975.

Q What will the program have cost by that time?

A Well, our educated guess when it started in 1955 was 27 billion dollars. The most recent estimate is about 58 or 60 billion.

The way construction wages are going up, I would venture the guess that the final figure will be closer to 70 billion. But remember that this started out to be a 40,000-mile system, and it is now being expanded to 42,500 miles.

Q Won't you have to keep on extending this highway program indefinitely as travel increases?

A Not necessarily the Interstate network. We will be building highways as long as you and I are alive—and then some. However, I think the emphasis will probably be shifted from the Interstate System to the urban arterial highways and the rural secondary roads, which have, in many cases, not had sufficient attention.

Q What part of the cost of improving these roads will be paid for by the Federal Government?

A As you know, we now have the Government paying 90 per cent of the cost of the Interstate System and 50 per cent of the cost of building other roads. There is some sentiment for having just one formula for all construction, once the Interstate program is completed. It could be 65 or 70 per cent federal.

Q Who will pay to widen the Interstate highways which already are becoming crowded in some places?

A It has been proven that you just are not going to get the job done with highways alone. You can lay down a 12-lane expressway and still not do the job. As a matter of fact, what you do is just make more congestion. We can't tear down half our cities, and that is what you probably would end up doing if you tried to take care of this job with highways alone. That's why I'll be fighting so hard for public transportation—because this is the way we've just got to travel.

That isn't to say we stop the highway program. There are some places where it would seem that we ought to build more highways or widen those we have, but in many cases the answer will be public transportation without expanding the highway networks any great amount beyond what has already been projected.

SAFER HIGHWAYS, DRIVERS

Q Are there ways to make highways safer?

A The statistics speak for themselves: For every five miles of the Interstate Highway System we complete, we save one life per year. That is because we have eliminated the hot-dog stands, the access is limited to the interchanges, and so on.

The bigger area where we can effect a saving in lives is in the education of the driver and in the vehicle itself.

Q Which is more important?

A They have to go hand in hand. But if you ask me which has the most potential for saving lives, I would say it is the driver. Just about half of the 55,000 people who were killed on the highways last year were killed because of alcohol.

We have made some advances in the car. For example, there have been no fatal injuries from impact with the new energy-absorbing steering columns. The old-type steering column was responsible for spearing half the drivers who were injured in crashes.

Q Are motor-vehicle inspections effective?

A I think they could be made more effective in some cases. Especially in those States where the inspections are done by a public agency, they are pretty good. I don't say they can't be improved. That is one of the things our National Highway Safety Bureau is looking at.

Q Can anything really be done about the drunken driver?

A I think you ought to have a breath-analyzer test in every State. You can't force a man to take the test—that isn't constitutional. But if he objects to taking the test, he automatically has his license suspended for a period of months. You don't have to do this many times before the word gets around. That approach has worked in Britain. It has reduced traffic accidents and the death rate considerably.

By the way, though I hope we can reduce our annual toll of 55,000 lives considerably, the fact is that our safety record per 100,000 miles of travel is better than that of any other nation in the world.

PLANS FOR THE "SST"

Q Are you going to continue with the development of the supersonic transport, and, if so, how do you propose to pay for it?

A I don't think that in a risk venture involving the large amount of money that is involved here, you can do it without Government guarantee.

Now, although some people are in favor of suspending work on the SST, that raises a number of problems:

You would scatter to the winds 20,000 people who have been gathered over the last eight years to work on this project. If you lose that group, it would take a couple of years to assemble a new one. So that if you suspend the program for a year or two, you end up losing three or four years.

Then there is the cost factor. Your cost at the end of this period will be even higher than it is today. We are trying to develop ways and means of financing the SST that will be more acceptable than a simple appropriation of funds by Congress, though all of us recognize that the straight-appropriation method probably is the cheapest, in the final analysis.

We might set up a corporation like Comsat [Communications Satellite Corporation] that could raise the money by selling stock and bonds, with some federal guarantee of the bonds. The ultimate cost might be no more than 300 or 400 millions in excess of the straight-appropriations method.

I feel we ought to give consideration to the construction of the prototypes. If we develop a plane that is economically viable, that holds the noise down to a level that is acceptable, then there is no question in my mind that American and foreign airlines will buy this plane and pay enough so that further Government backing will not be needed from that point on.

Q Would the Government have to invest any cash during the development phase?

A No, but remember you haven't arrived at the point today where you can guarantee a plane that will work. So the Government would be taking the risk. But, after all, this is the kind of risk that the governments of England and France are taking.

Q All things considered, would you say an American SST is going to be built?

A I am not sure of that. The British and French together are going to build an SST, and Russia has one. I don't see how the United States of America —supposedly the leading power in the world—can stop aeronautical research and progress in this country, though I know what the other needs are, in terms of feeding the poor and so on.

I think of all the technological "fallout" that comes from the SST program to the Defense Department and the National Aeronautics and Space Administration, the number of jobs it will provide—anywhere from 50,000 to 100,000 over the entire country.

Q Do you expect to invest more money on the development of high-speed trains like the Metroliner?

A We will spend a few millions more on demonstrations, but I am satisfied that the railroads are going to be able to make money on these trains, or at least break even. And the railroads will keep these new trains going if they can get a break-even proposition.

VIOLENCE: INNATE OR LEARNED

Time

Violent behavior is as old as man yet the debate over whether violence is learned or innate continues. Perhaps some combination of the above may be true. Man may well possess the capacity for violence, yet something is needed to set off this violence. Certainly there are causes of violence and certainly violence can be lessened. It is up to man to find a way to control or positively channel this emotion.

Violence is not only an urban but overwhelmingly a lower-class phenomenon. In Atlanta, for example, neighborhoods with family incomes below $3,000 show a violent-crime rate eight times higher than among $9,000 families. In the middle class, violence is perhaps sublimated increasingly in sport or other pursuits. Says one sociologist: "The gun and fist have been substantially replaced by financial ability, by the capacity to manipulate others in complex organizations, and by intellectual talent. The thoughtful wit, the easy verbalizer, even the striving musician and artist are equivalents of male assertiveness, where broad shoulders and fighting fists were once the major symbols."

What are the seeds of violence? Freud found "a powerful measure of desire for aggression" in human instincts. He added: "The very emphasis of the commandment "Thou shalt not kill" makes it certain that we are descended from an endlessly long chain of generations of murderers, whose love of murder was in their blood, as it is perhaps also in ours." Further, Freud held that man possesses a death instinct which, since it cannot be satisfied ex-cept in suicide, is instead turned outward as aggression against others. Dr. Frederic Wertham, noted crusader against violence, disagrees sharply and argues that violence is learned behavior, not a product of nature but of society: "The violent man is not the natural but the socially alienated man."

The fact is that if violence is not innate, it is a basic component of human behavior. The German naturalist Konrad Lorenz believes that, unlike other carnivores, man did not at an early stage develop inhibitions against killing members of his own species—because he was too weak. As he developed weapons, he learned to kill, and he also learned moral restraints, but these never penetrated far enough. Writes Lorenz: "The deep emotional layers of our personality simply do not register the fact that the cocking of a forefinger to release a shot tears the entrails of another man."

The yearning for nonviolence is as real as the yearning for love but, East or West, no religion has succeeded in establishing a society based on it. When trying to point to a really nonviolent community, anthropologists are usually forced to resort to the Arapesh of New

Guinea or the Pygmies of the Ituri rain forest in the Congo. The human impulse to violence cannot be completely denied or suppressed. When that is tried, the result is often an inner violence in man that can burst out all the more fiercely later. At times the U.S. displays a kind of false prudery about violence to the point where in the words of psychiatrist Robert Coles, "almost anything related to forcefulness and the tensions between people is called violent." While this attitude (including Dr. Wertham's frequent blasts at anything from military toys to Batman) is plainly unrealistic, there is no denying that a gruesome violence on screens and in print is threatening to get out of hand. According to one theory, such vicarious experience of violence is healthy because it relieves the viewer's own aggressions. But recent tests suggest the opposite.

Violence can be a simple, rational reaching for a goal, in its legal form of war or its illegal form of crime. It can often be irrational, as in a seemingly senseless killing or quarrel. But the distinction between irrational and rational violence is not easily drawn. Even the insane murderer kills to satisfy a need entirely real to him. Violence is often caused by "displaced aggression," when anger is forced to aim at a substitute target. Every psychologist knows that a man might beat his child because he cannot beat his boss. And a man may even murder because he feels rejected or "alienated." But what leads one man in such a situation to kill and another merely to get drunk is a question psychologists have never really answered. There is no doubt that violence has a cathartic effect, and the pressures that cause it must find an outlet of one kind or another. (Japan's Matsushita Electric Company has set up a dummy of the foreman that workers can beat up on a given day once a week, thereby presumably releasing their aggressions.)

But the aims of violence are usually mixed. Several violent codes combine a functional purpose with an emotional mystique. This was true of the aristocratic dueling code, which served to maintain a social hierarchy that became enshrouded in trappings of honor and death. It is true of the city gang, which functions as a rough and ready community but also includes a mystique in which violence is equated with courage and crime with merit. It is, finally, true of revolutionary ideology, which combines the brutal but often practical belief that only violence can pull down the existing order through a crude poetry about the purifying properties of blood and fire. "I believe in the cutting off of heads," proclaimed Marat during the French Revolution, and his contemporary, the Marquis de Sade, preached, in the duller pages of his books, the virtue of murder as policy. Explains Brandeis University sociologist Lewis Coser: "The act of violence commits a man symbolically to the revolutionary movement and breaks his ties with his previous life. He is, so to speak, reborn." The late Frantz Fanon, a polemicist for anti-colonial revolution, wrote: "Violence is a cleansing force. It frees the native from his inferiority complex."

It is something resembling this revolutionary mystique that Stokely Carmichael and a few others are trying to impose on the American Negro movements. Mixed with the anarchical slogans of "Burn, baby, burn!" and "Tear down the courthouses," there is a calculated conviction that violence is above all else a language, and that this language, through fear, will persuade white society to give things to the Negro that it would not otherwise give. Says Lester McKinney, Washington head of S.N.C.C.: "In the minds of the people, history has proved that any meaningful social change has come through a bloody revolution." Many Negro leaders point to the violent tactics of the labor movement in gaining its ends. Even Negro sociologist Kenneth Clark, no advocate of black power, calls violence "the cutting edge of justice." Social change for Negroes is moving faster than at any time in 100 years; for that very reason, Negroes were able to lament that things were still moving too slowly. The riots, as the President's Crime Commission report puts it, are a way to "let America know."

But the language of violence is crude and dangerous for those who use it. As Hannah Arendt notes, the Western tradition is full of violence and its legend seems to say, "whatever brotherhood human beings may be capable of has grown out of fratricide"; yet she also points out that neither wars nor revolutions are "ever completely determined by violence. Where violence rules absolutely, everything and everybody must fall silent." Violence is not power. In the last analysis it is an admission of failure, a desire for a magical shortcut, an act of despair. Shameful though conditions in the Negro ghettos are, violence is not really the only language left in which to appeal for improvement.

Dealing with violence, the U.S. faces several tasks, none easy. One is to provide more intelligent, effective law enforcement and, through legislation, to do away with the dangerous unfettered sale of firearms. Another is nothing less than the elimination of the ghetto and what it stands for—an increasingly disaffected population. Though probably there will always be violence—out of anger or greed, love or madness—large-scale, socially significant violence is usually caused by authentic grievances, and the U.S. should be able to narrow if not eliminate these. But that leaves, finally, the individual flash or explosion of violence; and to deal with this, man must learn more about man —the mystery that can turn creative energy into brute force, a peaceful crowd into a mob, and an ineffectual weakling into a mass murderer.

THE INALIENABLE RIGHT TO A DECENT ENVIRONMENT

Gaylord Nelson

Senator Nelson has long been a leader in the field of pollution control. This article clearly summarizes the many sources of pollution that have escalated in direct proportion to our advancing technology. The air we breathe, our lakes and rivers, and our once beautiful countryside are being polluted at a rate that is rapidly destroying our environment. "Standing knee deep in garbage, throwing rockets at the moon" by the American balladeer, Pete Seeger, is not far off target. The trend must be reversed *now*. Senator Nelson has proposed an amendment to

Senate Joint Resolution 169, "Introduction of a Joint Resolution Relating to an Environmental Agenda for the 1970's," *Congressional Record*, Jan. 19, 1970.

our Constitution which states simply that: "Every person has the inalienable right to a decent environment. The United States and every State shall guarantee this right." The program is now gathering speed—the battle must be won.

Mr. President, in the nearly 40 years since Franklin D. Roosevelt said in his first inaugural address that "this great Nation will endure as it has endured, will revive and will prosper," our economy has soared to levels that no one in the 1930's could have imagined. In these past four decades we have become the wealthiest nation on earth by almost any measure of production and consumption.

As the economic boom and the post war population explosion continued to break all records, a national legend developed: With science and technology its tools, the private enterprise system could accomplish anything.

We assumed that, if private enterprise could turn out more automobiles, airplanes, and TV sets than all the rest of the world combined, somehow it could create a transportation system that would work. If we were the greatest builders in the world, we need not worry about our poor and about the planning and building of our cities. Private enterprise with enough technology and enough profit would manage that just fine.

In short, we assumed that, if private enterprise could be such a spectacular success in the production of goods and services, it could do our social planning for us, too, set our national priorities, shape our social system, and even establish our individual aspirations. . . .

In the 1960's the era of fantastic achievement marched on to levels unprecedented in the history of man. It was the decade when man walked on the moon—when medical magic transplanted the human heart—when the computer's mechanical wizardry be-

came a part of daily life—and when, instead of "a chicken in every pot," the national aim seemed to be two cars in every garage, a summer home, a color television set, and a vacation in Europe.

From the small farmers and small merchants of the last century, we had become the "consumer society," with science and technology as the New Testament and the gross national product as the Holy Grail.

One might have thought we would have emerged triumphantly from the 1960's with a shout: "Bring on the next decade."

We have not. For, in addition to the other traumatic national and international events, the 1960's have produced another kind of "top of the decade" list. It has been a decade when the darkening cloud of pollution seriously began degrading the thin envelope of air surrounding the globe; when pesticides and unrestricted waste disposal threatened the productivity of all the oceans of the world; when virtually every lake, river, and watershed in America began to show the distressing symptoms of being overloaded with polluting materials.

These pivotal events have begun to warn the Nation of a disturbing new paradox: The mindless pursuit of quantity is destroying—not enhancing—the opportunity to achieve quality in our lives. In the words of the American balladeer, Pete Seeger, we have found ourselves "standing knee deep in garbage, throwing rockets at the moon."

Cumulatively, "progress—American style" adds up each year to 200 million tons of smoke and fumes, 7 million junked cars, 20 million tons of paper, 48 billion cans, and 28 billion bottles.

It also means bulldozers gnawing away at the landscape to make room for more unplanned expansion, more leisure time but less open space in which to spend it, and so much reckless progress that we face even now a hostile environment.

As one measure of the rate of consumption that demands our resources and creates our vast wastes, it has been estimated that all the American children born in just one year will use up 200 million pounds of steel, 9.1 billion gallons of gasoline, and 25 billion pounds of beef during their lifetimes.

To provide the electricity for our air conditioners, a Kentucky hillside is strip-mined. To provide the gasoline for our automobiles, the ocean floor is drilled for oil. To provide the sites for our second homes, the shore of a pristine lake is subdivided.

The unforeseen—or ignored—consequences of an urbanizing, affluent, mobile, more populous society have poisoned, scarred, and polluted what once was a beautiful land "from sea to shining sea."

It is the laboring man, living in the shadows of the spewing smokestacks of industry, who feels the bite of the "disposable society." Or the commuter inching in spurts along an expressway. Or the housewife paying too much for products that begin to fall apart too soon. Or the student watching the university building program destroy a community. Or the black man living alongside the noisy, polluted truck routes through the central city ghetto.

There is not merely irritation now with the environmental problems of daily life—there is a growing fear that what the scientists have been saying is all too true, that man is on the way to defining the terms of his own extinction.

Today it can be said that there is no clear air left in the United States. The last vestige of pure air was near Flagstaff, Ariz., but it disappeared 6 years ago.

Today it can also be said that there is no river or lake in the country that has not been affected by the pervasive wastes of our society. On Lake Superior, the last clean Great Lake, a mining company is dumping 60,000 tons of iron ore process wastes a day directly into the lake.

Tomorrow? Responsible scientists have predicted that accelerating rates of air pollution could become so serious by the 1980's that many people may be forced on the worst days to wear breathing helmets to survive outdoors.

It has also been predicted that in 20 years man will lived in domed cities.

Dr. S. Dillon Ripley, Secretary of the Smithsonian Institution, believes that in 25 years somewhere between 75 and 80 percent of all the species of living animals will be extinct.

Dr. Paul Ehrlich, eminent California ecologist, and many other scientists predict the end of the oceans as a productive resource within the next 50 years unless pollution is stopped. The United States provides an estimated one-third to one-half of the industrial pollution of the sea. It is especially ironic that, even as we pollute the sea, there is hope that its resources can be used to feed tens of millions of hungry people.

As in the great depression, America is again faced with a crisis that has to do with material things—but it is an entirely different sort of dilemma. In effect, America has bought environmental disaster on a national installment plan: Buy affluence now and let future generations pay the price. Trading away the future is a high price to pay for an electric swizzle stick—or a car with greater horsepower. But then, the environmental consequences have never been included on the label.

It is a situation we have gotten into, not by design, but by default. Somehow, the environmental problems have mushroomed upon us from the blind side—although, again, the scientists knew decades ago that they were coming.

What has been missing is the unity of purpose, forged out of a threat to our national health or security or prestige, that we so often seem to have found only during world war.

But there is now, I think, a great awakening underway. We have begun to recognize that our security is again threatened—not from the outside, but from the inside—not by our enemies, but by ourselves. As Pogo quaintly put it, "We have met the enemy and they is us."

A Gallup poll taken for the National Wildlife Federation last year revealed that 51 percent of all persons interviewed were deeply disturbed about the grim tide of pollution.

Growing student environmental concern is a striking new development. A freshman college student attitude poll, conducted last fall by the American Council on Education, found that 89.9 percent of all male freshmen believed the Federal Government should be more involved in the control of pollution. And a Gallup poll published in late December found that the control of air and water pollution is fast becoming a new student cause, with students placing this issue sixth on a list of areas where they felt changes must be made.

Other national and local polls, the rising citizen attendance at public hearings on polluters, the letters that are pouring into congressional offices—all indicate a vast new concern.

As a dramatic indication of the degree the new citizen concern has reached Congress, a daily average of 150 constituent requests on environmental questions is coming into the Legislative Reference Service, the research arm of Congress, from Members of Congress. This is a request rate second only to that for crime.

In the *Congressional Record,* the amount of environmental material inserted in the first 6 months of last year by Senators and Congressmen was exceeded only by material on the issue of Vietnam.

Congress last year took the major initiative of appropriating $800 million in Federal water pollution control funds —nearly four times the request of the present and previous administrations.

And environmentalists across the country have been heartened by the reports that the President will devote major attention to the environmental crisis in his state of the Union message later this week. All conservationists applaud the President's interest and commitment.

In short, I believe that today we are at a watershed in the history of the struggle in this country to save the quality of our environment.

With the massive new coalition of interests that is now forming, which is including the urbanite and the student, it is possible to wage war on our environmental problems and win. In any such effort the continued commitment of millions of people is the most essential resource of all.

But, lest anyone be misled or caught unaware, this war will be lost before it is begun if we do not bring other massive resources to it as well. A victory will take decades and tens of billions of dollars. Just to control pollution, it will take $275 billion by the year 2000. Although that sounds like a lot of money, it will be spent over the next 30 years and is equivalent to the Defense expenditure for the next 4 years.

More than money, restoring our environment and establishing quality on a par with quantity as a goal of American life will require a reshaping of our values, sweeping changes in the performance and goals of our institutions, national standards of quality for the goods we produce, a humanizing and redirection of our technology, and greatly increased attention to the problem of our expanding population.

Perhaps, most of all, it will require on the part of the people a new assertion of environmental rights and the evolution of an ecological ethic of understanding and respect for the bonds that unite the species man with the natural systems of the planet.

The ecological ethic must be debated and evolved by individuals and institutions on the terms of man's interdependence with nature. Institutions such as our churches and universities could be of important assistance in providing increased understanding of these ethical considerations. . . .

American acceptance of the ecological ethic will involve nothing less than achieving a transition from the consumer society to a society of "new citizenship"—a society that concerns itself as much with the well-being of present and future generations as it does with bigness and abundance. It is an ethic whose yardstick for progress should be: Is it good for people?

American college students—thousands of whom are now actively planning a teach-in on the crisis of the environment April 22 on hundreds of campuses —are in the forefront in expressing the terms on which we will need to meet this critical challenge.

Students, scientists, and many others are saying that we must reject any notion that progress means destroying Everglades National Park with massive airport development—or that it is progress to use the American public as an experimental laboratory for artificial sweeteners, food additives, or other products without understanding the "technological backlash" that may come from their unmeasured dangers —or that it is progress to fill hundreds of square miles of our bays and coastal wetlands, destroying natural habitat for thousands of species of fish and wildlife, polluting our waters; and in many other ways wreaking havoc with this fragile ecological system in the name of providing new space for industry, commerce, and subdivisions.

There is a great need, and growing support, for the introduction of new values in our society—where bigger is not necessarily better—where slower can be faster—and where less can be more.

This attitude must be at the heart of a nationwide effort—an agenda for the 1970's—whereby this country puts gross national quality above gross national product.

AN ENVIRONMENTAL AGENDA FOR THE 1970'S CONSTITUTIONAL AMENDMENT

The first item I suggest for this agenda will be the introduction of an amendment to the U.S. Constitution which will recognize and protect the inalienable right of every person to a decent environment.

In its degradation of the quality of American life—in its danger to the future of man himself—I believe the environmental crisis is the greatest single threat to our pursuit of those inalienable rights—life, liberty, and the pursuit of happiness—which we have recognized as a society.

The amendment will be brief. It will state:

Every person has the inalienable right to a decent environment. The United

States and every State shall guarantee this right.

Now, the tragedy is that the citizen has little clear, legal, or explicit constitutional avenue to protect the sensitivities and well-being of himself, his family, or his community from environmental assault.

Far too frequently, the citizen finds himself left with no remedy, in the face of the pollution of a lake which belongs to the public, or the poisoning of the air which he must breathe, or the shattering din which is imposed upon him with no choice.

This is because, in the development of our Anglo-Saxon common law, our protections have traditionally focused on economic or personal injury, with the subordination of other damages that we are finding are just as much a threat to the quality of life.

Although I believe we must explicitly establish environmental right and protection as a fundamental doctrine of our society, it is clear that any such right, and the terms of its protection, must be enumerated in statutes at the Federal and State level and further defined in the courts.

I will introduce this constitutional amendment today.

As the second item for an agenda, I propose immediate action to rid America in the 1970's of the massive pollution from five of the most heavily used products of our affluent age. For each of these products, I am convinced that it can be done—with firm Federal action to assure it.

The five areas are: Internal combustion engine, hard pesticides, detergent pollution, aircraft pollution, and non-returnable containers.

INTERNAL COMBUSTION ENGINE

Phase out the internal combustion automobile engine by January 1, 1978,

unless it can meet national emission standards by that time.

I have already introduced this legislation—the Low Emission Vehicle Act. It is imperative that a near pollution-free automobile be developed and put into use as quickly as possible. Present exhausts are causing up to 90 percent of the air pollution problem in some areas of the Nation.

This proposal would also initiate a Federal research and subsidy program to find an alternative to the internal combustion engine or improve the performance of existing alternatives.

ELIMINATE HARD PESTICIDES

Eliminate persistent, toxic pesticides —the "chlorinated hydrocarbons"—by 1972.

Because of the grave, worldwide environmental dangers from these long-lasting, poisonous compounds, this step was proposed as a national goal 7 years ago by the President's Science Advisory Committee. There is growing agreement that the persistent pesticides are expendable, because of less persistent substitutes and the development of other means of pest control.

A recent decision by the U.S. Department of Agriculture to eliminate all nonessential uses of DDT by the end of this year was a step forward. Yet the pesticide industry's continued unwillingness to initiate or accept reform, coupled with the Agriculture Department's historic hesitancy to improve pesticide regulation, makes it mandatory that Congress set a deadline on banning the persistent pesticides.

REDUCE DETERGENT POLLUTION

Set strict antipollution standards on detergents, including a ban on their phosphorous "builders" that have contributed so much to the pollution of our lakes all across the Nation.

Detergents are one of the major pollution problems in the country today. Six years ago I sponsored legislation which prompted an industry changeover to a new ingredient which cut the massive mountains of foam detergents were causing on our waters. Now, another important step is needed: elimination of the detergent's polyphosphate "builders" that pass through sewage treatment systems into our lakes and rivers, stimulating the growth of algae.

Most recently at House committee hearings, scientists testified that nonpolluting substitutes for these detergents are now within reach. Industry, however, continues to resist such a move. Congress must act to require the substitution and, in addition, to set national standards on the water eutrophication ability, biodegradability, toxicity, and health effects of detergents.

JET AIRCRAFT POLLUTION

To dramatically reduce pollution from jet aircraft, establish a deadline of December 1972 for the installation of smokeless combustors on their engines.

Industry has produced a combustor that makes jet engines smokeless and significantly cuts their other pollution. At the rate the airlines have agreed to install these devices, it would take until the middle of the decade to make the changeover. It will soon be possible to install the combustors at the rate of 200 a month, which would accomplish the changeover in 2 years, but the industry is refusing to do so.*

With jets in the country pouring 78 million pounds of pollutants into the atmosphere each year, there is every reason for the combustors to be installed as quickly as possible. Congress should act to require this and to pro-

* The airlines have now agreed to complete the program by the end of 1972.

vide Federal assistance for research to make the combustors even more effective and easier to install.

Aircraft noise is another area which is in need of urgent action. As just one example, the supersonic transport plane, when flying at a height of 65,000 feet, will lay down a path of sonic booms 40 to 50 miles wide. This is a massive intrusion into human life which we cannot tolerate.

ELIMINATE NONRETURNABLE CONTAINERS

Eliminate bottles, jars, and cans from the American landscape through a combination of effluent charges, development of reusable or degradable containers, and packaging standards.

In the comprehensive solid waste management legislation that has already been introduced in this Congress, provision should be made for standards which will require reusable or degradable consumer product containers, as soon as it is proven technically feasible. In addition, our solid waste control program should be financed in part by effluent charges paid by industry for packaging that will not degrade or cannot be reused.

It is my conviction that the long run answer to our solid waste problem must be a massive effort to turn our wastes into valuable new products that can be recycled into the economy.

With these five actions, we would be taking great strides toward establishing the principle that industry's responsibilities for the human and environmental effects of its products do not stop at the end of the production line. The only way to assure this is through national laws that establish performance standards, so that products will be tested and environmental and health protections built in before, not after, they reach the marketplace.

FAMILY PLANNING

The third item on an agenda for quality of American life should be establishing and protecting the right of every citizen to plan his family. The funds and coordination must be made available for conducting necessary research into population problems and providing family planning services.

The statistics are deeply disturbing. It took until 1850 for the world population to reach 1 billion. By 1930, 80 years later, that figure had doubled, and by the year 2000, the world population is expected to reach 6 to 8 billion. Some ecologists see that population level as the "crash point," beyond which the natural environment will not be able to cleanse and restore itself from the massive pressure of exploitation and pollution.

At the December meeting of the American Association for the Advancement of Science, in Boston, there was general agreement that the world's optimum population limit has already been passed. Measured in terms of our past performance in protecting our environment, the United States is already overpopulated. If we cannot manage the wastes produced by 200 million people, it will be a catastrophe when we reach 300 million, as predicted within the next 30 years.

ENVIRONMENTAL ADVOCATE AGENCY

The fourth item on an agenda for the 1970's must be involving the citizen in environmental decisionmaking through new mechanisms, including establishment of new channels and forums for public participation, creation of a citizen environmental advocate agency, and creation of an environmental overview committee in Congress.

As a start, industry must consult with the community on the pollution controls needed to protect and enhance the environment. It must make a full disclosure of facts before, not after, the decisions are made that affect the consumer and his environment.

Although it is ironic that it needs to be said, public participation in environmental decisionmaking must also be extended to our government. The sorry history is that, through rhetoric, inaction, and compromise with special interests, our public institutions have been accomplices in frittering away the quality of American life.

The infusion of a spirit of advocacy and environmental ombudsmanship is urgently needed at every level of government, and I will propose a citizen environmental advocate agency at the Federal level. This independent office would represent the public interest in matters before every Federal department and in the courts.

With strong support, the National Environmental Policy Act recently signed into law and a complementary proposal now pending in Senate-House conference that would provide staff support should be major steps forward in achieving in the White House an independent overview of Federal activities as they affect the American environment. Hopefully, one of the most frequently used provisions of the National Environmental Policy Act will be the one which makes available to the public the agency reports required where a Federal program or project would significantly affect the environment.

Finally, Congress itself could profit greatly by the establishment of a non-legislative environmental committee that would provide all committees with a continuing assessment of the state of the environment and of Federal environmental activities.

MORATORIUM ON UNDERSEA OIL PRODUCTION

A fifth item on an environmental agenda for the 1970's should be the launching of a broad-scale effort to halt the pollution of our sea. Municipalities and industries must be required to halt their wholesale dumping of wastes into the ocean environment. And we should declare a moratorium on new leases or permits for oil production and other activities on the undersea Outer Continental Shelf until criteria are established for its protection.

The oceans, man's greatest asset, are being degraded at an alarming rate, hurling us toward worldwide catastrophe. In addition to dramatic oil pollution incidents, there are the less visible forms of pollution—from pesticides that are accumulating in the sea and from raw industrial wastes and sewage. In the United States, some 27 million tons of wastes were dumped at sea from barges and ships in 1968 alone.

These activities have their most immediate effect on our very limited continental shelves, the most productive area of the sea. If this sensitive environment is destroyed, sea life will rapidly diminish and a major source of food protein will be lost in a world that is searching for resources to feed its exploding population.

In a glimpse into the future, the recent report of the President's Panel on Oil Spills predicts we can expect a Santa Barbara-scale pollution incident once a year by 1980, if offshore oil development continues at the present rate.

To meet this problem, Congress should declare a moratorium on further Outer Continental Shelf development until the ground rules are established. Recreation, esthetics, fishery resources, and natural ecology must not be sacrificed in the interest of mineral and other development.

A high-level commission should be established and given the 2-year task of conducting an inventory of our offshore resources and recommending criteria by which we can achieve a harmonious relationship with the ocean environment. Upon the establishment of such criteria, the moratorium would be lifted.

ENVIRONMENTAL EDUCATION

The sixth item on the agenda should be the establishment of an environmental education program which will make the environment and man's relationship to it a major interdisciplinary subject at every level of public education.

No country can maintain its vigilance in protecting its environment without a broad education for understanding of man's relationship to his land, air, water, and to other living creatures.

To help achieve this, I introduced the Environmental Quality Education Act in November. A companion bill was introduced in the House. The legislation would provide support for the development of new environmental education curriculums from preschool through college, adult education, and community programs.

TRANSPORTATION FOR PEOPLE

As a seventh item for an environmental agenda, we must utilize the billions of dollars a year that could be made available on completion of the Interstate Highway System to provide new transportation alternatives, including mass transit, in our polluted, congested, highway-choked urban areas.

This year, about $3.3 billion of the $4.4 billion administered by the highway trust fund will be spent on the

Federal Interstate System, which is scheduled for completion in the mid-1970's. Instead of being used to lay new blankets of asphalt and concrete from coast to coast in another round of massive highway building, as has already been suggested, the Interstate Highway portion of the fund that could be made available in 1975 must be put to work alleviating the gargantuan transportation problems of our American cities. A major emphasis of those funds should be the provision of adequate mass transit systems, as well as developing and refining other transportation alternatives.

NATIONAL LAND USE POLICY

As an eighth item, a national policy on land use must be delineated and implemented that will halt the chaotic, unplanned combination of urban sprawl, industrial expansion, and air, water, land, and visual pollution that is seriously threatening the quality of life of major regions of the Nation.

The nationwide land use policy must comprise and effectively use all the tools available to Federal, State, and local governments to establish rational planning, management, and controls.

Such a policy must deal with the massive strip mining operations that are ravaging and polluting vast acreages; the reckless draining and filling of wetlands that are destroying wildlife habitat and polluting vital coastal and inland areas; the helter-skelter development of our coastal and inland lakes shoreline that is eliminating a vital national asset from any future public use; the widespread land erosion in urbanizing areas that is silting and polluting our rivers and lakes; and the disruption of communities and destruction of marshlands and other scenic and naturally valuable areas that are brought about by our gigantic highway program

where building in the fastest, cheapest "point to point" fashion has invariably been the rule, despite the consequences.

I should add that an integral part of our land resource and environmental heritage is the national park, lakeshore, and seashore system that we have established over the past decades. In this area, we have fallen tragically short of carrying out the congressional intention of providing $200 million a year for the land and water conservation fund through 1973. Land purchase for our national parks and other Federal wildlife and recreation areas is critically dependent on this fund. Yet for last year, only $124 million was sought and appropriated. Meanwhile, Outer Continental Shelf oil revenues intended to bring the fund to a $200 million a year level have been accumulating in trust year after under-funded year, unappropriated and unspent.

It is urgent that this year we provide not only the annually authorized $200 million, but the additional $164.5 million in Outer Continental Shelf funds now sitting in trust.

A NATIONAL MINERALS AND RESOURCES POLICY

A ninth item must be the establishment of a national minerals and resources policy.

Vital resources are already being exhausted because of our fantastic rate of consumption and our indiscriminate national waste. In addition, the extraction of our natural resources for our raw material has more often than not been done in such a way as to wreak violent and lasting environmental destruction.

A part of this national policy must be replacing the U.S. mining law of 1872 with a modern system of mineral leasing. As it is now, the 1872 law is a major obstacle to wise and effective land management in a world where the best kind of multiple use management is imperative. The present policy, based on that antiquated law, gives blind priority to mineral resources and makes any consideration of wildlife, recreation, esthetic or urban land values impossible. I have introduced legislation to establish a modern mineral leasing system, and a companion bill has been introduced in the House.

NATIONAL AIR AND WATER QUALITY POLICY

As a 10th and highly important item, America must establish a national air and water quality policy and commitment which will restore and enhance the quality of these critical natural resources. Our dirtied rivers and poisoned air are dramatic evidence of the desperate need to take action on a national unprecedented scale.

The fuel funding of present pollution control programs—closing the environmental money gap—is a fundamental and urgent requirement of a national policy. Despite the congressional initiative last year in Federal water pollution control aid, our national water quality program still faces the danger of total collapse. While the Federal aid has been trickling to the critical municipal sewage treatment program in the millions of dollars, applications for aid from cities and towns across the country are in the billions.

In this perilous situation, it is essential that we appropriate the full authorization of $1.2 billion in the Federal water pollution control grant program for sewage treatment plants for fiscal 1971. Other means of long-range financing are being considered, but we cannot afford a delay in already authorized water quality funding while the alternatives are being debated.

A national air and water quality policy must also dramatically expand our present program of research and development of ways to neutralize, dispose of, and recycle all wastes, and require all governmental units and all industries and municipalities to comply with the highest state of the art in treating their wastes. We must also require that, as new, more effective pollution control equipment is developed, it be installed as a matter of course.

ENVIRONMENTAL POLITICAL ACTION

The 11th item on an agenda for the 1970's must be the creation of a nonpartisan national environmental political action organization, with State and local organizations providing the foundation.

The organization will give the public the day to day involvement that is essential to achieving environmental solutions.

CONCLUSION

Our efforts to meet a broad-gaged agenda such as I have outlined above will require a vast increase in spending for environmental programs. At least $20 to $25 billion per year over present expenditures is essential. A major portion of this could come from existing sources of revenues by reordering national priorities and diverting funds to environmental programs. New resources must also be tapped. . . .

A casual look at the deterioration that has come about over the past 30 years is a frightening prologue to a disaster of inestimable dimensions if the accelerating rate of the environmental crisis continues.

It is not, however, a trend that cannot be reversed. If we have the will, the environmental challenge can be met. But in doing so, it will take significant modifications in our way of life. It will mark the beginning of a period when all of the institutions of our society—social, political, and economic—must readjust their philosophical attitudes toward man's relationship to his environment and all other living creatures.

Our environmental problems are man made. The solutions must be man made as well.

Mr. President, at this time I introduce, for appropriate reference, a constitutional amendment to guarantee every person the right to a decent environment and ask unanimous consent that the text of the amendment be printed in the *Record*, at the conclusion of my remarks.

NEW YORK: FRAGRANT DAYS IN FUN CITY

Time

The difficulty in dealing with local strikes is brought into sharp focus by a look at the garbage strike of New York City. However, it would be more useful to view this strike in terms of the increase in strikes among public employees. Autumn teachers' strikes are common, and other public employees are taking their cues from these first attempts to force collective bargaining.

It is imperative that local governments find effective legal means in dealing with this problem. The New York City garbage strike should give some insight into the problems which must be faced.

For New York City's 8,000,000 adversity-tempered citizens, the sanitation workers' strike was merely a nuisance at first. By the end of last week, it had turned into a genuine crisis. Nearly 100,000 tons of uncollected garbage lay in noisome heaps on sidewalks and in doorways. Trash fires flared all over town. Rats rummaged through pyramidal piles of refuse. Public-health authorities, warning of the danger of typhoid and other diseases, proclaimed the city's first general health emergency since a 1931 polio epidemic.

The confrontation between Mayor John Lindsay and the Teamster-affiliated Uniformed Sanitationmen's Association had been building for months. The

Mayor thought that he had a tacit understanding with Union President John DeLury for a reasonable settlement. The city was willing to give an annual increase of $350, plus fringe improvements, to the 10,000 workers who now receive $7,956 after three years' service. But DeLury, apparently unable to sell those terms to his men, demanded $600. After sporadic negotiations, the union staged a wild rally at city hall two weeks ago, virtually forced DeLury to call a strike. Said he, ducking an egg thrown at him: "I accept the motion to go-go-go."

Immediate rebuff. Next day, the strike was on. Refusing to knuckle under to what he called "blackmail, brute force and muscle," Lindsay fought back as best he could with legal action and calls for unity. He was determined to bring order into the city's chaotic labor relations and to counter the threat of public strikes that, though banned by state law, have been used to win fat contract settlements. "Now is the time and here is the place," he declared, "for the city to determine what it is made of."

Lindsay had DeLury jailed for ignoring a court injunction issued under a new state law, but this merely solidified the union. The mayor's pleas for help from other city employees were immediately rebuffed. On the strike's seventh day, Lindsay was forced to turn to his fellow liberal Republican, Governor Nelson Rockefeller. The mayor wanted the National Guard called in to clean up the city, and Rockefeller was the only man who could do it.

Rockefeller's relationship with Lindsay has never been more than coldly cordial, but even if it were warm, it is doubtful whether Rockefeller would have agreed to mobilize the Guard. The Governor has considerable rapport with labor, and particularly DeLury's union, which strongly supported him for re-election in 1966. Though he insists he is not a presidential candidate, he was loath to become a strikebreaking Governor (though such stern action would probably have helped among conservatives, who most distrust him). There were also material arguments against calling out the Guard: the cost to the city would have been far more than a contract settlement; the troops' effectiveness would have been limited by lack of training; and most persuasive, the city's million-member Central Labor Council might have called a general strike.

A LITTLE BLACKMAIL   Rockefeller, with control over the Guard his trump,

seized the initiative from Lindsay by taking over the negotiations. He named his own mediation panel to supplant the mayor's and treated the outlaw union with unwonted deference. Rockefeller's mediators proposed a pay increase of $425. The union accepted immediately, and the Governor hailed the proposal as "fair and reasonable." Lindsay rejected it out of hand. Though the difference over wages had become seemingly insignificant, Lindsay was determined not to reward the strikers with a figure above what the union leadership had been willing to accept earlier. "A little blackmail," he said, was still blackmail.

For nearly 48 hours after Lindsay's veto, the impasse persisted, and 20,000 more tons of garbage piled up in the city's streets. While Lindsay enjoyed considerable moral support for his stand, the city's three major daily papers attacked Rockefeller. Even the New York Times, normally a Rockefeller supporter, flayed the Governor in uncharacteristically harsh terms, indicting him for "sabotage," "appeasement," "bad politics and bad government."

ULTIMATUM   By the weekend, the fight was clearly lost. Parts of the city were reeking, and Lindsay could do nothing except stand on principle. At the end of the strike's ninth day, Rockefeller announced a settlement that was really an ultimatum to Lindsay. The union agreed to send its men back to work immediately in exchange for the $425 pay raise that Lindsay had earlier rejected. The city would either agree to pay it or the state, by means of a special measure that Rockefeller will request of the legislature this week, would assume temporary control of the Sanitation Department and fulfill the new contract terms—with city funds.

New Yorkers were doubtless relieved

that their latest crisis had eased before turning into an outright calamity. But in the long run, Rockefeller's solution seemed to offer little consolation for a city already traumatized by excessively high taxes and strike-happy unions. As written by Rockefeller, the moral of New York's latest step toward chaos seemed to be that it pays to strike.

A TRILLION DOLLARS TO SAVE THE CITIES?

U.S. News & World Report

The trillion dollar figure is widely quoted as the amount of money needed in the metropolitan areas over the next dozen years. The cities are dogged with crisis that stagger the imagination. Industry and middle-income residents are moving out, reducing the tax base available to the cities. The needs of the cities increase day by day and the cities are no longer able to provide this support. The state governments are unable to support the deficit, even should it be politically acceptable. This article clearly states the case that, if the cities are to be saved, massive financial assistance must come from the federal government.

Seven out of 10 Americans—nearly 140 million out of 197 million—are crowded into just 1 per cent of this nation's land.

Three out of 10—or some 57 million —enjoy the remaining 99 per cent of the diverse and beautiful U.S. country-side.

Now it's predicated that in the next 25 years, 100 million additional American will try to pile in on top of the 140 million already in the cities and their suburbs.

If that happens it would mean nearly a quarter of a billion people crowded into areas already staggering under their problems.

So what to do? A Senate subcommittee, headed by Abraham Ribicoff (Dem.), of Connecticut, is trying to find some answers.

From a conference of experts on city problems, just held, have come other ideas.

A first suggestion: Spend 1 trillion dollars—1,000 billion—trying to save present cities by reorganizing, redesigning, rebuilding. One trillion dollars, it's explained, would give a "good start" toward bringing order out of impending chaos.

A second suggestion: Create as many as 1,000 "new cities" all across the country—modern cities designed for a modern kind of America, not those built for the horse-and-buggy age.

New cities would be built from scratch in parts of the nation where people could enjoy living. These cities would grow around the needs and desires of people for recreation, as well as for work; for beauty as well as for utility; for easy access to all means of communication.

The cost? Nobody is suggesting a figure, but all agree it would be staggering.

How financed? By expanding industry, just as some "new towns" already are being financed, and by use of some forms of subsidy from the Federal Government.

A NEW ERA   America is seen as moving steadily toward the era when it must provide for half a billion people. Those studying city needs insist there is no time to waste and that the nation must begin soon in earnest to deal with the problems of its big cities and its expanding population.

A dream? Far from it, say those who see problems even today overwhelming city and State governments.

New York City's Mayor John V. Lindsay told the Senate Subcommittee on Executive Reorganization that his city alone needs 50 billion dollars to try to cope with its local problems.

Jerome P. Cavanagh, mayor of Detroit, put a price tag of 15 billions on the needs of his city, and one of 250 billions, over the next 10 years, to help out all major cities of the U.S.

The veteran mayor of New Haven, Conn., Richard C. Lee, said that it is "impossible" to put a price tag on what it is going to cost to save the cities.

When Robert F. Kennedy, New York Senator, added up suggested costs of federal aid for cities, he concluded that, if figures for major cities were extended to all, the total for the next 10 years would be 1.1 trillion dollars.

From the National Planning Association, a private research organization backed by business and labor, comes the prediction that it will take 2.1 trillion dollars, spent over a 20-year period, to make cities "viable."

"I admit that the figure is a very staggering one," says Detroit's Mayor Cavanagh.

Others, however, see in the vast spending that city officials regard as necessary not only a great expense but a tremendous opportunity.

Building on the scale now being talked about, as they see it, could keep the people of the nation—and their industries—fully occupied for as far ahead as anyone would try to look.

Costs of a war on the scale of Korea or Vietnam, by comparison, appear almost trivial.

And what would the country get in return for the trillion dollars paid out to save the cities?

The Constitution Plaza in Hartford, Conn., is referred to as one example of what can be done when a city faces up to a problem.

An older downtown area of Hartford now is restored into a beautiful pedestrian plaza with hotels and shops and an expressway close by, and with parking underground. This development, in turn, is generating adjacent renewal projects, opening more of the downtown area to new business and residential facilities.

Philadelphia showed earlier what could be done by moving rail yards out and reclaiming large areas for redevelopment. In Pittsburgh, one of the pioneers in urban renewal, the Pennsylvania Railroad is planning a 40-square-block "business and residential park" where rail yards now stand, next to the city's famed Golden Triangle.

SLUMS WIPED OUT   In Washington, D.C., a blighted area in the Southwest section is being reclaimed. Where there had been slums are now apartments and hotels, office buildings, Government buildings, a theater and plans for a refurbished waterfront with restaurants. Private and Government capital is involved.

The Rosslyn area in nearby Arlington County, Virginia, is cited as a spectacular example of redevelopment with private capital.

Not all of the plans for larger cities now being discussed as essential call for wiping out old areas and starting over.

In many neighborhoods, it is pointed out, if an investment would be made to get parked cars off the streets, really tidy up those streets and add benches and trees, a much more attractive appearance would result.

Georgetown, in Washington, D.C., and some areas of Philadelphia and San Francisco are referred to as examples of what can be done to bring back decaying areas through renovation rather than large-scale rebuilding.

Those who look ahead say that population densities in some sections of the major cities probably will have to be lowered, or at least prevented from growing more dense. This would be true of Manhattan. Space in present cities is described as often poorly used.

More than downtown areas will have to be redeveloped. Those areas between the central business district and the suburbs, as planners see it, will also have to be rebuilt in many cases to wipe out slums, build new schools, provide open space and recreation areas.

Plans to do just that are underway already in Detroit, Baltimore, St. Louis, Boston and many other cities.

In New York City, State and local officials are thinking of locating government buildings and encouraging a large private business complex in the heart of Harlem, the famed Negro area, as a way of "bringing the jobs to where the workers are," as one official put it.

BETTER TRANSIT   Subways and other forms of rapid transit are coming to be accepted as a necessary supplement to autos and highways to beat rising traffic congestion in big cities.

These transit systems, in turn, are expected to touch off a boom in new office and apartment building, reshaping the living patterns of city dwellers.

Edgardo Contini, partner in Victor Gruen Associates, a Los Angeles land-planning firm, looks for stores, restaurants and other commercial facilities to be built right into subway terminals and thus help turn decaying areas into new business centers.

An official of an economic-research organization had this to say:

"We are trying to get along with a completely obsolete idea of how we can live, an obsolete structure of Government and obsolete methods of planning.

"The remedy lies in taking a national view of our urban problems, in developing regional and metropolitan organizations of government that are capable of planning and executing development programs.

"That means, whether we like it or not, more controls on where buildings are established, on where homes are built or autos can drive.

"It also means revising the structure of Government so that people do not flee from the cities with their tax money and then expect to come back during the day to earn their living—leaving the poorer people in the cities without the tax base needed to correct the city's deficiencies."

"IF WE REBUILD. . . ."   From Wilfred Owen, economist and senior staff member of Brookings Institution:

"If we are going to rebuild existing cities to standards that will provide for the kind of life our wealth and increasing leisure permit, then we will be forced to put a limit on the extent to which the city sprawls and extends to meet with contiguous cities.

"We are going to be forced to limit densities of people, because, when we bring in trees and open space and more recreational facilities, we are going to have a looser fabric.

"So there will be an overflow of people from the renewal of existing cities. On top of that, we are told that there will be another 100 million more Americans to provide for in the not too distant future.

"This new population and the overflow from cities will require us to think about new urban centers—and these should be planned communities."

It is from this analysis that the idea of 1,000 new cities springs.

NEW-CITY SYMBOLS   Is the vision of new cities on that scale taken seriously? Those who are thinking of the problem ahead say that it is a very serious proposal. They say that two communities growing near Washington, D.C., are symbols of what can be expected on an expanding scale.

These cities are Reston, 25 miles west of the nation's capital, and Columbia, midway between Washington and Baltimore to the northeast. One is designed for about 75,000 people; the other for about 100,000.

Already scores of towns, on roughly the same scale as Reston and Columbia, are being planned on land that only yesterday was farmland. Urban planners say new cities of even larger size will be needed to meet the mounting pressure of urban growth.

The maximum size suggested for new cities is set by many planners at about 300,000. Beyond that figure, according to an urban economist, "the cost of providing public services for each inhabitant tends to rise quickly while the standard of living may drop."

Cities to be created would not, in most cases, be around the metropolitan areas of today. Instead, they would be located in open areas of the country that meet peoples' tastes with respect to climate, recreation or geography.

In fact, says Joseph Timan, head of the Committee for National Land Development Policy, Chicago-based group of builders, bankers and real estate men, new cities are going to have to be hundreds of miles from present population centers or they will be overwhelmed as the big cities spread outward.

"WONDERFUL PLACES"   Ian C. McHarg, urban expert at the University of Pennsylvania, says:

"There is no difficulty at all about finding wonderful places where you could put a thousand new cities."

Mentioned were places near the Cascade Range in the Northwestern U.S.; sparsely settled areas in Hawaii and Minnesota, in Texas and other parts of the Southwest.

New England, with its opportunities for summer and winter sports, is frequently cited as an ideal place for new cities. So are areas in Utah, Idaho and Wyoming, where people could enjoy the mountains or fishing and yet be within easy reach of business centers in San Francisco or Los Angeles by high-speed air transportation.

Says Mr. Owen: "We are reaching the point where we can locate new cities wherever we please. New developments in highway and air transport and in communications, here and on the way, make it no longer necessary for cities to be located in specific places, such as the confluence of a river or a railroad junction or a deep seaport.

"What we now have the opportunity to do is to take advantage of this country and the space that is one of our big assets. Every part of the U.S. is going to be on the main stream."

SELF-CONTAINED   Talk to urban planners and other authorities on new cities and you find broad agreement on what these places will be like.

Most will be self-contained. Some residents might still commute to other cities, but the idea is to have people live, work and play all in one area—"to close the gap between home and work, as in the preautomobile age," one architect explained.

Housing, business and industry, schools, churches, recreation all would be within walking distance or only a short, enjoyable trip away. Around these cities, land would be preserved for farming, forests and recreation.

New cities, as now visualized, would be architecturally pleasing and orderly, with far more open space, trees and greenery than found in present cities. The pedestrian would be king.

Traffic ways would be made less obvious. Main routes, for example, would be run around a community or be depressed or tunneled under it. Human traffic would be separated from motorized traffic as much as possible.

"Separate rights of way for pedestrians" is the idea of C. McKim Norton, president of the New York Regional Plan Association. Pedestrian underpasses might be built at potentially busy corners when the city is laid out.

UNDERGROUND PARKING Businesses would be centered around pedestrian plazas, an outgrowth of today's shopping centers, but with parking underground. The same would apply to industrial parks on new-city outskirts.

Small electric carts that create no air-pollution problem, according to Mr. Contini, would be ideal for daily trips too far for walking.

Special roads, in addition, would be reserved for public transportation, with nearly everybody within minutes' walk of a bus stop.

The kinds of industry now growing fastest in the U.S.—research and light industry—are expected to be attracted to new cities. The promise of greater efficiency in modern new plants with a good deal of space, it is claimed, will make such a move by industry economical in the long run.

In some cases, new cities may turn out to be "college towns," built around large universities. Right now, for example, the new town of Irvine is going up near Los Angeles around a branch of the University of California.

Private funds—from builders, bankers, big corporations—are expected to finance these new cities in major part. Yet there is general agreement among urban authorities that Government aid, of one sort or another, will be needed to get new urban settlements under way.

State and local governments, it is said, will have to take over and assemble large tracts of land. Tax concessions by federal and State governments will have to be made to lure the first industries. There may be need for federal "seed money" and for other financial aid to developers of new communities.

One suggestion often made, in the words of an economist for a major research organization: "Let the Federal Government, in distributing money for education, hospitals and highways or in putting up federal buildings, focus on those places where the new cities of tomorrow will be built."

An example cited is the decision to move the headquarters of the U.S. Geological Survey, with its 4,000 workers, from downtown Washington to Reston.

Many specific moves of this kind will be taken in coming years, specialists in urban problems are convinced.

TIME IS SHORT Their basic point is that time is running out. People have been talking about the plight of the city for decades, but doing little.

But doing nothing, these authorities say, can be costly too—in terms of congestion, noise, pollution, traffic snarls, slums, crime, welfare loads.

Now Congress is showing signs of concern. Money is beginning to pour out to stimulate mass transit. There are proposals by President Johnson for money to remake "demonstration cities" and for new towns.

Planners see changes ahead for urban America in the coming decades—changes that will be vast and costly.

PART X

QUESTIONS FOR DISCUSSION

1. How important is clean air and clean water to your community, to your very way of life?
2. What is your community doing to insure clean air and clean water for future generations?
3. Do you favor open housing legislation? Examine the results of open-housing in terms of immediate economic effects in contrast to the fullfillment of human rights.
4. What can be done to insure that strikes of public employees will no longer be allowed to cripple the public welfare?

VOCABULARY

alienated   aggression
paranoid   anarchy
pollutant   learned behavior
decibel   exodus
psyche

THE CITY OF TOMORROW

After a thorough study of urban problems, a student may begin to feel that it is an impossible task for him to influence the course of urban development. As an individual this may be true, but, as current research is showing, effectively organized interest groups can play a major role in bringing about change. Of the current community organizers, perhaps best known is Saul Alinsky who has effectively united groups of formerly politically impotent people. As they become organized and form significant constituency, politicians and, more importantly, the power structure begin to listen. One might ask what does this have to do with the person who simply wants to make the cities and the lives of the people in them more productive and allow them to enter the mainstream of American life.

Every two years, candidates for national, state, and local political offices will be seeking your vote in your area. As you review the major problems confronting our cities, what will be the position you will ask the candidate to take? Are you going to demand minimum housing standards, as well as open-housing legislation, so that all people in your community can enjoy the basic necessities of decent housing in keeping with their ability to pay? Will you support a basic minimum subsistance for all people in the areas of health, nourishment, and clothing? Are you in favor of programs that will adequately provide for those unable to work because of age, physical, or social disability in a manner which allows the recipient to retain his dignity and self-respect? Do you personally know the shortcomings of education in your schools and will you support the candidate willing to finance the needed improvements? Do you understand the impact of overpopulation in local, national, and world perspectives, and will you demand that your candidate take a stand on population controls? Does your candidate take a position on air and water pollution, and specifically, will he act in the interests of all the people or will he be unduly influenced by industrial pressure groups? Will your candidate work to find means of relieving automobile, air, and rail transportation deficiencies?

Will you ask your candidate for his specific program for beautifying your cities? What are your candidate's views on alleviating the burden of regressive sales and property taxes and incorporating more progressive and equitable systems of taxation? Does your locality and state have active human-relations councils and is your candidate actively supportive of them? Has your candidate taken a strong stand on law and order, tempered with justice, for all members of the community? Will he work to establish programs designed to develop greater understanding between minority groups and the police? Lastly, has he developed a firm, realistic, and comprehensive program to deal with community problems?

The above problems are ones on which you should take a firm position, and will you demand and work for candidates who advocate similar views? Once your candidate is elected you must understand that he cannot accomplish these ends without your active support and participation on the local level. These are things you must actively join in if our cities are to survive.

THE FREE CITY

Lawrence Haworth

The need for a city which would enlarge human freedoms seems almost a mad hatter's dream. Yet the city must remain free if its inhabitants are to realize their potential worth. Indeed, in view of our increasing urbanization, the need for maintaining a free people in the face of increasing bureaucracy becomes a matter of primary concern.

In answering this dilemma, the author recommends a city with flexibility of alternatives and openness of its system. Politically, he speaks of neighborhood centers in direct communication with the city government. Most importantly, he stresses that institutionalism need not signify a loss of freedom, rather it may be a necessary part of life to preserve the free city.

I

Individual growth presupposes individual freedom. Only when the inhabitant of the city participates in its affairs through personal choice rather than from compulsion or habit can we properly say that he has grown through such participation. To have a complete notion of the form of a good city, it is necessary, therefore, to grasp not only the traits that give it moral power, but the traits that make it free. We must discover that kind of urban structure implied by the idea that the direction of the city dweller's life should be in his own hands.

During the middle ages, the city was regarded as a bastion of freedom. The slogan *Stadt macht frei* expressed the aspiration of peasants throughout Europe to shed feudal restraints by escaping to a city and remaining there for a year. More recently the exurbs have come to be regarded as places of escape from the bondage of the city. This new image has been brought under attack, but only the openness and autonomy of life outside the city have been challenged, not the assumption of deadness and restraint within. If the city is to recover the image of a bastion of freedom, then we must understand the form it would take if it were to deserve the image.

The concept of an urban institutional structure that grounds freedom may seem strange. Structure, institution, and organization are often regarded as opposed to freedom, at least when freedom is understood, as it is here, to mean personal choice. Many imagine that in a thoroughly institutionalized urban life there would be no room for choice—that insofar as his activity follows an institutional pattern the affairs of the city dweller are directed by social forces outside himself. It might seem that if the whole course of family life, for example, were institutional, then every family process would follow a previously fixed pattern. The motions family members go through might testify to the fact that the city is well ordered, and even that its order is distinctively human and beneficial. But is it not true that when family members act in terms of an institutional pattern they are not spontaneous, and that to that extent personal choice does not figure in the family process? Choice and spontaneity would seem to require that the behavior of the members deviate from the established pattern; but were this to happen the family would not be an institution. One might conclude that order is capable of being grounded in the institutionalization of urban affairs, but that life can exhibit choice only by resisting the drift toward institutional standardization. Order requires organization; personal choice and freedom appear to exist only in the interstices of organized life.

This antithesis of freedom and organization is almost wholly false. Certain kinds of social organization do threaten individual freedom, but other kinds promote it: organization as such is not at fault. The technique of freedom does not lie in fighting organization, in resisting the fact that urban life has a structure. Individual freedom for the inhabitant of the city will not be found outside this structure, but, if at all, within it. Freedom has an institutional ground. The problem of freedom is that of discovering this ground, and of conceiving programs by which urban institutions may be led to acquire traits that establish self-determination.

II

The notion that freedom and organization are opposed to each other is based on the belief that for the inhabitant of the city, organization means role-playing. A consideration of the limitations of this belief will enable us to develop the idea of a free city. Though the term "role-playing" is cumbersome and, in some of its con-

notations, misleading, it conveys an important truth. The individual's role, in a family, government, industry, or church, is always defined with some precision. It sets limits on what he can and cannot do as long as he retains his connection with the institution. The factors that fix these limits conspire to keep him from stepping outside of his role. And all the ways of acting that the role *excludes* tend to be excluded also from the role-player's life.

But the fact that the individual's role is limited does not automatically imply that it limits his freedom of choice. For the role, if it is of the right sort, is also an opportunity and a source of power. Whether participation in the structured life of the city limits the individual's freedom of choice depends upon three additional factors. The first is the width of the limits imposed by the role. The office of President of the United States is a role, and a very well defined one. But not all Presidents act alike as President. The office, though well defined, is *broadly* defined. Each occupant brings to the task a unique personality, and within the conditions of his office expresses himself in ways which differentiate his tenure from that of every other President. The role is wide enough to tolerate alternative interpretations, a latitude that permits personal decision on the part of the office-holder. This is true of all forms of institutional participation. In every case, the role has a certain breadth or flexibility. It does not follow that the organization within which the role occurs is incomplete, or that there are areas of urban life that the structure of affairs does not reach. The definition of the role provides for breadth or flexibility. Often, as in the case of the Presidency, there are positive arrangements designed to enable the individual to exercise wisely the freedom of choice permitted by such flexibility.

Regular channels are established for providing him with information necessary for reaching intelligent decisions.

To the extent that the structure of urban affairs incorporates broad, flexible modes of institutional participation, the inhabitant of the city finds room in his life for deliberation and decisive action. Institutional flexibility is thus one of the traits of a free city.

Second, there is a vital difference between institutional participation, however flexible, that is imposed on the inhabitant of the city, and participation that he may accept or reject at his discretion. If in any event his affairs will be institutionalized, then by being able to choose the activities that are to form his life, the inhabitant is able to introduce personal direction into it. Whether he has the opportunity to make such choices depends upon the order of affairs—upon the way the city is organized, not upon the presence or absence of organization. A free city then, is also one wherein institutional participation is voluntary.

Third, it is relevant to ask whether the institutional structure that settles the form of the inhabitant's life is any way subject to his control. Does he exercise supervision over the specific patterns of family and economic life in the city? Are these left to drift with the currents of the times? Or does a narrow group or a particular institution shape the form of life for the whole? To the extent that the city dweller controls the growth of his institutions, the limitations inherent in the idea or organization are self-imposed limitations and do not form genuine restrictions on individual freedom. When the inhabitant controls the growth of urban institutions, they become in a real sense *his*, and the fact that they shape his destiny becomes one with the fact that he shapes his own destiny. Institutions have not been dissolved, but they have

been made to take on a certain form. They have become controllable. Controllability is a third trait of a free city.

The free city, then, is one whose institutions are flexible, voluntary, and controllable. When modes of participation in the settled life of the city are broadly defined, when individual participation in urban affairs is discretionary, and when the structure of those affairs is controlled by the inhabitants, then individual freedom is woven into the fabric of urban life. When moral power and community are added to the traits that make the city free, it becomes in every dimension a good city.

III

Of the three traits of a free city, flexibility is probably the most direct and familiar. If an organized activity follows a narrowly standardized pattern, the obvious means of bringing freedom to the participant is to broaden the pattern. As a result, personal decision in the role of the individual will not only be permitted but required. He can and must decide how, within the framework of his role, to conduct himself.

Inflexibility in human settlements takes various guises. In the city it typically results from bureaucratic modes of social organization; in settlements like the village community and manor, from custom. Customs are specific; they imply a form of ritual and exact observances. The individual bound by custom has not latitude but must reproduce prescribed movements. The mechanism that underlies inflexibility in a custom-bound settlement is psychological in nature: deference to the past. By contrast, the inflexibility of life in the modern city arises from the systematic character of joint activity, extensive differentiation, and the intricate interdependence of functions.

The operator of a machine in a factory may find that the physical design of the machine and its place in the over-all productive process determine with some precision how he must spend his working day.

The bureaucratization of industry has meant that the necessity for personal decision in the minute activities of the industrial process has been eliminated. Automation—the use of machines to tend machines—has thus become possible. But the development of automation in industry is not nearly as noteworthy as the development of bureaucracy. Automation is nothing more than a refinement. There is no great difference to the productive process between using men in a machine-like way, so that on the job they function as automatons, and using actual machines to perform the same tasks. No difference to the productive process, that is. For the employee, the difference is great indeed. Automation liberates him from the necessity to occupy himself with an inflexible activity and thus creates the possibility of his finding more satisfactory work. It is when this possibility is not realized that technical unemployment is the only result of replacing men with machines.

Bureaucracy and inflexibility in urban affairs are not limited to industrial relations. The machinery of urban government—as the proliferation of bureaus, departments, agencies, and commissions testifies—closely parallels the organization of urban industry. Inflexibility here, as in industry, results from the attempt to *rationalize* organized activity in the interests of efficiency. If the ideal were achieved, the entire operation could be summed up in advance in a code of operation that precisely detailed the responsibilities associated with each role. The bureaucrat would need only to refer to

the code, and all occasion for deliberation and decision would be removed.

Unquestionably, urban government is moving in this direction. The bureaucrat in a tightly organized office increasingly resembles the factory worker in a highly mechanized plant. And just as the inflexibility of the latter's role makes it feasible to replace him with a machine, the inflexibility of the bureaucrat's role makes it feasible to replace him with an electronic computer. The use of computers for administrative decision-making, a science-fiction phantasy only a few years ago, is now a reality, and there is no reason to doubt that it will increase. In large cities where government employees make up a significant proportion of the population, this trend may be expected to have considerable impact upon the quality of urban life. It is a trend toward the automation of government.

The efficiency of organized activity often increases with the inflexibility of institutional roles. But is the gain in efficiency worth the loss of flexibility? Actually, this is not one problem but many, since inflexibility may not be as intolerable in some institutions as it is in others. Moreover, if total automation were to come about, human beings would be released from the burdens inflexibility imposes. If urban industry, for example, were to become completely automatic, the question of whether the city's inhabitants had gained or lost by the transformation would depend upon the quality of the activity which replaced that turned over to the machines. This is the problem of leisure time: whether automation in industry is a blessing depends on people's ability to find satisfying ways of occupying themselves during the time they are not at work.

When this nest of problems is viewed

from the vantage point of the conception of a good city, two conclusions suggest themselves. First, extreme inflexibility throughout the structure of urban life would be intolerable, for it would leave the inhabitant no satisfying means of utilizing his increased leisure time. It is obvious that in a good city the institutions of education, religion, science, art, and family life should remain, as far as possible, flexible.

On the other hand, there appears to be no alternative to increased inflexibility, since it is encouraged by the products of our industrial system which enter into every phase of urban life. By "packaging" activity, the products of this system do for the individual what he otherwise would do for himself, and as a result, his position becomes more passive than active. Prepared foods, for example, eliminate all but the most elementary steps in cooking. Television sets imply a passive mode of recreation, by contrast with the activities they ordinarily replace. The automatic starter and automatic transmission do for the motorist what prepared foods do for the cook.

Some of these "conveniences" we cannot but regard as absurd; others represent significant advances. My reason for mentioning them is neither to decry present trends nor to extol technology, but only to emphasize that, on the whole, the age of commodities portends inflexibility in institutional life. Though doubtless there are ways of minimizing the undesirable effects of commercialization, it is not realistic to suppose that cities in the future can be made any less commodity-ridden. Consequently, we must base our hopes for a free city largely on making urban institutions voluntary and controllable.

It is fortunate, therefore, that the three traits which form the freedom dimension of a good city are alternatives. In this respect, the dimension of freedom is unlike that of moral power. Openness, richness, and person-centeredness are "ingredients" of moral power in the same way that length, width, and depth are "ingredients" of space. Just as space is unthinkable without all three, in the sense that the elimination of any one would mean the elimination of space itself, so in the absence of openness, richness, or person-centeredness the city would entirely lack moral power. A deficiency of openness, for example, is not remedied by added richness, since that addition does not touch those city dwellers to whom urban institutions are closed.

The traits that form a free city represent three distinct routes to the same end. Different cities are free mainly by virtue of having followed one or another of these routes. Once a human settlement, largely because of the limited development of industry, could stake its claim to being free on the fact that there was considerable flexibility in its institutions. In such a time, even political autocracy could not drastically jeopardize the inhabitants' self-determination. Now, however, we must ordinarily look elsewhere for freedom in the city. We must not give up the attempt to salvage flexibility wherever possible and desirable, but we have to recognize that voluntary institutions, subject to human control, are indispensable to the modern city.

IV

The notion of a voluntary institution, one which is not imposed on the individual but in which participation is discretionary, is closely related to that of an open institution. A little reflection will show that though to be voluntary an institution must be open, the reverse does not hold. It is possible, and indeed it frequently happens, that an institution will be open but not voluntary. During times of national crisis, military service is open to everyone who can meet minimum standards of fitness; yet for most of those who meet such standards, whether they enter military service is determined by persons other than themselves. The element that distinguishes a voluntary institution from an open institution is choice.

The idea of making or having a choice is often oversimplified. We habitually assume that there are only two alternatives: one is either permitted or not permitted to choose one's own course of action. Actually, choice, and therefore the extent to which an institution is voluntary, are matters of degree. Whether an individual is genuinely free to decide to participate in some activity or to remain aloof from it depends upon whether there are feasible alternatives to participation. The question of whether an inhabitant of a one-factory town is compelled to take a job at that factory has no simple answer. It does not suffice to observe that he may legally refuse to accept employment there, or that his neighbors are unconcerned about his activities. More than social and legal permission is needed if the factory is to be in a meaningful sense voluntary. For all practical purposes, the individual must eat. If the only means to that end is accepting a job at the factory, then employment there is not voluntary. Since no actual human situation is as uncomplicated as this, however, the voluntariness of an institution is always a matter of degree. One could accept the consequences of refusing employment at the factory, and thus in effect choose starvation. One could steal bread rather than work for it. Or one could, by making more or less severe sacrifices, move to an area where other jobs are available.

The degree to which an institution is voluntary is a function of the extent and seriousness of the sacrifices the individual will make if he decides not to participate in it. Even legal restraint is encompassed in this formula, since as a rule the law does not preclude but only imposes a penalty for noncompliance. Draft-dodgers are not physically compelled to report for military service; they are only penalized for failing to report. The severity of the penalty measures the degree to which military service is involuntary. When an institution is truly voluntary, the sacrifices the individual makes in consequence of his decision not to participate are minimal: no legal penalties are imposed; and the city is so rich in institutional opportunities that the individual does not, by excluding himself from one activity, deny himself the opportunity to live a good life.

There are, therefore, two sides to the question of making urban institutions more voluntary. On one hand is the problem of minimizing legal and customary restraints. If there are laws or informal social pressures that impose certain forms of institutional participation on the city's inhabitants, the strategy of freedom lies in changing the laws and eliminating the pressure. Though in some instances the indirect values of these restraints may outweigh the immediate sacrifice of freedom they entail, ideally the city would dispense with all of them.

On the other hand, the problem of making urban institutions more voluntary is one with the problem of nurturing the moral power of the city. By becoming more open and richer in opportunities for significant action, the city assures a wide range of alternatives to participation in any one of its institutions. As the range of these alternatives widens, the voluntary character of the city's institutions is enhanced.

V

Voluntary and flexible institutions can make no more than a partial contribution to the formation of a free city. These traits appear within the framework of an urban structure not of the individual's devising, and it is only, in a sense, by submitting to this structure that he enjoys freedom of choice. The order of affairs in the city, including the flexibility and voluntary character of its institutions, is, from the standpoint of the maturing individual, fixed. The shape of the city as he enters into its life, the opportunities it affords for significant action and personal decision, form his fate, as they do the fate of all others who are born and mature, willy-nilly, in the same city. He does not choose but merely comes upon the ground conditions of his life. By an accident of birth he is fated to be free or unfree. The limitations on personal freedom implied by the element of fate are overcome only when the individual achieves significant control over the structure of the city—when his fate becomes, in some measure, self-imposed.

Consequently, institutional control figures in the idea of a good city in two distinct ways. We are led to conceive a good city so that our attempt to control institutional developments will be pointed at a proper object; but we find in the course of working out this conception that institutional control is one of its ingredients. Thus, control of institutions is both a means and an end: it is indispensable for the building of a good city, since we cannot suppose that institutional drift will have a happy result; and it is part of the end for whose sake control is undertaken. If we could think of control as merely a means, then the question of who should be responsible for building a better city could be answered by determining who is best qualified. This would probably result in some form of control by experts. But when control is seen to be an intrinsic trait of a good city—an end as well as a means —then we are led to consider a more democratic approach. By opening the control function to all competent persons, an immediate and certain contribution to the freedom of the city is made; on the other hand, closing the control function to all but a narrow group of experts does not merely jeopardize but detracts from this freedom.

The major problem created by accepting the ideal of democratic institutional control is whether existing urban political machinery can provide a satisfactory means of pursuing that ideal. Are the avenues that traditionally lend substance to political democracy in the city—the vote, public meetings, the voicing of complaints to precinct committeemen and other party officials— still adequate? Many observers argue that they are not. It is said that urban government has begun to seem remote and foreign to the ordinary citizen. To be sure, he possesses the right to vote, and though this is a significant activity, in a larger city it is scarcely sufficient to make political democracy a reality. At the most it means that in some sense the people rule. "The people," however, like "the average man," is a statistical abstraction. In large cities, where government is highly bureaucratic, rule by "representatives" of the people may assure a measure of responsibility, at least in the sense that the government will not tyrannize the inhabitants. But it seldom echoes the voice of the ordinary citizen, either in matters of day-to-day policy or in the larger issues of government. The citizen will often agree with what is being done by "his" government, but as a rule he will regard the agreement as a happy accident and in no way indicative of his political effectiveness. Only in city hall is the possessive pronoun used in speaking of urban government; on the streets it is always "they."

The present alienation of the inhabitants of large cities from their government does not mean, however, that democratic control of urban institutions should take place entirely outside of normal governmental channels. As much use as possible should be made of nongovernmental citizens groups. But these lack both the financial resources and the comprehensive viewpoint that might be expected of a governmental agency. What seems indicated is some form of partnership between urban government and citizens groups functioning on the neighborhood level. In this partnership, the primary contributions of government would be to define, by referring to the over-all needs of the city, the framework within which the neighborhood should undertake to control its structure; and to provide the resources, in the form of skilled personnel as well as money, that the neighborhood requires to rebuild itself. When democratic social control is established in this manner, the machinery of democracy not only serves the inhabitant's need to control his own destiny, but advances the cause of person-centeredness and community.

VI

In analyzing the ideas of moral power and freedom, I have sought to discover an exhaustive list of institutional traits which, taken all together, form the objective ground of individual freedom and individual power in the city. So far as the city possesses these traits, it is itself free and morally powerful. Implicit in this approach, then, is a distinction between the freedom and power of the person and the freedom and power of the city. This distinction creates certain problems. Shall we say that the individual automatically becomes free when the objective ground of freedom is built into the structure of urban affairs? Does individual freedom inevitably result from the acquisition by the city's institutions of flexibility, voluntariness, and controllability? A similar question might be asked regarding moral power. The issue is whether the individual can fail to be free even though the formal ground of freedom is present in the city; or, more generally, whether he can fail to grow, to realize his nature, even though the city itself is both free and morally powerful. If this is possible, then one must inquire whether there are not certain subjective conditions of growth that must be met as well before the good life can become a reality.

When the city is free and morally powerful, the inhabitant finds there genuine opportunity for personal growth. Whether he does in fact lead the good life is another matter. The freedom and power of the city denote opportunities that are, from the standpoint of the individual, possibilities. The freedom and power of the individual is something actual. An individual enjoys freedom and power by acting in certain ways; a city possesses freedom and power by grounding the possibility for acting in those ways. To be sure, the existence of the possibility depends upon a number of actualities, including the personal characteristics of the city's inhabitants. Whether the inhabitant will in fact participate in the rich life of the city is in no way assured by the existence of an opportunity to do so.

But to supplement our conception of the good city with arrangements designed to induce the inhabitants to realize the opportunities it offers would be disastrous—a violation of the ideal it was intended to serve. If such inducements were successful, they would, in effect, impose the city on its inhabitants, and in so doing they would jeopardize the voluntary character of the city's institutions. The point is a fundamental one. A city becomes good by opening vistas, by widening and intensifying opportunity, not by narrowing and restricting life, by imposing arrangements, however desirable, upon the individual. What the individual makes of this open environment, assuming that he is mature and mentally competent, is entirely his own affair and quite beyond the legitimate domain of those who would build a better city.

THE CITY OF COLUMBIA

James W. Rouse

This selection, by the President of Community Research and Development, Inc., the builders of Columbia, forecasts the population growth of the United States to the end of this century. It clearly points to the need for farsighted planning if we are to build an aesthetic and satisfying environment for our people. The author reviews the entire planning cycle for Columbia. Although it is a bit early to say with certainty, it does appear that the goal of building an "ideal" city for 100,000 people will be met in an orderly and satisfying manner.

I think that, although belated in our attention to the problems of the inner city, we are beginning now to pay the kind of attention that is required if we are going to make these old cities fit places for people to live in.

But there is danger that we will become so preoccupied that we will lose sight of the fact that at least half of the problem of the metropolitan areas of the United States will be expressed in what happens in the areas not now built upon.

Half of the dwelling units that will exist in the State of California in 1988 have not yet been started.

The New York Regional Planning Commission made a report recently showing the prospect of 11 million people being added to the New York Region in the course of the next 32 years.

It is fairly generally predicted, even with a declining birth rate, that we will add something like 60 to 70 million people to the cities of the United States over the next 20 years.

This means that we add a new Toledo each month to the population of the United States.

We add a new Denver, Dallas, and Atlanta every year.

A whole new Denver, Dallas, and Atlanta every year to the population of the United States.

In the last 20 years the metropolitan

From *Housing and Urban Development Legislation and Urban Insurance,* Hearings before the Subcommittee on Housing of the Committee on Banking and Currency, House of Representatives, Ninetieth Congress, Part 2, pp. 962–971.

area of Baltimore has added a population larger than that of San Diego to its size, and in the next 20 years it will add a city larger than Kansas City.

In those same 20 years, the metropolitan area of Washington will be adding a city bigger than Baltimore. Thus we are in the midst of growth which is transforming the shape, size, and the complexity of the American metropolis.

This is an area which we can do something about much more easily than we can about reshaping the heart of the old city. We can do something about it, if we will. But currently we are not.

I think it is a fair statement to say that with the powers and processes that now exist in America it is impossible to provide in an orderly and intelligent way for the metropolitan growth which we know will occur.

I don't believe there is one single metropolitan area in the United States that has a plan for accommodating the growth that it knows will occur in communities of a quality which we know how to create.

I don't think there exists in local government the powers or the processes to account for our growth and I don't think there exists outside of local government the system, the organization, the corporations, the enterprises to undertake the job that needs to be done.

It is a phenomenon of American business and industry that the largest single industry in the United States is the business of city building. The end product production of the American city is the single biggest industry in the United States—the building of houses, apartments, service stations, factories that constitute the growth of the American city—and yet there is not one single major corporation engaged in this enterprise as its major undertaking. There are no corporations, no

private business enterprises in America that have the financial capacity within their own resources to go out and acquire the land, do the planning, conduct the research to bring about orderly new communities in the United States.

The growth of the American city depends in America upon a vast proliferation of small enterprises in the home-building industry, a great industry and great people, but by American business standards very small and with limited capital.

We depend upon a combination of these, upon this proliferation of small business for the end product of city building in partnership with the huge financial institutions of America—the life insurance companies, the savings banks, the pension funds. This combination produces the American industry.

Our cities grow today really by sheer chance. A farm begins growing houses instead of potatoes, and if it does it successfully pretty soon another farm is bought and a homebuilder starts building houses on it, then another, and soon major development begins to spring up across the landscape.

As it does, the school board has to rush in and provide an elementary school. Now that there is a school there is an inducement for more housing; with more housing there begins to be more traffic along the old two-lane highway, the country road, that served the area; with more traffic it becomes a good place for hamburger stands and Tastee Freez and a service station. This induces further traffic. Then we have to cut back the front yards and widen the old road to a four-lane road. Now we have a typical American highway leading out from an old city. This provides the avenue to more housing. High schools and junior high schools and churches become scattered across the landscape. We need a freeway. So we hack a freeway through the landscape. It intersects the old highway with a cloverleaf. This is a spot for a regional shopping center and an office building. This is the way a city grows.

This is the business I am in. Financing on the one hand and developing on the other these pieces that make up a city.

We all know how to do it better. This committee could go out and plan tomorrow the growth of the American city far better than we do it. It is not new knowledge, not new technological breakthroughs that we need to discover. I doubt if there is any other phase of American life in which the gap is so great between what we now know how to do and what we are doing as in the growth of the American city. And we don't do it better because you can't grow a good city in piecemeal development with small land parcels of 100 or even 1,000 acres of land.

It was out of this awareness and this background that we as a company began asking ourselves half-a-dozen years or more ago isn't it possible somehow to do this thing better?

Wouldn't it be possible to assemble a large enough area of land to plan the pieces of a city in better relationship to one another? The housing, the stores, the schools, the churches, the highways, the recreation areas, the downtown, and might it not be very profitable to do this? Might there not be a very special capability between the public interest in a better environment and private interest in a better profit in producing a better accommodation for the growth of a metropolitan area?

We began exploring this in hypotheses. We built an economic model of what it would take to build a city of 100,000 people. What it would consist of in terms of primary industry, of

dependent and following industry, how many jobs, how many dwelling units, what the income level of the people would be, and therefore what the rents and placing of the housing would have to be, how many schools and churches and theaters and concert halls and hospitals. What would be the whole fabric of a new city of 100,000 people? How many acres of land would this take? What would it cost to acquire it and develop it and over what period of time could it occur and would it work out economically to undertake this?

And as we built this model, with no tract of land in sight we came to the conclusion that it would be very profitable indeed to do it, that it would be more profitable to do it, in fact, than to build the pieces in fractured fashion around the city. We started looking in the Baltimore-Washington corridor until we found an area where we felt it might be possible to assemble the 12,000 acres of land it would take to build a new city of 100,000 people.

We tested the market, bought 1,000 acres of land and at that point, with our model and our location, went to a great life insurance company, the Connecticut General of Hartford. We laid on the line the model and the hypotheses that there was special compatibility between public purpose and private profit—that this could make money. But we also laid on the line the simple fact that there are no development corporations in the United States that could undertake the task. Not one single developer in the United States has the financial resources to go out and acquire that land. Therefore, to do this required a very unique relationship between the great financial institution and the developer.

You can't build a city with a bootstrap. If this was going to be done Connecticut General would have to put up all the money to buy the land. We would share the ownership with them, 50–50. We would produce the plan and zoning and then come back with proposals for its development.

They agreed to this. They made the largest single investment in the history of Connecticut General in order to provide us with the money to assemble all that land.

In the course of 9 months in 1963 we assembled 14,000 acres of land in Howard County, Md., midway between Baltimore and Washington, 165 separate farms and parcels that we put together into a piece of Swiss cheese, the holes of which were existing subdivisions through the area that we didn't acquire. Then went back with a new economic model in which we projected the full cost of carrying this city through to completion in 13 years—of building a city of 100,000 people in 13 years.

Through market studies we estimated what the pace of development could be. We divided up the land into business and industry and recreation and into all of its uses. We got our zoning, which is another story. We went back and showed that it would take $50 million, to carry this project forward to completion. When we put in our economic model the full cost of everything that it would take, including streets and utilities, parks and playgrounds and a bus system, interest and carrying charges and promotion and administration—and the whole works, and when we deducted from those costs the revenues from the sale of land year by year we showed that our peak debt requirements would reach about $50 million.

We asked Connecticut General to participate with us in a new financing that would refinance there then $23.5 million of investment in the land into a new $50 million financing, and we would find two other institutional partners to share this new financing with them.

The Teachers Insurance and Annuity Association and the Chase Manhattan Bank joined Connecticut General in December of 1965 and together the three companies committed $50 million to us to permit this development to go forward.

In the summer of 1966 we commenced construction and in the summer of 1967 we opened Columbia to the first residents. Now after 9 months there are some 1,200 people living there: the first four industries are operating. We have created more jobs than dwelling units in our first 9 months, and we look forward by 1980 to the completion of this city of 110,000 people.

The lessons that we have learned from this are important, I think. There are a great many things that we have been able to accomplish through large-scale acquisition and land ownership and planning that simply aren't possible on the basis of typical piecemeal 100, 500, even a thousand-acre development, and these things are important to the future of America.

In the first place, the only reason in the world we could ever assemble this land—we had no power of eminent domain and no large single ownership from which to work—was that we had the financial resources to do it. If we had had to go out and buy this land on 10 percent down and 10 years to pay the typical developer-financing relationship with a land owner, the land could never have been assembled. We were successful because of our ability to pay cash for the land, and the fact that we were acquiring so much land that we could make a variety of tenure relationships with the people who were selling—we could buy the land, lease it back to a farmer for 3 years or 5 years and simply plan to defer that part of the development. We gave life estates— we had flexibility because of the scale of the development and we had the financial resources that let us do the assembling.

Many people would say that even if you could acquire the land, you couldn't get the zoning. But the fact that we were planning on this large scale, let us get the zoning. This was a county in which the Republicans had thrown out the Democrats in 1962 for the first time in 40 years there and the whole issue in the campaign was zoning. It was typical of a threshold county on the edge of urban growth—the Republicans alleging that the Democrats were being too free with the home builders, allowing quarter-acre zoning, and that the only way to protect Howard County was through the maintenance of low density zoning, half-acre zoning. This is a typical state of mind in a threshold county because there are no other devices for protecting against urbanization, but the device of low-density zoning simply spreads a thin coat of suburban paint over the whole landscape instead of providing a real community.

Anyway, the Republicans won and 1 year later we arrived in the county, having acquired 10 percent of the county, and saying we wanted to build a city. This was a pretty horrendous political fact to face in this county and we were warned by the people of their skepticism and disbelief in what we were doing. But we kept saying "You have all the cards, we have to produce either a better image of urban growth than you have in mind or we will get turned down. We will plan for a year and a year from now we will be back and present our plans to you."

And a year later we did. We presented our plans to the county. We set up models, invited people to come and meet with us in groups of 1 to 100,

from 10 in the morning to 10 at night, 7 days a week. We met with over 5,000 people about their individual needs, before we filed for our zoning. We then filed for a whole new kind of zoning, called "New Town District" zoning, a complete amendment to the zoning laws of the county.

It provided all kinds of things that still can't be done anywhere else in Howard County—townhouses, high-rise apartments—uses that hold out prospects to the people in isolated form, but were acceptable within the context of a whole city in which we were preserving the stream valleys, and the open spaces; building lakes; providing public transportation; providing a city. When we went in for our final critical zoning hearing in July of 1965 the hearing was set up to go from noon until midnight. That was the custom. We presented our case and they then called on the opposition and not one single person in Howard County opposed the zoning. Not a single person. This was only possible because the size of our land holding and the scale and comprehensiveness of the plan made sense in a suburban location typically frightened by piecemeal urbanization. There was nothing unusual about these people except they were people of good will who would listen—and that is not really unusual—given the choice between the continuance of suburban sprawl, or a city that would work, those people chose a city that would work.

This is a very significant fact in the growth of the American city.

The next thing that happened was that we were able to do things again because of our land holding that a builder with 100 or 500 acres couldn't do.

We extended sewers 7 miles at a cost to us of $1,750,000. We extended the water 4 miles at a cost of $600,000. This is $2,300,000 to get sewer and water to the land. But this was only $160 an acre on 14,000 acres of land.

We were able to take U.S. 29 between Baltimore and Washington, which is right on its way to being the kind of road that I described, a two-lane road that is now getting a lot of traffic and filling stations and being pockmarked. We were able to acquire the commercial clutter along 29. We paid $75,000 an acre for 2 acres of land. We paid $135,000 for a 1-acre parcel on which we are tearing down the building and turning it back to open space.

We were able to do this kind of thing, able to remove this commercial clutter, in the 5 miles that 29 goes through Columbia, and convert it into a landscaped parkway and spread the cost over the 14,000 acres.

We have been able to concentrate the development where it ought to occur. We were able to take the 14,000 acres of land and identify all the major stream valleys, all the major forests, all the significant historic buildings, all of the country lanes that ought to be preserved. We were able to identify these things and provide for them and to concentrate the development where it ought to occur in the open areas and leave alone the stream valleys that ought to be left alone.

In fact, we were not only able to leave them alone but dam them up and create five lakes through the city.

We were able to provide 3,200 acres of permanent open space. And it is land that ought to be open space. We concentrated the development when it ought to occur. We were able to do it because it was prudent to do it, because we put the development where it was more economic to put it.

It made for shorter streets, shorter runs of sewer and water and underground utilities. And we were only able

to do this because of developing and planning on a large enough scale.

As a matter of fact, a study was recently published by the Howard County Planning Commission that has received very little attention and is tremendously important. They took the future growth of Howard County to 1985. This is a county now with 60,000 people—pre-Columbia. They traced the pattern of growth that has occurred over the last decade and they then built three models of the future growth of Howard County. One model assumed what they call the continuance of trend development and no Columbia. What would it cost? The second model was Columbia with 110,000 people, and the rest of the county in trend development, what would that cost? The comparison of those two nearly showed that the development of Columbia would save Howard County in 20 years $135 million and that at the end of that time nearly $1 million a year would be saved in school bussing and nearly $1 million in road maintenance because of the compact development that occurs as a result of this kind of planning.

We were able to provide a public transportation system in Columbia because we have a large enough area to locate the employment centers and downtown and village centers in such a way that the bus system can relate to those destinations and we are able to plan the location of the high density housing in such a way that it is along the bus line. But running the bus line on its own right-of-way, separated from the regular road system we are able to get 40 percent of the dwelling units in Columbia within a 3 minutes' walk of a bus stop.

This is yet to be proven, but all of our studies say that this bus system can operate on a self-sustaining basis by our 5th year and on a headway of, say,

20 minutes. This only possible because we were able to plan over a large enough area.

We show about $2,800,000 in the cost of lakes in Columbia, five lakes with roughly 500 acres of water in the town.

This is $200 an acre it is costing us to do this. This is a public gain but economical to do when we can spread it over a 14,000-acre development.

We were able to provide roads of higher specifications than required in the county. We were able to provide roads that were wide enough to account for the population of this area 20 years from now, not to build a little road today for 100 acres of land that you know is going to have to be widened in 20 years.

We were able to landscape our roads, able to provide a path system separate from the roads that serve the houses and schools and neighborhood and village centers.

But most important, really, in this whole enterprise is that, having created this blueprint for a new city, and therefore a new opportunity for the institutional life of that city to take new form, the response we have received from the institutions, from the school system, from the churches, from the health system, from the cultural institutions, has been perfectly extraordinary.

They are in Columbia in a new way.

The 13 major Protestant denominations formed a single Religious Facilities Corporation to own all church buildings in order that they can double the amount of money going into the church program and cut half the amount that goes into brick and mortar. The Catholic Archdiocese has joined the Religious Facilities Corporation and abandoned parochial schools in Columbia. The Catholic physical facilities, will be owned by a corporation not controlled by the Catholic Church but

controlled jointly by 13 Protestant denominations and the Catholic Church. This is a miracle because of the opportunity to bring religion to people in a new form. The Jewish community has agreed to join this religious facilities corporation and the Jewish, the Catholic, and the Protestants together will own the church buildings in Columbia.

The Catholics and Protestants and Jews have formed an innerfaith housing corporation to build housing for low-income families and by this fall there will be available in Columbia two-bedroom apartments at rents of under $75 a month to families of low and moderate income, using the 221(d) (3) as the financing device.

In the educational system in a threshold county such as this the county school board has little choice but to go out and build a consolidated school and bus kids in from wherever they are going to come.

In Columbia we have been able to provide for 15 years for this growth. We will add 40,000 schoolchildren to a school system that now has 13,000. That is the impact of this growth. But we have been able to provide in advance every single school site. Every elementary school is at the heart of the neighborhood and every kid can walk to school. Every middle and junior high school is at the heart of a village and we have accounted for it before the city is built.

The net result is that the school board responding to this has obtained grants to reexamine curriculums in the public schools, and grants to design schools that are responsive to the curriculum studies. The first elementary school in Columbia will have open classrooms, will be ungraded, with team teaching, and emphasis on growth of the individual child instead of jamming knowledge at kids.

In the field of health, Johns Hopkins

has sat down with us and worked for the creation of a program of comprehensive health care.

Johns Hopkins announced its intention of being in Columbia with a comprehensive health care system to be known as Columbia Medicine in which, for the first time in the history of this country, a great university hospital would be providing facilities to make available to the people, on a monthly payment prepaid basis, home nursing care, group medical practice, hospitalization, psychiatric service—all on a monthly payment basis and on a voluntary basis to every family in Columbia.

The estimated cost of this program per capita is less than the average per capita cost of health care in the United States today.

The point being that this great medical institution says:

If we could deliver to a population the knowledge that exists about preventive medicine and health care rather than just treating sickness, we could build the health of a community and save money in hospitalization and crises care; that those dollars saved at that end would more than pay for the cost of preventive medicine and health education at the beginning of the pipeline.

This is their conviction born of data which they consider to be convincing.

The very first thing that happened in our new city never would have been possible, but for the fact that Columbia was planned as a new city. We signed a 30-year lease with the Washington National Symphony to provide a summer home for the National Symphony. We built the Merriweather Post Pavilion of Music and opened up last summer in the midst of a violent rainstorm. But, this summer, in this new city with only 1,200 people there are over 50 events scheduled by the National Symphony,

the New York City Ballet, and others— a whole variety of first-rate cultural events for this community.

The Cochran Gallery will be in Columbia with an art school. The Peabody Conservatory of Music, we hope, will be there with a music school. These things could never occur, rationally in the fractured growth of sprawl. They can only occur within the framework of comprehensive planning and development.

Now, this gets to the financing provisions of title IV.

We have been able to do this without the benefits of that title, therefore, why is it needed? We were very lucky. We were in a very fortunate position. We had represented the Connecticut General Life Insurance Company in the mortgage banking business for 25 years. We also happen to be a developer who had financed a great many projects with the Connecticut General. Our relationship was very intimate. They obviously had confidence in what we might be able to do, and they therefore supported this venture through its first critical phase of land acquisition and into its development.

But this economic model that we were able to prepare with no special things going for us showed that the full cash requirements of building a new city could be advanced by three great institutions, the Teachers Insurance Annuity, The Chase Manhattan Bank, and the Connecticut Life Insurance Company, because the value added by the acquisition, planning and zoning process gave them sufficient margins to advance that money.

The credit of our company wasn't even pledged to that debt.

The Harvard Research & Development Corp., which is the developer, is the borrower. And the prospective full cash requirements are advanced by those three great institutions. This same arithmetic is reproducible over and over again in America.

The homebuilders may not feel the need for this. The homebuilders may feel that they can prosper building 100-acre or perhaps 500-acre developments. The great financial institutions may not feel the need for this. They have more places to put their money than they can possibly use. That is the expression of the congestion that exists in the money market. But the country needs it. The country can't afford to grow with no alternatives to sprawl. This is the only real prospect we have today. But the passage of this bill and the setting up of these insurance provisions will bring out money from the insurance companies and the pension funds to serve individual developers or groups of developers to allow the kind of comprehensive planned development in the metropolitan areas that this country must have.

We can't afford to add 11 million people to the New York region with the same unplanned sprawl. We can't afford the growth in California without doing this job better. This legislation should be completely self-sustaining and ought to be mandatory that it is. The insurance premiums that the developer ought to have to pay, and that he can afford to pay, should more than cover the cost of this program. It is an ideal relationship between the Federal Government and the entrepreneural forces and capital forces of the country in meeting a national need that can't otherwise be met.

URBAN COALITION: TURNING THE COUNTRY AROUND

Urban America Inc.

On the night of July 31, 1967 over 1,000 leaders of religion, business, unions, local government, and civil rights organizations met in a Washington hotel ballroom. Their task was to organize a national program and enlist the aid of all Americans in rectifying the underlying troubles causing "the long hot summers." That summer Newark and Detroit had borne the brunt of riots occurring in eighty cities. A convocation followed on August 24 at which goals were established under an organization called the Urban Coalition. The agreement provided for eight broad goals expressing the "sense" of the body. It enumerated seven specific programs for the federal government, five specific programs for the private sector, and for the nation as a whole to provide decent housing and a suitable living environment. The Urban Coalition then pledged itself to see the goals through to success no matter how long it took.

The platform was 96 feet long, stretching from wall to wall of the third largest ballroom in Washington. At its center stood Andrew Heiskell, hands on the podium, and beside him sat A. Philip Randolph, frail but firm and

"Urban Coalition: Turning the Country Around," *City* (October 1967), pp. 1–3, 15–16. Copyright 1967 by Urban America Inc. Reprinted by permission.

resonant of voice. To their right were
I. W. Abel of the Steelworkers; Mayor
Ivan Allen of Atlanta; Arnold Aronson
of the Leadership Conference on Civil
Rights; Mayor Joseph Barr of Pitts-
burgh; Mayor Jerome Cavanagh of
Detroit; Frederick Close of Alcoa;
Mayor John Collins of Boston; Mayor
Richard Daley of Chicago; Gilbert Fitz-
hugh of Metropolitan Life; Henry Ford
II; Mayor Milton Graham of Phoenix;
Joseph Keenan of the Electrical Work-
ers; Mayor John Lindsay of New York.
To their left were George Meany of the
ALF-CIO; J. Irwin Miller of Cummins
Engine Company; Mayor Arthur Nafta-
lin of Minneapolis; Gerald Phillippe
of General Electric; Walter Reuther of
the United Auto Workers; David
Rockefeller; Rabbi Jacob Rudin; Asa
Spaulding of the North Carolina Mutual
Insurance Company; David Sullivan of
the Building Service Employees; Mayor
James Tate of Philadelphia; John
Wheeler of the Southern Regional
Council; Roy Wilkins of the NAACP;
Whitney Young of the National Urban
League.

"In this room," said Heiskell, "the
leadership of religion, business, unions,
local government, and the civil rights
organizations is meeting to make a
major commitment . . . to turn law and
principles into reality, to bring equality
of opportunity to every one of our citizens." His listeners filled 1,000 chairs
and lined the room's perimeter. Those
registered included Gen. James M.
Gavin (and Richard Belford of the
New Haven Jewish Community Council), Leon Keyserling (and William J.
Born of the Urban League of Greater
Hartford), August Heckscher (and Mrs.
Robert Hoyt of Church Women United
in Georgia), Oveta Culp Hobby (and
Mayor Walter J. Kelliher of Malden,
Mass.), Dore Schary (and Matthew J.
Stevens of the Essex-West Hudson
Labor Council). There were the presi-

dents or board chairmen of Standard
Oil, DuPont, Sears Roebuck, Morgan
Guaranty Trust, American Airlines,
among other corporations, and there
was Dr. Nathan Wright, chairman of
the Black Power conference in Newark.

There was, in this Emergency Convocation August 24 at the Shoreham
Hotel, "enough power to turn this
country around," according to Whitney
Young. It was a precise statement of
the Convocation's purpose.

PROLOGUE: A JOINING
OF POWER AND CONCERN,
OUT OF A SENSE OF
EMERGENCY

Those on the platform were members
of the steering committee of the Urban
Coalition, formed four weeks earlier,
while Detroit still was smoldering and
glass still littered the streets of Newark.
The Coalition had been conceived, however, in the chill and inattentive winter.
In January, the late Stephen R. Currier,
founder and president of Urban America Inc., had invited a group of mayors
to Washington to discuss the national
social crisis that had developed in the
cities.

The mayors came from Atlanta,
Baltimore, Boston, Denver, Detroit,
Miami, Milwaukee, New York, Philadelphia, Pittsburgh, and Tacoma, Washington. All told much the same story.
Their cities faced increasing welfare
loads, high rates of concentrated unemployment, deterioration of the housing
supply—and a rising sense of alienation in ghetto areas. At the same time,
local tax bases were dwindling as the
federal share of tax revenue increased,
and the shortage of operating revenue
had become chronic.

The mayors felt that it was time for
those who shared a stake in the cities'
well-being to join in a coalition to
alert the nation to the critical urgency

of urban needs. They asked Mr. Currier and Urban America, together with the U.S. Conference of Mayors and the National League of Cities, to act as catalysts in forming such a coalition.

A steering committee of mayors was established as the coalition's first component. Last spring, a series of meetings was begun with representatives of business, civil rights, labor, and religion. The timetable called for the coalition of these groups to be completed in the fall to launch a long-range attack on urban problems.

Then came summer. Outbreaks of violence in more than 80 cities, and the evidence of a hardening national reaction, clearly called for emergency action. In three days of the week following the riots in Detroit, Mayors Barr and Lindsay called upon leaders in the five fields to meet July 31 in the Washington offices of Urban America. Thirty-four attended or sent assurances of their support. At the July 31 meeting, the Urban Coalition became a reality, and these men its steering committee.

The meeting, as one participant commented, was held under "battlefield conditions." The night was appropriately hot, and the building's air conditioning had chosen the occasion to malfunction. All day there had been rumors of violence, first in one part of the edgy capital, then another.

There was tension in the room, too, at the outset: some of the participants —business and labor, mayors and civil rights leaders—were used to sitting opposite the table from each other, rather than side by side. But there was also a tangible sense of urgency, commonly felt. It was this sense of urgency that held the Urban Coalition together, that night and in the weeks thereafter.

The unspoken question was how far this disparate group of powerful individuals could go toward specific agreement on the nature of the crisis and proposed solutions. The discussion began with diagnosis, and the word alienation was spoken repeatedly. The discussion turned to prescriptions, and the group found agreement that not nearly enough had been either proposed or accomplished. Andrew Heiskell read a statement of concern which he had drafted in preparation for the meeting: "The tangible results of the urban riots in terms of death, injury, and property damage are horrifying in themselves," it began. "The intangible damage in terms of the riots' effects on men's minds may yet be even greater." John Lindsay began writing swiftly on a small tablet; Walter Reuther, then David Rockefeller, handed him paragraphs they had composed; others voiced suggestions and amendments.

The result of this high-level draftsmanship was the first statement of the Urban Coalition, and it went further toward specificity than even those who called the meeting had anticipated. The statement called for a reordering of national priorities to provide the cities with resources in scale with their problems. It called on Congress to act immediately on urban programs. It proposed immediate enactment of a federal emergency work and training program for the urban poor, and at the same time pledged a massive expansion of private sector employment efforts. It pointed to the need for a long-range commitment to the physical and social reconstruction of American cities.

And, in conclusion, it called for an Emergency Convocation of a thousand leaders in the five segments of society before the end of August. The Convocation was not to be a deliberative session. Those invited by and from the five segments were to attend on the basis of commitment to the Coalition's stated purposes. The objectives of the Convocation were to expand the circle of the concerned, and to plan how the Coalition's purposes could be carried forward.

The Convocation was organized in exactly three weeks from the time the August 24 date was chosen. Staff representatives of the steering committee members met almost daily to plan arrangements, and to expand the original statement into a full-fledged program. It was agreed that the steering committee itself would meet on the night of August 23 to act upon the program document, and to resolve any major differences that remained.

The room was larger this time, and air conditioned; Washington had made it through the summer without a major disturbance; Detroit, in fact, had been the last full-scale summer riot. Yet somehow, the sense of urgency remained. One by one, the remaining issues were discussed. Traditional differences came to the surface; traditional positions were challenged and stretched to the breaking point. Each time, viewpoints were reconciled. If anything, the program statement was stronger, went further, when it emerged from the meeting than before.

It was printed and ready for the opening of registration the next morning.

THE CONVOCATION CALLED FOR, AND ITSELF PLEDGED, VAST NEW COMMITMENTS

"We are here, representing many aspects of our society, because we know that the problem is too vast and complex to be resolved by any one sector," said Co-chairman Heiskell from the podium. "Our joint presence is testimony to that realization."

The first order of business was the Coalition's program for proceeding beyond just joint presence at the one-day Convocation. The document adopted

the night before, the Coalition's "Statement of Principles, Goals, and Commitments," was presented to the Convocation by Co-chairman Randolph . . .:

We are experiencing our third summer of widespread civil disorder. In 1965, it was Harlem, and the disaster of Watts. In 1966, it was the Hough area of Cleveland, Omaha, Atlanta, Dayton, San Francisco, and 24 other cities. This summer, Newark and Detroit were only the most tragic of 80 explosions of violence in the streets.

Confronted by these catastrophic events, we, as representatives of business, labor, religion, civil rights, and local government, have joined in this Convocation to create a sense of national urgency on the need for positive action for all the people of our cities.

We are united in the following convictions:

We believe the tangible effects of the urban riots in terms of death, injury, and property damage, horrifying though they are, are less to be feared than the intangible damage to men's minds.

We believe it is the government's duty to maintain law and order.

We believe that our thoughts and actions should be directed to the deep-rooted and historic problems of the cities.

We believe that we, as a nation, must clearly and positively demonstrate our belief that justice, social progress, and equality of opportunity are rights of every citizen.

We believe the American people and the Congress must reorder national priorities, with a commitment of resources equal to the magnitude of the problems we face. The crisis requires a new dimension of effort in both the public and private sectors, working together to provide jobs, housing, education, and the other needs of our cities.

We believe the Congress must move

without delay on urban programs. The country can wait no longer for measures that have too long been denied the people of the cities and the nation as a whole—additional civil rights legislation, adequately funded model cities, anti-poverty, housing, education, and job-training programs, and a host of others.

We believe the private sector of America must directly and vigorously involve itself in the crisis of the cities by a commitment to investment, job-training, and hiring, and all that is necessary to the full enjoyment of the free enterprise system—and also to its survival.

We believe the sickness of the cities, including civic disorder within them, is the responsibility of the whole of America. Therefore, it is the responsibility of every American to join in the creation of a new political, social, economic, and moral climate that will make possible the breaking of the vicious cycle of the ghetto. Efforts must be made to insure the broadest possible opportunity for all citizens and groups, including those in the ghetto, to participate fully in shaping and directing the society of which they are a part.

This Convocation calls upon the nation to end once and for all the shame of poverty amid general affluence. Government and business must accept responsibility to provide all Americans with opportunity to earn an adequate income. Private industry must greatly accelerate its efforts to recruit, train, and hire the hard-core unemployed. When the private sector is unable to provide employment to those who are both able and willing to work, then in a free society the government must of necessity assume the responsibility and act as the employer of last resort or must assure adequate income levels for those who are unable to work.

This Convocation calls upon the federal government to develop an emergency work program to provide jobs and new training opportunities for the unemployed and underemployed consistent with the following principles:

1. The federal government must enlist the co-operation of government at all levels and of private industry to assure that meaningful, productive work is available to everyone willing and able to work.

2. To create socially useful jobs, the emergency work program should concentrate on the huge backlog of employment needs in parks, streets, slums, countryside, schools, colleges, libraries, and hospitals. To this end an emergency work program should be initiated and should have as its first goal putting at least one million of the presently unemployed into productive work at the earliest possible moment.

3. The program must provide meaningful jobs—not dead-end, make-work projects—so that the employment experience gained adds to the capabilities and broadens the opportunities of the employees to become productive members of the permanent work force of our nation.

4. Basic education, training, and counseling must be an integral part of the program to assure extended opportunities for upward job mobility and to improve employee productivity. Funds for training, education, and counseling should be made available to private industry as well as to public and private nonprofit agencies.

5. Funds for employment should be made available to local and state governments, nonprofit institutions, and federal agencies able to demonstrate their ability to use labor productively without reducing existing levels of employment or undercutting existing labor standards or wages which prevail for comparable work or services in the

area but are not less than the federal minimum wage.

6. Such a program should seek to qualify new employees to become part of the regular work force and that normal performance standards are met.

7. The operation of the program should be keyed to specific, localized unemployment problems and focused intially on those areas where the need is most apparent.

All representatives of the private sector in this Urban Coalition decisively commit themselves to assist the deprived among us to achieve full participation in the economy as self-supporting citizens. We pledge full-scale private endeavor through creative job-training and employment, managerial assistance, and basic investment in all phases of urban development.

The alternatives to a massive and concerted drive by the private sector are clear. They include the burden of wasted human and physical potential, the deterioration of the healthy environment basic to the successful operation of any business, and the dangers of permanent alienation from our society of millions of citizens.

We propose to initiate an all-out attack on the unemployment problem through the following steps:

1. In cooperation with government, to move systematically and directly into the ghettos and barrios to seek out the unemployed and underemployed and enlist them in basic and positive private training and employment programs. We will re-evaluate our current testing procedures and employment standards so as to modify or eliminate those practices and requirements that unnecessarily bar many persons from gainful employment by business or access to union membership.

2. To create a closer relationship between private employers and public training and emergency employment programs to widen career opportunities for our disadvantaged citizens. To this end, we will proceed immediately to promote "Earn and Learn Centers" in depressed urban areas that might well be the joint venture of business, labor, and local government.

3. To develop new training and related programs to facilitate the early entry of under-qualified persons into industrial and commercial employment.

4. To develop large-scale programs to motivate the young to continue their education. Working closely with educators, we will redouble our efforts to provide part-time employment, training, and other incentives for young men and women. We also pledge our active support to making quality education readily accessible to deprived as well as advantaged young people.

5. To expand on-the-job training programs to enhance the career advancement prospects of all employees, with particular emphasis on those who now must work at the lowest level of job classifications because of educational and skill deficiencies.

We pledge to mobilize the managerial resources and experience of the private sector in every way possible. We will expand part-time and full-time assistance to small business development. We will strive to help residents of these areas both to raise their level of managerial know-how and to obtain private and public investment funds for development. We will work more closely with public agencies to assist in the management of public projects. We will encourage more leaders in the private sector to get directly and personally involved in urban problems so that they may gain a deeper understanding of these problems and be of greater assistance.

We pledge our best efforts to develop means by which major private investment may be attracted to the renovation of deteriorating neighborhoods in our cities. We will explore and encourage governmental incentives to expedite private investment. We will develop new methods of combining investment and managerial assistance so that the residents may achieve a leadership position in the development of their areas.

This Convocation calls upon the nation to take bold and immediate action to fulfill the national need to provide "a decent home and a suitable living environment for every American family" with guarantees of equal access to all housing, new and existing. The Urban Coalition shall, as its next order of business, address itself to the development of a broad program of urban reconstruction and advocacy of appropriate public and private action to move toward these objectives, including the goal of rehabilitation and construction of at least a million housing units for lower-income families annually.

This Convocation calls upon the nation to create educational programs that will equip all young Americans for full and productive participation in our society to the full potential of their abilities. This will require concentrated compensatory programs to equalize opportunities for achievement. Early childhood education must be made universal. Work and study programs must be greatly expanded to enlist those young people who now drop out of school. Financial barriers that now deny to youngsters from low-income families the opportunity for higher education must be eliminated. Current programs must be increased sufficiently to wipe out adult illiteracy within five years.

This Convocation calls upon local government, business, labor, religions, and civil rights groups to create counterpart local coalitions where they do not exist to support and supplement this declaration of principles.

This Convocation calls upon all Americans to apply the same determination to these programs that they have to past emergencies. We are confident that, given this commitment, our society has the ingenuity to allocate its resources and devise the techniques necessary to rebuild cities and still meet our other national obligations without impairing our financial integrity. Out of past emergencies, we have drawn strength and progress. Out of the present urban crisis we can build cities that are places, not of disorder and despair, but of hope and opportunity. The task we set for ourselves will not be easy, but the needs are massive and urgent, and the hour is late. We pledge ourselves to this goal for as long as it takes to accomplish it. We ask the help of the Congress and the Nation.

HOUSING: A PLAN FOR ACTION

President's Commission on Civil Disorders

The effects of restricted housing patterns on the Negro have generally been well known. However, little has been done to provide true open-housing legislation. So long as patterns of housing are continued along racial lines, the frustration of

From the President's Commission on Civil Disorders, *Report of the National Advisory Commission on Civil Disorders*, March 1, 1968.

the Negro, which is inherent in such patterns, will mount. This selection provides a comprehensive plan for dealing with racial patterns in housing as well as the public-private controversy in urban renewal.

INTRODUCTION

The passage of the National Housing Act in 1934 signaled a new Federal commitment to provide housing for the Nation's citizens. Congress made the commitment explicit 15 years later in the Housing Act of 1949, establishing as a national goal, the realization of "a decent home and suitable environment for every American family."

Today, after more than three decades of fragmented and grossly under-funded Federal housing programs, decent housing remains a chronic problem for the disadvantaged urban household. Fifty-six percent of the country's nonwhite families live in central cities today, and of these, nearly two-thirds live in neighborhoods marked by substandard housing and general urban blight.[1] For these citizens, condemned by segregation and poverty to live in the decaying slums of our central cities, the goal of a decent home and suitable environment is as far distant as ever.

During the decade of the 1950's, when vast numbers of Negroes were migrating to the cities, only 4 million of the 16.8 million new housing units constructed throughout the Nation were built in the central cities. These additions were counterbalanced by the loss of 1.5 million central-city units through demolition and other means. The result

was that the number of nonwhites living in substandard housing increased from 1.4 to 1.8 million, even though the number of substandard units declined.

Statistics available for the period since 1960 indicate that the trend is continuing. There has been virtually no decline in the number of occupied dilapidated units in metropolitan areas, and surveys in New York City and Watts actually show an increase in the number of such units. These statistics have led the Department of Housing and Urban Development to conclude that while the trend in the country as a whole is toward less substandard housing, "There are individual neighborhoods and areas within many cities where the housing situation continues to deteriorate."[2]

Inadequate housing is not limited to Negroes. Even in the central cities the problem affects two and a half times as many white as nonwhite households. Nationally, over 4 million of the nearly 6 million occupied substandard units in 1966 were occupied by whites.

It is also true that Negro housing in large cities is significantly better than that in most rural areas—especially in the South. Good quality housing has become available to Negro city dwellers at an increasing rate since the mid-1950's when the postwar housing shortage ended in most metropolitan areas.

Nevertheless, in the Negro ghetto, grossly inadequate housing continues to be a critical problem.

---

[1] The Department of Housing and Urban Development classifies substandard housing as that housing reported by the U.S. Census Bureau as (1) sound but lacking full plumbing, (2) deteriorating and lacking full plumbing, or (3) dilapidated.

[2] Hearings before the Subcommittee on Executive Reorganization of the Committee on Government Operations, U.S. Senate, 89th Cong., 2d sess., Aug. 16, 1966, p. 148.

Substandard, Old, and Overcrowded Structures

Nationwide, 25 percent of all non-whites living in central cities occupied substandard units in 1960, compared to 8 percent of all whites. Preliminary Census Bureau data indicate that by 1966, the figures had dropped to 16 and 5 percent respectively. However, if "deteriorating" units and units with serious housing code violations are added, the percentage of nonwhites living in inadequate housing in 1966 becomes much greater.

In 14 of the largest U.S. cities, the proportions of all nonwhite housing units classified as deteriorating, dilapidated, or lacking full plumbing in 1960 (the latest date for which figures are available), were as follows:

City	Percentage of Nonwhite Occupied Housing Units Classified Deteriorating, or Dilapidated, 1960	Percentage of Nonwhite Occupied Housing Units Classified Deteriorating, Dilapilated, or Sound, but Without Full Plumbing, 1960
New York	33.8	42.4
Chicago	32.1	42.8
Los Angeles	14.7	18.1
Philadelphia	28.6	32.0
Detroit	27.9	30.1
Baltimore	30.5	31.7
Houston	30.1	36.7
Cleveland	29.9	33.9
Washington, D.C.	15.2	20.8
St. Louis	40.3	51.6
San Francisco	21.3	34.0
Dallas	41.3	45.9
New Orleans	44.3	56.9
Pittsburgh	49.1	58.9

Source: U.S. Department of Commerce, Bureau of the Census.

PERCENTAGE OF HOUSING UNITS
DILAPIDATED OR DETERIORATED IN
SELECTED AREAS OF NEWARK, 1960

Area Number	Population	Percentage Nonwhite	Percentage of All Housing Units Dilapidated or Deteriorating
1	25,300	75.5	91.0
2	48,200	64.5	63.8
3A	48,300	74.8	43.1

Source: George Sternlieb, The Tenement Landlord, New Brunswick, New Jersey: Rutgers (1966) pp. 238–241.

Conditions were far worse than these city-wide averages in many specific disadvantaged neighborhoods. For example, a study of housing in Newark, N.J., before the 1967 disorders, showed the following situation in certain predominantly Negro neighborhoods as of 1960.

These three areas contained 30 percent of the total population of Newark in 1960, and 62 percent of its nonwhite population.

The Commission carried out special analyses of 1960 housing conditions in three cities, concentrating on all Census Tracts with 1960 median incomes of under $3,000 for both families and individuals. It also analyzed housing conditions in Watts. The results showed that the vast majority of people living in the poorest areas of these cities were Negroes, and that a high proportion lived in inadequate housing:

Item	Detroit	Washington, D.C.	Memphis	Watts Area of Los Angeles
Total population of study area	162,375	97,084	150,827	49,074
Percentage of study area, nonwhite	67.5%	74.5%	74.0%	87.3%
Percentage of housing units in study area:				
Substandard by HUD definition	32.7	23.9	35.0	10.5
Dilapidated, deteriorating or sound but lacking full plumbing	53.1	37.3	46.5	29.1

Source: U.S. Department of Commerce, Bureau of Census.

Negroes, on the average, also occupy much older housing than whites. In each of 10 metropolitan areas analyzed by the Commission, substantially higher percentages of nonwhites than whites occupied units built prior to 1939.

Finally, Negro housing units are far more likely to be overcrowded than those occupied by whites. In U.S. metropolitan areas in 1960, 25 percent of all nonwhite units were overcrowded by the standard measure (that is, they contained 1.01 or more persons per room). Only 8 percent of all white-occupied units were in this category. Moreover, 11 percent of all non-white-occupied units were seriously overcrowded (1.51 or more persons per room), compared with 2 percent for white-occupied units. The figures were as follows in the ten metropolitan areas analyzed by the Commission.

PERCENTAGE OF WHITE AND NONWHITE OCCUPIED HOUSING UNITS BUILT PRIOR TO 1939 IN SELECTED METROPOLITAN AREAS

Metropolitan Area	White Occupied Units	Nonwhite Occupied Units
Cleveland	33.2	90.6
Dallas	31.9	52.7
Detroit	46.2	86.1
Kansas City	54.4	89.9
Los Angeles— Long Beach	36.6	62.4
New Orleans	52.9	62.2
Philadelphia	62.0	90.8
Saint Louis	57.9	84.7
San Francisco— Oakland	51.3	67.6
Washington, D.C.	31.9	64.9

Higher Rents for Poorer Housing

Negroes in large cities are often forced to pay the same rents as whites and receive less for their money, or

PERCENTAGE OF WHITE AND
NONWHITE OCCUPIED UNITS WITH
1.01 OR MORE PERSONS PER ROOM
IN SELECTED METROPOLITAN
AREAS

Metropolitan Area	White Occupied Units	Nonwhite Occupied Units
Cleveland	6.9	19.3
Dallas	9.3	28.8
Detroit	8.6	17.5
Kansas City	8.7	18.0
Los Angeles— Long Beach	8.0	17.4
New Orleans	12.0	36.1
Philadelphia	4.9	16.3
Saint Louis	11.8	28.0
San Francisco— Oakland	6.0	19.7
Washington, D.C.	6.2	22.6

Source: U.S. Department of Commerce, Bureau of Census.

pay higher rents for the same accommodations.

The first type of discriminatory effect —paying the same amount but receiving less—is illustrated by data from the 1960 Census for Chicago and Detroit.

In certain Chicago census tracts, both whites and nonwhites paid median rents of $88, and the proportions paying various specific rents below that median were almost identical. But the units rented by nonwhites were typically:

Smaller (the median number of rooms was 3.35 for nonwhites versus 3.95 for whites).

In worse condition (30.7 percent of all nonwhite units were deteriorated or dilapidated units versus 11.6 percent for whites).

Occupied by more people (the median household size was 3.53 for nonwhites versus 2.88 for whites).

More likely to be overcrowded (27.4 percent of nonwhite units had 1.01 or more persons per room versus 7.9 percent for whites).

In Detroit, whites paid a median rental of $77 as compared to $76 among nonwhites. Yet 27.0 percent of nonwhite units were deteriorating or dilapidated, as compared to only 10.3 percent of all white units.

The second type of discriminatory effect—paying more for similar housing —is illustrated by data from a study of housing conditions in disadvantaged neighborhoods in Newark, N.J. In four areas of that city (including the three areas cited previously), nonwhites with housing essentially similar to that of whites paid rents that were from 8.1 percent to 16.8 percent higher. Though the typically larger size of nonwhite households, with consequent harder wear and tear, may partially justify the differences in rental, the study found that nonwhites were paying a definite "color tax" of apparently well over 10 percent on housing. This condition prevails in most racial ghettos.

The combination of high rents and low incomes forces many Negroes to pay an excessively high proportion of their income for housing. This is shown by the following chart showing the percentage of renter households paying over 35 percent of their incomes for rent in 10 metropolitan areas.

The high proportion of income that must go for rent leaves less money in such households for other expenses. Undoubtedly, this hardship is a major reason many Negro households regard housing as one of their worst problems.

Discrimination in Housing Code Enforcement

Thousands of landlords in disadvantaged neighborhoods openly violate building codes with impunity, thereby

442

THE CITY OF TOMORROW

PERCENTAGE OF WHITE AND
NONWHITE OCCUPIED UNITS WITH
HOUSEHOLDS PAYING 35 PERCENT
OR MORE OF THEIR INCOME FOR
RENT IN SELECTED METROPOLITAN
AREAS

Metropolitan Area	White Occupied Units	Nonwhite Occupied Units
Cleveland	8.6	33.8
Dallas	19.2	33.8
Detroit	21.2	40.5
Kansas City	20.2	40.0
Los Angeles— Long Beach	23.4	28.4
New Orleans	16.6	30.5
Philadelphia	19.3	32.1
St. Louis	18.5	36.7
San Francisco— Oakland	21.2	25.1
Washington, D.C.	18.5	28.3

Source: U.S. Department of Commerce, Bureau of Census.

providing a constant demonstration of flagrant discrimination by legal authorities. A high proportion of residential and other structures contain numerous violations of building and housing codes. Refusal to remedy these violations is a criminal offense, one which can have serious effects upon the victims living in these structures. Yet in most cities, few building code violations in these areas are ever corrected, even when tenants complain directly to municipal building departments.

There are economic reasons why these codes are not rigorously enforced. Bringing many old structures up to code standards and maintaining them at that level often would require owners to raise rents far above the ability of local residents to pay. In New York City, rigorous code enforcement has already caused owners to board up and

abandon over 2,500 buildings rather than incur the expense of repairing them. Nevertheless, open violation of codes is a constant source of distress to low-income tenants and creates serious hazards to health and safety in disadvantaged neighborhoods.

Housing Conditions and Disorder

Housing conditions in the disorder cities surveyed by the Commission paralleled those for ghetto Negroes generally.

Many homes were physically inadequate. Forty-seven percent of the units occupied by nonwhites in the disturbance areas were substandard.

Overcrowding was common. In the metropolitan areas in which disorders occurred, 24 percent of all units occupied by nonwhites were overcrowded, against only 8.8 percent of the white-occupied units.

Negroes paid higher percentages of their income for rent than, whites. In both the disturbance areas and the greater metropolitan area of which they were a part, the median rent as a proportion of median income was over 25 percent higher for nonwhites than for whites.

The result has been widespread discontent with housing conditions and costs. In nearly every disorder city surveyed, grievances related to housing were important factors in the structure of Negro discontent.

Poverty and Housing Deterioration

The reasons many Negroes live in decaying slums are not difficult to discover. First and foremost is poverty. Most ghetto residents cannot pay the rent necessary to support decent housing. This prevents private builders from constructing new units in the ghettos or from rehabilitating old ones, for either action involves an investment that would require substantially higher rents than most ghetto dwellers can pay. It also deters landlords from maintaining units that are presently structurally sound. Maintenance too requires additional investment, and at the minimal rents that inner-city Negroes can pay, landlords have little incentive to provide it.

The implications of widespread poor maintenance are serious. Most of the gains in Negro housing have occurred through the turnover which occurs as part of the "filtering down" process— as the white middle class moves out, the units it leaves are occupied by Negroes. Many of these units are very old. Without proper maintenance, they soon become dilapidated, so that the improvement in housing resulting from the filtering-down process is only temporary. The 1965 New York City survey points up the danger. During the period that the number of substandard units was decreasing, the number of deteriorating units increased by 95,000.

Discrimination

The second major factor condemning vast numbers of Negroes to urban slums is racial discrimination in the housing market. Discrimination prevents access to many nonslum areas, particularly the suburbs, and has a detrimental effect on ghetto housing itself. By restricting the area open to a growing population, housing discrimination makes it profitable for landlords to break up ghetto apartments for denser occupancy, hastening housing deterioration. Further, by creating a "back pressure" in the racial ghettos, discrimination keeps prices and rents of older, more deteriorated housing in the ghetto higher than they would be in a truly free and open market.

Existing Programs

To date, Federal building programs have been able to do comparatively little to provide housing for the disadvantaged. In the 31-year history of subsidized Federal housing, only about 800,000 units have been constructed, with recent production averaging about 50,000 units a year. By comparison, over a period only 3 years longer, FHA insurance guarantees have made possible the construction of over 10 million middle and upper-income units.

Federal programs also have done little to prevent the growth of racially segregated suburbs around our cities. Until 1949, FHA official policy was to refuse to insure any unsegregated housing. It was not until the issuance of Executive Order 11063 in 1962 that the Agency required nondiscrimination pledges from loan applicants.

It is only within the last few years that a range of programs has been created that appears to have the potential for substantially relieving the urban housing problem. Direct federal expenditures for housing and community development have increased from $600 million in fiscal 1964 to nearly $3 billion in fiscal 1969. To produce significant results, however, these programs must be employed on a much larger scale than they have been so far. In some cases the constraints and limitations imposed upon the programs must be reduced. In a few instances supplementary programs should be created. In all cases, incentives must be provided to induce maximum participation by private enterprise in supplying energy, imagination, capital and production capabilities.

Federal housing programs must also be given a new thrust aimed at overcoming the prevailing patterns of racial segregation. If this is not done, those programs will continue to concentrate the most impoverished and dependent segments of the population into the central-city ghettos where there is already a critical gap between the needs of the population and the public resources to deal with them. This can only continue to compound the conditions of failure and hopelessness which lead to crime, civil disorder and social disorganization.

BASIC STRATEGIES

We believe the following basic strategies should be adopted:

The supply of housing suitable for low-income families should be expanded on a massive basis.

The basic reason many Negroes are compelled to live in inadequate housing is the failure of the private market to produce decent housing at rentals they can afford to pay. Programs we have recommended elsewhere are directed toward raising income levels. Yet it is obvious that in the foreseeable future there will continue to be a gap between the income of many Americans and the price of decent housing produced by normal market mechanisms. Thus, the implementation of the strategy depends on programs which not only generate more lower cost housing but also raise the rent paying capability of low-income households.

Areas outside of ghetto neighborhoods should be opened up to occupancy by racial minorities.

Provision of decent low-cost housing will solve only part of the problem. Equally fundamental is the elimination of the racial barrier in housing. Residential segregation prevents equal access to employment opportunities and obstructs efforts to achieve integrated education. A single society cannot be

achieved as long as this cornerstone of segregation stands.

SUGGESTED PROGRAMS

We are proposing programs in 10 areas to illustrate how we believe basic strategies we have outlined can be put into effect:

Provision of 600,000 low- and moderate-income housing units next year, and six million units over the next 5 years.

An expanded and modified below-market interest rate program.

An expanded and modified rent supplement program and an ownership supplement program.

Federal write-down of interest rates on loans to private builders.

An expanded and more diversified public housing program.

An expanded Model Cities program.

A reoriented and expanded urban renewal program.

Reform of obsolete building codes.

Enactment of a national, comprehensive and enforceable open-occupancy law.

Reorientation of Federal housing programs to place more low and moderate-income housing outside of ghetto areas.

The supply of housing suitable for low-income families should be expanded.

THE COMMISSION RECOMMENDS

Provision of 600,000 low- and moderate-income housing units next year and six million units over the next 5 years.

Some 6 million substandard housing units are occupied in the United States today, and well over that number of families lack sufficient income to rent or buy standard housing, without spending over 25 percent of their income and thus sacrificing other essential needs. The problem promises to become more critical with the expanded rate of family formation on the immediate horizon and the increasing need to replace housing which has been destroyed or condemned.

In our view, the dimension of the need calls for an unprecedented national effort. We believe that the Nation's housing programs must be expanded to bring within the reach of low and moderate-income families 600,000 new and existing units next year, and 6 million units over the next 5 years.

This proposal can only be implemented if present subsidy programs are extended so that (*a*) a part of the existing housing inventory can be brought within the reach of lower income families, and (*b*) private enterprise can become a major factor in the low-cost housing field, both in terms of the construction capabilities of private developers and the capital of private institutional lenders.

In the sections that follow, we discuss specific programs that must be part of this expanded national effort.

An expanded and modified below-market interest rate program.

The below-market interest rate program, which makes long-term, low-interest financing available to nonprofit and limited profit sponsors, is the best mechanism presently available for engaging private enterprise in the task of providing moderate and lower income housing.

Several limitations, however, prevent the program from providing the quantity of housing that is needed. Funding levels are inadequate to launch a national program, nonprofit sponsors are deterred by lack of seed money to finance preconstruction costs and limited profit corporations are deterred by the statutory prohibition on transfer or refinancing projects for 20 years without FHA permission.

We recommend that funding levels of the program be substantially increased. We also recommend that legislation be enacted to permit interest-free loans to nonprofit sponsors to cover pre-construction costs, and to allow gram, which makes long-term, low-limited profit corporations to sell projects to nonprofit corporations, cooperatives, or condominiums.

Though the potential of the program is great, it presently serves few truly low-income families. Current costs average $14,400 per unit, making the typical rental for a two-bedroom unit $110 per month, thereby in effect requiring a minimum annual income of $5,300. Only with rent supplements can poor families afford housing commanding rents of this amount, but the amount of rent supplement funds which can be used in such developments is limited by statute to 5 percent of the total appropriation for the rent supplement program.

In order to make below-market interest rate housing available to low as well as moderate-income families, we recommend that the 5 percent limitation be removed, and that the overall funding of rent supplements be greatly expanded. We also recommend that serious consideration be given to expanding the interest subsidy under the program in order to lower the rate for sponsors.

An expanded and modified rent supplement program and an ownership supplement program.

The rent supplement program offers a highly flexible tool for subsidizing housing costs, because it permits adjustment of the subsidy according to the income of the tenant. The project financing is at market rates, so that tenants who do not qualify for supplements must pay market rentals. Potentially, therefore, these developments can provide an alternative to public housing for low-income families, while still attracting middle-income families.

We believe, however, that several changes are necessary if the full potential of this program is to be realized.

First, we recommend that existing regulations restricting architectural design, imposing rigid unit cost standards, and limiting tenant income to amounts lower than required by statute be removed. These regulations diminish the attractiveness of the program to private developers, and represent a major barrier to substantial expansion of the program.

Second, the statutory limitation of rent supplements to new or rehabilitated housing should be changed to permit use of rent supplements in existing housing. In many areas, removal of the restriction would make possible a major increase of the program without requiring investment in new construction. This option must be made available if the program is to be expanded to its fullest potential.

Third, the rent supplement concept should be extended to provide home ownership opportunities for low-income families. The ambition to own one's own home is shared by virtually all Americans, and we believe it is in the interest of the Nation to permit all who share such a goal to realize it. Home ownership would eliminate one of the most persistent problems facing low-income families in rental housing—poor maintenance by absentee landlords —and would provide many low-income families with a tangible stake in society for the first time.

The Senate Banking and Currency Committee recently approved a bill that would establish a program to pay a portion of the mortgage payments of low-income families seeking to purchase homes. As with rent supplements, subsidy payments would decrease as the purchasers income rose. The income limits of the program—70 percent of the below-market interest rate eligibility limits—would greatly impair its usefulness, in our opinion, and should be eliminated. With that reservation, we strongly endorse the concept, urge that such a program of ownership supplements be enacted, and recommend that it be funded on a basis that will permit its wide use in achieving the goal of 6 million units for low- and moderate-income families over the next 5 years.

Federal write-down of interest rates on loans to private builders.

To make private loan capital available, we recommend direct Federal write-down of interest rates on market rate loans to private construction firms for moderate-rent housing. This program would make it possible for any qualified builder to enter the moderate-rent housing field on the basis of market rate financing, provided that the project meets necessary criteria. The Federal Government would enter into a contract with the financing institution to supply the difference between the mortgage payment at the market interest rate and 20 percent of the tenant's monthly income, to a specified maximum write-down which would make the interest rate paid by the tenant equivalent to 1 or 2 percent.

An expanded and more diversified public housing program.

Since its establishment in 1937, the public housing program has produced only some 650,000 low-rent housing units. Insufficient funding has prevented construction of a quantity more suited to the need, and unrealistic unit-cost limitations have mandated that most projects be of institutional design and mammoth size. The resulting large concentration of low-income families has often created conditions generating great resistance in communities to new projects of this type.

We believe that there is a need for substantially more public housing, but we believe that the emphasis of the program should be changed from the traditional publicly built, slum-based, highrise project to smaller units on scattered sites. Where traditional high-rise projects are constructed, facilities for social services should be included in the design, and a broad range of such services provided for tenants.

To achieve the shift in emphasis we have recommended, we urge first, expansion of present programs under which public housing authorities lease existing scattered site units. Present statutory restrictions on long-term leasing should be eliminated to provide incentives for private construction and financing. Families whose incomes increase above the public housing limit should be permitted to take over the leases of their units from the housing authority.

We also urge expansion of present "turnkey" programs, under which housing authorities purchase low-rent units constructed by private builders instead of constructing the units themselves. Here too, families whose incomes rise above the public housing limits should be permitted to stay in the units at market rentals.

An expanded Model Cities program.

The Model Cities program is potentially the most effective weapon in the Federal arsenal for a long-term, comprehensive attack on the problems of American cities. It offers a unique means of developing local priorities, coordinating all applicable government programs—including those relating to social development (e.g., education and health) as well as physical development —and encouraging innovative plans and techniques. Its "block grant" multipurpose funding feature allows the city to deploy program funds with much greater flexibility than is possible under typical categorical grant programs, and the statutory requirement that there be widespread citizen participation and maximum employment of area residents in all phases of the program promises to involve community residents in a way we think most important.

The full potential of the program can be achieved, however, only if (*a*) the Model Cities program is funded at a level which gives the cities involved an opportunity and incentive to produce significant results, and (*b*) the various programs which can be brought into play under Model Cities, such as urban renewal, below-market interest rate housing, and health, education and welfare programs, are independently supported at levels which permit Model Cities' funds to be used for essentially innovative purposes. Appropriations must also be sufficient to expand coverage far beyond the 63 cities that currently are funded.

The President has recommended that $1 billion be appropriated for Model Cities. We strongly support this recommendation as a minimum start, noting that a much greater scale of funding will ultimately be necessary if the program proves successful and if it is to be made available to all the cities that require such aid.

A reoriented and expanded urban renewal program.

Urban renewal has been an extremely controversial program since its inception. We recognize that in many cities it has demolished more housing than it has erected, and that it has often caused dislocation among disadvantaged groups.

Nevertheless, we believe that a greatly expanded, though reoriented, urban renewal program is necessary to the health of our cities. Urban renewal is an essential component of the Model Cities program, and in its own right is an essential tool for any city attempting to preserve social and economic vitality. Substantially increased funding will be necessary if urban renewal is to become a reality in all the cities in which renewal is needed. A reorienting of the program is necessary to avoid past deficiencies. The Department of Housing and Urban Development has recognized this, and has promulgated policies giving top priority to urban renewal projects that directly assist low-income households in obtaining adequate housing. Projects aimed primarily at bolstering the economic strength of downtown areas, or at creating housing for upper income groups while reducing the supply of low-cost housing, will have low priority, unless they are part of balanced programs including a strong focus on needs of low-income groups. With these priorities in mind, we recommend substantial expansion of the program.

Reform of obsolete building codes.

Approximately 5,000 separate jurisdictions in the United States have building codes. Many of these local codes are antiquated and contain obsolete requirements that prevent builders from taking advantage of new technology. Beyond the factor of obsolesence, the very variety of the requirements prevents the mass production and standardized design that could significantly lower building costs.

Opinions differ as to whether a uniform national code is yet feasible, but it is clear that much greater uniformity is possible than presently exists. We urge state and local governments to undertake the task of modernizing their codes at once, and recommend that the Department of Housing and Urban Development design for their guidance a model national code. We can no longer afford the waste caused by arbitrary and archaic building codes.

Areas outside of ghetto neighborhoods should be opened up to occupancy by racial minorities.

THE COMMISSION RECOMMENDS

Enactment of a national, comprehensive and enforceable open-occupancy law.

The Federal Government should enact a comprehensive and enforceable open-occupancy law making it an offense to discriminate in the sale or rental of any housing—including single family homes—on the basis of race, creed, color, or national origin.

In recent years, various piecemeal attempts have been made to deal with the problem of housing discrimination. Executive Order 11063, issued by President Kennedy in 1962, provided that agreements for federally assisted housing made after the date of the Order must be covered by enforceable nondiscrimination pledges. Congress, in enacting Title VI of the Civil Rights Act of 1964, promulgated a broad national policy of nondiscrimination with respect to programs or activities receiving Federal financial assistance—including public housing and urban renewal. Eighteen states and more than 40 cities have enacted fair housing laws of varying degrees of effectiveness.

Despite these actions, the great bulk of housing produced by the private sector remains unaffected by anti-discrimination measures. So long as this continues, public and private action at the local level will be inhibited by the argument that local action produces competitive disadvantage.

We have canvassed the various alternatives and have come to the firm opinion that there is no substitute for enactment of a Federal fair housing law. The key to breaking down housing discrimination is universal and uniform coverage, and such coverage is obtainable only through Federal legislation.

We urge that such a statute be enacted at the earliest possible date.

Open housing legislation must be translated into open housing action. Real estate boards should work with fair housing groups in communities where such groups exist, and help form them in areas where they do not exist. The objective of voluntary community action should be (1) the full dissemination of information concerning available housing to minority groups, and (2) providing information to the community concerning the desirability of open housing.

Reorientation of Federal housing programs to place more low- and moderate-income housing outside of ghetto areas.

Enactment of a national fair housing law will eliminate the most obvious barrier limiting the areas in which nonwhites live, but it will not deal with an equally impenetrable barrier, the unavailability of low and moderate income housing in nonghetto areas.

To date, housing programs serving low-income groups have been concentrated in the ghettos. Non-ghetto areas, particularly suburbs, have for the most part steadfastly opposed low-income, rent supplement, or below-market interest rate housing, and have successfully restricted use of these programs outside the ghetto.

We believe that federally aided low- and moderate-income housing programs must be reoriented so that the major thrust is in nonghetto areas. Public housing programs should emphasize scattered site construction, rent supplements should, wherever possible, be used in nonghetto areas, and an intensive effort should be made to recruit below-market interest rate sponsors willing to build outside the ghettos.

The reorientation of these programs is particularly critical in light of our recommendation that 6 million low- and middle-income housing units be made available over the next 5 years. If the effort is not to be counterproductive, its main thrust must be in nonghetto areas, particularly those outside the central city.

THE CITIES—YOUR CHALLENGE TOO

Institute of Life Insurance

This selection briefly reviews some of the problems of our cities. It reports on current action programs being conducted by individuals and groups in their communities whose goals are the enrichment of the lives of our underprivileged of all races and age groups. It suggests what skills, training, materials, and personal participation are needed in programs which should be in existence throughout our nation. It would be most difficult for an individual to review these opportunities for personal participation and then say he has no way to help—the opportunities are almost limitless. Do you have the will to help?

I visit cities and walk through their streets, breathing air that's not fit for anyone to breathe; I hear the constant rumble of traffic and I feel its vibration in the soles of my feet; I see the grime caked on windows, walls, sidewalks, and parked cars and shudder as I realize that this dirt is going into our lungs; then I think that life in today's cities is no picnic for anyone . . . black or white. You're a second-class citizen when you live like this.

Polluted air . . . traffic congestion . . . dirt . . . grime . . . behind each of the problems cited by social worker Mary Pegram in the previous paragraph lie dozens of others. Unemployment. Crowded schools. Housing shortages. Crime. Delinquency. Urban decay. And the inescapable fact is that they are beginning to affect each one of us in one fashion or another, wherever we live. Mrs. Pegram went on to discuss many of them in a letter to the Institute of Life Insurance. She was concerned. And a concern similar to the one expressed by Mrs. Pegram was voiced by more than 40,000 other Americans—Americans of all races, creeds and colors, and representative of all age groups. These were the persons who wrote the Institute in response to a campaign on behalf of the life insurance companies in America asking all Americans to help in turning the tide of decay and despair that was beginning to engulf the cities of this great nation. The need continues for Americans to volunteer their time, their efforts, their talents, their resources, in the battle to help resolve the nation's

ills. There is the highest need for all of us—government, labor, private business, private citizens—to work together in resolving this major challenge of our time. In fact, it is absolutely necessary if we are to overcome it. On the following pages, we have identified, with the aid of the Office of Economic Opportunity, some of the ways in which you can help to meet the challenge.

If You Have Skills in

Homemaking—Driving—Typing—Bookkeeping—Building or Repair Work—Interviewing—Office Procedures—First-aid—Foreign Languages—Sewing—Games and Sports—Cooking—Needlecraft—Knitting—Music—Arts—Crafts—Photography—Story-telling—Dramatics—Gardening—Writing

If You Have Professional Training in

Business—Nursing—Teaching—Accounting—Psychology—Group Recreation—Medicine—Dentistry—Physical Sciences—Sociology—Administration—Ministry—Economics—Library Sciences—Law—Journalism

If You Can Contribute

Materials—Tools—Transportation—Buildings—Outdoor or Indoor Space—Furniture—Facilities—Machinery—Toys—Clothes—Food—Books—Services—Entertainment

If You Belong to a

Religious Group—Professional Association—Business Organization—Labor Union—Youth Group—Parent-Teachers Association—Social Club—Service Group—Civic Association—Political Party—Fraternity—Sorority—Ethnic Organization—Special Interest Group

If Your Organization Can Supply

Willing Hands—Financial Resources—Moral Support—Facilities—Sponsorship—Direction—Know-How

If Your Organization Can Use Its Influence on

Elected Officials—Other Groups—Existing Agencies—The Public at Large
. . . YOU CAN HELP

But no matter what you can offer—as an individual or as a member of a group—the most important ingredient is your desire to help
. . . YOU CAN HELP

WHERE DO YOU START?

Approach familiar, nearby sources first. Your clergyman, the head of your civic association, teachers, your local legislator or precinct leader will know something of your area's needs and will be able to put you in touch with others already organized or equally concerned.

If you've already chosen your field of interest but need information on how to contribute, consult the yellow pages of your telephone directory for a listing of "Social Service Organizations." A simple call may supply the answers.

Your local or area Health and Welfare Council can also be located through the yellow pages. Volunteer Bureaus are operated by 110 Councils throughout the country. In other cities, privately-supported bureaus

may exist. Both types coordinate activities with other social and welfare groups and assist in the training and placement of volunteers.

Check with your local newspaper, radio or television stations, the Mayor's office or other local officials for names of area community programs. Whether these operate as anti-poverty programs or for other civic purposes they have need of dedicated volunteer help.

Check with the same local sources for information on efforts in your area of organizations such as the Urban Coalition and Urban League, which are attempting to meet the needs of the cities and have established many local affiliates. You can find more about these and other national-local efforts by writing:

The Urban Coalition
1819 H. Street, N.W.
Washington, D.C. 20006

National Urban League, Inc.
55 East 52nd Street
New York, New York 10022

Urban America, Inc.
1717 Massachusetts Avenue, N.W.
Washington, D.C. 20036

HERE IS WHAT SOME PEOPLE LIKE YOURSELF ARE DOING

Hundreds of volunteers joined with representatives of business, public and private agencies and churches in Minneapolis to help raise $100,000 in funds so that an additional 100 children could be enrolled in the city's Head Start program.

In Florence, Ala., senior citizens give four hours per week, serving as aides in day care centers, teaching home-making skills, and visiting other older persons served by the programs of the Florence-Lauderdale Community Action Committee, Inc.

Two young Washington, D.C., attorneys, with the help of other volunteers, are devoting three nights a week to a program they organized to provide recreation, instruction and friendship for some 100 youngsters.

A suburban California housewife has become the dynamic leader of a council which coordinates the activities of more than 20 fair housing groups in the San Francisco Bay Area.

A Massachusetts grandmother and her friends spend four afternoons a week tutoring boys at a Job Corps Conservation Center.

Twenty-three Atlanta, Ga., poverty area residents got together and organized slum tours in the city to teach others about poverty. The thousands taking the tours range from housewives to lawyers and from young to old.

Individual volunteers have enabled a new community center in Madison, Wis., to fill the educational and recreational needs of a disadvantaged area. The center conducts programs during the week, in the evenings, and on weekends largely through the efforts of the volunteers.

Two Tennessee life insurance underwriters have seen their efforts as members of the all-volunteer Memphis Committee on Community Relations help in the formation of a permanent human relations organization. Both are now appointed members of the new and official Memphis and Shelby County Human Relations Commission. The old volunteer organization was set up in 1927.

An Indiana dentist takes appointments for Head Start children on his day off, then offers to examine and x-ray all Head Start children in his town free of charge. His wife delivers the children to their homes after treatment.

A midwest farmer and his wife invite underprivileged children to their farm. The youngsters ride ponies, see the cows milked, play with kittens, climb into the hayloft and are treated to a picnic.

Two Colorado mothers led a group of parents in establishing and managing a recreation center in an old store building for their school age youngsters, then helped set up a Head Start program and an adult education course in early childhood development with the aid of their local antipoverty agency.

A Miami, Fla., teacher who teaches underprivileged children during the day, conducts evening basic education classes at Dade County Jail for inmates who want to work toward a high school diploma.

After the Mayor of Lima, Ohio, proclaimed "Upward Bound Week" citizens responded with an auction to raise scholarship money. But one volunteer, a mother on welfare, started and ran it all through to success. She had two children in Upward Bound—one a graduate, one entering Ohio State University. She's a volunteer member of the Allen County Action Commission.

HERE IS WHAT SOME ORGANIZATIONS ARE DOING

A nonsectarian, nonprofit organization called Full Circle Associates is actively bringing together 5,000 white suburbanites with black and

Puerto Rican residents of 43 New York City blocks. Through a series of projects, it is helping them to work together to close the gap between races and classes in America and raise the quality of life for everyone.

A group of employers in Riverside, Calif., has organized the Job Opportunities Council to provide employment counselling and placement services to benefit seriously disadvantaged people.

The Catholic Diocese, Council of Jewish Women and the Junior League are helping to strengthen family life in the Hough area of Cleveland by lending their support to the new Hough Parent and Child Center.

Members of two New Hampshire Girl Scout troops are helping in their town's Head Start program. The girls come in every day after school to work in the kitchen, play with the children, help with inventory and perform many other useful tasks.

In Detroit, Mich., Wayne State University students have formed a Coalition for Youth Action, utilizing not only students but former Peace Corps and current VISTA Volunteers in continuing service to the community.

In Seattle, Wash., the Volunteer Services of America has recently expanded its usual program by building a home for the aged with the aid of government funds.

In Knoxville, Tenn., the local association of life underwriters assumed the responsibility of buying and paying off the mortgage on additional property for the Girl's Club in the community. It will be used for girls between the ages of six and twelve who are underprivileged or from broken homes or homes where both parents are away working most of the time.

Nationwide action is being taken by the National Council of Churches, the National Council of Catholic Women, the National Council of Jewish Women, and the National Council of Negro Women to recruit and screen Job Corpswomen.

In Anchorage, Alaska, the PTA has furnished over 30,000 books and much-needed school supplies for funded and unfunded Head Start programs. They are also working closely with VISTA Volunteers.

A group of men from a Norwalk, Conn., church has been spending several days a month helping to tutor young school students from the inner city.

In Kansas City, Mo., representatives of 54 big business or industrial firms launched a massive drive to employ at least 1,000 "hard core" unemployed. In cooperation, the Urban League scheduled a Career Fair to make the jobs available to persons wanting them.

In Newark, N.J., the Fair Housing and Equal Opportunities Council of Maplewood, South Orange, Millburn and Short Hills has helped to establish a dental clinic; is providing money for alterations and equipment of a community center; and sponsors an urban-suburban dialogue to encourage support of the Community Action programs.

Throughout the country, SCORE, a volunteer program begun by the Small Business Administration, brings retired businessmen into contact with others who need advice. Approximately 2500 volunteers are now enrolled.

In Dayton, Ohio, the Jaycees instituted Half-Way Houses to provide follow-through for young persons just leaving correctional institutions.

SOME OF THE MANY ORGANIZATIONS YOU CAN OFFER YOUR WILL AND SKILLS TO

Your children's school or a "sister" school in less fortunate parts of the city—Your own place of worship or another that needs your help—Hospitals and Clinics—Community Action Agencies—Settlement Houses—Legal Services—Schools for the Handicapped—Health and Welfare Agencies—Head Start—Specific Charity Organizations—Neighborhood Centers—Homes for the Aged or Infirm—Day Care Centers—Maternity Homes—Family Planning Clinics—Orphanages—Recreation Centers—Police Athletic League—Neighborhood Youth Corps Projects—Youth Clubs or Organizations—Upward Bound—Service Organizations—Migrant Programs—Civic Associations—Job Corps Centers—4-H Club Foundation—Health Centers—Urban Coalition—American Bar Association—National Council on the Aging—Urban League—League of Women Voters—American Legion—AFL-CIO—YMCA—JAYCEES.

Utilize helpful booklets. The following contain much useful information:

"The Turning Point," published by Urban America, Inc., 1717 Massachusetts Avenue, N.W., Washington, D.C. 20036.

"Voluntary Help Wanted," published each spring by the Information Center, Office of Economic Opportunity, Washington, D.C. 20506.

"Where To Turn Directory," available through the Health and Welfare Councils for a minimum charge.

"Now We Need An Army to Fight Poverty," published by VISTA, Office of Economic Opportunity, Washington, D.C. 20506.

"Low-Cost Homes . . . through group action," a consumer guide, published by the Department of Housing and Urban Development, Washington, D.C. 20506.

"HEAD START," A Community Action Program, published by Head Start, Office of Economic Opportunity, Washington, D.C. 20506.

Many service organizations publish similar booklets which relate specifically to the projects they sponsor.

PROJECT IDEAS

1. Found, contribute to, or staff a community center for youth, the elderly, or the neighborhood as a whole.

2. Provide space in your office, yard, home or shop for group activities.

3. Organize your neighbors to set up day-time centers for children of working mothers.

4. Organize, direct, or teach tutorial or remedial education classes.

5. Organize a network of interested individuals or groups to attack a specific problem and coordinate the various lines of action. Your civic or service organization could take on a particular project—housing, delinquency, the aged, pollution, health care—and become a local source of information and help.

6. Conduct survey work to determine the needs, the conditions, and the current action being taken.

7. Sponsor recreational or cultural enrichment projects.

8. Initiate a paint-up, clean-up, fix-it campaign with donated materials and labor.

9. Conduct homemaker, handicraft, carpentry or other classes relating to your skills.

10. Collect and distribute needed materials, clothing, books, food.

11. Form a legislative committee to write letters, prepare testimony, and consult with elected officials.

12. Open up job opportunities in your business or office and encourage others to do the same.

13. Serve as a Foster Grandparent in hospitals, schools, and city institutions or locate other senior citizens to do so.

14. Develop Citizen Communication Bureaus for housing complaints, inadequate city or town services, and emergency aid or referral service.

15. Organize empty land into "tot lots" or play areas.

16. Investigate investment opportunities in the inner city.

17. Start a fund-raising campaign for better street lighting, school materials, playground equipment, a new library or project of your choice.

18. Let the community know what you're doing; let others know how they can help by publicizing both the needs and the efforts through contacting editors of student, business, organization or other newsletters and magazines. Organize conferences; speak in behalf of the programs or projects; devote space or special issues to project news in your organization newsletter or business house organ; edit or contribute to a project newsletter, radio, or TV.

The list is endless—and so is the need. YOU can begin today.

PART XI

QUESTIONS FOR DISCUSSION

1. What problem of the city seems of greatest concern to you today?
2. As our population becomes more urbanized what effect do you think this will have on your way of life?
3. Assuming a reasonable amount of money and cooperation, what immediate steps would you take to solve the problems of the cities today?
4. What do you, as a private citizen, plan to do to make your community a better place in which to live?

VOCABULARY

exurbs	openness
spontaneity	statutory limitation
role-playing	discrimination
bureaucratization	"color tax"

SUGGESTED READINGS

Alex, Nicholas. *Black in Blue: A Study of the Negro Policeman.* New York: Appleton-Century-Crofts, 1969.

Arensberg, Conrad M., and Solon T. Kimball. *Culture and Community.* New York: Harcourt, Brace & World, Inc., 1965.

Bailey, Harry A., Jr., and Ellis Katz. *Ethnic Group Politics.* Columbus, Ohio: Charles E. Merrill Company, 1969.

Banfield, Edward C., and James Q. Wilson. *City Politics.* New York: Vintage Books, 1963.

Barron, Milton L. (ed.). *Minorities in a Changing World.* New York: Alfred A. Knopf, Inc., 1967.

Bellush, Jewel, and Murray Hausknecht (eds.). *Urban Renewal: People, Politics, and Planning.* New York: Anchor Books, 1967.

Bernstein, Abraham. *The Education of Urban Populations.* New York: Random House, Inc., 1967.

Berry, Brian J. L., and Jack Meltzer (eds.). *Goals for Urban America.* Englewood Cliffs, N.J.: Prentice-Hall, Inc., 1967.

Berube, Maurice R., and Marilyn Gittell (eds.). *Confrontation at Ocean Hill-Brownsville.* New York: Frederick A. Praeger, Inc., 1969.

Budd, Edward C. (ed.). *Inequality and Poverty: An Introduction to a Current Issue of Public Policy.* New York: W. W. Norton & Company, Inc., 1967.

Caplovitz, David. *The Poor Pay More.* New York: The Free Press, 1967.

Churchill, Henry S. *The City Is the People.* New York: W. W. Norton & Company, Inc., 1962.

Cole, William E. *Urban-Society.* Cambridge, Mass.: Houghton Mifflin, 1958.

Coles, Robert. *Children of Crisis: A Study of Courage and Fear.* New York: Dell Publishing Company, Inc., 1967.

Coulter, Philip B. (ed.). *Politics of Metropolitan Areas: Selected Readings.* New York: Thomas Y. Crowell Company, 1967.

Cox, Harvey. *The Secular City.* New York: The Macmillan Company, 1965.

Danielson, Michael N. (ed.). *Metropolitan Politics: A Reader.* Boston: Little, Brown & Company, 1966.

Dentler, Robert A. *American Community Problems.* New York: McGraw-Hill Company, Inc., 1968.

———. Bernard Mackler, and Mary Ellen Warshauer (eds.). *The Urban R's: Race Relations as the Problem in Urban Education.* New York: Frederick A. Praeger, Inc., 1967.

The Editors of Fortune. *The Exploding Metropolis,* 2nd Edition. New York: Time, Inc., 1958.

Eldredge, H. Wentworth (ed.). *Taming Megalopolis: Volume I, What Is and What Could Be.* New York: Anchor Books, 1967.

———. *Taming Megalopolis: Volume II, How to Manage an Urbanized World.* New York: Anchor Books, 1967.

Elias, C. E., Jr., James Gillies, and Svend Riemer, *Metropolis: Values in Conflict.* Belmont, Calif.: Wadsworth Publishing Co. Inc., 1964.

Fava, Sylvia Fleis (ed.). *Urbanism in World Perspective: A Reader.* New York: Thomas Y. Crowell Company, 1968.

Fiser, Webb S. *Mastery of the Metropolis.* Englewood Cliffs, N.J.: Prentice-Hall, Inc., 1962.

Frazier, E. Franklin. *Black Bourgeoisie.* New York: The Free Press, 1957.

French, Robert Mills. *The Community: A Comparative Perspective.* Itasca, Ill.: F. E. Peacock Publishers, Inc., 1969.

Friedman, Lawrence M. *Government and Slum Housing: A Century of Frustration.* Chicago: Rand McNally & Company, 1968.

Fuchs, Estelle. *Pickets at the Gates.* New York: The Free Press, 1966.

Glaab, Charles N., and Theodore Brown. *A History of Urban America.* New York: The Macmillan Company, 1967.

Glaser, Daniel (ed.). *Crime in the City.* New York: Harper and Row, Publishers, Inc., 1969.

Glazer, Nona Y., and Carol F. Creedon (eds.). *Children and Poverty: Some Sociological and Psychological Perspectives.* Chicago: Rand McNally & Company, 1968.

Goodall, Leonard E. *The American Metropolis.* Columbus, Ohio: Charles E. Merrill Company, 1968.

Gordon, Mitchell. *Sick Cities: Psychology and Pathology of American Urban Life.* Baltimore: Penguin, 1963.

Greer, Scott. *Urban Renewal and American Cities.* Indianapolis: Bobbs-Merrill Co., Inc., 1965.

Hadden, Jeffrey K., Louis H. Masotti, and Calvin J. Larsen (eds.). *Metropolis in Crisis.* Itasca, Ill.: F. E. Peacock Publishers, Inc., 1967.

Hall, Peter. *The World Cities.* New York: McGraw-Hill Company, Inc., 1966.

Handlin, Oscar. *The Newcomers: Negroes and Puerto Ricans in a Changing Metropolis.* New York: Anchor Books, 1962.

Harrington, Michael. *The Other America: Poverty in the United States.* Baltimore, Md.: Penguin Books, Inc., 1962.

Havighurst, Robert J. *Education in Metropolitan Areas.* Boston: Allyn & Bacon, Inc., 1967.

Hawley, Willis D., and Frederick M. Wirt. *The Search for Community Power.* Englewood Cliffs, N.J.: Prentice-Hall, Inc., 1968.

Hoover, Edgar M., and Raymond Vernon. *Anatomy of a Metropolis.* Cambridge, Mass.: Harvard University Press, 1959.

Hunter, David R. *The Slums: Challenge and Response.* New York: The Free Press, 1968.

Jacobs, Jane. *The Death and Life of Great American Cities.* New York: Vintage Books, 1961.

Jacobs, Paul. *Prelude to Riot: A View of Urban America from the Bottom.* New York: Vintage Books, 1967.

Kammerer, Gladys M., Charles D. Farris, John M. DeGrove, and Alfred B. Clubok. *The Urban Political Community: Profiles in Town Politics.* Boston: Houghton Mifflin Company, 1963.

Keller, Suzanne. *The Urban Neighborhood: A Sociological Perspective.* New York: Random House, Inc., 1968.

Kramer, Ralph M. *Participation of the Poor: Comparative Community Case Studies in the War on Poverty.* Englewood Cliffs, N.J.: Prentice-Hall, Inc., 1969.

Leacock, Eleanor Burke. *Teaching and Learning in City Schools.* New York: Basic Books, Inc., Publishers, 1969.

Leinwand, Gerald (ed.). *The Negro in the City.* New York: Washington Square Press, Inc., 1968.

Levenson, William B. *The Spiral Pendulum: The Urban School in Transition.* Chicago: Rand McNally & Company, 1968.

Levine, Naomi, and Richard Cohen. *Ocean Hill-Brownsville: Schools in Crisis.* New York: Popular Library, 1969.

Liston, Robert A. *Downtown: Our Challenging Urban Problems.* New York: Dell Publishing Company, Inc., 1968.

Lowe, Jeanne R. *Cities in a Race with Time.* New York: Vintage Books, 1967.

Mahood, H. R., and Edward L. Angus (eds.). *Urban Politics and Problems: A Reader.* New York: Charles Scribner's Sons, 1969.

McCord, William, John Howard, Bernard Friedberg, and Edwin Harwood. *Life Styles in the Black Ghetto.* New York: W. W. Norton & Company, Inc., 1969.

Meissner, Hanna H. (ed.). *Poverty in the Affluent Society.* New York: Harper and Row, Publishers, Inc., 1966.

Miller, Harry L., and Marjorie B. Smiley (eds.). *Education in the Metropolis.* New York: The Free Press, 1967.

Minar, David W., and Scott Greer (eds.). *The Concept of Community: Readings with Interpretations.* Chicago: Aldine Publishing Company, 1969.

Moore, William, Jr. *The Vertical Ghetto: Everyday Life in an Urban Project.* New York: Random House, Inc., 1969.

Mumford, Lewis. *The City in History: Its Origins, Its Transformations, and Its Prospects.* New York: Harcourt, Brace & World, Inc., 1961.

Okun, Arthur M. (ed.). *The Battle Against Unemployment.* New York: W. W. Norton & Company, Inc., 1965.

Parsons, Talcott, and Kenneth B. Clark (eds.). *The Negro American.* Boston: Beacon Press, 1967.

Resh, Richard (ed.). *Black America.* Boston: D. C. Heath & Company, 1969.

Rudman, Herbert C., and Richard L. Featherstone (eds.). *Urban Schooling.* New York: Harcourt, Brace & World, Inc., 1968.

Schnore, Leo F. (ed.). *Social Science and the City: A Survey of Urban Research.* New York: Frederick A. Praeger, Inc., 1968.

Schulz, David A. *Coming Up Black: Patterns of Ghetto Socialization.* Englewood Cliffs, N.J.: Prentice-Hall, Inc., 1969.

Scientific American, Inc. *Cities.* New York: Alfred A. Knopf, Inc., 1965.

Sennett, Richard (ed.). *Classic Essays on the Culture of Cities.* New York: Appleton-Century-Crofts, Inc., 1969.

Shank, Alan (ed.). *Political Power and the Urban Crisis.* Boston: Holbrook Press, Inc., 1969.

Shostak, Arthur B., and William Gomberg (eds.). *New Perspectives on Poverty.* Englewood Cliffs, N.J.: Prentice-Hall, Inc., 1965.

Smiley, Marjorie B., and Harry L. Miller (eds.). *Policy Issues in Urban Education.* New York: The Free Press, 1968.

Speizman, Milton D. (ed.). *Urban America in the Twentieth Century.* New York: Thomas Y. Crowell Company, 1968.

Starr, Roger. *The Urban Choices: The City and Its Critics.* Baltimore, Md.: Penguin Books, 1966.

Steffens, Lincoln. *The Shame of the Cities.* New York: Hill and Wang, 1904.

Stein, Maurice R. *The Eclipse of Community: An Interpretation of American Studies.* New York: Harper and Row, Publishers, Inc., 1964.

Stringfellow, William. *My People Is the Enemy.* New York: Holt, Rinehart and Winston, Inc., 1964.

Thernstrom, Stephan, and Richard Sennett (eds.). *Nineteenth-Century Cities: Essays in the New Urban History.* New Haven, Conn.: Yale University Press, 1969.

Thomlinson, Ralph. *Urban Structures: The Social and Spatial Character of Cities.* New York: Random House, Inc., 1969.

Tietze, Frederick T., and James E. McKeown (eds.). *The Changing Metropolis.* Boston: Houghton Mifflin Company, 1964.

Toffler, Alvin (ed.). *The Schoolhouse in the City.* New York: Frederick A. Praeger, Inc., 1968.

Tunnard, Christopher. *The Modern American City.* Princeton, N.J.: D. Van Nostrand Company, Inc., 1968.

Urban America, Inc. and The Urban Coalition. *One Year Later.* New York: Frederick A. Praeger, Inc., 1969.

Von Eckardt, Wolf. *A Place to Live: The Crisis of the Cities.* New York: Dell Publishing Company, 1967.

Wagar, W. Warren. *The City of Man.* Baltimore, Md.: Penguin Books, Inc., 1963.

Warren, Roland L. *The Community in America.* Chicago: Rand McNally & Company, 1963.

——— (ed.). *Perspectives on the American Community.* Chicago: Rand McNally & Company, 1966.

Weber, Max. *The City.* New York: The Free Press, 1958.

Weimer, David R. *City and Country in America.* New York: Appleton-Century-Crofts, 1962.

Will, Robert E., and Harold G. Vatter. *Poverty in Affluence.* New York: Harcourt, Brace & World, Inc., 1965.

Williams, Oliver P., and Charles Press. *Democracy in Urban America.* Chicago: Rand McNally & Company, 1969.

The following journals regularly contain material of significant value in viewing urban problems.

Urban Affairs Quarterly   *The American City*
Urban Studies   *Communities in Action*
Urban   *Education and Urban Society*
Urban Research News   *Environment and Behavior*
Urban Renewal Review   *Trans Action*
Urban Crisis Monitor

DATE DUE			
GAYLORD			PRINTED IN U.S.A.